Cockpit Resource Management ————————➤

Cockpit Resource Management ✈

Edited by

Earl L. Wiener
Department of Management Science
University of Miami
Coral Gables, Florida

Barbara G. Kanki
Aerospace Human Factors Research Division
NASA-Ames Research Center
Moffett Field, California

Robert L. Helmreich
Department of Psychology
University of Texas at Austin
Austin, Texas

ACADEMIC PRESS

An Imprint of Elsevier

Amsterdam   Boston   Heidelberg   London   New York   Oxford   Paris   San Diego
San Francisco   Singapore   Sydney   Tokyo

Permissions may be sought directly from Elsevier's Science and Technology Rights Department in
Oxford, UK. Phone: (44) 1865 843830, Fax: (44) 1865 853333, e-mail: permissions@elsevier.co.uk.
You may also complete your request on-line via the Elsevier homepage: http://www.elsevier.com by
selecting "Customer Support" and then "Obtaining Permissions".

Academic Press
An Imprint of Elsevier
525 B Street, Suite 1900, San Diego, California 92101-4495, USA
http://www.academicpress.com

Academic Press
84 Theobolds Road, London WC1X 8RR, UK
http://www.academicpress.com

Library of Congress Cataloging-in-Publication Data

Cockpit resource management / edited by Earl L. Wiener, Barbara G. Kanki,
    Robert L. Helmreich ; with a foreword by John K. Lauber.
        p.   cm.
    Includes bibliographical references and index.

    ISBN-13: 978-0-12-750026-3   ISBN-10: 0-12-750026-X

    1. Flight training. 2. Aeronautics-Human factors. I. Wiener, Earl L.
    II. Kanki, Barbara G., date III. Helmreich, Robert L..
TL712.G62   1995
6629.132'52–dc
                                        92-28741
                                        CIP
ISBN-13: 978-0-12-750026-3   ISBN-10: 0-12-750026-X

PRINTED IN THE UNITED STATES OF AMERICA
05   06   07   SB   20   19   18

Contents

_____ *I The Nature of CRM*

1 Why Crew Resource Management? Empirical and Theoretical Bases of Human Factors Training in Aviation

Robert L. Helmreich and H. Clayton Foushee

5 *Decision-making in the Cockpit*

Judith M. Orasanu

6 *Crew Resource Management Training Assessment*

Steven E. Gregorich and John A. Wilhelm

II Perspectives

10   *The Accident Investigator's Perspective*

Phyllis J. Kayten

11   *Critical Issues for CRM Training and Research*

Thomas R. Chidester

12   *Training and Research for Teamwork in the Military Aircrew*

Carolyn Prince and Eduardo Salas

13   *CRM: Cross-Cultural Perspectives*

Neil Johnston

14   *Keeping CRM Is Keeping the Flight Safe*

Hisaaki Yamamori and Takao Mito

15   *Developing and Implementing CRM Programs: The Delta Experience*

Robert E. Byrnes and Reuben Black

III   Conclusions

16   *Airline Pilot Training Today and Tomorrow*

Harry W. Orlady

17   *The Future of Crew Resource Management in the Cockpit and Elsewhere*

Robert L. Helmreich, Earl L. Wiener, and Barbara G. Kanki

Contributors

Numbers in parentheses indicate the pages on which the authors' contributions begin.

Richard A. Birnbach (263), Federal Aviation Administration, Great Lakes Region, Des Plaines, Illinois 60018

Reuben Black (421), Delta Airlines, Hartsfield Atlanta International Airport, Atlanta, Georgia 30320

Roy E. Butler (231), NASA/UT Aerospace Crew Research Project, University of Texas at Austin, Austin, Texas 78701

Robert E. Byrnes (421), Delta Airlines, Hartsfield Atlanta International Airport, Atlanta, Georgia 30320

Thomas R. Chidester (315), Crew Resource Management, American Airlines, Dallas-Fort Worth International Airport, Texas 75261

H. Clayton Foushee (3), Northwest Airlines, St. Paul, Minnesota 55111

Robert C. Ginnett (71), Center for Creative Leadership, Colorado Springs, Colorado 80906

Steven E. Gregorich (173), San Jose State University, San Jose, California 95192

J. Richard Hackman (47), Department of Psychology, Harvard University, Cambridge, Massachusetts 02138

Robert L. Helmreich (3, 479), Department of Psychology, University of Texas at Austin, Austin, Texas 78712

Neil Johnston (367), Aerospace Psychology Research Group, Trinity College, Dublin 2, Ireland

Barbara G. Kanki (99, 479), Aerospace Human Factors Research Division, NASA–Ames Research Center, Moffett Field, California 94035

Phyllis J. Kayten (283), Federal Aviation Adminstration, Washington, D.C. 20591

Thomas M. Longridge (263), Federal Aviation Administration, Headquarters, Washington, D.C. 20041

Takao Mito (399), Japan Airlines, Tokyo International Airport, Haneda Ota-ku, Tokyo 144, Japan

Judith M. Orasanu (137), Aerospace Human Factors Research Division, NASA–Ames Research Center, Moffett Field, California 94035

Harry W. Orlady (447), Orlady Associates, Los Gatos, California 95032

Mark T. Palmer (99), Department of Communication Studies, Northwestern University, Evanston, Illinois 60201

Carolyn Prince (337), Human Factors Division, Naval Training Systems Center, Orlando, Florida 32826

Eduardo Salas (337), Human Factors Division, Naval Training Systems Center, Orlando, Florida 32826

Earl L. Wiener (199, 479), Department of Management Science, University of Miami, Coral Gables, Florida 33124

John A. Wilhelm (173), Department of Psychology, University of Texas at Austin, Austin, Texas 78712

Hisaaki Yamamori (399), Japan Airlines, Tokyo International Airport, Haneda Ota-ku, Tokyo 144, Japan

On the night of December 29, 1972 a Lockheed L-1011 with 163 passengers and 13 crewmembers aboard crashed 19 miles west–northwest of the Miami International Airport. Ninety-nine passengers and five crewmembers were fatally injured in this accident, which the National Transportation Safety Board (NTSB) attributed to "the failure of the crew to monitor the flight instruments during the final four minutes of flight, and to detect an unexpected descent soon enough to prevent impact with the ground." The Board further cited "preoccupation with a malfunction of the nose landing gear position indicating system [which] distracted the crew's attention from the instruments and allowed the descent to go unnoticed." Some, myself included, consider this to be a prototypical cockpit resource management (CRM) accident: A professional, well-trained, experienced flightcrew allowed a modern, well-equipped, well-designed, and well-maintained jet transport to fly into the ground because of a burned-out "59-cent" light bulb. Nobody was minding the store.

On June 19, 1989 a DC-10 crashed during an attempted emergency landing at Sioux City, nearly 45 minutes after a catastrophic, uncontained failure of the fan disk in the center engine severed lines in all three hydraulic systems, resulting in a total loss of the aircraft's hydraulically powered flight control systems. Fatal injuries were sustained by 110 of the 285 passengers and by 1 of the 11 crewmembers aboard the crippled aircraft. In its report on this accident, the NTSB commended the crew for its performance, noting that the pilot, copilot, flight engineer, and a DC-10 flight instructor who had been riding in the passenger cabin managed to devise a crude but workable method for partially controlling the control-less aircraft. Working together as a highly integrated team, this flightcrew salvaged much of what could have been a total disaster. Because of their performance, 185 people survived an otherwise unsurvivable situation.

Why the difference? What factors explain why the crews of these two widebody airliners behaved in starkly contrasting styles even though they had roughly comparable levels of flight experience and technical training?

Captain Al Haynes, the pilot of the DC-10, has frequently and publicly cited the training they received in "cockpit resource management" (CRM) as one of the most important ingredients in his crew's successful performance. He has described how he and his fellow crewmembers actively and consciously utilized the principles of CRM as the event was unfolding, and how this enabled these four skilled aviators to function as one skilled crew.

This book is about an unfolding but already proven human factors success story. It is a story of close collaboration between cognitive, behavioral, social, and organizational psychologists on the one hand, and airline pilots and training experts on the other; between the government and academic research communities, and private industry. From these diverse, and occasionally divergent, points of view has emerged a training concept and operational philosophy now being applied widely (but not universally) around the world, not only by civilian airlines, but by military operators as well. Furthermore, the lessons learned in the aviation context are now being applied in other fields including operations in nuclear power plants and surgical theaters. Other domains include law enforcement, space launches, and marine operations, just to name a few.

Like most good concepts, CRM is not new. Although I believe I was the first to use the phrase, some time around 1977 or so, antecedents abound. Many airlines had realized that safe and successful operation of commercial jet transport airplanes required more than the traditional "stick-and-rudder" skills, and that a "good stick" did not necessarily a good captain make. For example, Pan Am had incorporated "crew concept" into its training programs and operating manuals. Northwest had developed "coordinated crew training," or CCT, now known universally by another acronym, LOFT—line-oriented flight training. KLM and Lufthansa had both tackled the problem of flightcrew coordination and discipline, and Japan Airlines had formed a human factors working group to look at these and closely related issues. But none of these or many other early efforts had explicitly recognized that at heart, many crew-caused accidents resulted directly from the failure of flight crewmembers to identify and utilize resources—the hardware, software, and liveware, to borrow from Elwyn Edwards—readily available to them.

In the mid-1970s, there were several activities under way at NASA's Ames Research Center that played a strong role in the early history of CRM. With the cooperation and support of Pan Am management and pilots, Charlie Billings, George Cooper, and I had conducted a series of structured interviews with line pilots and flight engineers, primarily to learn their perceptions about human factors issues and how these affected their operations. One persistent comment we heard during these interviews was a general dissatisfaction with flightcrew training. However, this dissatisfaction was not directed toward the technical side of flight training; crewmembers felt that in general, they were well trained on aircraft systems and operating procedures. Rather, their concerns were directed toward something a bit more difficult to pin down, but which often included reference to leadership, command, communications, decision making, and similar concepts. Often, the most vocal complaints were from newly upgraded captains, who were learning the hard way that being a captain involved something considerably more than adding some gold braid to their uniforms and moving across the cockpit from the right to the left seat.

About the same time, George Cooper and Maury White did a detailed analysis of wordwide commercial jet transport accidents from 1968 to 1976. They noted that a large proportion of these accidents were associated with various failures of command, communication, and crew coordination. Miles Murphy did a similar analysis of several hundred incident reports which had been submitted to NASA's Aviation Safety Reporting System, with similar results.

And finally there was the now-classic "Ruffell Smith study." This landmark full-mission simulation study of airline flightcrew performance, conducted by the late H.P. Ruffell Smith, was instrumental in focusing our developing notions about the role of management skills in cockpit operations.

Based on these converging lines of research, we identified several factors common to aircrew performance observed in incidents, accidents, and simulator experiments:

1. Preoccupation with minor mechanical problems
2. Inadequate leadership
3. Failure to delegate tasks and assign responsibilities
4. Failure to set priorities
5. Inadequate monitoring
6. Failure to utilize available data
7. Failure to communicate intent and plans

In June, 1979 NASA sponsored a NASA/industry workshop on "Resource Management on the Flight Deck." This widely attended meeting served to focus the attention of the airline training community on some of the issues we had identified in our research, and also served as a forum for discussions between that community and others, including the academic community. Among those who actively participated in that meeting were Bob Helmreich from the University of Texas and one of his graduate students, Clay Foushee. Representatives from the FAA, NTSB, Air Line Pilots Association, Allied Pilots Association, and most major U.S. and several foreign airlines were in attendance. United Airlines had the largest group present, and left the meeting well prepared to push ahead with the development of their landmark CLR—Command, Leadership, and Resource Management—program.

Today it is difficult to pick up any publication dealing with aviation human factors or flightcrew training which does not contain some reference to CRM. Tremendous progress has been made in refining the concept and in the development of new ways to teach the skills necessary for good CRM. Success stories are becoming more frequent, but it does not take many instances like the story of United 232 at Sioux City to validate these concepts and methods. And yet we continue to have accidents and incidents caused by failures of *crew*, as opposed to *individual*, performance: Two weeks before these words were written, the NTSB found the probable cause of a fatal runway collision between two airline aircraft to be "a lack of proper crew coordination." Although much has been done, much remains to be done.

This book brings together for the first time the complex and rapidly changing developments in CRM and associated areas such as LOFT and the new advanced qualification program (AQP). The chapters that follow chronicle the emergence and continued development of the CRM concept. Although the authors are the leaders in this field, hundreds, if not thousands, of others in laboratories, classrooms, and cockpits are also key players. It is an exciting story, and one which offers great personal gratification: There are few more rewarding efforts than those which result in the saving of lives.

John K. Lauber, Member
National Transportation Safety Board
Washington, D.C.

Preface

When our late colleague H. Patrick Ruffell Smith launched his classic study of flightcrew performance in a Boeing 747 simulator in the late 1970s, he could not have dreamed of what would come of that project. The experiment was originally planned to investigate pilot vigilance, workload, and response to stress. A thorough exploration of those variables would have been enough of a contribution: They are still poorly understood today, despite the best efforts of many talented researchers. What Ruffell Smith did was to open the door to a new realm of human factors, which the author of our Foreword, John Lauber, later named "cockpit resource management" (CRM).

Although crew coordination and teamwork had always been a part of military and airline training, the emphasis was primarily on individual skilled behavior. The CRM movement, while in no way diminishing the importance of traditional pilot skills and airmanship, has brought into focus the necessity for highly trained individual crewmembers to work together as a team. This lesson is dramatically documented in the chapters by Kayten on the role of CRM, or lack of it, in aircraft accidents, and by Byrnes and Black on the experience of their company, which had prided itself on being a "captain's airline." Just what it means to be a captain's airline is not clear. One interpretation could be that in their decision-making capacity, captains are not second-guessed by management, which is healthy. Another interpretation could be that only the captain asserts him- or herself in the cockpit, which is a position that probably calls for a CRM program.

CRM training, like any novel approach to a well-established, tradition-bound enterprise, was not universally acclaimed in its early years. Many airline managements dragged their feet; they claimed that they were doing it anyway, just not under the name of CRM. And besides, who had any proof that the new training was effective? The Federal Aviation Administration (FAA) viewed the field with a degree of skepticism and did not react to a string of recommendations from the National Transportation Safety Board (NTSB) that CRM training be required of the nation's airlines.

Even today CRM is not a training requirement, though it is encouraged by an FAA Advisory Circular (AD 120-35A). More positive steps have come from the FAA in requiring stringent CRM training, evaluation, and database management under its Advanced Qualification Program, which will reshape the nature of aircrew training as we head into the next century. The FAA has wisely avoided telling the airlines *how* to conduct CRM training and evaluation, recognizing that the field is in its infancy and concluding that it would be better to encourage creativity and imagination, rather than strict adherence to a set of regulations. Airline training departments are free to devise their own programs, to borrow from each other, and to enlist talented academicians and government scientists, whose research took off where Ruffell Smith's had ended.

As cockpit technology leaped ahead, driven by the microprocessor revolution, and duties previously performed by three-pilot crews were assumed by two-pilot crews, effective crew coordination, communication, and leadership skills became even more important. Parallel developments occurred in the design and proliferation of simulators. Modern simulators have permitted use of full-mission simulation, or LOFT (line-oriented flight training). LOFT provides the organizations with a means of creating conditions requiring the practice of effective crew coordination to resolve complex emergency situations. It is also the instrument for reinforcing and evaluating the concepts learned in the CRM classroom. Video recordings taken during the LOFT furnish the instructors with a tool capable of providing trainees with a richer form of feedback than had ever been available.

As the field of CRM grew in importance, an ever-expanding literature emerged from several universities and government research installations, primarily the University of Texas and NASA–Ames Research Center, whose work has dominated the field in the last decade. The research reports flowing from this effort were inevitably scattered through journals and government documents, while organizational experience tended not to be documented at all.

So we decided that it was time for a book that would gather the research, organizational experience, and government activities in one place. We have assembled a team of contributors who are not only experts in their field, but who constitute the first generation of experts. We feel that the book is a "balanced portfolio": Our contributors are about evenly divided between academia, government, and private enterprise. Although the United States has been the leader in the field, significant advances have been made in other nations. Johnston's chapter gives a view from Europe, Yamamori and Mito's from Asia.

The design of the book is such that the chapters can be read in order, moving from broad treatments of the general nature of CRM to specific perspectives and application areas, and finally to two concluding chapters. Or the chapters can be read in any order as stand-alone treatises.

Our aim has been to produce a book that would appeal to a wide audience:

pilots, government officials, training experts, and safety personnel and management, whether airline, military, or corporate, just to name a few. Our contributors have minimized the use of arcane jargon, writing for an audience interested in, but not necessarily trained in, human factors. We hope that the book will also appeal to students and practitioners of applied social psychology and human factors engineering. Although not written as a textbook, it could be used as such in courses in applied psychology and aviation technology.

We are pleased with our choice of John K. Lauber to write the Foreword. No single person has done more, both as a NASA researcher and a member of the NTSB, to advance the field of CRM throughout the world, and to gain recognition of the contribution of the behavioral sciences to flight safety.

The editors recognize the many persons, too numerous to name, at the University of Miami, NASA–Ames, and the University of Texas who have supported and encouraged us. We also acknowledge the support for our research efforts of many airlines in the United States and elsewhere, and the Air Line Pilots Association. We are also grateful to the staff of Academic Press for their very professional help.

We dedicate this volume to the thousands of aircraft crewmembers throughout the world whose participation and experiences have made CRM research and training possible.

Earl L. Wiener
Barbara G. Kanki
Robert L. Helmreich

I

The Nature of CRM

Why Crew Resource Management? Empirical and Theoretical Bases of Human Factors Training in Aviation

Robert L. Helmreich
Department of Psychology
University of Texas at Austin
Austin, Texas 78712

H. Clayton Foushee
Northwest Airlines
St. Paul, Minnesota 55111

INTRODUCTION ✈

One of the most striking developments in aviation safety during the past decade has been the overwhelming endorsement and widespread implementation of training programs aimed at increasing the effectiveness of crew coordination and flightdeck management. Civilian and military organizations have developed programs that address team and managerial aspects of flight operations as complements to traditional training that stresses the technical, "stick-and-rudder" aspects of flight. The original, generic label for such training was *cockpit resource management*, but with recognition of the applicability of the approach to other members of the aviation community including cabin crews, flight dispatchers, and maintenance personnel, the term *crew resource management* (CRM) is coming into general use.

Just as CRM has evolved from "cockpit" to "crew" over its short history, the field of human factors has similarly changed in its scope. From an initial marriage of engineering and psychology with a focus on "knobs and dials," contemporary human factors has become a multidisciplinary field that draws on the methods and principles of the behavioral and social sciences, engineering, and physiology to optimize human performance and reduce human error (National Research Council, 1989). From this broader perspective, human factors can be viewed as the applied science of people working together with devices. Just as the performance and safety of a system can be degraded because of poor hardware or software design and/or inadequate operator training, so too can system effectiveness be reduced by errors in the design and management of crew-level tasks and of organizations. CRM is thus the application of human factors in the aviation system. John K. Lauber (1984), a psychologist member of the National Transportation Safety Board (NTSB), has defined CRM as "using all available resources—information, equipment, and people—to achieve safe and efficient flight operations" (p. 20). CRM includes optimizing not only the person–machine interface and the acquisition of timely, appropriate information, but also interpersonal activities including leadership, effective team formation and maintenance, problem-solving, decision-making, and maintaining situation awareness. Thus training in CRM involves communicating basic knowledge of human factors concepts that relate to aviation and providing the tools necessary to apply these concepts operationally. It represents a new focus on crew-level (as opposed to individual-level) aspects of training and operations.

This chapter's title inquires why an industry would embrace change to an approach that has resulted in the safest means of transportation available and has produced generations of highly competent, well-qualified pilots. In seeking the answer, we examine both the historic, single-pilot tradition in aviation and what we know about the causes of error and accidents in the system. These considerations lead us to the conceptual framework, rooted in social psychology, that encompasses group behavior and team performance. In this context we can look at efforts to improve crew coordination and performance through training. Finally, we discuss what research has told us about the effectiveness of these efforts and what questions remain unanswered.

THE SINGLE-PILOT TRADITION IN AVIATION ——— ✈

The evolution of concern with crew factors must be considered in the historical context of flight. In the early years, the image of a pilot was of a single, stalwart individual, white scarf trailing, braving the elements in an open cockpit. This stereotype embraces a number of personality traits such as independence, machismo, bravery, and calmness under stress that are more associated with individual activity than with team effort. It is likely that, as with many stereotypes, this one may have a factual basis, as individuals with these attributes may have been disproportionately attracted to careers in aviation, and organizations may have been predisposed to select candidates reflecting this prototype.

As aircraft grew more complex and the limitations and fallibility of pilots more evident, provision was made for a co-pilot to provide support for the pilot, to reduce individual workload and decrease the probability of human error. However, these additional crewmembers were initially perceived more as redundant systems to be used as backups than as participants in a team endeavor. Ernest K. Gann (1961) and other pioneers of air transport have documented the distinctly secondary role played by the co-pilot in early airline operations.

The tradition in training and evaluation has similarly focused on the individual pilot and his or her technical proficiency (Hackman & Helmreich, 1987). This begins with initial selection and training, which have historically used aptitude and performance standards developed for single-pilot operations. Indeed, the first critical event in a pilot's career is the solo flight. Even in multipilot operations, the major emphasis continues to be on evaluating the individual proficiency of crewmembers. Regulations surrounding the qualification and certification of pilots reinforce these practices and can even result in negative training. For example, if crewmembers are cautioned not to provide assistance to pilots whose proficiency is being evaluated, a model of individual instead of team action is being reinforced. Indeed, in 1952 the guidelines for proficiency checks at one major airline categorically stated that the first officer should not correct errors made by the captain (H. Orlady, personal communication cited in Foushee & Helmreich, 1988). The critical point is that the aviation community has operated on the assumption that crews composed of able and well-trained individuals can and will operate complicated aircraft in a complex environment both safely and efficiently.

HUMAN ERROR IN FLIGHT OPERATIONS ———— ✈

The introduction of reliable turbojet transports in the 1950s was associated with a dramatic reduction in air transport accidents. As problems with airframes and engines diminished, attention turned to identifying and eliminating other sources of failure in flight safety. Figure 1.1 gives statistics on the causes of accidents from 1959 through 1989, indicating that flightcrew actions were causal

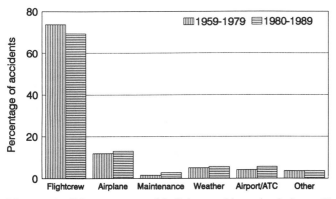

Figure 1.1 Primary causes of hull loss accidents (excluding military and sabotage): worldwide commercial jet fleet, 1959–1989. Data from Boeing Aircraft Company.

in more than 70% of worldwide accidents involving aircraft damage beyond economical repair. Recognition of this human performance problem stimulated a number of independent efforts to understand what the term "pilot error" encompassed and what could be done to reduce it.

The formal record of investigations into aircraft accidents, such as those conducted by the NTSB, provides chilling documentation of instances where crew coordination has failed at critical moments.

- A crew, distracted by the failure of a landing gear indicator light, failing to notice that the automatic pilot was disengaged and allowing the aircraft to descend into a swamp.
- A co-pilot, concerned that take-off thrust was not properly set during a departure in a snowstorm, failing to get the attention of the captain with the aircraft stalling and crashing into the Potomac River.
- A crew failing to review instrument landing charts and their navigational position with respect to the airport and further disregarding repeated Ground Proximity Warning System alerts before crashing into a mountain below the minimum descent altitude.
- A crew distracted by nonoperational communications failing to complete checklists and crashing on take-off because the flaps were not extended.
- A breakdown in communications between a captain, co-pilot, and Air Traffic Control regarding fuel state and a crash following complete fuel exhaustion.
- A crew crashing on take-off because of icing on the wings after having inquired about de-icing facilities. In the same accident, the failure of a flight attendant to communicate credible concerns about the need for de-icing expressed by pilot passengers.

The theme in each of these cases is human error resulting from failures in interpersonal communications. By the time these accidents occurred, the formal study of human error in aviation had a long tradition (e.g., Fitts & Jones, 1947; Davis, 1948). However, research efforts tended to focus on traditional human factors issues surrounding the interface of the individual operator with equipment. This type of investigation did not seem to address many of the factors identified as causal in jet transport accidents, and researchers began to broaden the scope of their inquiry.

In the United States, a team of investigators at NASA–Ames Research Center began to explore broader human factors issues in flight operations. Charles Billings, John Lauber, and George Cooper developed a structured interview protocol and used it to gather firsthand information from airline pilots regarding human factors in crew operations and "pilot error" accidents. At the same time, George Cooper and Maurice White analyzed the causes of jet transport accidents occurring between 1968 and 1976 (Cooper, White, & Lauber, 1980), while Miles Murphy performed a similar analysis of incidents reported to NASA's confidential

Aviation Safety Reporting System (Murphy, 1980). The conclusion drawn from these investigations was that "pilot error" in documented accidents and incidents was more likely to reflect failures in team communication and coordination than deficiencies in "stick-and-rudder" proficiency. A number of specific problem areas were identified, including workload management and task delegation, situation awareness, leadership, use of available resources including other crewmembers, manuals, air traffic control, interpersonal communications (including unwillingness of junior crewmembers to speak up in critical situations), and the process of building and maintaining an effective team relationship on the flightdeck.

In Europe, Elwyn Edwards (1972) drew on the record of accident investigation and developed his SHEL model of human factors in system design and operations. The acronym represents *software*, usually documents governing operations; *hardware*, the physical resources available; *liveware*, consisting of the human operators composing the crew; and *environment*, the external context in which the system operates. Elaborating his model to examine the functioning of the liveware, Edwards (1975) defined a new concept, the trans-cockpit authority gradient (TAG). The TAG refers to the fact that captains must establish an optimal working relationship with other crewmembers, with the captain's role and authority neither over- nor underemphasized.

In the operational community in the early 1970s, Pan American World Airways management became concerned about crew training issues following several "pilot error" accidents in the Pacific. In 1974, a flight operations review team headed by David D. Thomas, retired Deputy Administrator of the Federal Aviation Administration (FAA), examined all aspects of flightcrew training and made a number of significant recommendations. The foremost of these was to utilize "crew concept training." Under this approach, both simulator training and checking were to be conducted not as single-pilot evolutions but in the context of a full crew conducting coordinated activities. At the same time, Pan Am manuals were revised to incorporate crew concepts and to explain more completely responsibilities for team activities and communications. These actions represented a fundamental change in the operating environment and provided an organizational framework for more effective crew coordination. Although the focus in training was now on crew activities, the shift was not accompanied by a program of formal instruction in communications and coordination. Crewmembers were mandated to operate as effective teams but were left to develop means of achieving this goal without formal guidance and instruction.

Identifying crew-level issues as central to a high proportion of accidents and incidents was a significant achievement in the process of understanding the determinants of safety in flight operations. However, development of successful strategies to improve crew performance requires an understanding of the determinants of group behavior and how they can be influenced. In the following section we describe a model of group processes and performance and its implications for training and organizational actions.

GROUP PROCESSES AND PERFORMANCE IN THE AVIATION ENVIRONMENT ✈

The study of group behavior has historically been the province of social psychology and provides the conceptual basis for the three-factor model of the determinants of group performance we presented in an earlier discussion of flightcrew interaction and performance (Foushee & Helmreich, 1988; McGrath, 1964). Subsequent research has enabled us to expand and refine the model, and we present it as a framework for discussing issues surrounding CRM training. The model defines three major components of group behavior: *input factors*, which include characteristics of individuals, groups, organizations, and the operational environment; *group process factors*, which include the nature and quality of interactions among group members; and *outcome factors*, which include primary outcomes such as safety and efficiency of operations and secondary outcomes such as member satisfaction, motivation, attitudes, and so on. The underlying assumption of the model is that input factors both provide the framework and determine the nature of group processes that lead, in turn, to the various outcomes. Figure 1.2 shows the three factors and their interrelationships. A central feature of the model is feedback loops among the factors. Outcomes (right side of figure; either positive or negative) may change components of input factors (left side; e.g., attitudes and norms), and these changes may alter subsequent group processes (middle) and outcomes. Outcomes may theoretically also influence group pro-

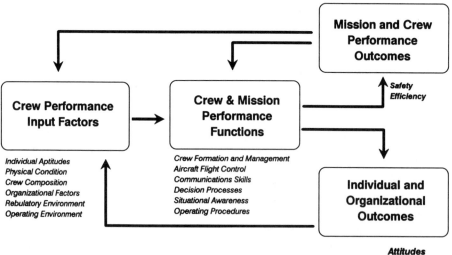

Figure 1.2   Flightcrew performance model.

cesses without being directly mediated by input factors. It is the iterative nature of the factors determining group performance that makes its study both complex and challenging.

Outcome Factors

Primary outcome factors are readily recognizable and relatively easily quantifiable. In flight operations safety is paramount, but the efficient completion of missions and compliance with organizational and regulatory requirements are also important. Both experience and training can create changes in crew attitudes and norms regarding appropriate flightdeck management. The quality of group processes, influenced by organizational, group, regulatory, and environmental factors, determines the satisfaction crews experience with operations and their motivation for future operations.

Outcome factors form the criteria against which the impact of interventions such as training or organizational policy changes are measured. While the most compelling measure of effectiveness in aviation would be a decrease in the frequency of accidents, such events are (happily) already so infrequent that reliable statistical evidence can only be found by aggregating data over extremely long periods of time. Accordingly, criteria of group performance need to be drawn from surrogate measures such as records of operational errors, expert ratings of crew effectiveness, and measures of attitude and job satisfaction.

Input Factors

A number of qualitatively different variables form the inputs to group processes. These have multiple components that, singly and in combination, influence the way teams interact. Figure 1.3 expands the input factors portion of the model to include lower-order variables that have a demonstrated influence on group processes and outcomes.

Individual Factors

Consideration of a flightcrew's job in today's airspace brings to mind a number of background or input factors that can influence the effectiveness of crew activities even before an engine is started. Teams are composed of individuals who bring to the flightdeck their knowledge, skills, personalities, motivation, and physical and emotional states. Each of these characteristics has been identified as causal in one or more aircraft accidents.

Physical condition includes fatigue, which can undermine vigilance in a knowledgeable and motivated pilot. Emotional state is determined by a variety of life stresses (for example, marital discord or worries about the financial condition and viability of an airline) that cannot be left at the gate and can subtly undermine effectiveness. Aptitude (including intelligence and psychomotor skills) has

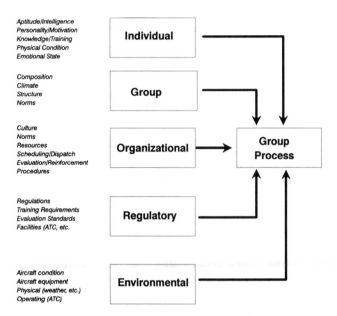

Figure 1.3 Flightcrew performance model: expanded input factors.

long been recognized as critical to success as a pilot, and selection has emphasized these attributes. Recent research has also confirmed that personality factors are significant determinants of individual and team performance. A full-mission simulation study was run with volunteer, three-person crews in the NASA–Ames Boeing 727 simulator. The study explored the impact of leader personality factors on crew performance (Chidester, Kanki, Foushee, Dickinson, & Bowles, 1990). Crewmembers participating in the study were pretested on a personality battery that had been validated as predictive of flightcrew behavior (Chidester, Helmreich, Gregorich, & Geis, 1991). Three experimental groups were composed on the basis of the captain's personality constellation. One group was led by captains high on both goal orientation and interpersonal skills. A second group had captains who were high on goal orientation but relatively low on the interpersonal dimension. The third group was led by captains who were quite low on both goal orientation and positive interpersonal dimensions.

Each crew flew five complete flight segments spread across two days. On two of the legs, mechanical malfunctions occurred which were compounded by poor weather conditions at the destination airport. Crew performance was rated by expert observers, and technical errors were coded from computer records and videotapes of the flights. The data showed significant differences in performance between groups that could be attributed to the leader's personality. Crews led by captains high in both achievement needs and interpersonal skills performed uniformly well across all segments. In contrast, crews led by captains low on both of these dimensions were significantly less effective across all flights. Those in the third group, with captains high in achievement needs but low in interpersonal traits, were given poorer performance ratings initially but improved substantially by the fifth leg. One interpretation of this finding is that crews in this condition learned over time how to adapt to this difficult but motivated type of leader. The point relevant to this discussion is that a single input factor (personality) can be isolated as an influence on the performance of a well-trained and qualified crew in a controlled research setting.

Attitudes serve as guides for behavior and are another of the input factors that crews bring to the flightdeck. The *Cockpit management attitudes questionnaire* (*CMAQ*, Helmreich, 1984; Helmreich, Wilhelm, & Gregorich, 1988) is a 25-item, Likert-scaled battery that allows quantification of attitudes regarding crew coordination, flightdeck management, and personal capabilities under conditions of fatigue and stress. Attitudes measured by the *CMAQ* have been validated as predictors of outcome factors in the form of expert ratings of performance in line operations (Helmreich, Foushee, Benson, & Russini, 1986), thus demonstrating the linkage between input and outcome factors. Measures such as the *CMAQ* can be used both to assess input factors in organizations and as measures of outcomes to determine whether programs such as CRM can change attitudes.

Group Factors

Crews are composed of individuals who bring with them all the attributes noted above. They may be cohesive and effective or divisive, rancorous, and ineffectual depending on the mix of individuals and their states that comes together at any given time. The climate that develops in a group is multiply determined by the characteristics of individual members, by the structure imposed by the formal and informal norms of the organization, and by the quality and style of leadership present. Because of the many individual and group factors identified, research into these issues and their effects is difficult and time-consuming. As a result there is not an extensive literature on the outcome effects of systematically varying multiple individual- and group-level variables, especially in the aviation environment.

Organizational Factors

The culture of an organization is a critical input factor. If an organization sanctions individual actions rather than team coordination, both processes and outcomes are likely to have a very different flavor from those in organizations that stress crew actions and responsibility. The level of training and type of formal evaluation given to crews are also influential. Manuals and formal procedures also form part of the operational setting, as do the resources that the organization has and makes available for crews (including crew scheduling practices, maintenance support, flight planning, dispatching, etc.).

Another NASA simulation study examined the performance implications of several individual- and group-level factors. Foushee, Lauber, Baetge, & Acomb (1986) examined the interactions and performance of experienced two-person jet transport crews flying a realistic scenario in a Boeing 737 simulator. NASA was directed by the U.S. Congress to investigate the operational significance of pilot fatigue—an individual factor driven by organizational and regulatory practices. The experimental design reflected this concern and divided crews into two groups, pre-duty (defined as flying the scenario after a minimum of two days off as if it were the first leg of a three-day trip) and post-duty (flying the scenario as the last segment of a three-day trip). The scenario was characterized by poor weather conditions that necessitated an unexpected missed approach that was complicated by a hydraulic system failure. Following the hydraulic failure, crews were faced with a high-workload situation involving the selection of an alternate destination while coping with problems such as the requirement to extend gear and flaps manually and fly an approach at higher than normal speed.

Crews in the post-duty condition had less pre-simulation sleep and reported significantly more fatigue, as expected from the research design. The surprising finding, however, was that fatigued crews were rated as performing significantly better and made fewer serious operational errors than the rested, pre-duty crews. This finding was counterintuitive but had major implications relevant to the importance of team formation and experience. By the nature of the scheduling of flight operations, most crews in the post-duty condition had just completed three days of operations as a team, while those in the pre-duty condition normally did not have the benefit of recent experience with the other crewmember. When the data were reanalyzed on the basis of whether or not crews had flown together recently, the performance differences became even stronger. The findings suggest that crew scheduling practices that result in continuing recomposition of groups and a need for frequent formation of new teams can have significant operational implications. For example, three recent takeoff accidents in the United States (one involving a stall under icing conditions, one an aborted takeoff with an over-run into water, and one a runway collision after the crew became lost in dense fog) involved crews paired together for the first time.[1] The implications of crew pairings are discussed further in the chapter by Hackman.

Environmental Factors

Weather conditions constitute an environmental input factor outside the control of flightcrews. The ability of organizations and the government to provide accurate, timely information on weather constitutes one of the factors governing

[1]One involved a DC-9 taking off in a snowstorm at Denver, the second a rejected take off by a B-737 at New York–LaGuardia, and the third a DC-9 that erroneously taxied onto the active runway and collided with a B-727 taking off.

both group processes and outcomes. The physical condition of the aircraft (including inoperative equipment, etc.) also determines part of the field in which the crew must operate as does the availability and quality of navigational aids.

Regulatory Factors

Regulatory practices also influence the nature of crew interaction and performance. For example, the "sterile cockpit" rule in the U.S. proscribes non-operational communications below 10,000 feet. As described above, the focus of regulation has been on individual training and evaluation, and this has been echoed in organizational policies (recall the prohibition on first officers correcting captain's mistakes during proficiency checks). Ambiguity in regulations can also impact crews' decisions and actions. If the regulations governing an operation are unclear, responsibility shifts to the organization that can direct operations to meet operational goals and to the captain who must take ultimate responsibility for decisions regarding the safety of flight.

A Case Study: The Interplay of Multiple Input Factors in a Crash

Investigation of the human factors surrounding the crash of a Fokker F-28 on takeoff in Canada demonstrates the interplay of input factors at the regulatory, organizational, environmental, and individual levels. In this accident it can be seen how all of these can intersect to create an operational environment that fails to provide needed safeguards against pilot error (Helmreich, 1992; Moshansky, 1992). On a snowy winter afternoon the crew of Air Ontario Flight 1363 attempted a takeoff from Dryden, Ontario, with an accumulation of snow and ice on the wings and crashed because the aircraft could not gain enough lift to clear trees beyond the end of the runway. In the crash and resulting fire, 29 passengers and crewmembers, including both pilots, were killed. In attempting to understand how a crew with many years of experience operating in the severe winter weather of northern Ontario could make such a serious operational error, a number of input factors were uncovered which, operating in concert, set the stage for a tragically wrong decision.

At the *environmental* level, the weather was poor and deteriorating, forcing the crew to select distant alternate landing sites and to carry extra fuel. Because of the poor weather, the flight was operating more than an hour late and was full, operating at maximum gross weight. The aircraft itself had a number of mechanical problems, the most serious of which was an inoperative auxiliary power unit (APU). With an inoperative APU, it was necessary to keep an engine running during stops at airports without ground start capabilities. Dryden had no such facilities.

At the *regulatory* level, the Canadian regulations regarding de-icing prohibited an aircraft from commencing a flight "when the amount of frost, snow, or ice adhering to the wings, control surfaces, or propeller of the aeroplane may adversely affect the safety of flight" (Moshansky, 1989).[2] The problem facing the crew under existing regulations was how, under time and operational pressures, to determine what constituted enough contamination to "adversely affect" safety of flight. The regulation as written made the takeoff decision at the captain's discretion and, at the same time, failed to provide safeguards against personal and organizational pressures to complete the mission at all costs.

The regulatory agency's surveillance of the airline had not focused on the newly initiated jet operation. While an audit of the airline's operations had been completed during the preceding year, the audit did not include the F-28 operation. A more complete examination might have revealed procedural and organizational discrepancies in the F-28 operation, as noted below.

A number of *organizational* factors served to increase the stress level of the crew. The airline had just begun operating jet transports and had little operational experience with this type of equipment. Initial crews for the Fokker had been trained at two different U.S. airlines before the operation was initiated. The airline had not developed its own operating manuals, and some crewmembers were carrying manuals from one airline and others from another. The organization had not developed an approved minimum equipment list (MEL) specifying what equipment could be inoperative in normal passenger operations. Dispatchers had received only minimal training for this type of aircraft and were experienced only with small propeller-driven equipment. The flight release for the day of the accident contained a number of errors. In sum, the crew was operating without a high level of organizational support and resources.

The airline itself was the product of the merger of two regional airlines with very different operational cultures. One had operated in the north of Canada as what was often called a "bush" operation. The other had operated in southern Ontario in a more traditional airline environment. The chief pilot of the Fokker fleet had come from the northern operation and had himself had two serious incidents involving take-offs with ice on the wings—experiences that had earned him the nickname of "Iceman." These practices suggest the possibility that norms and pressures existed to operate with wing contamination. The ambiguous regulation (see p. 13) provided no safeguard against such norms and pressures.

As *individuals*, both crewmembers had extensive experience in Canadian operations. The captain had more than 24,000 flight hours and the co-pilot more than 10,000. However, neither had much experience in jet transport operations, the captain having accumulated 81 hours in the F-28 and the first officer 65. The captain had been a chief pilot and instructor and was known for adherence to procedures. The first officer was a former captain described as having a somewhat abrasive personality. He also had a history of difficulties in completing some stick-

---

[2]In response to a recommendation by the Commission of Inquiry into the crash, the regulation was changed to prohibit operation with *any* contamination of lifting surfaces.

and-rudder maneuvers and had required additional supervision and training before qualifying in new aircraft.

As a *group*, the crew had only flown together for two days. The fact that the crew lacked operational familiarity with each other and with the aircraft, along with the fact that both were accustomed to flying as captains, may have influenced the processes surrounding their conduct of the flight. In addition, the captain came from the more structured southern airline, while the first officer's experience was in the less formal northern operation.

When the aircraft landed to pick up passengers at Dryden, the crew faced a complex and stressful situation. Weather was deteriorating further, with heavy snow falling. Refueling was needed before departure, but this would necessitate keeping an engine running because of the inoperative APU. The cabin manual prohibited refueling with passengers aboard and an engine running, but the cockpit manuals were silent on this issue. The flight attendants were not alerted to the need to refuel with an engine running. The manufacturer's manual further prohibited de-icing with an engine running because of possible ingestion of fluid into the powerplant. The flight was falling further behind its schedule, and many passengers were facing the prospect of missing connecting flights if there was an additional delay for de-icing.

Faced with these contingencies, the crew chose to refuel with passengers aboard and an engine running. It is known that the captain considered de-icing, because he inquired about the availability of equipment and was told that it could be provided. Ultimately, however, the crew chose to take off without de-icing. Having reached this decision, a further environmental factor intervened in the form of a small plane, flying under visual flight rule (VFR) conditions, which made an emergency landing, causing additional delay until the runway was cleared.

There were also several experienced pilots, including two airline captains, seated as passengers in the main cabin. They survived and testified to being aware of the need for de-icing and the associated threat to safety. One of them expressed his concerns about icing to the lead flight attendant but was told (falsely) that the aircraft had automatic de-icing equipment. These credible concerns were never communicated to the flightdeck by the flight attendants. This failure in communication is understandable in light of organizational norms regarding cabin–cockpit communication on safety issues. One of the managers of flight attendant training testified that flight attendants were trained not to question flightcrews' judgment regarding safety issues.

Because the cockpit voice recorder was destroyed in the fire following the crash, it is impossible to reconstruct the interaction processes that led to the decision to depart Dryden without de-icing. While there was unquestionably human error in that decision, to stop at this conclusion would be to ignore the extent to which the input factors set the stage for the outcome.

Group Process Factors

Group process factors have historically been the least studied and least understood aspects of team performance. Much of the research that has been done, especially in operational settings, has looked at input and outcome factors, leaving the intervening process as a block box (e.g., Foushee, 1984: Foushee & Helmreich, 1988: Hackman & Morris, 1975). Input factors are manifested in the types of interactions that occur when individuals and machines come together to execute complex tasks in a complex environment. The fact that process variables have been largely ignored in research does not indicate a lack of awareness of their importance; rather, it reflects the difficulty of conceptualizing and measuring them. There are a number of important and theoretically interesting questions regarding flightcrew group processes: (1) How do individuals come together as strangers and forge a cohesive team that can operate effectively after only a brief acquaintance? (2) How is team workload managed and delegated? (3) What means are used to integrate ambiguous and incomplete data to reach optimum decisions? (4) How does stress induced by fatigue, emergencies, and personal experiences influence the way teams communicate and operate? (5) What is the nature of effective and ineffective leadership among flightcrews?

Group processes are manifested primarily through verbal communications, and these provide the record that we can use to understand how teams function in flight operations. Fortunately, there is a growing base of empirical research on group processes among flightcrews, much of it from experimental flight simulations. As Foushee (1984) has pointed out, modern flight simulators provide investigators with an extraordinarily useful research setting. Simulation provides high experimental realism including visual, motion, and auditory cues. Major aspects of flight operations can be reproduced, including mechanical problems, weather, air-to-ground communications, and cabin–cockpit interactions. Flight-plans can be generated and normal and abnormal operations between real air-ports simulated. Having experienced crews "fly" familiar equipment using nor-mal procedures and manuals further enhances the external validity and generality of findings from simulations. Participants in experimental simulations report that realism is high and that motivation is comparable to that in regular line opera-tions. Because simulators can be programmed to provide an identical operating environment for each crew, it is possible to gain statistical power by exposing many crews to the same conditions. To isolate causal factors, operational factors can be experimentally varied for different subgroups of participants: for example, the manipulation of recent experience in the simulation addressing fatigue. The simulator computer provides a record of the crew's physical actions controlling the aircraft, while video and audio recordings capture the interpersonal aspect of flight. The simulations described earlier have yielded important data on the impact of input factors such as operational experience and personality and have also allowed quantification of the processes involved.

Although not designed as a study of group processes, an experimental simulation sponsored by NASA and conducted by the late H. Patrick Ruffell Smith (1979) is a powerful demonstration of the operational significance of crew interactions. Eighteen airline crews flew a two-segment flight in a Boeing 747 simulator. The scenario consisted of a short flight from Washington, D.C., to John F. Kennedy Airport in New York and a subsequent leg from New York to London. After departing from New York, the crew experienced an oil pressure problem that forced them to shut down an engine. Because the flight could not be completed with a failed engine, the crew had to decide where to land. This decision was complicated by the further failure of a hydraulic system, deteriorating weather at possible landing sites, complex instructions from air traffic control, and a cabin crewmember who repeatedly requested information and assistance from the flightdeck at times of high workload. The study showed a remarkable amount of variability in the effectiveness with which crews handled the situation. Some crews managed the problems very well, while others committed a large number of operationally serious errors, including one miscalculation of more than 100,000 pounds in dumping fuel. The primary conclusion drawn from the study was that most problems and errors were induced by breakdowns in crew coordination rather than by deficits in technical knowledge and skills. For example, many errors occurred when individuals performing a task were interrupted by demands from other crewmembers or were overloaded with a variety of tasks requiring immediate action. In other cases, poor leadership was evident and resulted in a failure to exchange critical information in a timely manner.

The cockpit voice data from the study were subsequently analyzed by Foushee & Manos (1981) to quantify the processes related to variability in group performance. Their approach grew out of social psychological research into information flow within groups (e.g., Bales, 1950) and involved classifying each speech act as to type (i.e., observations regarding flight status, inquiries seeking information, etc.). The findings were clear: crews who communicated more overall tended to perform better and, in particular, those who exchanged more information about flight status committed fewer errors in the handling of engines and hydraulic and fuel systems and the reading and setting of instruments.

This methodology has been subsequently refined by Barbara Kanki and her colleagues at NASA–Ames Research Center and applied to communications records from additional experimental simulations. Kanki, Lozito, & Foushee (1989) and Kanki & Foushee (1989) examined communications patterns among crews in the previously described fatigue simulation (Foushee et al., 1986). For example, in the Kanki et al. study, sequences of communications were classified in terms of initiator and target as well as content. Initiating communications were classified as *commands, questions, observations,* and *dysfluencies* (e.g., ungrammatical or incomplete statements), while responses were classified as *replies* (responses greater than simple acknowledgments), *acknowledgments,* or *zero response*. Over and above the typical (and prescribed) occurrences of command–acknowledgment sequences, this study found that greater information transfer in the form of "commands" structuring activities and acknowledgments validating actions was associated with more effective crew performance.

Communications sequences were contrasted between crews committing a large number of operational errors and those making few. Although some specific patterns (such as that noted above) are worth special note, the primary finding of the study was the homogeneity of patterns characterizing the low-error crews. This was interpreted as the adoption of a more standard, hence more predictable form of communication. High-error crews, in contrast, showed a great diversity of speech patterns. Kanki and Palmer further discuss the status of communications research as it relates to flightcrews in their chapter.

Orasanu (1991) has conducted additional analyses of decision-making by crews in this simulation and has identified four components that support the decision process and differentiate effective from ineffective crews. This decision strategy includes *situation assessment, metacognitive processes* in forming action plans, *shared mental models* based on intra-crew communication of both situation assessment and plans, and *resource management* that encompasses task prioritization and delegation of specific responsibilities. Orasanu's formulation is congruent with basic principles of CRM and can be translated into prescriptive training. Several airlines have incorporated these findings and concepts into their CRM training. This research and a growing empirical and theoretical literature question traditional theories of decision making that are based on the assumption of a "rational," but biased, Bayesian decision maker (e.g., Klein, Orasanu, Calderwood, & Zsambok, in press). In particular, this approach emphasizes differences between decision-making by experts in natural settings with high stakes and time pressure, and the processes employed by naive subjects in the constrained, laboratory environments frequently employed in decision research. Orasanu summarizes the state of knowledge in this area in her chapter.

Data from the Chidester et al. (1990) simulation involving personality factors were coded and analyzed to isolate decision-making processes while crews dealt with multiple inflight abnormalities—a jammed stabilizer and low oil pressure on one engine (Mosier, 1991). It was found that the majority of crews utilized a strategy consistent with Thordsen & Klein's (1989) team decision model. Sampling of information and repeated verification of the accuracy of situation assessment continued throughout the decision process. Many crews made preliminary, revocable decisions as soon as they felt they had enough critical data about the problem. The implication of this finding is that, while thorough assessment of the situation is critical, crews make decisions without having all relevant information. Indeed, the best-performing crews collected information pertinent to situation evaluation *after* making a final decision as a means of confirming the decision. In contrast, high-error crews showed a diverse pattern of interactions.

In a field investigation of group formation and interaction processes among three-person airline crews, Ginnett (1987) observed crews from their formation on the ground prior to the first flight of a multi-day trip, and in the cockpit on each flight segment. He found that the quality of the initial briefing was associated with better crew performance throughout the trip. Captains of effective crews communicated the team concept and elaborated or affirmed the rules, norms, and task boundaries that constitute the organizational structure (what Hackman, 1987, has called the "organizational shell") in this first encounter. Leaders of less effective crews showed a variety of interaction patterns. Thus in both studies there was consistency among crews rated as performing well and diversity among the less effective teams. These team issues are discussed in the chapter by Ginnett.

Elaborating Group Process Factors

Building on research with flightcrews and theoretical conceptions of group process mediators of aircrew performance, we should be able to fill in the black box with a more complete description of the processes that influence outcomes. Helmreich, Wilhelm, Kello, Taggart, & Butler (1991) have developed an evaluation system for systematic observation of flightcrews in line operations and simulations. The methodology grew out of findings from small group research and investigations of accidents and incidents. Group processes identified during flight operations fall into two broad categories. One consists of the *interpersonal and cognitive functions*. The second includes *machine interface tasks*. The latter category reflects the technical proficiency of the crew. It is a given that optimal team interactions and decision-making will be of little value if the crew cannot also integrate them with technical execution of maneuvers and procedures needed for safe flight. There is also ample evidence from review of the accidents cited earlier that competence in machine interface tasks alone does not guarantee operational safety.

Figure 1.4 shows the expanded group process model as it flows into outcome factors. In theory, the two categories of group processes containing human factors and technical components must be integrated operationally to produce effective overall performance. Note that the final box in Figure 1.4 is labeled "Integrated CRM and Technical Functions" to emphasize the fact that the two components need to come together in the group process phase, which then flows into desired outcomes of safe and efficient mission completion.

Breaking the subordinate categories down further, the interpersonal and cognitive functions can be classified into three broad clusters of observable behaviors: team formation and management tasks, communications processes and

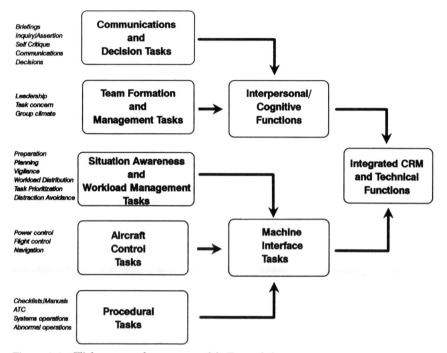

Figure 1.4 Flightcrew performance model: Expanded group process factors.

decision tasks, and workload management and situation awareness tasks. The machine interface tasks fall into two clusters, the actual control of the aircraft (either manually or through computer-based flight management systems) and adherence to established procedures for the conduct of flight.

Team Formation and Management Tasks

The first cluster deals with the formation of the crew as an operating team, including cabin as well as flightdeck personnel. As Ginnett's (1987) research has demonstrated, there is a formation process for teams during which patterns of communication and interaction are established. Once established, the process continues and leads to activities that can maintain patterns of effective (or ineffective) group interaction. The process of formation and maintenance can be categorized into two broad areas, *leadership, followership, and task concern;* and *interpersonal relationships and group climate.*

Flightcrews are teams with a designated leader and clear lines of authority and responsibility. Not surprisingly, the captain, as leader, can and should set the tone of the group. Effective leaders use their authority but do not operate without the participation of other team members. As demonstrated in the Chidester et al. (1990) simulation study, captains' attributes such as personality play a role in determining group processes and outcomes. Two negative patterns of leadership have been isolated in the investigation of accidents. One consists of a strong, autocratic leader who chills input from subordinates and conducts operations as if the flightdeck were a single-seat fighter. The "macho pilot" tradition discussed by Foushee & Helmreich (1988) represents the prototype of such a leadership style and is typified by an incident reported by Foushee (1982) in which a co-pilot's attempts to communicate an air traffic control speed restriction were met with an order to "just look out the damn window." Equally destructive are leaders who abdicate responsibility and fail to control activities on the flightdeck. An example of this type of leadership is seen in the crash of a B-727 at Dallas–Fort Worth because the crew was distracted and failed to confirm that flaps were set prior to take-off (NTSB, 1989). In this case, the first officer became involved in a lengthy social conversation with a flight attendant during taxi. Although not participating extensively in the conversation, the captain failed to control the group processes and did not establish work priorities or demonstrate a concern for operational duties.

One of the observable components of group processes is the quality of interpersonal relationships and the resulting group climate. Effective crews maintain a group climate that encourages participation and exchange of information. The group climate does not reflect the crew's concern with effective accomplishment of required tasks, but it is axiomatic that, other things being equal, crews functioning in a positive environment will be more motivated and will participate more fully in team activities.

Communications Processes and Decision Tasks

As data from experimental simulations have shown, the processes of information transfer and decision-making are prime determinants of crew performance, and higher levels of communication are associated with fewer operational errors. Critical elements in this process include *briefings* and the extent to which free and open communications are established and practiced. Briefings need to address team formation issues as well as technical issues anticipated during operations. Although categorized as part of the communications cluster, briefings are one of the demonstrated means of forming effective teams and establishing a positive group climate.

Inquiry, advocacy, and *assertion* define behaviors meant to ensure that necessary information is available and that required communications are completed at appropriate times (for example, initiating and completing checklists, alerting others to developing problems). The accident literature is replete with examples of crewmembers failing to inquire about actions being taken by others. It is critical to safety and team action that crewmembers request clarification when they are unclear about the current operational situation or planned actions. Paralleling the need to gain operational data is the willingness of crewmembers to advocate effectively courses of action that they feel essential to safe and efficient operations. In cases such as the Air Florida crash in Washington, D.C. (NTSB, 1982). The voice recorder shows that one crewmember is uneasy about the take-off but fails to express his concern strongly and to advocate an alternative action strategy. Concerns and suggestions for needed actions must be communicated with sufficient assertiveness to ensure that others are aware of their importance. It is noteworthy that the NTSB's first call for something like CRM was in the form of a recommendation for "assertiveness training" for junior crewmembers after investigation of a crash that was caused by fuel exhaustion during a hold to investigate a warning light (NTSB, 1979). In this accident, the second officer repeatedly reported that the fuel state was critical, but without sufficient assert-iveness to elicit action on the part of the captain. The willingness of crewmembers to advocate the course of action they feel best, even when it involves disagreements with others, is an essential attribute of an effective team. When crewmembers have differing views of proper courses of action and advocate their preferred course of action, interpersonal conflict may result. The observable behaviors resulting from disagreement are the means used for conflict resolution. Conflict may result in either careful consideration of alternatives, or a polarization of positions and a negative group atmosphere. Effective conflict resolution is focused on *what* is right rather than *who* is right.

   Active participation in decision-making processes should be encouraged and practiced, including questioning actions and decisions. When decisions are made, they need to be clearly communicated and acknowledged. *Crew self-critique* is another essential component of effective group processes. Teams need to review their decisions and actions with the goal of optimizing future team ac-tivities. Effective critique includes the *product or outcome*, the *process*, and the *people involved*. Critique can and should occur both during and after completion of activities. Critique is not the same as criticism. Indeed, review of effective team performance is a powerful reinforcer.

Situation Awareness, Workload Management Tasks

   The third grouping of crew effectiveness markers is labeled Workload management and situation awareness. The crew's awareness of operational condi-tions and contingencies, usually defined as situation awareness, has been impli-cated as causal in a number of incidents and accidents. However, situation awareness is an outcome rather than a specific set of mission management behav-iors. The specific factors that are defined for this cluster are *preparation/ plan-ning/vigilance, workload distribution,* and *distraction avoidance.*

   Preparation, planning, and vigilance behaviors reflect the extent to which crews anticipate contingencies and actions that may be required. Excellent crews are always ahead of the curve while poor crews continually play catch-up. Vig-ilant crews devote appropriate attention to required tasks and respond immediately to new information. However, a crew indulging in casual social conversation during periods of low workload is not lacking in vigilance if flight duties are being discharged properly and the operational environment is being monitored; the crew may be using this time for team formation and maintenance.

As the Ruffell Smith (1979) study demonstrated clearly, when abnormal situations arise during a flight, particular crewmembers may become overloaded with multiple tasks and/or become distracted from primary responsibilities. One of the observables of group process is how well crews manage to distribute tasks and avoid overloading individuals. By prioritizing activities, teams can avoid becoming distracted from essential activities, as was the crew whose concentration on a burned-out light bulb kept them from noticing that the autopilot had become disengaged and that the aircraft was descending below the proper flight path (NTSB, 1972).

Machine Interface Tasks

The flight control and procedural tasks that constitute the machine interface portion of group processes represent the traditional model of flight training and evaluation. The model proposed here, with its inclusion of interpersonal and cognitive processes, in no way downplays the continuing importance of these activities. Rather it reflects the fact that both are essential to safe and efficient operations.

If the proposed model does indeed reflect the major input and process determinants of flightcrew performance, it should provide insights into how training programs can best address the group processes of flight. In the following section we discuss theoretical approaches to maximizing the impact of CRM.

THEORETICAL LEVERAGING OF CRM TRAINING — ✈

The model indicates that there are multiple determinants of crew effectiveness among both input and process factors. In theory, organizations should achieve the greatest impact on crew performance when they address and optimize as many input and group process factors as possible. In this section we consider how programs can be designed to accomplish this. This discussion is cast in terms of an integrated approach to technical and human factors training.

Optimizing Input Factors

Individual Factors

We suggested in an earlier article on crew interaction and performance that the selection of individuals more predisposed toward team activity and crew coordination concepts could provide one means of achieving more effective crew performance (Foushee & Helmreich, 1988). Subsequent research has supported this contention as personality factors have been linked to crew performance in experimental simulations (Chidester et al., 1990), to acceptance of CRM training and changes in attitudes regarding flightdeck management (Chidester et al., 1991; Helmreich & Wilhelm, 1989, 1991; Helmreich, Wilhelm, & Jones, 1991), and to fatigue and health complaints in short- and long-haul operations (Chidester, 1990). The chapters by both Hackman and Chidester discuss the need for innovations in this area. Selection represents a long-term strategy, but one that should be entertained. In the short term, however, efforts should concentrate on enhancing training for the existing workforce.

All effective training programs have an information base. In the case of CRM, the goal is to communicate new knowledge about effective team performance and, concurrently, to change or reinforce attitudes regarding appropriate flightdeck management. Changed attitudes, in turn, should be reflected in improvements in group process and ultimately in better crew performance.

Organizational Factors

There are a number of issues that organizations can address that should, in theory, increase crew effectiveness. Foremost, of course, is to demonstrate a commitment to developing and implementing training of the highest quality. However, unless the concepts presented in training are consistent with the organization's culture and practices, they are not likely to have a major impact. Several steps are necessary to ensure that the culture and norms are congruent with CRM. One is to stress training using a crew rather than an individualistic model. Another is to make checklists and other cockpit documents consistent with crew concepts (Pan American Airways took this step in the early 1970s in response to a number of crew-induced accidents). An additional step is to address communications issues between flightcrews and other operational units including dispatchers, cabin crews, and the maintenance force. The interface between the cockpit and these elements forms a significant component of group processes and can either support or hinder effective team performance.

An essential means of making organizational culture and norms congruent with CRM concepts is by providing role models who practice and reinforce them. In most organizations, check airmen, instructors, and chief pilots are highly respected and experienced pilots who are looked to as exemplars of the organization's norms and requirements (Helmreich, 1991a, 1991b; Helmreich, Wilhelm, Kello, Taggart, & Butler, 1991). Selection of individuals for these positions should include assessment of interpersonal as well as technical expertise. Special training in evaluating and debriefing group processes can help them establish and maintain norms supportive of good CRM practices.

Regulatory Factors

In 1986, following a crash caused by a crew's failure to complete pre–takeoff checklists and to extend flaps, then FAA Administrator T. Allen McArtor called a meeting of airline managers to discuss the implementation of human factors training. This resulted in the formation of a government–industry working group that drafted an Advisory Circular (AC) on cockpit resource management (FAA, 1989; in press). The AC defines the concept, suggests curriculum topics, and recognizes that initial CRM training provides only basic awareness of CRM issues. It further points out that awareness must be followed by a practice and feedback phase and a continual reinforcement phase. Full mission simulation training (line-oriented flight training, LOFT) is highly recommended as the most effective means of continual reinforcement. The content of the AC is consistent with generally accepted principles of learning and reinforcement and with the the-oretical model of flightcrew performance being discussed here. Although CRM has not been mandated as a requirement for air carriers, the AC clearly encourages U.S. carriers to develop such programs. Efforts are further under way to mandate CRM training for all air transport.

Also growing out of this government–industry collaboration has been a Special Federal Aviation Regulation–Advanced Qualification Program (FAA SFAR 58, AQP) issued in 1990. AQP is described in detail in the chapter by Birnbach & Longridge. It is a voluntary regulation for airlines that allows much more flexibility and innovation in training. In exchange for this flexibility in conducting training, participating airlines are required to provide CRM training, LOFT, and to initiate formal evaluation of crew as well as individual proficiency. Organizations that operate under AQP should find the regulatory environment supportive of CRM training efforts.

Enhancing Group Process Factors

In theory, the point of greatest impact on flightcrew behavior should be the group process itself. This should be accomplished effectively by full mission simulation training (LOFT), where crews have an opportunity to experiment with new interaction strategies and to receive feedback and reinforcement. The FAA supported this approach and issued an Advisory Circular (FAA, 1978) establish-ing guidelines for the conduct of LOFT. NASA hosted an industry conference on LOFT in 1981 that resulted in two volumes providing a review of techniques and formal guidelines for its conduct (Lauber & Foushee, 1981). The principles espoused include establishing high levels of realism, conducting normal flight operations as well as creating emergency and abnormal situations, and non-intervention by instructors into group processes, decisions, and actions. CRM LOFT is defined as training rather than formal evaluation, with the goal of allowing crews to explore the impact of new behaviors without jeopardizing their certification as crewmembers.

LOFT should influence subsequent behavior most strongly when scenarios are crafted to require team decision-making and coordinated actions to resolve in-flight situations. The debriefing of LOFT is also a critical element in achieving impact. Skilled instructors should guide crews to self-realization rather than lecture them on observed deficiencies. Instances of effective team behavior should be strongly reinforced. The use of videotapes of the simulation can provide crews with the opportunity to examine their own behavior with the detachment of observers (Helmreich, 1987). Butler discusses the status of contemporary LOFT programs in his chapter and Wiener discusses the peculiarities of LOFT in the high-technology cockpit in his chapter.

In addition to the practice and reinforcement provided later by LOFT, initial CRM training, usually conducted in a seminar setting, should allow participants to observe and experiment with behavioral strategies and to receive individual and group feedback. Instruction that allows participants to experience processes is more meaningful than lectures where ideas are presented to a passive audience. Introductory training in CRM provides the conceptual framework needed to understand the processes that will later be encountered in LOFT.

It is also necessary to identify and reinforce effective group processes in normal line operations as well as in the training environment. We earlier identified check airmen as key agents and role models. To help transfer concepts from training to the line, check airmen should address not only technical performance but also interpersonal and cognitive issues in their conduct of periodic evaluations of crew performance line operations (line checks).

As we pointed out in describing Figure 1.4, process factors from both the interpersonal and machine interface components need to be integrated as the team performs its duties. The corollary of this is that the most effective training should bring together technical and human factors aspects of each maneuver taught, so crewmembers can recognize that every technical activity has team-level components essential to its successful completion. For example, the V_1 cut[3] is a maneuver in which crews are required to demonstrate proficiency. It involves the loss of power at a point when it is too late to abort the take-off. Crews are required to climb out, reconfigure the aircraft, communicate with the tower, and return for landing. While this is often seen as primarily a technical exercise, in fact it requires concerted activity by the full crew along with rapid, accurate information transfer within the cockpit and between cockpit and cabin and cockpit and ground. If training in basic flight maneuvers stresses the human factors as well as technical components, the likelihood that crews will demonstrate effective, integrated group processes should be increased.

In a similar vein, the specificity of concepts communicated and reinforced should determine their acceptance and adoption. Individuals may accept, in principle, abstract ideas of open and complete communication, team formation, situation awareness, and workload management, but may find it difficult to translate them into concrete behaviors on the flightdeck. In theory, individuals

---

[3]V_1 is the decision speed for take-off. When an aircraft reaches V_1 the crew is committed to take-off. It is a function of runway length and condition, aircraft weight, temperature, etc. We are indebted to Captain Kevin Smith for his analysis of actions required during the maneuver.

- **Avoids "tunnel vision", being aware of factors such as stress that can reduce vigilance**
- **Actively monitors weather, aircraft systems, instruments, and ATC, sharing relevant information**
- **Stays "ahead of curve" in preparing for expected or contingency situations**
- **Verbally insures that cockpit and cabin crew are aware of plans**
- **Workload distribution is clearly communicated and acknowledged**
- **Ensures that secondary operational tasks are prioritized**
- **Recognizes and reports work overloads in self and others**
- **Plans for sufficient time prior to maneuvers for programming of automation**
- **Ensures that all crewmembers are aware of status and changes in automation**
- **Recognizes potential distractions caused by automation and takes appropriate preventive action**

Figure 1.5   Behavioral markers for workload distribution/situational awareness.

who understand both the conceptual bases of effective crew coordination and their specific behavioral manifestations should be able to put them into practice readily and should be able to evaluate their success in accomplishing them.

As part of a research effort to evaluate the impact of CRM training and to train observers to judge crew effectiveness, Helmreich, Wilhelm, Kello, Taggart, and Butler (1991) have attempted to define behavioral markers of the three clusters of interpersonal and cognitive tasks. These are observable behaviors that reflect the concepts central to CRM training. Forty discrete markers have been isolated and utilized in observations of line operations and LOFT (Clothier, 1991a). The data suggest that these behaviors can be reliably measured. Figure 1.5 shows the ten markers associated with the Situation Awareness/Workload Management cluster. It can be argued that programs that employ concrete, behavioral examples should have a greater impact on crew processes and outcomes than those that deal with abstract concepts.

In this section we have tried to derive approaches to CRM training that should theoretically have the greatest leverage on crew performance. This analysis suggests that programs need to attack a number of areas in concert if they are to achieve maximum influence on behaviors and attitudes. In the following section we discuss efforts to achieve these goals and describe some of the major developments in CRM training over the last decade.

THE EVOLUTION OF CRM TRAINING ─────── ✦

Formal training in human factors aspects of crew operations was beginning to take root by the 1970s. For example, the late Frank Hawkins (1984) had initiated a human factors training program at KLM, Royal Dutch Airlines, based on Edwards' (1972, 1975) SHEL model and trans-cockpit authority gradient. Operational and theoretical concerns with human factors aspects of flight came together in a NASA/Industry workshop held in 1979. At this gathering, managers from worldwide aviation met with the members of the academic and government research community concerned with human performance. Research into the human factors aspects of accidents was reviewed (e.g., Cooper, White, & Lauber, 1980) along with the seminal findings from the Ruffell Smith (1979) study. Many of the participants left the meeting committed to developing formal training in crew coordination.

A number of different CRM courses began to emerge in the early 1980s. The focus of most early training was on input factors, especially in the areas of knowledge and attitudes. Much of the emphasis was on the review of human factors aspects of accidents, with the goal of changing attitudes regarding appropriate flightdeck management. Many of these courses were presented in a lecture format, and some consisted only of videotaped presentations. Other training, growing out of management development programs, included tests and exercises designed to provide self-awareness and to demonstrate general concepts of group processes. What was not present in early efforts was a focus on organizational issues and flightcrew group processes, including reinforcement of effective process behavior. Many early CRM courses faced considerable resistance from crewmembers who expressed concerns about both the motivation for and possible outcomes of the training. Some saw it as unwarranted psychological meddling, equating the training with clinical psychology or psychotherapy. Others feared that captains' authority would be eroded by a kind of Dale Carnegie charm school approach to developing harmonious interpersonal relations, without regard for operational effectiveness.

The first CRM course integrated with LOFT was developed by United Airlines following the NASA workshop. The course, called Command, Leadership, and Resource Management, was the result of a collaboration among United flight training personnel, members of the Air Line Pilots' Association, and Drs. Robert Blake and Jane Mouton. Blake and Mouton were social psychologists who had developed training programs aimed at improving managerial effectiveness for a number of major corporations. The centerpiece of their training approach is providing participants with insights into their personal managerial styles (an individual input factor) using the managerial grid (Blake and Mouton, 1964) as a means of classifying managers along independent dimensions of task and interpersonal orientations. The multi-day training program that emerged is intensive and interactive, requiring participants to assess their own behaviors and those of peers. Operational concepts stressed in the training include process factors such as inquiry, seeking of relevant operational information; advocacy, communicating proposed actions; and conflict resolution, decision-making, and critique, reviewing actions taken and decisions reached. The unique aspect of the United approach was that the initial training was followed by recurrent review of CRM concepts. The program also demonstrated a major commitment to group process factors by providing annual CRM LOFT sessions. These allow crews to practice the human factors concepts covered in the seminar and recurrent training. One of the major innovations in United's LOFT was the use of a video camera in the simulator to record crew interactions. By replaying the tape of their LOFT, crews gain the ability to review their actions and decisions and to obtain insights into their behavior, guided by the LOFT instructor.[4] This program represents the first integration of multiple input and group process factors that also recognized the need for continuing practice and reinforcement.

NASA and the Military Airlift Command of the U.S. Air Force jointly sponsored a workshop on developments in CRM training in May, 1986 (Orlady & Foushee, 1987). This conference demonstrated the striking spread of CRM training throughout the world since the first workshop in 1979. Reports were presented on the implementation of CRM courses at United Airlines (Carroll & Taggart, 1987), Pan American World Airways (Butler, 1987), People Express Airlines (Bruce & Jensen, 1987), Continental Airlines (Christian & Morgan, 1987), Japan Air Lines (Yamamori, 1987), Trans Australia Airlines (Davidson, 1987), in units of the Military Airlift Command (Cavanagh & Williams, 1987; Halliday, Biegelski, & Inzana, 1987), and in corporate and regional operations (Mudge, 1987; Schwartz, 1987; Yocum & Monan, 1987).

In the late 1980s a second generation of CRM training began to emerge in the United States. Pan American World Airways and Delta Airlines both initiated CRM courses that included recurrent classroom training and LOFT. In addition, these programs addressed organizational input factors by providing additional training for check airmen and instructors with the goal of increasing impact on group process factors through reinforcement of effective behaviors both in LOFT and in line operations. Black and Byrnes discuss the implementation of the Delta program in their chapter.

Although there has been a great proliferation of CRM courses, there has not been a parallel growth in the use of CRM/LOFT to provide practice and reinforcement. At the time this is written, in the United States only United, Horizon Airlines, Delta, Continental, and units of military aviation have integrated CRM/LOFT programs, although a number of other organizations including Northwest Airlines, USAir, and Comair are in the process of implementing them. There are a number of reasons why more comprehensive programs have been slow in emerging. One is certainly economic. As Chidester points out in his chapter, at a time of great financial distress in the industry, innovative and relatively expensive programs that are not formally mandated by regulations must

---

[4]The videotape is always erased following the LOFT debriefing to preserve the confidentiality of the training and behaviors observed.

compete with other operational needs for scarce resources. Indeed, regulations in the U.S. have tended to operate against the adoption of LOFT because it is necessary to meet many formal, technical requirements each year and because requirements for recurrent training for captains are semi-annual but annual for first officers and flight engineers, making it difficult to schedule complete crews for LOFT.[5] The previously mentioned Advanced Qualification Program both removes some of the regulatory barriers to comprehensive CRM/LOFT and provides incentives for their adoption. Additional resistance to changes in training may also come from awareness that the aviation system has an excellent safety record when compared with all other forms of transportation and from the fact that empirical evidence for increased safety of flight as a result of CRM training has been lacking until very recently.

At the present time a third generation of CRM training is emerging. This approach continues the practices of integrating CRM with LOFT but also takes a systems approach to multiple input factors including organizational cultures and group and individual factors. Evaluation and reinforcement in line operations are also cornerstones of this approach. In addition, new programs are becoming more specific in focus and are defining and directly addressing optimal behaviors (e.g., behavioral markers). Efforts are underway in several organizations (stimulated in part by requirements of AQP) to remove the distinction between technical training and evaluation and CRM, with the goal of implementing a training philosophy where both components are addressed in every aspect of pilot qualification.

An additional characteristic of evolving programs is the extension of CRM training beyond the cockpit to other operational areas. Joint training for cabin and cockpit crews has been initiated at America West Airlines, and programs are being developed at a number of other carriers. American Airlines is including dispatchers in CRM training in recognition of common concerns and responsibilities and the need for effective, open communication. Pan American and later Continental Airlines developed CRM programs for maintenance personnel. Efforts are also underway to implement similar training within the FAA for Air Traffic Control personnel who also operate in a team environment but have historically received little or no formal instruction in human factors issues relating to their jobs.

Looking at the growth and evolution of CRM training, one is struck by the willingness of very disparate organizations to embrace a training concept that counters many of the traditions of an industry. In the following section we consider factors that may have facilitated this acceptance.

[5]United Airlines, Pan American Airlines, and Delta Airlines have received exemptions from some training requirements to facilitate training complete crews on an annual basis in exchange for implementation of integrated CRM/LOFT programs.

CRM AND TRADITIONAL MANAGEMENT
DEVELOPMENT TRAINING ────────────────── ✈

From an observer's perspective, the philosophical and pragmatic bases of CRM are consistent with programs that have been used in management development training for several decades. Concerns with self-assessment, managerial styles, interpersonal communications, and organizational influences on behavior have academic roots in social, industrial, and clinical psychology, sociology, and schools of business. Programs to translate empirical and theoretical knowledge about groups into practical training have been employed with differential acceptance in many segments of industry and government. Indeed, many of the initial CRM programs, such as that at United Airlines, were adaptations of existing management training courses. What is striking about CRM is the rapidity of its spread and the enthusiasm with which it has been accepted. What is unique about its implementation in this setting? What can convince fiscally conservative managers to commit scarce resources and highly experienced crewmembers to re-evaluate their approach to a highly structured task?

Part of the answer rests in the nature of the flight environment. Operating an aircraft with a multi-person crew is a structured and bounded endeavor with clear lines of authority and responsibility. The inherent activities involved in taking an aircraft from one point to another are similar in organizations throughout the world. Although aircraft differ in design and sophistication and in number of crewmembers required for operation, the basic tasks are generic. One implication of this is that the types of problems in flightdeck management found in one organization or flightcrew have a high probability of occurring in others. Findings regarding crew contributions to accidents can be easily recognized as generic rather than as unique occurrences in unique organizational cultures and operating environments. It can be inferred that similar approaches to improving crew effectiveness should work throughout the industry despite differences in the culture, history and health of organizations. The chapters by Johnston; Yamamori & Mito; and Helmreich, Wiener, & Kanki provide additional perspectives on cross-national issues in human factors.

In aviation the results of breakdowns in flightcrew group processes are dramatic and highly visible and provide an unequivocal outcome criterion. In contrast, outcome criteria in industry such as profits or productivity are relatively diffuse and subject to qualification by industry-specific and organization-specific factors. Given an overall performance criterion that represents a common, desired outcome, it is understandable that a similar approach would be recognized and embraced.

Again, in contrast to the diversity found outside aviation, the range of decisions and behaviors that faces flightcrews is constrained and can be incorporated in a fairly simple model. Because of this behavioral specificity, training can be more sharply focused than it normally is in courses developed for generic managers. This clearer definition of issues and processes should lead both to greater acceptance by participants and to more tangible, positive outcomes.

Another distinctive feature of the aviation environment is the ability to use highly realistic simulation to practice behaviors and receive feedback and reinforcement. Unlike many of the exercises that are used in general management training, LOFT provides a valid representation of the actual task setting with measurable outcomes. This allows crews to observe the discrete components of group processes as they flow into outcomes. LOFT provides compelling evidence of the validity of the concepts being trained.

The ultimate question, of course, is how well the training achieves its stated goals. In the following section we review preliminary results from evaluation of CRM courses in a number of organizations.

RESEARCH FINDINGS ————————————————— ✦

Although the process of research is necessarily slow and incremental, a number of consistent findings have emerged regarding the effects of CRM programs. Our goal is to provide a brief overview of what research has told us about the impact of CRM and to point out some of the gaps in current knowledge. It should be noted that the research to be discussed regarding the effectiveness of CRM training comes from evaluation of intensive programs integrated with LOFT and not from brief lecture or discussion sessions called CRM that may be included in crew training. Strategies for the investigation of CRM-related behaviors and concepts are discussed further in Helmreich (1991b).

1. *Crewmembers find CRM and LOFT to be highly effective training.* Survey data from more than 20,000 flight crewmembers in civilian and military organizations in the United States and abroad show overwhelming acceptance of the training. The vast majority of crewmembers find the training both relevant and useful (Helmreich & Wilhelm, 1991). Figure 1.6 shows the distribution of responses in five airlines to a post-training survey question regarding the utility of the training.

A similar pattern of endorsement is found in evaluations of the value of LOFT. Wilhelm (1991) has analyzed reactions to LOFT from more than 8,000 participants in the training at four organizations. Crewmembers overwhelmingly feel that it is important and useful training and that it has value on the technical as well as the human factors dimensions. Figure 1.7 shows the distribution of mean ratings of the usefulness of LOFT in four airlines, broken down by crew position.

Clearly, acceptance of training is a necessary but not sufficient indicator of

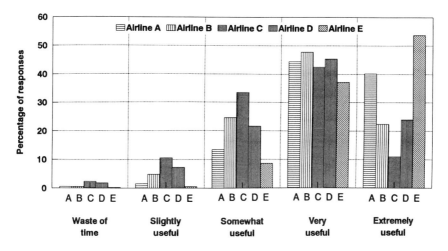

Figure 1.6 Responses to the question, "Overall, how useful did you find the CRM training?" in five organizations (A, B, C, D, E).

its effectiveness. If crews do not perceive training as useful, it is unlikely that it will induce behavioral change. On the other hand, the training may be perceived as useful, but because behavioral tools are not provided to help participants apply the concepts, the result may be increased awareness of CRM concepts but little change in observable behavior.

   2. *There are measurable, positive changes in attitudes and behavior following the introduction of CRM and LOFT.* Changes in attitudes regarding

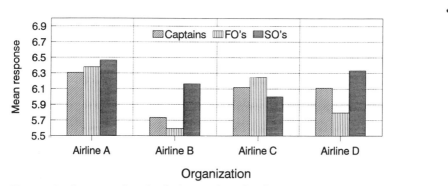

Figure 1.7 Average ratings for the item, "Overall, LOFT is an extremely useful training technique," in four organizations (A, B, C, D). Scale: 1, strongly disagree; 4, neutral; 7, strongly agree.

flightdeck management measured by the *CMAQ* (Helmreich, 1984) can be used as a measure of training impact. Typically, attitudes show significant positive shifts on the three scales of the *CMAQ*, Communications and Coordination, Command Responsibility, and Recognition of Stressor Effects (Helmreich & Wilhelm, 1991). As Figure 1.8 illustrates for the Communications and Coordination scale in six organizations, there is a consistent increase in the positivity of reactions, although the magnitude of change (along with the baseline attitudes) varies between organizations. The *CMAQ* findings suggest that participants do relate the concepts being taught to specific attitudes regarding the conduct of flight operations.

Because the linkage between attitudes and behavior is less than perfect (e.g., Abelson, 1972), it is critical to the validation of CRM training effectiveness that there be observable changes in crewmembers' behaviors on the flightdeck. Data have been gathered both by independent observers and by check airmen and instructors given special training in observational methodology (e.g., Clothier, 1991b). Data collected across time show changes in behavior in the desired direction. Figure 1.9, for example, shows shifts in observed behavior during line operations over a 3-year period on 14 observed categories of process behavior following the introduction of CRM and LOFT in one major airline. All mean differences are statistically significant. It can be noted that the behavioral effects continue to grow across time. A reasonable interpretation of this trend is that, as concepts become more widely accepted, organizational norms shift and exert pressure on crewmembers to conform to the new standards of behavior.

Significant differences have also been found when crew behavior is aggregated and contrasted in terms of the level of flightdeck automation (Butler, 1991; Clothier, 1991a). Crews observed in advanced technology aircraft are rated as

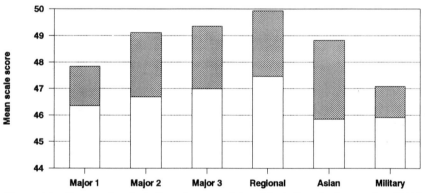

Figure 1.8 Pre-test (unshaded) and post-training (shaded) attitudes on the *CMAQ* Communications and Coordination scale. All differences significant ($p < .01$); scale range, 11–55.

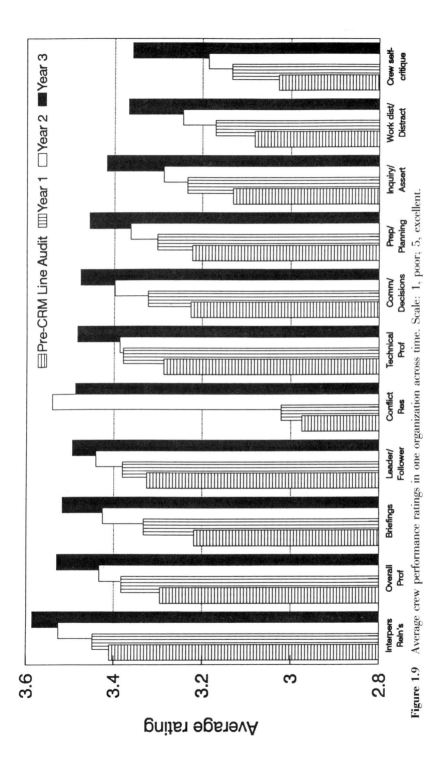

Figure 1.9 Average crew performance ratings in one organization across time. Scale: 1, poor; 5, excellent.

more effective in LOFT than those flying conventional aircraft on a number of human factors dimensions. The causes and extent of these differences remain for further research to clarify. Issues surrounding cockpit automation, crew coordination, and LOFT are discussed in the chapter by Wiener.

As we have noted, the number of accidents involving crews with formal training in CRM and LOFT is too small to draw any statistical inferences regarding the role of these experiences in helping crews cope with serious emergency situations. There are, however, a growing number of anecdotal reports that the training does provide valuable resources for crews faced with major inflight emergencies. Two recent accidents have involved United Airlines crews with both CRM and LOFT experience. In one, a cargo door blew off in flight on Flight 811, a Boeing 747, causing considerable structural damage and the loss of two engines. In the other, the catastrophic failure of the center engine on a McDonnell Douglas DC-10, Flight 232, resulted in the loss of all hydraulic systems and flight controls. Both crews were able to minimize loss of life by coping effectively with the problems, and both acknowledged the role of CRM in enabling them to cope with their novel emergencies. Crew communications taken from the cockpit voice recorder transcripts have been coded in terms of content and frequency and analyzed by Steven Predmore (1991). The coding system classifies communications in terms of CRM concepts including inquiry, command and advocacy, reply and acknowledgment, and observation (communication of operational information). Both crews maintained a high level of communication and verification of information throughout the emergencies. Figure 1.10 shows the pattern of communications over time in both accidents.

3. *Management, check airmen, and instructors play a critical role in determining the effectiveness of CRM training.* Hackman's (1987) delineation of the "organizational shell" as a critical determinant of the success of CRM training has been borne out by operational experience and research. Organizations where senior management has demonstrated a real commitment to the concepts of CRM and its importance for safety and crew effectiveness by providing intensive and recurrent training have found greater acceptance than those which have simply provided a brief introduction to the concepts. Indeed, several organizations in which flight operations management made a concerted effort to communicate the nature of CRM training and the organization's dedication have noted significant improvement in cockpit management attitudes even before formal training was instituted.

The pivotal position of check airmen and instructors as primary role models and agents of reinforcement has also become increasingly recognized (Helmreich, 1987; Helmreich, Wilhelm, Kello, Taggart, & Butler, 1991). Consistent with the theoretical model, the extent to which these key individuals endorse, practice, and emphasize CRM concepts both in the training and checking environment seems largely to determine program acceptance.

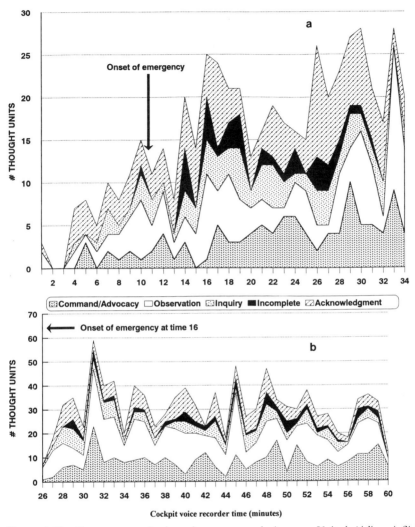

Figure 1.10 Crew communications, by category, during two United Airlines inflight emergencies. (a), Flight 811; (b), Flight 232.

4. *Without reinforcement, the impact of CRM training decays.* Data indicate that even intensive, initial CRM training constitutes only an awareness phase and introduction to the concepts, and that continuing reinforcement is essential to produce long-term change in human factors practices. Some of the most compelling evidence of the need for ongoing emphasis on CRM comes from revisiting

organizations where well-received initial CRM training has not been accompanied by an organizational commitment to continuing the effort (Helmreich, 1991a). In one organization, when the *CMAQ* was re-administered more than a year after the completion of initial training, attitudes had reverted to near their baseline, pre-CRM levels. In this organization many open-ended comments written by respondents expressed concern over the fact that some outspoken opponents of CRM concepts continued management styles antithetical to good human factors practice. In another organization, recurrent CRM and LOFT were provided, but management support was weak, there was high turnover in training and checking personnel, no formal human factors training for new check airmen and instructors, and limited efforts to revise and update LOFT scenarios. When attitudes regarding the value of CRM training and LOFT were assessed more than two years later, they had become significantly less positive than in the first year. These longitudinal findings have major operational significance as they reinforce the notion that organizations desiring to maintain the momentum provided by initial CRM training must make a formal commitment to provide the resources necessary for continuing training and reinforcement.

5. *A small but significant percentage of participants "boomerang" or reject CRM training.* Although the self-report reactions and attitude change findings discussed above show the overall positive impact of initial CRM training, some participants fail to see its value and some even show attitude change in a direction opposite to that intended. These individuals have been described as showing a "boomerang effect" (Helmreich & Wilhelm, 1989). Similarly, some crews observed in line operations following initial CRM seminars do not practice the concepts espoused in training. The fact that reactions to CRM are not uniformly positive does not negate the value of the training, but this undesired outcome is reason for some concern.

Research has shown that there are multiple determinants of the boomerang effect (Helmreich & Wilhelm, 1989). Some resistance to the training is rooted in individual personality characteristics. Crewmembers who are lacking in traits associated with both achievement motivation and interpersonal skills are initially more prone to reject CRM concepts. In addition, the group dynamics of particular seminars also appear to influence reactions. The presence of a charismatic participant who openly rejects the training can influence the level of acceptance by other crewmembers and poses a major challenge to those conducting the training.

OPEN ISSUES FOR RESEARCH ✈

There are a number of open questions that require sustained research efforts to assist CRM training in reaching its full potential. One is to determine the long-term impact of the training on crew behavior and system safety. Many of the measures employed to evaluate crew performance and attitudes are still under development and require refinement through research (see the chapter by Gregorich & Wilhelm). Part of the measurement effort has been directed toward the development of consistent classification strategies for human factors aspects of aviation incidents and accidents. These can generate extremely important research databases, and investigations supporting this effort are much needed.

Chidester describes many of the critical issues facing those trying to develop effective CRM programs in his chapter. All of these can be addressed more effectively with continuing research into the impact of programs and careful assessment of participant reactions. Such data should facilitate continual refinement of programs and will take into account changes in the aviation system itself (for example, the development of more digital data links between aircraft and Air Traffic Control).

Another urgent need is to learn how to maximize the role of LOFT in reinforcing and extending human factors training. Recent data suggest that there are great differences in the perceived value of different scenarios and in the quality of their implementation (Wilhelm, 1991). The chapter by Butler discusses critical research issues that need to be addressed in LOFT design and execution.

Several critical topics need much additional research before they can be translated into basic CRM training. Research into fundamental aspects of interpersonal communications, such as that described in the chapter by Kanki & Palmer, has much to offer those developing CRM programs, but the knowledge base remains relatively undeveloped. Another critical area is decision-making. As Orasanu points out in her chapter, substantial progress has been made toward understanding decision-making in natural situations, but much remains to be done before full operational benefits can be gained. In particular, additional research into individual and group decision-making under highly stressful conditions (such as high time pressure, fatigue, life stresses, and life-threatening emergencies) should have high priority. Indeed, the whole topic of psychological stress and its behavioral impact has languished in the research community and needs renewed attention. Not until the research base is extended will we be able to mount effective programs of stress management and evaluate their operational impact.[6]

Given the lack of empirical data on the impact of system automation on crew coordination, it is also difficult to specify how best to train crewmembers to interact most effectively with "electronic crewmembers." The chapter by Wiener provides a summary of the state of our knowledge about behavioral effects of

[6]A related question is what level of stress needs to be imposed on training to maximize the probability that human factors concepts will generalize to operational emergencies. See the chapter by Butler for further discussion of this topic with regard to LOFT.

automation, and Byrnes & Black describe the first course attempting to integrate automation issues with CRM training in their chapter. Clearly this effort will be enhanced by further research.

We also need to know whether the boomerang reaction to CRM training is transitory or enduring. It is characteristic of human nature to question new and alien concepts on first encounter. Some exposed to CRM for the first time may show initial hostility to the concepts but may, after time and with peer pressure, later become enthusiastic advocates of CRM concepts. Only longitudinal research strategies that revisit and reassess individual reactions across time can determine the long-term reactions of the "boomerang" group. An associated question is whether different training strategies or interventions may be needed to gain acceptance from this subset of individuals.

Human factors concepts and training need to be further integrated with traditional technical training. To a considerable extent, CRM has developed outside the boundaries of the traditional training and evaluation of technical proficiency. As CRM has matured and become a part of organizational cultures, awareness of the fact that there are vital human factors components of all aspects of flight training has grown. As the theoretical model suggests, the effectiveness of both CRM and technical training should be enhanced when trainers stress the human factors components of every aspect of flight. Only basic research and operational evaluation can optimize these efforts. In the same vein, such research should provide guidance for incorporating human factors training into initial pilot training as well as training for experienced crewmembers.

CONCLUSIONS ─────────────────────────────────────→

Recognizing the critical role of human factors in determining the effectiveness of technically proficient flightcrews in both normal and emergency situations, the aviation community has embraced the concept of CRM training. The spread of CRM programs has proceeded faster than the accumulation of knowledge regarding their operational impact, reflecting the perceived importance of the issues. However, research findings to date suggest that this faith has not been misplaced. Crewmembers value the training, and available data suggest that it does have a positive impact on crew behavior and, by inference, on the safety of the aviation system.

The theoretical model of flightcrew group processes suggests that the most effective CRM courses will simultaneously address multiple input and group process factors and will be developed with awareness of the particular cultures in which they are embedded. Impact should also be enhanced when participants are not forced to make large generalizations from abstract concepts to their normal work setting, but rather receive training that communicates psychological concepts in terms of shared everyday experiences and clearly defined behaviors. Successful programs appear to provide not only basic psychological concepts, but their translation into operational terms.

It seems likely that if research and evaluation proceed in tandem with the implementation of continuing human factors training, courses of the future will evolve continually and make today's efforts look as antiquated as the Link Trainers of World War II. The open exchange of information that has developed surrounding CRM training has provided an environment conducive to rapid evolution.

Acknowledgments

Research by the first author has been supported by a Cooperative Agreement with NASA–Ames Research Center, NCC2-286, Robert L. Helmreich, Principal Investigator, and by a contract with the Federal Aviation Administration, DTFA-90-C-00054. The cooperation of many airlines and flightcrews in the United States and around the world allowed the research for this chapter to take place. Special thanks are due John K. Lauber, who motivated us both to enter this research area and who has served as mentor for many years. Don Burr, former CEO of People Express Airlines, provided great assistance by opening the organization for research into determinants of crew performance. Captain Roy E. Butler, formerly of Pan American World Airways, assisted in the design and execution of research into the impact of CRM and LOFT and has subsequently become a colleague. Captain Reuben Black of Delta Airlines has also been instrumental in the implementation of integrated CRM/LOFT and the collection of data to assess the process. Captain Milt Painter and the CRM team at Southwest Airlines contributed their time and talent to the development of LOFT videos for calibrating evaluators. John A. Wilhelm has been a close collaborator for many years and remains master of the data, while William R. Taggart has provided invaluable counsel and assistance in the design and delivery of training for evaluation of crew performance. Finally, current and former graduate students at the University of Texas have been instrumental in all stages of the project. This group includes Cathy Clothier, Thomas R. Chidester, Steven E. Gregorich, Cheryl Irwin, Sharon Jones, Randolph Law, Terry McFadden, Ashleigh Merritt, Steven Predmore, and Paul Sherman.

References

Abelson, R. (1972). Are attitudes necessary? In B. T. King & E. McGinnies (Eds.), *Attitudes, conflict, and social change.* New York: Academic Press.

Bales, R. F. (1950). *Interaction process analysis: Theory, research, and application.* Reading, MA: Addison-Wesley.

Blake, R. R., & Mouton, J. S. (1964). *The managerial grid.* Houston: Gulf Press.

Bruce, K. D., & Jensen, D. (1987). Cockpit Resource Management training at People Express: An overview and summary. In H. W. Orlady & H. C. Foushee (Eds.), *Cockpit resource management training: Proceedings of the NASA/MAC workshop* (NASA CP-2455) (pp. 50–55). Moffett Field, CA: NASA–Ames Research Center.

Butler, R. E. (1987). Pan Am flight training—A new direction: Flight Operations Resource Management. In H. W. Orlady & H. C. Foushee (Eds.), *Cockpit resource management training: Proceedings of the NASA/MAC workshop* (NASA CP-2455) (pp. 61–67). Moffett Field, CA: NASA–Ames Research Center.

Butler, R. E. (1991). Lessons from cross-fleet/cross airline observations: Evaluating the impact of

CRM/LOS training. *Proceedings of the Sixth International Symposium on Aviation Psychology* (pp. 326–331). Columbus: Ohio State University.

Carroll, J. E., & Taggart, W. R. (1987). Cockpit resource management: A tool for improved flight safety (United Airlines CRM training). In H. W. Orlady & H. C. Foushee (Eds.), *Cockpit resource management training: Proceedings of the NASA/MAC workshop* (NASA CP-2455) (pp. 40–46). Moffett Field, CA: NASA–Ames Research Center.

Cavanagh, D. E., & Williams, K. R. (1987). The application of CRM to military operations. In H. W. Orlady & H. C. Foushee (Eds.), *Cockpit resource management training: Proceedings of the NASA/MAC workshop* (NASA CP-2455) (pp. 135–144). Moffett Field, CA: NASA–Ames Research Center.

Chidester, T. R. (1990). Trends and individual differences in response to short-haul flight operations. *Aviation, Space, and Environmental Medicine, 61,* 132–138.

Chidester, T. R., Helmreich, R. L., Gregorich, S., & Geis, C. (1991). Pilot personality and crew coordination: Implications for training and selection. *International Journal of Aviation Psychology, 1,* 23–42.

Chidester, T. R., Kanki, B. G., Foushee, H. C., Dickinson, C. L., & Bowles, S. V. (1990). *Personality factors in flight operations: Vol. 1. Leader characteristics and crew performance in full-mission air transport simulation* (NASA Technical Memorandum 102259). Moffett Field, CA: NASA–Ames Research Center.

Christian, D., & Morgan, A. (1987). Crew coordination concepts: Continental Airlines CRM training. In H. W. Orlady & H. C. Foushee (Eds.), *Cockpit resource management training: Proceedings of the NASA/MAC workshop* (NASA CP-2455) (pp. 68–74). Moffett Field, CA: NASA–Ames Research Center.

Clothier, C. (1991a). *Behavioral interactions in various aircraft types: Results of systematic observation of line operations and simulations.* Unpublished Master's thesis, The University of Texas at Austin.

Clothier, C. (1991b). Behavioral interactions across various aircraft types: Results of systematic observations of line operations and simulations. *Proceedings of the Sixth International Symposium on Aviation Psychology* (pp. 332–337). Columbus: Ohio State University.

Cooper, G. E., White, M. D., & Lauber, J. K. (Eds.). (1980). *Resource management on the flightdeck: Proceedings of a NASA/Industry workshop* (NASA CP-2120). Moffett Field, CA: NASA–Ames Research Center.

Davidson, J. (1987). Introduction to Trans Australia Airlines CRM training. In H. W. Orlady and H. C. Foushee (Eds.), *Cockpit resource management training: Proceedings of the NASA/MAC workshop* (NASA CP-2455) (pp. 88–89). Moffett Field, CA: NASA–Ames Research Center.

Davis, D. R. (1948). *Pilot error: Some laboratory experiments.* London: His Majesty's Stationery Office.

Edwards, E. (1972). Man and machine: Systems for safety. In *Proceedings of British Airline Pilots Association Technical Symposium* (pp. 21–36). London: British Airline Pilots Association.

Edwards, E. (1975). *Stress and the airline pilot.* Paper presented at British Airline Pilots Association Medical Symposium. London.

Federal Aviation Administration. (1978). *Line oriented flight training* (Advisory Circular AC-120-35A). Washington, DC: Author.

Federal Aviation Administration. (1989). *Cockpit Resource Management* (Advisory Circular 120-51). Washington, DC: Author.

Federal Aviation Administration. (in press). *Crew resource management* (Advisory Circular 120-51A). Washington, DC: Author.

Fitts, P. M., & Jones, R. E. (1947). *Analysis of 270 "pilot error" experiences in reading and interpreting aircraft instruments* (Report TSEAA-694-12A). Wright-Patterson Air Force Base, OH: Aeromedical Laboratory.

Foushee, H. C. (1982). The role of communications, socio-psychological, and personality factors in the maintenance of crew coordination. *Aviation, Space, and Environmental Medicine, 53,* 1062–1066.

Foushee, H. C. (1984). Dyads and triads at 35,000 feet: Factors affecting group process and aircrew performance. *American Psychologist, 39,* 886–893.

Foushee, H. C., & Helmreich, R. L. (1988). Group interaction and flight crew performance. In E. L. Wiener & D. C. Nagel (Eds.), *Human factors in aviation* (pp. 189–227). San Diego, CA: Academic Press.

Foushee, H. C., Lauber, J. K., Baetge, M. M., & Acomb, D. B. (1986). *Crew performance as a function of exposure to high density, short-haul duty cycles* (NASA Technical Memorandum 88322). Moffett Field, CA: NASA–Ames Research Center.

Foushee, H. C., & Manos, K. L. (1981). Information transfer within the cockpit: Problems in intracockpit communications. In C. E. Billings & E. S. Cheaney (Eds.), *Information transfer problems in the aviation system* (NASA TP-1875). Moffett Field, CA: NASA–Ames Research Center.

Gann, E. K. (1961). *Fate is the hunter.* New York: Simon and Shuster.

Ginnett, R. C. (1987). *First encounters of the close kind: The first meetings of airline flight crews.* Unpublished doctoral dissertation, Yale University, New Haven, CT.

Hackman, J. R. (1987). Organizational influences. In H. W. Orlady & H. C. Foushee (Eds.), *Cockpit resource management training: Proceedings of the NASA/MAC workshop* (NASA CP-2455) (pp. 23–39). Moffett Field, CA: NASA–Ames Research Center.

Hackman, J. R., & Helmreich, R. L. (1987). Assessing the behavior and performance of teams in organizations: The case of air transport crews. In D. R. Peterson & D. B. Fishman (Eds.), *Assessment for Decision* (pp. 283–316). New Brunswick, N.J.: Rutgers University Press.

Hackman, J. R., & Morris, G. (1975). Group tasks, group interaction process, and group performance effectiveness: A review and proposed integration. In L. Berkowitz (Ed.), *Advances in Experimental Social Psychology* (Vol., 8, pp. 45–99). New York: Academic Press.

Halliday, J. T., Biegelski, C. S., & Inzana, A. (1987). CRM training in the 249th military airlift wing. In H. W. Orlady & H. C. Foushee (Eds.), *Cockpit resource management training: Proceedings of the NASA/MAC workshop* (NASA CP-2455) (pp. 148–157). Moffett Field, CA: NASA–Ames Research Center.

Hawkins, F. H. (1984). *Human factors of flight.* Aldershot, England: Gower Publishing Co.

Helmreich, R. L. (1984). Cockpit management attitudes. *Human Factors, 26,* 583–589.

Helmreich, R. L. (1987). Exploring flight crew behaviour. *Social Behaviour, 21,* 63–72.

Helmreich, R. L. (1991a). The long and short term impact of crew resource management training. In *Proceedings of the AIAA/NASA/FAA/HFS conference, Challenges in aviation human factors: The national plan.* Vienna, VA, January 1991.

Helmreich, R. L. (1991b). Strategies for the study of flightcrew behavior. *Proceedings of the Sixth International Symposium on Aviation Psychology* (pp. 338–343). Columbus: Ohio State University.

Helmreich, R. L. (1992). Human factors aspects of the Air Ontario crash at Dryden, Ontario: Analysis and recommendations. In V. P. Moshansky (Commissioner), *Commission of Inquiry into the Air Ontario Accident at Dryden, Ontario: Final report. Technical appendices.* Ottawa, ON: Minister of Supply and Services, Canada.

Helmreich, R. L., Foushee, H. C., Benson, R., & Russini, W. (1986). Cockpit management attitudes: Exploring the attitude-performance linkage. *Aviation, Space, and Environmental Medicine, 57,* 1198–1200.

Helmreich, R. L., & Wilhelm, J. A. (1989). When training boomerangs: Negative outcomes associated with cockpit resource management programs. *Proceedings of the Sixth International Symposium on Aviation Psychology* (pp. 92–97). Columbus: Ohio State University.

Helmreich, R. L., & Wilhelm, J. A. (1991). Outcomes of crew resource management training. *International Journal of Aviation Psychology, 1,* 287–300.

Helmreich, R. L., Wilhelm, J. A., & Gregorich, S. E. (1988). *Revised versions of the cockpit management attitudes questionnaire (CMAQ) and CRM seminar evaluation form* (NASA/The University of Texas Technical Report 88-3–revised 1991). Austin.

Helmreich, R. L., Wilhelm, J. A., & Jones, S. G. (1991). *An evaluation of determinants of CRM outcomes in Europe* (NASA/University of Texas Technical Report 91-1). Austin.

Helmreich, R. L., Wilhelm, J. A., Kello, J. E., Taggart, W. R., & Butler, R. E. (1991). *Reinforcing and evaluating crew resource management: Evaluator/LOS instructor reference manual* (NASA/University of Texas Technical Manual 90-2). Austin.

Kanki, B. G., & Foushee, H. C. (1989). Communication as group process mediator of aircrew performance. *Aviation, Space, and Environmental Medicine, 60,* 402–410.

Kanki, B. G., Lozito, S., & Foushee, H. C. (1989). Communication indices of crew coordination. *Aviation, Space, and Environmental Medicine, 60,* 56–60.

Klein, G., Orasanu, J., Calderwood, R., & Zsambok, C. (Eds.). (in press). *Decision making in action: Models and methods.* Norwood, NJ: Ablex.

Lauber, J. K. (1984). Resource management in the cockpit. *Air Line Pilot, 53,* 20–23.

Lauber, J. K., & Foushee, H. C. (1981). *Guidelines for line-oriented flight training* (Volume 1, NASA CP-2184). Moffett Field, CA: NASA–Ames Research Center.

McGrath, J. E. (1964). *Social psychology: A brief introduction.* New York: Holt, Rinehart, and Winston.

Moshansky, V. P. (1989). *Commission of Inquiry into the Air Ontario Accident at Dryden, Ontario: Interim report.* Ottawa, ON: Minister of Supply and Services, Canada.

Moshansky, V. P. (1992). *Commission of Inquiry into the Air Ontario Accident at Dryden, Ontario: Final report* (Volumes 1–4). Ottawa, ON: Minister of Supply and Services, Canada.

Mosier, K. (1991). Expert decision making strategies. *Proceedings of the Sixth International Symposium on Aviation Psychology* (pp. 266–271). Columbus: Ohio State University.

Mudge, R. W. (1987). Cockpit management and SBO's. In H. W. Orlady & H. C. Foushee (Eds.), *Cockpit resource management training: Proceedings of the NASA/MAC workshop* (NASA CP-2455). Moffett Field, CA: NASA–Ames Research Center.

Murphy, M. (1980). Review of aircraft incidents. Cited in Cooper et al.

National Research Council. (1989). *Human factors research and nuclear safety.* Washington, DC: National Academy Press: Author.

National Transportation Safety Board. (1972). *Aircraft Accident Report: Eastern Airlines, Inc., Lockheed L-1011, N310EA, Miami, Florida, December 29, 1972* (Report No. NTSB-AAR-73-14). Washington, DC: Author.

National Transportation Safety Board. (1979). *Aircraft Accident Report: United Airlines, Inc., McDonnell Douglas DC-8-61, N8082U, Portland, Oregon, December 28, 1978* (Report No. NTSB-AAR-79-2). Washington, DC: Author.

National Transportation Safety Board. (1982). *Aircraft Accident Report: Air Florida, Inc., Boeing B-737-222, N62AF, Collision with 14th Street Bridge, Near Washington National Airport, Washington, D.C., January 13, 1982* (Report No. NTSB-AAR-82-8). Washington, DC: Author.

National Transportation Safety Board. (1989). *Aircraft Accident Report: Delta Air Lines, Inc., Boeing 727-232, N473DA, Dallas–Fort Worth International Airport, Texas, August 31, 1988* (Report No. NTSB-AAR-89-04). Washington, DC: Author.

Orasanu, J. (1991). Information transfer and shared mental models of decision making. *Proceedings of the Sixth International Symposium on Aviation Psychology* (pp. 272–277). Columbus: Ohio State University.

Orlady, H. W., & Foushee, H. C. (Eds.). (1987). *Cockpit Resource Management training.* (NASA CP 2455). Moffett Field, CA: NASA–Ames Research Center.

Predmore, S. C. (1991). Microcoding of communications in accident analyses: Crew coordination in United 811 and United 232. *Proceedings of the Sixth International Symposium on Aviation Psychology* (pp. 350–355). Columbus: Ohio State University.

Ruffell Smith, H. P. (1979). *A simulator study of the interaction of pilot workload with errors, vigilance, and decisions.* (NASA Technical Memorandum 78482). Moffett Field, CA: NASA–Ames Research Center.

Schwartz, D. (1987). CRM training for FAR Parts 91 and 135 operators. In H. W. Orlady and H. C. Foushee (Eds.), *Cockpit resource management training: Proceedings of the NASA/MAC workshop* (NASA CP-2455). Moffett Field, CA: NASA–Ames Research Center.

Thordsen, M. L., & Klein, G. A. (1989). Cognitive processes of the team mind. *1989 IEEE International Conference on Systems, Man, and Cybernetics Proceedings, 1,* 46–49.

Wilhelm, J. A. (1991). Crewmember and instructor evaluations of Line Oriented Flight Training. *Proceedings of the Sixth International Symposium on Aviation Psychology* (pp. 362–367). Columbus: Ohio State University.

Yamamori, (1987). Optimum culture in the cockpit. In H. W. Orlady and H. C. Foushee (Eds.), *Cockpit resource management training: Proceedings of the NASA/MAC workshop* (NASA CP-2455) (pp. 75–87). Moffett Field, CA: NASA–Ames Research Center.

Yocum, M., & Monan, W. (1987). CRM training in corporate/regional airline operations: Working group V Report. In H. W. Orlady and H. C. Foushee (Eds.), *Cockpit resource management training: Proceedings of the NASA/MAC workshop* (NASA CP-2455) (pp. 238–240). Moffett Field, CA: NASA–Ames Research Center.

2

Teams, Leaders, and Organizations: New Directions for Crew-oriented Flight Training

J. Richard Hackman

Department of Psychology
Harvard University
Cambridge, Massachusetts 02138

INTRODUCTION ✈

Consider three facts about cockpit crews. One, cockpit crews are teams. Two, the captain is the team leader. And three, cockpit crews are richly entwined with the organizational, technological, and regulatory contexts in which they operate. None of these three facts is controversial. If taken seriously, however, they call into question a number of widely accepted policies and practices about how pilots and flight crews are trained and managed. And they suggest a number of new directions—some of which may be controversial indeed—for how cockpit resource management (CRM) programs are designed, taught, and supported.

The ideas explored in this chapter are based on data our research group has collected over the last several years about the behavior of cockpit crews on the line. The premise of our research is that understanding the behavior and performance of cockpit crews requires careful attention to team-as-a-whole issues, not just to the behaviors of individual team members. Therefore, we followed intact crews through their entire life cycles, from the moment members first met prior to a trip until the team eventually disbanded, sometimes several days later. In addition, we asked members of the crews we observed to give us their views (on a standardized survey administered at the end of the trip) about how their crews had operated. We supplemented these data by meeting members of many other crews at check-in and asking them to take the survey along on their trip and complete it when the rotation was finished. Overall, we collected data from well over 300 crews who flew 10 different aircraft types in 10 different organizations—three U.S. airlines, three U.S. military units, and four overseas airlines.

Cockpit Resource Management
Copyright © 1993 by Academic Press, Inc. All rights of reproduction in any form reserved.

FACT ONE: COCKPIT CREWS ARE TEAMS ————— ✈

It can be inspiring to watch a superb team in action. One wonders, as members of a jazz ensemble pass solos back and forth without missing a beat, how they *do* that. The same feeling can come while watching a great basketball team. A player feints in one direction, moves three strides in another, and, at the precise moment he has broken free, the ball reaches his outstretched hands. The subsequent shot is anticlimactic: the awesome part is how it happened that the player and the ball arrived at the same place at the same instant.

The other side of the coin is the empathic embarrassment one feels when watching a team that does not work. The ball is passed but no one is there to catch it and it bounces untouched out of bounds. There was supposed to be someone there, of course, but the play fell apart and the passer, who actually did what he was supposed to do, looks like a fool. Or the amateur jazz group finishes one passage, the drummer keeps on beating out the rhythm, but no one picks up the solo line. Members of the audience look away as the players frantically signal one another with their eyes to try to recapture the music that they somehow lost.

Anyone who has logged much time watching cockpit crews has experienced both kinds of feelings. The first officer, who is flying the leg, calls for retraction of the flaps even as the captain's hand is moving toward the lever. The coordination is smooth and seamless. Or the captain, reflecting privately on the deteriorating weather at the destination, muses, "Probably we ought to take a look at the approach plates for the alternate," and the first officer, without a moment of hesitation, responds "Yes, I've got them right here. . . ." Watching a great crew operate can be as impressive as watching a superb dance company perform a well-rehearsed ballet.

Watching other crews can make you wish you were somewhere else. The captain's hand moves toward the lever and then stops halfway, waiting, while the first officer pointedly keeps his eyes outside and his mouth shut. After some seconds of awkward silence, the first officer announces, "When I'm ready for flaps, I'll call for them." And things go downhill from there. Or when a last-minute runway change results in both pilots, heads down, flipping pages hurriedly to find the new plate while the observer, his eyes alternating between the gauges and the traffic outside, hopes that one of them finds it soon.

Cockpit crews are teams. The extremely low accident rate in commercial aviation testifies to just how well those teams perform day in and day out. Yet when an incident does occur, more often than not it is because the team broke down, because members somehow "lost the music." In reviewing the causes of accidents and reportable incidents, Helmreich (1991) has concluded that in the great majority of cases, the aircraft was mechanically capable of flying out of the situation, all crew members were well trained and in good health, and yet the crew got itself into trouble. It is the team, not the aircraft or the individual pilots, that is at the root of most accidents and incidents.

Of the many factors that differentiate outstanding crews from those that get into trouble, three bear directly on the design and support of CRM activities. The first is pilots' skills as team members. Although team skills are critical to crew performance, they cannot be assumed to be present. People are not born with them, nor do they necessarily develop them at flight school. Therefore, special training can be useful in helping pilots hone their skills as team members. The second is the criteria airlines use to select pilots for employment. Even with training, not everyone is able to work well in a team. Current selection practices, however, do little to identify such individuals and weed them out of the applicant pool. Third is airline scheduling and rostering practice. Time and experience are required for a new crew to develop itself into a flexible, self-correcting team—and the policies and practices of most airlines fail to provide pilots with that opportunity. I explore each of these three factors below.

Training in CRM Skills

Despite the increased acceptance in the aviation community that flying a commercial aircraft is a team task, and despite all the talk one hears these days about crew coordination and team dynamics in the cockpit, CRM training programs still tend to focus mainly on improving the attitudes, behavior, and performance of individual pilots. Even those CRM courses that specify improved team functioning as a major educational objective often pursue that objective by attempting to change individual attitudes and behavioral styles. The hope seems to be that improved team functioning will come about more or less automatically if each individual in the cockpit understands his or her personal style as a leader or follower and recognizes the need for good communication and coordination.

Although the characteristics of individual team members are indeed important, there is more to the story. It is not uncommon, for example, for an athletic team consisting of several individual stars to be defeated by a less illustrious set of players who work well together. And if I were a passenger on an aircraft that developed serious mechanical problems, I would greatly prefer a cockpit populated by average pilots who work well as a team over one filled with superb technical flyers who do not.

What is required to help pilots develop their skills as team leaders and members? Most important is that the training include significant amounts of hands-on practice, feedback, and reinforcement in using team skills. Early CRM programs, however, tended to place less emphasis on skills than on behavioral styles. In those programs, each participant typically took a paper-and-pencil test that, when scored, revealed his or her characteristic style of operating in teams. Instructors then showed participants that certain styles are better than others for promoting team effectiveness. Students often were taught, for example, that captains should foster task accomplishment and interpersonal harmony simultaneously, and that they should avoid both autocratic and relentlessly democratic leadership styles. And they learned that first officers and flight engineers should be assertive (but not excessively or unpleasantly so) with their captains when something occurs that concerns them. In full-fledged programs, participants also had the opportunity to experiment with their new styles. The hope was that the styles taught in the classroom would be used to good effect when the pilot-students returned to the line.

Although trainees invariably find tests of behavioral style interesting and informative, I have a number of concerns about such devices.[1] For one thing, they perpetuate the assumption that crew effectiveness will improve if the styles of individual members become better aligned with what is viewed as desirable by the theorists who construct the tests. I know of no empirical evidence that supports this assumption.

Moreover, changes in style that are learned in the classroom may not generalize to the cockpit. Indeed, those times when a newly learned style would be most valuable are precisely the times when it is least likely to appear. Research has shown that when a person becomes highly aroused (as typically happens under stress), he or she reverts to well-learned behaviors, exhibiting whatever response is most dominant for that person in that situation (Zajonc, 1965). Learning a new behavioral style in a CRM course does not immediately change someone's dominant responses; they are too deeply ingrained for that. Therefore, when a crew encounters a highly stressful situation, such as an engine fire followed by numerous secondary problems, each crewmember is likely to revert to his or her old, tried-and-true way of dealing with such events. The new style learned in the classroom is unlikely to be seen—at least not until the immediate crisis has passed.

This phenomenon is nicely illustrated in a story told by Captain Reuben Black of Delta Airlines. Some years ago, an instructor was attempting to get his students to memorize the 13 steps that were to be taken in the event of a heater fire on a certain aircraft. The students were having trouble committing the list to memory, but the instructor persisted. Finally one veteran captain captured the essence of the problem when he exploded, "How the hell do you expect me to remember all this shit when I'm *scared?*" How, indeed?

[1]My credibility on this topic may be lessened somewhat by what happened when I participated as a guest in one carrier's CRM program. I took the test that was offered and, upon plotting my scores, discovered that my characteristic behavioral style was most similar to that of "housewife." Moreover, I was predicted to behave even more like a "housewife" when under stress. This category was not viewed by other participants as among the most desirable. Although they acknowledged that a university professor might well fall into it, a real pilot surely would not. We all laughed about the episode, but I could not help wondering about the feelings of those pilot participants who shared the category with me.

If paper-and-pencil tests of individual behavioral styles do not do the trick, what alternatives are there for helping crewmembers learn the skills that can help a team function effectively? To frame the question that way is to begin to answer it: Learning a new skill is a very different—and more tractable—enterprise than is changing one's characteristic behavioral style. Crewmembers can learn how to get a team off to a good start, how to deal with a change of membership in the cockpit (or a new cabin crew in the back), how to negotiate with uncooperative ramp or maintenance personnel, how to address conflicts among members constructively, and how to draw out and use the full range of expertise that exists in the cockpit. "Ah," a crewmember may reflect, "I know how to do *that*." And then he or she may proceed to do it, using his or her own, idiosyncratic style.

The skills that are needed to help a team become a self-correcting performing unit are known (see Hackman, 1987, or Hackman & Walton, 1986, for an overview), and a number of airlines have stepped up to the challenge of designing training that helps pilots become expert in using those skills on the line (see the chapter by Helmreich & Foushee). All skills, even relatively simple ones such as starting aircraft engines, require practice and feedback before becoming settled in a pilot's repertoire. How can practice and feedback be provided for interpersonal and team skills such as those listed above?

There is no better alternative than line-oriented flight training (LOFT) (see, for example, the chapter by Butler; Wilhelm, 1991). In LOFT training, pilots operate as a real team in a setting that is uncanny in its realism—but that also provides a safe site for experimentation with new or unfamiliar behaviors. Video feedback, a key component of LOFT training, allows pilots to review their behavior and to assess its effects on the crew and its work. Moreover, the instructor and the other crewmembers are in the same room during videotape playback, available to help each pilot explore the positive and negative effects of his or her behaviors. Together, a well-designed scenario, video feedback, and an expert facilitator can provide a pilot with precisely the kind of experience that is needed to hone a new skill and to become comfortable using it.

Let me emphasize once again that the intent of team-oriented skill training is not to get people to change their styles to match a template that has been prespecified as "best" for cockpit crews. The focus, instead, is on how each pilot can exploit the strengths, and contain the weaknesses, of his or her own characteristic way of behaving in teams. Although air transport organizations are still learning how best to exploit LOFT for such training, the potential benefits of this educational device over the long term are enormous.

Pilot Selection Criteria

Extensive evaluation research on pilot responses to CRM training, collected by Helmreich and his associates (e.g., the chapter by Chidester; Helmreich &

Wilhelm, 1991), shows that most pilots benefit greatly from participation in such programs. There are some pilots, however, whose CRM skills do not improve by the end of the training and even a few who exhibit what Helmreich calls the "boomerang" effect: they reject the lessons taught and leave the course even more strongly opposed to CRM values than they were when they arrived.

There are a handful of such individuals in every airline. What is to be done about them? The question is important, because the effectiveness of an entire team can be undermined by a single person who is unwilling or unable to work collaboratively with other members. And, as Helmreich's data show, there are some people, even some pilots, who are just not cut out for working in teams.

Clearly, the stance of an airline must be to work with such individuals and help them develop team skills. I doubt that any airline would terminate a pilot solely because he or she was not a good "team player," nor would I advocate such action. Moreover, the threat of negative outcomes (such as being fired) makes it harder, not easier, to learn new skills. Far preferable, then, is for organizations to reinforce positive team behavior whenever it is seen, and to coach individuals who have trouble working in teams so that they become as skilled as possible in team work.

The time when choices *can* be made is not after someone is already on the line, but when he or she initially is considered for employment. If every individual selected had at least rudimentary skill in working in teams, then the total population of pilots in an organization, over time, would become increasingly amenable to team-oriented resource management training and to regular use of that training on the line.

Although assessing the interpersonal or team skills of prospective pilots is not simple, it is no more difficult or dubious an enterprise than using personality tests for selection—a routine practice at many airlines. Interviews and paper-and-pencil tests can be helpful in measuring team skills, but data about actual behavior are also needed. Perhaps most informative would be observations of prospective pilots operating in a team setting (for example, performing a group task assigned to them by selection staff). Observers could be trained to assess the skills that each participant demonstrates in the group setting, and those data could be combined with information from tests and interviews to arrive at employment decisions.

Such procedures would be unusual in most airlines. Yet the potential benefits of basing pilot selection for crewed aircraft partly on team skills are considerable. Organizations surely should do whatever they can to ensure that each flight crew begins its work atop the highest possible platform that the organization can provide. A key feature of such a platform is a pilot population that is composed, to the greatest extent possible, of people who find teamwork agreeable—and who have at least the basic interpersonal skills needed for teamwork.

Scheduling and Rostering Practices

Even when members of a team have abundant technical and interpersonal skills, it takes time for them to develop into a superb performing unit. This is true for athletic teams and for musical ensembles (recall the basketball team and the improvisational jazz group described earlier), for industrial production teams, and for decision-making committees (Hackman, 1990). It also is true for cockpit crews, as is neatly illustrated in an experimental study by Foushee, Lauber, Baetge, & Acomb (1986).

Foushee and his colleagues originally set out to assess the effects of fatigue on crew performance. To accomplish this, they recruited a number of crews as they returned from several days on the line, and compared their performance on a moderately demanding LOFT-type scenario with that of crews whose members had just completed several days off duty. As one would expect, the pilots returning from multiple-day trips were indeed tired. The surprising finding was that the fatigued crews, as crews, made significantly fewer errors than did crews composed of rested pilots who had not yet flown together. Having experience flying together more than overcame the debilitating effects of individual fatigue.

In an ideal world, then, crews would remain intact for a considerable period of time, giving members the opportunity to develop themselves into the best performing unit that they are able to become. Moreover, on any given trip they would fly the same aircraft and work with the same cabin crew. Current practice in the U.S. airline industry, reinforced by provisions in most contracts with pilot unions, is significantly at variance from this ideal (although some military organizations, such as the U.S. Air Force Strategic Air Command, closely approximate it). In one organization we studied, for example, a normal day's flying could involve two or even three changes of aircraft and as many different cabin crews. In another carrier, it was not uncommon for cockpit crews themselves to have one or two changes in composition during their one- or two-day life spans.

Perhaps the most vivid example of crew instability that we observed occurred when a crew lost one of its members (for personal reasons) in mid-trip. While we waited for a reserve pilot to appear, I asked the captain if he was concerned about having a change of membership halfway through the trip. "No problem," he responded. "Every pilot in this company knows his job, and the new first officer will pick up right where Bob left off." Because we were already quite late departing, the captain called for pushback and the pre-start checklist immediately after the reserve pilot arrived. Engine start, taxi, and take-off proceeded normally, and only when we were well into the climb were introductions made all around.

Was there anything wrong here? Should the captain have taken a further delay to repair the damage done to his team by the unexpected, last-minute departure of one of its members? In this particular instance, the fact that the work began the moment the reserve pilot arrived did not result in any discernible problems. But what if something unusual and challenging had occurred during taxi, take-off, or initial climb? Our research suggests that having taken a few moments before pushback to get the boundaries of the team re-established, to clarify the basic norms and expectations that would guide behavior in the cockpit, and to review together the strategy for taxi and take-off (including contingencies if problems should develop) would have helped had something gone wrong. I also predict, based on conversations with pilots in a number of carriers, that many pilots—perhaps most—would disagree with this conclusion.

Constant changes in cockpit crew composition deprive members of the time and experience they need to build themselves into a good team. Frequent changes of equipment tempt crews to take shortcuts in accepting an aircraft (for example, when the crew has to dash down the concourse from a late-arriving inbound flight to pick up a new airplane for an already-late outbound flight). And frequent switches of cabin crew decrease the chances that the captain will conduct a proper briefing of the lead flight attendant of yet another new cabin crew. Overall, scheduling and rostering instabilities constrain a crew's ability to settle in and develop performance strategies and routines that are uniquely suited to the partic-ular demands and opportunities of a given day's work.

Some real efficiencies in the use of personnel and equipment can be achieved if pilots, flight attendants, and aircraft are switched around from day to day, or even within a given day. The financial benefits of these efficiencies can, with a little effort, be calculated—and they are substantial. Moreover, the bidding systems that are in place at most U.S. carriers provide individual pilots with greater latitude in choosing work schedules than would be possible under a system that promoted crew integrity and stability. These are real benefits, but they must be assessed against the costs to crew performance that are incurred when airline scheduling and rostering practices make it next to impossible for a crew to become established as a stable task-performing unit. Our research suggests that these costs also are substantial—and, indeed, that the full benefits of CRM training may never be realized if crews are kept constantly in a state of flux.

Summary

It is now generally recognized throughout the aviation community that cockpit crews are task-performing teams. This legacy of the first generation of resource management training is something of which members of that community justifiably can be proud. The challenge, now, is to bring both CRM training and organizational policies into better alignment with what is required for team effec-tiveness.

Accomplishing this will require, first, that we continue to move beyond old-style, individual-oriented CRM programs to training that provides explicit practice, feedback, and reinforcement of team skills. Moreover, it will require a fresh look at the criteria used to select pilots for airline employment, and at the ways organizations schedule pilots and form them into teams. If it is true that the difference between a great crew and a mediocre one, between a crew that is self-correcting and one that risks falling victim to cascading exogenous problems, lies in a crew's skill in drawing on and coordinating the full set of resources available to it, then these matters are worthy of serious attention both from airline managements and from pilots' unions.

As is documented in other chapters in this book, a number of airlines already have made great strides in meeting the challenges of team-oriented CRM training. Now, perhaps, is the time to mount an equally vigorous attack on the organization-level issues that must be resolved for the full benefits of that training to be harvested.

FACT TWO: THE CAPTAIN IS THE TEAM LEADER ✈

Let us return to the parallel between cockpit crews and athletic teams and consider a basketball team that includes a player-coach. There are, without question, a number of constructive things a playing coach can do on the floor during a game—such as adjusting team strategy in response to opponents' behaviors, reinforcing high effort and enthusiasm, and keeping play well coordinated. Yet what can be done on the court with the clock running is necessarily limited. Imagine a situation in which there are 40 seconds to play, you are three points down, and you have no timeouts left. That situation is akin to being over the marker with no autopilot in rapidly deteriorating weather and having a flight attendant appear in the cockpit door to say, "Captain, we have a very serious problem in the cabin." All one can do in either case is to hope the team is ready to handle the challenge it faces, and then proceed to deal with it in real time.

Happily, there is a great deal that can be done beforehand to increase the chances that a team will be able to handle a tight situation well. Consider, for example, some of the things that good athletic coaches do off the court: They build the team in practice sessions, they have a pre-game warmup and strategy-setting session, they use halftime to review what has happened so far and to lay plans for the second half of play, and the day after the game they review the films with the players to see what can be learned that may be helpful in future games. A coach that does these things, and does them well, substantially increases his or her team's capability to deal competently with time-critical situations such as the one I described above.

The analogy is obvious, is it not? The captain is the playing coach on the aircraft and may need to do some of the same kinds of things that athletic coaches do. In our research on crew behavior, we document all acts of leadership that occur in the crews we observe, including team-building initiatives that take place outside the cockpit or during low-workload times as well as actions intended to fine-tune crew performance in real time. So far, we have found that just over 70% of all leadership acts fall into the fine-tuning category—that is, managing crew effort, strategy, or the use of knowledge and expertise in flight. Less than 30% of the leadership acts we have observed deal directly with building or strengthening the team as a performing unit.

Yet this 30%, the things captains do when not pressed by flying duties, are just as important to team functioning, if not more so, as are their actions when things get demanding in flight. These team-building activities typically involve establishing team boundaries (including how the cockpit crew and cabin crew will relate), helping the crew come to terms with any special requirements of the day's work, and establishing the basic norms of conduct that will guide behavior in the crew.

Research by one member of our team (Ginnett, 1986, 1990; see also his chapter) found that captains who had been identified (by check airmen familiar with their work) as excellent team leaders engaged in significantly more of these team-building activities during the first few minutes of a crew's life than did captains who had been rated as equally good technical flyers but as less expert in team leadership. Moreover, what happened in the first few minutes carried forward throughout a crew's life: Those that had a good "pre-game" briefing generally fared better than did those that received no briefing at all, or a briefing that undermined rather than affirmed the integrity of the crew as a performing unit. Our recent research has built on Ginnett's findings by seeking to determine what captains can do later in the life of a crew to further strengthen its capabilities. Preliminary results suggest that other low-workload times, such as extended cruise and overnights, also provide good opportunities for captains to take initiatives to strengthen their crews as performing units.

Team Leadership Training for Captains

The research reviewed above has at least two implications for the design of team-oriented CRM training for captains. First, captains could be helped to see that there are many different occasions when they can provide constructive leadership to their crews—including times other than the high-workload periods that so often are the focus of attention in accident and incident analyses, and that occupy center stage in many CRM programs. And they could learn that leadership intended to fine-tune crew performance both is easier and has greater impact if a crew already has been built into a basically sound performing unit.

Moreover, captains could be taught specific skills that are useful in exploiting the opportunities that low-workload times offer. For example, they could learn how to efficiently form their crews into teams; how to conduct initial briefings that get teams off to good starts; how to take advantage of the "halftime" represented by overnights on multi-day trips; how to use extended cruises to further strengthen their crews; and so on. They could be shown that these kinds of activities are precisely what great athletic coaches do, that great captains do them too, and that—in truly superb crews—such acts of leadership are also initiated from time to time by members other than the captain.

Crew-oriented leadership training has a good chance of generalizing from the classroom to the line because it does not require change in one's preferred personal or interpersonal style. Instead, trainees learn how to use their own styles to put in place conditions that build and sustain effective teamwork. Still, training in crew-oriented leadership is sure to require repetition and opportunities for practice, since many captains will find team-building skills unfamiliar and awkward when they first try them. Because LOFT provides a relatively safe site for behavioral experimentation, it can provide an especially good vehicle for such training.

The potential benefits of crew-oriented leadership training are great. If a captain has done a good job in forming and building his or her crew as a team, then the chances are good that the resources needed to deal with significant problems and opportunities will be both available and deployable. Then, even if the captain slips into an ineffective style of leadership during a crisis, help still may be forthcoming from his or her colleagues, precisely because he or she previously took the trouble to build the crew into a strong performing unit whose members are prepared to share responsibility for the crew and its work.

As was the case for training crew members in team skills, discussed earlier, there are many things that organizations can do to increase the chances that leadership training for captains will be used to good effect on the line. Two of the greatest points of leverage are (1) what senior managers communicate to captains about *direction*—that is, what is expected of them and their crews, and (2) the degree to which captains are given sufficient *latitude* to achieve those directions.

Clear and Challenging Direction

We were surprised by the number of captains who reported that they were not entirely clear about what they were supposed to accomplish in their leadership role. Individual captains reacted in various ways to that ambiguity. At one extreme, some captains explicitly abdicated much of their leadership responsibility. These individuals were ready, at the slightest provocation, to issue the well-worn Bus Driver's Affirmation: "I'm just a bus driver here. They own the bus, they tell me where they want it driven, and I do it. So long as the bus doesn't break down, we don't have any problems." Other captains took the opposite tack and exploited the ambiguity about direction to strengthen their own authority. In effect, these captains crowned themselves King of their Domain, where that domain was defined as the aircraft, its crew, the passengers, and anyone else encountered along the way—gate agents, dispatch staff, mechanics, and even, on a couple of occasions, Federal Aviation Administration (FAA) inspectors.

When we asked airline managers about such variation in leadership behavior, the explanation invariably had to do with differences in the personalities of various captains—often accompanied by a shrug to signal that there is not much one can do about someone's personality. Although personality clearly does influence behavior, I would argue that the considerable variation we observed also depends heavily on the kind of leadership provided to captains by senior flight operations managers.

Management does, of course, provide great clarity about the task responsibilities of captains (and other crew members), and those duties are explicated in detail in flight operations policy manuals. In many airlines, however, management provides little specific direction for captains about the kind of crew leadership they are expected to provide, in effect leaving the matter open to interpretation by individual captains. Psychologists learned long ago that the more ambiguity there is in a situation, the more personality differences show themselves. That is why they use ambiguous stimuli such as inkblots to diagnose personalities. It is also one reason why we saw so much variation in the character of the leadership that was provided by the captains of the crews we observed.

Had the managements of the airlines we studied provided their captains with clearer direction, then we surely would have seen fewer instances of captains tending toward either the "abdicrat" or the "autocrat" pole. Research suggests that the optimum strategy is for management to provide clear and challenging direction about desired end-states, to be equally clear about the outer-limit constraints on what can be done to achieve those ends, and then to let leaders do whatever needs to be done to achieve the aspirations without violating the constraints (see, for example, Hackman, 1986). When this is done, then one tends to obtain, simultaneously, greater attention to leadership tasks, greater motivation and engagement with the work, and fewer leaders either abdicating their leadership responsibilities or taking unto themselves authority that they do not really have.

One airline in our study accomplished this in a way that also added an element of surprise to pilots who were attending their captain upgrade course. Managers at this airline were intent on providing clear and challenging direction but also were worried about the risk of emphasizing any single objective, for fear that captains would focus on it to the detriment of other important outcomes. After a senior manager had welcomed the new captains to the "partnership," the head of flight operations stood up to talk about what was expected of them. Their main job, he said, was to maximize simultaneously three outcomes: one, safety; two, efficiency and economy; and three, passenger comfort and service.

The new captains nodded in agreement; all three aspirations struck them as both worthy and appropriate. Then, gradually, furrows began to appear on brows as they realized that what was being asked of them is impossible to achieve: one cannot, simultaneously, maximize safety *and* efficiency *and* passenger comfort. One must, instead, make constant trade-offs among them as one goes about one's flying duties. And that, of course, was the point the senior manager wanted to make. To promote the overall well-being of the organization and its people, captains must understand the critical importance of all three objectives, accept that trade-offs must be made among them, and expertly mobilize all the resources at their disposal to manage those tradeoffs well in real time.

Latitude to Act

Even when management provides captains with clear, challenging direction for their leadership responsibilities, restrictions on captains' latitude to act can seriously limit what they are able to accomplish. The increasing standardization of cockpit procedures provides a case in point. Although unquestionably standardization has contributed to the safety of flight, there is reason to believe that we may now be starting to see some unanticipated negative effects of a very good idea.

Those who study the effects of public policies use the concept "perverse effects" to describe what can happen when one tries too hard to accomplish something that is, on its own merits, entirely worthy (Hirschman, 1989). Public programs to reduce poverty, for example, sometimes can unintentionally encapsulate poor people in a state of poverty rather than help them work their way out of it. The same phenomenon often is seen when individuals try too hard to achieve something about which they care intensely: The result, to the performer's dismay, can be the opposite of that which was sought. "Just relax," we say to such people. "Quit trying so hard, give yourself some room." In many instances, that advice works.

Perhaps we need some more room in the cockpit. In reflecting on that possibility, consider what happens after an aircraft accident or serious incident. The National Transportation Safety Board invariably identifies one or more proximal causes of the event and recommends changes to minimize the chance that the same thing can happen again. Often, this involves introducing a technological safeguard (such as a warning signal or a guard on a switch), a new component of initial or recurrent training, or an additional procedure that crews subsequently are required to follow. Each of these actions, by itself, is invariably a good idea. But no one ever examines their collective impact on crews and their work.

There is at least a possibility that all the well-intentioned additions to procedure manuals, together with all the automated devices that have been introduced into cockpits and all the management directives intended to promote efficiency or passenger service, have significantly eroded the latitude that captains have to do what needs to be done to accomplish their overall objectives. Or, in other words, the industry may be limiting, gradually and entirely unintentionally, the ability of captains to provide to their crews the very kind of leadership that everyone agrees is needed.

One airline we studied went to great lengths to impress upon captains that they held the pivotal role in the entire airline, that their behavior was the most critical of all in helping the airline weather these difficult economic and operational times. "If there is a delay before pushback," captains were told, "get out of the cockpit and see if you can help resolve the problem. You may be the one person who can really do something about it." It is ironic that these same captains, exhorted to exercise their authority to deal with problems formally beyond the bounds of their own job, found their latitude in doing their real work ever more limited.

The evidence is clear: what is needed is balance between standardization of cockpit procedures and that which captains are trained and paid to do—that is, to lead their crews. Too much standardization results in crews merely monitoring systems and executing, sometimes without as much thought as one would wish, pre-specified procedures. Too much latitude can result in a poorly disciplined cockpit in which members are unable to predict who is going to take what action next. We have seen the sometimes tragic outcomes of both extremes. When a good balance is achieved, all crewmembers tend to be alert and proactive in managing the aircraft and its systems. And the likelihood increases that, when extraordinary leadership is in fact required—that is, when circumstances are such that standard procedures are inadequate—the captain will be both ready and able to lead the crew through the difficulties to a successful outcome.

Summary

Competent, well-trained captains who are skilled in crew leadership are among the most valuable assets an airline has. We have seen that there is much that airlines can do to further develop those assets. Training in crew-oriented leadership, with special emphasis on actions captains can take during low-work-load times to build and strengthen their crews as teams, can significantly enhance the likelihood that a crew will be ready to handle demanding, time-critical episodes when they do occur.

Yet more than training is required. We have seen that the quality of the leadership provided by captains also depends on their having received from management a clear and challenging statement of direction, coupled with sufficient latitude to take the actions that are needed to meet those expectations and confident knowledge of the outer-bound limits on their authority. Wisdom and leadership are required, then, not just by captains, but also by senior flight operations managers, who must negotiate questions of direction and authority with their own colleagues and managers. It is a significant leadership challenge to achieve balance between laissez-faire management that can invite anarchy and relentless standardization that can risk eroding the ability of captains to develop and lead their cockpit teams.

FACT THREE: CREWS OPERATE IN ORGANIZATIONAL CONTEXT ⎯⎯⎯⎯⎯⎯⎯⎯⎯→

We can view the major influences on cockpit crew performance as three concentric circles (see Figure 2.1). The innermost circle is what happens in real time, on the line. To return to our basketball analogy, these are the acts of

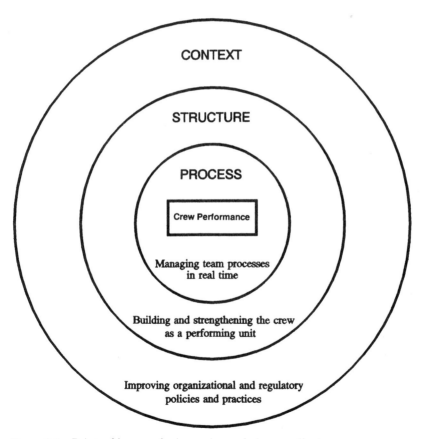

Figure 2.1   Points of leverage for improving cockpit crew effectiveness.

leadership that crewmembers exhibit on the court while the game is underway. Although important, they are far from the whole story. The next circle is team-building and team-strengthening activities, the acts of leadership I just discussed, the ones that typically take place out of the cockpit or during low-workload times. If these activities are done well, then less real-time management of a crew may be necessary—and the hands-on management that *is* done is likely to unfold more smoothly and with greater success.

Let us turn now to the outermost circle. This is the context within which the crew operates. New skills learned in training are like the sprouts of plants that emerge in the spring. If the climate is unfavorable, or if someone inadvertently steps on them, they do not survive. For this reason, crew resource management cannot stop at the schoolhouse door. A full-fledged CRM program also must ensure that the organizational context supports rather than undermines the use of resource management skills.

We have seen in previous sections how specific organizational policies and practices, ranging from scheduling and rostering to the level of authority assigned to captains, moderate the impact of both team member and team leader training. Now we turn to the overall policies of the organization where the crew works, and to those of the government agencies that monitor and regulate flight operations. If what is taught in CRM training conflicts with either organizational or regulatory influences, then training is almost certain to come out the loser. The research literature is full of studies in which well-conceived and well-executed training fails because what is taught is poorly aligned with the culture of the organization where the work is done.

Among the contextual features—the factors in the outermost circle—that are especially powerful in either reinforcing or compromising what is taught in the CRM classroom are (1) those that determine the consequences of performance, and (2) those that provide crews with the information and material resources they need to do their work.

The Consequences of Performance

Pilots receive feedback constantly as they go about their work. Simply flying an aircraft provides abundant data about how, and how well, a crew is performing. These data are supplemented by signals or remarks from the many other people a crew encounters in its work: gate and ramp agents, air traffic controllers, cabin crewmembers, and sometimes even passengers. Moreover, a pilot in his or her career receives periodic feedback of potentially great conse-quence from trainers, FAA inspectors, physicians, and managers in the chief pilot's office. Pilots do not suffer from an absence of feedback.

One group of feedback-providers merits special comment because it is positioned to significantly reinforce—or undermine—crew resource management values. This is the flight standards staff, whose job it is to ensure that pilots and crews operate at the highest possible level of professionalism. Ideally, check airmen would be fully conversant with, and supportive of, what is taught in resource management courses. Debriefings from a check ride would review how the crew operated as a team as well as members' technical performances, and check airmen would both reinforce constructive team behavior and help members identify behaviors that may have detracted from good team functioning (for details, see the chapters by Helmreich & Foushee and by Butler).

Standard practice at a number of the airlines we studied was at variance from this ideal. Check airmen typically were selected on the basis of their technical skills (coupled, in many cases, with being in the right network and known to chief pilots or flight standards managers). We also found considerable variation in the degree to which check airmen themselves understood and practiced good crew resource management. Some were deeply knowledgeable about such matters and took it as a personal responsibility to share their knowledge with other pilots and to reinforce behaviors that contributed to effective teamwork. Others viewed CRM as mere pop psychology; they focused exclusively on the technical aspects of flying, confident that one day CRM, like so many previous airline programs, would be history.

The damage that can be done by even one individual with this attitude is considerable. One captain told us of an instance when a colleague, fresh from CRM training, noticed an anomalous instrument reading while being given a check ride. He turned to the first officer and asked for his views about what might be responsible for the strange behavior of the instrument. "Just a moment," interjected the check airman. "I'm checking *you*, not him. You figure it out." That kind of intervention by someone who has influence over your career can undo days of first-rate CRM training.

In all the organizations we studied, check airmen, like regular line pilots, participated in whatever CRM training the organization offered. We did not, however, find that either selection for the role or continued occupancy of it required that check airmen demonstrate expertise in CRM in their own behavior. Nor did the airlines we studied explicitly require check airmen to address CRM items in their debriefings. The situation is now improving. As Helmreich & Foushee point out in their chapter, a number of airlines have instituted special training and quality control procedures for check airmen and flight instructors. In addition, the FAA's draft advisory circular on crew resource management training explicitly highlights these issues (FAA, in preparation). I applaud this movement, because CRM can never become deeply rooted in an airline, let alone in the industry as a whole, until and unless those who are on the front line of quality control endorse and behaviorally reinforce CRM values.

Beyond the reinforcement that can be provided by check airmen, excellent team performance could be regularly and explicitly recognized and rewarded by airlines. Such rewards would signal to pilots the importance that the organization places on teamwork and would provide an incentive for continued striving for excellence. In the airlines we studied, recognition was always provided to crews that had surmounted an extraordinary performance challenge such as a hijacking or a catastrophic mechanical failure.[2] But what about crews that turn in consistently first-rate performance every day? How might an airline recognize a team that has become expert in doing the quiet persuading of others that so often is needed to achieve on-time departures, that routinely deals well with passengers, that operates the aircraft with great efficiency, and that takes a multitude of small extra steps to promote safety and comfort?

Indeed, is it even possible for an organization to recognize and reward routine excellence by flightcrews? Or is it necessary to rely exclusively on rewards that are self-administered by teams—that is, on the collective pride that comes when a team knows that it has done a first-rate job? Clearly, it is not practical for an airline to recognize and reward crew performance if crew composition is constantly changing: By the time relevant data become available, the crew no longer exists.

If crews are relatively stable, however, a number of possibilities become available. For example, information that is routinely collected for use by management (such as data about fuel burn, passenger complaints and compliments, on-time pushbacks, and so on) could be summarized and passed on to crews as a matter of course. These data would serve two purposes. First, members would have the data they need to monitor their own effectiveness over time, to initiate corrections of chronic problems, and to seek ways of operating that generate performance improvements. Moreover, crews would experience that special good feeling that comes when members know that others in the organization are aware of, and appreciate, their efforts and accomplishments.

Information and Resources

Ideally, a cockpit crew would never encounter a delay or an unsafe situation merely because the information or material resources needed for the work (for example, equipment, paperwork, supplies) were not available. Among the saddest of all crew failures we observed were those that occurred when a crew was well composed, well led, and ready to go out and do a first-rate job—but was unable to do so because information or resources were late or inadequate, or because crewmembers became frustrated and angry in trying to obtain them.

Providing such support, in ample supply and on time, is especially challenging for managers of air transport organizations. Information is a problem, because

[2]Once again, some military organizations have an advantage: Not only do crews remain intact, but training missions are scored on objective criteria (such as bombs on target), and teams that perform well are explicitly recognized and rewarded.

the nature of the work requires that most pilots be "out of the office" most of the time. Moreover, the current competitive situation in the airline industry has prompted many airlines to define even information about performance trends, not to mention plans for routes and equipment, as proprietary. Such information, therefore, is not shared even with captains, who surely would be in a stronger leadership position with their crews if they did have knowledge about what was happening, and what was about to happen, in their own companies.

At one airline in our study, a group of senior managers were debating precisely this issue. "We cannot possibly tell our people about such important matters," one executive declaimed. "Everybody around here has a neighbor who has a brother-in-law who works for [a competitor airline]. We tell our employees, and it will be in their executive offices within a day." After a moment's reflection, another manager responded, "That may be true, but which would be worse, for [the competitor] to know, or for our own people *not* to know?" Which, indeed?

Other resources are also a problem, largely because so many diverse items must be made available and coordinated for a trip to unfold smoothly. Too often it falls on the crew to try to figure out how to deal with the absence or tardiness of such basic resources as weather information, catering, fuel, de-icing, a tug, or even the aircraft itself. It is hard to focus on achieving superb team performance when you do not even have what you need to accomplish your most basic responsibility—namely, getting an aircraft away from the gate and flown safely to its destination.

Providing crews with timely information and ample material resources is complicated by the pattern of inter-group relationships that develops in some airline organizations. When airlines are structured along strictly functional lines, for example, different groups can easily fall into conflict with one another, especially if resources are scarce. In one airline we studied, it seemed as if the last thing members of one department wanted was to do anything that might make life a little easier for members of another.

Because inter-group conflict is both self-fueling and destructive, managers often try to smooth out problems between groups—for example, by making sure everyone realizes that their prosperity and continued employment depends on company-wide cooperation or by convening meetings to improve inter-department communication. If the conflict stems from basic problems such as resource scarcity or poor organizational design, however, such remedial efforts are unlikely to succeed. The result can be cockpit crews who become increasingly frustrated that they do not have, and cannot readily get, the wherewithal to do their work.

Resolving such difficulties requires flight operations managers to use sophisticated political and interpersonal skills in dealing with other departments and in resolving emerging inter-group tensions before they spiral into flaming conflicts that defy containment. Managers who have such skills, and who use them well in negotiating with their peers and bosses, can do much to empower the crews for which they are responsible, enabling those crews to give full attention to their own special responsibilities—without constant distractions and irritations from resource problems that are properly someone else's concern.

CONCLUSION ————————————————————————— ✈

Resource management training is moving to the next stage in its evolution. While training that focuses on individual attitudes and skills continues to be important in CRM programs, there is increasing emphasis on what is required to build, lead, and organizationally support crews as teams. It is noteworthy, for example, that the FAA has titled its new advisory circular on the topic *Crew* [formerly *Cockpit*] *Resource Management Training* (FAA, in preparation). In this chapter I have identified some factors suggested by our research that may be worth considering in helping CRM become established on this next, higher plateau.

In the early days of CRM, attention appropriately was focused on basic questions of course design, on the construction of LOFT scenarios, and on ways to persuade both airline managers and pilots that CRM activities were worth the trouble and expense. There continue to be opportunities to refine and improve instructional materials and techniques, and there are always some recalcitrant individuals who need to be convinced that resource management is not just an expensive and irrelevant feel-good activity. But it is now time to move on to new challenges.

Our research shows that those challenges have much to do with how well crews are composed, structured, and supported by their organizations. Indeed, I suspect that among the highest leverage activities managers can undertake to reap the benefits of their investments in crew resource management are those that seek to improve the basic design of crews as performing units and the supportiveness of the organizational context within which crews operate.

Yet progress along these lines will not be easy, a lesson we learned with some pain as our research progressed. To assess the effects of crew design and organizational context on crew behavior and performance, we initially sought the cooperation of three carriers in the United States: A new entrant that was in serious economic difficulty; an established carrier that recently had experienced considerable stress from mergers, acquisitions, and labor-management turbulence; and an airline that was relatively stable both organizationally and financially.

We encountered two significant problems with this research design. One was that it was difficult even to *find* a successful airline that also was stable during the late 1980s when the data were collected. More serious was the fact that the differences we expected to find across the three airlines in how crews were structured, managed, and organizationally supported were simply not present to any-where near the extent that we had anticipated. There was variation in how different crews performed, to be sure. But our data showed that there was at least as much variance in crew behavior within carriers as between them, and that organization-level factors were remarkably similar across airlines. Since these were the factors in which we were especially interested, we decided to invite a number of European carriers to also participate in the research. That, surely, would give us the variation we were seeking.

We selected three carriers on the other side of the Atlantic that we expected to be quite different from one another and, as a group, different from our three U.S. carriers. The route structures of the European carriers differed significantly from one another and from those of our domestic carriers; the airlines were located in three different countries where three different languages were spoken; and two of the three trained all of their new pilots ab initio, sharply contrasting with U.S. practice. Nevertheless, we still found few differences among carriers in how crews were composed, in their in-flight procedures, in airline organizational structures, or in the reactions of pilots to their work environment.

At this point, we began to take more seriously the commonalities that we were discovering across carriers—and, now, across nations. We finally did obtain a bit more variation (by adding one last airline, an Asian carrier, to our sample), but the dominant phenomenon we had to contend with, and to explain, was one of similarity rather than difference. So we began to dig deeper and to look historically at how it came to pass that organizational structures and systems are as similar worldwide as they are. What we found, in retrospect, makes sense; but neither we nor our advisors in the industry, in NASA, or in the FAA had anticipated it. (For additional perspectives on cross-cultural similarities and dif-ferences, see the chapters by Helmreich, Wiener, & Kanki; Johnston; and Yama-mori & Mito).

It turns out that there are three dominant influences on how the work of cockpit crews is designed and managed, none of which is directly under the control of the management of any given airline. One is the relatively standard cockpit technology that has been generated by designers and engineers at three corporations: Airbus, Boeing, and Douglas. Although crews did react differently to various aircraft types, we did not obtain significant differences between standard and advanced technology cockpits, as a group, on any of our measures—some-thing that was quite surprising at the time, albeit less so now, given the recent findings of Wiener and his colleagues on this issue (Wiener, Chidester, Kanki, Palmer, Curry, & Gregorich, 1991). Clearly, there is a philosophy of cockpit design, deeply rooted at all three manufacturers, that provides the technological platform on which airline operating policies and practices are erected. The com-monalities in that platform—across manufacturers, aircraft size, and level of cockpit automation—overwhelm the differences associated with particular aircraft types and significantly shape and constrain the operating policies and practices of individual airlines.[3]

The second influence is the set of regulatory procedures and standards that have been developed over the years by the U.S. FAA in cooperation with aircraft manufacturers and the flight operations departments of U.S. airlines. It turns out that these procedures and standards have been adopted, often with only minor modifications, by a number of airlines and regulatory agencies around the world. It makes sense: Why start from scratch when the largest and arguably most sophisticated regulatory agency in the world, the FAA, has already done the bulk of the work? The result, however, is both fatter procedure manuals and more commonality among them than otherwise might have been the case.

Third is the culture of flying that pervades both civilian and military aviation worldwide. That culture, which can be traced back to the earliest days of flying, is highly individualistic in character. No pilot forgets his or her first solo flight, for example, nor does any pilot fail to worry, from time to time, about his or her upcoming medical check. This individualistic orientation is reinforced continuously throughout a pilot's career, both formally (in training and proficiency checks) and informally (through a status system that accords the highest respect to great "stick-and-rudder" pilots). The strength of the culture is such that attempting to develop team-oriented pilot selection, training, and management is, to some unknown but clearly considerable extent, like swimming upstream against a strong and consistent current.

Together, cockpit technology, the regulatory environment, and the culture of flying significantly constrain the latitude of any airline to design and manage its crews differently from the rest of the industry. That is why the structural and contextual factors that we were studying varied so little across carriers, countries, and aircraft types. And, finally, that is why it will be necessary to involve the manufacturers, the regulators, and the aviation community as a whole if, in the years to come, the industry is to accommodate to the three facts with which I began this chapter—and with which I now end it. One: Cockpit crews are teams. Two: The captain is the team leader. And three: Crews are richly entwined in—and constrained by—their technological, organizational, and regulatory contexts.

Acknowledgments

This chapter is based, in part, on presentations made at the International Civil Aviation Organization Human Factors Seminar, Leningrad (April, 1990) and at the Flight Crew Training Meeting of the International Air Transport Association, New Orleans (February, 1988). The research on which the paper is based was conducted under Cooperative Agreement NCC 2-457 between the

[3]The Airbus 320, which was not in our sample, does seem to require a different way of thinking about crew factors.

Ames Research Center of NASA and Harvard University, with support from the NASA Office of Space Science and Applications and the Federal Aviation Administration. Principal members of the research team were Robert Ginnett (formerly with the U.S. Air Force Academy, now at the Center for Creative Leadership) and Linda Orlady (now with United Airlines). Research assistance on the project at Harvard University has been provided by Leslie Grubb, Lynn Hilger, and Erin Lehman. Valuable counsel has been provided by Clay Foushee (formerly with NASA and the FAA and now at Northwest Airlines), Barbara Kanki (NASA), and Robert Helmreich (University of Texas).

References

Federal Aviation Administration. (in preparation). *Crew resource management training* (Advisory Circular No. 120-51a). Washington, DC: Author.

Foushee, H. C., Lauber, J. K., Baetge, M. M., & Acomb, D. B. (1986). *Crew factors in flight operations III: The operational significance of exposure to short-haul air transport operations* (Technical Memorandum #88342). Moffett Field, CA: NASA–Ames Research Center.

Ginnett, R. C. (1986). *First encounters of the close kind: The first meetings of airline flight crews.* Unpublished doctoral dissertation, Yale University, New Haven, CT.

Ginnett, R. C. (1990). Airline cockpit crew. In J. R. Hackman (Ed.), *Groups that work (and those that don't).* San Francisco: Jossey-Bass.

Hackman, J. R. (1986). The psychology of self-management in organizations. In M. S. Pallack & R. O. Perloff (Eds.), *Psychology and work: Productivity, change, and employment.* Washington, DC: American Psychological Association.

Hackman, J. R. (1987). The design of work teams. In J. W. Lorsch (Ed.), *Handbook of organizational behavior.* Englewood Cliffs, NJ: Prentice-Hall.

Hackman, J. R. (Ed.). (1990). *Groups that work (and those that don't).* San Francisco: Jossey-Bass.

Hackman, J. R., & Walton, R. E. (1986). Leading groups in organizations. In P. S. Goodman (Ed.), *Designing effective work groups.* San Francisco: Jossey-Bass.

Helmreich, R. L. (1991). The long and short term impact of crew resource management training. *Proceedings of the AIAA/NASA/FAA/HFS conference on challenges in aviation human factors: The national plan.* Vienna, VA.

Helmreich, R. L., & Wilhelm, J. A. (1991). Outcomes of crew resource management training. *International Journal of Aviation Psychology, 1,* 287–300.

Hirschman, A. O. (1989, May). Reactionary rhetoric. *The Atlantic Monthly,* pp. 63–70.

Wiener, E. L., Chidester, T. R., Kanki, B. G., Palmer, E. A., Curry, R. E., & Gregorich, S. E. (1991). *The impact of cockpit automation on crew coordination and communication: I. Overview, LOFT evaluations, error severity, and questionnaire data* (Contractor Report 177587). Moffett Field, CA: NASA–Ames Research Center.

Wilhelm, J. (1991). Crew member and instructor evaluations of line oriented flight training. *Proceedings of the Sixth International Symposium on Aviation Psychology.* Columbus: Ohio State University.

Zajonc, R. B. (1965). Social facilitation. *Science, 149,* 269–274.

3

Crews as Groups: Their Formation and Their Leadership

Robert C. Ginnett
Center for Creative Leadership
Colorado Springs, Colorado 80906

INDIVIDUAL VERSUS CREW ORIENTATION ✈

A crew is a group and arguably the most critical resource in Cockpit Resource Management. It is also the primary and fundamental issue if we are to improve the work outcome for those who fly airplanes in the crew environment. But it goes far deeper than just the work in crew-served aircraft. Across America, we are discovering the difficulty of making the transition from *individual work* to *group work* in many of our industrial settings.

Our tendency not to think in group concepts is itself a group issue. We are an individualistic culture. From birth through college, we nurture and praise the individual accomplishments of our offspring. Whether in academics or athletics, in myth or in history, we focus on and reinforce individual accomplishment. This is not to say that group-oriented activity is ignored, but rather to say that we do not focus as much attention on the accomplishments of groups as we do on the accomplishments of individuals. Being a member of the NCAA championship football team is obviously cause for celebration. But are we more inclined to remember the team that won the national championship five years ago or the winner of the Heisman trophy from five years ago? Being a member of the national collegiate debate team is something to be proud of—but in our culture being a Rhodes Scholar carries more prestige.

Even our educational systems are based upon individual competition rather than group collaboration. At the U.S. Air Force Academy a group of fellow faculty members and I came to believe that the entire system—from elementary school through undergraduate pilot training—evaluated and rewarded individual performance. At the same time, we began to recognize and acknowledge that once finished with the formal "training" portion of the lives of our pilots, the subsequent "work" which was to be done depended largely on the ability to work in a group. This notion was reinforced in the extreme when F-16 pilots from Nellis Air

Force Base requested our research results on crew performance. As they noted, F-16 pilots work in "two-ships" or "four ships," and even though they were in separate cockpits, they needed to work as a group or team to be effective.

We have imported and strengthened this individualistic orientation in the aviation community. From the early days of flight training, the goal is to "solo." I am hard pressed to come up with a more individualistic term than "solo." Historically, the airline industry and those responsible for its oversight have been primarily interested in the qualifications and performance of the individual even though the individual was to be inserted into a crew-served cockpit. Airline companies have traditionally hired many of their pilots from the military, which assured them some reasonable minimum standard of training and experience in flying modern aircraft. Other pilots hired by the major companies have had to demonstrate comparable levels of qualifications. Likewise, the Federal Aviation Administration (FAA) certifies individual pilots on their technical skills at flying the airplane (for the captain and the first officer) or at managing the aircraft systems (for the flight engineer). For example, pilots are asked to demonstrate in recurrent simulator training procedures for difficult and infrequently encountered conditions, such as steep turns, multi-engine failures, recovery from wind shear stalls on take-off, and go-arounds in weather conditions with less than minimum visibility. Scheduling in most major airlines is driven by individual considerations, with seniority of the individuals in each of the positions being the principal factor. Only within the last decade have we begun to consider this issue of crews and groups (which is quite foreign to our culture) in the training of teams that fly commercial aircraft.

Before one gets the idea that this chapter is "anti-individual," let me lay those fears to rest. Nothing in this chapter suggests we need any less individual competence if we are to enhance crew performance. As we shall see later, individual skills are critical in aviation performance and should continue to be developed and rewarded. However, we have reached a point in aviation history (and in America as well, I might argue) where we need to take the next step and go beyond the individualistic focus. That next step requires that we learn about groups.

Sometimes we hear the argument that "groups are nothing more than the collection of individuals making up the groups." Such statements ignore a growing body of evidence in both the research literature and in the annals of aviation mishaps. Rather than citing evidence from both of these sources, let me provide a very simple example to show how group work can be quite different (and to someone with little group experience, even counterintuitive) from individual work. Again this example comes from athletics.

As a culture built on valuing individual performance, we are sometimes given individual advice which will not necessarily result in quality team outcomes.

For example, often team members are told by their coach that they all need to do their absolute best if the team is going to do well (at least, that is what my coaches told me on more than one occasion). But from systems theory we know that for a team to do well, sometimes the individuals comprising the team must not maximize their individual effort. Referred to as subsystem non-optimization, this concept is not intuitively obvious to many team members or their coaches either. But consider a high school football team which has an extremely fast running back and some very good, but measurably slower, blocking linemen. If our running back does his absolute best on a sweep around the end, he will run as fast as he can. By doing so, he will leave his blocking linemen behind. The team is not likely to gain much yardage on such a play, and the back, who has done his individual best, is apt to learn an important experiential lesson about teamwork. The coach would get better results if he or she worked out an integrated coordination plan between the back and the linemen. In this case, the fast running back needs to slow down (i.e., not perform maximally) to give the slower but excellent blockers a chance to do their work. After they have been given a chance to contribute to the play, the back will have a much better chance to then excel individually, and so will the team as a whole. Good teamwork is sometimes on a different plane (no pun intended) from good individual work.

Unfortunately, we find repeated evidence of poor crew work resulting in errors, accidents, and incidents in the aviation community. Three of the more publicized examples should be sufficient to illustrate this problem. The first example is taken from a National Transportation Safety Board investigation (NTSB, 1979, pp. 23–29). It illustrates both the pervasiveness of the captain's authority and the group's failure to demand that attention be focused on a critical aspect of the flight.

> The crew of Flight 173 had experienced only routine conditions as they brought the four-engine DC-8 into the Portland, Oregon traffic pattern. However, on final approach as they lowered their gear for landing, they heard a dull thump from what seemed to be the main gear area. The captain elected to abort the landing and was put into a holding pattern until they could determine if there was a problem and whether or not it warranted further emergency precautions.
>
> The aircraft proceeded in a large holding pattern while the captain directed the crew in attempting to determine the possible cause of the noise. This pattern was maintained for approximately one hour at the captain's insistence. During this time, both the first officer and the flight engineer warned the captain on four separate occasions that they were running out of fuel and needed to make a decision about landing. In spite of these repeated cautions, the captain insisted that they continue to circle. Finally,

as the first of the four engines flamed out, the captain ordered the plane toward the field while demanding that the flight engineer explain the cause of the engine failure. With all fuel tanks now dry, the other engines began to fail in sequence and the DC-8 nosed downward.

About 1815 PST, Flight 173 crashed into a wooded, populated area, killing 8 passengers and 2 crew members, and seriously injuring 21 passengers and 2 other crew members. The National Transportation Board determined that the probable cause of the accident was the failure of the captain to monitor properly the aircraft's fuel state and to properly respond to the low fuel state and the crew members' advisories regarding fuel state. This resulted in fuel exhaustion to all engines. Contributing to the accident was the failure of the other two flight crew members to fully comprehend the criticality of the fuel state or to successfully communicate their concern to the captain.

The Safety Board believes that this accident exemplifies a recurring problem—a breakdown in cockpit management and teamwork during a situation involving malfunctions of aircraft systems in flight. To combat this problem, responsibilities must be divided among members of the flight crew while a malfunction is being resolved. . . .

Admittedly, the stature of a captain and his management style may exert subtle pressure on his crew to conform to his way of thinking. It may hinder interaction and adequate monitoring and force another crew member to yield his right to express an opinion.

The second example, taken from a confidential report submitted to the NASA/FAA Aviation Safety Reporting System (ASRS) (Foushee, 1984, p. 888) describes a more blatant example of an overbearing and intimidating captain.

I was the first officer on an airline flight into Chicago O'Hare. The captain was flying, we were on approach to 4R getting radar vectors and moving along at 250 knots. On our approach, Approach Control told us to slow to 180 knots. I acknowledged and waited for the captain to slow down. He did nothing, so I figured he didn't hear the clearance. So I repeated, "Approach said slow to 180," and his reply was something to the effect of, "I'll do what I want." I told him at least twice more and received the same kind of answer. Approach Control asked us why we had not slowed yet. I told them we were doing the best job we could and their reply was, "You almost hit another aircraft." They then asked us to turn east. I told them we would rather not because of the weather and we were given present heading and to maintain 3000 ft. The captain descended to 3000 ft. and kept going to 2500 ft. even though I told him our altitude was 3000 ft. His comment was, "You just look out the damn window."

This last example illustrates the tragic consequences of a captain from the other extreme—one who would not make a decision when one was required (NTSB, 1982; Burrows, 1982; Foushee, 1984).

> "Slushy runway. Do you want me to do anything special for it or just go for it?" asked the First Officer of Air Florida's Flight 90, as he peered into a snowstorm at Washington National Airport. . . .
>
> "Unless you got anything special you'd like to do," quipped the plane's 34-year old captain. Shortly after brake release, the first officer expressed concern with engine instrument readings or throttle setting. Four times during takeoff roll he remarked that something was "not right," but the captain took no action to reject the takeoff. (Air Florida operating procedures state that the *captain alone makes the decision to reject.*)
>
> Seconds later, Flight 90 came back down, hitting the 14th Street Bridge before it crashed into the ice covered Potomac River, killing 74 persons on the aircraft and four motorists on the bridge.
>
> The NTSB ruled that the captain of the aircraft did not react to the copilot's repeated, subtle advisories that all was not normal during the takeoff. Moreover, in recommending that pilot training include "considerations for command decision, resource management, role performance, and assertiveness," the Board implied that the copilot's lack of assertiveness (possibly induced by the inherent role structure of the cockpit) may have been a causal factor. (NTSB, 1982, pp. 67–68)

It is painfully obvious that some crews do not do as well as they should. Yet in the course of our research on crews we have seen evidence of crews that go well beyond the call of duty—crews that do better than the collection of individual skills available to them. If we are to understand effective crew performance, it is essential that we move beyond our focus on the individual to a broader level. We must begin to pay serious attention to the crew as a group if we are to optimize cockpit resources.

CREWS, GROUPS, AND TEAMS ⟶ ✦

Groups fly crew-served airplanes, for a number of reasons. "As a direct result of the limitations and imperfections of individual humans, multi-piloted aircraft cockpits were designed to ensure needed redundancy" (Foushee, 1984). Furthermore, the Federal Aviation Regulations require at least a second in command if the aircraft is designed to carry more than 10 passengers (FAR 135.99). At a minimum then, commercial flights will have a dyad (the smallest group) in the cockpit. The other extreme observed in our research was a crew of 25 aboard a military C-5 Galaxy. Whether a dyad, a triad, or a crew of 25, these are all groups and as such share the potential strengths and weaknesses that are inherent in groups.

As illustrated earlier, groups are something more than merely a collection of the individuals comprising them. Some groups do remarkably well with no particularly outstanding individuals. Other groups, made up almost exclusively of high-performing individuals, do not do at all well as a team. A review of the performance of some of the U.S. Olympic teams illustrates this phenomenon quite well. The 1988 U.S. Olympic basketball team is remembered, if at all, for *not* winning the gold medal. Yet the team had high-performing individuals, many of whom are currently playing in the National Basketball Association, and the coach was highly respected. How could this happen, many asked? In the view of color commentator and former coach Al McGuire, the problem was that they did not have a "team," but merely a collection of high-performance individuals. As McGuire recalls, the United States had a history of putting together basketball teams by selecting the best individuals available but doing little to foster or coordinate teamwork. In previous Olympics, when our individuals were much superior to the rest of the world's individual players, we could win in spite of our lack of true teamwork. But as the rest of the world improved, particularly in the work of their teams as a whole, individual ability could no longer do the job. In what may be McGuire's most remembered quote, he said "You have to remember, there's no 'I' in team." He also noted that if we want to win, we have to quit building "all-star teams" and instead, build a team.

That is precisely what was done with the famous 1980 U.S. Olympic hockey team, which is remembered for "the impossible dream come true" as it beat the Soviet team. Here was a team of no overwhelmingly great individuals— but a great team. They practiced over one hundred games together as a team. Rather than being rewarded solely as individuals for goals, assists, saves, and the like, they were rewarded for the play of their lines (the five-man sub-groups that take the ice together) and for the performance of the team as a whole (see the chapter by Hackman on structuring an organization to reinforce group work). They learned to work as a team and found that a team can overcome individual inadequacies, deficiencies, and errors.

Although these are excellent examples of team performance (or lack thereof), one does not have to go to the intense level of Olympic competition to demonstrate the same phenomenon. A technique used widely in helping groups to understand the value added from team performance is a classroom exercise designed to demonstrate synergy. In this exercise, individuals are presented with a hypothetical scenario which places them in an uncommon setting and asks them to rank-order a limited number of items critical to their ultimate survival. While the specific task can very widely (from "Lost on the Moon" to "Desert Survival"), the procedures remain common. After the individuals have completed their own rank orderings, they are placed in a group which represents the other survivors in this unique setting. The group's task is to arrive at a consensus rank ordering of the same set of critical items. Upon completion of the rankings, both the individual and group rankings are compared to an ordering by experts in the particular setting (e.g., desert survival experts). Regardless of the specific nature of the setting, the results are virtually always the same. The most common result is that all of the groups' performances will exceed the performance of any individual in any group.

The parallel between lessons learned from this exercise and those learned in many aircraft accidents is more than casual. The characteristic of the classroom task that results in such predictable outcomes is its high degree of ambiguity to the participants. None of us has been lost on the moon, and it is such a strange environment that our experiences as individuals are not particularly useful. Only when we integrate a number of varied experiences are we likely to arrive at a high-quality solution. Similarly, we seldom crash airplanes when we know exactly what the problem is and how to handle it. Even with major problems in critical periods of flight (such as loss of one engine at V_r), we are trained to handle them. In many accidents in today's complex systems and environment, it is common to find that some aspect of the environment or situation created ambiguity which, by definition, eliminates a structured solution. After all, if you do not know what the problem is, it is unlikely that you know what the solution is! But if you can get two or three independent critical thinkers involved, you will have a better chance of ruling out individual biases and will be on the road to a more effective solution. It is important to acknowledge, even in these hypothetical examples, that there must be time available to have effective group work. As I note in a later section, time-critical emergencies drive different strategies.

In order to better understand group behavior and the impact of the group on the individual, it is necessary to become familiar with conditions that are uniquely associated with groups themselves. These are characteristics that either can only be defined relative to the group or, if associated with individuals, only make sense in a group setting.

Boundaries

Boundaries for a group are like the fence around a piece of property. A group boundary allows us to know who is in the group and who is not, whether we are a member of the group or not. It defines both physically and psychologically who the members of the group might rely on within their own group's boundaries and thus indicates when it may be necessary to go beyond their own group for assistance or resources. A cockpit crew has a number of members defined by the design of the aircraft. A Boeing 727 has seats for three cockpit members, and hence there is an expected boundary of three for the crew of that airplane.[1] A psychosocial boundary might also define the limits of tolerable deviance for group members. For example, all the types of socially acceptable and unacceptable behaviors are never made absolutely clear and are seldom written down. Thus if a group can identify a boundary maintainer (usually someone close to the edge of acceptable behavior), they will have some means of gauging their own behavior as to its acceptability or not.

Roles

A role is a set of expected behaviors associated with a particular position (not person) in a group or team. In any group setting over time, various roles will emerge. Some people will assume roles that are focused on accomplishing the task while others will take on behaviors associated with maintaining relationships within the group. Still others may take on roles that are counterproductive or even destructive to the group. Examples of some of the group roles which have been identified are listed in Table 3.1.

Airline crews have clearly defined roles for the most part. The captain is the leader of the crew, followed by the first officer and second officer in turn. The lead flight attendant occupies a similar leadership position for the flight attendants. Some aspects of these roles are defined by law. Federal Aviation Regulation 91.3 states, "The pilot in command (i.e., the captain of a commercial aircraft requiring more than one pilot) of an aircraft is directly responsible for, and is the final authority as to, the operation of that aircraft." Other role expectations are defined by the organization, or even by the crew itself.

To the extent roles are clear and independent, the group will tend to function well, at least from a role standpoint. However, there can be role problems which will cause stress for the individuals involved and typically decreased performance from the group. Two kinds of role problems are most common.

Role Conflict

When the individual is getting contradictory messages or expectations about his or her behavior, he or she is experiencing role conflict. These conflicts can come from several different sources. Perhaps most common is where the person is receiving two different signals about the expectations for a particular role. We can attach a label to this kind of role conflict depending on where the signals are emanating from. If the same person is giving you conflicting signals, we call that *intra-sender role conflict.* ("I want you to do a high-quality, detailed job and I need it in two minutes.") If two different people are providing differing expecta-

---

[1] Sometimes technology overtakes original design. For example, on a C-141 aircraft there is a seat and workstation for a navigator. But the incorporation of inertial navigation systems has eliminated the requirement for the navigator position. Interestingly, this crew restructuring has also changed the social dynamics of the crew as predicted by sociotechnical systems theory, but that is another chapter.

Table 3.1
Commonly Identified Group Roles

Task roles	Maintenance roles	Blocking roles
Initiator contributor	Harmonizer	Dominator
Information seeker	Encourager	Blocker
Information giver	Gatekeeper	Aggressor
Evaluator	Compromiser	Disruptor
Summarizer		

tions about your role, that is labeled *inter-sender role conflict*. Sometimes the conflict can be between two different roles held by the same person. For example, a newly upgraded first officer may have conflicts between his role as father and Little League baseball coach and his flying schedule, which is now based on low seniority. This is referred to as *inter-role conflict*. Last is the situation where the expectations of a role violate the role occupant's personal expectations or values. This is known as *person-role conflict*. An example of this type of conflict from the Vietnam era was when intelligence specialists were instructed by their superior officers to falsify reports on bombing targets. When this practice violated an individual's personal values, he or she would experience conflict. This type of conflict is also experienced by people who are labeled by the press as "whistle-blowers."

Role Ambiguity

In role conflict, one receives clear messages about expectations but the messages are not all congruent. In situations of role ambiguity, the problem is that one cannot be sure what the expectations are at all. The information about the role is either lacking or not clearly communicated. Role ambiguity is more apt to occur in management positions than in traditional cockpit crew roles.

Norms

Norms are the informal rules that groups adopt to regulate group members' behaviors. Although these norms are infrequently written down or openly discussed, they often have a powerful, and consistent, influence on group members' behavior (Hackman, 1976). One might reasonably ask, "if norms are powerful (so they are something I *need* to know about) but they aren't written down and aren't discussed, how am I supposed to figure them out?" Fortunately, most of us are rather good at reading the social cues that inform us of existing norms. When we first enter a work situation, even though there may not be a dress code, we are fairly astute at determining that "everybody around here wears a suit." We also are apt to notice a norm if it is violated, even though we may have been unable to articulate the norm before its violation was apparent (e.g., the guy wearing jeans when everybody else is wearing a suit).

Another fortunate aspect of norms is that they do not govern all behaviors, just those behaviors that the group feels are important. Feldman (1984) has outlined four reasons why norms are likely to be enforced. He suggests norms are more apt to be enforced if they (1) facilitate group survival; (2) simplify, or make more predictable, what behavior is expected of group members; (3) help the group avoid embarrassing interpersonal problems; or (4) express the central values of the group and clarify what is distinctive about the group's identity.

An outsider is often able to learn more about norms than an insider for several reasons. First, the outsider (not necessarily being subject to the norms himself) is more apt to notice them. In fact, the more "foreign" the observer is, the more likely the norms are to be perceived. If one is accustomed to wearing a tie to work, one is less likely to notice that another organization also wears ties to work, but more likely to note that a third organization typically wears sweaters and sweatshirts around the office. Another lesson the outsider can learn by observing other groups' norms is something about his or her own group's norms. In a recent consulting project, our research team was struck by the failure of the client organization to share information with us—not proprietary information, but information that impacted our own ability to work with them. In a moment of reflection on this situation, we realized that *our* work group norm was very different from theirs. Our team had a norm that encouraged open sharing of information with each other—but prior to seeing a very different norm in a different group, none of us could have articulated our own norm of openly sharing information.

Status

Status is the relative ranking of individuals within a group setting. In an airline cockpit crew, status is typically associated with the roles of captain, first officer, and second officer. In these cases, status comes with the position. Status, like roles, determines appropriate behaviors for all group members. Usually a high-status person has more power and influence, and thus the lower-status members of a group tend to defer to the higher-status members. Again, crossing cultures gives us interesting insights into status impact. In Eastern cultures, age is given status and younger people will bow to older people. Since Western culture lacks castes or clear-cut status lines, it is sometimes difficult to figure out who has the most status. Status incongruence can result in stress for the individuals and less than satisfactory work outcomes. Tom Wolfe in *The Right Stuff* (1979) describes the status incongruence that occurred between the flight surgeons (who believed they were the most important people in the manned space flight program—after all, they could reject an unfit "subject" with the stroke of a pen), and the test pilots who were to become the astronauts (who believed they were the very reason there was a manned space flight program).

Authority

Technically, authority is the right to use power and influence. People derive authority in the group setting from the legitimate power given them by the organization. The captain has the authority to order a drunken or abusive passenger off of the airplane or to not accept a flight that he or she believes is unsafe. Authority can also be granted on the basis of recognized expertise or expert power. Again, the group can get into trouble when differing sources of authority clash. There have been numerous reports of accidents caused by confused authority dynamics in the cockpit. For example, several accidents have occurred in military cockpits when a higher ranking (status) officer was assigned as a check pilot for a junior ranking crew and then became involved in giving directions during an actual emergency. The confused authority dynamics were directly responsible for accidents of this nature. Such confusion is also possible in the case of the senior captain who is forced to retire at age 60 by FAA rules but then decides to assume the position of flight engineer. Even though that former captain may be entirely clear on the limits of his authority in his own mind, his former status may create confusing authority dynamics for his younger crewmates.

Authority dynamics have their roots in the dependency relationships we have developed from birth. As children, we were dependent on our parents and accepted their authority. As we grew and became more independent, we had to work through the evolving authority relationships. Even today, we are all dependent at certain times. Passengers in commercial aircraft are dependent on the crew. A "dead-heading" first officer with 10,000 hours of flying time is still dependent on the crew flying in the cockpit. There is nothing good or bad about being dependent unless we mismatch the degree of dependency and the situation. A passenger who decides to take over the airplane has inappropriately usurped authority. At the other extreme, a first officer who becomes overly dependent on the captain for decision-making is not likely to help the crew either. Yet authority dynamics can result in just such occurrences. In an investigation conducted by Harper, Kidera, & Cullen (1971) at a major air carrier, captains feigned incapacitation at a predetermined point during final approach in simulator trials characterized by poor weather and visibility. In that study, approximately 25% of these simulated flights "hit the ground" because, for some reason, the first officers did not take control even when they knew the plane was well below glide slope. We can assume from this research and from other artifacts (see below) that the authority dynamic surrounding the role of the captain must be extremely powerful. Figure 3.1, which depicts a sign found on a bulletin board in a commercial carrier's operations room, is only partly facetious.

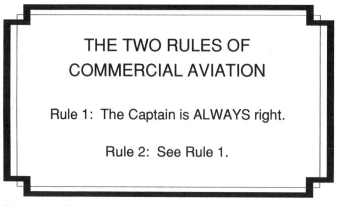

Figure 3.1   Sign posted on an airline's bulletin board.

Group Dynamics

Clearly all the topics in this section on groups could fall under the general heading of group dynamics, since they are all dynamic characteristics that only occur in a group setting. Recognizing the confusing nature of groups themselves, especially in our culture, it seems best to discuss a few group dynamics topics separately. There are, of course, many more group topics than I have space to discuss here. However, in closing we should note two remaining dynamics of groups.

Social influence is a by-product of group activity. Unfortunately, it has both positive and negative components. On the positive side is an effect labeled "social facilitation." This construct suggests that, in general, people are aroused by the presence of others and more motivated to perform well, knowing that others are evaluating them. On the dark side of social influence is what Latane, Williams, & Harkins (1979) have called "social loafing." Here the individual members of the group feel less pressure to perform when they are working with others. The researchers believe this may happen when the individuals are only carrying part of the load and no one can tell which member is loafing.

Groupthink is another flaw of highly cohesive groups, discovered by Janis (1982). He found that when people became deeply involved in a highly cohesive group, they often became more concerned with striving for unanimity than in realistically appraising alternative courses of action. This condition can be exacerbated when the leader promotes his or her preferred solution and when the group is insulated from expert opinions outside the group. Janis believed that groupthink accounted for a number of historic fiascoes, including the United States' failure to heed warnings of the impending attack on Pearl Harbor, the decision processes leading up to the failed Bay of Pigs invasion, and the Watergate cover-up.

GROUP PROCESS AND LEVERAGE ——————— ✈

Having briefly discussed some of the characteristics associated with groups, teams, and crews, we may now begin to consider a model for improving their output. Merely the mention of the word "output" leads us to begin thinking in the language and models of systems theory with its familiar terminology of "input–throughput–output." While that concept may be useful for considering group work, interventions or corrections based on systems theory have not been too successful. In systems theory, inputs are generally "givens" and outputs are "desired." If the outputs are not meeting expectations, then the corrective intervention most typically occurs somewhere in the "throughout" or process stage of the system. In the 1970s, much of our group-oriented corrective interventions pursued that course of action by attempting to intervene in the process stage of the group's work (see Schein, 1969, for a discussion of process interventions). After all, that is where the problems were most obvious—why not fix them where you see them? Unfortunately, years of evidence did not support that concept (Kaplan, 1979). That does not mean that process interventions cannot be helpful, but they should not be expected to fix all the problems encountered by groups either. If one buys an extremely cheap automobile, no amount of work by a mechanic will make it perform and ride like a Mercedes-Benz. Some things are far better incorporated in the design (input) phase than in the maintenance (process) phase.

Hackman (1987) has proposed a model to design groups for output effectiveness. His model suggests that the organization should be set up to support group work and also that the group should be designed to accomplish output objectives. Two important points should be noted in his model. First, the output is not unidimensional—it is not exclusively focused on satisfying the organizational or client (whoever that may be) needs. Certainly that is an important consideration, but Hackman also notes that the group must be able to continue to perform in the future, and the individuals making up the group should obtain at least as much satisfaction as dissatisfaction from working in the group. For example, if a cockpit crew flies a "safe and efficient" leg in a trip, that would meet the first criterion. But if, in the process of the trip, there was so much interpersonal tension that the crew felt they could no longer work together on subsequent legs, the output of the group would not be labeled as effective.

Most organizations (airlines included) cannot afford to wait until their teams disintegrate or fail to perform their required tasks successfully before taking corrective action. This is where process criteria can be helpful, not as points for intervention but as points for diagnosis. By paying attention to how the group is going about its work, we may infer that their ultimate performance may have problems as well. But rather than intervening first at the process level, it makes more sense to use leverage at the input level. The chapter by Hackman discussed factors at the organizational level which can support group-level work. There are also factors at the group design level that should lead to better group outcomes. It is at this level of leverage, the group design level, that we will focus our attention.

LEADERSHIP ————————————————————— ✈

Having just stated the focus to be group design and then labeling this section "leadership" might trigger a few questions if not alarms. Two such questions might be: (1) How can we do anything about group design—aren't cockpit crews based on the design of the cockpit? and (2) What does leadership have to do with groups—I thought leadership was about leaders?

Let me address the second question first. Leadership *is* about leaders. But it is not about leaders in a vacuum—it is about leaders in relation to followers in a particular setting. Is there such a thing as leadership without followers? And since we have already agreed that any two people comprise a group, if there is a leader and at least one follower, we are in the group realm. The fact is, leadership is a group phenomenon.

This contributes directly to our answer to the first question. Anyone who has spent much time watching groups operate in organizational environments will tell you that they do not all work equally well. Some cockpit crews cause accidents (as we have already noted), yet other cockpit crews exceed our greatest expectations. As one example, Captain Al Haynes and the crew of United 232 enroute from Denver to Chicago suddenly found themselves in a situation that was never supposed to happen. After a catastrophic failure of the DC-10's number 2 engine fan disabled all three hydraulic systems, this crew was left with little or no flight controls. Captain Haynes enlisted the assistance of another captain traveling in the passenger cabin and, with his newly expanded crew, literally developed their own emergency procedures on line. In the midst of crisis the crew of United 232 managed to get the crippled airliner within a few feet of the Sioux City airport before impact. Remarkably, this crew performed even better than subsequent crews in simulator re-enactments. If some crews work better than others in the same organizational setting, then something about those crews must be different, and it must have something to do with the design of the groups. For airline crews, this "crew design" begins to occur when the crew first forms. But what is responsible for the difference?

In numerous interviews with crew members about this variation among crews, the same consistent answer emerged. Whether a crew works well or not is a function of the captain. One typical example of interviews of subordinate aircrew members conducted by this author (Ginnett, 1987) illustrates this point.

> RCG: Are all the [captains] you fly with pretty much the same?
> PILOT: Oh no. Some guys are just the greatest in the world to fly

with. I mean they may not have the greatest hands in the world but that doesn't matter. When you fly with them, you feel like you want to do everything you can to work together to get the job done. You really want to do a good job for them. Some other guys are just the opposite . . . you just can't stand to work with them. That doesn't mean you'll do anything that's unsafe or dangerous but you won't go out of your way to keep him out of trouble either. So you'll just sit back and do what you have to and just hope that he screws up.

  RCG: How can you tell which kind of guy you're working with?
  PILOT: Oh, you can tell.
  RCG: How?
  PILOT: I don't know how you tell but it doesn't take long. Just a couple of minutes and you'll know.

Not only does this illustrate the perception of the impact of the leader (the captain), but it also points to the critical nature of the crew formation (i.e., "Just a couple of minutes and you'll know").

The pervasive impact of the leader has been demonstrated in controlled research settings as well. I have already cited the feigned incapacitation study by Harper et al. (1971), in which the authority dynamics associated with the captain's role impacted the performance of the first officers. In another simulator study, Ruffell Smith (1979) designed an experiment where crews were given an interactive problem soon after departing on an intercontinental flight. The problem required a return to a short, wet runway with a number of interrelated mechanical problems and a critical fuel dump. The workload burden fell on the engineer, so the most obvious predictions about which crews would be able to safely return centered around the engineer's performance. A very detailed analysis of the number and type of errors showed great variations among the crews. As it turned out, the variable of most significance was not the flight engineer's behavior but the behavior of the captain. If the captain recognized the problem as a crew problem and managed the problem accordingly, the crew did well. However, if the captain handled the problem as "a piloting problem," the crews did not fare as well. Apparently the captain's behavior carries considerable weight in the way the crew works. And if the interview data are valid, the leadership impact begins early in the crew's life.

LEADERSHIP AT FORMATION: A CRITICAL LEVERAGE POINT ✈

  The first phase of our NASA research set out to address the question of what actually goes on in the formation process of cockpit crews (Ginnett, 1987).

Of particular interest was the behavior of captains who, prior to observation, were assessed by check airmen as being exceedingly good at creating highly effective teams (the HI-E captains) versus their counterparts who received low ratings on this same ability (LO-E captains). In accordance with accepted research procedures, the category of the captain to be observed was not revealed until after all data collection and content analyses were completed.

It may be helpful to briefly explain the context within which the first phase of the research occurred. Phase One was conducted entirely with crews assigned to 727-200 aircraft so the technology, crew size, and training were standardized. The particular airline company in which these first data were collected used a fairly typical bid system for crew scheduling. As a result, the crews were quite likely never to have worked together prior to coming together for an assigned trip. Of the 20 different three-person crews observed in the first phase of the research, none had ever worked together prior to the observation period. In fact, of the 60 dyads within the 20 crews, only 8 had ever flown together before, and 7 of those 8 had done so only once. Their operations manual required a formal crew briefing before the first leg of each new crew complement. This briefing, conducted one hour before scheduled departure, was held in a designated room in the terminal unless there were late arrivals, in which case the briefing would occur on the aircraft. It is important to note that whether an organization requires a formal briefing or not (as was the case in subsequent organizations researched), there *will* be a crew formation process. If the organization does not legitimize this process with a required briefing, then whether the formation process occurs by design or by chance is very much up to the captain.

Based on extensions of the normative model by Hackman and Walton (1986) and observations of team formations in organizations other than airlines, I had certain expectations of what effective leaders would do when forming a team that had never worked together before. It seemed reasonable to expect a team leader to:

1. Discuss the task to be accomplished by the group.
2. Discuss the relevant team boundaries. Since this was a team that had never worked together before, I expected the leader to build a tight-knit working group.
3. Discuss relevant norms for the group's effective performance.

There were some surprises in what I found.

Task

Contrary to expectations, the HI-E captains hardly discussed tasks at all. Even when tasks were mentioned (e.g., closing the cabin door, retracting the aft air stairs, or keeping the cockpit door open prior to pushback), they were more about boundary issues (to be discussed in the next section) than about the tasks themselves. The only other exceptions which generated some task discussion occurred when there were unusual conditions such as weather or performance limitations due to deferred maintenance items on the aircraft. In contrast, some of the LO-E captains spent inordinate amounts of time discussing minute task requirements for the flight attendants which had little to do with boundary requirements or any other critical aspect of team performance. One LO-E captain went into great detail about procedures for bagging the cabin garbage!

But the general absence of task discussion was far from the predicted behavior—or from behavior exhibited by leaders in other task groups. For example, in problem-solving groups (often assembled in organizational settings as ad hoc committees), the bulk of the first meeting is spent in defining and clarifying the task at hand. How can we explain the lack of task discussion by HI-E captains, and in sharp contrast, the focus on even trivial tasks by LO-E captains?

Boundaries

As noted earlier, it might appear that an airline cockpit crew, or even the total crew including the attendants, is a fairly well defined and bounded group. After all, when you seal a work team in a pressurized aluminum cabin at 35,000 feet, there is little chance of someone leaving the group. In fact, based on the behaviors of the HI-E captains, they felt the groups were potentially over-bounded. The HI-E captains worked both in the briefing and at other opportunistic times to expand the relevant team boundary and to make the boundary more permeable. They always talked about "we" in terms of the total flightcrew, as opposed to some of the LO-E captains who referred to the cockpit crew as "we" and the flight attendants as "you." The HI-E captains also worked to create a larger vision of the relevant work group—one that exceeded the bounds of the aircraft. They took pains to include (at least psychologically) gate personnel, maintenance, and air traffic controllers as part of the group trying to help them— not as an outside hostile group trying to thwart their objectives. One HI-E captain routinely reminded the crew that the passengers could be a relevant part of their team if the crew made the effort to listen to passengers, particularly if they were expressing some concern about the aircraft.

Norms

Norms can be communicated in a variety of ways. Certainly the captain can make explicit the standards and expected behaviors of the crew. He or she can communicate the importance of a subject merely by including it in the briefing, or he or she can talk explicitly about its importance. The captain can also communicate normative information through a modeling process. This may include specific descriptions of intended behaviors or, more subtly, be expressed through actual behavior in the briefing and at other times in the presence of the crew. For example, a captain may quite subtly transmit the importance of exchanging information as the group goes about its work by merely taking time to exchange information (two-way communication) in the time allotted for the crew briefing. The norm that "communication is important" is expressed in the series of exchanges including: (1) I need to talk to you; (2) I listen to you; (3) I need you to talk to me; or even (4) I expect you to talk to me.

There was no single norm that was explicitly communicated by all of the highly effective captains. However, there were three norms most frequently communicated as important to the effective work of the group. These were the importance of safety, effective communication, and cooperation between crew members. Perhaps most surprising is that "safety" should need to be mentioned at all! Is that not the most important consideration anyway? That safety should be emphasized also seems to be contrary to the finding regarding tasks which were not mentioned much at all by the HI-E captains. These apparently conflicting and confounding findings are explained later in the section on "group shells."

Authority Dynamics

While not a factor outlined in Hackman & Walton (1986) as something to which the leader should attend in group formation, the authority dynamic was such a powerful finding that it could not be overlooked. Certainly, the use of influence and authority are common issues in leadership writings as far back as Lewin, Lippitt, & White (1939) and often are an integral part of leadership definitions. And, as alluded to earlier, the history, regulations, and even characteristics of the crew members themselves impact authority relationships. To understand the authority dynamics for airline cockpit crews it will first be necessary to provide a small amount of background information. The authority relationship between the captain and the rest of the crew is inexorably bound to aviation history, regulations, and often to the characteristics of the crewmembers themselves. This combination of history, regulation, and crewmember characteristics has established an authority dynamic that has undoubtedly positively impacted the aviation safety record. In those situations requiring immediate response to a single authoritative command, airline crews work particularly well. However, this tendency toward the high-authority end of the continuum has resulted in crewmembers not speaking up when necessary, as in the previously cited study and accident investigation. This inclination may also result in excessive psychological dependence on the captain as leader to the extent that individual contributions to problem-solving are neither voiced nor attempted. For example, one captain with whom I flew made a particularly poor approach which resulted in an excessive dive on short final, thus setting off numerous alarms. In reviewing the crew members' inactions afterward, the young second officer (who literally said nothing during the final approach) admitted that he had never seen an approach quite like that, but figured "the captain must know what he's doing."

If we plot authority dynamics along a continuum (as opposed to Lewin et al., 1939, who used nominal categories), the history, regulations, and individual characteristics of crew members all tend to be forces pushing toward the high end of authority use and response (Figure 3.2).

As noted above, there are occasions in aviation where the extreme high end is appropriate, and most of us would agree that we cannot afford (nor do we personally want) the low end to occur. Given the existing history, regulations, and backgrounds, the latter condition is unlikely to occur. In fact, a review of the records of aviation accidents cannot produce a single incidence of "accident due to mutiny."

Establishing Appropriate Authority

One might expect HI-E captains to deliberately move the authority dynamic back down from its pre-existing extreme point to a level more appropriate for group level work (i.e., somewhere in the middle of the continuum). Under such a hypothesis, the leader might operate solely in a more democratic or participative fashion. Such a finding would be simple and prescriptive. Unfortunately, that simplistic approach is not what happens.

Rather than operating at some specific point between complete democracy and complete autocratic behavior, the highly effective captains shifted their behavior during the formation process along the continuum between the extremes of the effective range. Again note, the highly effective captains never exhibited laissez-faire behaviors. Three methods were used to build an effective leader–team authority relationship: (1) establish competence, (2) disavow perfection, and (3) engage the crew.

1. *Establish competence.* In addition to the other statements made by the HI-E captains during their briefings (like establishing norms for crew behavior),

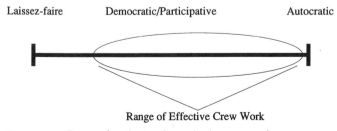

Figure 3.2   Range of authority dynamics in crew work.

they demonstrated their capability to assume the legitimate authority given them in three ways. First, the briefing was organized along some logical parameter (e.g., temporal, criticality, etc.). This helped to establish competence by demonstrating the captain had given some thought to the work they were about to engage in and he or she was able to present this in an organized manner, thus indicating rationality. Second, the briefing always contained elements of technical language specific to the vocation of flying. And finally, they were comfortable in a group setting—the environment of leadership. This fact escaped recognition until its absence was observed among some of the LO-E captains.

2. *Disavowing perfection.* All the HI-E captains established competence by exhibiting the above behaviors, but that only provided their crews with evidence that there was cause for the captain to exercise legitimate authority. They then balanced the leader–crew relationship by having the crewmembers take responsibility for the work of the group as well. This is important if the crew is not to completely rely on the captain, especially when he or she is in error.

This was first noted in a captain's statement prior to an extremely effective crew performance in a simulator: "I just want you guys to understand that they assign the seats in this airplane based on seniority, not on the basis of competence. So anything you can see or do that will help out, I'd sure appreciate hearing about it."

As simple as that sounds, it seems to underlie the basic behavior that HI-E captains use in disavowing perfection. They make a statement suggesting they don't know something about a particular issue even though the information is often quite readily available. They do not contradict the competence they have established regarding their ability as a captain. Rather, they typically make some comment about their lack of knowledge (although not on a critical task) or about some personal shortcoming. They are open about dealing with their own vulnerabilities.

3. *Engaging the crew.* The HI-E captains became involved with and included the crews in the process of the briefing and in the social process of group formation. Content analysis of the briefing process showed specific instances where the HI-E captains were engaging the crew through real-time interactions. They dealt with the situations that could potentially impact the particular crew they were briefing as they learned about them in the course of their interactions. They interacted on a personal level with the other people who were filling the crew roles. They did not present a "canned briefing," nor did they provide a briefing that could just as well have been given to a group of mannequins. They interacted in the here and now with the other people with whom they would work. By dealing in real time with the people who were filling the roles, they conveyed important normative information about themselves and the value of the individuals who made up this particular group. They often did this with humor but it was not humor to isolate (canned jokes) but rather humorous responses to real-time interactions.

The HI-E captains also spent more "non-directive" time with the group. It is not the case that these captains spent significantly more total time in the briefing with the crew than did the LO-E captains. Nor is it the case that they spent more time than the LO-E captains actually talking to the crew. There was, however, a significant difference between the HI-E captains and the LO-E captains in the amount of time that other members of the crew talked while the captain was present. The highly effective captains allowed and encouraged conversation by the other crew members, particularly if it was related to the task. They always asked if there were any questions, and several of them solicited comments about any behaviors on other crews or with other captains that might be troublesome.

By establishing their competence, disavowing perfection, and engaging the crew in the course of the briefing, the HI-E captains actually covered the range on the continuum of authority in which groups most effectively operate. Rather than demonstrate only one type of leadership authority which would be inappropriate across the range of requirements in a typical line operation (see Ginnett, 1990), these captains established, early on, an authority basis that would change according to the situation. This contingent authority pattern ranged from direct statements by a competent, legitimate authority figure to a human who recognized and was comfortable with his own imperfections. They further provided a mechanism for correcting these errors by ensuring that the crew was engaged and active in the task group work already begun in the briefing.

In summary, the HI-E captains did not dwell on the task, expanded the boundaries to include others who could help the group in its work, made explicit certain important performance norms, and created an expectation of flexible authority contingent upon the situation.

What remains unresolved are (1) explanations of the unexpected or surprising findings concerning the absence of task discussion in contrast to the explicit discussion around norms associated with safety, (2) some understanding of how the leaders of these groups were able to accomplish the formation process so quickly, and (3) what the differing leadership behaviors had to do with subsequent performance. Fortunately, the concept of organizational shells[2] can help answer these questions.

GROUP SHELLS ⟶

The origin of group shells is similar in concept to shells in chemistry or shells in computer science. In chemistry, a shell is a space occupied by the electrons or

---

[2]The concept of organizational shells emerged in a working session between this author and Richard Hackman. Although we both remember that the concept first appeared "on the flip-chart on the back of the door," neither of us recalls who used the term first. Hence we agreed to jointly assume responsibility for the concept.

protons and neutrons in an atomic structure. The shell can be qualitatively pictured as the region of space where there is a high probability of finding the particle of interest. Similarly, the organizational shell for a group will not guarantee that every component for its formation will be established. It merely suggests that somewhere within the bounds of the shell, one might expect to find certain behaviors, roles, norms, or dynamics occurring.

In computer science, a shell provides a predefined set of interactions between various aspects of the system. Typically, these predefined sets of interactions occur between the computer and the operator. Analogously in organizational settings, a shell serves the same function—it provides a predefined or expected set of interactions between various elements of the system which permits simpler and more efficient interactions. With these two concepts as background, it is now possible to examine the data in light of the concept of the shell.

The research described in part here was designed to examine the captain's behavior during the formation process of crews *in* their organizational setting *with* all the relevant contextual information in place. This pre-existing context provides critical information for the forming group. Just as it was important for the reader to have some understanding of the relevant background of aviation-related authority dynamics to make sense of the findings in that area, so too is it important to recognize that all the task work described here occurs in an ongoing organizational and environmental context. The crews do not form in isolation but rather in an embedded system of intra-organizational, industry, and environmental conditions (see Figure 3.3).

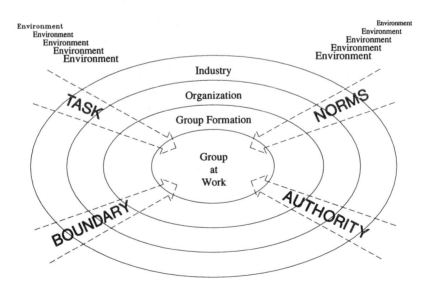

Figure 3.3   Organizational shells.

One can see from this diagram that information critical to group work can come from a variety of sources and in varying amounts. For example, the environment and industry may provide a sufficient guarantee of capability such that the organization (or lower levels) need not expand upon these. In the case of the airlines, industry-level agencies such as the FAA and the Air Line Pilots Association provide minimum certification requirements for commercial pilots. Other requirements for effective group work may be left solely to the crew, and these elements may be added at the formation or other opportunistic moments later in the crew's life. In light of this understanding of the concept of the shells, let us examine a few of the apparent anomalies in the data.

How is it that HI-E captains forming their crews for the first time do not spend much time at all discussing the task? In contrast, since safety would seem to be the most important factor for commercial air travel (at least from the perspective of passengers), why is it that the HI-E captains do take time to discuss safety? And how is it that even the LO-E captains produce teams that, under normal conditions, perform satisfactorily?

The answer to the first question lies in the nearly total fulfillment of task information from the shells outside of crew formation. All the individuals coming together to form the crew bring with them the knowledge, skill, and training necessary to perform the group's work. At increasingly redundant levels, the environment, the industry, and the organization test and certify these abilities. Unlike a randomly selected group of college sophomores forming to complete a novel task in a social science laboratory, all these crew members were highly qualified in the task requirements of a role that was designed to enable the group to work. Knowing that the outer shells have satisfied these task requirements, it would be extremely redundant for the leader to further discuss them. This is also consistent with the predictions of leader effectiveness according to path–goal theory as described by House and Mitchell (1974). In fact, when a LO-E captain spends time discussing obvious tasks, the crew begins to develop a very different picture of how life will be with him or her as their leader.

But this explanation might seem to confound expectations regarding the time spent by the leaders in explicitly discussing safety. Certainly the outer shells contain some normative expectations concerning safe operations. And if one were to ask any individual crewmember whether safety was important, it is reasonable to assume they would answer affirmatively. Then why spend time talking about a norm everyone accepts? The answer again is found in the shells, but in a more complex and ambiguous manner. Within the various shells there are numerous normative expectations for performance, among them safety. Unfortunately, not all the norms are congruent. A specific example will help to clarify this.

Beyond the norm of safety which exists in all the shells, a highly supported norm from airline management (within the organizational shell) is fuel conservation. For a commercial carrier, fuel is typically the second highest expense, so anything that can be done to save fuel is reinforced. Thus, when take-off delays are anticipated, captains will instruct their crews to delay starting all engines as a fuel conservation measure. This tactic has virtually no confounds with safety. But another fuel conservation technique might be to keep the airplane "as clean as possible for as long as possible." Pushing this technique to the extreme, a crew may delay extension of flaps and gear until late in the approach. The problem is that this practice might be in conflict with safety, which might prescribe an earlier and more gradual configuration for landing. By prioritizing potentially conflicting norms, the HI-E captains have clarified in advance their expectations, thus reducing ambiguity and potentially enhancing performance on the line. This will help the crew in routine operations and will be critical to effective performance in demanding or emergency situations.

Lastly, the shells for airline crews provide sufficient structure to allow them to perform at some minimal level in spite of ineffective leader behavior. It is important to note in this context that we are not considering "optimal" group performance across normal line operations, but rather "satisficing" group performance (cf. the chapter by Orasanu). This type of minimally acceptable behavior may well be less than necessary in demanding situations where crew resource management is essential.

It is critical to stress the importance of understanding the contribution made by the shells for the particular group under examination. This means that the particular findings from these groups should not be extrapolated directly to other groups unless their shells are similar. In these airline crews, the HI-E captains did not spend much time in the formation process dealing with the task because the task information was imported from the shells. However, in the first meetings of other groups (e.g., B-1 bomber crews on a new low-level night mission, or ad hoc task groups) it may be most appropriate for the leader to spend considerable time discussing the task to be performed, since the shells offer insufficient information about the group's impending assignment.

If we return to Hackman & Walton's (1986) normative model, which suggests the leader can make a contribution to the group at the critical formation period by discussing the task, the boundaries, and the norms of the group, we may now be able to improve those prescriptions. First, authority dynamics must be added to the list. The leader needs to consider the pre-existing (shell-provided) authority issues and modify them in the direction of group effectiveness. For airline captains, the shell structure for authority was almost exclusively in the direction of the autocratic power of the leader. While that is sometimes appropriate, it may not be the best for effective group work, and so the leader should attempt to shift authority down the continuum while maintaining a contingency approach. Second, rather than suggesting the leader spend time discussing tasks, boundaries, norms, and authority issues, it is more appropriate to say the leader should consider these issues and ensure information about them is provided in sufficient quantities for the group to get started and work effectively. The shells may provide all the necessary information for some groups and virtually none for others. In the former groups, discussion might be redundant, while in the latter case, discussion (in the absence of information) or clarification (in the event of conflicting information) may be the most important function the leader can perform at the group's formation. Which behavior is most important can only be determined by understanding the data inherent in higher levels of the shells.

IMPLICATIONS FOR EFFECTIVE
CREW LEADERSHIP ─────────────────────────── ✈

From the research described here, it should be fairly obvious that the captain can make a difference. Assuming we have an organizational context that supports and sustains crew and team effectiveness (as described in the chapter by Hackman), the captain has available to him or her the critical period of crew formation. This is where the captain breathes life into the shell which is filling with others who will play predefined roles. How well or how poorly the crew performs is, in large part, established in the course of the first meeting (Weick, 1985; Ginnett, 1987).

I have already detailed four specific areas in which the captain can create effective conditions for crew work. Beyond this are four more general categories which describe the captain's overall response to the shells at the group level.

Undermining

A captain who "undermines" actively countermands the conditions inherent in the shell that each member imports to the crew situation. These are the captains who, through their behaviors (including explicit statements), redefine in a more restrictive and unconstructive manner the tasks, boundaries, norms, and authority dynamics which will guide the crew's operations. These captains create conditions that undermine crew effectiveness. In an organization with established shells that foster effective crew work, undermining captains negate the preexisting and positive shells. Not only can they reduce and restrict positive aspects of the shell by explicitly undermining them, but their general tendency to undermine is extrapolated to other areas of the shell they do not mention. If a captain says he does not want flight attendants to get off the aircraft to talk to gate personnel without his permission, the flight engineer who overhears this may well wonder whether he or she needs the captain's specific approval to conduct a walk-around inspection of the aircraft. Worse yet, should he or she take the initiative to plan ahead for the crew's benefit or wait to see if it is "what the captain wants?" If captains go against procedures on one aspect of performance, what can they be expected to do on others? The most widespread negative effect of undermining behavior is that, like a cancer, it metastasizes throughout the organization. Unfortunately, the reduced shells that result from interaction with an undermining captain may be subsequently imported to other crews with the same potential negative impact. If a captain can behave inappropriately (as defined by existing organizational shells) and the organization fails to correct that inappropriate behavior, the other members of the crew will doubt the validity of the shells and hence expect less of subsequent captains and crews.

Abdicating

Captains who "abdicate" neither confirm the pre-existing shell nor deny it. They add nothing to the shell, nor do they confirm what the environment and organization have put in place. Crews under these kinds of captains are "not sure"—they are left with whatever shell they arrived with, minus any confirmation of its current utility or appropriateness. Not only is the shell for this particular crew left unverified, but each crewmember's shell used for defining the role of "captain" is reduced because of this particular captain's performance. They leave with a "less clearly defined and potentially poorer" shell of what the organization expects of its captains. This is because it is very likely the organization, if not the environment, has authorized the captain to clarify and even modify the shell, and this captain has failed to do that. Therefore, extrapolations regarding his or her self-imposed diminished authority in a more general sense are apt to be the result. By abdicating, the captain has unwittingly exhibited some of the behaviors inherent in the previous category.

Affirming

At a minimum for crew effectiveness, the captain should affirm the constructive task definitions, boundary conditions, norms, and authority dynamics that the environment and the organization have structured into the shell. These behaviors would not expand the shell but would help solidify the crew's understanding and acceptance of it. In effect, each crew member arrives with a shell that has generally defined appropriate crew behaviors in the past. The "affirming" captain "fills in the existing dotted lines" so the crew can proceed with behaviors based on their imported expectations. To the extent the organization and the environment have provided a shell appropriate for crew effectiveness, then the crew under an affirming captain can be expected to perform well.

Elaborating and Expanding

These are the behaviors of the best captains. They appreciate and exploit the opportunity for crew effectiveness provided them at the time of crew formation. They expand the existing shell and create new ways to operate within and outside of its boundaries. They are the ones who expand and create new opportunities for constructive interactions among crew members. They tend to elaborate and enlarge the boundaries of the individual roles and of the crew as a whole. They also create semipermeable boundaries for the crew (not so under-bounded that the crew operates only as individuals, but not so over-bounded that they exclude information or assistance available outside their group per se) which can be useful later in the conduct of work on the line. They elaborate and expand the norms regarding safety, cooperation, and communication. Under their leadership, new ways to share their authority emerge, and hence the total authority of the cockpit and cabin expands and becomes more effective. They create conditions which can lead to better crew performance by expanding previously defined shell structures. These behaviors also tend to enlarge each crew member's concept of what the shell can be for an effective crew, and this improved image can be imported into the shells of subsequent crews of which they will be a member.

CONCLUSION ✈

Prior to the first meeting of the crew, we find a series of individuals, each with his or her own perception of the shells for crew behavior. That imported shell is only that—a shell which the captain can enhance or diminish. Captains can expand it or undermine it; they can affirm it or abdicate. But when the first meeting is over and the crew goes to work, they are some sort of a team. They may start work envisioning new and creative ways to improve team effectiveness, or they may be wondering what this crew is really going to be like. In one form or another, this new team now has its own shell, one shaped by the captain's behavior regarding the tasks, by the boundary definitions the captain described, by the transmission of implicit and explicit norms, and by the authority dynamics demonstrated by the captain. If we assume that the company believes in CRM and provides sufficient shell support for crew work, then whether the captain enhances or impedes a crew's ability to perform well is really up to him or her.

Acknowledgments

The research reported here was supported by Cooperative Agreement NCC 2-324 between NASA–Ames Research Center and Yale University.

References

Burrows, W. E. (1982, December). Cockpit encounters. *Psychology Today*, pp. 42–47.
Feldman, D. C. (1984, January). The development and enforcement of group norms. *Academy of Management Review*, pp. 47–53.
Foushee, H. C. (1984). Dyads and triads at 35,000 feet: Factors affecting group process and aircrew performance. *American Psychologist*, *39*, 885–893.

Ginnett, R. C. (1987). *First encounters of the close kind: The formation process of airline flight crews.* Unpublished doctoral dissertation, Yale University, New Haven, CT.

Ginnett, R. C. (1990) Airline cockpit crews. In J. Richard Hackman (Ed.), *Groups that Work.* San Francisco: Jossey-Bass.

Hackman, J. R., (1976). Group influences on individuals. In M. Dunnette (Ed.), *Handbook of industrial and organizational psychology* (pp. 1455–1525). Chicago: Rand McNally.

Hackman, J. R. (1987). The design of work teams. In Jay W. Lorsch (Ed.), *Handbook of organizational behavior.* Englewood Cliffs, NJ: Prentice-Hall.

Hackman, J. R., & Walton, R. E. (1986). Leading groups in organizations. In P. S. Goodman & Associates (Eds.), *Designing effective work groups* (pp. 72–119). San Francisco: Jossey-Bass.

Harper, C. R., Kidera, G. J., & Cullen, J. F. (1971). Study of simulated airline pilot incapacitation: Phase II, subtle or partial loss of function. *Aerospace Medicine, 42,* 946–948.

House, R. J., & Mitchell, T. R. (1974). Path-goal theory of leadership. *Contemporary Business, 3,* 81–98.

Janis, I. L., (1982). *Groupthink,* 2nd ed. Boston: Houghton Mifflin.

Kaplan, R. (1979). The conspicuous absence of evidence that process consultation enhances task performance. *Journal of Applied Behavioral Science, 15,* 346–360.

Latane, B., Williams, K., & Harkins, S. (1979). Social loafing. *Psychology Today, 13,* 104.

Lewin, K., Lippitt, R., & White, R. K. (1939). Patterns of aggressive behavior in experimentally created social climates. *Journal of Social Psychology, 10,* 271–301.

National Transportation Safety Board. (1979). *Aircraft Accident Report: United Airlines, Inc., McDonnell-Douglas DC-8-61, N8082U, Portland, Oregon, December 28, 1978.* (NTSB-AAR-79-7). Washington DC: Author.

National Transportation Safety Board. (1982). *Aircraft Accident Report: Air Florida, Inc., Boeing 737-222, N62AF, Collision with 14th Street Bridge, Near Washington National Airport, Washington D.C., January 13, 1982* (NTSB-AAR-82-8). Washington DC: Author.

Ruffell Smith, H. P. (1979). *A simulator study of the interaction of pilot workload with errors, vigilance, and decisions* (Report No. TM-78482). Moffett Field, CA: NASA–Ames Research Center.

Schein, E. H. (1969). *Process consultation: Its role in organization development.* Reading, MA: Addison-Wesley.

Weick, K. E. (1985). Systematic observational methods. In G. Lindzey & E. Aronson (Eds.), *Handbook of social psychology, Vol. 2* (3rd ed.). New York: Random House.

Wolfe, T. (1979). *The right stuff.* New York: Farrar, Straus, and Giroux.

4

Communication and Crew Resource Management

Barbara G. Kanki
Aerospace Human Factors Research Division
NASA–Ames Research Center
Moffett Field, California 94035

Mark T. Palmer
Department of Communication Studies
Northwestern University
Evanston, Illinois 60201

INTRODUCTION ✈

Communication is one of those sprawling, complex topics that has many faces and many uses because it is fundamental to all social process. Whether in its written or verbal form, communication and language topics are related to nearly every social science: philosophy, psychology, sociology, education, political science, geography, and so on. Academic mergers such as philosophy of language, psycholinguistics, and sociolinguistics have become legitimate fields in their own right. In spite of all these possibilities, it is important to think of communication in a pragmatic way; that is, we communicate in order to acquire what we need and to accomplish cooperative tasks. Thus, we are likely to think of communication in all-or-nothing terms: you are understood or misunderstood; information is transmitted or it is not; you are persuaded or unmoved. In short, communication can determine the success or failure in achieving goals, and when the goals are attached to high stakes, communication effectiveness is essential.

There can be no doubt that operating modern aircraft is a high-stakes profession with lives invested in every flight. It is therefore reasonable to assume that communication plays an important part of this human activity as it does in all others where individuals are trying to accomplish common goals and integrate separate tasks. In this chapter, we would like to underscore the importance of communication for efficiency and safety in aviation and to describe how specific communication practices help to achieve particular task goals.

A HISTORICAL VIEW OF COMMUNICATION AND
FLIGHT SAFETY ─────────────────────────────────── ✈

National Transportation Safety Board Accident Reports

Probably the most dramatic and compelling demonstrations of the link between communication and flight safety come from the accident investigations carried out in the United States by the National Transportation Safety Board (NTSB). Although there are many components of such an investigation, Kayten asserts in her chapter, "Today, DFDR [digital flight data recorder] and CVR [cockpit voice recorder] data are the primary resources for learning what happened in the accident sequence" (p. 287).

A recent example is the NTSB investigation of the crash of Avianca Flight 052, a Boeing 707B from Bogotá to Medellín, Colombia, to John F. Kennedy International Airport (JFK), New York, which ran out of fuel over Long Island on January 25, 1990 (NTSB, 1991). Even at the most cursory level, it is clear there were critical failures in communication. Specifically, the crew failed to communicate to ATC the information that they were desperately low on fuel and needed immediate clearance to land. A closer look at the events and conditions surrounding the accident reveals that several critical information links were lacking.

Poor weather conditions led to the flight being held three times by air traffic control for a total of about 1 hour and 17 minutes. Not until the third period of holding did the flightcrew report that (1) the airplane could not hold longer than 5 minutes, (2) it was running out of fuel, and (3) it could not reach its alternate airport, Boston–Logan International. Following the execution of a missed approach to JFK, the crew experienced a loss of power to all four engines and crashed approximately 16 miles from the airport.

The NTSB attributed probable cause of the accident to the failure of the flightcrew to manage the airplane's fuel load adequately and their failure to communicate an emergency fuel situation to air traffic control before fuel exhaustion occurred. Contributing to the accident, in the NTSB's view, was the flightcrew's failure to use an airline operational control dispatch system for assistance under these difficult conditions. Traffic flow management by the Federal Aviation Administration (FAA) and the use of standard terminology for pilots and controllers during emergency were also called into question. Safety issues enumerated in the executive summary follow:

1. Pilot responsibilities and dispatch responsibilities regarding planning, fuel requirements, and flight following during international flights.
2. Pilot to controller communications regarding the terminology to be used to convey fuel status and the need for special handling.

3. ATC flow control procedures and responsibilities to accommodate aircraft with low fuel state.
4. Flightcrew coordination and English language proficiency of foreign crews. (NTSB, 1991, p. v)

In Figure 4.1, critical communication links are depicted by bi-directional arrows. Although probable cause of the accident is shown in Link #2, at least 4 sets of communication/information links were called into question by the investigators.

Effective communication among crewmembers has always been an essential component of the concept of crew coordination. The chapter by Kayten reports that the first NTSB mention of "flight deck resource management" was made in the report filed on the crash in 1978 in Portland, Oregon, of United Airlines Flight 173 (NTSB, 1979). Probable cause was determined to be failure of the captain to monitor aircraft fuel state, which resulted in total fuel exhaustion. Contributing causes included "the failure of the other two flight crewmembers either to fully comprehend the criticality of the fuel state or to successfully communicate their concern to the captain" (NTSB, 1979, p. 29.)

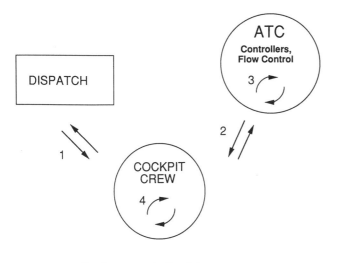

Key to communication links:

1. Between pilot and dispatchers
2. Between pilot and ATC controllers
3. Within ATC flow control teams
4. Within cockpit crew

Figure 4.1   Critical information links in Avianca 052 accident.

Furthermore, one of the results of that investigation was the FAA Air Carrier Operations Bulletin Number 8430.17 (Change 11), which gave instructions regarding resource management and interpersonal communications training for air carrier flightcrews. This action was taken in response to one of the four recommendations made by the NTSB that focused on both participative management for captains and assertiveness training for other cockpit crewmembers. Since 1979 the NTSB has continued to consider the possible impact of crew resource management (CRM) and crew communication in accident sequences. The communications contained in CVR data have pointed to a wide range of CRM problems related to command authority, maintenance of vigilance, monitoring and cross-checking, briefings, planning, and crisis management in addition to assertiveness and participative management.

However, it is one-sided to focus only on communication inadequacies. NTSB reports also acknowledge instances of exemplary CRM practices in their findings (see the chapter by Kayten). Communication data provided by CVR recordings have provided evidence of good cockpit management in the face of challenging emergency conditions. Possibly the most dramatic cases are United 811 (NTSB, 1990a) and United 232 (NTSB, 1990b), in which flightcrew interactions were "indicative of the value of cockpit resource management training, which has been in existence at UAL for a decade." (NTSB 1990b, p. 76). Although there was no specific mention of communication practices in the NTSB reports, these two accidents have been analyzed by researchers and specific communication patterns have been identified (Predmore, 1991). The use of accident reports in research is discussed in a later section.

NTSB accident reports provide case studies in which several critical communication problem areas can be identified. They inform us who is involved, and more importantly, how those involved could have provided the critical resources needed to keep a crew on top of a difficult but otherwise manageable situation. We are given real-time accounts of events unfolding and problems escalating. We are shown how safety margins are chipped away until no system redundancies remain.

Because these reports represent single cases in which conditions are to some extent unique, and because they represent complex, multi-factor situations, it is difficult if not impossible to make direct comparisons across accidents or incidents. The projected likelihood of a particular kind of accident is not immediately obvious, nor can we make predictions from a dataset of one. Nevertheless, such detailed accident reports represent an in-depth view of an event and clearly identify the most safety-critical items.

Incident Reports

In contrast to accident reports, incident reports are generated and gathered in far greater numbers by a variety of organizations (e.g., airlines, unions, and neutral government agencies such as NASA's Aviation Safety Reporting System, ASRS). These reports may not always represent the most critical problems to flight safety, because the data are voluntarily submitted and cannot be assumed to represent an unbiased perspective on all parts of the aviation system. Nevertheless, greater frequencies of certain classes of events can indicate recurrent trouble spots. Furthermore, the large sample of reports illustrates a range of occurrences that tell us whether these problems occur under many circumstances, or whether they are specific to particular conditions such as geographic locations, aircraft type, weather, and so on.

Because voice recordings are unavailable in incident reports, the role of communication is less easy to discern. For example, an incident classified as a "distribution of workload" problem may be, in part, brought about by a pilot's ineffective communication style. Face-to-face communications within the flight-crew or between flight crewmembers and other ground support teams may not be so easily recognized and/or described as a communication problem. As Foushee & Manos (1981) note in their analysis of within-cockpit communication problems, "the [ASRS] narrative descriptions are sometimes not specific enough with respect to antecedent conditions to allow classification" (p. 67). Complex or subtle points of an incident may be lost because the analytic value of incident report data is limited by the degree of detail, objectivity, and skill of the individual submitting the narrative. However, simple incidents that are easy to explain and classify can provide reliable data. For instance, miscommunications between pilots and controllers are often concrete events that can be explicitly characterized and related to standards.

Billings & Cheaney (1981) discuss problems in the transfer of information within the aviation system that represented over 70% of 28,000 reports submitted by pilots and air traffic controllers to the ASRS during the 5-year period 1976–1981. Reports focus on pilot–controller interactions and controller communication more often than on within-cockpit communication. Nevertheless, the conclusions are consistent with the Foushee & Manos (1981) analyses of within-cockpit communication from research and ASRS reports.

> Close examination of ASRS reports led to the finding that information transfer problems, as we have come to call them, did not ordinarily result from an unavailability of information nor because the information was incorrect at its source (although there are certain exceptions to this generalization). Instead, the most common findings showed that information was not transferred because (1) the person who had the information did not think it necessary to transfer it or (2) that the information was transferred, but inaccurately. (Billings & Cheaney, 1981, p. 2)

Figure 4.2 represents the primary communication links discussed by Billings & Cheaney (1981, p. 87) in their discussion of information transfer problems

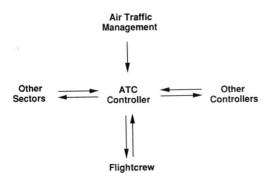

Figure 4.2   The role of the controller in information transfer (Billings & Reynard, 1981).

in today's aviation system. In this representation, the air traffic controller is depicted in the pivotal role.

In spite of limitations in the system for some kinds of research, incident reports are extremely informative with respect to locating problem areas in specific parts of the aviation system. Findings may include a summary of enabling factors that indicate types of behaviors (e.g., distraction, failure to monitor, complacency, etc.), and systems factors (e.g., frequency saturation, high workload, and inadequately presented data) that interfere with information transfer (see Billings & Cheaney, 1981, p. 86). The identification of such behaviors and systems factors not only is important for the operational community, but also assists systems designers and researchers by pointing them toward critical issues. For instance, how are communications affected in an automated environment, using datalink, or in conjunction with visual displays, or with aural warning systems? Or, how do information transfer problems surface under conditions of work overload, ambiguous data, or failing equipment?

> Based on reports to ASRS, it is concluded that information transfer problems are responsible for many potentially serious human errors in aviation operations. Voice communications, in particular, are a pervasive problem. Technological solutions exist for many problems related to information transfer. These solutions, however, may give rise to serious new problems unless they are implemented with an understanding of the capabilities and limitations of the humans who operate the aviation system. (Billings & Reynard, 1981, p. 13)

Early Communication Research

The primary advantage of research over case reports is that, by design, the data represent specific contrasts between specific conditions. In addition, data can sometimes be recorded on audio/videotape so that repeated viewing and detailed analyses can be performed. It is in this research context that we can validate what we learn from observations in actual operations and accident and incident reports. We can also try to disentangle some of the variables that influence crew coordination and flight safety by systematically manipulating or contrasting variable conditions and studying their effects. Unlike accident investigations which are specifically focused on answering why events occurred in a particular case, research looks for generalizable answers. Hypotheses are often generated on the basis of case studies and nonsystematic observations, but they are tested systematically upon a theoretical basis.

The following section describes early research into communication processes that used three data sources: (1) accident CVR data, (2) systematic field observations, and (3) full-mission simulations. Each of these sources is useful, and each requires a different research approach; but most important, they are complementary, and their findings support each other.

Case Studies of Accident CVR Transcripts

One of the first systematic looks at communications from CVR data was undertaken by Goguen, Linde, & Murphy (1986). Hypotheses grew out of the growing recognition that assertiveness training may be needed for junior crewmembers, as recommended by the NTSB (NTSB, 1979). A linguistic methodology was developed for analyzing small-group discourse and applied to CVR transcripts from commercial air transport accidents.

In order to entertain hypotheses regarding crewmember assertiveness, a classification scheme distinguished levels of mitigation (i.e., direct vs. softened), and included speech types such as planning, explanation, and command/control. For example, a command stated in the imperative form is less mitigated than a suggestion which is usually spoken as a question. Finally, because problems had been noted where captains did not solicit crewmember participation/information sharing, levels of mitigation were compared across positions (captain vs. first officer, FO, or second officer, SO).

Results (based on eight transcripts and 1725 speech acts) included the following: (1) subordinate crewmembers were characterized by a more mitigated (softened) style of making requests. (2) Mitigated speech was associated with subsequent changes of topic and unratified commands, indicating that mitigated communications were less successful. (3) However, requests were less mitigated during conditions of recognized emergencies or problems. Thus, while mitigated requests may not offer the most effective means of eliciting a standard validation response, this relationship may be flightphase-critical under limited conditions. Finally, insofar as other speech types show patterned use (more planning and explanation during problem-solving but less during emergencies), mitigated requests may serve a different function under different conditions or in other cultures. For example, the use of suggestions rather than commands during a prebriefing may be a means of encouraging crewmember participation.

Field Studies

Field studies have the advantage of having uncompromised face validity; that is, there is no question that the operations observed are relevant to the domain of interest. (This does not imply that inaccurate observations cannot be made or inappropriate conclusions drawn!) However, it is very difficult to collect communication data systematically during actual operations because: (1) Control is minimal; many conditions cannot be controlled (e.g., weather) or assumed to be standard (e.g., routing and air traffic control (ATC) operations). (2) Most observed operations will consist of normal conditions that will not allow examination of abnormal or emergency procedures. (3) One can typically make online observations only; that is, whatever can be documented must be done so in real time or immediately after the fact. Audio or video recording is not usually possible or allowed. Still, it is from observations during actual operations that we can specifically define problem areas and generate hypotheses.

Field studies can go beyond mere observations. For example, a methodology developed for collecting real-time communication data under normally occurring, contrasting conditions constitutes a more focused approach in a field setting. Costley, Johnson, & Lawson (1989) were among the first to develop an online communication coding system for making systematic observations during flight. Their contrast conditions were aircraft types: B737-200, B737-300, and B757, which represented three different levels of aircraft automation.[1] Total observation flights numbered 19. The coding system included speech categories such as commanding, reacting, information processing, giving explanation, checking, summarizing, asides (jokes, quips), and questioning, seeking information, and testing understanding.

From a communications point of view, several potential problem domains were identified:

1. Lower communication rates in more automated aircraft (B737-200 vs. B757) with no accompanying decrease in operational actions. Of the categories of speech affected, questioning seems to be the primary difference; that is, less questioning in more automated aircraft.
2. Lower communication rates during night operations (day vs. night hours).

While these data are suggestive of potential problem areas, many factors may be coming into play to produce these results. For instance, a B737 cockpit may be more conducive to face-to-face communication than that of a B757 because the B737 cockpit is smaller and quieter. Furthermore, these flights were

[1]Because of its relevance to automation and CRM, Wiener has described this study in some detail in his chapter.

"normal," and differences in communication were not linked to observed differences in performance. Although Costley et al. felt there were no grossly distorting factors confounded with aircraft type to draw conclusions about performance, we need to investigate whether (1) abnormal conditions produce very different communication patterns and (2) performance is linked to any such differences.

These questions can be tested by conducting more focused research either in further field studies or in a more controlled experimental setting. If performance differences are not found to be linked to differences in communication rates, then we need not be concerned about implications for flight safety. Rather we would conclude that these are harmless, stylistic differences. However, if lower communication rates are linked to performance decrements under certain operational conditions (as discussed by Costley et al.), there could be serious implications for communication training and interventions.

Simulation Studies

Although accident and incident reports have provided compelling evidence that communication processes are linked to performance outcomes and flight safety, it was in simulation research that evidence moved beyond the case study methodology. Because flight scenarios and conditions could be controlled and variables manipulated, flightcrew performances could be legitimately, statistically compared. Unlike any previous source of flight data, the entire flight performance (even pre-pushback) could be videotaped. This provided far greater research opportunities for analyzing communications than did accident CVRs, incident reports, and field study data. Because communication patterns could be analyzed in great detail and related to differences in performance, full-mission simulation has become a unique tool for communication researchers.

The Ruffell Smith (1979) simulation at NASA–Ames Research Center was a landmark in identifying issues related to mission performance. In addition to proving the yet untapped potential of high-fidelity, full-mission simulation design for experimental purposes, it confirmed what instructors, practitioners, and accident investigators already knew: Technical skills alone were not enough to guarantee effective crew performance. More important, it proved that specific CRM behaviors could be clearly identified and characterized for incorporation into a training curriculum.

Foushee & Manos (1981) extended the research by analyzing communication behaviors generated in a simulation setting. In many ways, this study provided a model for most of the systematic communication research mentioned in this chapter. The methodology consists of the following: (1) a systematic "speech act" coding of verbatim transcribed speech; (2) an exploration of communication patterns that reliably distinguish between qualities of crew performance; (3) testing for patterned differences among crew factors at the individual, organizational, environmental, training, or task levels; and (4) a means of identifying conditions (e.g., normal vs. abnormal operations, flight phases, etc.) that influence the use of particular speech patterns. The overall goal is to provide specific characterizations of communication patterns associated with effective CRM principles so that appropriate training implementations can be made.

Controlled research is critical for teasing apart the effects of multiple factors inherent in complex operations. It is also critical for delineating the communication processes that account for the differences in crew coordination and overall flightcrew performance. But the results of any particular research study must, at some point, be interpreted within the total operational context. Conclusions drawn from experiments must undergo whatever adaptation is needed to be training-ready at an appropriate cost, within technological constraints, in harmony with organizational policies, and supported by government regulation.

In conclusion, it should be noted that data from sources discussed above are generated to satisfy different ends and are obtained under very different conditions. As such, they provide different but complementary types of information. For instance, incident reports may define for us the range of conditions that appear relevant to a problem, while a simulation study can quantitatively determine the importance of particular conditions. Each data source has its strengths and weaknesses, but taken together, accident reports, incident reports, and human factors research provide ample evidence that communication practices are closely linked to flight safety.

THE COMMUNICATION CONCEPT ⟶

While it may be possible to differentiate dozens of communication functions ranging from pragmatic to poetic, there are two aspects of communication that are particularly relevant to aircrew performance. First, communication is clearly a means by which crews accomplish tasks. They coordinate actions by issuing commands, stating intentions, and sending and receiving information. In this sense, communication behavior is a skill that can be structured by organizational policy (i.e., by standard operating procedures) and shaped by training. The second aspect of communication is more descriptive than prescriptive. This aspect refers to "how" things are communicated (as opposed to "what" is said) and refers to qualities or styles of crewmember interaction. Therefore, communication variations can have two slightly different interpretations. They may be (1) solutions that represent the means by which tasks are carried out verbally; or (2) symptoms representing behavioral styles that distinguish various ways in which crewmembers interact and coordinate their work. Thus, while one goal of research is to be able to provide guidance for training communication skills (solutions), another goal is to determine how crew-linked communication variations (symptoms) relate to performance.

The relationship between communication variations and crew performance constitutes two parts of a three-part conceptual model of factors affecting group performance processes. This model is derived from McGrath's (1984) theoretical framework, altered to fit the aircrew work environment, and consists of input, process, and output variables. See the chapter by Helmreich and Foushee for a discussion and depiction of the model (Figure 1.2).

To briefly review the model, input variables refer to attributes of individuals, characteristics of the group itself, and factors related to the environment, including specific task parameters that define the work environment. Individual-level input factors include any aspect of a group member that would conceivably affect that person's ability to be an effective group member, such as flying skills, personality traits, motivation, interests, and relational skills that affect his or her ability to participate in group-level communication and decision-making processes. Complementing individual-level factors are effects characteristic of groups. Bringing various individuals together to create a flight team means fitting together individual personalities to form a single group identity. Thus, there is an interpersonal component to groups as well as a group structure defined by the integration of task responsibilities.

Environmental input factors are focused on characteristics of the task itself, such as level of difficulty, amount of stress involved, and rewards intrinsic or extrinsic to the task. Design factors such as flightdeck configuration characteristics, including displays, specialized equipment, and so on, also fall in this category. It is in this area that we find research examining the effects of automation on performance and crew communication (Wiener, 1989; Wiener, Chidester, Kanki, Palmer, Curry, & Gregorich, 1991).

Outcome variables refer to aspects of the group performance, such as productivity and efficiency, but they also refer to how safely the crew performed and how satisfied they felt about their performance. Clearly the most salient output concern is the relative success or failure of a group in achieving formal objectives. Performance errors and successes have typically been the chief outcome measures in communication research.

Process variables represent mediators between inputs and outcomes; they refer to the dynamics of the team performance itself and the means by which crews achieve specific performance outcomes. Communication processes are of central importance to group activities that rely on verbal exchanges. Many aspects of crew coordination, such as decision-making, problem-solving, and managerial processes are chiefly analyzed in terms of communication data.

While a great deal of research has focused primarily on the relationship between input and performance variables, a body of research is growing that suggests the critical importance of group processes as intermediate or immediate predictors of group success (Foushee & Manos, 1981; Foushee, Lauber, Baetge, & Acomb, 1986; Kanki, Lozito, & Foushee, 1988). Group process variables are behavioral sequences that describe the interaction of group members. These include communication patterns as well as resource management strategies and processes (e.g., decision styles including collaboration and cooperation, and management strategies including consensus or strong leadership).

Process variables may be thought of as mediating input effects on performance. Communication patterns, for example, may be driven by individual personality types. Analyses of a subset of the full mission simulation conducted by Chidester, Kanki, Foushee, Dickinson, & Bowles (1990), and by Kanki, Palmer, & Veinott (1991) revealed that captains whose personalities reflected high levels of both achievement motivation and concern for others and whose crews were rated the best performers in the scenario initiated communication to crewmembers only slightly more often than crewmembers initiated communication to the captain. Thus, communication appeared to have a generally balanced, two-way flow among high-performing crews. Captains whose crew performance was rated less well, and whose personalities were more authoritarian and less interpersonally sensitive, received more commands from their first officers than did captains of other personality types. In this case, an authoritarian atmosphere created by the captain appears to have driven the cockpit communication. Therefore, to the extent that communication styles affect performance, personality effects may be mediated through communication. Although these results are preliminary, they illustrate the potential for increasing our understanding of how input factors affect outcomes.

Process variables have also been directly associated with performance as predictors of outcomes, independent of input variables. For example, Foushee et al. (1986) demonstrated that patterns of communication among air transport crews that had recently flown together were more clearly associated with higher levels of performance than patterns among crews that were flying together for the first time. These have been further investigated and described in research by Kanki & Foushee (1989), Kanki et al. (1989), and Kanki, Greaud, & Irwin (1991) which indicates that crews that share similar communication patterns appear to perform better as a team. Thus, group process analyses have shown how communication sequences in the interactions of flightcrews produce effects on performance.

Communication analyses involve exploring relationships between group processes and both input and output variables. Although the overall direction of influence in the model (chapter by Helmreich and Foushee, Figure 1.2) flows from left to right (i.e., culminating in outcome), it must be noted that group processes are dynamic and can change over time. The model also contains a continual feedback loop because performance outcomes can and do reflect back onto ongoing group processes.

As crewmembers individually and jointly perform sequences of tasks, information must be sent and received in a timely and accurate fashion. The dynamic nature of communication arises from the changing state of the aircraft and conditions affecting flight. Even with the highly standardized and routinized forms of communication used in operating aircraft, unexpected events and differences among crewmembers' styles and attitudes create the need for versatile and adaptable communication skills.

With respect to aircrew performance, the way in which teams perform early in flight can have significant effects on their later behaviors. For instance, crews that plan ahead may never experience high workload, whereas crews that allow themselves to "get behind the aircraft" may have to redouble efforts in order to "get everyone back in the loop." Thus, an early outcome consisting of an organized contingency plan may lead to one type of group process, whereas an early outcome consisting of ill-timed preparations may lead to a process of a very different type.

Furthermore, changes in crew and aircraft dynamics may also require changes in content and style of communication. For example, sudden emergency conditions or developing problems may create a cockpit environment where authoritarian control and management of resources temporarily define the ideal model. In fast-changing situations where quick decisions are required, control and direction "from the top" may be in order. The following is a mild, but highly relevant example from the NASA ASRS files in which a first officer describes a situation in which some authoritarian control would have been helpful (names of places are marked xxxx to maintain confidentiality).

> The Captain had the flight plan and I tried to ask him what our route was after xxxx VOR. A flight attendant was in the cockpit insisting that the Captain radio ahead to xxxx about connections since we were late. Every time the Captain tried to answer my question the flight attendant interrupted. The flight attendant was so into her problem she didn't seem to care that I had a more urgent need. By this time we were at least 10 miles past xxxx, and xxxx Center came onto the radio and gave us radar vectors onto the correct course. It was no problem, just embarrassing to have Center tell you that you are starting to go off in the wrong direction. We should have handled it by not being nice guys and telling the flight attendant in a loud voice to "shut up, we are trying to fly the plane."

In another notable ASRS report, a first officer attempted to assist an extremely "negative" captain by reminding him of the correct speed, heading, and altitude during an approach into Chicago–O'Hare. The captain's response, "You just look out the damn window," is a good example of a situation in which authoritarian control was clearly excessive, inappropriate, and unsafe (see Foushee & Manos, 1981, p. 70).

Thus, the communication concept is one that describes a dynamic process in which the transfer of information is affected by and affects crewmembers as well as the crew as a whole. Communication is a primary means by which individuals develop and coordinate activities in order to achieve goals. Variations in communication patterns are useful indicators of effective crew solutions as well as symptoms of crew problems, but in any case must be interpreted within a task, environment, and interpersonal context which can change dramatically over time.

THE FUNCTIONS OF COMMUNICATION ⟶ ✈

The philosopher John L. Austin in an entertaining book called *How to Do Things with Words* (1962) described how words can be "used" in much the same way bricks and boards are used to build things. Austin discussed the ability of language not only to "say" things but to "do" things as well. For instance, saying "I promise to do X" means you have actually "made a promise" (as long as you were being sincere and understood what you were saying). Speech not only accompanies actions but is action itself.

Because communication serves so many functions, it provides an effective index of crew performance. Just by listening to the communications during a flight, we get many indicators of whether tasks are being performed uneventfully according to normal procedures or whether problems are occurring. We can also tell, when problems do occur, if they are handled in a timely way or are leading to greater problems. With respect to CRM, there are at least five significant ways that communication affects crew performance. In some cases, it is the actual communication content that is most important, and in other cases, it is the way in which communication is used:

1. Communication provides information.
2. Communication establishes interpersonal relationships.
3. Communication establishes predictable behavior patterns.
4. Communication maintains attention to task and monitoring.
5. Communication is a management tool.

Although each of these communication functions can be studied as a topic in its own right, in reality, most communications fulfill several functions at the same time. For example, if a captain makes it a point to bring flight and cabin crews together for a pre-departure briefing, his or her communications serve several functions simultaneously. First, they provide important operational information for all crewmembers. Second, they provide a means for the captain to establish an interpersonal tone with the rest of the crew. Third, they help to establish predictability, because the crewmembers now know something about the captain's management style and expectations of them and are provided a preview of how they will work together.

In communication research, any one or more of these functions may be investigated, or, as in case studies, all functions may be considered together. To return to the Avianca Flight 052 example, four of the five functions are illustrated in the safety issues raised. (1) The communication link between pilots and dispatch points to a failure on the part of the pilots to manage or effectively utilize their resources from dispatch. (2) The communication link between pilots failed in terms of situation awareness and monitoring. (3) The communication link between pilots and ATC illustrates the simple lack of information transfer. The pilots failed to communicate "emergency" to the controllers. (4) It exemplifies a lack of predictable behavior patterns, since the language difference between pilots and controllers failed to provide the usual redundancy of information (via intonation and other paralinguistic cues) pertaining to emergency states.

Communications are typically multi-functional, and any given flight may be analyzed on any or all of these dimensions. However, each of the communication functions is typically associated with somewhat different potential problems, inadequacies, or omissions that can result in a less than efficient use of resources and can degrade crew coordination (see Figure 4.3). The following sections discuss each of the communication functions and its associated problems and describe research that addresses them. There will be overlap across topics, but each function is so critical to CRM principles that it is discussed separately.

The Informational Function

The traditional view of communication highlights the informational function of language or information transfer. In the cockpit there is an overwhelming number of settings, conditions, navigational fixes, and status markers to monitor.

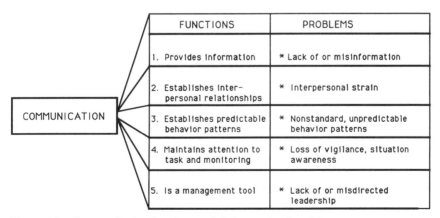

	FUNCTIONS	PROBLEMS
COMMUNICATION	1. Provides information	* Lack of or misinformation
	2. Establishes inter-personal relationships	* Interpersonal strain
	3. Establishes predictable behavior patterns	* Nonstandard, unpredictable behavior patterns
	4. Maintains attention to task and monitoring	* Loss of vigilance, situation awareness
	5. Is a management tool	* Lack of or misdirected leadership

Figure 4.3   Communication functions and their associated problems.

This information is provided by a variety of sources including air traffic controllers, company dispatch, procedures, manuals, maintenance records, and checklists. In addition, information is obtained from aircraft instruments and from the outside world (e.g., visual inspection). Information from instruments is often communicated in terms of numbers and is so critical to the safety of flight that some information is required to be discussed and implemented in a pre-defined, standardized manner (e.g., briefings and checklists). Standard operating procedures not only specify when information must be obtained and acted upon, but often include a verification component as well (e.g., cross-check, or readback).

However, when operations are normal and repetitive, the entire information exchange can become more like a verification of expectations and can degrade into rote recitations. Although the actual words may be exactly the same, the placement, accuracy, attention, and consequences may alter the function of the communication dramatically. There is a critical difference between simply repeating a statement versus verifying the statement versus questioning the statement. Take the following statement as an example: "This reads in the normal range." If the statement was repeated by the FO with a questioning intonation, it may be that FO did not hear the captain. If it was said with the same rising intonation by the FO but it was not a simple repetition, it may mean the FO was questioning whether the reading is "normal." If the FO said the statement after the captain actually reads an instrument, it may have been a verification or cross-check of the captain's reading. In short, intonation and many other contextual features contribute to the functional interpretation of a statement.

The informational function is particularly crucial in problem-solving situations because crewmembers must gather extra or non-routine information and use this information to resolve an ongoing or potential problem. The types of speech act that become particularly salient in "metacognitive" or problem-solving talk include statements that (1) recognize problems, (2) state goals and subgoals, (3) plan and strategize, (4) gather information, (5) alert and predict, and (6) explain (see Orasanu, 1990). Based on transcribed and coded communication from two simulation studies (Foushee et al., 1986; Chidester et al., 1990), these categories of problem-solving talk were compared across normal and abnormal phases of flight for high-performing crews versus low-performing crews.

In highlighting the informational function of communication, it is not the simple gathering of task-relevant information that ensures good performance, but the patterning of these communications that is critical. In Orasanu's (1990) study, good performing teams generated communication patterns showing problem-solving talk during low-workload phases and increased interchanges of planning and reflecting strategy formation. Poorer teams failed to engage in planning communication during low-workload periods. Thus, when workload became high, the information-gathering increased but was not as effective.

The picture we get here is of good Captains who are planful, anticipate difficulties, use time during the normal phase to prepare for higher work-load periods, and who are ahead of the curve. . . . I suggest that the good Captains, by articulating plans and strategies, create a context in which their commands and information requests take on meaning. This articulation helps to build a shared mental model for the situation. It enables the first officer to make suggestions, coordinate actions, and offer information that contributes to solving the problem and making the decisions. (Orasanu, 1990, pp. 13–15.)

Related to problem-solving are decision-making processes that accompany problem solution. Again, the informational aspect of communication is called into play, and the speech categories most of interest are functions related to situation assessment. Some relatively generic speech categories include (1) situation awareness, (2) information requests, and (3) notifications to ground (Orasanu, 1990). However, each scenario and specific problem generates its own list of pertinent information, and speech categories are typically tied directly to these points. For example, in her analysis of expert decision-making strategies, Mosier (1991) developed an information transfer matrix containing "items evaluated as important to making the critical decisions of each flight segment, as well as the checklists and procedures associated with the abnormalities of that scenario. . . . Information solicitation and transfer were coded on the matrices beginning with the onset of the abnormal situation" (p. 268). The general strategy was (1) to consider how correctly and completely the communication data from each flightcrew filled out the matrix, and (2) to assess whether performance and correctness of decision outcomes were related to this measure of situation assessment.

Both studies above are excellent examples of how communications serve an informational function critical to problem-solving and decision-making. Communication analyses help to delineate what information is critical, when it should be solicited, the best way in which it should be integrated, who the possessors of information are, and whether specific patterns can be linked to more effective crew communication and coordination. The chapter by Orasanu provides more detailed discussions of the work in this area.

The Interpersonal/Expressive Function

Communication serves an expressive function when it helps to form interpersonal relationships or creates a relational environment which affects how crews perform their duties. Pilots may possess exceptional "stick-and-rudder" skills, but in complex, modern aircraft pilots must also possess the ability to utilize and manage a large variety of informational inputs, including verbal and non-verbal channels of intercrew communication. Should crewmembers fail to maintain these channels, they may find themselves in information deficits at critical times. To maintain these channels, crewmembers must feel that it is beneficial to provide and receive information through them. If the interpersonal environment in the cockpit deteriorates to a point where crewmembers decide to withhold or are reluctant to seek information, the potential for failure is increased. Conversely, when interpersonal relationships among team members are positive, the desire to seek and provide information is likely to be increased, resulting in a complimentary increase in chances for success.

One important input to the interpersonal–communication–performance formula is the personality of each individual making up the crew. The separate personalities of crewmembers must be integrated to create a single, effective team with a positive orientation toward sharing tasks and information relevant to those tasks. Recent research has focused on the links between personality and performance, and between personality and communication.

The link between personality and performance of flight crews has been established by Helmreich and his associates (Gregorich, Helmreich, Wilhelm, & Chidester, 1989; Helmreich, Foushee, Benson & Russini, 1986; Helmreich & Wilhelm, 1989) and by Chidester (Chidester, 1990; Chidester et al. 1990). Three major personality groups have been identified in flightcrew composition research. First, *positive instrumental skill/expressive* pilots are highly motivated, goal-oriented achievers who are also concerned with the interpersonal aspects of crew performance. Second, *negative instrumental* captains tend to have a very high goal achievement orientation with little regard for interpersonal skills. Third, *negative expressive* captains have lower motivation toward achieving goals and toward enhancing their interpersonal relations with other crewmembers. As mentioned earlier, studies have indicated that captains who are characterized by the positive instrumental/expressive trait tend to consistently lead crews at a high performance level in full-mission LOFT scenarios (Chidester & Foushee, 1988; Chidester et al., 1990).

What might the high-performing, highly concerned pilots consider good skills? In a survey conducted by Helmreich et al. (1986), pilots rated "above average" by check pilots reported that: (1) a first officer should be encouraged to question a captain and procedures; (2) pilots should make their personal problems known to other crewmembers; (3) first officers may assume control of an aircraft in situations other than total incapacitation of the captain; and (4) the pilot flying should verbalize plans and maneuvers and make sure that they are acknowledged and understood. Thus, pilots who tend to get highest ratings from observers recognize the value of encouraging two-way communication in the cockpit and the importance of the interpersonal relationship between crewmembers.

A preliminary study of the links between captains' personalities and communication was conducted by Kanki, Palmer, & Veinott (1991) on a subset of crews from the full mission simulation reported in Chidester et al. (1990). In this simulation study, 23 three-person crews flew flight segments over 2 days in a high fidelity Boeing 727 simulator at the NASA Man–Vehicle Systems Research Facility at Ames Research Center.

This communication analysis involved 12 of the original 23 three-person crews who flew five flight segments over 2 days. The 12 crews were divided into three groups of four. In one group, the crews were led by captains from the positive instrumental/expressive personality group described above. The other two groups were led by captains from the negative instrumental and the negative expressive groups. Captains were assigned to these groups based on a battery of personality instruments filled out before participating in the simulation. The battery included the Expanded Personal Attributes Questionnaire (Spence, Helmreich, & Holahan, 1979), the Work and Family Orientation Questionnaire (Spence & Helmreich, 1978), and the Revised Jenkins Activity Survey C.

The scenario used for the communication analysis was a single flight segment from the second day of the mission. This flight left Los Angeles bound for Sacramento under rapidly deteriorating weather conditions. Ultimately diverted to San Francisco and then San Jose, crews experienced a hydraulic failure that necessitated manual extension of landing gear and alternative flap configurations.

Comparisons were made between crews led by each personality type, and preliminary communication analysis revealed several interesting findings. One set of results centered around who initiated communications: Negative expressive captains initiated less total speech than did other types of captains, and these were the same crews who made the most errors in the original study (Chidester et al., 1990). Thus, captains who were characterized as having less achievement motivation in interpersonal and flying skills were also the captains who initiated communications the least and who led crews that performed least well. Considering the ratio of initiations (captain compared to crew), negative expressive captains initiated less often than their crews. In contrast, positive instrumental/expressive captains initiated speech marginally more often than their crews. Therefore, in crews led by captains who had reported high interest in interpersonal and technical tasks, the flow of information was encouraged but not dominated by captains. These crews were the consistently high performers in the original study.

Further analysis broke down the initiating speech into commands, questions, and observations. First, the lower ratio of initiating speech by negative expressive captains and the marginally higher ratio of initiating speech by Positive Instrumental captains were primarily due to how often questions and observations were used. It could be inferred from these data that the negative expressive captains showed less initiative in providing and seeking information, while positive instrument/expressive captains took a slight lead in this regard. Furthermore, first officers paired with negative expressive captains asked more questions than other first officers, possibly compensating for the behaviors of negative expressive captains who initiated less speech overall. In other words, first officers may have had to seek out information from negative expressive captains since these captains offered less information on their own. Finally, first officers initiated more commands to negative instrumental captains than first officers paired with any other captain type. If it is true that captains can set the interpersonal communication style for an entire crew (Ginnett, 1987), then the negative instrumental captains may have invited more authoritarian behaviors from their subordinates.

Because of the small number of crews used in these preliminary analyses, the findings remain tentative. However, the general picture emerging from these studies of crew composition focusing on leader personality is one that fits with the general concept of CRM and with communication evidence from other areas. The notion being developed is that the effective management of important information resources in the cockpit requires open channels of communication among crewmembers. Each member of the crew must feel that his or her input will be welcomed and seriously evaluated. Clearly, the interpersonal styles and attitudes that a crewmember brings to each flight will predispose him or her to participate in this type of communication. Gaining a greater understanding of those personality factors and how they relate to effective communication is therefore an important goal of human factors research.

Establishing Predictable Behavior

Effective team performance in complex task environments requires team members to integrate their activities in an ordered, timely fashion and to make their actions and intentions known to others. Tasks need to be completed simultaneously (as in setting altimeters for captain and first officer) or in sequence (as in performing normal and emergency procedures), and they need to be completed at the appropriate times. For example, descent requires a sequence of events performed by pilot-flying and pilot-not-flying that allow changes in aircraft configuration, altitude, speed, and course in a gradual, controllable manner.

This type of coordination of tasks among crewmembers is facilitated by the fact that pilots share the same knowledge and skills. Standard operating procedures (SOPs) extend the shared knowledge base by setting up expectations about who is doing what and when. To the extent that both pilots have the same cognitive or mental representation regarding the general state of the aircraft (i.e., location, course, altitude, weather, flaps and slats configuration, etc.), the simultaneous or sequential coordination of tasks is made easier. Second-guessing other crewmembers is not an efficient way of gaining information, especially in high-workload, critical phases of flight or during emergency situations. Using SOPs frees busy crewmembers from having to spend valuable time searching for and validating routine information. For example, a pilot busy with landing an aircraft may know that the pilot-not-flying will be making regular call-outs for altitude and speed. Checklists are a means of bringing both pilots to the same sequence of tasks and same levels of knowledge about the state of the aircraft.

Communication is an important aspect of SOPs because in some cases it defines the procedures formally, and in other cases it is used informally to create or access a shared knowledge base. Checklists and written procedures are two cases in which communication is used to define or specify what tasks need to be done, who should do them, what order they should be done in, and when they should be done (see Degani & Wiener, 1990). When checklists and procedures are performed, pilots also become aware of various aspects of aircraft systems, and in many cases crewmembers are forced to participate in tasks or to monitor other crewmembers' performance.

SOPs may also arise out of company policies that become conventionalized ways of performing tasks and/or communicating. For example, the task of operating radios during flight typically falls to the pilot-non-flying. The pilot-flying will assume that all in-coming and out-going communication is being dealt with and that he or she can count on the other pilot to relay relevant information. This division of labor is useful because it prevents the flying pilot from being overloaded with tasks, but on some occasions the pilot-flying may operate the radios (e.g., when the non-flying pilot is performing an abnormal procedure).

From a communication perspective, conventionalized patterns of information exchange serve the same purpose; i.e., to create expectations about how and when important information is made available. When information is made available in a predictable way, more efficient understanding and utilization of that information is accomplished. For example, the use of formulaic statements like "positive rate, gear up," makes accurate information transfer easier. Even if only part of the phrase is heard in a noisy cockpit, pilots will know what is being communicated and can act accordingly.

The notion of conventionalized communication patterns also refers to accepted and typical exchanges between pilots. For example, captains may be expected to issue more commands than first officers, and first officers may be expected to use more acknowledgments of communications (e.g., of commands) than do captains. Other less obvious, but no less conventionalized, patterns may distinguish high-performance crews from less effective crews.

Foushee & Manos (1981) demonstrated associations between specific types of speech acts and performance outcomes. Using the database generated by Ruffell Smith's (1979) simulation study, these researchers found that increased performance (i.e., fewer errors) among crewmembers was associated with increases in observations about flight status, in acknowledgments of messages received from other crewmembers, and the number of agreements between crewmembers. Increases in crew errors were also associated with increases in the amount of communication in which one or more crewmembers expressed uncertainty about what the others were talking about. In other words, crews appear to perform best in a cockpit environment in which pilots share and acknowledge information about the state of the aircraft and minimize the amount of uncertainty about communication.

In another study, communication processes were associated with crew familiarity. Foushee et al. (1986) conducted a full mission simulation study and found that crews that flew the simulation immediately after completing a trip together (post-duty condition) performed better than crews that had the benefit of rest before the simulation but had not flown together (pre-duty condition). Expanding on these findings, post-duty crews in general used more statements of intent to perform actions, more acknowledgments of others' communication, and a greater amount of communications overall. Also, first officers in post-duty crews expressed more disagreements with captains than first officers in pre-duty crews.

It has been suggested (Foushee et al., 1986; Kanki & Foushee, 1989) that the time spent flying together before the simulation increased the ability of crewmembers to anticipate each other's actions and interpret the style and content of their communication. Post-duty crews therefore could adopt a more informed or "familiar" style in which first officers might be more willing to initiate directives or question captains' decisions. Furthermore, while there may have been a stronger flow of "bottom-up" communication (i.e., from first officer to captain), the authority structure was not impaired (captains still issued more commands than first officers), and overall, recent experience enhanced performance.

Taking a different approach with these data, Kanki et al. (1989) and Kanki, Greaud, & Irwin (1991) have shown that similarity of communication patterns may be a distinguishing feature of high-performance crews. This research has attempted to demonstrate that high-performance crews (regardless of whether or not they had flown together) share similar communication patterns, while low-performing crews show more heterogeneous patterns. For example, consistent with the earlier findings (Foushee et al., 1986), in four of five best-performing crews, captains and first officers generated essentially the same proportions of speech types (commands, questions, acknowledgements, etc.). The five low-performing crews used in these analyses showed no consistent pattern of speech types. These analyses suggest that high-performance crews share similar patterns of communication. Thus, regardless of amount of time spent flying together, high-performance crews appear very quickly to reach levels of efficient information transfer and crew coordination because they share basic knowledge and skills of communication.[2]

[2]It should be noted that several communication analyses have used a subset of the original data from Foushee et al. (1986). The first analysis (Kanki et al. 1989) included 10 of the total 20 flightcrews: the 5 highest and 5 lowest performances. The later analysis (Kanki, Greaud, & Irwin, 1991) added the 8 middle-performing crews. Communications from two of the original 20 crews were not analyzable due to irregularities in the simulation flight.

It should be noted that in none of the simulation experiments cited here has a direct causal link been claimed between communication and performance. The evidence is mounting that a strong correlation exists between certain patterns of communication and the regularity of those patterns and performance in the cockpit. However, it is unclear which comes first, performance or communication—whether high-performing pilots develop regular patterns of communication due to their efficient flying skills, or whether their efficient flying skills have developed as result of certain communication patterns and skills. The growing evidence of the association of communication and performance suggests that, in either case, there is enormous value in discovering relationships and their causal links so that trainers and evaluators can develop guidelines and criteria for improving crew coordination (discussed in the chapter by Gregorich and Wilhelm).

Maintaining Task Attention and Situation Awareness

It should be obvious by now that many of the preceding communication functions overlap. For instance, problem-solving and decision-making requires correct situation assessment and the planned, sequential acquisition of pertinent information. Furthermore, CRM principles that underlie good managerial and leadership skills are very much linked to achieving situational awareness across all crewmembers, particularly in a problem-solving situation. However, safe operations depend on maintaining vigilance during normal and abnormal operations alike; from extremely low workload (i.e., "boring" conditions) to extremely high workload (i.e., juggling of many complex tasks and operations at once). From a communication standpoint, we are interested in what kinds of communication patterns contribute to maintaining attention to task and effective monitoring under any of these various conditions.

As mentioned earlier, NTSB investigations have acknowledged several instances of exemplary CRM behaviors in the face of extreme emergency. United Flight 811 (NTSB, 1990a) and United Flight 232 (NTSB, 1990b) were two such flights. In both cases the captain cited training in CRM as contributing significantly to the overall effectiveness of the crews. With these characterizations in hand, an analysis of the verbal behavior of each crew was undertaken to explore how catastrophic events impacted the dynamics of crew interaction, and how CRM principles contributed to successful crew performance under stressful, high-workload conditions (Predmore, 1991).

Similar to other studies mentioned, the verbatim transcripts were broken into units of analysis classified by speaker, target (of the communication), time of onset, and speech type. Categories of speech acts included: (1) command-advocacy, (2) incomplete-interrupted, (3) reply-acknowledgement, (4) observation, and (5) inquiry. Larger units of speech were then delineated called action decision sequences (ADSs, roughly representing topics or types of operational subtasks). These included: (1) flight control, (2) damage assessment, (3) problem solution, (4) landing, (5) emergency preparations, and (6) social.

Once all speech was categorized in this way, the distribution of communication was graphically presented on timelines in a variety of ways. For example, a graph depicting speech act categories is shown in the chapter by Helmreich and Foushee (Figure 1.10). Timelines were constructed that depicted action decision sequences (ADSs) broken down by crewmembers (captain, first officer, flight engineer, check airman). These graphs show that the distribution of topics or attention shifts drastically over time. As one would expect, some topics (such as social) completely drop out because other ADSs, such as flight control and landing, are assigned higher priorities by pilots. This form of analysis allows us to see where problem solution and damage assessment fall in the timeline and how they gained attention without loss of attention to other ADSs. While we already know something about effective communication patterns related to problem-solving (see prior discussion on the informational function), these patterns are concerned with how several tasks are distributed and monitored in a multiple-task situation. As stated by Predmore (1991), "The interactions of the crew of United Flight 232 were marked by an efficient distribution of communications across multiple tasks and crewmembers, the maximum utilization of a fourth crewmember, the explicit prioritizing of task focus, and the active involvement of the captain in all tasks throughout the scenario" (p. 355).

Clearly, we need to extend this methodology beyond the few available case studies in order to make contrasts among different levels of performance under controlled conditions. However, this study presents yet another productive technique for analyzing communications and identifying effective patterns for training purposes.

The Managerial/Directive Function

In a real sense, the managerial function of communication is the heart of CRM. Consider the following characteristics of a hypothetical crew: (1) The interpersonal atmosphere of the cockpit is conducive to a good working relationship among crewmembers. (2) Standard procedures and crewmember expectations are known to be reliable. (3) Information is available and easily accessible. (4) Crewmembers are in the loop and ahead of the airplane (i.e., situationally aware). In short, we have a "CRM-ready" crew. All that is lacking is the actual implementation of the plans, problem solution, decisions; that is, "CRM in action." To state it according to fixed-sequence theory, crews "form, storm, and norm" and are now ready to "perform" (see Ginnett, 1987; Tuckman, 1965). To enable performance a manager is needed who can lead, distribute tasks, oversee, and monitor the whole process. Enter the captain who holds command authority and ultimate responsibility.

The above situation, while not incorrect, is somewhat limited in scope. The other side of leadership is followership. There is a strong implication that all crewmembers participate to some extent in the managerial function, since each must contribute to the coordination of the crew as a team. Consider a multiple team environment such as the C-5 military transport (U.S. Air Force Military Airlift Command), in which there are several levels of "teams." The entire flightcrew, led by the aircraft commander (AC), consists of at least two pilots (AC and copilot), two flight engineers (FE and scanner), and as many loadmasters as are needed to carry out the mission. However, the crew is also composed of three operational subgroups, each of which has its own leader, namely, the AC, the primary engineer, and the primary loadmaster who oversees the others. There are many periods during operations (prior to, during, and after flight) when these subteams work autonomously, while at other times the team is called together into a single unit led by the AC. For instance, before take-off and on approach, the AC makes a "headsets on" call and "crew report call to stations," which assemble the team as one, while at other times individual tasks define the composition and authority structure for sub-teams. In short, there are times for individual and sub-team autonomy, and throughout a flight crewmembers shift from working alone to working with various subsets of the crew.

Even within a two-person cockpit, there are constant shifts between times when both pilots are working together and when each is working alone (e.g., one flying the airplane and the other interfacing with ATC). Each of these team variations consists of pre-defined roles and tasks and makes up what Hackman (1987) and Ginnett call the organizational "shell"; that is, "a predefined or expected set of interactions between various elements of the system which permits simpler and more efficient interactions" (Ginnett, chapter 3, p. 92). Every flight depends on the shell as a foundation that ensures standard and predictable behavior and safe and efficient ways of operating. But flight operations include more than the single-unit task definition. Each subteam and each individual must also define its roles and tasks within the team as well as how they will relate to interfacing teams (e.g., ATC, maintenance, dispatch, etc.).

Whether the actions taking place are produced by a single team unit or by many subunits working in parallel, they must be choreographed into a single flow. It is to this end that communication takes a directive function, coordinating the crew's actions. We typically think of directive speech acts as commands and suggestions, but this should not imply that managers and leaders necessarily accomplish their own overseeing jobs by dictating crew actions in an authoritarian way. In fact, recalling the results of Orasanu's work (discussed earlier), directive speech during abnormal operations will not promote smooth crew coordination if the proper groundwork (e.g., planning and sharing of information) has not been accomplished earlier. The good manager knows when to take the controls and when to let the crew do their job; when to direct and when to monitor. Probably most important is that the good manager accomplishes much of his or her work in creating a CRM-ready team.

Ginnett's field study of team-building[3] further emphasizes this notion. Briefly, the attributes that described the more effective captains included the following: (1) Effective leaders explicitly affirmed or elaborated on the rules, norms, task boundaries, and so on that constituted the "normative" model (or "shell") of the organizational task environment. Specifically, captains briefed both flightdeck and cabin crews about interface tasks, physical and task boundaries, and other norms for performing their task (regarding safety, communication, and cooperation). (2) They established clear authority dynamics, as well as their own technical, social, and managerial competence. Each effective leader covered these areas in the process of team creation prior to flight (e.g., early crew briefings) and behaved consistently with this model during task execution.

It appears that the effective leader is one who helps crewmembers minimize ambiguities in task and allocation of resources. An effective captain may also expand on the "shell" so that predictability based on standard procedures (written and unwritten rules alike) is enhanced for his or her flightcrew. As stated by Ginnett (1987):

> Captains can also do much more than affirm the shell. . . . They can "expand" the shell. That larger definition, while providing the potential for more effective crew work, is nonetheless, quite fragile. In fact, the "expanded" definition is, itself, a new "dotted line" of how the group will work. Just as the "dotted line" of imported definitions for all forming crews requires some work by the leader, so too will the expanded shell require reinforcement. Some of that reinforcement is provided by the congruence between that which the captain "says" in the briefing and how he "behaves" in the briefing. Even more importantly is how he behaves during line flying. If he supports the expanded definition of crew work which he created, the "dotted lines" will fill in and more effective crew work will result. But if he should behave in a manner inconsistent with the expanded shell, its newly formed and fragile outer boundaries will collapse. Effective

[3]This study was a part of a larger cross-organizational investigation (see the chapters by Hackman and Ginnett). Focusing on one particular organization, the research goal was to identify behavioral variations in the team formation process that correspond with variation in leadership effectiveness; in short, to be able to behaviorally define differences between effective leaders and less effective leaders. From observations made during actual operations of ten (B-727) crews, Ginnett was able to differentiate variations in leadership effectiveness, and using an inductive method he integrated these observations and constructed "behavioral profiles" corresponding to each type.

team work doesn't just happen—it takes effort by everyone, but especially by the leader. (pp. 404–405)

While Ginnett's study was not strictly a communication study (i.e., it did not look at communications on an utterance-by-utterance level), his work highlights the critical managerial functions that occur during team formation prior to flight. Communication, in the form of briefings and in-flight task discussions, was the focus of his analyses and the core of team-building behaviors. If we are to analyze communication specifically on the managerial function, we should consider that crew management is not the sole responsibility of the captain. Communication from all crewmembers carry the potential for directing actions toward a single coordinated effort. Just as there may be metacognitive speech acts that are "problem-solving" talk, speech acts may be categorized in terms of "task management" talk. For example, Conley, Cano, & Bryant's (1991) analysis of communication takes a task management perspective, and all communications were coded into a 3 × 3 matrix that differentiated among coordination techniques (i.e., planning, acting, and evaluating/monitoring) and content domain (i.e., aircraft, environment, and people). See also Conley, Cano, Bryant, Kanki, & Chidester (1990). In Conley et al. (1990), a matrix of process (coordination techniques) and content area dimensions was depicted with illustrations of a typical activity for each category (as adapted in Figure 4.4). Task management talk is best represented by the three coordination techniques under the "people" content domain (highlighted in the figure). Note that commands probably fall most often in the "action" cell of the matrix, while the planning and evaluating cells may contain any variety of speech act type.

	Aircraft	Environment	People
Planning	Studying approach procedures	Planning routes	Prioritizing tasks
Acting	Following glideslope	Implementing routes	Assigning tasks
Evaluating/ Monitoring	Assessing pitch of aircraft	Reporting a navigational fix reached	Evaluating crew experience with task

Figure 4.4 Typology of management strategies. (Adapted from Conley, Cano, Bryant, Kanki, & Chidester, 1990.)

Managing crew resources in modern aircraft is a complex task which may
involve coordinating teams within teams and tasks within tasks. The ability to
manage communication in complex operations must be cultivated, for it is
through good communication skills that effective leaders can both invite the
willing participation and contributions of a diverse group of team members and
also direct and order a complex flow of enabling acts.

RESEARCH ISSUES AND APPLICATIONS ───────── ✈

Much of this chapter has discussed communication research conducted over
several years using a variety of approaches (e.g., field studies, full-mission simulations, etc.). While support for many of the conclusions drawn from this work is
growing, it is extremely important that the reader understand something about the
nature of the research and the limitations on its implications. This explanation is
not meant to diminish in any way the importance of recent findings. On the
contrary, the true value of communication research can be best understood and
implemented in the context of the issues discussed here.

A primary issue in discussions of CRM research findings is the degree to
which results are generalizable; specifically, how certain can we be that research
results can be applied to any cockpit situation in the "real world"? The ultimate
goal of communication research is to create a reliable body of knowledge about
how crews communicate that will enable researchers, trainers, line pilots, government regulators, engineers, and designers to make recommendations that enhance
the safe and efficient operation of aircraft. The question here is whether this is a
realistic goal for communication researchers and what are the limitations. How far
can we generalize the results of a study with confidence? The following discussion
addresses limitations to generalizability that are tied to three factors: (1) research
approaches, (2) research focus, and (3) problem focus.

Limitations Imposed by Research Approach

It is obvious that studies conducted during actual operations (as in Ginnett's study discussed above) have a great deal of face validity. Generalizing from
line flights to other line flights will not stretch the credibility of scientist or
professional. However, field studies are often constrained in ways that reduce their
scope. For example, a study that requires researchers to spend many hours
traveling with flight crews may limit the number of crews that can be reasonably
sampled. While the analyses are intensive, their generalizability is diminished
because the sample is small. Furthermore, in a field setting there is no way for
researchers to exercise any control over environmental or operational conditions.
Thus, if a study is concerned with emergency conditions, a researcher would have

to fly many hours before finding even one such incident to analyze. (This is a mixed blessing!) Therefore, while field studies allow a close look at a small part of the "real world," their results also address a subset of research questions.

On the other hand, laboratory studies (especially full-mission simulations) offer an excellent opportunity to exercise control over test conditions. To the extent that these conditions can realistically simulate actual flight, the advantage of control is gained at only a small loss to the generalizability inherent in field studies. Clearly, the more closely a research situation in a laboratory replicates conditions in the "real world," the more generalizable the research will be. However, every scientist knows that in the laboratory he or she is forced to reduce the "real world" to a number of manageable parameters which can be controlled and measured.

Limitations Linked to Research Focus

The high-fidelity full-mission simulation paradigm introduced by Ruffell Smith (1979) represents the state of the art in aviation crew research, and the level of realism achieved far exceeds that found in many other domains of human factors research. Flight scenarios are designed to replicate real flight with the subtle effects of aircraft motion, a wide range of weather conditions, high resolution visual displays, and realistic communications for air traffic control. To the extent that these realistic conditions are maintained, it is tempting to make strong recommendations based on the results of this paradigm. However, it is important to keep in mind that even in the best full-mission simulation, choices have been made by researchers based on both simulation limitations and research focus. These choices result in the selection of particular conditions and design manipulations that best fit the research questions but at the same time limit the generalizability of the findings to a reduced description of "real world" line operations.

For example, specific kinds of problems are built into scenarios to create opportunities to observe pilots' decision-making and crew coordination skills. Limitations to the generalizability of findings occur in every case because each scenario is different to some degree. Researchers' main emphases or reasons for doing a particular study may differ across studies, and as a result scenarios will differ. In any given study, only one or two central problems are examined, and these are the problems that are emphasized in the scenario. Therefore care must be taken to qualify the conclusions made on the basis of a single full-mission simulation study, and researchers should take greater advantage of the growing number of simulation studies which can be compared.

In both field and simulation settings, generalizability is limited by the fact that research is conducted on different aircraft types using different equipment and crew configurations. For example, crew studies have been performed in 747 and 727 simulators requiring three-person crews, while others have been conducted on 737, DC-9, and MD-88 simulators requiring two-person crews. Also, different levels of automation exist in these different aircraft, and the levels of activities pilots are engaged in will differ in quality if not in quantity. In addition to the issue of different flight scenarios in simulation, and different flight operations in the field, it is also possible that different crew compositions and equipment may yield differences in communication patterns and as a result limit the generalizability across such configurations.

Limitations Imposed by Problem Focus

Generalizability is limited when we constrain the problem focus to a single operation that actually occurs within a larger system of operations. For example, when we investigate within-cockpit communication and its relationship to flight safety but do not consider the pilot–ATC linkages that have been shown to be so crucial from accident and incident reports, we must qualify our results to reflect this omission.

For example, a rare study focusing on both controllers and pilots was conducted by Morrow, Lee, & Rodvold (1991). This study of controller–pilot collaboration used field data obtained from four of the busiest terminal radar approach control facilities in the United States. It was found that when controllers economized workload by composing longer messages including those that require more than one kind of readback (e.g., readback and answer request), pilots used more procedural deviations, such as partial readbacks. In short, a decreased workload for controllers appeared to increase the "memory load" for pilots. In addition, procedural deviations were associated with nonroutine transactions (e.g., clarifications, interruptions/repeats, corrections, etc.). Therefore, while on the one hand, a correction of a readback error improves accuracy, it also reduces communication efficiency by lengthening the transaction.

The results point to potential trade-offs inherent in the interactive process between controllers and pilots and the importance of bearing in mind both speaker and addressee perspectives. As Morrow et al. state (p. 17), "ATC communication depends not only on individual skills and capacities (e.g., processing speed and working memory capacity), but on how smoothly controllers and pilots collaborate during routine communication." There are at least two lessons to be learned: (1) Studies of communication, pilot workload, and cockpit crew performance may be defining the problem space too narrowly and should be aware that controller–pilot collaborations affect both controller and pilot performances. While this does not imply that all studies must include controller–pilot interactions, it does imply that the interpretation of research results should bear these relationships in mind. (2) There are important CRM training implications for both pilots and controllers, and the incorporation of such findings may be fruitfully incorporated into a CRM curriculum. Chidester describes in his chapter how numerous other work groups (e.g., flight attendants, dispatchers, ATC, and others) need to become a part of the crew coordination picture.

Summary

The limitations described do not in any way diminish the value of current communication research. Important findings are being discovered with each new study. These cautions are offered here to help the reader better interpret and integrate findings from this growing body of information. If there is any message here, it is that the work must proceed with an open dialogue among researchers and the CRM community so that an increasing number of studies may be meaningfully compared at various levels of analysis. In time, these analyses will reveal a common set of findings and conclusions with an undeniable increase in generalizable power.

COMMUNICATION SKILLS TRAINING WITHIN CRM PROGRAMS ✈

By now it should be evident that communication at its simplest is a multifaceted, slippery concept. It is clearly a means to an end; that is, communication is required in accomplishing the flying task. But it is also a means to another end in the same sense that it is a tool by which many of the CRM principles are implemented (e.g., conduct briefings and debriefings, solve problems, make decisions, assume leadership, etc.). Furthermore, communication is an indicator of a person's role, attentional focus, personality, state of mind, expertise, experience level, style of operating, level of professionalism, and many other personal attributes that can influence how smoothly crewmembers interact and coordinate their actions together.

For this reason, there can be many different approaches to "teaching" communication as part of a CRM curriculum. Most practitioners agree that like other critical elements of CRM, there are (1) concepts to be learned, (2) skills to be practiced, and (3) performance to be assessed. "Communication" can be considered a stand-alone topic or as instrumental toward achieving other CRM skills such as decision-making or leadership.

Learning the Concept

In the curriculum suggested in the NASA/MAC CRM Workshop (Orlady & Foushee, 1987), communication skills is listed as one of seven major topic areas:

1. Communication
2. Situation awareness

3. Problem-solving/Decision-making/Judgment
4. Leadership/Followership
5. Stress management
6. Critique
7. Interpersonal skills

As a stand-alone "skills area," communication was described as follows:

> Specific skills associated with good communication practices include such items as polite assertiveness and participation, active listening, and feedback. In order to improve the communication channel, cultural influences must be taken into account as well as factors like rank, age, and flight position which can create barriers to communication in the cockpit situation. Polite assertiveness is a skill frequently ignored in communications training but vital to a healthy cockpit. A single hesitant attempt to communicate important data fails to discharge individual responsibility. A captain/aircraft commander may be open to communication but be temporarily unable to receive and comprehend. Information possessors must be aware of the importance of their information and have a strong feeling of self-value. Captains must constantly strive to emphasize this in their team-building efforts. The concept of "legitimate avenue of dissent" (which deserves further development) won instant approval from both groups as an important vehicle for "clearing the air", maintaining lines of communication, and maintaining self-image. The problem comes in attempting to define specific avenues or tools of dissent, both during in-flight problem-solving and after the flight. (Orlady & Foushee, 1987, p. 199)

However, communication easily extends into the other six topics. Other participants in the CRM Workshop consistently included communication in their discussions. For instance, Schwartz's discussion of situational awareness (Schwartz, 1987, p. 173–174) states that the key to safety lies within the group's level of situational awareness rather than the cumulative awareness of individual crewmembers. The dynamics involved in "group situational awareness" hinge on cockpit management skills such as communication, managing people, command, and leadership.

It is easy to see that all seven topics overlap, with communication as the tool used in all. Problem-solving, leadership/followership, critique, and interpersonal skills are all clearly enhanced or limited by one's communication skills. Even stress management includes not only one's ability to perceive and accommodate to stress in oneself and others, but to communicate this potential problem to the other crewmembers in an appropriate way. Most of this chapter has illustrated the interrelationships between communication and these other aspects of CRM.

The newest proposed draft of the FAA Advisory Circular on Crew Resource Management (FAA, in preparation) combines communication processes and decision behavior into a single category and lists five subtopics contained within it:

(1) briefings, (2) inquiry/advocacy, (3) crew self-critique, (4) conflict resolution, and (5) communications and decision-making. This particular classification scheme mirrors the evaluation system based on behavior markers discussed by Helmreich and Foushee in their chapter and represents a useful way of thinking of these concepts. For instance, if one is developing advanced CRM training for check airmen and evaluators, it is efficient to teach the concepts in the same way that they will be used for assessment. Nevertheless, different organizations must tailor programs to fit their own specific needs and design curricula to emphasize their most critical communication concerns.

It is not surprising that CRM training programs incorporate communication concepts in a variety of ways. It may (1) constitute a topic on its own (i.e., a communication module), (2) be incorporated into every other topic of the curriculum (i.e., interwoven into every other module), and/or (3) be treated as a special topic, such as one that focuses on the interface between teams (e.g., pilot–ATC, pilot–flight attendant, pilot–dispatch coordination). All three strategies are being effectively used in currently implemented CRM training programs.

Practicing the Skill

Like other skills, communication requires active practice beyond simple concept learning. Classroom work may include an experiential component (including team exercises, role playing, demonstrations, video feedback), but there is no substitute for exercising these skills during actual operations and, when possible, during line operational simulation (LOS) or line-oriented flight training (LOFT). Many other chapters discuss LOFT, particularly that by Butler. It is clearly a technology with tremendous potential because of the opportunity it provides for crewmembers "to practice line operations . . . with a full crew in a realistic environment. Crewmembers learn to handle a variety of scripted real-time scenarios which include routine, abnormal, and emergency situations. They also learn and practice cockpit resource management skills, including crew coordination, judgment, decision-making, and communication skills" (FAA, 1990, p. 1).

Part of LOFT's potential is inherent in flight scenario design. Although there are some generic guidelines that should not be violated (e.g., crew integrity should be maintained, interruptions by the instructor should be avoided, etc.), there are yet untapped opportunities for designing scenarios with very specific training objectives, integrating both technical and CRM functions. Communication skills are central to LOFT because they are associated with so many different functions. As described earlier, communication skills are fundamental to the practice of CRM behaviors such as leadership, situational awareness, problem-solving, and workload management. While it is therefore assumed that communications will be practiced in every LOFT, it is critical to delineate just what type of communication function is of major interest and to pay careful attention to the sometimes multiple ways in which communications are used. For instance, a crewmember may have excellent interpersonal communication skills in promoting a cooperative atmosphere in the cockpit. However, this does not imply that the same person will exhibit excellent communication skills in advocating a position in a problem-solving situation. In short, one must design scenarios with these distinctions in mind in order to delineate among the many types of communications skills that make up "good" CRM.

Another area in which LOFT can tap its great training potential is in enhancing the effectiveness of evaluators to debrief crewmembers. While it is the ultimate goal for crewmembers to self-debrief, the way in which LOFT is debriefed by an evaluator can make all the difference in whether or not crewmembers direct their attention to the most critical elements of their performance. It is important for evaluators to delineate the functions of communication with tangible evidence.

Assessing Communication Effectiveness

The sections above have discussed many communication patterns associated with effective versus less effective CRM. Accident and incident reports, field and simulation research have all contributed to our knowledge about many varieties of communication skills. However, the critical operational question regarding CRM is whether measurable improvements in the way crews perform flight operations result from the training. Motivated by this concern, the NASA/University of Texas/FAA Aerospace Crew Performance Project developed the Line-LOS Checklist (Helmreich, Wilhelm, Kello, Taggart, & Butler, 1991) for assessing the human factors components of flightcrew performance. Crew performance markers are defined for each of the three interaction and cognitive functions as well as for the two machine interface (or technical skills) functions (see the chapter by Helmreich and Foushee). Following this schema, communications processes and decision tasks are combined as one of the three interpersonal functions. "Team formation and management tasks" and "workload management and situational awareness tasks" form the other two interpersonal functions. However, the evaluator must also remember that communication serves in a double capacity, (1) as a skill in itself and (2) and as an indicator of other CRM processes. Communications are important components of all three interpersonal functions as well as several of the machine interface tasks such as checklists and ATC communications.

SUMMARY ————————————————————→

Although we are interested in fundamental principles that differentiate effective versus ineffective communications, actual patterns observed in the research have shown a great amount of variation. The short explanation for this is simply that there is a trade-off between standardization and flexibility, and every flightcrew performance needs both (see the chapter by Hackman). Standardization in communicating has obvious benefits—less ambiguity, more efficiency, greater case in teaching and evaluating. And there are many specific communication tasks that cannot tolerate deviation from SOPs. However, flexibility is needed so that crewmembers can maximize their resources in a variety of situations and solve problems creatively in novel conditions.

A longer explanation for why standard communications alone will not ensure flight safety includes some of the following reasons.

1. *Communication is an interactive process.* Therefore, variations are generated because each interactant has a different personal style, different role, and different tasks and goals. As interactants become more familiar with each other's communication style, roles, and tasks, the predictive strength of their mutual understanding increases.

2. *Communication processes vary within and between teams.* Some communication links involve participants within a team or subteam, while other links involve participants from other interfacing teams in the system.

3. *Communications serve many functions simultaneously.* Variations exist because communication not only conveys particular pieces of flight information but is an instrument for accomplishing many other tasks (both interpersonal and technical) at the same time. One speech act can serve many functions.

4. *Communications vary because situations change dynamically over time.* Over the course of a flight, task conditions change and different phases are marked by different goals (e.g., the communication context is different for pilots at cruise under normal conditions in contrast to pilots on short final under difficult weather conditions and a mechanical malfunction).

5. *Communications adapt themselves to task differences imposed by cockpit design,* equipment, levels of automation, and other significant hardware and software differences. As crewmembers adapt their behaviors to take advantage of (or compensate for) changes in the equipment, communication patterns may also require adjustments.

The above assertions do not imply that there are no general communication principles to be found. Rather, they point out that in addition to such principles, actual patterns may take many forms. Because some variations are simply stylistic and others are critical performance indicators, we need to disentangle the significance of these variations in order to understand and teach specific skills.

"Communication" as a topic is one of such depth and breadth that we will never run out of research opportunities or lessons to learn. In operations of great complexity, high risk, and changeable conditions, a fuller understanding of how enhanced communication skills can be trained and extended to more of the aviation system is needed. We cannot assume that one or two findings will apply across all tasks and conditions, or that we have identified the full range of communications problems. Our knowledge of communication processes beyond the cockpit is relatively undeveloped in spite of the evidence from accidents and incidents that there are critical links in the system that need to be understood. In short, we need to expand our horizons with respect to identifying communication links among teams and disentangling both the functions and variations associated with speech act patterns. We need more expertise in interpreting what is revealed in accident and incident reports and continued research into these issues. Finally, we need to transform what we have learned into tangible training products for the classroom, the simulator, and the line.

Acknowledgments

We thank NASA–Ames Research Center, Northwestern University, and the National Research Council for their support in the belief that communication research is necessary and valuable. Our work has been jointly funded by NASA (the Office of Space Science and Applications) and the Federal Aviation Administration. Special thanks also go to all the research assistants who have spent countless hours listening to, transcribing, and coding videotapes, as well as to our colleagues whose own work has sparked our ideas and enthusiasm. In particular, we owe a debt to Clay Foushee, who established the Crew Factors program of CRM research at Ames. Finally, we acknowledge the generous participation and advice from the airline industry, without which our work might have strayed from critical, real-life issues.

References

Austin, J. L. (1962). *How to do things with words.* London: Oxford University Press.

Billings, C. E., & Cheaney, E. S. (1981). *Information transfer problems in the aviation system.* (NASA Technical Paper 1875). Moffett Field, CA: NASA–Ames Research Center.

Billings, C. E., & Reynard, W. D. (1981). Dimensions of the information transfer problem. In Billings, C. E. & Cheaney, E. S. (Eds.), *Information transfer problems in the aviation system* (NASA Technical Paper 1875). Moffett Field, CA: NASA–Ames Research Center.

Chidester, T. R. (1990). Trends and individual differences in response to short-haul flight operations. *Aviation, Space, and Environmental Medicine, 61,* 132–138.

Chidester, T. R., & Foushee H. C. (1988). Leader personality and crew effectiveness: Factors influencing performance in full-mission air transport simulation. *Proceedings of the 66th Meeting of the Aerospace Medical Panel on Human Behavior in High Stress Situations in Aerospace Operations.* The Hague, Netherlands: Advisory Group for Aerospace Research and Development.

Chidester, T. R., Kanki, B. G., Foushee, H. C., Dickinson, C. L., & Bowles, S. V. (1990). *Personality factors in flight operations I: Leader characteristics and crew performance in full-mission air transport simulation* (NASA Technical Memorandum 102259). Moffett Field, CA: NASA–Ames Research Center.

Conley, S., Cano, Y. & Bryant, D. (1991). Coordination strategies of crew management. *Proceedings of the Sixth International Symposium on Aviation Psychology* (pp. 260–265). Columbus: Ohio State University.

Conley, S., Cano, Y., Bryant, D., Kanki, B., & Chidester, T. (1990). *Beyond standard operating procedures: Crew dynamics in the B-727.* Unpublished technical report. Moffett Field, CA: NASA–Ames Research Center.

Costley, J., Johnson, D., & Lawson, D., (1989). A comparison of cockpit communication B737–B757. *Proceedings of the Fifth International Symposium on Aviation Psychology* (pp. 413–418). Columbus: Ohio State University.

Degani, A. S., & Wiener, E. L. (1990). *Human factors of flight-deck checklist: The normal checklist* (NASA CR 177549). Moffett Field, CA: NASA Ames Research Center.

Federal Aviation Administration. (1990). *Line operational simulations,* (Advisory Circular 120-35B). Washington, DC: Author.

Federal Aviation Administration. (in preparation). *Crew resource management training.* (Advisory Circular 120-51A). Washington, DC: Author.

Foushee, H. C., Lauber, J. K., Baetge, M. M., & Acomb, D. B. (1986). *Crew factors in flight operations III: The operational significance of exposure to short-haul air transport operations.* (NASA Technical Memorandum 88322). Moffett Field, CA: NASA–Ames Research Center.

Foushee, H. C., & Manos, K. (1981). Information transfer within the cockpit: Problems in intra-cockpit communications. In C. E. Billings & E. S. Cheaney (Eds.), *Information transfer problems in the aviation system.* (NASA Technical Paper 1875). Moffett Field, CA: NASA–Ames Research Center.

Ginnett, R. G. (1987). The formation of airline flight crews. *Proceedings of the Fourth International Symposium on Aviation Psychology* (pp. 399–405). Columbus: Ohio State University.

Goguen, J., Linde, C., & Murphy, M. (1986). *Crew communication as a factor in aviation accidents.* (NASA Technical Report 88254). Moffett Field, CA: NASA–Ames Research Center.

Gregorich, S. E., Helmreich, R. L., Wilhelm, J. A. & Chidester, T. R. (1989). Personality based clusters as predictors of aviator attitudes and performance. In *Proceedings of the Fifth International Symposium on Aviation Psychology* (pp. 686–691). Columbus: Ohio State University.

Hackman, J. R. (1987). Group level issues in the design and training of cockpit crews. In H. W. Orlady & H. C. Foushee (Eds.), *Proceedings of the NASA/MAC workshop on cockpit resource management.* (NASA Conference Publication 2455). Moffett Field, CA: NASA–Ames Research Center.

Helmreich, R. L., Foushee, H. C., Benson, R., & Russini, R. (1986). Cockpit management attitudes: Exploring the attitude–performance linkage. *Aviation, Space and Environmental Medicine, 57,* 1198–2000.

Helmreich, R. L., & Wilhelm, J. (1989). *Validating personality constructs for flightcrew selection: Status report on the NASA/UT Project.* NASA/UT Technical Memorandum, 89–3, Austin: University of Texas.

Helmreich, R. L., Wilhelm, J. A., Kello, J. E., Taggart, W. R., & Butler, R. E. (1991). *Reinforcing and evaluating crew resource management: Evaluator/LOS instructor reference manual.* NASA/UT Technical Manual 90–2. Austin: University of Texas.

Kanki, B. G., & Foushee, H. C. (1989). Communication as group process mediator of aircrew performance. *Aviation, Space and Environmental Medicine, 60,* 5, 402–410.

Kanki, B. G., Greaud, V. A., & Irwin, C. M. (1991). Communication variations and aircrew performance. *International Journal of Aviation Psychology, 1*(2), 149–162.

Kanki, B. G., Lozito, S. C., & Foushee, H. C. (1989). Communication indices of crew coordination. *Aviation, Space and Environmental Medicine, 60*(1), 56–60.

Kanki, B. G., Palmer, M. T., & Veinott, E. (1991). Communication variations related to leader personality. In *Proceedings of the Sixth International Symposium on Aviation Psychology* (pp. 253–259). Columbus: Ohio State University.

McGrath, J. E. (1984). *Groups: Interaction and performance.* Englewood Cliffs, N.J.: Prentice-Hall.

Morrow, D. G., Lee, A. T., & Rodvold, M. (1991). Collaboration in pilot–controller communication. *Proceedings of the Sixth International Symposium on Aviation Psychology* (pp. 278–283). Columbus: Ohio State University.

Mosier, K. (1991). Expert decision making strategies. *Proceedings of the Sixth International Symposium on Aviation Psychology* (pp. 266–271). Columbus: Ohio State University.

National Transportation Safety Board. (1979). *Aircraft Accident Report: United Airlines, Inc., McDonnell-Douglas DC-8-61, N8082U, Portland, Oregon, December 28, 1978.* (NTSB-AAR-79-7). Washington DC: Author.

National Transportation Safety Board. (1990a). *Aircraft Accident Report: United Airlines Flight 811, Boeing 747-122, N4713U, Honolulu, Hawaii, February 24, 1989.* (NTSB/AAR/90/01). Washington DC: Author.

National Transportation Safety Board. (1990b). *Aircraft Accident Report: United Airlines Flight 232, McDonnell Douglas DC-10-10, Sioux Gateway Airport, Sioux City, Iowa, July 19, 1989.* (NTSB/AAR/90/06). Washington DC: Author.

National Transportation Safety Board. (1991). *Aircraft Accident Report: Avianca, The Airline of Columbia, Boeing 707-321B, HK2016, Fuel exhaustion, Cove Neck, New York, January 25, 1990.* (NTSB/AAR/91/04). Washington DC: Author.

Orasanu, J. M. (1990). *Shared mental models and crew decision making* (Cognitive Science Laboratory Report #46). Princeton, NJ: Princeton University.

Orlady, H. W., & Foushee, H. C. (Eds.) (1987). *Proceedings of the NASA/MAC workshop on cockpit resource management* (NASA Conference Publication 2455). Moffett Field, CA: NASA–Ames Research Center.

Predmore, S. C. (1991). Microcoding of communications in accident investigation: Crew coordination in United 811 and United 232. *Proceedings of the Sixth International Symposium on Aviation Psychology* (pp. 350–355). Columbus: Ohio State University.

Ruffell Smith, H. P. (1979). *A simulator study of the interaction of pilot workload with errors, vigilance, and decisions* (NASA Technical Memorandum 78482). Moffett Field, CA: NASA–Ames Research Center.

Schwartz, D., (1987). CRM training for Parts 91 and 135 operations. In H. W. Orlady & H. C. Foushee (Eds.). *Proceedings of the NASA/MAC workshop on cockpit resource management* (pp. 170–177) (NASA Conference Publication 2455). Moffett Field, CA: NASA–Ames Research Center.

Spence, J. T., & Helmreich, R. L. (1978). *Masculinity and femininity: Their psychological dimensions, correlates, and antecedents.* Austin: University of Texas Press.

Spence, J. T., Helmreich, R. L., & Holahan, C. K. (1979). Negative and positive components of psychological masculinity and femininity and their relationships to self-reports of neurotic and acting out behaviors. *Journal of Personality and Social Psychology, 37,* 1673–1682.

Tuckman, B. W. (1965). Developmental sequence in small groups. *Psychological Bulletin, 63,* 384–399.

Wiener, E. L. (1989). *Human factors of advanced technological ("glass cockpit") transport aircraft* (NASA Contractor Report No. 177528). Moffett Field, CA: NASA–Ames Research Center.

Wiener, E. L., Chidester, T. R., Kanki, B. G., Palmer, E. A., Curry, R. E., & Gregorich, S. E. (1991). *The impact of cockpit automation on crew coordination and communication: I. Overview, LOFT evaluations, error severity, and questionnaire data* (NASA Contractor Report No. 177587). Moffett Field, CA: NASA–Ames Research Center.

5

Decision-making in the Cockpit

Judith M. Orasanu
Aerospace Human Factors Research Division
NASA–Ames Research Center
Moffett Field, California 94035

INTRODUCTION ✈

Cockpit crews make decisions all the time, from the captain's acceptance of the aircraft and flight plan prior to departure to docking at the gate after landing. Unfortunately, the ones that get the most attention are those that result in disasters—for example, the decision to take off with snow and ice on the plane and engine power lower than needed for takeoff at Washington National Airport (NTSB, 1982), or the decision to take off without being sure the runway was clear of traffic in heavy fog at Tenerife, Canary Islands (Dutch Aircraft Accident Inquiry Board, 1979).

While an industry-wide analysis has shown that over 70% of aviation accidents result from crew coordination or communication problems (as opposed to lack of individual technical skills, Lautman & Gallimore, 1987), Diehl has found that over 50% of accident-related human errors in the military and civil aviation industry from 1987 to 1989 were decisional errors (Diehl, 1991). The aviation industry and the U.S. Federal Aviation Administration (FAA) are both concerned with improving the quality of decisions made in the cockpit. The importance accorded cockpit decision-making is reflected in its inclusion as a recommended topic in the revision of the FAA Advisory Circular on crew resource management (CRM) (FAA, in preparation). Decision-making modules are already included in the CRM courses run by most of the major air transport carriers. Another FAA Advisory Circular deals specifically with Aeronautical Decision Making (FAA, 1991). This circular is aimed mainly at general aviation, corporate, and commuter flying, but its concerns about hazardous attitudes apply to all pilots.

Because decision-making takes mental energy and because a large body of research suggests that people do not always make optimal decisions, aircraft builders and flying organizations try to reduce crew decision-making as much as

possible. This is done by automating systems and by establishing standard procedures and checklists to cover anticipated failures or emergencies (Billings, 1991;
Wiener, 1988). However, poor decisions may occur even when situations are
fairly straightforward because of the presence of conditions that increase risk,
often weather and/or heavy air traffic. In other cases, simple problems cascade or
interact, precluding "by-the-book" solutions. In still rarer cases, completely un-
foreseen catastrophic problems arise, like the loss of all hydraulic systems due to
an engine explosion (NTSB, 1990; see the chapter by Kayten). Given the impossibility of designing error-proof or fully automated systems that can cope with any
emergency, the only way to maintain or increase safety is to train crews to make
the best decisions possible under difficult circumstances. The question is how to do
that. What skills should be trained and how should they be trained?

The short answer to these questions is the following: crew decision-making
is not one thing. Crews make many different kinds of decisions, but all involve
situation assessment, choice among alternatives, and assessment of risk. However,
the decisions differ in the degree to which they call on different types of cognitive
processes. A decision to abort a take-off requires different decision processes from
choosing an alternate airport for landing with a system failure or determining the
cause of a master caution warning light. The nature of the processes involved in a
decision depends on the structure of the decision task and the conditions surrounding it. How familiar is the problem? Is a response prescribed or must it be
generated? How many options are readily available? How clear is the nature of
the problem? Is time limited? Given the variety of decisions that are made
routinely in the cockpit, no single approach can be prescribed for training crews in
decision-making skills. No silver bullet exists to make crews better decision-
makers.

The long answer to the above questions is addressed in the five issues that
follow. Brief sketches of the topics to be discussed under each are provided below
and elaborated in the remainder of this chapter.

➤ *What is cockpit decision-making?* Six different types of decisions are made by
crews in the cockpit (Cf. Rasmussen, 1983).
   1. Rule-based decisions (condition-action rules): (a) go—no go decisions and
      (b) recognition-primed decisions
   2. Knowledge-based decisions (well-defined problems): (a) option selection
      decisions and (b) scheduling decisions
   3. Knowledge-based decisions (ill-defined problems): (a) procedural man-
      agement and (b) creative problem-solving

These six types of decisions impose different processing demands on the decision-
maker and imply different types of training.

➤ *How can we recognize good decisions in the cockpit?*
   1. Good cockpit decisions support effective task performance (judged by safe-

ty, efficiency, and effectiveness). Consequently, cockpit criteria are not the same as laboratory criteria, where logical consistency and optimality prevail.

2. Cockpit decision criteria include cognitive economy (least mental effort), working within time limits, and constraint satisfaction.
3. Formal normative decision models do not fit conditions in the cockpit, which are dynamic, reactive, action-oriented, and time-pressured.
4. Cockpit decisions are heuristic. Grounded in expert knowledge and experience, heuristics work most of the time. They are shortcuts that reduce the mental work involved in making decisions and yield decisions that are good enough rather than optimal. Expertise contributes to rapid situation assessment, retrieval of candidate solutions, and guidance based on past experience. Expertise does not, however, insulate crews from bad decisions. It may lead to rigid expectations, biases, overconfidence, and greater risk-taking.

✈ *How does crew decision-making differ from individual decision-making?*

1. Crew decision-making is managed decision-making. The captain has responsibility for making the decisions but is supported by input from the crew, both in the cockpit and on the ground (air traffic control, dispatch, maintenance).
2. Crews may do *better* than individuals: (a) Multiple eyes, ears, hands, and minds increase available cognitive capacity, increasing the potential for better decisions. (b) Crews can consider a larger picture, contribute more viewpoints, offer multiple options, use more information, share workload, critique proposals, and avoid traps.
3. Crew may do *worse* than individuals: (a) Through poor communication, crews may not share an understanding of the problem or how to go about solving it; they may not understand the captain's intentions. (b) Errors can propagate through the crew, while increasing their collective confidence in their correctness. (c) Crewmembers may abdicate responsibility, leaving work to others, or can perform poorly due to interpersonal conflicts.

✈ *What ingredients contribute to effective crew decision-making?*

1. Situation awareness: Crews are alert to developing situations, sensitive to cues, and aware of their implications.
2. Planfulness: Crews work out plans and strategies for reaching their goals, prepare for contingencies, figure out what information they need, and evaluate their progress.
3. Shared mental models: Crews communicate efficiently to create a shared big picture: What's the problem? What are we going to do about it? Who does what? Through shared models crews utilize all available resources,

make sure that they're all solving the same problem, and assure coordination.

4. Resource management: Resources are used efficiently and explicitly. Crews set priorities, schedule tasks, allocate responsibilities, and build in thinking time, especially for the captain.

The above four ingredients do not in themselves constitute decision-making, but create a context within which effective decisions can be made.

➔ *Implications for training: What skills should be trained and how?*
  1. What to train? (a) Situation assessment: based on considerable pattern recognition practice and development of models of the systems and tasks in the cockpit. (b) Risk assessment: recognizing risk factors associated with various malfunctions and situations. (c) Planning: strategizing, anticipating future events and outcomes of actions, critiquing plans. (d) Resource management: prioritizing tasks, estimating time requirements, scheduling, allocating responsibilities. (e) Communicating: Building shared models for the problems through explicit communication about goals, plans, strategies, expectations, and reasons. (f) Specialized skills should be trained to meet the specific demands of each of the six decision types.
  2. How to train? Train crews under time-pressured high workload conditions representative of those under which they will be expected to make difficult decisions.

WHAT IS COCKPIT DECISION-MAKING? ─────── ➔

Cockpit decision-making is many things, but all types of decisions have at least three elements in common: choice among options, situation assessment, and risk assessment. First, by definition, all decisions involve choice among alternatives. However, the nature of the choice depends on task conditions. Some decisions do not appear to be choices because only one option is considered (e.g., deciding to descend to a lower altitude following loss of cabin pressure). Sometimes the choice is to stop doing something already in progress (e.g., aborting a take-off or landing). In still other cases, the manner in which an action is performed must be determined (e.g., deciding on a cruise speed when the landing gear will not retract). And finally, the choice may be about the sequence and timing of a set of actions, all of which must be accomplished in a limited time period (e.g., manually lowering landing gear and extending flaps following a hydraulic failure). These various types of choices are considered in this chapter. No one type is more important than any other. However, very different kinds of cognitive work must be done for each of them, as is described shortly. Furthermore, differences in requisite cognitive processes mean that each will be vulnerable to disruption or increases in difficulty from different sources. Likewise, each requires a specific focus in training.

Prior to making a choice among options, however, the nature of the problem must be accurately assessed. Whereas the choice aspect of decision-making has been the focus of most laboratory research, decision-making in naturalistic situations requires people first to recognize that a problem exists that may require a decision, and then to define the nature of the problem. Based on his observations of decision-making by fire fighters and tank commanders, Klein and his colleagues (Brezovic, Klein, & Thordsen, 1987; Calderwood, Crandall, & Klein, 1987) have concluded that the biggest difference between experts and novices was in their ability to evaluate the situation rather than in their ability to choose among options.

Third, all cockpit decisions involve risk assessment, whether it is explicit or not. Safety is the overriding concern behind every decision, but other values on occasion are pitted against safety considerations. These frequently are subtle pressures resulting from organizational policies and goals. For example, according to a NASA Aviation Safety Reporting System report (ASRS, 1991), one pilot described pressure from the company ground agent after an hour's delay at the gate to depart with an incompletely locked forward cargo door. The agent justified it by saying, "We release planes like this all the time." Certain decisions are programmed as responses to specific conditions to eliminate the need for the crew to assess risk and make a decision, especially in time-critical situations. Some of these are triggers to abort take-offs or landings. But in many cases, borders blur and gray areas emerge in which the captain's assessment of the conditions— visibility, runway conditions, the aircraft, and his own skill—determines the choice of action. Judging by confidential reports to ASRS, pilots are often quite conscious of the trade-offs involved in their decisions. For example, one pilot reported that, following a loss of cabin pressure, he descended to a lower altitude and continued to the original destination. He noted that this decision was not as conservative as landing immediately, but since no passenger injuries were evident, he felt the passengers' convenience would be served better by continuing to the destination than by diverting.

Beyond these three common elements of situation assessment, choice, and risk assessment, the types of decision problems in the cockpit differ in their underlying structure, time parameters, and information characteristics. They require different kinds of mental work and consequently are susceptible to different types of failures. Six different types of decisions have been identified. These are illustrated in the double boxes in Figure 5.1. This figure shows the relationships among the different types of decisions, based on problem definition, information, and option availability. It is not a flowchart of human information processing, but a depiction of decision categories. These six categories differ in the degree to which they call on cognitive components, such as cue or situation interpretation, problem

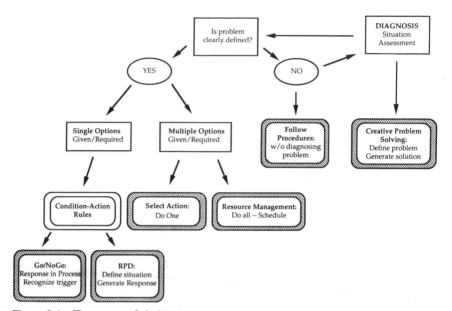

Figure 5.1   Taxonomy of decision types.

structuring, option generation, option assessment, probability estimation, constraint satisfaction, priority setting, time estimation, causal reasoning (diagnosis), risk assessment, planning, forward reasoning, and information integration. This figure will be discussed from top to bottom, left to right.

While various types of decisions can be distinguished for analytical purposes, in practice any given flight situation may require use of several different decision strategies. Making one decision or taking the prescribed action may present a new set of conditions requiring a different type of decision. To an observer, these may appear as a smooth flow of action, although decisions are hidden behind the actions.

Well-defined versus Ill-defined Problems

Most cockpit decisions are triggered by conditions falling outside normal ranges. A light flashes, an indicator drops to the yellow or red range, a strange vibration is felt. Some of these cues are unambiguous in the context and in the phase of flight in which they occur. Any pilot experienced in flying that plane would interpret certain cues to mean the same thing. Many instrument readings fall into this category. The displays of newer planes ("glass cockpits") are even more explicit in telling the crew what they mean. When the problem is clear from the display or cue configuration, the crew does not need to expend energy trying to discern what it is. We refer to these as well-defined problems. But sometimes displays do not unambiguously indicate the nature of the problem. Then the crew must engage in diagnostic efforts to figure out what triggered the signal or cue. How they do this depends on the nature of the specific signal—whether a check-list exists for addressing that particular problem or whether the crew literally has to fly by the seat of its pants to determine the underlying cause of the signal. This second category is what we mean by ill-defined problems. The highest branch of the taxonomy in Figure 5.1 distinguishes between well-defined and ill-defined problems. Well-defined problems will be described first.

Single versus Multiple Response Options

Given that the nature of the problem is clear, decision tasks differ in the information available about response options. Certain cue sets offer or require just a single response, while in other cases, multiple response options are immediately available or required. Single-response situations in the cockpit appear to fit what Rasmussen (1983, 1993) has called rule-based decisions, while multiple-response problems invoke knowledge-based reasoning. Single-option cases can be defined as condition–action pairs and are perhaps the simplest decisions because they require the least cognitive work. When multiple options are immediately available, as when choosing an alternate airport, choice is involved and additional cognitive work is usually required to select one option from among the set.

Rule-based Decisions

In rule-based decisions, the primary decision is whether circumstances meet the conditions for a pre-set response. Condition-action rules specify that a particular action should be taken when a certain stimulus condition exists. Little reasoning or deciding about the nature of the response is required. Most effort focuses on whether circumstances fit a specified pattern. Two different types of rule-based decisions can be distinguished. In the first case the response is antici-pated or already in process and a stimulus condition arises that triggers a decision to terminate that response. These tend to be decisions to reject take-offs or to go around on an approach. This type of decision is called a *go/no-go* decision. In the second type of rule-based decision, the appropriate response must be generated by the decision-maker. It is not already in process but must be generated, evaluated and implemented. These decisions are referred to as *recognition-primed* decisions (Klein, 1989, 1993).

1. *Go/no-go decisions.* In go/no-go decisions, an action is in progress, a pattern is recognized that signals danger, and the response is pre-set: stop the action. The cognitive work that must be done is essentially perceptual and in-

terpretive. The crew must recognize a stimulus configuration as a signal to initiate the designated "Stop" response. No choice of response type is required. However, the stimulus conditions that elicit this response may actually be quite diverse. For example, ASRS reports of rejected take-offs include as triggers explosive engine failures, cargo door lights, runway traffic, compressor stalls, and overheat lights (also see Chamberlin, 1991). Likewise, missed approaches, which consist of a decision to terminate a descent to landing, were most often triggered by inability to see the runway at decision height but were also triggered by traffic (air or ground), autopilot disengagement, and unstable approaches (e.g., off glide slope). Decisions of this type involve risk assessment, particularly when ground speed or altitude are near a decision threshold. Certain conditions, like a wet runway or system malfunctions resulting in poor braking, will complicate the decision and may shift it across the threshold. Decisions in this category are in general the most time-critical because of the severe consequences of mistakes. As a result, this is the type of decision that is most proceduralized. Companies want their crews to act quickly and think as little as necessary in these conditions. However, given the need to assess the risks and interpret conditions that may be changing rapidly, this type of response must clearly be defined as a decision.

   2. *Recognition-primed decisions.* The second category of rule-based decisions is what Klein (1989, 1993) has called recognition-primed decisions (RPDs). Like go/no-go decisions, these also involve condition–action pairings. The crew first interprets the cue configuration as a particular type and then generates an appropriate response. The response is not ongoing, as it is in the go/no-go case. According to Klein's research, once the situation has been properly assessed, responses are retrieved on the basis of their past success. In airline cockpits, however, these responses are often prescribed as standard procedures. For example, following loss of cabin pressure, the response is to descend to a lower altitude. Or when the terminal collision avoidance system (TCAS) indicates traffic, the crew attempts to locate the traffic visually, using their TCAS screen as an aid. These two cases require rapid responses. Not all responses in this category are as time-sensitive, but many are. For example, in the case of a fuel leak, the crew must calculate the fuel remaining, the rate of loss, and how long they can continue flying; identify the closest appropriate airport; and perhaps declare an emergency. These tasks must be handled expeditiously, but not in the same time frame as collision avoidance.

   The cognitive work that must be done in recognition-primed decisions includes situation recognition, response generation, and response evaluation. Response evaluation involves simulating the consequences of taking the candidate action and determining whether the response will satisfy the crew's goals. If so, the action is accepted. If not, another option is generated and evaluated, or the situation definition is reassessed. Risk assessment is involved in the response evaluation.

Multiple-Option Decisions

The next major category of decisions includes those that are made when the situation is clearly defined and multiple response options are available or required. In one case multiple options are present and the pilot must choose one (*option selection* decisions). In the other case multiple options are present and all must be accomplished within a limited time frame (*resource management* decisions). The first type are true choices and map most closely onto our everyday notion of decision-making. The second type are usually scheduling decisions and involve resource allocation and management. Both are cases of knowledge-based reasoning (Rasmussen, 1983).

1. *Option selection decisions.* On occasion the crew must select one option from among a set of alternatives, meeting certain constraints active in the situation. Cockpit selection decisions often involve selection of an alternate landing site. The conditions demanding such a decision may be bad weather at the original destination or an in-flight problem that requires a diversion. Alternates are prescribed in the flight plan if weather conditions are bad or deteriorating at the original destination and may be needed in the case of a missed approach. For discussion purposes, I deal here with weather-induced diversions. The choice decision process is triggered when the pilot first decides that the original destination may not be suitable for landing (a no-go decision). The decision to abort the landing should generate the alternate, a recognition-primed decision. Consequences of going to the alternate are considered, and if no reason is found to reject it, that option will be accepted and the decision is done.

However, if situational factors prevent a clean decision, conditions such as bad weather at the alternate or an aircraft system malfunction that creates special requirements, such as a long, dry runway, emergency or medical equipment, Category II instrument landing systems, and so on, then the choice process is opened up. Malfunctions during flight also may require a search for an appropriate airport. The first step in the choice process is to generate a set of options that meet a minimum criterion, such as finding airports within fuel range. Usually weather conditions are considered next. Then the options are evaluated in terms of specific requirements, such as runway length, approach path, equipment available, familiarity to the crew, or maintenance capability. The actual strategies used by crews to select an alternate vary, but observations to date (Klein, 1993; Orasanu, 1990) suggest that they do not correspond to a full analytical procedure, such as a multi-attribute utility analysis (Edwards & Newman, 1982). A full analysis would involve evaluation of *each* option in terms of every variable relevant to the decision (e.g., weather, fuel consumption, runway length, airport facilities), and a mathematical formula would be used to combine all the information to yield the optimal choice. In fact, crews appear to make decisions in the most economical way, taking shortcuts in this process. They work toward a suitable decision in the shortest time, investing the least possible cognitive work. Options are often eliminated on the basis of one feature, such as weather, and are out of the running thereafter, unless no suitable alternate can be found and the process must be reopened. This pruning may leave only one acceptable option, which is chosen. (This is essentially an elimination by aspects strategy, Tversky, 1972.) However, if a few candidates are available, usually only two or three, one is chosen to match the constraints of the circumstances and the crew's preferences. Usually the most safety-critical constraint prevails; however, organizational policy also plays an important role here. The crew may try to choose an alternate that has a company maintenance facility or where replacement planes will be available for passengers to continue their flight. For example, in an ASRS report, a crew reported losing a tire during take off. Subsequently, the captain lost his heading information display and the first officer lost his attitude indicator. These problems were rectified after level-off and the crew decided to head for a company mainte-nance facility. However, as they climbed to flight level (FL) 180, cabin pressure went out of control, and they ultimately decided to return to their departure airport.

Decision difficulties arise when goals conflict or when no good choice is available. For example, the assigned or most desirable alternate might be satisfac-tory when the plane takes off, but the weather may deteriorate rapidly and may be below minimums by the time the flight arrives. The second-choice alternate may have clear weather, but it may be more distant, straining fuel resources. All options are evaluated in terms of their level of risk, but sometimes no low-risk option is available. Then risk must be played off against what will be gained in each case, factoring in the crew's level of confidence that they can follow through with the choice. In these cases, "what if?" reasoning may be needed. The crew needs to think about what might happen down the line. They are in a dynamic state: Their equipment may be changing over time (e.g., a fuel leak or a conse-quent system problem may develop with some probability), the weather is chang-ing over time, and their location is changing over time.

Unfortunately, the scientific literature is quite barren with respect to guid-ance about how to make decisions under such circumstances. Obviously, many factors need to be taken into consideration, and the crew need to use all the knowledge and experience they possess collectively. Certain rules of thumb have been shown to be effective in time-pressured complex decision situations. These strategies may include elimination by aspects (described above, Tversky, 1972) or satisficing (Simon, 1955). Satisficing means stopping the search for an option as soon as the first acceptable option is found (rather than thoroughly evaluating all options to choose the best). Doing a full analysis of all options in a complex situation takes considerable time, which often is not available during flight.

2. *Resource management.* The second type of decision involving multiple options is the scheduling or resource management problem. These are situations in

which several time-consuming tasks must be performed during a limited time frame. Tasks may include diagnosis of a system malfunction using checklists, radio communication with dispatch or ground controllers to evaluate alternates, and manual efforts, such as lowering gear or flaps. A decision has already been made that each of these individual tasks must be done. The issue is how to coordinate them, that is, how to accomplish them all so that their products are available when they are needed.

The cognitive work that must be done for this type of decision includes establishing priorities among the various tasks, assessing available resources, both equipment and human (in the cockpit and on the ground), estimating the amount of time available and the amount that will be consumed performing the various tasks, and developing a plan that integrates goals with resources, taking into account relevant constraints. This type of activity is considered decision-making because choices are made about what to do, who will do what tasks, and when they will be done. More properly, it should be called a complex of decisions that constitute a plan. Others call this a scheduling task (Moray, Dessouky, Kijowski, & Adapathya, 1991).

Perhaps most critical to this type of decision is priority setting. Certain actions must be accomplished within the time frame, such as extending the landing gear. Other tasks may be less critical. Diagnosing a problem may be desirable for safety reasons, but fixing the problem during flight may not be possible, so this task may be given lower priority. Plans need to be flexible. Certain actions may uncover other difficulties that require attention or may take longer than expected. Or air traffic delays may disturb the plan. Plan execution must be monitored for progress and revised as necessary to meet changing conditions. If it looks like everything will not be done in time (e.g., prior to landing), the captain may need to request vectors that will give him more time to complete tasks that must be done, or less critical tasks may be eliminated altogether.

Ill-defined Problems

The other two types of decisions hardly look like decisions at all. They consist of ill-defined problems that may or may not be clarified in the process of dealing with them. Ill-defined problems are ones resulting from ambiguous cues that make it impossible (initially) to say what the problem is that needs fixing. No match can be made to the condition side of a condition–action rule to trigger a response. Two strategies may be used to cope with this type of situation: manage the situation as though it is an emergency without clearly defining the problem, or diagnose and define the problem, and then work out a solution. The second type is more complex because no prescribed procedures exist for solving the problem. In addition, because of the ambiguity of the conditions, no single correct or best solution exists.

1. *Procedural management.* Certain cues leave the crew without a clear idea of the nature of the underlying problem. Various noises, thumps, vibrations, rumblings, pressure changes in ears, or control problems indicate that something has happened, but not necessarily what. Certain cues signal potentially dangerous conditions that trigger emergency responses, regardless of the source of the problem. Smoke, loss of pressure, an acrid smell, an explosion, or loss of control all signal "Land now." Little time is devoted to determining the source of the cues. All energies are devoted to finding an appropriate airport, running necessary checklists, getting landing clearance, declaring an emergency, dumping fuel, and landing. In a sense, these problems are treated as RPD situations, with the condition broadly labeled as "emergency landing" conditions.

The cognitive work done for this class of decision is primarily situation and risk assessment. Responses are clearly prescribed and highly procedural—once the situation is defined as an emergency. If the risk is judged to be high, then emergency procedures are undertaken. If the risk is not immediately defined as an emergency, then additional energy may be devoted to situation assessment.

Diagnosis of the cause underlying ambiguous cues can serve two purposes. It can clarify exactly what the problem is so that an appropriate specific action can be taken, and it can provide information that may be useful for fixing the problem. Particularly while in cruise, when workload is relatively low, the crew may devote time to diagnosing and fixing the problem. Risk assessment determines whether or not such efforts will be attempted, as diagnosis takes time and crew resources. But even if diagnosis does not lead to fixing the malfunction, it can turn the problem into one with a well-defined response (essentially a recognition-primed decision). Defining the problem clearly may lead to a more specific response than simply treating it as an emergency. For example, one crew reported to ASRS a high-frequency flutter through the airframe. A company mechanic on board visually inspected the craft and noticed that the right outboard aileron balance tab was loose. The crew consulted with flight control and company maintenance who recommended that they reduce their speed. When they did, the problem disappeared, and they were able to continue their flight without further difficulties. Had they not diagnosed the problem, they would probably have made an emergency landing, with its attendant cost and inconvenience for passengers.

Diagnosis does not always succeed (even with the help of ground maintenance), and the crew may have few choices other than to proceed to their destination without fixing the problem, or to make an emergency landing. For example, one crew reported that they had an anti-ice problem compounded by a pressurization problem. Cues were ambiguous as to the source of the problems. They divided the workload to try to figure out what was wrong, and when they couldn't diagnose the situation, they made an emergency descent. Another crew reported an unfamiliar rumbling and pressure in their ears that signaled a high rate of climb. Efforts at diagnosis were unsuccessful, so they too decided to land.

Subsequent maintenance discovered that the Electrical and Electronics compartment was not secured and the switch that should have signaled this problem was not working.

2. *Creative problem-solving.* Perhaps the most difficult types of decisions are embedded in complex situations that require creative problem-solving. Problem-solving means that in addition to defining the nature of the situation, response options must be generated that will lead to the goal. In other words, procedures do not exist to meet the needs of the situation. These cases tend to be extremely low frequency events; no one imagined such situations would arise, so no procedures were designed to cope with them. Perhaps the most extreme and celebrated case of a non-routine emergency was United Airlines flight 232 (NTSB, 1990), the DC-10 that lost all hydraulic systems at FL 330. An explosion in the number 2 engine caused debris to cut the hydraulic lines. The crew realized that they had no flight controls except engine power and then had to experiment to find any manner of controlling the plane in order to land it. Both situation assessment and response generation are required in such cases.

The cognitive work required by ill-defined problems is most varied of all the decision types. Diagnosis is critical. Often the problems that fall into this category are low-frequency events, which may mean that they are more difficult to diagnose. Diagnosis typically involves causal reasoning, which is reasoning backward from effects to cause. Hypothesis generation and testing are often involved. Depending on the nature of the problem, the range of tests that can be performed will vary. For example, in response to a power loss indication for one engine, the crew can manipulate the throttle to see its effect. If they find no effect, they may shut down the engine since it is not working. They may check to see if fuel is flowing to the engine. Tests are often embedded in checklists.

Even after the nature of the problem has been determined, no ready solutions are prescribed. In the case of UAL 232, the captain spent considerable energy on situation assessment, determining what capability he had left after the hydraulic failure (Predmore, 1991). The two outboard engines were still running, but no flight controls were operative. His goal was to control the direction and level of flight. Knowing that the only control he had was engine thrust, he and his crew determined that they could use asymmetrical engine thrust to turn the plane. The power level controlled altitude. Continuous monitoring was required to adjust the power to keep the plane from rolling over on its back and to control oscillation.

While the case of UAL 232 is extreme, ASRS reports indicate that crews do, in fact, encounter situations that are not covered by the Federal Aviation Regulations, minimum equipment lists, or checklists. In these cases crews must use their ingenuity, experience, and creativity to deal with the problem. For example, a captain of a large transport on a cross-country flight reported a low level of oxygen in the crew emergency tanks while at FL310. No guidance concerning how to proceed was available in company manuals. The cause of oxygen depletion could not be determined in flight, nor could the problem be fixed. Regulations require emergency oxygen in case of rapid decompression, so the crew came up with a creative solution. They descended to FL250 and borrowed the flight attendants' walk-around oxygen bottles. (Different O_2 requirements are specified for flight attendants above and below FL250.) This solution allowed them to continue to their destination rather than to divert to a base that had O_2 bottles for the cockpit system or to descend to 10,000 feet, eliminating the need for the O_2. The latter option would have meant that the flight would not have had sufficient fuel to reach their destination because of rerouting around bad weather.

This example is interesting because it illustrates consideration of multiple options, creation of a novel solution, sensitivity to constraints, and explicit risk assessment. In creating his solution, the captain was aware that he would not be able to communicate with ATC in an emergency if he was using the walk-around O_2 bottle, as it has no microphone. But he judged the likelihood of a rapid decompression to be sufficiently low that he chose this option. Another constraint was fuel: the captain wanted to conserve fuel because of bad weather at his destination. He was concerned about the possibility of a missed approach or further diversion. An early decision to divert would have been the most conservative decision, but it would not have met the goal of getting the passengers to their destination in a timely manner. This example also indicates that there is no right or wrong solution; there is only a solution that works given the conditions that exist.

This effort at classifying decisions in terms of situational demands is a first step toward understanding what makes certain kinds of decisions difficult and where the weak links are. The six types of decision fall on a continuum ranging from simple to complex, requiring little cognitive work to considerable effort. One reason for laying out these differences is to create an appreciation for the fact that no single unified method for improving decision-making will work. A number of heuristics have some general power, but the specific requirements of each type of decision problem differ considerably. This issue is addressed in the final section on training.

HOW DO WE RECOGNIZE A GOOD DECISION IN THE COCKPIT? ✈

Criteria for judging the quality of decisions in the cockpit are not necessarily the same as those for judging decisions in the laboratory. Decisions in the laboratory are judged on the basis of logical consistency and optimality, two highly valuable criteria. However, reaching an optimal decision is cognitively demanding and time-consuming. It means using all available information, which may exceed the mental capacity of the unaided human decision-maker (Simon, 1955). Decisions in the laboratory can be evaluated against abstract criteria because the problems are solved outside of any meaningful context and nothing hinges on the outcome. The goal of laboratory tasks is to make a decision. However, the goal in the cockpit is to fly the plane safely from point A to point B in accord with regulations and company policy, while satisfying passengers' comfort and convenience needs. Decisions are embedded in and support that primary task.[1] Crews are judged on how well they perform their task, and decisions should be evaluated in terms of their contributions to overall task performance: safety, efficiency, effectiveness. Effectiveness includes satisfying multiple goals such as company policy and customer comfort and convenience; efficiency includes fuel economy and timeliness.

Unfortunately, at present no theory relates decision quality to overall task performance. In principle, we expect that a series of good decisions will lead to a highly successful flight (i.e., safe, effective, efficient). All we know with confidence is that bad decisions contribute to accidents (Diehl, 1991; the Chapter by Kayten). We have no evidence that improving the quality of decisions from "good enough" to optimal would buy more safety, efficiency, or effectiveness.[2] Christensen-Szalanski (1986, 1993) examined the quality of medical decisions and the quality of resulting diagnosis and treatment and found only a loose relationship. Because diagnoses and treatments are categorical, slight improvements in the quality of a decision had little effect on outcomes. The only case in which decision improvements affected performance was when they pushed a decision over a threshold that distinguished treatment A from treatment B.

Clearly, we want crews to make the best decisions they possibly can make, but they must operate with the resources available to them—specifically, time, mental capacity, and information. Performing a full analysis to evaluate all options (e.g., using a multi-attribute utility analysis, Edwards & Newman, 1982) costs a lot in time and mental resources (Payne, Bettman, & Johnson, 1988; Tolcott, 1991). Normative decision models ignore this practical reality, but crews cannot afford to. Costs are associated with generating all options, gathering all relevant information, evaluating the options in light of relevant attributes, and integrating the data to yield the optimal decision. These costs are measured in crew time and workload. A decision strategy that is "good enough," though not optimal, and is low in cost may be more desirable than a very costly, and perhaps only marginally better, decision. In addition, the appropriateness of applying normative models to decision-making in dynamic, time-pressured, action-oriented situations has been questioned (Brehmer, 1991). Given the inap-

---

[1]For a discussion of the differences between decision-making in the laboratory and in naturalistic environments, see Orasanu and Connolly (1993).

[2]One exception may be the case of flight replanning, in which an optimal flight plan can be selected to provide maximum fuel economy, smoothest flight (avoiding weather), or fastest arrival. Computer devices are required to assist such efforts, however (see Smith, McCoy, Layton, & Bihari, 1992).

propriateness of normative criteria, process criteria might be considered instead. That is, decision quality may be judged by asking how the decision was made. Actually, two questions are embedded in this one. The first concerns how decisions are made in dynamic natural environments. The second concerns how crews collaborate in making decisions (as opposed to individuals). I return to these questions in the next section.

A sizable literature shows unaided human decision-making in formal laboratory tasks to be nonoptimal and to violate logical principles, compared to normative standards (Kahneman, Slovic, & Tversky, 1982). Instead, people tend to use heuristic strategies, or mental shortcuts. Optimality requires that all available information be factored into the decision, but heuristics ignores some information. Options are pared down and the problem is simplified to reduce the information-processing load. Heuristic strategies yield adequate but not optimal decisions. In Simon's (1955) term, people often "satisfice," settling for the first choice found to be acceptable. Many people concerned with decision-making want to stamp out heuristics as defective forms of reasoning. Yet there is little evidence that they are bad under some everyday reasoning circumstances. To the contrary—under time pressure certain heuristic strategies have been found to yield better outcomes than truncated (and therefore incomplete) full analysis of options (Payne et al., 1988).

Research grounded in normative decision models tends to ignore the enormous power conferred by domain expertise. Research on expertise has focused mainly on problem-solving rather than on decision-making per se. However, the findings are relevant to the broad set of cockpit decisions described in this chapter (Johnson, 1988). Experts differ from novices mainly in the structure and richness of their knowledge bases. They have more complete and accurate "mental models" for the domain which allow them to interpret cues and to predict what will happen in the future (Johnson-Laird, 1983; Rouse & Morris, 1986). Expertise may be expected to contribute to cockpit decision-making in three ways (Chi, Glaser & Farr, 1988). First, expert knowledge facilitates rapid and accurate perception and interpretation of problems. Experts can "see" problems in terms of their underlying structure, which enables them to frame appropriate solutions. They can size up situations quickly. This type of knowledge is needed to recognize the conditions that trigger go/no-go or RPD decisions. Experts' mental models of aircraft systems also contribute to diagnostic situation assessment, used to clarify ambiguous problems (Cannon-Bowers, Salas, & Converse, 1991). Second, experts have more specific knowledge in their memory storehouses. This knowledge should include stored condition–action patterns corresponding to go/no-go and RPD decisions. These patterns are similar to the thousands of patterns chess masters have in memory (Chase & Simon, 1973). Experts should have to do little work to retrieve these stored condition–action rules. Third, expert knowledge provides a basis for risk assessment. Because of their experience with aircraft systems and routes over many hundreds or thousands of flight hours, expert pilots can assess the likelihood of various kinds of problems occurring. They can infer likely causes and project what is likely to happen in the future, given no action or as a consequence of actions they might take. Finally, experts have more problem "cases" or stories in memory, based on their own experience or professional lore, that guide their search for information or suggest solutions.

It should be pointed out that knowledge is not a shield against errors. Actually, expert knowledge is the foundation for heuristics, which sometimes result in poor judgments. (For a thorough treatment of the role of knowledge in heuristics and biases, see Cohen, 1993a, 1993b). That same knowledge is responsible for efficient functioning most of the time, but occasionally it leads one astray. For example, Maher (1991) reports on a flight destined for Lexington, Kentucky, that actually landed at Frankfort, Kentucky. He attributed this error to the heuristics of availability and representativeness and suggested that training should try to eliminate their influence. However, it makes little sense to try to get people not to use their knowledge. Instead, it might be more productive to help people avoid traps by using other kinds of strategies, such as checking, monitoring, and verifying ambiguous information.

Two other points about expertise: First, expert knowledge only confers an advantage on problems that are meaningful within the expert's domain. For example, chess masters show remarkable memory for the location of chess pieces that represent positions during play (Chase & Simon, 1973). But if those same pieces are placed randomly on the chessboard, the masters' recall is no better than that of novices. The message is clear for decision-making in the cockpit: expertise may reach its limits on problems that are so low in frequency that they are unfamiliar to the crew, and new systems that violate long-term pilots' mental models may interfere with effective decision-making involving malfunctions in those systems. Evidence supporting these predictions is found in McKinney (1992), who reported that expertise conferred no advantage to Air Force pilots making decisions about unique system malfunctions; it did lead to better decisions in more routine cases. A second implication from the expertise literature is that pilots who are relative novices to the plane, company, or routes will probably not be as efficient or effective as more experienced pilots in assessing situations, making quick condition–action decisions, predicting future events, or selecting decision-relevant information. Vast amounts of experience are necessary to get to the point.

HOW DOES CREW DECISION-MAKING DIFFER FROM INDIVIDUAL DECISION-MAKING? ✈

So far the discussion has been about decision-making in the cockpit, without specific reference to who is making the decision. Cockpit decision-making is defined as a team task, yet it is the captain who has ultimate responsibility for decisions that are made. The crew provides input from a variety of information sources: personal experience, aircraft systems, weather, air traffic control (ATC), and dispatch. The presence of multiple eyes, ears, heads, and hands would lead one to expect crews to make better decisions than individuals. Additional cognitive resources can monitor changing conditions more carefully, back each other up, assess the situation, provide alternate perspectives, reduce workload, generate options, suggest strategies, and identify obstacles. Yet research on group problem-solving and decision-making indicates that groups often do worse than individuals solving the same problems (Orasanu & Salas, 1993). Individuals do as well as groups on tasks for which there is a right or best answer, or those for which an effective strategy will lead to a good answer. However, teams do better in situations like the cockpit, where the solution depends on contributions from multiple sources and where coordination is required (Mullen & Goethals, 1987).

Even when the task is one that depends on team effort, there are many ways in which a team can perform in a less than ideal manner. Factors that detract from team efforts are either process failures or performance failures. *Process failures* (Steiner, 1972) are those stemming from the team's interpersonal processes: the intellectual and communicative processes by which members pool and assemble their resources, allocate responsibilities, and evaluate each other's contributions. A number of process failures stem from failure to question assumptions: Crew members assume they know each others' goals, or one person thinks he or she is the only one who sees the situation differently from others. A second process failure is based on shared misconceptions: Shared experience leads the crew to see a situation similarly, but incorrectly, and they have greater confidence in that wrong view because of their numbers. Third, a lack of cohesion may interfere with a crew's performance: Interpersonal conflict may lead to a refusal to cooperate. In a related vein is "social loafing": A crew member may abdicate responsibility because he or she thinks someone else will take care of the problem. Finally, some research suggests that groups make riskier decisions than individuals, perhaps because of dilution of responsibility, but this depends on the nature of the tasks (Davis & Stasson, 1988). Unfortunately, little experimental research exists on decision-making by teams of professionals like cockpit crews, so many of the findings reported here are based on work with ad hoc groups of college students performing laboratory tasks (Druckman & Bjork, 1991).

Performance failures are due to problems in accomplishing the task rather than to interpersonal process factors. These include interruptions from other tasks (e.g., ATC calls that must be answered); failure to communicate critical information in a timely manner (e.g., reporting on actions taken or sharing of information obtained); failure to complete critical tasks in time, usually due to poor task prioritization (e.g., computing landing weight or fuel consumption); and ambiguous goals or task assignments (not enough information is provided by the captain to enable each crew member to carry out the assigned task) (Leedom, 1991).

A third factor that pertains to individuals rather than the crew as a whole, but that is important in determining the decisions that may be made in critical circumstances, is *hazardous attitudes* (Diehl, 1991; FAA, 1991). These include: *antiauthority* (Don't tell me what to do), *impulsivity* (I must do something now), *macho* (I can do anything), *invulnerability* (Nothing will happen to me), and *resignation* (What's the use of trying?). Diehl (1991) has prescribed antidotes for each of these and reports reductions in accident rates as a result of training to overcome these attitudes in military and general aviation environments.

All three factors can contribute to poor decisions because they interfere with doing the work needed to make a good decision. In addition, hazardous attitudes may increase the amount of risk that crews will accept. The critical question remaining, however, is what features contribute to *effective* crew decision-making? This question is addressed in the next section.

WHAT CONTRIBUTES TO EFFECTIVE CREW DECISION-MAKING? ⎯⎯⎯⎯⎯⎯⎯⎯⎯⎯⎯⎯⎯⎯ ✈

Given that the issue of defining good cockpit decisions was bypassed in an earlier section, the question of what contributes to effective crew decision-making may seem somewhat strange. The earlier discussion concluded with the suggestion that decision-making may be evaluated in terms of its contribution to overall *task performance*, that is, safety, effectiveness, and efficiency. Furthermore, attention should be paid to the *process* by which a crew reaches its decisions. Considerable data exist on crew performance in high-fidelity full-mission simulations (e.g., Oser, McCallum, Salas, & Morgan, 1989), and several studies have examined decision-making in those contexts. Relations have been identified between features of crew processes and overall levels of crew performance (Kanki, Lozito, & Foushee, 1989; Murphy & Awe, 1985; Orasanu & Fischer, 1991; Stout, Cannon-Bowers, Salas, & Morgan, 1990). While these findings are all correlational, they at least provide a basis for describing decision-relevant behaviors characteristic of crews that perform more or less effectively in simulated flight. Causal models have not yet been validated.

Four aspects of crew behavior that support cockpit decision-making have been identified (Orasanu, 1990). They are associated with effective crew performance, where performance is judged by operational errors (mainly violations of standard procedures and aircraft control problems such as altitude deviations). These features pertain to the crew as a whole, rather than to individual crew members. Effective crews are characterized by the following features, which will be described in some detail: good situation awareness, high levels of metacognition, shared mental models based on explicit communication, and efficient resource management.

Situation Awareness

Situation awareness involves interpreting situational cues to recognize that a problem exists which may require a decision or action. Crews must go beyond merely noticing the presence of cues; they must appreciate their significance. Doing so successfully depends on knowledge and experience in similar situations. For example, recorded weather information at airports is available to all pilots. Hearing that there is less than a 5° spread between temperature and dew point means that fog is likely, although there may be no mention of fog in the report. An alert pilot will recognize this potential problem for landing and seek further information.

Recognizing and defining the nature of a problem encountered in a dynamic environment such as flying is the first and perhaps most critical step in making an effective and safe decision. The significance of situation awareness is clear in Freeman & Simmon's (1991) analysis of 244 in-flight incidents reported to a major carrier. Of that entire set of incidents, 143 of them (or 59%) were classified either as problems in perceiving that a problem existed ($n = 81$) or in recognizing the significance of the cues for the safety of the flight ($n = 62$). If a crew does not realize they have a problem, they surely are not going to begin trying to solve it. Unfortunately, problems have a way of evolving, and by the time less sensitive crews are aware that a problem exists, the situation may be much more risky.

Sometimes cues are subtle and do not signify a problem at the moment, but forewarn that conditions may deteriorate in the future. For example, turbulence en route may remind a crew that a weather front is moving in to their destination. They may begin to consider the possibility of a missed approach or diversion if weather drops below minimums. Situation awareness allows crews to plan ahead and prepare for contingencies, which is an element under the next component.

Metacognition

Metacognition is a word from the research world that means, literally, thinking about thinking. It refers to reflection on and regulation of one's own thinking (Brown, Armbruster, & Baker, 1986; Flavell, 1981; Garner, 1987). In the cockpit, where thinking is a collective activity, metacognition involves defining the problem and working out a plan to solve it, determining that a decision must be made, and deciding what information and resources are needed and what are available. As used here, metacognition refers broadly to a reflective executive function, as opposed to a narrower definition sometimes adopted in the decision literature which focuses on degree of confidence in one's judgments (Evans, 1989).

A metacognitive framework was used by Orasanu (1990) to analyze crews that differed in their overall performance in a full-mission simulated flight at

NASA–Ames Research Center (Foushee, Lauber, Baetge, & Acomb, 1986). Analysis of crew communication showed that higher and lower performing crews differed in their levels of metacognitive activities when faced with in-flight abnormalities. All crews (flying a simulated B-737) encountered turbulence en route to their destination. (See Figure 5.2 for a schematic of the scenario.) High cross-winds made the landing illegal, so a missed approach was required. During climb-out one of the hydraulic systems failed, which increased workload and complicated the choice of an alternate. The hydraulic failure meant that braking power would be reduced, and gear and flaps would need to be lowered manually. Because the gear could not be retracted once lowered, a second go-around was not desirable. None of these problems in itself was difficult, but their confluence increased the workload substantially and seemed to increase the difficulty of both the choice decision (the alternate landing site) and the scheduling decision (task prioritization and resource management) for some of the crews.

More effective crews paid attention early on to the turbulence and to the possibility of a missed approach. They reviewed the approach plates, checked to see whether Category II instrument landing equipment was available and working, and considered possible alternates. They also checked weather frequently and realized the cross-wind problem before going down to decision height. Following the missed approach and hydraulic failure, more effective crews all adopted a conservative strategy: They requested a holding pattern to buy time while they collected information about weather at possible alternates, checked on runway lengths and approaches, and calculated fuel availability. When low-error crews made their choice of an alternate, they used more safety-relevant information. All these behaviors can be considered evidence of metacognition. The crews reflected on what they were trying to do, how they could do it, what additional information they needed, and what the likely results might be.

Several recent studies of cockpit crews support Orasanu's (1990) conclusions concerning the role of metacognitive processes in effective crew performance. The importance of planning to overall mission effectiveness was demonstrated by Pepitone, King, & Murphy (1988), who found fewer operational errors among crews that made more contingency plans. Also supporting the importance of a broad plan was the Smith, McCoy, Layton, & Bihari (1992) finding that more effective crews emphasized strategies that kept open more options in a flight replanning problem. A second metacognitive factor is sensitivity to information needed to solve a problem. Cohen (1992) found that more experienced captains faced with a flight replanning task paid more attention to recommendations from dispatchers than did less experienced captains. While this finding might be explained on the basis of the senior captains' greater organizational integration, it could also reflect their greater appreciation of the value of this source of information. Dispatchers have a broad view of the entire system, both weather and traffic, and can provide more optimal suggestions.

SIMULATION SCENARIO

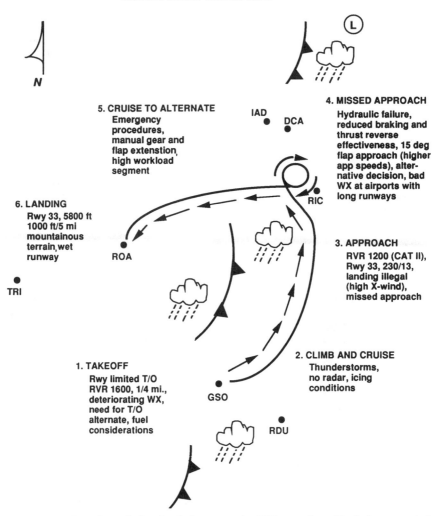

N

5. CRUISE TO ALTERNATE
Emergency
procedures,
manual gear and
flap extenstion,
high workload
segment

IAD ● DCA ●

4. MISSED APPROACH
Hydraulic failure,
reduced braking and
thrust reverse
effectiveness, 15 deg
flap approach (higher
app speeds), alter-
native decision, bad
WX at airports with
long runways

RIC ●

6. LANDING
Rwy 33, 5800 ft
1000 ft/5 mi
mountainous
terrain, wet
runway   ROA ●

● TRI

3. APPROACH
RVR 1200 (CAT II),
Rwy 33, 230/13,
landing illegal
(high X-wind),
missed approach

1. TAKEOFF
Rwy limited T/O
RVR 1600, 1/4 mi.,
deteriorating WX,
need for T/O
alternate, fuel
considerations

GSO ●

2. CLIMB AND CRUISE
Thunderstorms,
no radar, icing
conditions

RDU ●

Figure 5.2 Overview of the simulation scenario. WX, weather; X-wind, cross-wind. (Originally from Foushee, Lauber, Baetge, & Acomb, 1986.)

Shared Mental Models

When a crew encounters a problem in flight, two kinds of shared knowledge may contribute to effective solution: shared background knowledge and
shared problem models. Shared background knowledge refers to the knowledge
the crews bring with them to the cockpit based on common training and experi-

ence: knowledge of aircraft systems, standard procedures, regulations, company policy, and crewmember roles and responsibilities (chapters by Ginnett and Hackman; Cannon-Bowers et al., 1990). This kind of shared knowledge allows the crew to function efficiently in routine situations because it allows them to anticipate events and each others' actions. Hutchins & Klausen (1991) have shown how shared knowledge allows one crew member to interpret ambiguous gestures, facial expressions, and utterances of the other crew member while making a change in heading. When a flight is uneventful, little communication is required beyond the standard monitoring, callouts, and sharing of weather and clearance information obtained over the radio to assure crew coordination. All crew members play their assigned roles in synchrony, like a string quartet (cf. Hackman, 1987).

However, when a problem arises, especially one that is ambiguous and cannot be solved "by the book," or when multiple problems co-occur, then the crew needs to get organized. Communication is needed to assure that each crew member understands basic information about the situation: what the problem is, what the plan is for solving it, who does what. In this case, the crew needs to create a shared problem model. This model uses shared background knowledge but is specific to the immediate problem and its solution. A shared problem model is necessary to assure that all crew members are solving the same problem and have the same understanding of priorities, urgency, cue significance, what to watch out for, who does what, and when to perform certain activities.

Note that each participant can have his or her own understanding of the situation and plan for coping with it. The captain can give commands and the crew members can carry out their jobs. But without shared understanding of the overall goal, there is no guarantee that all crew members will be working toward the same ends. Obviously, the degree of communication required depends on how familiar the problem is to the crew and how complex it is. The greatest amount of communication is required in ill-defined or non-routine problems. For routine problems, crews may show implicit coordination and little overt discussion of what to do (Kleinman & Serfaty, 1989).

Shared problem models are created through communication—all crew members may contribute to them, depending on who has relevant information. Certain types of utterances contribute specifically to building shared problem models and working out solutions. These utterances are distinct from standard cockpit talk required to fly the plane, namely, call-outs, check lists, system monitoring, ground communication, and associated acknowledgements and replies, but are clearly built on these. This distinct type of talk enables the crew to get organized when a problem is encountered.

Model-building utterances perform the following functions: recognize and define the problem, state goals, state or suggest plans or strategies, offer explanations, and predict outcomes. Other utterances are more action-oriented but still augment the problem model by making explicit what is to be done and who is to do it. These include specific task assignments and commands. Orasanu & Fischer (1991, 1992) analyzed the performance of 2-member (B-737) and 3-member (B-727) crews in full mission simulations at NASA–Ames Research Center. Both simulations used the same complex scenario described earlier (weather-induced missed approach followed by a hydraulic system failure). (For full descriptions of the original studies, see Chidester, Kanki, Foushee, Dickinson, & Bowles, 1990, and Foushee et al., 1986).

The Orasanu & Fischer (1992) analysis showed that crews talked more overall during the abnormal phase than in the normal phase of the flight, as would be expected. However, the increase in their talk was concentrated in certain categories. Both captains and first officers stated more goals and plans/strategies during the abnormal phase and made more explicit task assignments. These data support the notion that crews in fact respond to the exigencies of the situation and organize themselves to cope. Moreover, Orasanu & Fischer (1992) found that captains of higher performing crews (those who made fewer procedural or aircraft handling errors) were more explicit in their problem-related talk than were captains of lower performing crews. They stated more plans or strategies and made more explicit task assignments. This study showed that the captains set the tone and contributed disproportionately to creating the shared model. They created the context that allowed other crewmembers to participate. This pattern is confirmed by an analysis by Murphy & Awe (1985), who found that the quality of decision-making in 16 air transport crews (in simulated flight) was a function of the decision efficiency and the quality of the captain's communication. The decision efficiency measure reflected the degree to which the problem was clearly defined and relevant information was obtained. In turn, decision efficiency was predicted by quality of decision communication, command reversal, and crew coordination. Command reversal refers to the first officer taking over the captain's usual duties; it was negatively related to decision efficiency, meaning that when the captain was clearly in command, decision-making was more efficient.[3]

What these findings suggest is that shared problem models serve as organizing frameworks within which crews solve problems and make decisions. By articulating goals, plans, and strategies, effective captains create a context for interpreting their commands, observations, and information requests. The shared model enables other crewmembers to make suggestions, to offer information useful for solving the problem, and to coordinate their actions. Good crews also use resources outside the cockpit, such as ground controllers and company dispatchers, who can provide assistance.

[3]This finding should not be taken to mean that first officers should not take responsibility for managing a situation in the cockpit if conditions warrant it. Sometimes command reversal is the best way for a crew to manage a situation.

Resource Management

Resource management is itself a type of decision-making, but it also bears on the quality of other decisions that must be made during the critical time period. Crews that manage their resources well reduce the demands on their own cognitive resources, especially during high-workload phases of flight, freeing them to deal with other complex decision requirements. Resource management involves the management of information, cognitive work, communication, and actions that must be accomplished within a fixed time or event window. Effective resource management requires an understanding of what must be done, what resources are available, the time required to carry out various tasks, and the cognitive and non-cognitive demands of various events. In addition and most important, the captain must clearly understand the relative priorities associated with each task and use this information to schedule tasks and assign crewmembers responsibility for accomplishing them. Well-managed crews look as if they are guided by an overall plan that matches resources to goals, and everything fits in. All tasks are accomplished in a well-coordinated manner. Poorly managed crews are constantly playing catch-up and appear poorly coordinated. Often important tasks do not get done.

What accounts for these differences between more and less well managed crews? First, it appears that captains with good metacognitive skills have a better overall picture of their strengths and weaknesses and potential problems. Armed with this information, they develop overall time and resource management strategies designed to give themselves clear thinking time and flexibility. They either use low-workload periods to do contingency planning, or explicitly structure tasks to give themselves time to work on problems. Strikingly different overall strategies appear to be optimal depending on crew size, and thus the total cognitive resources available (Orasanu, 1990; Orasanu & Fischer, 1992). In two-member (B-737) crews, more effective captains used low-workload periods to prepare for possible high-workload periods. Specifically, with bad weather at their destination, they reviewed approach plates early and often, included missed approach guidance, and considered the possibility of needing an alternate. When workload became intense, these captains talked very little. They stated their goals and plans and assigned the first officer to work on the system malfunction, while they (the captains) flew the plane. Those captains gave few commands during the high-workload period. Instead, they spelled out overall priorities and sequences for completing various tasks. They created a shared problem model within which the first officer could work out details of how to get the tasks done. In contrast, captains in lower performing crews gave many commands during the high-workload phase but provided no overall plan or strategy for getting the work done. Coordination of these crews was very disjointed; first officers seemed to have trouble completing one task before they were called on to do another.

In three-member crews, a very different resource management strategy was associated with effective crew performance. More effective captains assigned flying the plane to the first officer while they, the captains, worked on the system malfunction problem and decision about an alternate with the second officer. These captains' rate of talk, including goals, plans, commands, and explicit task assignment, went up significantly during the abnormal or high-workload phase. Less effective captains of three-member crews flew the plane themselves and assigned the task of working out the problems to the first and second officers. But those captains still tried to manage the problem-solving activities. It appears that managing problem-solving and complex decision-making while flying a plane is difficult to do. So we see very different patterns associated with effective performance depending on the crew resources available.

Further support for the importance of good resource management to overall flight performance comes from research by Wickens & Raby (1991), who examined performance of single pilots flying low-fidelity simulators. They found that high performers (defined by low frequency of errors such as altitude deviations) carried out critical tasks (e.g., landing gear and flaps) earlier than low performers and scheduled other "must do" tasks at more optimal times. Clearly, the better performers showed greater sensitivity to timing and better planning. Presumably, their effective task management contributed to their high performance.

Unfortunately, life sometimes presents challenges for which no specific training or planning can prepare one. Such a case was the loss of all hydraulic systems at 33,000 feet in United Airlines flight 232 (NTSB, 1990), referred to earlier. The captain's management of that crew and the level of crew coordination (including ground personnel) contributed to saving lives that surely would have been lost otherwise. Predmore (1991) analyzed the tapes of the last 32 minutes of that flight. His analysis showed that during the high-workload period after the failure, the captain used his crew resources in an efficient manner. A check airman happened to be a passenger on the flight and was recruited to assist in situation assessment by visually inspecting the nature of the damage. Then he was used to manipulate the throttles (once the crew discovered they could control the plane somewhat using that mechanism). That left the captain free to manage the situation, which he did with the aid of ground controllers and the company dispatcher. Through composure, good crew coordination and communication, and a heavy dose of luck, that plane was brought to earth, though not without some loss of life.

How do the four components I have described contribute to decision-making? Situation assessment is necessary for recognizing that a decision must be made or an action must be taken. Metacognition is involved in determining an overall plan and the information needed to make the decision. Shared situation models are needed to exploit the cognitive capabilities of the entire crew. Shared models also assure that all participants are solving the same problem. And resource management assures that time, information, and mental resources will be available when they are needed.

CAN WE TRAIN CREWS TO MAKE BETTER DECISIONS? ✈

If we want to improve performance by cockpit crews, should we focus training efforts on helping them to be more rational decision-makers? Or should we train them to interpret cues, be metacognitive, make plans, build shared problem models, and manage their resources? Recent research findings suggest that the latter might be more productive. Evidence is accumulating on the lack of success of "debiasing" efforts (Fischhoff, 1982) and efforts to improve statistical reasoning (Cheng, Holyoak, Nisbett, & Oliver, 1986).[4] On the other hand, positive evidence is accruing on training in perceptual skills needed for situation assessment (Getty, Pickett, D'Orsi, & Swets, 1988), on metacognitive skills (Nickerson, Perkins, & Smith, 1985), and on crew resource management skills (Chidester, 1987; Helmreich, 1987; Helmreich, Chidester, Foushee, Gregorich, & Wilhelm, 1989; Helmreich & Wilhelm, 1991).

At this point in research history, no basis exists for believing that it is possible to develop training techniques to improve all-purpose decision-making skills. The problem is that different component skills are involved in the six types of decisions described earlier in this chapter. Efforts at training general-purpose cognitive skills have notoriously met with failure (Bransford, Arbitman-Smith, Stein, & Vye, 1985; Sternberg, 1985, 1986). Conclusions from a large body of research show that cognitive skills are specific to the domain in which they are to be practiced. Strategies are learned most effectively in conjunction with the domain-specific content (Glaser & Bassok, 1989).

Consider the six decision types discussed earlier. The cognitive work required by each type demands different types of training. Following is a sketch of what organizations might want to teach for each type of decision.

1. *Go/no-go decisions.* Since these decisions usually must be made under severe time pressure and involve considerable risk, the amount of thinking should be minimal. Essentially, crews must be taught to recognize the sets of conditions that trigger the response, Stop what you are doing! (usually taking off or landing). The other necessary element is risk assessment, especially when conditions are borderline. Training should focus on developing perceptual patterns in memory that

---

[4]"Debiasing" efforts attempt to help people use all available information which they might otherwise ignore, resulting in biased judgments. For example, people tend to give little weight to the base rate frequency of certain outcomes or events (e.g., the rate at which certain systems fail in the cockpit) (Kahneman & Tversky, 1982).

constitute the conditions for aborting an action. Such training should be conducted under realistic time pressure and should include cases that are borderline or have additional contingencies that require more complex risk assessment.

2. *Recognition-primed decisions.* As with go/no-go decisions, crews must be trained to recognize situational patterns that serve as input to condition–action rules. But in this case they must also learn the response side of the rule and its link to the condition. For example, if a rapid depressurization occurs, the crew must know to descend immediately to a lower altitude. Evaluation skills also must be trained: The crew must ask, What will happen if I take this action? What will happen if we do not take this action? Is there a reason not to take this action?

3. *Response selection decisions.* When a single option must be selected from a set, crews must recognize multiple options and evaluate them in terms of how well they satisfy the goals and meet constraints. Often they must consider trade-offs among competing goals which are satisfied by different options. A traditional decision-analytic approach would be to train crews to perform a multi-attribute utility analysis. However, this is a very costly procedure in terms of time and resources. A more efficient approach might be to train crews to use "satisficing" (Simon, 1955) or other heuristic strategy that yields a satisfactory, though not optimal, solution. Two heuristic strategies that may be appropriate in certain environments are elimination-by-aspects (Tversky, 1972) or dominance-structuring (Montgomery, 1989, 1993). In the former, options are eliminated if they fail on one criterion (e.g., weather or runway length) and are not evaluated on other criteria. In the ideal situation, only one acceptable option remains. Dominance-structuring proceeds in the opposite direction. Evidence supporting various options is reevaluated to support a single choice.

4. *Resource management decisions.* The relative priorities of various tasks, especially critical ones, must be part of the basic knowledge of all crewmembers. Skills that enter into this type of decision include estimation of the time required to complete various tasks, knowledge about the interdependencies among tasks, and scheduling strategies. An important strategy for captains appears to be structuring activities to free up time for thinking. When problems are ambiguous, requiring diagnosis or creative problem-solving, captains may manage best by off-loading some of their own tasks, like flying the plane, to other crew members.

5. *Non-diagnostic procedural decisions.* This is the least clearly defined type of decision. It involves a cue pattern that falls into a category with no prescribed response. The nature of the problem is unclear. Many different types of ambiguous cues (e.g., loud noise from air rushing in the cockpit, strange vibrations, smells) may signal dangerous conditions. The prescribed response for many of these cases would be to land as soon as possible (essentially a procedural solution). This type of decision may be a variant of the RPD category, but with a non-specific condition side. Training for these cases would involve mainly situation assessment and risk assessment. Cues that signal possible emergencies need to

be distinguished from those that are troublesome but not severe enough to precipitate an emergency landing. Knowledge of the specific aircraft type and its systems would be most useful in this case.

6. *Problem-solving.* These tasks are the most complex, because they involve both diagnosis to determine the nature of the situation and response generation. Once the nature of the problem has been determined, there are no recommended solutions "in the book." Crews must determine what their goals are, develop a plan and candidate strategies, and evaluate the strategies and planned actions based on projections of outcomes. General reasoning strategies such as means–ends analysis may be appropriate for very unfamiliar problems. Alternatively, the crew may try to think of similar or related cases in their own experience or in aviation lore. Case-based reasoning using analogies can offer suggestions for proceeding when little specific knowledge is available (Kolodner, 1987). Solutions that worked in the past are evaluated by imagining their consequences in the present situation. Training for case-based reasoning involves presenting many examples of other people's experiences, as is currently done in many CRM courses. Videotaped reenactments of in-flight emergencies are used to illustrate how those crews coped with the problem. "Hangar flying" provides an informal means for crews to share experiences that may help each other cope with unexpected events.

The above recommendations are based on the structure of the specific types of decision presented by the environment. Different situations demand different kinds of strategies. However, training suggestions also derive from the analysis of factors contributing to effective crew performance. These suggestions cut across all types of problems but may be more significant for one type than others.

The first step in all decisions is *situation assessment*. Both rapid pattern recognition and diagnostic skills are needed. Crew recognition of danger cues should be automatic. Crews also need training to pay attention to ambiguous or worrisome cues. Diagnostic skills may be needed to figure out what the situation is before a decision can be attempted. For example, split flap and asymmetrical flap configurations impose different landing requirements in a B-727. Considerable diagnostic effort may be required to distinguish between them. This is an example of a rare occurrence but one that crews must master.

A second general skill that is a component of all decisions is *risk assessment*. Often safety is pitted against other goals such as saving fuel or getting the passengers to their destinations on time. Organizational policy plays a critical role in these trade-offs and should be explicitly acknowledged when goals may conflict. Organizations and crews must recognize that some level of risk always exists and that there are always trade-offs. Both explicit policy guidance from the organization and reinforced practice by the crew are needed so that crews will be able to achieve solutions that optimize safety and other goals. Training should also emphasize using ground support (dispatch and ATC) to get a bigger picture of the crew's situation in order to minimize risk.

Perhaps the most trainable decision-related skill complex is *metacognition* (see Means, 1993). Abundant research exists supporting the trainability of these skills across wide ranges of populations (Brown et al., 1986; Garner, 1987). A study supported by the Department of Defense to improve decision-making by senior executives found that metacognitive skills were most affected by training (Laskey, Leddo, & Bresnick, 1989). However, learners must have a repertoire of relevant strategies; what they learn is how best to use them. Metacognitive training involves problem analysis (the demands of the problem, information needs, and resources available), strategy development, and the conditions under which various strategies can best be used. The goal is to encourage crews to be reflective and planful–to stop and think. This should overcome what Diehl (1991) calls the hazardous attitude of impulsiveness. Obviously, the crew must still first evaluate the situation and ask, Is a quick response necessary? If yes, do it! If not, buy time and develop a plan. For example, a crew might need to request a holding pattern or longer vectors to give them time to gather needed information or to fix a problem. Candidate decisions need to be evaluated by "what if" reasoning—If we do (or don't do) X, what will happen? A critical issue is how to teach good judgment. The crew must figure out how much information is needed, how many options should be considered, and when to say, "This decision is good enough," and stop deliberating. An equally important goal is cognitive economy, that is, training crews to make the best decision with the least cost in terms of effort and time.

A related issue pertains to encouraging crews to use communication to build *shared problem models.* The intent is not simply to get crews to talk more; more is not necessarily better. High levels of talk contribute to workload. What is desired is explicit discussion of the problem: its definition, plans, strategies, and relevant information. Current training programs that are integrating CRM with technical training encourage crews to use pre-briefings to assure that all members know what to do in case of time-critical emergencies, such as how to handle aborted take-offs. All crewmembers need encouragement to contribute to these shared models because most cockpit situations are dynamic and conditions may change rapidly. The entire crew needs to be kept up to date, and plans may need to be revised. The consequences of failed communications are evident in accident reports; specific findings have been summarized by Goguen, Linde, & Murphy (1986).

The possibility of training crews to communicate more effectively was demonstrated by Lassiter, Vaughn, Smaltz, Morgan, & Salas (1990). Instructors demonstrated various aspects of communication, including those we have defined as relevant to building shared problem models—closed-loop communication, mission-relevant talk, timeliness, volunteering of necessary information, requesting clarification, providing reinforcement, feedback, and confirming vital information. Demonstration of these skills was found to be more effective than didactic classroom instruction (simply telling the students what they should do). Line-oriented flight training or line-oriented simulation training provides crews opportunities to practice these communication skills.

A final set of skills that support the decision-making process is task and *resource management* skills. Overall crew performance depends on the captain's ability to prioritize tasks and allocate duties. But decision-making per se appears to depend more on the captain's ability to free him or herself from demanding tasks, like flying the plane. If they cannot do so, as in a two-member crew, they need to devise other strategies to keep themselves free and delegate tasks to the first officer. Demands can be managed by contingency planning, but this depends on the captain having a long enough time horizon and anticipating possible problems. This in turn depends on good situation awareness and metacognitive skill.

Two other general points about training skills that support decision-making:

1. Most critical is crew performance under time pressure, high workload, and other stressful conditions. If we expect crews to function well under those conditions, they must be trained under those conditions, as Butler points out in his chapter. Various levels of simulated environments could be used to create appropriate conditions without incurring risks.
2. If airlines are concerned about crew decision-making, then they must train crews, not individuals, to make decisions together (Hackman, 1987). Crew training is critical because of the communication, coordination, and task allocation aspects of performance. However, certain component skills that should be practiced until they are automated, such as pattern recognition, could probably be trained individually.

CONCLUSIONS: WHAT DO WE STILL NEED TO KNOW? ✈

While research has yielded knowledge about how people make decisions in dynamic natural contexts and about how to train certain categories of complex skills, efforts to improve crew decision-making are hampered by a lack of specific research knowledge.

• We still need a better understanding of the structure of decision tasks in the cockpit, the kinds of knowledge, skills, and strategies needed to meet those demands, and the potential weak links in responding to each of the decision types.
• We need better definitions of performance standards and criteria for

judging the quality of each type of decision. Normative models are convenient but inappropriate to the dynamic time-pressured, knowledge-based reasoning in the cockpit. Reliable and valid measures of the skills that support decision-making are also needed.

   • A better definition of which decision-relevant skills can be automated is needed.

   • More knowledge is needed about the effects of various stressors, such as workload, fatigue, boredom, noise, or temperature extremes on crew (as opposed to individual) decision performance.

   One final cautionary note: Formal decision models are seductive as the basis for training crew decision-making. These models offer optimal decisions and can be used as a benchmark against which to evaluate crew performance. The problem is that the assumptions of the formal models do not fit the conditions of the cockpit (especially the dynamically changing information, multiple goals, and lack of complete information). Furthermore, there is no evidence that using formal models will result in better crew performance. Encouraging crews to approximate normative reasoning in training programs (or stamping out useful heuristics) could undermine crews' positive use of their experience, knowledge, and skill. More fruitful approaches will build on the strengths the crews bring to the tasks and emphasize decision-making that supports effective flight performance.

Acknowledgments

   The author's research was supported by the National Aeronautical and Space Administration (NASA), Office of Space Science and Applications, and by the Federal Aviation Administration (FAA).

References

Aviation Safety Reporting System (1991). *FLC Decision-Making Situations* (ASRS SR No. 2276). Moffett Field, CA: Author.

Billings, C. E. (1991). *Human-centered aircraft automation: A concept and guidelines* (Tech. Mem. No. 103885). Moffett Field, CA: NASA–Ames Research Center.

Bransford, J. D., Arbitman-Smith, R., Stein, B. S., & Vye, N. J. (1985). Improving thinking and learning skills: An analysis of three approaches. In J. W. Segal, S. F. Chipman, & R. Glaser (Eds.). *Thinking and learning skills*, (Vol. 1, pp. 133–208). Hillsdale, NJ: Erlbaum.

Brehmer, B. (1991). Strategies in real-time dynamic decision making. In R. Hogarth (Ed.), *Insights in decision making: A tribute to the late Hillel J. Einhorn* (pp. 262–279). Chicago: University of Chicago Press.

Brezovic, C. P., Klein, G. A., & Thordsen, M. (1987). *Decision making in armored platoon commanders* (KATR-858(b)-87-05F). Yellow Springs, OH: Klein Associates Inc. Prepared under contract #MDA 903-85-C-0327 for the U.S. Army Research Institute.

Brown, A. L., Armbruster, B. B., & Baker, L. (1986). The role of metacognition in reading and studying. In J. Orasanu (Ed.), *Reading comprehension: From research to practice* (pp. 49–76). Hillsdale, NJ: Erlbaum.

Calderwood, R., Crandall, B., & Klein, G. A. (1987). *Expert and novice fireground command decisions* (KATR-858(d)-87-02F). Yellow Springs, OH: Klein Associates Inc. Prepared under contract #MDA 903-85-C-0327 for the U.S. Army Research Institute.

Cannon-Bowers, J. A., Salas, E., & Converse, S. (1990). Cognitive psychology and team training: Training shared mental models of complex systems. *Human Factors Society Bulletin, 33*(12), 1–4.

Chamberlin, R. W. (1991). Rejected takeoffs: Causes, problems, and consequences. In *Proceedings of the Sixth International Symposium on Aviation Psychology* (pp. 993–998). Columbus: The Ohio State University.

Chase, W. G., & Simon, H. A. (1973). The mind's eye in chess. In W. G. Chase (Ed.), *Visual information processing.* New York: Academic Press.

Cheng, P. W., Holyoak, K. J., Nisbett, R. E., & Oliver, L. M. (1986). Pragmatic versus syntactic approaches to training deductive reasoning. *Cognitive Psychology, 18,* 293–328.

Chi, M. T. H., Glaser, R., & Farr, M. J. (1988). *The nature of expertise.* Hillsdale, NJ: Erlbaum.

Chidester, T. R. (1987). Selection for optimal crew performance: Relative impact of selection and training In R. S. Jensen (Ed.), *Proceedings of the Fourth International Symposium on Aviation Psychology* (pp. 473–479). Columbus, OH: The Ohio State University.

Chidester, T. R., Kanki, B. G., Foushee, H. C., Dickinson, C. L., & Bowles, S. V. (1990). *Personality factors in flight operations: Volume 1. Leadership characteristics and crew performance in a full-mission air transport simulation* (NASA Tech. Mem. No. 102259). Moffett Field, CA: NASA–Ames Research Center.

Christensen-Szalansky, J. J. J. (1986). Improving the practical utility of judgement research. In B. Brehmer, H. Jungermann, P. Lourens & G. Sevon (Eds.), *New directions for research in judgement and decision making* (pp. 383–410). New York: North-Holland.

Christensen-Szalansky, J. J. J. (1993). A comment on applying experimental findings to naturalistic environments. In G. Klein, J. Orasanu, R. Calderwood, & C. Zsambok (Eds.). *Decision making in action: Models and methods.* Norwood, NJ: Ablex.

Cohen, M. S. (June, 1992). *Taking risks and taking advice: The role of experience in airline pilot diversion decisions.* Technical Report. Fairfax, VA: Decision Sciences Corporation.

Cohen, M. S. (1993a). The naturalistic basis of decision biases. In G. Klein, J. Orasanu, R. Calderwood, & C. Zsambok (Eds.). *Decision making in action: Models and methods.* Norwood, NJ: Ablex.

Cohen, M. S. (1993b). Three paradigms for viewing decision biases. In G. Klein, J. Orasanu, R. Calderwood, & C. Zsambok (Eds.). *Decision making in action: Models and methods.* Norwood, NJ: Ablex.

Davis, J. H., & Stasson, M. F. (1988). Small group performance: Past and present research trends. *Advances in Group Processes, 5,* 245–277.

Diehl, A. (1991). The effectiveness of training programs for preventing aircrew "error." In *Proceedings of the Sixth International Symposium on Aviation Psychology* (pp. 640–655). Columbus: The Ohio State University.

Druckman, D., & Bjork, R. A. (1991). *In the mind's eye: Enhancing human performance.* Washington, DC: National Academy Press.

Dutch Aircraft Accident Inquiry Board. (1979). *Verdict of the aircraft accident inquiry board regarding the accident at Los Rodeos Airport, Tenerife (Spain).* The Hague: Dutch Government.

Edwards, W., & Newman, J. R. (1982). *Multiattribute evaluation.* Beverly Hills, CA: Sage.

Evans, J. St. B. T. (1989). *Bias in human reasoning: Causes and consequences.* London: Erlbaum.

Federal Aviation Administration. (1991). *Aeronautical Decision Making* (Advisory Circular No. 60–22). Washington, DC: Author.

Federal Aviation Administration. (in preparation). *Crew Resource Management (CRM) Training* (Advisory Circular No. 120–51). Washington, DC: Author.

Fischhoff, B. (1982). Debiasing. In D. Kahneman, P. Slovic, & A. Tversky (Eds.), *Judgement under uncertainty: Heuristics and biases* (pp. 422–444). Cambridge: Cambridge University Press.

Flavell, J. H. (1981). Cognitive monitoring. In W. P. Dickson (Ed.), *Children's oral communication skills.* New York: Academic Press.

Foushee, H. C., Lauber, J. K., Baetge, M. M., & Acomb, D. B. (1986). *Crew factors in flight operations: Vol. 3. The operational significance of exposure to short-haul air transport operations.* (Tech. Mem. No. 88322). Moffett Field, CA: NASA–Ames Research Center.

Freeman, C., & Simmon, D. A. (1991). Taxonomy of crew resource management: Information processing domain. In *Proceedings of the Sixth International Symposium on Aviation Psychology* (pp. 391–397). Columbus: The Ohio State University.

Garner, R. (1987). *Metacognition and reading comprehension.* Norwood, NJ: Ablex.

Getty, D. J., Pickett, R. M., D'Orsi, C. J., & Swets, J. A. (1988). Enhanced interpretation of diagnostic images. *Investigative Radiology, 23,* 240–252.

Glaser, R., & Bassok, M. (1989). Learning theory and the study of instruction. *Annual Review of Psychology, 40,* 631–666.

Goguen, J., Linde, C., & Murphy, M. (1986). *Crew communications as a factor in aviation accidents* (NASA Tech. Mem. No. 88254). Moffett Field, CA: NASA–Ames Research Center.

Hackman, J. R. (1987). Group-level issues in the design and training of cockpit crews. In H. W. Orlady & H. C. Foushee (Eds.), *Cockpit resource management training: Proceedings of the NASA/MAC workshop* (CP-2455). Moffett Field, CA: NASA–Ames Research Center.

Helmreich, R. L. (1987). Theory underlying CRM training: Psychological issues in flightcrew performance and crew coordination. In H. W. Orlady & H. C. Foushee (Eds.), *Cockpit resource management training: Proceedings of the NASA/MAC Workshop.* Moffett Field, CA: NASA–Ames Research Center, CP-2455.

Helmreich, R. L., Chidester, T. R., Foushee, H. C., Gregorich, S., & Wilhelm, J. A. (1989). *How effective is cockpit resource management training: Issues in evaluating the impact of programs to enhance crew coordination.* (NASA/UT Tech. Report No. 89). Moffett Field, CA: NASA–Ames Research Center.

Helmreich, R. L., & Wilhelm, J. A. (1991). Outcomes of crew resource management training. *International Journal of Aviation Psychology, 1,* 287–300.

Hutchins, E., & Klausen, T. (1991). *Distributed cognition in an airline cockpit.* Unpublished manuscript. University of California, San Diego, CA.

Johnson, E. J. (1988). Expertise and decision under uncertainty: Performance and process. In M. Chi, R. Glaser, & M. Farr (Eds.), *The nature of expertise.* Hillsdale, NJ: Erlbaum.

Johnson-Laird, P. (1983). *Mental models.* Cambridge, MA: Harvard University Press.

Kahneman, D., Slovic, P., & Tversky, A. (Eds.) (1982). *Judgment under uncertainty: Heuristics and biases.* New York, NY: Cambridge University Press.

Kahneman, D., & Tversky, A. (1982). Intuitive prediction: Biases and corrective procedures. In D. Kahneman, P. Slovic, & A. Tversky (Eds.) *Judgment under uncertainty: Heuristics and biases.* New York, NY: Cambridge University Press.

Kanki, B. G., Lozito, S., & Foushee, H. C. (1989). Communication indices of crew coordination. *Aviation, Space and Environmental Medicine, 60,* 56–60.

Klein, G. A. (1989). Recognition-primed decisions. In W. B. Rouse (Ed.), *Advances in man–machine system research, 5,* 47–92. Greenwich, CT: JAI Press.

Klein, G. A. (1993). A recognition-primed decision (RPD) model of rapid decision making. In G. Klein, J. Orasanu, R. Calderwood, & C. Zsambok (Eds.), *Decision making in action: Models and methods.* Norwood, NJ: Ablex.

Kleinman, D. L., & Serfaty, D. (1989). Team performance assessment in distributed decision making. In R. Gilson, J. P. Kincaid, & B. Goldiez (Eds.), *Proceedings: Interactive networked simulation for training conference.* Orlando, FL: Naval Training Systems Center.

Kolodner, J. L. (1987). Extending problem solving capabilities through case-based inference. In *Proceedings of the 4th Annual International Machine Learning Workshop.*

Laskey, K. B., Leddo, J. M., & Bresnick, T. A. (1989). *Executive thinking and decision skills: A characterization and implications for training* (Tech. Rep. No. TR89-12). Reston, VA: Decision Science Consortium.

Lassiter, D. L., Vaughn, J. S., Smaltz, V. E., Morgan, B. B., Jr., & Salas, E. (1990). *A comparison of two types of training interventions on team communication performance.* Paper presented at the 1990 meeting of the Human Factors Society, Orlando, Florida.

Lautman, L. G., & Gallimore, P. L. (1987, April–June). Control of the crew caused accident: Results of a 12-operator survey. *Airliner.* Seattle: Boeing Commercial Airplane Co., pp. 1–6.

Leedom, D. (1991). Aircrew coordination for Army helicopters: Research overview. In *Proceedings of the Sixth International Symposium on Aviation Psychology* (pp. 284–289). Columbus: The Ohio State University.

Maher, J. (1991). Why pilots are least likely to get good decision making precisely when they need it most. In *Proceedings of the Sixth International Symposium on Aviation Psychology* (pp. 1032–1037) Columbus, OH: The Ohio State University.

McKinney, E. (1992). *Uniqueness of task, experience, and decision making performance: A study of 146 U.S. Air Force Mishaps.* Unpublished report. Colorado Springs: U.S. Air Force Academy.

Means, B. (1993). Training decision makers for the real world. In G. Klein, J. Orasanu, R. Calderwood, & C. Zsambok (Eds.), *Decision making in action: Models and methods.* Norwood, NJ: Ablex.

Montgomery, H. (1989). The search for a dominance structure: Simplification and elaboration in decision making. In D. Vickers & P. L. Smith (Eds.), *Human information processing: Measures, mechanisms, and models* (pp. 471–483). Amsterdam: North Holland.

Montgomery, H. (1993). The search for a dominance structure in decision making: Examining the evidence. In G. Klein, J. Orasanu, R. Calderwood, & C. Zsambok (Eds.), *Decision making in action: Models and methods.* Norwood, NJ: Ablex.

Moray, N., Dessouky, M. I., Kijowski, B. A., & Adapathya, R. (1991). Strategic behavior, workload, and performance in task scheduling. *Human Factors, 33,* 607–629.

Mullen, B., & Goethals, G. R. (1987). *Theories of group behavior.* NY: Springer-Verlag.

Murphy, M. R., & Awe, C. A. (1985). Aircrew coordination and decision making: Performance ratings of video tapes made during a full mission simulation. In *Proceedings of the 21st Annual Conference on Manual Control.* Columbus: Ohio State University.

National Transportation Safety Board. (1982). *Aircraft Accident Report: Air Florida, Inc., Boeing 737-222, N62AF, Collision with 14th Street Bridge near Washington National Airport, Washington, DC, January 13, 1982* (NTSB/AAR-82-8). Washington, DC: Author.

National Transportation Safety Board. (1990). *Aircraft Accident Report: United Airlines Flight 232, McDonnell Douglas DC-10-10, Sioux Gateway Airport, Sioux City, Iowa, July 19, 1989* (NTSB/AAR-91-02). Washington, DC: Author.

Nickerson, R. S., Perkins, D. N., & Smith, E. E. (1985). *The teaching of thinking.* Hillsdale, NJ: Erlbaum.

Orasanu, J. (1990). *Shared mental models and crew decision making* (Tech. Rep. No. 46). Princeton, NJ: Princeton University, Cognitive Science Laboratory.

Orasanu, J., & Connolly, T. (1993). Reinventing decision making. In G. Klein, J. Orasanu, R. Calderwood, & C. Zsambok (Eds.). *Decision making in action: Models and methods.* Norwood, NJ: Ablex.

Orasanu, J., & Fisher, U. (1991). Information transfer and shared mental models for decision making. In *Proceedings of the Sixth International Symposium on Aviation Psychology* (pp. 272–277). Columbus: The Ohio State University.

Orasanu, J., & Fischer, U. (1992). Team cognition in the cockpit: Linguistic control of shared problem solving. In *Proceedings of the 14th Annual Conference of the Cognitive Science Society.* Hillsdale, NJ: Erlbaum.

Orasanu, J., & Salas, E. (1993). Team decision making in complex environments. In G. Klein, J. Orasanu, R. Calderwood & C. Zsambok (Eds.). *Decision making in action: Models and methods.* Norwood, NJ: Ablex.

Oser, R., McCallum, G. A., Salas, E., & Morgan, B. B. (1989). *Toward a definition of teamwork: An analysis of critical team behaviors* (Tech. Rep. No. TR-89-0043). Orlando, FL: Naval Training Systems Center.

Payne, J. P., Bettman, J. R., & Johnson, E. (1988). Adaptive strategy selection in decision making. *Journal of Experimental Psychology: Learning, Memory and Cognition, 14,* 534–552.

Pepitone, D., King, T., & Murphy, M. (1988). *The role of flight planning in aircrew decision performance* (SAE Technical Paper Series No. 881517). Warrendale, PA: Society for Advanced Engineering.

Predmore, S. C. (1991). Microcoding of communications in accident analyses: Crew coordination in United 811 and United 232. In *Proceedings of the Sixth International Symposium on Aviation Psychology* (pp. 350–355) Columbus: The Ohio State University.

Rasmussen, J. (1983). Skill, rules, and knowledge: Signals, signs and symbols, and other distinctions in human performance models. *IEEE Transactions on Systems, Man and Cybernetics,* Vol. *SMC-13,* No. 3.

Rasmussen, J. (1993). Deciding and doing: Decision making in natural context. In G. Klein, J. Orasanu, R. Calderwood, & C. Zsambok (Eds.). *Decision making in action: Models and methods.* Norwood, NJ: Ablex.

Rouse, W. B., & Morris, N. M. (1986). On looking into the black box: Prospects and limits in the search for mental models. *Psychological Bulletin, 100,* 359–363.

Simon, H. A. (1955). A behavioral model of rational choice. *Quarterly Journal of Economics, 69,* 99–118.

Smith, P., McCoy, E., Layton, C., & Bihari, T. (1992). *Design concepts for the development of cooperative problem solving systems* (Technical Report #CSEL-1992-09). Columbus: The Ohio State University.

Steiner, I. (1972). *Group process and productivity.* New York: Academic Press.

Sternberg, R. J. (1985, November). Teaching critical thinking, Part 1: Are we making critical mistakes? *Phi Delta Kappan,* pp. 194–198.

Sternberg, R. J. (1986). *Intelligence applied: Understanding and increasing your intellectual skills.* San Diego: Harcourt, Brace, Jovanovich.

Stout, R., Cannon-Bowers, J. A., Salas, E., & Morgan, B. B. (1990). Does crew coordination behavior impact performance? In *Proceedings of the 34th Annual Meeting of the Human Factors Society* (pp. 1382–1386). Santa Monica, CA: Human Factors Society.

Tolcott, M. A. (1991). *Understanding and aiding military decisions.* Paper presented at the 27th International Applied Military Psychology Symposium, Stockholm, Sweden, June, 1991.

Tversky, A. (1972). Elimination by aspects: A theory of choice. *Psychological Review, 79,* 281–299.

Wickens, C., & Raby, M. (1991). Individual differences in strategic flight management and scheduling. In *Proceedings of the Sixth International Symposium on Aviation Psychology* (pp. 1142–1147). Columbus: The Ohio State University.

Wiener, E. (1988). Cockpit automation. In E. L. Wiener & D. C. Nagel (Eds.). *Human factors in aviation.* San Diego: Academic Press.

6

Crew Resource Management Training Assessment

Steven E. Gregorich
San Jose State University
San Jose, California 95192

John A. Wilhelm
Department of Psychology
University of Texas at Austin
Austin, Texas 78712

OVERVIEW ✈

Considerable evidence from experimental simulations suggests that air crews vary in their coordination and resource management skills (e.g., Ruffell Smith, 1979; Foushee, Lauber, Baetge, & Acomb, 1986). More recent observational data (e.g., Butler, 1991; Clothier, 1991; chapter by Helmreich and Foushee) suggest that substantial variability is also found in line operations and in simulator-based training—even after the implementation of special training designed to enhance crew resource management (CRM). In an industry that prides itself on standardization, this is a cause for concern. The thesis of this discussion is that this concern can be addressed through continued development of assessment strategies for CRM training programs.

CRM training is designed to add a team focus to the training of air transport professionals. These programs target knowledge, skills, and abilities (KSA) as well as mental attitudes and motives related to cognitive processes and interpersonal relationships that influence crew coordination and the management of resources in civil and military flight operations. (For our purposes, the acronym KSA includes mental attitudes and motives.) CRM training programs are designed to build awareness and provide for the practice of related KSAs. The ultimate goal of this training is the increased safety, effectiveness, and efficiency of operations.

Although formal CRM training has existed for more than a decade, guidelines for its initial and continuing development and delivery have been slow to evolve. Strategies to evaluate whether these training programs fully realize their goals are not yet mature. Undoubtedly, CRM training can be advanced with the aid of general research that investigates curriculum, instruction, and measurement theory. However, insights can be more directly derived from assessments of existing CRM training programs. Training program assessment encompasses both the evaluation of training program outcomes and the evaluation of the curricula and instructional technique. Put another way, assessment refers to efforts to evaluate all aspects of training programs. It does not refer to the evaluation of aviators for the purposes of certification or licensure. A careful and thorough program of CRM training assessment that includes systematic collection and analysis of appropriate data can increase understanding of CRM principles and training outcomes. Evaluations of current training programs provide insights for the construction of future programs. In turn, the insights gained provide reciprocal guidance for improved evaluation efforts (e.g., Cannon-Bowers, Tannenbaum, Salas, & Converse, 1991; Helmreich, Chidester, Foushee, Gregorich, & Wilhelm, 1989b). Currently, there are many opportunities to learn from existing training programs.

CRM training program assessment is not without its difficulties. The state of the art of CRM evaluation methodology and the logistical constraints of the training environment introduce real challenges. A comprehensive assessment of any large-scale training program can become a complex and involving task. Organizations involved in CRM training need to make difficult decisions regarding assessment strategies. This chapter presents possibilities for CRM training assessment programs as an aid to those decisions.

After discussing preliminary issues, we present a framework for criteria useful in the assessment of existing CRM training programs. This framework extends previous efforts in this area (Cannon-Bowers, Prince, Salas, Owens, Morgan, & Gonos, 1989; Helmreich et al., 1989b; Kirkpatrick, 1976). It considers the main targets of assessment efforts as well as other sources of information that are likely provide insight into the processes and outcomes of training. After the framework is introduced, a model for the systematic integration of these criteria is presented. Only through integration of assessment criteria can the full benefit of assessment efforts be realized. Together, the framework and model comprise useful tools with which to view the current state of CRM training program assessment and to guide future training efforts.

Finally, although the current chapter focuses on CRM programs designed to address the needs of aviators, similar issues pertain to training programs designed for other aviation populations (e.g., dispatch, maintenance, flight attendants) or other fields (e.g., nuclear power plant control room teams and surgical teams). For simplicity however, this chapter focuses on training programs designed for cockpit crew members.

Background of CRM Training

Because most recent air transport accidents have been attributable, in part, to deficiencies in CRM, it makes sense to assume that if CRM KSAs could be advanced, air safety would follow suit (Cooper, White, & Lauber, 1980; Orlady

& Foushee, 1987). Broadly speaking, CRM KSAs can be grouped into three clusters (Federal Aviation Administration, FAA, in press). *Communication processes and decisions* involve listening, scrutiny, inquiry, advocacy, and conflict resolution, as well as operational problem-solving and decision-making. *Team building and maintenance* focuses on interpersonal relationships and effective team practices, including leadership and followership. *Workload management and situational awareness* reflects the extent to which crewmembers maintain awareness of the operational environment, anticipate contingencies, and plan and allocate activities so as to manage stress and workload.

As outlined in the pending revision of the FAA CRM Advisory Circular (FAA, in press), fully implemented CRM training programs are delineated by three components: *initial indoctrination/awareness, recurrent practice and feedback*, and *continuing reinforcement*. Initial indoctrination/awareness is typically provided by a CRM course where students are introduced to specific CRM KSAs. It usually takes place in a seminar setting with one or more instructors or facilitators. Some original CRM seminars emphasized intra-crew communications, personality, leadership and followership, and group synergy. More recent seminar modules have included group decision-making, team formation and maintenance, situational awareness, stress management, and workload distribution. The curriculum may include a combination of lectures, group activities, group discussions, and role-playing exercises. The last of these instructional techniques may have more impact, but they also place more demands on the facilitative skills of instructors.

The recurrent practice and feedback component is typically associated with recurrent line-oriented flight training (LOFT). During recurrent LOFT a full crew complement takes part in a full-mission, high-fidelity simulator session. The LOFT scenario is designed to present situations requiring the coordinated efforts of all crewmembers for optimal mission completion. LOFT emphasizes training, not checking, and is provided on a no-jeopardy basis. Within this component of training, aviators can practice their CRM skills in a realistic setting and receive feedback about their performances from the LOFT instructor and from reviewing selected segments of a videotape of the simulated flight leg (see the chapter by Butler). To protect anonymity, videotapes are erased after each session. Challenges for this component of training include the development of training scenarios that present optimal circumstances for the practice and learning of CRM KSAs and the selection and training of instructors who can effectively administer and debrief these crew-level exercises.

During continuing reinforcement, CRM KSAs are reinforced on a recurrent basis. Actually, the continuing reinforcement is equivalent to a recurrent cycle of the first two components with the important addition that check pilots should provide additional feedback and reinforcement to crewmembers when debriefing line checks. Through recurrent classroom curricula and LOFT in combination with line checks, crewmembers regularly receive feedback on CRM KSAs. The most important aspect of this component of training is the opportunity to reinforce CRM behaviors in the operational setting.

Why Assess CRM Training Programs?

Generally, the CRM training outcomes that have been evaluated suggest past successes (e.g., Helmreich et al., 1989b; Helmreich & Wilhelm, 1991). These findings raise questions about the role of assessment in CRM training programs. After all, if CRM training programs have been generally successful, why make further efforts to assess them? First, it is critical to determine whether the specific goals of the current training program are met. CRM training programs and the operational environments they are designed to address are not static. Therefore, training programs are continually modified to address past deficiencies, changing operational environments, and changing needs of the organization. In those organizations that have adopted CRM training on a recurrent basis, new curriculum materials are continually generated. Furthermore, changes in the aviation system, such as the transition from three- to two-position cockpit crews as well as evolving flight management systems and air traffic control (ATC) technology, require modifications in CRM training programs. As training programs change, their resemblance to their predecessors diminishes and new assessment efforts are warranted.

Second, a better understanding of CRM training curriculum and instruction can be developed through assessment. While the industry is happily on the right track with CRM training, there are still improvements to be made. For example, although CRM training programs have existed in various forms for more than a decade and have demonstrated potential, there is "insufficient guidance in the industry with respect to the key elements of CRM and for developing operationally relevant training and evaluation programs for CRM" (FAA, in press). This finding is congruent with the perception that training practices are often not grounded in theory (Tannenbaum & Yukl, 1992).

Finally, training program outcomes are affected by more than their curriculum and instruction. The predispositions of individual students and the organizations they represent can promote varied reactions to a single training program (e.g., Chidester, Helmreich, Gregorich, & Geis, 1991; Helmreich & Wilhelm, 1991; Mathieu, Tannenbaum, & Salas, 1992). Therefore, program modifications designed to make training more widely accepted are needed. There is still much to learn about this form of training.

Evaluation without Jeopardy

No discussion of CRM training assessment would be complete without emphasizing the need for anonymity of students and organizations. Training program assessment requires that highly detailed information about individual aviators be collected regarding their reactions to—and behaviors in—training and in line operations. However, CRM training is designed to provide a no-jeopardy environment where individuals and crews learn how to improve their performance. When records of performance are made to provide program evaluation information, crewmember and organizational anonymity must be maintained. Hence, data must be de-identified. An important consideration in the design of evaluation is how to collect specific information that will prove useful in evaluating the long-term effectiveness of the training without providing so much information that individuals and organizations can be identified. A balance must be struck between the organization's evaluation needs and those of crewmember and organizational privacy (e.g., the chapter by Birnbach and Longridge).

The reasons behind this are compelling. First, data that are not carefully de-identified may find their way into accident investigations and the courtroom. Legitimate or not, such practices might put individual aviators and organizations in jeopardy. Under this circumstance, the desire of crewmembers and organizations to participate in such training would likely wane. Second, under less extreme circumstances, parties other than the specific organizations providing the training are involved in routine evaluations making comparisons across different organizations. Comparisons of the strategies used in implementing CRM training and their outcomes are often central to these programs. These comparisons allow for organizations to learn from the experiences of others. However, when any two organizations are compared, some aspects will necessarily look worse in one than the other. Thus, it is imperative to maintain organizational confidentiality for these "friendly" purposes as well. Organizational anonymity can be ensured through maintenance of de-identified, off-site archives and by reporting cross-organizational comparisons that contain only summary-level data from de-identified individuals and organizations (e.g., Helmreich et al., 1989b).

MODES OF ASSESSMENT ➔

As implied above, training program assessment is conceptualized to have two modes: evaluation of training program outcomes and evaluation of training program elements (e.g., curriculum and instruction). Evaluation of outcomes focuses on determining the extent to which training programs were successful in achieving their intended results (e.g., establishment of a pre-defined level of proficiency). Program outcomes concern the effects of training on the CRM KSAs targeted by the curriculum. These outcomes may be assessed during, immediately following, or at any point after training. Delayed assessment of training outcomes helps to determine the extent to which CRM KSAs are transferred to line operations and retained between recurrent visits to the training center. Additionally, assessment of training program outcomes can focus on the individual student, the crew, the training session, the aircraft fleet, or the organization. Complete evaluation of training outcomes should focus on each of these levels of organizations.

In contrast to the evaluation of outcomes, the evaluation of training program elements goes beyond the identification of training program successes and failures. It is concerned with modifying and enhancing existing training programs through recommendations based on observations. This mode of assessment relies on the evaluation of the curriculum materials and instructional behaviors, as opposed to program outcomes. In short, it focuses on the "how?" and "why?" of training program outcomes. Additionally, evaluation of instructional behaviors is useful for the initial training and standardization of instructors.

Characteristics of students, instructors, and their organizations that exist before the onset of particular training components may moderate the effects of training program elements on training outcomes. These characteristics should be identified and investigated for a more complete understanding of training processes and outcomes. The consideration of individual and organizational characteristics constitutes an additional mode of assessment.

ASSESSMENT CRITERIA ➜

Each mode of assessment requires that specific evaluation criteria be identified and developed. Existing and proposed criteria for each mode are discussed in turn.

Training Program Outcomes

The ultimate criteria for assessing CRM training program outcomes are measures of their effectiveness in improving the safety and efficiency of air transport operations. Therefore, one obvious criterion of CRM training evaluation would be the air transport accident rate. In fact, substantial reductions in accident rates following CRM training have been reported among several rotorcraft operators as well as US Navy A-6, F-14, and Military Airlift Command operations (Alkov, 1991; Diehl, 1991). However, the use of accident rate data for the evaluation of CRM training programs has two distinct disadvantages. The first is its lack of immediately useful statistical data. The accident rate in commercial air transport operations is so low that it does not provide an immediately useful test of the effectiveness of training programs. Because of the low incidence of air accidents, data must be aggregated over many years before changing trends can reliably be determined. Therefore, the use of accident rate data requires the passage of many years between the implementation of training programs and the opportunity to assess them, leaving many unanswered questions about training program effectiveness in the interim period. The second disadvantage of this form of data is that, for this purpose, it introduces an element of ambiguity. Over time, many aspects of the air transport system are likely to change (e.g., ATC systems, CRM training, routing, regulations, equipment flown, crew complement). These changes complicate attempts at exact determination of the causal forces behind any historical trends identified in the accident rate.

These circumstances led to a search for more immediate measures of training outcomes that unambiguously targeted CRM training programs (e.g., Helmreich et al., 1989b). CRM training assessment requires more refined techniques to assess the direct or indirect effects of training programs on the KSAs they targeted (e.g., team building and maintenance, workload management, situational awareness, assertiveness, communication, and decision-making). Unfortunately, current knowledge is not advanced enough to establish definitive standards for these concepts. Lacking defined standards for CRM training outcomes, a logical alternative was to adopt the use of relative measures. Within this approach, CRM training outcomes are not judged against an external standard, but are gauged relative to their prior levels or those of a comparison group. In this way training programs can be assessed without the benefit of absolute standards.

The complexity of the training context also suggests that the use of multiple measures provides less ambiguous assessment of training program elements and outcomes as well as more reliable and more interpretable findings (Helmreich & Wilhelm, 1986, 1987). However, with the collection of multiple criteria, the issue of cost is important. Cost-effective measurement systems should provide ease of use, flexible use across training contexts, and reliable and valid data (Meister, 1985). These concerns can be met with carefully selected paper-and-pencil data collection forms (questionnaires). Questionnaires can be quickly and easily administered, (for example, to participants in training), reducing the need for extra work force for data collection. Additionally, specific questionnaires can be used in a variety of training settings or can easily be modified to meet organizational needs. Finally, responses to the items of the questionnaires can be quantified, enabling estimation of their reliability and validity as well as promoting their continued development and refinement. The NASA/University of Texas/FAA Aerospace Crew Research Project (e.g., Helmreich et al., 1989b), the Naval Training Systems Center (e.g., Naval Training Systems Center, 1991), the Army Research Institute (e.g., Simon, 1991), investigations in the nuclear power plant industry (e.g., Harrington & Kello, 1991), and the Strategic Air Command (e.g., Povenmire, Rockway, Bunecke, & Patton, 1989) have made extensive use of questionnaires in their CRM assessment efforts.

Measures of training outcomes typically address four domains: (1) motivation, (2) learning, (3) change in mental attitudes among individual students, and (4) measures of crew behaviors in LOFT and line operations. The most common evaluations of training outcomes assess changes in attitudes that result from CRM seminars and evaluations of crews' CRM KSAs in LOFT.

Student Attitudes

Aviator attitudes are typically measured before and after CRM seminars with the Cockpit Management Attitudes Questionnaire (CMAQ: Gregorich, Helmreich, & Wilhelm, 1990; Helmreich, 1984; Helmreich & Wilhelm, 1991; Helmreich, Wilhelm, & Gregorich, 1988; Irwin, 1991) or a derivative tailored to the needs of a specific operational environment (e.g., Harrington & Kello, 1991; Naval Training Systems Center, 1991; Simon, 1991). The CMAQ is a self-report measure of aviator attitudes that are empirically or conceptually related to resource management on the flightdeck. On the CMAQ, students express the degree that they agree with a series of statements on a five-point Likert-type scale where 5 signifies strong agreement and 1 signifies strong disagreement with the statement. The following is an example item from the CMAQ: "A debriefing and critique of procedures and decisions after each flight is an important part of developing and maintaining effective crew coordination."

Crew Behaviors

Crew behaviors in LOFT are generally recorded with the aid of the Line/LOS[1] Checklist (LLC: chapter by Helmreich & Foushee; Helmreich, Wilhelm, Kello, Taggart, & Butler, 1990). The LLC is used by instructors in LOFT and other evaluators in line operations to rate full crews on a set of "behavioral markers." These behavioral markers are related to the clusters of CRM KSAs identified in the FAA's Advisory Circular on CRM (FAA, in press). The markers and their descriptions provide Likert-type rating scales that experts can use to rate crew performances in a much more descriptive way than the traditional binary system that considers crews only to be satisfactory or unsatisfactory. The LLC can be used to evaluate a crew's CRM KSAs, as an aid to an instructor's post-LOFT debriefing, and in the aggregate, evaluations of crew behaviors on the LLC can be used as one measure of organizational effectiveness.

Learning and Motivation

Learning and motivation resulting from CRM training have been investigated to a lesser degree. In CRM seminars, student learning has been addressed with tests that quiz students on curriculum content (e.g., Cannon-Bowers et al., 1989; Naval Training Systems Center, 1991). For example, students may be asked to list six warning signs of reduced situational awareness both before and after training. Comparisons of pre-training and post-training responses to these questions provide one indication of learning. Learning criteria in LOFT have received almost no attention. Data collection in LOFT has predominantly focused on crew behaviors as described above. In one sense, crew behaviors in LOFT can

[1]LOS is an acronym for line operational simulation. LOFT is one element of the larger set of LOS guidelines for simulation training and evaluation.

be considered as delayed outcomes of prior CRM seminars. But, LOFT also provides a learning experience, and efforts to measure what is learned by individual crew members in LOFT should be explored. In this setting the construction of tests of learning may be less straightforward than measuring the acquisition of concepts in CRM seminars, but possibilities exist. For example, tests asking students to identify the training objectives of the LOFT session easily could be constructed. Open-ended items that ask students what they have learned also should be considered. Additionally, LOFT instructors, through consideration of their pre-briefing and debriefing of crews (see the chapter by Butler), may gain valuable insight into the knowledge of crewmembers before and after LOFT. With this information, they could provide subjective evaluations of crewmember learning.

Student motivation to use and develop the KSAs targeted in training has been assessed with Likert-type questions that essentially ask how much the training will affect their behavior in line operations (e.g., "How much will this training affect your behavior on the flightdeck?" Helmreich et al., 1988). A related type of probe is called a *buy-on*. These items measure student orientation toward CRM training and reflect the belief that a desired outcome of training is its positive regard by students (e.g., "CRM training has the potential to increase safety and crew effectiveness"). The expression of motivation and agreement on these items does not guarantee changes in student behaviors, but it is unlikely that behavioral changes would occur without this type of endorsement. Buy-ons and measures of student motivation are therefore necessary but not sufficient evidence of program success (Helmreich & Wilhelm, 1987).

Training Program Elements

Student Preferences and Reactions

Evaluations of CRM outcomes have outpaced efforts to enhance training programs through formal data collection. Typically, efforts to evaluate training program elements have focused on students' post-training evaluations of curricula and instruction. For example, the CRM Seminar Evaluation Form shown in Figure 6.1 (from Helmreich et al., 1988) is often tailored to solicit student perceptions of the seminar modules with Likert-type questions (e.g., "The module on crew dynamics was extremely useful/a waste of time"). The Naval Training System Center has also made use of this type of query following their Aircrew Coordination Training seminars (Cannon-Bowers et al., 1989; Naval Training System Center, 1991). Additionally, following LOFT, students have supplied their perceptions of LOFT scenario contents and the perceived facilitative skills of LOFT instructors (e.g., "How would you rate the value of the scenario for crew coordination training?" "Our LOFT instructor was knowledgeable and helpful,"

For each of the topic areas or training techniques listed below, please rate the value of this aspect of the training to you. Rate each item by choosing the letter on the scale below that best describes your personal opinion and then write the letter beside the item.

A	B	C	D	E
A waste of time	Slightly Useful	Somewhat Useful	Very Useful	Extremely Useful

____1. Foundations of Human Factors

____2. Accident Analyses

____3. Crew Dynamics

____4. Leadership Styles

____5. Communications

____6. Conflict Resolution

____7. Decision Dynamics

____8. Stress Management

____9. Crew Effectiveness

____10. Overall, how useful did you find the training?

____11. How important is recurrent training in aircrew coordination?

____12. How useful will this training be for other crew members?

13. Crew resource management training has the potential to increase training and crew effectiveness. (circle one)

Disagree Strongly	Disagree Slightly	Neutral	Agree Slightly	Agree Strongly

14. How much will the training change your behavior on the flightdeck?

No change	Slight change	Moderate change	Large change

15. What aspects of the training were particularly good?

_____
_____
_____

16. What do you think could be done to improve the training?

_____
_____
_____

Figure 6.1 CRM seminar evaluation form. (From Helmreich, Wilhelm, & Gregorich, 1988.)

Wilhelm, Gregorich, & Tovani, 1992). These criteria reflect student reactions to—and preferences for—training program elements.

Auxiliary Evaluators

Curriculum and instruction can be evaluated on a variety of additional dimensions other than the reactions and preferences of students. For example, additional efforts to assess LOFT scenarios and instructional techniques have just gotten under way (Butler, 1991; Gregorich, 1991). One approach makes use of auxiliary evaluators who sit in on LOFT sessions to rate the scenario and the instructor's delivery of the training session. The LOFT Evaluator Survey (LES; Wilhelm, Butler, & Connelly, 1992) shown in Figure 6.2 was designed for this purpose. For example, on the LES, auxiliary evaluators rate scenarios on the time pressure generated, creative problem-solving required, the realism of the problem, and the value for crew coordination training. Instructors are rated on their administration of the simulation and their conduct of the briefing and debriefing. Compared to CRM seminars, LOFT typically makes use of several instructors and curricula (scenarios) within each training cycle and therefore offers more comparisons among training program elements. However, similar evaluations of curriculum and instruction could be conducted across CRM seminars.

Additional Criteria: Instruction

Although instructor practices should be standardized to ensure consistency across training sessions, some variation is inevitable because of individual styles and experiences. Some variation in instructional practices can actually benefit efforts to enhance training programs because the relative effectiveness of various styles can be compared. We propose criteria for the evaluation of instructional practices that fall into four domains: management, delivery, facilitation, and evaluation. Many of these dimensions are reflected in the items of the LES. *Management* of the training session includes the establishment and enforcement of ground rules and maintaining the time schedule for the training session. The notion of curriculum *delivery* includes: (1) the instructor's knowledge of curriculum materials; (2) whether the curriculum is delivered within stated guidelines; (3) the pace, timing, and realism of delivery; (4) the instructor's ability to respond to the dynamics of the training session; (5) the instructor's credibility; and (6) the use of humor by the instructor. Instructors also should be able to *facilitate* discussion, engage students in active participation, and debrief LOFT or role-playing exercises. Finally, especially in LOFT, instructors must *evaluate* crew behaviors so as to facilitate debriefing. Additionally, instructors are a source of data about training outcomes. Therefore, their ability to evaluate crew behaviors is another attribute requiring standardization.

Airline _____ Month ____ Year ____ Rater _____
LOS ID # _____ A/C & Series _____ Number of previous LOS's by instructor? ____
PF at start of Leg 1 ____ PF at start of Leg 2 ____

Scenario ratings:		Leg 1	Leg 2
1. Workload level appropriateness for trn'g	too low 1-2-3-4-5 too high		
2. Time pressure generated	too low 1-2-3-4-5 too high		
3. Radio/Flt. Attendant comm. required	too low 1-2-3-4-5 too high		
4. Checklist activity	too low 1-2-3-4-5 too high		
5. Creative problem solving required	too low 1-2-3-4-5 too high		
6. Mechanical condition of simulator	poor 1-2-3-4-5 excellent		
7. Realism of the problem	poor 1-2-3-4-5 excellent		
8. Scenario value for **crew coord** training	poor 1-2-3-4-5 excellent		
9. Scenario value for **technical** training	poor 1-2-3-4-5 excellent		
10. *Value for addressing advanced tech*	poor 1-2-3-4-5 excellent		

Briefing:		
11. Orientation to LOS training	poor 1-2-3-4-5 excellent	
12. Instructor enthusiasm for LOS	poor 1-2-3-4-5 excellent	
13. Description of ATC/company/Flt att.	poor 1-2-3-4-5 excellent	
14. Integration of crew into the briefing	poor 1-2-3-4-5 excellent	
15. Review of CRM components	poor 1-2-3-4-5 excellent	
16. Overall quality of the briefing	poor 1-2-3-4-5 excellent	

Instructor's administration of the simulation:		
17. Simulator operation	poor 1-2-3-4-5 excellent	
18. Radio roles and communications	poor 1-2-3-4-5 excellent	
19. Adherence to published script	poor 1-2-3-4-5 excellent	
20. Flight Attendant roles and communications	poor 1-2-3-4-5 excellent	
21. Overall simulation evaluation	poor 1-2-3-4-5 excellent	

Debriefing:		
22. Establishment of debriefing rules	poor 1-2-3-4-5 excellent	
23. Keeping focus of crew on self-appraisal	poor 1-2-3-4-5 excellent	
24. Comprehensiveness of debriefing	poor 1-2-3-4-5 excellent	
25. Mix of positive and negative critique	poor 1-2-3-4-5 excellent	
26. Integration of technical and CRM	poor 1-2-3-4-5 excellent	
27. Encourage participation of all crewmembers	poor 1-2-3-4-5 excellent	
28. Use of videotape	poor 1-2-3-4-5 excellent	
29. Use of behavioral markers and CRM skill	poor 1-2-3-4-5 excellent	
30. Summarization of key points at end	poor 1-2-3-4-5 excellent	
31. Linkage to line operations	poor 1-2-3-4-5 excellent	
32. Overall effectiveness of debrief	poor 1-2-3-4-5 excellent	

Crew evaluations:		
33. Crew knowledge of CRM at briefing	poor 1-2-3-4-5 excellent	
34. Crews performance on the LOS	poor 1-2-3-4-5 excellent	
35. CRM learning expressed by crew	poor 1-2-3-4-5 excellent	
36. Avoidance of crew-imposed workload	poor 1-2-3-4-5 excellent	

Overall evaluations:		
37. Instructor's conduct of entire LOS	poor 1-2-3-4-5 excellent	
38. Session's value for **crew coord.** training	poor 1-2-3-4-5 excellent	
39. Session's value for **technical** training	poor 1-2-3-4-5 excellent	
40. Quality of the **overall training experience**	poor 1-2-3-4-5 excellent	

Figure 6.2 LOS evaluator survey. (From Wilhelm, Butler, & Connelly, 1992.)

Additional Criteria: Curriculum

Additional evaluation criteria for curricula can be explored. Some of these include: (1) the degree to which topics covered are relevant to current line operations; (2) whether targeted objectives are clearly addressed; (3) whether emphasis is on crews or teams versus individuals; (4) level of challenge, complexity, and realism of curriculum materials; (5) whether student expertise is appropriately considered; (6) whether attention is paid to fundamental principles of learning and training; (7) whether seminar elements contain lectures, videotapes, group discussion, group activities, or role-playing exercises; (8) the extent that students are engaged in active participation (e.g., Smith & Salas, 1991); and (9) whether the curriculum provides for ample and timely feedback to students. Many of these issues were noted by Tannenbaum & Yuki (1992). Some of these issues have received attention in research efforts. In LOFT, student perceptions of challenge and realism have been assessed with Likert-type items on the NASA/UT/FAA LOFT Survey (e.g., "How realistic was the scenario with regard to the problems presented?" "How much time pressure did you feel?" Wilhelm, Gregorich, & Tovani, 1992).

Individual and Organizational Characteristics

Students

Because students may react differently to training, knowledge of some of their key characteristics may provide guidance in the development of training curricula and instructor training. Several student characteristics have been demonstrated to affect outcomes of CRM seminars. These characteristics include: pre-training attitudes concerning CRM-related KSAs (Gregorich et al., 1990; Helmreich et al., 1989b); personality traits (Chidester et al., 1991; Gregorich, Helmreich, Wilhelm, & Chidester, 1989; Helmreich & Wilhelm, 1989); experience (Gregorich et al., 1989; Helmreich et al., 1988); and general perceptions and expectations of training, including pre-training buy-on to CRM (Cannon-Bowers et al., 1989; Naval Training Systems Center, 1991). The effects of these student characteristics on the outcomes of LOFT have not yet been explored. However, there is evidence suggesting that personality traits (Chidester & Foushee, 1989) and the attitudes measured by the *CMAQ* (Helmreich, Foushee, Benson, & Russini, 1986; Taylor, 1992) do affect flightdeck crew resource management. It is therefore likely that these same individual factors affect behaviors in LOFT.

Instructors

Whether the individual characteristics of instructors affect training outcomes has received less attention. However, some obvious possibilities include instructional experience and their experience teaching the current curriculum (Naval Training Systems Center, 1991), the amount of instructor training and supervision received, and their orientation toward—and beliefs about—CRM and CRM training. The importance of employing instructors that are committed to CRM training and have demonstrated CRM skills has been emphasized (Helmreich, Chidester, Foushee, Gregorich, & Wilhelm, 1989a).

Organizational Factors

Additionally, the organization itself may have characteristics that affect the outcomes of training programs. For example, Helmreich et al. (1989a) found that demonstrated organizational commitment to CRM training and endorsement by pilot's organizations or unions were important first steps in the acceptance of CRM training. Further, in commercial air carriers that had undergone a merger, the culture of aviators' pre-merger affiliation had lasting effects on their CRM attitudes as measured by the CMAQ (R. L. Helmreich, personal communication, 1987). Another perspective on measuring organizational factors is presented in the chapter by Hackman. In a cross-organizational study, Hackman has collected data describing organizational educational systems, information systems, reward systems, and cultural climate. At this time these factors have not been related to CRM training program outcomes. However, it would be valuable to extend this work into the assessment of CRM training programs.

A Framework for Assessment Criteria

This discussion has considered multiple criteria for each of three modes of CRM training assessment. These three modes embody four targets of assessment: (1) outcomes, (2) curriculum, (3) instruction, and (4) individual and organizational characteristics. Implied within the discussion was the assumption that information about the criteria is available from three distinct sources: the students themselves, the instructors, and auxiliary evaluators. The roles of students and instructors are self-explanatory. Auxiliary evaluators come in many forms, such as research teams, members of curriculum review panels, as well as non-participating observers in CRM seminars, LOFT sessions, and line operations. The flexibility of auxiliary evaluators as sources of data comes at higher cost because they represent additional work force in the training setting. Therefore, their use should be limited to those areas where both students and instructors are imperfect sources of information because of their involvement in the training process. Auxiliary evaluators are also necessary where the goal of assessment is to determine levels of behavior between subgroups of organizations (such as aircraft fleets) and among organizations.

Each source of information brings the unique perspective of its role in the training process. A matrix of the possible target/source combinations is depicted

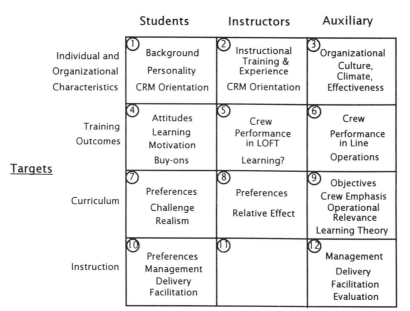

Figure 6.3 A framework for assessment criteria.

in Figure 6.3. Each cell of the matrix lists example criteria that are hypothesized to be best suited to the respective source/target pair. A rationale for the assignment of criteria to each cell of the matrix follows.

Individual and Organizational Characteristics

Especially in the measurement of their own internal states, such as personality traits and pre-training attitudes, students and instructors are especially valuable sources of information (Figure 6.3, cells 1 and 2). While they are not free of personal biases, students and instructors are obviously the most expedient source of this type of information. Other information, such as individual demographics, is also most expediently collected from students and instructors.

In some cases, data from a representative sample of students, taken in the aggregate, constitute one form of organizational-level measurement. For example, the average levels of CMAQ attitude scales within fleets and organizations have been used as one measure of organizational culture. Other measures of organizational factors are not efficiently derived from aggregating the data of individuals. Many constructs identified in the chapter by Hackman and mentioned previously are examples of non-aggregated organizational factors. In these cases, auxiliary evaluators can provide information about organizational factors of interest (cell 3).

Training Outcomes

In terms of training outcomes, students are the best source of information about their attitudes, motives, and learning (cell 4), but they are questionable sources of information about their own behavior in LOFT or in line operations (Helmreich & Wilhelm, 1988). In fact, a fundamental tenet of attribution theory is that individual appraisals of the causes of situational outcomes depend on the subject's role as an actor or observer in any given situation (Jones & Nisbett, 1972). Those with active roles are more likely to attribute their behaviors to situation factors, whereas observers are more likely to attribute the behaviors of actors to the actors themselves. Therefore, behavioral information is best collected from an observer, rather than an actor fully engaged in the situation at hand. In LOFT, the instructor can fill this observational role to assess the behaviors of the students (cell 5). In line operations auxiliary evaluators are observers (cell 6) and provide critical data on whether what was learned in training transfers to line operations and the degree to which CRM skills are retained between recurrent training cycles. For example, in line operations, check pilots can partially assume the role of an auxiliary evaluator by providing data on crew behaviors. As mentioned before, instructors and auxiliary evaluators also may be able to provide their subjective impressions about how much was learned by students in contexts where testing student knowledge is difficult or impractical.

Training Elements

In the evaluation of training program elements the situation becomes more complex because both the student and the instructor hold roles as actors and observers. Because of the role of students and their limited exposure to this form of training (at least initially), they are not qualified to evaluate objectively the instructor and curriculum materials. However, students' reactions to—and pref- erences for—curriculum and instruction are still important. Students' reactions to curriculum can include, but are not restricted to, measures of perceived challenge and realism (cell 7). Preferences and reactions to instructional behaviors could include ratings of instructor management, delivery, and facilitation of the training session (cell 10). These responses can indicate acceptance levels of the current training program to instructors and curriculum developers.

Experienced instructors bring an important perspective into the evaluation of curriculum materials. They have used various curricula and have witnessed their effects in many training sessions. Instructors therefore possess unique insight into the strengths and weaknesses of curriculum materials and their preferences for them (cell 8). This advantage increases when a variety of curricula are used within the same training cycle. Instructors may not always be able to separate the effects of curricula from their own instructional style, but their working knowledge of curricula makes them indispensable sources of information. LOFT probably has the greatest potential benefit from instructor evaluations of curricula because it typically entails the use of multiple scenarios within each training cycle. Therefore, instructors are able to compare the strengths and weakness of the scenarios they have administered.

Data describing instructor behaviors are important for both the standardization and evaluation of instructional practices. However, for the same reasons that students are poor judges of their own behaviors, instructors are in a poor position to assess their own behaviors (cell 11). Therefore, auxiliary evaluators should prove beneficial for the collection of data regarding instructional behaviors, as on the LOFT Evaluator Survey. Auxiliary evaluators are able to observe several instructors in action and can provide unique perspective into instructor evaluations (cell 12). Depending on their experience, they also may have observed a wider variety of curricula, across several fleets or organizations, than the typical instructor and may therefore bring valuable perspective in that regard (cell 9).

A MODEL OF CRM TRAINING ASSESSMENT ———— ➤

Cross-sectional and Longitudinal Designs

In the previous discussion, criteria for evaluating training outcomes within each component of training as well as the criteria for evaluating curriculum and instruction were considered independently. For training program assessment to reach its fullest potential, these criteria need to be considered more systematically. Because there are as yet no objective standards for levels of CRM KSAs, curriculum design, and instructional behaviors, assessment requires that comparisons be made to provide full benefit. Comparisons can be made with cross-sectional and longitudinal research designs. Cross-sectional comparisons are made across disparate groups (e.g., trained vs. untrained, curriculum A vs. curriculum B), whereas longitudinal analyses compare the data of individuals across time (e.g., pre-training and post-training attitudes, attitude change scores, and behaviors in LOFT). The ability to compare the outcome measures of various training sessions (cross-sectional) and the ability to track performances of individual students at various points in training (longitudinal) requires that the evaluation criteria be linked in the database.

Linking data cross-sectionally is relatively simple and inexpensive. All that is required to compare the outcomes of two curricula is that the outcome data from each training session be bundled and identified before they are entered into the database. Linking data longitudinally is more challenging. Although the cause of some confusion, the ability to link data longitudinally does not require that the anonymity of individuals or organizations be compromised. However, linking data in this way while still maintaining the confidentiality of individuals and organizations entails additional handling and is more costly than cross-sectional linking. For instance, in one organization, secret personal identification numbers were issued to crew members to link the data from individual students across various components of training while maintaining individual anonymity. With these distinctions in mind, a model for the assessment of CRM training programs is introduced (Figure 6.4).

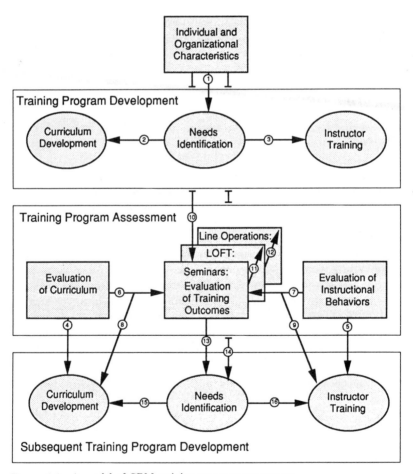

Figure 6.4   A model of CRM training program assessment.

The Model

Initial Training Program Development

Initially, an assessment of student and organizational characteristics, such as student attitudes, helps to identify the needs to be addressed by the training program (Figure 6.4, arrow 1). These identified needs in concert with training theory and the experience of experts in the training center provide guidance in the development of curricula and instructor training (arrows 2 and 3). Once the training program is initiated, data can be collected about its outcomes and elements.

Evaluations of Training Program Elements

Student reactions to CRM training and to open-ended requests for feedback have been major sources of information for enhancement of curriculum and instruction (arrows 4 and 5). Auxiliary evaluators should also be consulted for the evaluation of curriculum and instruction. By themselves, such evaluations can provide direct feedback for the design of future curricula and for instructor training. However, unless evaluations of training program elements are linked to outcome data from within the same component of training (arrows 6 and 7), feedback to training departments is of limited value. Data linked in this way allow for the establishment of cross-sectional relationships between instructional behaviors and the content of curricula with their respective outcomes. These relationships will provide more pointed and validated recommendations for enhancements of curriculum and instruction (arrows 8 and 9). Establishing relationships between training program elements and outcomes also can confirm or refute hypotheses and beliefs about CRM training. For instance, students and auxiliary evaluators may feel that instructors' use of humor facilitates student engagement and learning in a seminar, but until the use of humor is compared with its associated outcomes, the assumption is not well founded. Put another way, with cross-sectionally linked data, once more effective training sessions have been identified, the data can be used to determine the reasons behind their effectiveness.

Evaluation of Training Program Outcomes

The evaluation of training outcomes is most appropriately investigated with longitudinal designs. Training program outcomes are affected not only by training program elements, but also by individual and organizational characteristics. Individual and organizational characteristics must be longitudinally linked to training program outcomes if these relationships are to be determined (arrow 10). Further, unless outcomes of CRM training components are longitudinally linked, it will be uncertain whether what is learned in each component transfers to the next and, ultimately, to line operations (arrows 11 and 12). Although cross-sectional evaluations of training outcomes are possible, they do not provide the useful detail of longitudinal designs. Examples of cross-sectional and longitudinal designs from the evaluation of CRM seminars and LOFT illustrate this point.

In early research into CRM attitude change, as measured by the CMAQ, it was not possible to link students' pre- and post-training attitudes. Therefore, changes in attitudes resulting from CRM training could only be assessed in the aggregate; mean levels of pre-training and post-training attitudes were compared, and these analyses demonstrated positive overall attitude change. Later assessments of attitude change had the advantage of pre- and post-training measures that were linked at the individual level. Results from these data again demonstrated overall positive attitude change. However, it was also found that not all students reported positive change (Helmreich & Wilhelm, 1991). Some students did not manifest attitudinal change, while others changed in the opposite direction from that advocated in training. These data were also longitudinally linked to data describing students' characteristics. Further analyses showed that students with a particular constellation of personality traits were more likely to exhibit negative attitude change (Chidester et al., 1991; Helmreich & Wilhelm, 1991). These findings illustrate the fact that a particular pattern of aggregate or average change can coexist with highly varied patterns of individual change. Clearly, longitudinally linked data are superior in the evaluation of training outcomes. They allow for patterns of individual change to be identified, afford the potential for them to be better understood, and can provide insights into possible counter-measures that make training more universally accepted.

A somewhat different but related issue exists with respect to the evaluation of crew behaviors in LOFT. As mentioned earlier, crew behaviors in LOFT can be considered as delayed outcomes of CRM seminars. However, outcome data from CRM seminars have not been linked to evaluations of crew behaviors in LOFT. Because of this limitation, the effect of CRM seminar training on crew behaviors in LOFT was tested with a cross-sectional design. In a naturally occurring experiment, Helmreich, Wilhelm, Gregorich, & Chidester (1990) found that crews in which all members had completed a CRM seminar were more often rated as "above average" in terms of their CRM KSAs displayed in LOFT than were crews that had not completed a CRM seminar. This result provided evidence for the positive effect of CRM training on crew behaviors, but it, like early analyses of attitude change, only measured outcomes at the aggregate level. That is, specific outcomes of CRM seminars were not linked to behaviors in LOFT. Only the aggregate effects of training were tested. Many questions remain that can be addressed by linking individual outcome data across components of training: What seminar outcomes are associated with superior CRM KSAs exhibited in LOFT? Do CRM seminars enhance the CRM KSAs of all students in LOFT?

What characteristics of students are related to behaviors and learning in LOFT? Do outcomes measured in training correspond to behaviors in line operations?

Development of Subsequent Training Programs

Finally, training outcomes supplement the influence of individual and organizational characteristics on needs identification (arrows 13 and 14). These identified needs, in combination with the information available from the evaluation of training program elements, feed the development of subsequent training programs (arrows 4, 5, 8, 9, 15, and 16).

DISCUSSION ✈

CRM training continues to evolve. As experience with this form of training accumulates, the development, delivery, and assessment of CRM training will benefit. Systematic assessment plays a key role in the evolution of CRM training. We have identified three modes of CRM training program assessment, surveyed existing and proposed criteria for each, introduced a framework for the categorization of these criteria, and presented a model for their systematic integration. Taken together, the framework and model are useful for understanding the current state of efforts to assess CRM training and directions for expansion of those efforts. To date, evaluations of CRM programs across a variety of organizations have demonstrated positive impact. However, there exist opportunities for improvement in the assessment of CRM training programs, and such improvements should contribute to the understanding of current—and the development of future—training programs. Training program assessment could be advanced through the design of data collection efforts, inclusion of additional criteria, and refinement of existing criteria.

Design of Assessment

To understand patterns of the acceptance, impact, transfer, and retention of CRM KSAs, individuals' outcome measures need to be longitudinally linked across components of training. To date, this has occurred only to a limited degree. CRM seminars have demonstrated increases in targeted attitudes and motives as well as learning, but these successes have not yet been directly linked to behaviors in LOFT. What is more important, outcomes of CRM seminars or LOFT have not been linked to behaviors in line operations. Additionally, further exploration of the effects of individual and organizational characteristics on training outcomes requires linked data. Knowledge of these relationships will constitute important steps in understanding the effects of CRM training and the development of curricula and instructor training. Without the establishment of these relationships, evidence for the impact of CRM training on organizational effectiveness may be plentiful, but is indirect. Confidential, longitudinally linked data describing training program outcomes will provide direct evaluation of these crucial relationships.

Creating Additional Criteria

Besides a linked data structure, more complete evaluations of CRM training programs require that new criteria be considered. The training outcome that has received the least attention is student learning, whereas measures of student attitudes, motives, and behaviors have been more prevalent. This apparent bias against measures of learning may spring from the fact that CRM training is not academic, in the traditional sense. However, this imbalance in outcome criteria should be remedied with increased measurement of student learning that results from seminars and LOFT. Because they can be more objectively defined, measures of learning would also complement their more subjective counterparts, attitudes and motivation.

The ability of training programs to provide for both the optimal acquisition and practice of CRM KSAs is critical to the training mission. These goals require that curricula and instruction be fine-tuned to the needs of students and the organization. However, evaluations of training program elements have received less attention than outcomes. Additional opportunities exist for instructors and auxiliary evaluations to provide assessments of curricula and instructor behaviors. While these evaluations may provide key insights on their own, they also must be linked to outcome data to provide full benefit to the future development of training programs.

Refining Existing Criteria

In some cases, the identification of optimal criteria represents the fundamental challenge of assessment because the need to define and measure some CRM constructs exceeds current knowledge. Assessment must be viewed as a process of discovery, guiding future assessment. Improvements in the measurement of assessment criteria will result from better needs identification, enriched conceptualization of CRM KSAs, and advances in measurement as well as evaluation and training theories. Achieving the combination of better definitions of CRM KSAs and improved measurement methodologies will be important steps in the identification of definitive standards for CRM behaviors.

Currently, CRM assessment criteria are at various stages of development. We have discussed some criteria that have been used extensively and have been through many revisions; others have yet to be applied in training settings. Ideally, all existing and future CRM training assessment criteria will continue to evolve.

The Federal Aviation Administration's Advanced Qualification Program (AQP; FAA, 1991) promotes this process through its attention to a wide array of training issues, including the assessment of CRM KSAs (see the chapter by Birnbach & Longridge). Additionally, AQP has advanced the interaction of members of both the operational and research communities. This interaction has proven to be invaluable to the development of CRM training, including the measurement of CRM KSAs.

SUMMARY ────────────────────────────────── ✦

Assessment, when integrated into a training program, provides important information regardless of the success of that program. In the best-case scenario, assessment provides evidence that the objectives of training are being met efficiently and effectively. In the worst-case scenario, assessment can pinpoint the deficiencies of training programs and provide guidance for their improvement. Because CRM training brings many new challenges to training departments, there is much to learn from the successes and failures of current training programs. Assessment provides an important component in the development of CRM training. Each step toward more complete assessment of CRM training will provide meaningful information but will also incur additional costs. Organizations must weigh the costs and benefits of various assessment strategies to determine the system that best suits their needs. In the short term, assessment is often less expensive than the development and delivery of training. However, assessment in a recurrent training system is a long-term investment, and its value can only be gauged over the course of several training cycles.

Acknowledgments

Without the support of Federal agencies, this chapter would not have been written. Steven Gregorich's participation and research were supported by NASA (Office of Space Science and Applications) and the Federal Aviation Administration. John Wilhelm's research at The NASA/UT/FAA Aerospace Crew Research Project is supported by Cooperative Agreement NCC2-286 between NASA–Ames Research Center and the University of Texas at Austin and Federal Aviation Administration contract number DTFA-90-C-00054. Robert L. Helmreich is Principal Investigator for both research projects.

Many ideas generated in this chapter surfaced during the evaluation of components of CRM programs of both domestic and foreign major airlines, commuter carriers, freight carriers, and military units. Although complete acknowledgment would put us beyond our page limit, we acknowledge the contributions of the first individuals and organizations who trusted us with sensitive information and believed that the benefits of evaluation would outweigh the costs. Roy Butler of Pan American World Airways, Reuben Black of Delta Air Lines, Steve Walker of Alaska Airlines, and John Halliday of the 312th Military Air Squadron at Travis Air Force Base receive special thanks for their pioneering efforts at CRM training assessment.

References

Alkov, R. A. (1991). U.S. Navy aircrew coordination training: A progress report. In *Proceedings of the Sixth International Symposium on Aviation Psychology* (pp. 368–371). Columbus: Ohio State University.

Butler, R. E. (1991). Lessons from cross-fleet/cross-airline observations: Evaluating the impact of CRM/LOFT training. In *Proceedings of the Sixth International Symposium on Aviation Psychology* (pp. 326–331). Columbus: Ohio State University.

Cannon-Bowers, J. A., Prince, C. W., Salas, E., Owens, J. M., Morgan, B. B., & Gonos, G. H. (1989, November). *Determining aircrew coordination and training effectiveness.* Paper presented at the Eleventh Interservice/Industry Training Systems Conference, Fort Worth, TX.

Cannon-Bowers, J. A., Tannenbaum, S. I., Salas, E., & Converse, S. A. (1991). Toward an integration of training theory and technique. *Human Factors, 33,* 281–292.

Chidester, T. R., & Foushee, H. C. (1989). *Leader personality and crew effectiveness: A full-mission simulation experiment.* In *Proceedings of the Fifth International Symposium on Aviation Psychology.* Columbus: Ohio State University.

Chidester, T. R., Helmreich, R. L., Gregorich, S. E., & Geis, C. E. (1991). Pilot personality and crew coordination: Implications for training and selection. *International Journal of Aviation Psychology, 1,* 25–44.

Clothier, C. C. (1991). Behavioral interactions across various aircraft types: Results of systematic observations of line operations and simulations. In *Proceedings of the Sixth International Symposium on Aviation Psychology* (pp. 332–337). Columbus: Ohio State University.

Cooper, G. E., White, M. D., & Lauber, J. K. (Eds.) (1980). *Resource management on the flightdeck: Proceedings of a NASA/MAC industry workshop* (NASA Conference Publication No. 2120). Moffett Field, CA: NASA–Ames Research Center.

Diehl, A. (1991). The effectiveness of training programs for preventing aircrew "error." In *Proceedings of the Sixth International Symposium on Aviation Psychology* (pp. 28–37). Columbus: Ohio State University.

Federal Aviation Administration. (1991). *Advanced qualification program* (Advisory Circular AC 120-54). Washington, DC: Author.

Federal Aviation Administration. (in press). *Crew resource management training.* (Advisory Circular AC 120-51A). Washington, DC: Author.

Foushee, H. C., Lauber, J. K., Baetge, M. M., & Acomb, D. B. (1986). *Crew performance as a function of exposure to high density, short-haul duty cycles* (NASA Technical Memorandum 88322). Moffett Field, CA: NASA–Ames Research Center.

Gregorich, S. E. (1991). What makes a good LOFT scenario? Issues in advancing current knowledge of scenario design. In *Proceedings of the Sixth International Symposium on Aviation Psychology* (pp. 981–986). Columbus, Ohio: The Ohio State University.

Gregorich, S. E., Helmreich, R. L., & Wilhelm, J. A. (1990). The structure of cockpit management attitudes. *Journal of Applied Psychology, 75,* 682–690.

Gregorich, S. E., Helmreich, R. L., Wilhelm, J. A., & Chidester, T. R. (1989). Personality based clusters as predictors of aviator attitudes and performance. In *Proceedings of the Fifth International Symposium on Aviation Psychology* (pp. 686–691). Columbus: Ohio State University.

Harrington, D., & Kello, J. E. (1991). Systematic evaluation of nuclear operator team skills training. *Transactions of the American Nuclear Society, 64,* 182–183.

Helmreich, R. L. (1984). Cockpit management attitudes. *Human Factors, 26,* 583–589.

Helmreich, R. L., Chidester, T. R., Foushee, H. C., Gregorich, S. E., & Wilhelm, J. A. (1989a). *Critical issues in implementing and reinforcing cockpit resource management* (NASA/University of Texas Technical Report 89-5). Austin.

Helmreich, R. L., Chidester, T. R., Foushee, H. C., Gregorich, S. E., & Wilhelm, J. A. (1989b).

How effective is cockpit resource management training? Issues in evaluating the impact of pro-grams to enhance crew coordination (NASA/University of Texas Technical Report 89-2). Austin.

Helmreich, R. L., Foushee, H. C., Benson, R., & Russini, W. (1986). Cockpit resource manage-ment: Exploring the attitude-performance linkage. *Aviation, Space and Environmental Medicine, 57,* 1198–1200.

Helmreich, R. L., & Wilhelm, J. A. (1986). *Evaluating CRM training: Vol. 1. Measures and methodology* (NASA/The University of Texas Technical Report 86-8). Austin.

Helmreich, R. L., & Wilhelm, J. A. (1987). Evaluating cockpit resource management training. In *Proceedings of the Fourth International Symposium on Aviation Psychology* (pp. 440–446). Columbus: Ohio State University.

Helmreich, R. L., & Wilhelm, J. A. (1988). *Instructor and crewmember performance ratings in LOFT* (NASA/University of Texas Technical Report No. 89-4). Austin.

Helmreich, R. L., & Wilhelm, J. A. (1989). *Validating personality constructs for pilot selection: Status report on the NASA/University of Texas project* (NASA/University of Texas Technical Memorandum No. 89-3). Austin.

Helmreich, R. L., & Wilhelm, J. A. (1991). Outcomes of crew resource management training. *International Journal of Aviation Psychology, 1,* 287–300.

Helmreich, R. L., Wilhelm, J. A., & Gregorich, S. E. (1988). *Revised versions of the cockpit management attitudes questionnaire (CMAQ) and CRM seminar evaluation form.* (NASA/The University of Texas Technical Report 88-3). Austin.

Helmreich, R. L., Wilhelm, J. A., Gregorich, S. E., & Chidester, T. R. (1990). Preliminary results from the evaluations of cockpit resource management training: Performance ratings of flightcrews. *Aviation, Space, and Environmental Medicine, 61,* 576–579.

Helmreich, R. L., Wilhelm, J. A., Kello, J. E., Taggart, W. R., & Butler, R. E. (1990). *Reinforcing and evaluating crew resource management: Evaluator/LOS instructor reference manual.* (NASA/University of Texas Technical Manual No. 90-2). Austin.

Irwin, C. M. (1991). The impact of initial and recurrent cockpit resource management training on attitudes. In *Proceedings of the Sixth International Symposium on Aviation Psychology* (pp. 344–349). Columbus: Ohio State University.

Jones, E. E., & Nisbett, R. E. (1972). The actor and observer: Divergent perceptions of the causes of behavior. In E. E. Jones et al. (Eds.), *Attribution: Perceiving the causes of behavior* (pp. 79–94). Morristown, NJ: General Learning Press.

Kirkpatrick, D. L. (1976). Evaluation of training. In R. L. Craig (Ed.), *Training and development handbook: A guide to human resource development.* New York: McGraw-Hill.

Mathieu, J. E., Tannenbaum, S. I., & Salas, E. (1992). The influences of individual and situational characteristics on measures of training effectiveness. *Academy of Management Journal, 35,* 828–847.

Meister, D. (1985). *Behavioral analysis and measurement methods.* New York: Wiley.

Naval Training Systems Center. (July, 1991). *Lessons learned from the demonstration of aircrew coor-dination training methodology in the CH-53 community, 20–21 May, 1991.* Orlando, FL: Author.

Orlady, H. W., & Foushee, H. C. (1987). *Cockpit resource management training: Proceedings of the NASA/MAC workshop* (NASA Conference Publication No. 2455). Moffett Field, CA: NASA–Ames Research Center.

Povenmire, H. K., Rockway, M. R., Bunecke, J. L., & Patton, M. (1989). Cockpit resource management skills enhance combat mission performance in a B-52 simulator. In *Proceedings of the Fifth International Symposium on Aviation Psychology* (pp. 489–494). Columbus: Ohio State University.

Ruffell Smith, H. P. (1979). *A simulator study of the interaction of pilot workload with errors, vigilance, and decisions* (NASA Technical Memorandum No. 78482). Moffett Field, CA: NASA–Ames Research Center.

Simon, R. (1991). *Results of the data analysis: Army aircrew coordination measures testbed* (Dynamics Research Corporation Technical Report No. E-17639U). Wilmington, MA: Dynamics Research Corporation.

Smith, K. A., & Salas, E. (March, 1991). *Training assertiveness: The importance of active participation.* Paper presented at the 37th annual meeting of the Southeastern Psychological Association, New Orleans, LA.

Tannenbaum, S. I., & Yukl, G. (1992). Training and development in work organizations. *Annual Review of Psychology, 43,* 399–441.

Taylor, J. (1992). *The effects of crew resource management (CRM) training in maintenance: An early demonstration of training effects on attitudes and performance.* Washington, DC: Federal Aviation Administration.

Wilhelm, J. A., Butler, R., & Connelly, P. (1992). *The LOS evaluator survey.* (NASA/UT/FAA Technical Report 92-2). Austin.

Wilhelm, J. A., Gregorich, S. E., & Tovani, J. (1992). *The NASA/UT/FAA LOFT survey: A new version of an instrument to obtain participant crewmember evaluations of LOFT.* (NASA/UT/FAA Technical Report 92-3). Austin.

7

Crew Coordination and Training in the Advanced-Technology Cockpit

Earl L. Wiener
Department of Management Science
University of Miami
Coral Gables, Florida 33124

DC-9 pilots are men of steel on ships of wood. We set our sails and go. In the MD-88 you're always fiddling with something.

DC-9 Instructor

We live in a real schizophrenic situation. On one side, the aircraft industry is making full use of modern technology, integrating every possible type of computer in order to make the aircraft the safest, the easiest to fly, and the most economical, the fastest, and the most beautiful and so on. On the other side, you have the pilots, a very conservative corporation. They think they were born to fly and not to manage a modern cockpit!

Mollet (1988)

INTRODUCTION ✈

In January 1981 a group of leading authorities in the field of pilot training met at NASA–Ames Research Center to discuss the fairly recent concept of Line-oriented flight training (LOFT) (Lauber and Foushee, 1981). This meeting, which would later be regarded as a milestone in pilot training, came coincident-ally at a turning point in the history of cockpit automation. Just a few months earlier the first MD-80 (originally DC-9-80) aircraft had left Long Beach to join the fleets of regional carriers. The -80 brought to the short- and medium-haul carrier a level of cockpit sophistication previously found only in wide-body aircraft. Boeing's 767s were only months behind, propelling the aviation industry into an even higher level of flight-deck technology, the era of the "glass cockpit."

It is significant to note that at that historic meeting there was no discussion of the implications of the rapidly escalating sophistication of cockpit automation for pilot training or for LOFT. LOFT was seen as a boon to pilot training of all sorts, without regard for the level of cockpit technology. Even such esoteric topics as training for engine-out ferry flights were covered at this meeting, but the impact that automation would have on pilot training was yet to be recognized.

The participants of that meeting probably could not have imagined what lay ahead in the next decade of pilot training. In the years to follow, airline training departments throughout the world were to experience the birth pangs of the glass cockpit. They would learn that a 767 is not simply a 727 with some extra boxes, and they would struggle with higher failure rates in transition training than they had ever seen before. Not only were the world's airlines facing an industrial revolution in the cockpit, but they were simultaneously witnessing the beginning of the end of the era of the flight engineer and the three-pilot flight deck (Wiener, 1985a).

To the great credit of the industry, by the middle of the decade the problems were under control, and failure rates of crews transitioning to the glass cockpit aircraft were no greater than those usually found in conventional aircraft. The industry could begin to prepare for the rapid acquisition of new aircraft, route expansion, mixed fleets of derivative models, and equipment differences within the same models, extended twin-engine operations (ETOPS) of two-pilot aircraft over the ocean, and a tidal wave of newly hired pilots, many with less flying experience than those previously obtained. By the end of this century the glass cockpit aircraft will be not the oddballs of the fleets, but their mainstay.

All of this was occurring amid the economic uncertainties of airline deregulation, as industry and government were girding for the rapid expansion of traffic forecast into the next century (see Figure 7.1). Automation was expected to play its part by making flight not only economical of fuel and crew time, but also of that one irreplaceable asset, airspace. However, with carriers suffering from the sluggish economy in the United States, airline officials began to express doubt about the optimism of the Federal Aviation Administration's (FAA) forecasts, and some delayed or canceled deliveries of new aircraft (Ott, 1991).

Training Questions

The question that human factors professionals are most often asked by air carriers is, "What can you tell us about training for automation?" At this point, an honest answer is, "Not enough" (Lauber, 1984; Wiener, 1988b). The problem has not been systematically studied, although field studies by Renwick Curry and the author were a first step, providing insights into the difficulties and

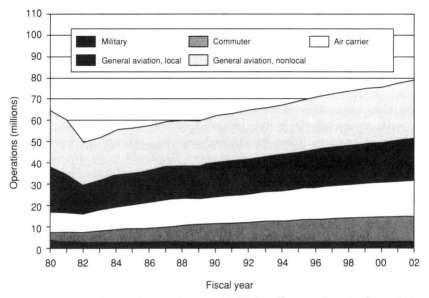

Figure 7.1 Aircraft operations at airports with FAA traffic control service from 1980 to present and forecast to 2002. (Source: FAA, 1991.)

opportunities present in training crews for highly advanced cockpit technology (see Curry, 1985; Wiener, 1985c, 1989). Now, over 10 years after the historic LOFT meeting at Ames, the question of LOFT for high-technology aircraft is only beginning to be addressed (Butler, 1991; Maurino, 1991). Helmreich summarized the situation:

> The impact of cockpit automation presents a number of challenges for future research. While we know that crews are behaving differently in advanced technology and standard aircraft, we do not yet know whether these differences are reflective of training or of characteristics of particular automation philosophies and aircraft designs. Most LOFT scenarios being used are "generic" in the sense of not being based on characteristics and capabilities of advanced technology aircraft. In particular, we know that a high percentage of incidents involving advanced technology aircraft involve interactions between the crew and Air Traffic Control [ATC]. Yet the ATC environment is not being effectively simulated in most LOFT scenarios. (1991, p. 5)

There are exceptions. LOFTs can be designed that are ATC-intensive. For example, one airline, America West, has produced an interesting scenario in which a line of thunderstorms tempts the crew to deviate from course toward a military operations area (MOA). In order to avoid penetrating the MOA, assistance from ATC is required. Realism is taken to the ultimate when a flight of fighters appears in the pilots' view.

Essentially the same argument that was made for LOFT could be made for crew resource management (CRM), although airlines are beginning to address the question of CRM programs for high-technology cockpits. Several carriers have begun to insert modules on the crew coordination and workload management required to successfully fly the high-technology cockpit into their CRM and recurrent training programs. These lessons emphasize not hardware and systems, but crew coordination demanded by automation. We should make the distinction between CRM LOFTs designed for recurrent training and those for transition training. For the sake of economy, airlines wish to keep recurrent LOFTs generic (model-independent). Transition training creates the opportunity to tailor a LOFT to the technology of the cockpit.

The following report from NASA's Aviation Safety Reporting System (ASRS) is illustrative:

> Descending on the CIVET profile descent (PD). Approx 4 NM east of CIVET, I realized we were about 13000' when, according to the PD, we should have been at or above 14000. The FMC [flight management computer] had been properly programmed for the routing, including alt instructions. Earlier in the descent the FMC, when programmed for 300 kts (per ATC), would not maintain the requested airspeed very well. At that time I requested vertical speed (VS) and used the [vertical speed control] wheel to control my descent at 1000 fpm and 300 kts. The next time I looked up the MCP [mode control panel] was operating with the speed mode selected, which confused me because I had not selected that mode. I reselected the VS mode. Again I looked back up in my scan and the speed mode had been reselected. I commented to the captain as to why the MCP kept going over to the speed mode and he informed me that he had selected it and preferred me to fly in that mode. We are both new in the aircraft. When the capt. selected SPD [speed] he had also set 10000' in the MCP, not understanding that the MCP would not capture at 14000. I was uncomfortable as well as confused, still thinking that CIVET would be captured at 14000. He went off the air to talk to company; I caught the alt deviation at 13000 and tried to correct. The controller issued instructions to amend alt to maintain 13000, and noted that on the profile CIVET should have been crossed at 14000. The capt. then proceeded to tell me how to fly every phase of the approach from then on. Contributing factors: 1) Capt. should not have been off the air at that phase of the flight. Calls should have been made earlier; 2) Two pilots fairly new to the aircraft; 3) Capt. punching buttons on the FMC without informing the PF [pilot flying]; 4)

Capt. not letting F/O fly the leg without constant flight instruction; 5) FMC should have been better understood. (ASRS No. 139884)

Philosophical Questions

The rapid development of cockpit automation, and the lack of operational doctrine by which it could be governed, led some airlines to formulate a "philosophy of automation" (Wiener, 1985a, 1985b). In 1990 Delta Air Lines adopted a one-page automation philosophy that would guide their approach to equipment acquisition, training, and operational doctrine for their rapidly growing fleet of modern aircraft. (The text can be found in the chapter by Byrnes and Black). Delta also implemented a new training course, "Introduction to Aviation Automation" ("IA^2"), which is required of all pilots transitioning to glass cockpit aircraft for the first time. It precedes ground school and is model-independent. The primary goals of the new course are to explain Delta's philosophy of automation and to relieve some of the anxieties and misconceptions that pilots often bring to ground schools for advanced technology aircraft. In 1991, prior to obtaining its first high-technology aircraft, the MD-11, Federal Express also adopted an automation philosophy and initiated a similar course, both based largely on Delta's work.

"Philosophy" may not be a familiar or comfortable word in the airline industry, but it will probably become more so in the years ahead, as airlines come to recognize that in order to manage technology successfully, policies and procedures must be based on a well-considered and consistent philosophical foundation (Degani & Wiener, 1991). To do otherwise may lead to inconsistent policies and procedures, and thence to inappropriate cockpit performance.

Automation: Human-centered or Technology-driven?

In 1979, NASA–Ames launched a program to study the human factors issues surrounding cockpit automation. Other automation research programs have been undertaken at NASA–Langley. For overviews of human factors in aircraft automation, see Billings, 1991; Chambers & Nagel, 1985; Norman, 1990; Wiener, 1988a; Wiener & Curry, 1980; Wiener & Nagel, 1988. For the views of three airline pilots regarding automation, see Demosthenes & Oliver, 1991, and Stone, 1991.

In the decade since this research began, considerable progress has been made toward understanding automation-related issues, though what has been accomplished to date is only a modest beginning. Researchers at Ames have committed themselves to a long-range effort to determine how the new cockpit environment can be made to be more human-centered (as opposed to "technology-driven"). The term "human-centered" is more than a slogan. It reflects a goal to be pursued in future generations of cockpit equipment, as well as a frustration that the present generation appears to be driven by the capabilities of technology, rather than by a careful consideration of the needs, capabilities, and limitations of the crew. As Graeber put it, "One is left with the nagging impression that the design of the cockpit is being led by technology available and not by the needs of the crew who occupy it" (1989, p. 68).

For a cockpit to be truly human-centered, not only must the hardware and software be properly designed and implemented, but also the crew must be supported by documents, checklists, procedures, operational doctrine, and training programs (including CRM and LOFT). These must be sensitive to crew needs, as well as the differences between traditional and modern cockpits.

Wiener (1989, p. 180) provides an example that he observed of the failure to heed this injunction. A computer-generated flight plan was delivered to the crew of a 757 departing Miami for Washington. The route portion read (in part), "AR-1 CLB . . . ILM . . . J-41 RIC . . ." (Atlantic route 1 to Carolina Beach, direct Wilmington, J-41 Richmond . . ."). In this form, the flight plan failed to recognize the fact that CLB is not a VHF omnirange (VOR), but a non-directional beacon (NDB), leading to confusion and high workload on the part of the crew as they attempted to enter the route into the control-display unit (CDU). What the flight management computer (FMC) wanted to see for Carolina Beach was "CLBNB," but this was not evident to the crew. The FMC repeatedly produced "not in the database" error messages each time "CLB" was entered. In brief, the ground-based computer had produced a flight plan that was not harmonious with the demands of the on-board computer of a glass cockpit aircraft. This was clearly not human-centered support of the flight crew.

Degani & Wiener (1990) point out the sensitivity of a seemingly mundane topic, checklists, to almost every aspect of equipment and procedural design. Checklists are also sensitive to certain ill-defined but nonetheless potent forces such as company philosophy and culture. In a follow-up paper, we discuss the role of procedures in flight deck management, providing an outline for procedure development based on the "Three P's": philosophy, policies, and procedures (Degani & Wiener, 1991). Our work on this is continuing, but now there are four P's, the fourth being "practices," that which actually occurs in the cockpit, which may, for a variety of reasons, differ from the stated procedures.

THE MARCH OF AUTOMATION ✈

Origins

Since the 1930s, aircraft have possessed some limited forms of cockpit automation; rudimentary autopilots were installed in aircraft of that decade.

These could hold the aircraft straight and level but could not do much more. (For a history of cockpit automation, see Billings, 1991). Progress was slow during the World War II years: scientific and engineering efforts were concentrated on airframes and power plants, which enjoyed rapid development. Avionics development brought about electronic navigational aids such as ADF (automatic direction finder) and ILS (instrument landing system), and later VORs, all of which improved navigational precision and system reliability, but these were essentially aids to manual flight. It was not until later that autopilots could acquire and track VOR radials and ILS beams. In the post-war period, flightdeck automation accelerated. Simple autopilots were replaced with more sophisticated models; later early forms of area navigation (RNAV) began to appear. Computer-based RNAV capability allowed aircraft to navigate over "oceans" of airspace rather than along "rivers" (airways). But it was not until the 1970s that cockpit automation saw explosive growth. The development of the microchip during that time brought about digital processors that were light, reliable, and flexible.

During this period integrated flight guidance systems replaced many individual boxes in the cockpit. Also, aircraft control systems became automated: autospoilers, autobrakes, and autothrottles joined hands with digital flight guidance systems that could steer an aircraft from waypoint to waypoint at a preset altitude and airspeed/Mach. More sophisticated warning and alerting systems as well as aircraft systems monitors became part of the picture. Automation was to play a major part in the emerging controversy over the two- versus three-pilot crew. With the growing sophistication of cockpit automation, there seemed less and less justification for the position of flight engineer. The issue is still debated today (Wiener, 1985a, 1988a, 1989). Although many pilots feel that two-person crews, especially on over-water flights of two-engine aircraft, represent a compromise with safety (Steenblik, 1991), most who have flown the high-technology aircraft are satisfied with the two-pilot crew station.

With the coming of ETOPS employing two-pilot, glass cockpit aircraft on long, transoceanic flights, new problems arose. Federal Aviation Regulations (FARs) call for "augmented crews" for extended flights. Flights planned for over 8 hours require a third pilot; flights over 12 hours require four. The FAR does not specify duties for the additional pilots, only that they must be there. Just what the role of the third and fourth pilot, especially the relationship between the two captains in some four-pilot operations, should be is an intriguing CRM question. The maintenance of pilot proficiency in these operations, in which pilots could make as few as one or two landings a month, is a research issue that has not been explored. At least one airline has decided not to let the two extra crew members make take-offs or landings at all, but only to fly at cruise. They have to maintain their proficiency in simulators and possibly limited flight training. These pilots have been dubbed "cruise buddies."

The Glass Cockpit

In the 1980s, with Boeing's introduction of the 767, the glass cockpit aircraft dictated the future direction of transport cockpits. These aircraft could navigate in both lateral and vertical modes and control airspeed or Mach with high precision. Traditional instrumentation gave way to computer-generated color graphics and text, and stored navigational information took much of the drudgery out of the pilot's task. Crews suddenly had available more information, more easily retrieved, than had ever been imagined. Perhaps the most remarkable feature of the glass cockpit is the ability of the crew to select or deselect features and modes of display, to configure their displays as they see fit. As an example, one of the most popular features of the glass cockpits is the pilots' ability to combine on a single display (the electronic map) both lateral navigational information and color radar. This provides the pilot with a graphic picture of the location of weather with respect to both the aircraft and the intended course of flight (or alternative courses or airports). Thus the pilot does not have to create a mental transformation of the location of the weather from one display and the world in which he or she is navigating from others, as is required in traditional aircraft.

The author (Wiener, 1988a) summarized the motivation for advancing cockpit automation, proposing eight explanatory factors:

1. Available technology
2. Concern for safety
3. Economy of operations
4. Workload reduction, and the crew complement issue
5. More precise flight maneuvers and navigation
6. Display flexibility
7. Economy of cockpit space
8. Special requirements of military missions

Questions about Automation

By the late 1970s some disturbing questions were being asked about the new technologies that were soon to appear. The House Subcommittee on Transportation, Aviation, and Weather held hearings on potential aviation safety problems that might appear at the turn of the century, and cockpit automation was listed by participants from the aviation industry and its unions. It was not clear to anyone what the "automation problem" consisted of, but only that, in the minds of the witnesses and groups that were canvassed, there existed some, albeit unspecified, potential safety problem. The Subcommittee issued its report in 1977 (U.S. House of Representatives, 1977). The question of human factors of automation was later referred to NASA and assigned to the Ames Research Center. In the summer of 1979, Renwick Curry and I were handed the task of determining just what the so-called "automation problem" entailed.

This period also saw the publication in the United Kingdom of a prophetic paper by Elwyn Edwards that alerted the human factors profession to the problems of automated flight (Edwards, 1977). Wiener & Curry (1980) later expanded on this topic in an early publication on flight-deck automation that attempted to clarify "the automation problem." This paper included 15 guidelines for cockpit automation. Shortly after the publication of this report we launched a series of field studies in cooperation with several U.S. airlines (Curry, 1985; Wiener, 1985c, 1989), focusing on the Douglas MD-80 and the Boeing 757/767. The observations and data from Wiener's (1989) field study of crews in glass cockpit aircraft form the basis for much of what appears in this chapter.

Three Pilots or Two? Or One? Or None?

The crew complement issue and its involvement with the development of cockpit automation has already been mentioned. A further discussion of this can be found in Wiener (1985a), so we need not belabor the issue here, except to say that the decision of the President's Task Force on Aircraft Crew Complement (1981) resolved one of the most important and controversial issues in modern aviation. The Task Force decreed that modern airliners, including wide-body models, could be staffed safely by two pilots, unaided by a flight engineer. Many of the functions performed by the flight engineer, primarily systems monitoring, could be turned over to computers.

The three-person crew is now a disappearing phenomenon in commercial aviation; three-pilot aircraft are being retired from airline fleets as modern, two-pilot models arrive. To speak of CRM is increasingly, and some day in the near future will be exclusively, to speak of a two-pilot crew.

At some distant time the possibility of a one-pilot crew for aircraft of the general type and size presently served by two or three pilots may surface. Indeed, Wiener & Curry (1980) have pointed out that an unmanned airliner is technologically, but not socially, feasible. For a concurring opinion, see Demosthenes and Oliver (1991). Technology notwithstanding, it seems safe to say that at least well into the next century, even with the potential of industry to develop intelligent computer capability not yet imagined, airliners will be flown by two pilots, and the remainder of this chapter is based on that assumption.

RESEARCH IN CRM AND COMMUNICATION IN THE HIGH-TECHNOLOGY COCKPIT ————————————————— ✈

The premise of this chapter is that the flightdeck equipment and configuration materially affect the quality and perhaps quantity of communication and crew coordination in the cockpit. And it does so in ways that at this date are not well charted. Unfortunately there is scanty literature on this subject, mainly based on observations taken during various field studies. Empirical investigations into the influence of cockpit technology on crew coordination are only now beginning to appear.

The presumption is that tasks involved in piloting a high-technology aircraft are substantially different from those of a traditional aircraft, and this in turn influences the crew's communication patterns, and perhaps more important, their coordination as a team.

Evidence for this assumption comes from five methodological sources.

1. Non-systematic observations of operations performed by human factors scientists in simulators and line flying (Curry, 1985; Wiener, 1985c, 1989). Let us be clear that information gained by observations is not in the usual sense "scientific data," but nonetheless it is valuable for gaining insights into crew behavior. These insights may provide the basis for experimental approaches, which will be discussed shortly.

2. It is possible for systematic observations to be taken in flight during actual revenue trips. These would shed light on the question at hand under the realistic line and ATC environments, which can be approximated but never truly duplicated in simulator experiments. See the chapters by Helmreich & Foushee and Butler for a discussion of the collection of observational data. The difficulties and disadvantages of obtaining data from line operations are obvious. For example, the experimenter and the data collection demands of the experiment must be totally unobtrusive; and in contrast to simulator experimentation, he or she must accept the conditions of the flight as they occur. Weather, ATC, diversions, mechanical problems, cabin problems, crew pairings, changes in procedures, and even on-board equipment are all part of the game. The experimenter may think that he or she has designed a "controlled experiment" but in fact has little control over what transpires. The experimenter must accept these conditions and adjust to deviations from the experimental plan as surely as the crew must adjust to changes in their flight plan. The cockpit of a revenue flight is no place for experimental purists.

Two examples are studies by Costley, Johnson, & Lawson (1989) on the quantity of cockpit communication as a function of cockpit type (757, 737-300-EFIS, and 737-200 traditional), and by Lyall (1990), who was investigating mixed-fleet operations of pilots who were flying both the B-737-200 and the more advanced -300 model.

3. Controlled experiments may be conducted in flight simulators. This approach allows the investigation of treatment variables that might not be feasible in line operations or even actual simulator training. A recent study by Wiener, Chidester, Kanki, Palmer, Curry, & Gregorich (1991) compared crew perfor-

mance on a specially written LOFT in two aircraft in the same family but with vastly different cockpit technologies: the traditional DC-9-30 and the glass cockpit MD-88 (DC-9 derivative). More is said about this experiment later in the chapter. Another study of note was conducted at Boeing by Rogers, Logan, & Boley (1989), in which crew error performance was compared in B-737 EFIS and traditional 737 simulators.

4. Questionnaires may be administered to airline pilots, either as stand-alone studies (James, McClumpha, Green, Wilson, & Belyavin, 1991), or as part of more inclusive field studies (e.g., Curry, 1985; Sarter and Woods, 1991; Wiener, 1985c, 1989).

5. Examination of accident and incident databases, such as the NASA ASRS database, provides investigators with insights into typical operational problems.

Examples of the use of each of these five methodologies follow.

Non-systematic Observations

From 1985 to 1988 the author undertook an extensive study with two airlines of the human factors of the glass cockpit (Wiener, 1989). One chapter of his report focused on crew coordination and communications and attempted to describe what the author believed to be genuine differences in this area between advanced and traditional-technology aircraft. As mentioned above, these are observations and generalizations, not experimentally generated data. There was no low-technology aircraft control group per se, only the author's familiarity with operations in both types of aircraft.

The following is taken from the 1989 report and summarizes crew coordination and communication observed in crews operating glass cockpit aircraft.

1. Compared to traditional models, it is physically difficult for one pilot to see what the other is doing. In first-generation jet aircraft, the setting of the autopilot and other modes could be observed easily by both pilots; likewise in the second generation, where most of the selections were made on a mode control panel (e.g., DC-10). But on the glass cockpit models, the important selections are made in the CDU, as well as the mode control panel (MCP), and this is not visible to the other crew member unless he or she selects the identical CDU page or leans across the pedestal to observe the first officer's CDU, as many captains do. Though some carriers have a procedure that requires the captain (or pilot-flying, PF) to approve any changes entered into the CDU before they are executed, this is seldom done; often he or she is working on the CDU on another page at the same time. Segal (1990) has discussed the communication inherent in observing the movements of another crew member as he or she interacts with cockpit devices and the impact of the new technology on this channel of communication. His

conclusions are essentially the same as mine: that the new technology diminishes this form of intra-cockpit communication.

2. It is more difficult for the captain to monitor the work of the first officer and to understand what he is doing, and vice-versa.

3. Automation tends to induce a breakdown of the traditional (and stated) roles and duties of the PF versus pilot-not-flying (PNF) and a less clear demarcation of "who does what" than in traditional cockpits. In aircraft in the past, the standardization of allocation of duties and functions has been one of the foundations of cockpit safety.

4. The modern cockpit seems to induce a redistribution of authority from the captain to the first officer. Automation may enable first officers, even when performing as PNF, to make decisions (e.g., when to slow the aircraft on descent into a terminal area) that previously were the prerogative of the captain. This is unintended and is a result of the fact that experienced first officers are often more proficient than their captains in data entry into the CDU. The captain, particularly in times of high workload, may surrender some authority to the first officer just to get the job done. Often the captain recognizes the superior CDU skills of the first officer and utilizes them to advantage.

For an experiment employing a GAT (general aviation trainer) simulator that tends to validate this finding, see Wickens, Marsh, Raby, Straus, Cooper, Hulin, & Switzer (1989). They showed that with use of the automation, the "authority gradient" between the pilot and copilot tends to be shallower.

5. There is a tendency for the crew to "help" each other with programming duties when workload increases. This may or may not be a good thing; it is difficult to say. But it clearly tends to dissolve the clear demarcation of duties when one pilot says "here, I'll do that for you" and rushes to the CDU or MCP. Computer-based systems seem to invite such behavior. The same pilot who gladly jumps in and performs duties assigned to the other pilot in a high-technology plane probably would not be tempted to do the same in a traditional aircraft, for example controlling cabin pressurization in a DC-9. Since there is usually little to do at cruise, when computer input is required there may be a race to see who gets to make the entry. A good example is an amended clearance direct to some waypoint, requiring an entry on the Direct Intercept page.

In summary, the highly automated cockpit may require special scrutiny for crew coordination and cockpit resource management, both in the assignment of tasks and standardization of their performance. This may prove to be particularly important in the likely event that pilots with the least experience may soon, at some carriers, be assigned to the most sophisticated cockpits (Wiener, 1989, pp. 177–178).

Indeed, this last prophecy has come to pass. British Airways has assigned a group of low-time, ab initio trainees as first officers in their most sophisticated aircraft, the A-320. Informal reports on this program indicate successful results.

The necessity for effective crew communication and coordination in the high technology aircraft was put well by an experienced 767 captain:

> Standardization of cockpit operations is critical in the new technology aircraft. More than ever, pilots can change configuration or operating parameters without the other pilot being aware of the change. This is not done out of maliciousness but rather as a consequence of system needs. ATC communications, aircraft reconfiguration, or other demands put pilots in a position where each must act independently at times. It is imperative in these occasions for each to understand what the other pilot has done. This type of cockpit communications is the essence of cockpit resource management courses prevalent in many air carrier training curricula. (Stone, 1991, p. 5)

Experimentation and Systematic Observation in Flight

The question of how cockpit configuration might affect in-flight communications was investigated on actual revenue flights in a study by Costley et al. (1989) in the United Kingdom. A trained observer rode in the jumpseat and recorded the frequency and classification of each type of oral communication. Three types of two-pilot aircraft were employed: 737-200 (traditional instrumentation), 737-300, and 757 (both with EFIS; electronic flight instrument system).[1]

We should regard these results as instructive, but, as previously discussed, studies involving line flights are difficult to control experimentally and cannot be judged by the rigorous standards of the laboratory. Two of the 19 flights were conducted at night. The durations of the flights varied from less than 1 hour to over 4 hours. Crews were not independently or randomly selected; one pilot flew as first officer on six of the seven B-757 flights and also flew as captain on one of the 737-300 legs. There were no statistical tests of contrasts between the three models studied.

Data were collected by the observer during three phases of flight: climb, cruise, and descent. Communications prior to "gear up" and following "gear down" were not recorded. Rates of communication for the two EFIS aircraft are provided in percentage relative to the baseline aircraft, the 737-200. Thus positive figures mean more utterances than the 737-200, negative per cent figures indicate fewer. These are displayed in Figure 7.2.

The results are somewhat difficult to interpret. The data indicate that

[1]The 757 was regarded by Costley et al. as a more automated aircraft than the 737-300 (EFIS). In fact, this is a difficult determination, as neither is uniformly "more automated." Each has capabilities that the other does not. For example, both have Category III approach capability, but only the 757 has the auto-rollout feature. Conversely, the 737-300 has 4-dimensional navigation capability (ability to arrive at a waypoint in 3-D space at a programmed time); the 757 does not.

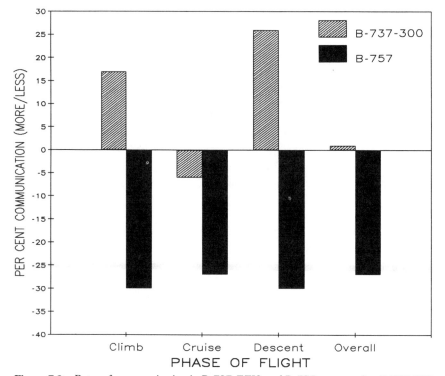

Figure 7.2 Rates of communication in B-737-EFIS and B-757 compared to B-737-200 baseline (traditional technology). (From data in Costley et al., 1989.)

overall there is far less communication in the advanced cockpit. However, the 737-300 data do not support this. Unlike the 757, the 737-300 crews showed considerably more communication during climb and descent than those flying the more primitive 737-200, but slightly less in cruise. The "overall" figure shows little difference between the aircraft probably because it is based on a lengthy cruise phase, which tends to dilute the influence of the more critical climb and descent phases. The authors report overall communication rates that are "almost identical." (Note: in constructing the graph I interpreted this as zero difference.)

It comes as no surprise that in the cruise phase of flight, pilots in both EFIS aircraft communicated less than those in the traditional-technology 737-200. This phenomenon has been noted by other observers, but it has never before been quantified. The automation of the EFIS aircraft reduces workload at cruise to a very low level. With pre-programmed lateral and vertical navigation and power plant control, crew duties are cut to a level probably not previously seen in aviation. In fact, the low workload at cruise for EFIS aircraft is of concern to manufacturers and operators because of the presumed vulnerability of crews to boredom and complacency (Wiener, 1987; Graeber, 1989).

It is intriguing and contrary to expectations that during the periods of high workload, climb and descent, the 737-300 pilots were more communicative than those in the 737-200. I recently observed a 757 crew on a flight from Atlanta to Washington National. From the "out of FL 180" call on climb-out until passing Richmond and preparing for the arrival into Washington, not a word was spoken! The only intra-cockpit communication the author could observe was between each pilot and his CDU.

We should recognize that it is a yet-unproven belief that the quality of crew performance is positively correlated with the amount of intra-cockpit communication. Foushee and Manos (1981), in their communication analysis of Ruffell Smith's (1979) tapes, first reported a correlation between the amount of crew communication and various measures of the quality of the crew. Although Helmreich, Chidester, Foushee, Gregorich, & Wilhelm (1989b), in their cogent review of CRM effectiveness, have stated (p. 8), "a fair summary of these findings would be that superior performing crews communicate more and better than less effective teams," I would raise two points of caution.

First, observers who rated the quality of the LOFT flights on which this conclusion is based may have viewed "more" and certainly "better" communication as a sign of superior crew performance per se. Thus, it may be tautologically true that "good" communication is correlated with "good" performance ratings. The quality and quantity of crew communication may be very different issues. I feel that as communication research continues, we will find this to be true.

Second, we should note that the studies from which Helmreich et al. reached this conclusion were all performed in simulators of traditional-technology cockpits, some two-pilot, some three. Even if their conclusion, particularly about the quantity of communication, is true for these aircraft, it may not hold for advanced-technology flight decks. The demands of the modern cockpits may simply be qualitatively different, so that higher amounts of conversation may be neither necessary nor desirable. As I have noted, much of the communication is between pilot and computer, and I am hesitant to conclude, pending further evidence, that quantity of communication is a hallmark of a good crew. Some answers to this question will come from the work of Barbara Kanki and her collaborators, to be reported in future volumes of the study by Wiener et al. (1991). See also the chapter by Kanki & Palmer.

Controlled Experiments in Simulators

In 1988 a team of human factors scientists from NASA–Ames Research Center and two contractors launched an experimental investigation into the effect of cockpit automation on crew communication, crew coordination, and performance (Wiener et al., 1991). The study was motivated by the unstructured observations (Wiener, 1989) previously mentioned. The goal was to provide experimental data that would examine those observations on the influence of automation on crew performance and communication and the conclusion that if there are differences in crew factors due to cockpit technology, they should be addressable by CRM training. This study also provides an example of a LOFT scenario that challenges the skills of the crews of both traditional and glass cockpit aircraft.

This discussion is included here only as an example of simulator-based experimentation into the influence of cockpit technology on crew factors, since the primary results, those dealing with crew communication and coordination, have not yet been published. Volume 1 (Wiener et al., 1991) covers the purpose and plan of the study, questionnaire data, and results from the LOFT experiment dealing with workload, self-reports of stress, and errors. Future volumes will deal more extensively with crew error, workload, procedures, and communication.

The purpose of this study was to examine jointly cockpit automation and group processes. Automation was varied by the choice of two radically different versions of the DC-9 series aircraft, the traditional DC-9-30 and its glass cockpit derivative, the MD-88.

The LOFT involved flights by DC-9-30 and MD-88 from Atlanta to Columbia, South Carolina. The crew is beset with electrical problems from the start, and an advancing cold front lay northwest of course, with deteriorating weather forward of the front (see Figure 7.3). During the flight to Columbia a generator constant speed drive overheats, which requires that the system be monitored by the crew. Then the weather at Columbia goes below Category II minimums during the approach. Due to a no-radio aircraft in the area, ATC gives the crew an unpublished missed approach and unpublished holding pattern on the Columbia VOR, creating, in combination with the electric problem, a critically high workload.

The goals of the study were achieved by comparing various performance measures of the crews in dealing with the situations introduced by the LOFT and particularly by examining the effect of the automation (two models of the same aircraft) on crew performance, coordination, and communication. The simulator runs were videotaped and examined in detail. In addition, two experts—the LOFT instructor and a line-qualified pilot-observer—rated crew performance, and the crew rated their own performance and perception of workload. Errors in procedures were also recorded, analyzed, and classified according to three levels of severity. Attitude questionnaires were administered to all members of the volunteer group, those who flew the LOFT as well as those who did not. The items on the attitude scale dealt primarily with cockpit equipment, automation, training, and CRM issues.

Results (Figure 7.4) show that the performance differences between the

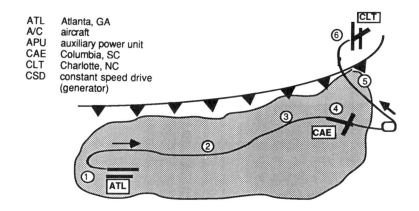

ATL	Atlanta, GA
A/C	aircraft
APU	auxiliary power unit
CAE	Columbia, SC
CLT	Charlotte, NC
CSD	constant speed drive (generator)

1 **Departure**	2 **Cruise to CAE**	3 **Initial Approach to CAE**	4 **Approach/Miss Approach**
1. Fog ahead of cold front causing low visibility in ATL (at alternate minimums) and CAE (CAT II). 2. Dual alternates: ATL, CLT (VFR). 3. At gate, A/C on ground electric power, APU, will not start until mechanic starts it.	1. Normal, low workload period.	1. Problem: left CSD temperature warning light illuminates. 2. Checklist completion indicates approach and CSD operation can continue but CSD temp. must be monitored.	1. Weather deteriorates requiring miss. Another A/C is in published holding pattern so crew must enter non-published holding. 2. CSD overheats and fails upon entering holding. APU will not restart. High workload begins.

5 **Cruise to Alternate**	6 **Landing**
1. Crew must choose an alternate: ATL or CLT. CLT is best (ATL will deteriorate if the crew heads there). 2. High workload period: completion of CSD shutdown, electrical off-loading, preparation for landing.	1. Relatively routine approach to Runway 5, if procedures have been completed effectively. 2. Concern about possible failure of second generator.

Figure 7.3 Schematic of LOFT scenario in experiment by Wiener et al. (1991).

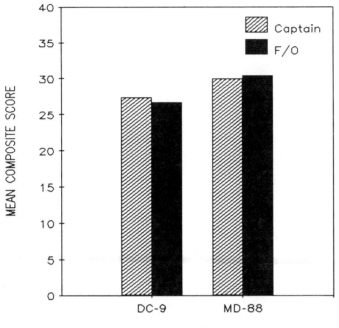

Figure 7.4 Results of self-assessed composite workload scale taken by crews of DC-9-30s and MD-88s in experiment by Wiener et al. (1989). High numbers indicate high workload. Differences between aircraft crews are small but statistically significant; differences between seats (captain vs. first officer) are not.

crews of the two aircraft were generally small, but where there were differences, they favored the DC-9. There were no measures on which the MD-88 crews performed better than the DC-9 crews. Furthermore, DC-9 crews rated their own workload as lower than did MD-88 pilots and reported less stress and less physical fatigue. While both groups were about equal in total flying experience, the experiment was confounded by the fact that the DC-9 pilots were more experienced in type, and it is difficult to isolate the effects of this factor. There were no significant differences between the two aircraft types with respect to the severity of errors committed during the LOFT flight. The attitude questionnaires provided some interesting insights but failed to distinguish any differences between DC-9 and MD-88 pilots.

Questionnaire Data

We shall briefly consider questionnaire data pertaining to pilot opinion on automation and crew coordination. This has been a topic of great interest in questionnaire research in recent years in the United States, Great Britain, Germany, New Zealand, and elsewhere. Unfortunately, for purposes of this chapter, most of the surveys have concentrated on cockpit equipment, attitudes toward automation, and pilot–machine relations, to the exclusion of queries about human–human interaction. Listed in Table 7.1 are a number of questionnaire studies either published or in preparation at this time.

It would be impossible to discuss all of these studies, which produced vast amounts of data; a representative sample is provided below. All the data displayed graphically are based on the use of Likert-type attitude scales. These are intensity scales which allow the respondent to indicate his or her agreement or disagreement with a statement ("probe"), which may be stated positively or negatively. The respondent replies as to his or her degree of agreement or disagreement, on an odd-numbered scale, with usually five or seven response categories ranging from strong agreement to strong disagreement. The middle response category does not have an exact meaning. It can represent neutrality, or no opinion, or equal agree/disagree sentiment.

Two almost identical probes from two studies by Wiener (1989) and Wiener et al. (1991) are displayed in Figure 7.5. In Figure 7.5a two variables represent two replications of surveys distributed to a single group of volunteer 757 pilots. The replications were separated by 14 months. In Figure 7.5b the two groups are pilots flying the DC-9-30 and MD-88 (DC-9 derivative) at one airline. In neither case was the difference between the groups statistically significant. (Note the inadvertent difference between the two probes, the words *easier* and *easy*).

The study by James et al. (1991) in the United Kingdom yielded a vast

Table 7.1

Questionnaire Studies in Cockpit Automation

Author	Date	Type of aircraft	Items on crew coord.?
Wiener	1985c	MD-80 (DC-9-80)	Yes
Curry	1985	B-767	Yes
Morters	1988	B-767	No
Wiener	1989	B-757	Yes
Heldt	1989	737-300, A310	No
Clothier	1991	Various	Yes
James et al.	1991	Various	Yes
Wiener et al.	1991	DC-9-30, MD-88	Yes
Sarter & Woods	1991	B-737-300	No
Helmreich et al.	1988	Various	Yes[a]

[a] Six items dealing with automation were added to the 1991 version of the NASA/University of Texas Cockpit Management Attitudes Questionnaire (CMAQ).

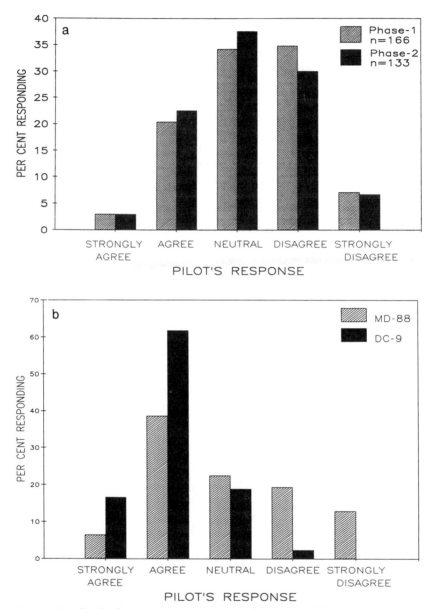

Figure 7.5 Results from questionnaires in two field studies. (a), "In the B-757, it is easier for the captain to supervise the first officer than in other planes" (Wiener, 1989). (b), "In the DC-9/MD-88, it is easy for the captain to supervise the first officer" (Wiener et al., 1991). Note the inadvertent use of (a) "easier" versus (b) "easy" in the two probes.

amount of questionnaire data from four groups of pilots: those currently flying helicopters, traditional cockpit transports, advanced (CDU but non-EFIS) transports, and advanced (EFIS) glass cockpit transports.

A total of 78 Likert probes were used, six of which dealt with crew coordination. I have plotted the data from one of the probes for the glass cockpit group in Figure 7.6. Note that the question and the data are not in the customary Likert scale form. The results of James et al. essentially agreed with those of Wiener (1989) and Wiener et al. (1991). Where there were differences, the pilots in the United Kingdom have expressed a somewhat more positive attitude toward automation than their U.S. counterparts.

As a final example of questionnaire data, a figure from Sarter & Woods's (1991) study of Boeing 737-300 (EFIS) pilots is included (see Figure 7.7). One of the aims of this study was to compare results of their attitude scales to data from Wiener's earlier (1989) study of B-757 crews. They plotted data for both experienced and less experienced pilots separately. Only one such plot is shown; it

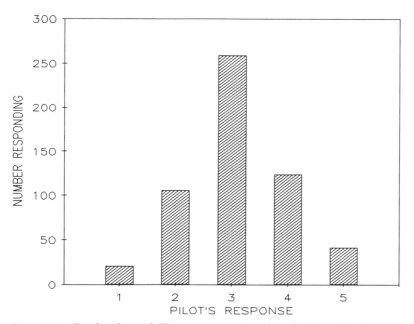

Figure 7.6 Results of one of 68 items on questionnaire administered to large sample of pilots by James et al. (1991). The probe read: "Automation greatly decreases/increases the quality of crew communication." The format was a modified semantic differential scale. At the left side, the probe contained the word "decreases," and on the right "increases." Numerals 1 to 5 lay between. Thus the low numbers represent belief that automation decreases communication, and vice versa. (From data supplied by M. James.)

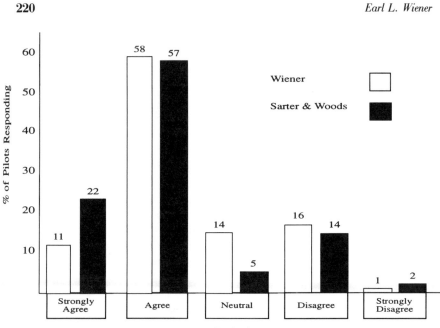

Figure 7.7 Data from Sarter & Woods (1991; $n = 97$), in which they compared results from their sample of B-737-300 pilots with Wiener's (1989; $n = 166$) results with B-757 pilots. The questionnaires were administered several years apart, at different airlines. The probe read, "In the -300 automation there are still things that happen that surprise me." (For Wiener, the probe substituted "B-757.")

indicates a high level of agreement between the two studies. Sarter & Woods's questionnaire data showed a striking similarity to that reported by Wiener, more so than did the British data reported by James et al. (1991).

Incidents from Reporting System Databases

The following example illustrates the type of report that can be accessed from various reporting system databases (e.g., NASA ASRS in the United States, CHIRP (Confidential Human Incident Reporting Program) in the United Kingdom.

Another altitude bust in a brand new aircraft! I've never in my career had so many alt busts until I got in this airplane. The scenario is all too familiar. One pilot involved in approach phases miscellany (ATIS, checklist, etc.), the other pilot trusting the autopilot to make the level off and getting involved in something else at the last minute. Next is the sound of the alt warning and a mad scramble to level the aircraft off before ATC notices. This time we made it down to 500′ too low due to a high rate of descent engendered by a crossing restriction given too close in by ATC. My fault for assuming that the F/O had it under control. His fault for assuming the autopilot had it. The designers/flight managers/flight instructors (etc.) fault for encouraging max utilization for the autopilot which has the net effect of taking the pilot out of the loop in spite of your best intentions. Human beings are not good "monitors" of machinery. The mind tends to wander if there is no need to actively control the process. (ASRS No. 144385)

AUTOMATION AND CREW COORDINATION ─────── ➔

Does Cockpit Technology Create a Difference?

Training experts in the airline industry and in government have generally assumed that CRM training programs are essentially model-independent: Identical training was delivered to all pilots at a given airline, regardless of the model they were or would be flying. The efficacy of this can no longer be accepted as true without proof, as there is mounting evidence that crew coordination and communication in the glass cockpit aircraft is qualitatively different from that in the traditional cockpit. If this proves to be the case, then at the least modules of CRM programs should be devoted to crew resource management in the advanced-technology aircraft. Such a move would be logical and consistent with Guideline Number 4 for CRM training proposed by Helmreich, Chidester, Foushee, Gregorich, & Wilhelm (1989a): "Customize the training to reflect the nature and needs of the organization." To their words I would only add, "and the generic type of cockpit technology as well."

Empirical Studies

The next step is to establish research that confirms the hypothesis that crew communication and coordination is indeed different in advanced cockpit aircraft, and that customized CRM is worthy of consideration. Regrettably the research to support this hypothesis has not advanced as rapidly as interest in this question. At this time there is no solid experimental evidence that these presumed differences actually exist, let alone that they are worthy of, or addressable by, a tailored CRM program for advanced-technology aircraft. The author's study of 757 crews points in this direction but could not by itself be taken as a warrant to launch a CRM program in automation.

Orlady (1989) has reported the results of a telephone survey of pilots of advanced-technology aircraft reporting incidents to the ASRS. About 40% of his respondents state the opinion that there are no differences in the CRM principles for advanced aircraft, while 40% report that there are "substantial differences." The remaining 20% did not hold an opinion. A typical example of lack of coordination in the advanced cockpit is seen in the following ASRS report. Such a problem might be addressable by a CRM program.

> Flt. was dispatched from Denver (DEN) to Burbank (BUR) with right wing/body overhead system inop. Continuously flickering caution lights associated with system were very distracting. Approaching the Palmdale (PMD) VOR we received a clearance from Los Angeles Center to descend from FL240 to 14000'. I initiated a V-nav [vertical navigation] descent predicated on crossing JANNY intersection at 8000 per the LYNXX 5 arrival to BUR. Shortly after the clearance was amended to cross 10 mi. E of PMD at 14000. I created a waypoint of 10 W of PMD. I immediately realized my error and attempted to put in corrected waypoint and re-strictions. My F/O, new on the aircraft, took over on the CDU and in trying to oversee her attempts to get the waypoint inserted I did not get the acft on the proper descent profile, resulting in crossing 10 E of PMD 1500–2000 feet high. The primary factor I feel was not flying the acft instead of attempting to program and/or supervise the F/O. A contributing factor was the constant distraction of the caution light. Caution: do not be dis-tracted by the FMC! (ASRS No. 139213)

Should the findings from the simulation experiment with the DC-9 and the MD-88 show significant differences in crew coordination and communication between the two aircraft, then these results would call into question the assump-tion of model independence in CRM training and possibly motivate the develop-ment of CRM modules tailored for the modern aircraft. Furthermore, this study may do more than simply justify the effort—we hope that it will point toward the directions the effort should take. Since this investigation involved a LOFT flight, it may also shed light on the manner in which LOFTs in high-technology aircraft might differ in design and conduct from the traditional aircraft.

Finally, we note that the answer may not lie in special CRM modules but in designing LOFT scenarios that are adaptable to and appropriate for a wide variety of cockpit environments.

IMPLICATIONS FOR LOFT ——————————————— ✈

Little has been written about the implications of the high-technology cock-pit for the design and conduct of LOFT (Butler, 1991 and his chapter; Helmreich et al., 1989b). I have argued in this chapter and elsewhere that the modern cockpit may require tailored CRM programs or modules. The same question must be raised about LOFT scenarios. Until this picture is clarified by a systematic approach, presumably involving cooperation between researchers and airline training centers, the incorporation of LOFT techniques tailored to the new cockpits may be difficult and may show slow progress.

Utilization of LOFT techniques may appear in transition training, where the issue may be forced by the needs to adapt to a new cockpit. Automation-specific scenarios will be adopted more slowly in recurrent training, where economic considerations continue to dictate model-independent scenarios.

Opportunities and Difficulties

The high-technology cockpit, with its strengths and weaknesses, offers novel opportunities for scenario design. For example, in traditional aircraft it has been necessary to induce abnormal conditions (e.g., system failures) in order to elevate the workload and stress on the crew in a realistic manner, in order to create a situation which demands crew coordination. Thus their proficiency at coping with these conditions can be evaluated as well as preserved on videotape for self-evaluation. The modern cockpit has enough normal, built-in stressors to do the job, particularly in the area of ATC instructions. (For a discussion of the mismatch between ATC capabilities and glass cockpit capabilities, see Wiener, 1989, chap. 9).

One cannot disagree with Foushee and Helmreich when they write (1988, p. 221), "unlike the real world, LOFT scenarios are usually designed to include emergency situations which require the coordinated actions of all crew members for success." However, the argument could be made that the glass cockpit presents new opportunities for scenario design that do not require emergencies per se, just difficult problems at the human–automation interface. Any pilot of a glass cockpit aircraft will be happy to tell you what they are.

Automation-Rich LOFT Scenarios

The resourceful LOFT designer therefore has new tools to work with, and these clearly meet the criteria of realism and line validity. One highly experienced LOFT designer (Neil Johnston, personal communication, 1991) remarked to me that the best LOFT he had ever constructed contained a single failure: The autopilot dropped off early in the flight and could not be restored. This failure produced implications for the remainder of the flight.

Consider the following example, which I observed in a glass cockpit aircraft departing San Jose, California (SJC) for a southeastern destination. After departing from SJC and completing the first part of the LOUPE departure (which in itself was at that time a tangled procedure creating a workload problem in any aircraft; it has since been somewhat simplified), the following clearance was issued: "After Wilson Creek, direct 37 degrees 45 minutes north, 111 degrees 05 minutes west, direct Farmington, as filed."

When the crew attempted to create the waypoint by entering the coordinates (latitude, lat; and longitude, lon) into the Legs page of the CDU, they experienced considerable trouble due to the fact that the sequence of the clearance did not conform to the format required by the CDU. For example the clearance as transmitted places the hemisphere ("N" and "W") *after* the coordinates; the CDU demands that it come first. The crew tried one format after another, with growing frustration. Both were "heads down" in the cockpit for a considerable time trying various formats for data entry. At one point the crew's input of the coordinates had five errors of three different types. Finally, the captain arrived at a solution: he told the first officer to fly the plane while he searched through other pages in the CDU, hoping to find the correct format for a lat and lon waypoint to use as a model. His solution represented true "resource management." Information readily at hand, several CDU pages containing lat/lon formats for another purpose, was used to solve the problem. In brief, the unexpected and unfamiliar lat and lon waypoint created a high workload and a compelling demand for effective crew coordination. Just why the controller felt the need to issue a lat and lon waypoint, when he could have given bearing and distance off of a nearby VOR (which is easy to enter into the CDU), is not clear. In issuing such a complex clearance, the controller was not only burdening the crew but was also making trouble for himself.

A LOFT designer could hardly improve on this "scenario." Of course, one could argue that the difficulty encountered here was a training problem, that the crew should have known how to enter a lat and lon waypoint. Others (including me) would reply that this is a human factors problem. First, there was no need for ATC to issue a waypoint in a complex and obscure form, requiring so many keystrokes, which must be entered in a rigid format, receptive to error. Second, it may have been months, or perhaps years, since the crew had attended ground school, where they had last been faced with entering coordinates into a CDU. Others might approach this as a problem-solving exercise, requiring that the pilots go beyond their present knowledge and find a solution (Spettell and Liebert, 1986). This demand on the part of the machine hardly qualifies as "human-centered automation" in any sense of the term. If the reader has had any experience with computers, he or she will know the frustration of struggling to enter information in the correct format and having seemingly correct inputs rejected.

Thus automation provides the LOFT designer with the opportunity to build scenarios that will directly address the problems and opportunities of two-pilot crews working in the advanced-technology cockpit, particularly those involving the aircraft automation/ATC interface as it exists today. The LOFT constructed for these aircraft can and should exercise those peculiar characteristics of the modern cockpits and can easily create situations that demand that one practice CRM principles. The LOFT designer can possibly be guided by incident reports of the type used as illustrations in this chapter.

IMPLICATIONS FOR GOVERNMENT ─────────── ✈

Clearly, advanced-technology aircraft provide novel challenges to the FAA in its regulation and supervision of training and raise difficult policy issues as well. Let us examine two examples.

1. Should the trainee, on a rating ride, or the qualified pilot on a proficiency check (PC) be allowed to select or deselect automatic devices as he/she sees fit? Or rather should the check airman or instructor have the authority to tell the crew what features to use to demonstrate their proficiency? Certainly the spirit of a realistic checkride or LOFT is violated if the second alternative is exercised. Indeed, the check airman who submits to the temptation of specifying equipment utilization sacrifices a priceless opportunity to observe a critical feature of operating the advanced aircraft: (1) the decision by the crew about what cockpit resources to employ, and (2) the coordination required once this decision is made. Communication of this decision and any required ensuing conversation on its implementation is a critical feature of CRM that should be observed by the examiner.

2. Presently captains are required to take training and evaluation twice a year and first officers only once. (There are some exceptions—a few airlines have been approved by the FAA to give annual training instead.) However, at most airlines the different annual requirements for checking captains and first officers impacts on the ability of training departments to schedule a realistic LOFT crew. Since captains must attend twice as often, about half the time two captains must fly together, and a great measure of realism is sacrificed. Such a checkride is simply not "real world." With two captains flying together on a checkride, the role relationship, duties, supervision, and authority of the captain–subordinate relationship is not faithfully represented. Should the FAA consider this?

IMPLICATIONS FOR THE FUTURE ─────────── ✈

With the vast number of two-pilot, advanced-technology aircraft currently on order, it would seem prudent to take stock of all training technologies and their interrelationships. In a few years, the glass cockpit aircraft will dominate the world's fleets; more advanced models with new automatic features are on the way (Scott, 1991). Furthermore, for reasons external to cockpit technology, these aircraft likely will be operated under more stressed conditions than we have known in the past. Airlines will face new demands to meet market conditions, adapt the modern aircraft to the ATC system (instead of the other way round, as it should be), and absorb new hires who may be quite inexperienced compared to those the airlines have previously attracted. The introduction of augmented crews (one or two additional pilots) into a two-pilot cockpit provides new challenges for crew coordination. All this will occur in an environment in the United States where there is continually expanding traffic, but only one new airport (Denver) under construction or even being planned (see Figure 7.1).

SUMMARY ─── →

Is the glass cockpit aircraft just another airplane, requiring no differential approach to CRM and LOFT training? Most researchers think not. But currently we are not able to produce an empirically based argument to support these beliefs. Field studies of the introduction of the new-technology aircraft lead me to believe that the demands on the pilot in the new aircraft are qualitatively different from those in the traditional models. If this is correct, it will call for qualitative changes in training methods and procedures. As we learn more about the crew coordination and communication requirements of the glass cockpits and sharpen our ability to provide effective CRM and LOFT training, we may be able to optimize training by tailoring the instruction and scenarios to recognize the great differences that exist between modern and traditional cockpits. Stone and Babcock wrote (1988, p. 552), "The use of LOFT-type training has changed the texture of airline training." I believe that with the growth of new cockpit technologies, that texture will continue to change, and possibly in ways that are not easily predicted at this time.

Acknowledgments

The author's work has been supported in part by a research grant, Number NCC2-581, from NASA's Ames Research Center to the University of Miami. It was jointly funded by NASA and the FAA. The author gratefully acknowledges the cooperation of Northwest, Eastern, and Delta Air Lines, and the safety committees of the Air Line Pilots Association at those carriers. Administrative support was provided at the University of Miami by Vanessa Donahue and Lynn Russell. The support of the staff of the NASA Aviation Safety Reporting System was also invaluable. The opinions expressed here are those of the author, and not of any organization.

References

Billings, C. E. (1991). *Human-centered aircraft automation: A concept and guidelines* (NASA Technical Memo 103885). Moffett Field, CA: NASA–Ames Research Center.
Butler, R. E. (1991). Lessons from cross-fleet/cross-airline observations: Evaluating the impact of CRM/LOFT training. *Proceedings of the Sixth International Symposium on Aviation Psychology* (pp. 326–331). Columbus: The Ohio State University.

Chambers, A. B., & Nagel, D. C. (1985). Pilots of the future: human or computers? *Communications of the ACM, 28,* 1187–1199.

Clothier, C. C. (1991). Behavioral interactions across various aircraft types: Results of systematic observations of line operations and simulations. *Proceedings of the Sixth International Symposium on Aviation Psychology* (pp. 332–337). Columbus: The Ohio State University.

Costley, J., Johnson, D., & Lawson, D. (1989). A comparison of cockpit communication B737–B757. *Proceedings of Fifth International Symposium on Aviation Psychology* (pp. 413–418). Columbus: Ohio State University.

Curry, R. E. (1985). *The introduction of new cockpit technology: A human factors study* (NASA Technical Memo 86659). Moffett Field, CA: NASA–Ames Research Center.

Degani, A. S., & Wiener, E. L. (1990). *Human factors of flight-deck checklists: The normal checklist* (NASA Contractor Report 177549). Moffett Field, CA: NASA–Ames Research Center.

Degani, A. S., & Wiener, E. L. (1991). Philosophy, policies, and procedures. *Proceedings of the Sixth International Symposium on Aviation Psychology* (pp. 184–191). Columbus: The Ohio State University.

Demosthenes, T. A., & Oliver, J. G. (1991, June). Design principles for commercial transport aircraft: A pilot's perspective. *Air Line Pilot,* pp. 22–25.

Edwards, E. (1977). Automation in civil transport aircraft. *Applied Ergonomics, 8,* 194–198.

Federal Aviation Administration. (1991). *FAA aviation forecasts* (FAA-APO 91-1). Washington, DC: Author.

Foushee, H. C., & Helmreich, R. L. (1988). Group interaction and flight crew performance. In E. L. Wiener & D. C. Nagel (Eds.), *Human factors in aviation* (pp. 189–227). San Diego: Academic Press.

Foushee, H. C., & Manos, K. L. (1981). Information transfer within the cockpit: Problems in intracockpit communications. In C. E. Billings and E. S. Cheaney (Eds.), *Information problems in the aviation system* (NASA TP-1875). Moffett Field, CA: NASA–Ames Research Center.

Graeber, R. C. (1989). Long-range operations in the glass cockpit: Vigilance, boredom, and sleepless nights. In A. Coblentz (Ed.), *Vigilance and performance in automated systems* (pp. 67–76). Dordrecht, Netherlands: Kluwer.

Heldt, P. (1989). Survey on cockpit systems B737-300/A310-200. *Flightcrew Info,* special edition. Frankfurt, Germany: Lufthansa German Airlines.

Helmreich, R. L. (1991). Strategies for the study of flightcrew behavior. *Proceedings of the Sixth International Symposium on Aviation Psychology* (pp. 338–349). Columbus: The Ohio State University.

Helmreich, R. L., Chidester, T. R., Foushee, H. C., Gregorich, S., & Wilhelm, J. A. (1989a). *Critical issues in implementing and reinforcing cockpit resource management training* (NASA/Univ. of Texas Technical Report No. 89-5). Austin.

Helmreich, R. L., Chidester, T. R., Foushee, H. C., Gregorich, S. A., & Wilhelm, J. A. (1989b). *How effective is cockpit resource management training? Issues in evaluating the impact of programs to enhance crew coordination.* (NASA/Univ. of Texas Technical Report No. 89-2). Austin.

Helmreich, R. L., Wilhelm, J. A., & Gregorich, S. A. (1988). *Measures of flightcrew attitudes.* (NASA/Univ. of Texas Technical Report No. 88-2, Revised 1991). Austin.

James, M., McClumpha, A., Green, R., Wilson, P., & Belyavin, A. (1991). Pilot attitudes to flight deck automation. *Proceedings of the Sixth International Symposium on Aviation Psychology* (pp. 192–197). Columbus: Ohio State University.

Lauber, J. K. (1984, July). *Cockpit resource management in the new technology aircraft.* Paper presented at Air Line Pilots Association Air Safety Forum, Washington, DC.

Lauber, J. K., & Foushee, H. C. (1981). *Guidelines for line-oriented flight training, Volumes I and II.* (NASA Conference Publication 2184). Moffett Field, CA: NASA–Ames Research Center.

Lyall, E. A. (1990). *The effects of mixed-fleet flying of the Boeing 737-200 and -300.* (Technical Report AWA01-90-01). Phoenix, AZ: America West Airlines.

Maurino, D. (1991, May). Training needs for advanced technology flight decks. *ICAO Journal,* pp. 20–21.

Mollet, C. (1988, February) *Training to and from the automated cockpit.* Paper presented at International Air Transport Association meeting on flight training. New Orleans.

Morters, K. (1988). *B-767 Flight-deck automation research* (Paper No. 32:420). Auckland, New Zealand: University of Auckland.

Norman, D. (1990). The "problem" with automation: Inappropriate feedback and interaction, not "over-automation." *Philosophical Transactions of the Royal Society of London, 327,* 585–593.

Orlady, H. W. (1989, October). *Selected human factors in aviation.* Paper presented at 6th Annual Meeting of the Mexican Association of Aerospace Medicine and the College of Professional Pilots of Mexico. Provencia Juriquilla, Mexico.

Ott, J. (1991, September 30). Airline officials fear forecasts of recovery were too upbeat. *Aviation Week and Space Technology,* p. 30.

President's Task Force on Aircraft Crew Complement. (1981). *Report of the President's Task Force on Aircraft Crew Complement.* Washington, DC: Author.

Rogers, W. H., Logan, A. L., & Boley, G. D. (1989). *Classification and reduction of human error* (NASA Contractor Report 181867). Hampton, VA: NASA–Langley Research Center.

Ruffell Smith, H. P. (1979). *A simulator study of the interaction of pilot workload with errors, vigilance, and decisions* (NASA TM-78482). Moffett Field, CA: NASA–Ames Research Center.

Sarter, N., & Woods, D. (1991). *Pilot interaction with cockpit automation* (Cognitive Systems Engineering Laboratory Report CSEL 91-017). Columbus: The Ohio State University.

Scott, W. B. (1991, June). 777's flight deck reflects strong operations influence. *Aviation Week and Space Technology,* pp. 57–58.

Segal, L. D. (1990). Effects of aircraft cockpit design on crew communication. In E. J. Lovesey (Ed.), *Contemporary Ergonomics 1990* (pp. 247–252). London: Taylor & Francis.

Spettell, C. M., & Liebert, R. M. (1986). Training for safety in automated person–machine systems. *American Psychologist, 41,* 545–550.

Steenblik, J. W. (1991, April). ETOPS: Is it overextended? *Air Line Pilot,* pp. 22–25.

Stone, R. B. (1991, May). *Automation: What have we learned so far as pilots?* Paper presented at first ICAO Human Factors Regional Seminar, Douala, Cameroon.

Stone, R. B., & Babcock, G. L. (1988). Airline pilots' perspective. In E. L. Wiener & D. C. Nagel (Eds.), *Human factors in aviation* (pp. 529–560). San Diego: Academic Press.

U.S. House of Representatives. (1977). *Future needs and opportunities in the air traffic control system* (Subcommittee on Transportation, Aviation, and Weather of the Committee on Science and Technology, Report No. 98-796). Washington, DC: Author.

Wickens, C. D., Marsh, R., Raby, M., Straus, S., Cooper, R. S., Hulin, C. L., & Switzer, F. (1989). Aircrew performance as a function of automation and crew composition: A simulator study. In *Proceedings of the Human Factors Society 33rd Annual Meeting* (pp. 792–796). Santa Monica, CA: Human Factors Society.

Wiener, E. L. (1985a). Beyond the sterile cockpit. *Human Factors, 27,* 75–90.

Wiener, E. L. (1985b). Cockpit automation: In need of a philosophy. In *Proceedings of Society of Automotive Engineers Aerotech 85 Symposium* (pp. 369–375). Warrendale, PA: SAE.

Wiener, E. L. (1985c). *Human factors of cockpit automation: A field study of flight crew transition.* (NASA Contractor Report No. 177333). Moffett Field, CA: NASA–Ames Research Center.

Wiener, E. L. (1987). Application of vigilance research: Rare, medium, or well done? *Human Factors, 29,* 725–736.

Wiener, E. L. (1988a). Cockpit automation. In E. L. Wiener & D. C. Nagel (Eds.), *Human factors in aviation* (pp. 433–461). San Diego: Academic Press.

Wiener, E. L. (1988b, February). *Training for high technology aircraft.* Paper presented at International Air Transport Association Conference on Pilot Training, New Orleans.

Wiener, E. L. (1989). *Human factors of advanced technology ("glass cockpit") transport aircraft* (NASA Contractor Report No. 177528). Moffett Field, CA: NASA–Ames Research Center.

Wiener, E. L., Chidester, T. R., Kanki, B. G., Palmer, E. A., Curry, R. E., & Gregorich, S. A. (1991). *The impact of cockpit automation on crew coordination and communication: I. Overview, LOFT evaluations, error severity, and questionnaire data* (NASA Contractor Report No. 177587). Moffett Field, CA: NASA–Ames Research Center.

Wiener, E. L., & Curry, R. E. (1980). Flight-deck automation: Promises and problems. *Ergonomics, 23,* 995–1011. Also published in R. Hurst & L. Hurst (Eds.). (1982), *Pilot error: the human factors* (pp. 67–86). New York: Jason Aronson.

Wiener, E. L., & Nagel, D. C. (Eds.). (1988). *Human factors in aviation.* San Diego: Academic Press.

8

LOFT: Full-Mission Simulation as Crew Resource Management Training

Roy E. Butler
NASA/UT Aerospace Crew Research Project
University of Texas at Austin
Austin, Texas 78701

INTRODUCTION ✈

Darkness falls early on Kennedy Airport. Visibility is obscured due to blowing snow that has been falling most of the day in the Northeast, causing numerous flight cancellations and diversions to alternate airports. After the first unexpected heavy snow the airport had been closed due to the inability of snow removal equipment to keep pace with the intensity of the storm. It has just re-opened for departing flights. Many of the runways at airports throughout the Northeast are closed, and most of the others are covered with packed snow, making the identification of taxiways and runways difficult.

The captain of today's flight on a Lockheed L1011-500 is reviewing the Automatic Terminal Information Service (ATIS) in-flight operations. Kennedy information Bravo is reporting an indefinite ceiling with visibility less than ¼ mile in blowing snow. The winds are out of the north at 10 miles per hour gusting to 20. The runway visual range (RVR) for runway 31R is 700 feet. The airport is still closed to arriving traffic—not the kind of day that even the most ardent of pilots looks forward to flying.

The captain, an experienced pilot with 22 years of service, is reviewing the dispatch release, weather, and Notice to Airmen (NOTAMS). He is satisfied that, though the flight is expected to be a little uncomfortable for the cabin crew and passengers, it is a safe operation, despite the poor weather. Due to the reported Kennedy weather, a take-off alternate airport is filed for this flight to Boston.

The preflight checklists and the cabin and cockpit crew briefings are complete. All systems are operational. The log book shows an engine instrument is unreliable. It has been placarded out of service, but the minimum equipment list indicates the flight can depart if all the other engine instruments are operating.

The crew is not expecting any taxi delays, and as soon as the wing de-icing is completed they will be ready to push back and start engines.

The startup is routine and, except for the weather and poor visibility, the taxi to runway 31R is not as difficult as they had anticipated. The cabin crew is notified they are number 1 for takeoff. The cabin is secure and the cabin crew seated.

With the takeoff checklist now complete, the captain makes a quick scan of the flight engineer's panel to see if all the switch lights are out and queries the crew to see if they are ready to go. The recently upgraded first officer is a little uncomfortable but feels secure in the knowledge that he is flying with one of the most experienced pilots in this fleet. The briefing had been thorough and he knows exactly what is expected from both him and the flight engineer.

As the thrust levers are advanced the captain calls, "Take-off thrust," and the flight engineer makes his final adjustments to the thrust levers. "Airspeed," the first officer calls out as the indicator moves off the peg and the aircraft begins its acceleration. The acceleration is a little slow due to the snow on the runway, but this had all been anticipated in flight operations earlier when the captain and first officer had reviewed the performance pages in the operating manual to determine what weight and performance penalties might apply. "Eighty knots." Everything looks good. "V_1." They are now committed to the takeoff. "V_r." The captain starts a slow, smooth rotation to the takeoff attitude. "V_2" is called as the L-1011 lifts off and begins its climb. "Positive climb," the first officer calls. The captain quickly responds, "Gear up." The first officer reaches for the gear handle and pulls it out of the down detent. The gear handle will not come up. The gear remains in the down position. "Captain, I can't raise the gear." The captain, continuing the climb and departure profile replies, "Let's leave the gear handle alone and we'll get back to it after we reach a comfortable altitude." The flight engineer notes and advises. "The gear not level light is illuminated."

The above scenario has taken place many times. This is line-oriented flight training (LOFT). Many crews flew this simulator scenario and, although the problem itself is not critical to flight, many different approaches were taken to finding solutions and making decisions.

The technical solution? Quite simple. The checklist requires that the gear be left down. Not a big problem. However, crew resource management (CRM) was more critical. The weather, the effect on fuel burn with the gear down, the distance to the take-off alternate, and the deteriorating weather at the destination were all considerations that had to be factored into the crew's decision on where to go and how far they could go with the fuel on board. All this was happening under time pressures that increased the level of stress imposed upon the crew.

Decisions had to be made. They could continue to the destination airport, go to the take-off alternate, or return and land at JFK with below minimum weather.[1] The flight management system could be reprogrammed, or they might revert to conventional cockpit navigation. They could climb to a higher altitude to reduce fuel burn but had to consider that they would burn more fuel in the climb because of the drag caused by the extended gear. Any or all decisions might be satisfactory. The problem ideally will involve all cockpit crewmembers, air traffic control (ATC), flight dispatch, operations control/maintenance, and the cabin crew. The airplane could easily make the approach and landing at JFK even though it is below minima. Should they declare an emergency and land? The fuel burn with the gear down allowed for continuation to the destination, but would there be enough for an approach with a miss and diversion to the alternate? They could proceed to the take-off alternate where the weather was good, but it was farther away than the destination and might leave them with minimum fuel on arrival. What information do you need—what would you do? Later we will see how the crew handled this problem and what decisions were made.

LINE OPERATIONAL SIMULATIONS ──────────── ✈

This chapter discusses LOFT and its relationship to CRM as defined in the Federal Aviation Administration's (FAA) Advisory Circular on Line Operational Simulations (LOS; Federal Aviation Administration, 1990). The chapter's focus is on the conduct of recurrent LOFT, one of several types of line operational simulations outlined in the LOS advisory circular. I discuss other types of flight simulation in the advisory circular, such as qualification LOFT, special purpose operational training (SPOT), and line operational evaluation (LOE) only to the extent that they relate to recurrent LOFT.

Qualification LOFT is part of a transition and upgrade training program designed to prepare a pilot in command for line operations. Its focus is on operational procedures, and it is the final step before releasing the pilot to the line. Although CRM is a factor it is not the primary purpose of this training.

[1]The Lockheed L-1011-500, an airplane designed for minimum visibility approaches, was approved for Category IIIa approaches down to 1000 feet RVR for this airline when the scenario was designed. Application for Category IIIb had been made and at a later date approaches were approved down to 600 feet RVR. British Airways had already been approved for landings with zero visibility at London–Heathrow Airport; however, they were limiting their approaches to an RVR of 300 feet for operational considerations. When the airplane was put in service the digital autopilot system represented the state of the art in automation, with sophisticated autoflight and flight controls designed to provide extremely stable auto approach, landing, and rollout capabilities. Direct lift control in the landing configuration allowed either the pilot or the autopilot to increase or decrease the rate of descent without changing the attitude of the airplane. By using spoilers that were partially extended, pitch inputs would either increase or decrease drag as required, providing very precise glide slope tracking.

SPOT is used to learn, practice, and accomplish specific CRM training objectives where crew performance is required. SPOT may contain full or partial flight segments similar to LOFT, using scenarios that are flown in real time. An example of SPOT would be the introduction of a problem requiring drift-down procedures over the North Atlantic in a two-engine aircraft operating under extended range operations (EROPS). This would evaluate crew decision-making, preparation and planning, and crew communications and coordination with ATC and other aircraft on the overseas tracks. It must be noted that under current regulations, SPOT cannot be substituted for recurrent or qualification LOFT.

LOE is designed for use as a formal crewmember evaluation under an Advanced Qualification Program (AQP). Its purpose is to check for both individual and crew performance and, unlike LOFT, it contains an element of jeopardy.

This chapter covers the philosophy, purposes, and procedures used in LOFT and LOFT evaluation programs. A review of the use of guidelines, surveys, and checklists is included to help understand how we can monitor the quality of LOFT designs. I discuss the use of the principles of CRM in the design, use, and evaluation of LOFT.

To address the issues of LOFT fully, we must take a broad human factors perspective to discuss the design considerations for LOFT and LOFT evaluation programs, recognizing that LOFT is most important as a training methodology for the reinforcement of CRM. We must also address check and supervisory pilot training as a key to effective reinforcement of CRM principles in LOFT.

CRM LOFT: AN OVERVIEW ——————————————— ✈

CRM LOFT training is systematic and is intended to simulate actual problem situations that require good crew skills for effective resolution and decision-making. It is best if LOFT scenarios are designed so that they are not only operationally relevant and believable but are also a good test of the cockpit crew's teamwork skills. One misconception that is periodically encountered is that LOFT should include continuously increasing the workload until the crew is overloaded. This is not the purpose or intent of LOFT training and can actually defeat its purpose.

LOFT scenarios are best if they provide an environment that will encourage good crew performance. For example, choosing a departure airport that requires an effective pre-flight briefing even under the best of conditions might be one way to begin. Providing an entry point that allows different options for the crew to choose from is also useful, since one scenario can have a wide variety of outcomes and choices depending on the decisions and courses of action that the crew decides on. Again, the scenario should be realistic and the situation should be one where the crew lives with whatever problems they have until the situation is either resolved or the airplane (simulator) is back on the ground.

The Need for LOFT

With the introduction of turbojet and turboprop airplanes and, more recently, the development of the advanced technology flightdeck ("glass cockpit"), a very real reduction in airplane accidents rates is now fact. This might prompt one to say, "If it ain't broke, don't fix it." Yet such conventional wisdom has proven to be a pitfall for airlines large and small. The data on accidents over the past two decades indicate that we do need to fix something. We are still bending metal.

In years past, technical proficiency was considered the sole factor in assessing a pilot's ability to perform safely, that is, having the "right stuff." Whoever possessed the "right stuff" was regarded in the highest esteem. Yet analysis of air carrier accidents and incidents over the past 20 years has confirmed that at least 65% (Sears, 1986; Nagel, 1988) can be attributed to inadequacies in leadership qualities, communications skills, crew coordination, or decision-making. In these accidents and incidents the lack of the "right stuff" was not a factor. Conversely, they were caused by poor management of resources readily available to the crew (see the chapter by Kayten).

Issues of safety are multi-faceted. The concept that safety in the cockpit rests solely on improving the equipment or on the pilot's technical proficiency is no longer valid. The scope of what comprises a safe cockpit has now expanded to encompass the equally important skill, CRM, discussed in the chapter by Helmreich & Foushee. However, the training programs of the past 40 years have not fully addressed the factors that affect the major causes of airplane accidents, primarily because they have not included human factors.

Training in aviation to develop human factors skills was almost nonexistent until just the past few years. Progress was slow because the change required in training is uncomfortable for many pilots and flight managers. Any way we look at it, the single biggest enemy in the training of cockpit crews has been inertia. Required was a major top-to-bottom change in attitude. We are beginning to see this change, and the word is out in many of the airlines worldwide that it's not business as usual.

Regulatory Involvement

As early as World War II, it was recognized that the limiting factor in the development and design of airplanes was the ability of the pilot to effectively operate and manage the resources provided. The human factors engineering lessons learned during this period were not lost and were incorporated in the development and design of military and transport aircraft.

As part of the FAA's responsibility to facilitate the introduction of the human factors concepts into flight training, it began to deal with two issues in pilot training and and checking in airline operations (Part 121, Federal Aviation Regulations). These issues were hardware requirements for total simulation and the redesign of training programs to deal with complex human factors problems. It is the issue of human factors errors, as it relates to management and leadership in the cockpit, that became an important part of the analysis of the use of total simulation in training and the introduction of line operational simulations using LOFT as the first introduction to CRM training in simulators.

FAA involvement in LOFT began in 1975 when a letter was received petitioning for an exemption from FAR 121.409 to permit a new type of training at Northwest Airlines. As a result of FAA evaluation of this petition, Exemption No. 2209 was issued that allowed a test program for LOFT, which at that time had not been named.

In 1977, a regulatory change was proposed that would permit any airline to utilize LOFT training as part of recurrent training. In 1978, a meeting of industry. FAA training personnel, instructors, and FAA inspectors was held in an attempt to determine guidelines for recurrent LOFT. This resulted in Advisory Circular 120-35a, which was published in May 1978. Also, FAR Part 121 was amended to allow LOFT to be a part of any airline's program. This was a significant change in training and dealing with crew coordination problems.

After the introduction of the advisory circular there was a slow response from industry in accepting the voluntary program. In 1979, the Air Transport Division issued a letter to the FAA regions and the industry soliciting comments about how to advance training in a progressive way so that we could meet the challenge raised by previous accidents. A 1981 NASA/Industry Workshop at the NASA–Ames Research Center, Moffett Field, California, and the resulting guidelines for LOFT were critical first steps in this program (Lauber & Foushee, 1981). At the workshop Charles Huettner (FAA) stated, "We are embarking on an adventure into the flight training techniques of the future" (Huettner, 1981).

In June 1988, the National Transportation Safety Board (NTSB) recommended that all major air carriers

> Review initial and recurrent flightcrew training programs to ensure that they include simulator or aircraft training exercises that involve cockpit resource management and active coordination of all crewmember trainees and that will permit evaluation of crew performance and adherence to those crew coordination procedures. (NTSB, 1988)

Current Federal regulations do not reflect recent advancements in aircraft technology or advancements in training methods and techniques. Certain training, checking, and testing requirements in the regulations are out of date for airline operations with advanced-technology aircraft. The joint FAA/industry approach for redesigning the training programs has been to maximize the benefits of advanced simulation and to deal with the increasing complexity of the cockpit human factors. They recognized that a dominant factor in accidents and incidents is the failure of flight crewmembers to engage in proper crew coordination during normal and abnormal inflight operations. It is now generally believed that advances in aircraft and cockpit technology and increased complexity in the airspace system will increase demands for crew coordination and effective cockpit management.

From this perspective, it is evident that manual manipulation of the aircraft through a fixed package of maneuvers trains and checks a pilot on less than the whole job. LOFT was initiated as a step toward more complete pilot training.

In the 1980s, the FAA accommodated air carriers desiring to address human factors training needs by issuing exemptions to their current training program requirements. In the past 5 years many airlines have started to introduce human factors training; however, it is important to note that at this writing only three airlines—United, Pan Am, and Delta—have fully integrated training with a recurrent CRM LOFT program in place for all crews.

In most cases the focus of training is still on the individual crewmember and not on the crew itself (Hackman and Helmreich, 1987; chapter by Hackman). Even in airlines with fully integrated CRM LOFT programs, those conducting the training tend to fall back to the concept of individual crewmember evaluation (Butler, 1991; Clothier, 1991b).

WAYS TO IMPLEMENT AND IMPROVE LOFT ── →

Nothing worthwhile can be accomplished without determination. In the early days of nuclear power, for example, getting approval to build the world's first nuclear submarine, the Nautilus, *was almost as difficult as designing and building it. Good ideas are not adopted automatically. They must be driven into practice with courageous patience.*

Admiral Hyman Rickover (quoted in Manske, 1987)

Preparation

In today's operating environment, one question that must be answered is how to get crew coordination or teamwork to happen. Is it the luck of the draw when monthly flying schedules are formed? Is it due to personality or other personal characteristics that crewmembers possess? Can crew coordination be trained into an operation, and if so, how can it best be accomplished? As we have already seen in the studies by the Boeing Commercial Airplane Company (Sears, 1986; Nagel, 1988), crew-caused accidents continue to dominate accident causes by a significant margin. These statistics, while sometimes controversial in the flightcrew community, are nonetheless consistent with the NTSB studies and NASA research into aviation safety issues.

To meet this challenge, three components of CRM training are identified in the FAA's CRM advisory circular (FAA, 1989; in preparation). They include awareness training, practice and feedback, and continuing operational reinforcement. In addition to these components of training, there must be organizational commitment and a training and checking environment that actively supports everyday use of CRM concepts. What this means in an operational context is that there needs to be an emphasis in training activities for using complete crews instead of individuals wherever possible (including proficiency checks). There also need to be quality control measures that go beyond traditional checking for technical competency. And finally, there needs to be management support for the changed approach to training and operations.

Training in these and other areas is a new challenge for many instructors and chief pilots who are accustomed to concentrating on the technical side of flight training. The good news, however, is that when exposed to these concepts in an operational context, most immediately see the benefits and wish they had received this type of training earlier in their careers. Research data show that training organizations using LOFT are enthusiastic about the potential of CRM training through LOFT as a means of effecting real change in the bottom line of safety and efficient operation (Wilhelm, 1991).

To develop an effective model for LOFT, there are several key components to consider. These include task and goal analysis, baseline CRM training, LOFT evaluation skills training for checking and instructional personnel, and a method for tracking and validating the training process (Helmreich, Wilhelm, & Gregorich, 1988; chapter by Gregorich and Wilhelm). This last item is particularly important if LOFT scenarios and procedures are to be improved and changed, as operating environments and crewmembers' needs change over time.

As a beginning step, an organization considering LOFT as a component of recurrent training might designate a steering or planning committee charged with gathering initial information regarding CRM in the organization. This committee or task force should be composed of individuals who represent a cross section of flight operations. It can include flight operations management, ground school instructors, curriculum developers, check airmen, pilots' association representatives, captains, first officers, and flight engineers. It is important that the individuals selected carry substantial credibility with the line pilot population. Many times, individuals are selected on the basis of availability or personal interest. It is critical that members of this initial work group carry the respect of their peers (see the chapter by Byrnes & Black).

The committee can be charged with diagnosing the current status of human factors training and procedures within the airline and within flight operations in particular. Once the current level of CRM practices is determined and a set of training objectives for LOFT is determined, a plan can be developed to close the gap between actual status and planned objectives. There are several advantages to using a work group approach for this first step. First, various segments of flight operations are represented. This avoids the perception that LOFT is a "management project" or that it is the work of one or two individuals. Another benefit is that there are likely to be different perceptions about the current state of CRM effectiveness and the desired goals in establishing the LOFT program. Being able to debate and discuss different perceptions can result in a better diagnosis and planning effort.

Another key part of assessing the organization is to identify limitations and restrictions (for example, crew time or funding) that need to be considered in planning. To deal with these negative issues and limitations, it is important to recognize that this training is an ongoing process and does not need to represent a significant investment in funds. Effective courses have been developed in-house by a variety of operators, and the ongoing research sponsored by NASA, the FAA, and others promises to make training information widely available.

The CRM and LOS advisory circulars provide many of the guidelines necessary to get started, and rules for the conduct of LOFT have been developed from Lauber & Foushee (1981). These meet the requirements in the LOS advisory circular and include instructions for LOFT facilitators and crews participating in LOFT.

CRM issues that should be addressed as part of the LOFT design and evaluation program are laid out in detail in Helmreich, Wilhelm, Kello, Taggart, & Butler (1991). This manual breaks down the human factors considerations into conceptual groupings or clusters of specific crew behaviors that reflect effective cockpit management. These behavioral markers are used as objective guidelines for evaluating CRM effectiveness. In addition to their use as tools for measuring crew performance, crew behavioral indicators can be used to help develop specific tasks and objectives for designing effective LOFT scenarios that integrate both technical and CRM skills. Even though many of the indicators are global in nature, good LOFT design deals in specifics rather than generalities.

To facilitate crew effectiveness in the use of CRM, some of the issues to be addressed as components of a scenario design might include the following:

1. Problems with several satisfactory solutions, to encourage crewmembers to propose various courses of action. Alternatives should be equally good or bad. One choice should not be so obviously correct as to preclude consideration of

other options available. This provides the proper environment to observe the
decision-making process and resolution of conflicts that may arise. The problems presented should be complex enough to challenge technical skills and
should provide the opportunity to confront problems and situations that are
not textbook solutions.

2. Weather requiring a quality pre-flight briefing of cockpit and cabin crew.
   Enroute turbulence, destination weather with the need to consider the possibility of a diversion, and standard instrument departures that demand good
   crew coordination are some ways to elicit thorough crew briefings.
3. Workload high enough to require tasks be distributed and communicated to
   achieve the most effective crew performance.
4. Some problems may be selected that will allow time for alternatives to be
   discussed and weighed before a final decision is required.
5. Scenarios that encourage participation in decision-making by all crewmembers.
6. ATC and environmental factors that require the crewmembers to stay ahead of
   the airplane to preclude being in a catch-up situation.

LOFT, through continuing training and rehearsal, will improve workload
management, problem-solving, and decision-making skills. LOFT is used in
learning CRM skills and is necessary to give practical application to the material
learned in the basic CRM training. Through LOFT, crews learn to make proper
reactions second nature so they are not required to consciously think about them.

The focus of LOFT is on how to practice and become equipped with a
better set of CRM skills to deal with the various types of crewmembers and
situations that will be faced in the line operation. In order to maximize the
benefits, guidelines must be written to enhance the line realism of LOFT. However, we may find that this does not preclude the employment of scenarios using
short segments beginning in an enroute environment.

It is important for the effectiveness of LOFT to create as much realism as
possible in the simulated trips. This requirement dictates that details such as pre-
flight activities, trip paperwork, manuals, communications, and so on be carefully
prepared if they are part of the scenario. If the scenario begins in an enroute
environment, enough quiet time for the crew to become acclimated to the flight
routine should be present. Previous experience with LOFT has shown that over-
looking the preflight details may destroy this illusion. The LOFT facilitator should
mention the necessity for the crew to treat the LOFT as though it were a line trip and
emphasize the importance of realistic role-playing to overall LOFT effectiveness.

The LOFT facilitator's goal is to produce crew performance and behavior
that would be typical for an actual line flight in the same set of circumstances as
those developed in the scenario. In keeping with this goal, it is essential that crews
have access to all the resources they would have on an actual line trip and be
allowed considerable latitude in their decisions.

Communications is an area vitally important to the assurance of realism in LOFT operations. Communications must be conducted in the manner normally found on a line flight (i.e., via radio from outside the "airplane," via interphone or normal conversations between cockpit crewmembers, or, in the case of cockpit–cabin, via the usual airplane equipment for this purpose). All external communications (ATC, ground crew, etc.) must be credible and realistic.

The LOFT scenario should foster an environment where free and open communication is practiced. This will encourage the crew to provide necessary information at the appropriate time (e.g., initiating checklists, alerting others to developing problems). Active participation in the decision-making process should be encouraged and practiced. Questioning of actions and decisions is proper. Decisions made need to be clearly communicated and acknowledged.

The entire simulator phase of the flight should, if equipment is available, be recorded on videotape. During the debriefing the videotape can be reviewed and discussed by the flightcrew with the main emphasis being placed on crew performance, including their use of the elements of CRM. Following review of the videotape, the tape will normally be erased and no record will be made of the items reviewed in the debriefing.

Pre-Flight Activities

For full mission simulations, LOFT facilitators should provide the crew with complete flight planning documentation. An effort should be made to duplicate as closely as possible the preflight and dispatch process used by the organization. The weather sequences, weight and balance, and other documents should be identical to those provided prior to line trips.

Adequate time must be provided for the crew to perform a normal cockpit pre-flight setup. If it is customary for the flight engineer to enter the cockpit before the captain and first officer, that sequence should be adhered to. However, to save time it is possible in some cases to modify the scenario to provide shorter ground times, such as are found on a through flight. It is desirable to provide a planned departure time toward which all preparations can be directed. This provision further enhances the realism of a LOFT scenario.

The role of the LOFT facilitator should be viewed as that of communicator, observer, and moderator in the debriefing process. During the simulator period he or she is not an instructor in the traditional sense. He or she is the "coordinator" or manager of the flight using appropriate radio calls or responses to direct the flight. Importantly, he or she must be prepared to accept and manage alternate courses of action that the crew may wish to follow. The LOFT facilitator should remain as unobtrusive as possible, within the physical limitations of the simulator, and should resist the temptation to "instruct."

Certain simulator problems that cause interference with the realism associated with LOFT can and will occur. If a component required for a given scenario is inoperative, that scenario should not be flown. However, minor simulator malfunctions (instruments, etc.) can be placarded just as the maintenance crew would do on the line. If an actual equipment failure occurs in flight and is consistent with failures that could occur in an airplane, the scenarios can proceed, with modification if necessary, just as would a line flight.

LOFT Facilitator Pre-Flight Briefing

It has been observed that inadequate briefings set the stage for problems that later interfere with LOFT realism. The most common difficulty is failure to convince the crew that the LOFT facilitator is functionally not present in the simulator—that he or she will not be available for communication except in roles as ATC, Company, Maintenance, or others. The latter fact cannot be overstressed in the briefing. Emphasis is needed to make certain the cabin crew is considered in operating the flight and that they are also a resource.

The philosophy underlying LOFT should be thoroughly explained before the crew begins to plan for the flight. To a considerable extent, the conflict between "training" and "checking" in a LOFT program can be offset by the manner in which the LOFT facilitator sets the scene during the preflight briefing.

In addition to establishing the rules for the conduct of LOFT, the LOFT briefing should include a reverse briefing on CRM factors affecting crew performance. The concept of reverse briefing is to elicit information from the crew by encouraging them to brief themselves, helping to determine their level of expertise. It makes them active participants rather than passive recipients of briefings on issues already understood. Questions using performance markers and behavioral indicators can effectively elicit the level of understanding that the crew has about human factors and technical proficiency issues. Preview of some of the behavioral indicators that are used for evaluating performance can be very useful as a tool to raise the crew's awareness that LOFT is an opportunity to practice CRM in the cockpit.

The crew could be asked to discuss the conduct and quality of an effective briefing. What can be said to create an atmosphere for establishing the team concept and environment within the cockpit and with flight service? What are the components of a briefing that is operationally thorough and interesting and addresses coordination, planning, and problems? Although primarily a captain's responsibility, what are the responsibilities of the other crewmembers and how may they add significantly to planning and definition of potential problem areas? What can be done to make the cabin crew feel they are part of the team? The importance of the crew briefing cannot be overstated. Crew performance is highly associated with the quality of the initial crew briefing (Ginnett, 1987).

How does the crew view inquiry and advocacy? To what extent should crewmembers advocate a course of action they feel best, even when it involves conflict and disagreements with others? What is their feeling toward the relationship between inquiry and advocacy and the captain's authority? How do they define the proper balance between authority and assertiveness? What are the indications that a crew is concerned with the effective accomplishment of necessary tasks? Can they give examples where poor workload management and the lack of situational awareness have contributed to accidents or incidents? Does casual social conversation during periods of low workload indicate a lack of vigilance? What can be done to avoid overloading individual crewmembers?

What is their understanding of the relationship between technical proficiency and CRM? Can CRM overcome a lack of technical proficiency? LOFT presupposes a knowledge of systems and an understanding of and proficiency in skills involving procedures and techniques. Training programs have always been concerned with developing the specialized skill required to be technically proficient crewmembers. However, how well the crew as a unit discharges the technical aspects of the flight reflects awareness that a high degree of technical proficiency is essential for safe and efficient operations. In the briefing it must be made very clear that demonstrated mastery of CRM concepts cannot overcome a lack of proficiency, but just as importantly, high technical proficiency cannot guarantee safe operations in the absence of effective crew coordination.

Discuss the crew's attitudes toward self-critique. What is their understanding of critique? Do they see any benefit in reviewing positive behavior? Have the crewmembers used critique on line operations? When do they feel critique appropriate?

These are just a few of the issues that can be addressed in a LOFT briefing that will set the stage for quality crew performance in LOFT and give focus to a positive debriefing after the LOFT is completed. The proper briefing will also act as a reinforcement of the CRM principles learned in initial and recurrent CRM training. Without a briefing that sets the stage for the use of CRM behavior, LOFT becomes a full mission simulation without a CRM focus. Though it can be a positive learning experience, it will usually be centered on individual technical proficiency and abnormal checklist usage.

The briefing that looks at CRM issues will also give direction to the LOFT facilitator's conduct of the LOFT. It will help focus his or her observations on the CRM behaviors that will later be highlighted in debriefing.

The L-1011 LOFT Revisited

The L-1011 is now established in the climb. The captain asks the flight engineer to check the aircraft operation manual to determine what their fuel burn will be with the gear down. This information is not in the manual, as the L-1011 cannot be dispatched with the gear fixed down. The flight engineer suggests calling the company to get a fuel burn figure. He has already started monitoring the fuel burn to see if he can get an estimate on what the fuel flow will be during the climb.

The first officer advises ATC of the problem and is trying to get an update on the destination and alternate weather and the latest forecast for Kennedy. They were cleared to level off at 10,000 feet. However, the first officer inadvertently sets 11,000 in the altitude reminder. The captain, distracted by the information he is getting from the flight engineer while trying to fly, did not confirm the altitude set by the first officer. It wasn't until they were approaching 10,000 feet that they realized the mistake setting the altitude. "We were lucky we caught that," stated the captain. His annoyance with the first officer is apparent, but in their discussion he acknowledges that he should have checked the altitude reminder. He also adds that the first officer should have made sure he received the clearance. The captain realizes that he had been trying to fly and monitor the activities in the cockpit. Accordingly, he decides to have the first officer fly so he can devote more attention to problem-solving and decision-making.

It is determined that the fuel burn will be 30% higher with the gear down. Even with the extra 3000 pounds of fuel the captain elected to have loaded prior to departure, the increased fuel burn will eat into their reserve to the point that if they continue to Boston, they will not have the fuel required to make a missed approach and go to the alternate. They would have to land at Boston with only one runway into the wind.

The company, concerned with the consideration of working on the mechanical problem at Boston or an alternate, is feeling out the crew's thoughts on holding for an improvement in the Kennedy weather. The Kennedy weather is now forecast to improve to landing minima in approximately 1 hour. They can hold for an hour but that will leave them with no options to go somewhere else.

The weather in Boston is reported to be 300 feet overcast with ½ mile visibility and forecast to remain that way for the next hour with gradual improvement after that. Fairly good weather is reported at the alternate airport, but they will have to make a decision soon if they are to have enough fuel to get there.

The lead flight attendant would have noticed the difference in the climb and the much higher noise level in the cabin. The LOFT facilitator, changing hats and playing the flight attendant role, is anticipating a call from the cockpit. The call from the cockpit was not forthcoming, so he initiated the call to the cockpit about the time the crew recognized their error in setting the altitude reminder. "Captain, what's happening? There seems to be a lot of noise back here." The captain advises him that they could not raise the gear, but it did not present a serious problem and he would make an announcement to the passengers. The captain also mentions that they might be returning to Kennedy and would advise the passengers as soon as a decision was made.

As we can see, the crew is faced with decisions under time constraints placed on them by the gear problem and the weather. Any decision made at this point in time would lead to a satisfactory conclusion of the flight scenario. But a decision has to be made.

The purpose of the LOFT is to not focus on which decision was made, but more on the decision-making process. We need to see how the crewmembers communicate with each other, ATC, the company, and the cabin crew. What is the level of situational awareness, and how are the distractions handled?

This crew decided to continue to Boston. After a short discussion to consider the flight engineer's concern about getting the gear problem fixed without a possible major delay of the airplane in Boston, the captain decided that no other solution was better than continuing the flight to Boston. The other crewmembers are in agreement. Other crews have made other decisions, but no matter what the decision was, most of the crews flying this scenario were able to gain a great deal of insight into their behavior.

In this scenario we have observed a crew that has done some things well, but there were areas where the crew's performance could certainly be improved. We noticed conflict in the cockpit and an attempt at resolution. We observed crew performance where workload distribution and distractions played a role. The LOFT facilitator's task is now to get the crewmembers to recognize for themselves what they did—what they did well, and what they could have done better.

During the debriefing the crew observed the first part of the scenario and some of the selected areas on the videotape highlighted by the facilitator. They were asked to disassociate themselves from the video and observe their performance as though they were the facilitator. Using a guide listing CRM performance indicators, they were asked to identify in the video playback those elements that were present and how well they were used. The discussion in the debriefing focused around the crew's observations.

Post-Flight LOFT Debriefing

After the LOFT is completed, the manner in which the debriefing is handled by the LOFT facilitator is of key importance if CRM skills are to be reinforced and improved. It is best if the LOFT facilitator does not handle the debrief in a "teacher-tell" manner but instead operates as a resource for the crewmembers to highlight different portions of the LOFT that may be suitable for review, critique, and discussion. It is best if the discussion is led by the crew themselves as a reverse briefing using the LOFT facilitator and the videotape as resources during the self-critique. If handled in this way, then perhaps crew-led debriefs will occur with increasing frequency on the line after a difficult segment or one where crew critique and review is called for.

It is important that debriefing and critique both in LOFT and line operations include review of areas where particularly effective CRM behavior is seen. This establishes the criterion that critique can and should be conducted for most flights and should not be limited to areas where improvement is needed. Critique that outlines specific positive behavior has been noticeably absent in most LOFT debriefings observed by the author (Butler, 1991).

When crewmembers have learned and appreciate the importance of open and direct critique, such operational review and analysis establishes a platform for effective post-LOFT discussion that consists of more than technical and "stick-and-rudder" issues. Because the focus of LOFT is on crew resource management skills, the LOFT debriefing session should concentrate on this area. Thus, key items for discussion include crew management, crew coordination, and crew communications. The use of behavioral indicators can provide assistance in identifying areas for review on the videotape. The utilization of systems and other resources is another area for attention. It should include the crew's use of ATC and company communications manuals, charts, and other software, the use of other crewmembers, and the use of autopilot, autothrottle, and other workload-reducing devices. It is the LOFT facilitator's responsibility to ensure that these items are fully explored during the debriefing sessions.

The attitudes expressed by the crew during the pre-LOFT briefing can provide additional information for the debriefing. During debriefing, both total crew performance and individual performances should be openly discussed and assessed by the LOFT facilitator. Critical assessment of individual performances can be conducted in the presence of the full crew.

To be effective, this critique must be descriptive, not evaluative, and should describe behavior, not judge it. It should be specific, not general. If, for example, one were trying to help crews improve approaches, it would be necessary to describe how they need to get the aircraft configured at certain points to allow the approach to be stabilized. Rather than just saying, "your approach wasn't stabilized!" one must be specific. The feedback should be focused on changeable behavior, not the person.

The critique must also account for needs of the receiver and sender. It is solicited, not imposed. It is not effective to order someone to listen to feedback. However, professional crewmembers are obligated to receive critique on job-related matters. The debriefing is the sharing of information, reporting something that one saw or heard and not telling others what one thinks they should do or say. It must be checked for clarity by asking the other person to state what they think was said.

Experience has shown that if crews are encouraged to critique themselves, self-criticism and self-examination are almost always present and in many cases are much more effective than instructor critique. Frequently, crews are more critical of themselves than the instructor would ever be. Thus, the LOFT facilitator should do everything possible to foster this sort of self-analysis while at the same time keeping it at a constructive level. The emphasis is on what is right, not who is right. In the role of moderator, the LOFT facilitator can guide the discussion to areas demonstrating effective crew performance as well as those areas needing attention. In particular, the discussion should be directed toward the CRM issues observed during the LOFT.

If the stage has been set during the pre-LOFT briefing, both the facilitator and the crew will be able to observe the LOFT with the CRM issues clearly in mind. The behavioral indicators can be used by the crew for their self-critique. These provide tools that can be used to objectively identify the presence or absence of good CRM.

Questions about certain procedures, decisions, and mistakes should be asked. However, unless absolutely necessary, the LOFT facilitator should avoid "lectures" about what is right and what is wrong. Obviously, the LOFT facilitator should avoid embarrassing crewmembers as much as possible. The LOFT facilitator should assure crews participating in LOFT that their jobs are not in jeopardy every time they enter the simulator for a LOFT session. While "satisfactory completion" is an inescapable aspect of LOFT, at the same time it is hard to imagine "unsatisfactory training" if conducted appropriately.

Each LOFT facilitator and check pilot must take cognizance of the successes and failures of the crewmembers and make sure that they also see them and their consequences as they relate to total crew performance. At this point, a difficult aspect of the role of evaluator arises. How can critique be impersonal and still be effective? How can a decision or technique be critiqued without the feeling that anyone is personally being demeaned? Only adequate communication can accomplish the above. The debriefing becomes extremely important and can make or break the effectiveness of LOFT.

The importance of adequate communication at this point is twofold. Not only may long-range damage be done to the crew's morale, but an immediate effect is often the crew's failure to accept the LOFT exercise as a useful training vehicle. It is too easy to produce antagonism and defensiveness when trying to be impersonal and to forget the human emotions and motives that are involved.

OTHER ISSUES ✈

Stress

Stress has become a common term in the airline industry, yet it remains an enigma to those trying to understand the implications and impact on flight safety and the incorporation of stress into human factors training.

In designing LOFT scenarios and developing the CRM objectives, it is important to be aware that there are many elements in the stress equation. Some relate directly to the cockpit environment and have short-term effect, such as discomfort and noise or the pressures of time and workload. However, "significant life events" such as marriage, job insecurity, or illness are much more subtle, have a long-term impact, and create a baseline of stress on which environmental factors build.

One key to designing good LOFT scenarios is the recognition that a moderate level of environmental stress will, in most cases, increase performance. A LOFT designed to elicit high levels of crew coordination must have the proper balance of low and high periods of stress.

The LOFT design should permit a more satisfactory conclusion if the crew is able to lessen the workload and reduce the effects of stress. The proper use of checklists and other ways of organizing or distributing the workload into smaller and more manageable parts will normally provide the tools for most crews to reach a successful conclusion of the LOFT period.

The effects of increasing stress in LOFT can account for an initial increase in crew performance when it is compared to that in a low-stress environment. This concept, embodied in the Yerkes–Dodson Law or inverted U function (O'Hare & Roscoe, 1990), states that performance improves with increased stress until stress reaches a critical level. Performance will then start to decline. The law also implies that performance will start to decline at lower levels of stress while performing difficult tasks as opposed to easy tasks. As stress increases, feelings of discomfort and anxiety build. These symptoms begin to take over to the exclusion of operation-related information. Since more difficult tasks require the processing of more operation-related information, some of this information will be displaced by stress effects and the pilot will suffer from what is commonly termed "tunnel vision." For example, a crew flying a non-precision approach in marginal weather conditions with critical fuel state will require an increased awareness of the situation. At the same time the stress associated with this situation will be high. The operation may suffer as the stress increases unless the approach is well planned and the workload is properly managed.

There are no absolute measures of crew reactions to stress. Each crewmember differs markedly, and reactions can vary depending on the outside stress level that crewmembers individually bring into the cockpit. A different mix of individual members can change the overall effectiveness (different captain or co-pilot). For example, the stress induced during a proficiency check will cause some crews to overreact (what we sometimes call "check-itis"). Others take stress in stride and perform better during a check than in a non-threatening environment, just as some athletes perform better in high-level competition. The crew that has a high level of technical and CRM skill will generally perform better under stressful situations. Some pilots even seem to enjoy the excitement and stimulation of the check environment.

In my observations of LOFT, it is apparent that, in most cases, stress has an activating function that leads to increased crew effectiveness consistent with the Yerkes–Dodson Law. However, at high levels of stress, an otherwise effective and orderly process can break down—checklist items can be skipped, and possible solutions to problems may remain unexamined (Ruffell Smith, 1979). Another result of stress is that crewmembers may revert to early response patterns. These patterns may be inconsistent with the CRM training they have received.

LOFT with sufficient and realistic stress designed into the scenario offers an opportunity to identify to the crew the effects of stress. It can show how well training has replaced deep-seated, undesirable responses, and how effective CRM practices can reduce the level of stress to acceptable levels. When observing LOFT, it is easy to identify the presence of too little or too much stress, but it is difficult to know how to design the appropriate level of stress into the scenario. With more evaluation and research into this difficult aspect of LOFT design we feel that some guidelines can be developed.

Line and LOFT Evaluation

In the development and improvement of LOFT programs, line and LOFT evaluation of CRM behavior plays an important role. Insight into the way crews behave in the real world and in the simulator allows the LOFT designers to tailor the scenarios to specific areas needing improvement. The NASA/University of Texas Line/LOS Checklist is one of the central parts of several CRM validation programs and is being used as the tool for evaluating and debriefing CRM and coordination by several airlines (Helmreich et al., 1991).

From the data collected to date, we see that the combination of a good CRM program and LOFT has produced positive changes in those airlines that have collected data from the inception of their CRM and LOFT programs (Taggart & Butler, 1989).

Evaluation of LOFT Conduct and Quality

In addition to programs that evaluate crew behavior during line and LOFT operations, observations of LOFT are being conducted at several airlines, by NASA/University of Texas expert evaluators. The data is collected using the LOFT Evaluator Survey described in the chapter by Gregorich & Wilhelm. This survey has been designed for the specific use of trained expert observers to evaluate the quality of LOFT scenarios and LOFT facilitation.

From these surveys it has been found that the design of LOFT scenarios varied considerably from one fleet to another and from one airline to another (Butler, 1991). The greatest difference noted is in the level of technical skills orientation. This varied from presenting no technical problems to extremely high technical orientation. Although the scenarios all deal with CRM issues in a global sense, few are designed to address specific CRM behaviors. Most designs did not have options available to the crews, so that decision-making was relatively simple and did not encourage interaction between crewmembers. The airports of intended landing were never in doubt. The decisions to be made were always quite obvious.

The most successful LOFT designs observed usually focused on relatively simple technical problems or systems failures, introducing additional complexities such as communications failures or ambiguous warning lights. Time compression and ATC restrictions also contributed effectively to the more successful LOFT scenarios.

Many scenarios observed were nothing more than a full mission simulation with a problem requiring the use of an abnormal checklist. No challenge, no decisions—yet the crews would say they got a lot out of the LOFT that they would take back to the line. Other scenarios presented so many unrelated technical problems that they became unrealistic.

One scenario I observed had been designed to conclude with a non-precision approach using a non-directional beacon (NDB approach)—no other option was allowed. This was done so that credit could be taken for the NDB approach that, if completed during the LOFT, would not be required on the proficiency check the next day. The problem the crew encountered was a runaway pitch trim. The captain, who was flying this leg, attempted to fly and work the checklist with the flight engineer during climb-out. Only after the captain had become completely overloaded and was over-controlling the aircraft did he bring the first officer into the loop. As a result, the checklist was not run properly and the problem that could have been easily resolved was not cleared.

The facilitator was so intent on getting the crew to accomplish the NDB approach at destination that when the crew requested a return to the departure airport, he reported it closed, even though the weather had been good when they departed. It should be noted that an NDB approach with the pitch trim inoperative would be difficult as it would require manual trimming of the airplane. During the course of the flight, no matter what option the crew put forth, it was denied. The LOFT facilitator, realizing the problem he faced, decided to intervene and prompted the crew to revisit the checklist. Given this guidance, they were able to restore the system immediately.

The LOFT facilitator was able to complete the scenario as designed. The crew, however, had been given so many unrealistic reasons as to why there were no other usable airports or approaches available that they gave up any attempts at decision-making. The problem? It was not the crew's failure to run a checklist correctly, but the inflexibility of the scenario design and the LOFT facilitator. The design philosophy had the scenario so tightly scripted that there was no room for any logical alternatives based on the crew's performance or decisions.

The debriefing of the above scenario was totally focused on the technical aspects of the flight and misuse of the checklist by the flight engineer. The videotape was not used to show how the captain had been a "one-man show" and contributed to the checklist problem, nor was it discussed. The crew did not feel the scenario was realistic.

Some of the LOFT scenarios included two legs. In two-leg LOFTS, the dynamics of the flight on some changed noticeably as a function of whether the pilot flying was the captain or the first officer. It appears (at least in the training environment) that when the first officer is flying, the captain, in an attempt to let the first officer have more autonomy, may not demonstrate advocacy or inquiry even where appropriate. A statement often heard in training from captains is, "I'm not a very good copilot," and from discussions with other check pilots, this conclusion seems to be proven on the line.

During the debriefing of a two-leg LOFT, the crew was asked if, in retrospect, they were aware of any difference in the level of CRM behavior while the first officer was flying. Both were able to recognize that there was less demonstration of leadership and effective inquiry and advocacy. In this case, close in on a non-precision approach with the first officer flying, the captain did not question the first officer's acceptance of a runway change (after receiving landing clearance) to a parallel runway. This resulted in an unstable approach and a landing well off the center line of the runway. In the self-critique, both crewmembers recognized that they should not have accepted the runway change. The captain said he was uncomfortable but wanted the first officer to have the opportunity to make the decisions, since this was his leg. They also agreed that after accepting the change, considering the difficulty the first officer was having stabilizing the approach, a decision to go around should have been considered. It also must be noted that this crew was above average when the captain was flying. He had abrogated his leadership role to the first officer, who did not have the experience to accept it and did not use advocacy as the pilot-not-flying to express his concerns and propose a different course of action.

Few of the LOFT facilitators observed were truly skilled at briefing for the LOFT period. The rules for conducting LOFT were covered to varying degrees (generally fairly well), but CRM issues were not a part of pre-LOFT briefings. This is not to say that they should be briefed on or have any knowledge of the types of problems they will encounter, but they certainly should know what CRM behaviors are being evaluated and will be reviewed after the LOFT. In most cases CRM concepts were not included in the LOFT facilitator guides. In some cases it seemed the policy was to not brief the crew on CRM prior to LOFT. This type of policy may be appropriate for LOE but disregards the fact that LOFT is a training environment where experiencing positive crew coordination results in a much more effective learning experience than reviewing mistakes. This policy toward LOFT is like asking a crew during training to fly through an engine failure after take-off and not discussing how to accomplish the maneuver until after it is completed. They could be told what they did wrong, but it would be much better to brief them on the maneuver before flying. It was as though CRM was intended to be a big mystery and only after the crew had completed the LOFT would they be given any hint as to what was being evaluated.

Many of the LOFT facilitators also fell short on debriefing and facilitation skills for the crew self-critique. Critiques centered more on technical proficiency and individual performance than on CRM and crew performance. Many debriefings were lectures or "teacher-tell" with little effort made to draw the crew out and get them to critique their own performance. Few examples of effective CRM behavior were highlighted on the videotape by the facilitator for later review. In a number of cases the videotape was not used at all. It appears that very little training has been given to the facilitators on the effective use of the video as a debriefing tool. Surprisingly, one of the best CRM debriefings was observed after a LOFT that was not videotaped.

Given the limited time available for debriefing, the effective use of video is extremely important. Unless LOFT facilitators are trained to use video effectively as a debriefing tool, the money spent on the equipment is only yielding a marginal payback to the company. This is why it is so important to use the pre-LOFT briefing to set the stage for effective use of the video during the debriefing. How can video be used more effectively? Let the crew view the first 15 minutes of the LOFT video uninterrupted. Observing routine activities in the beginning will prepare them to evaluate their own performance. During this first 15 minutes of the flight segment, over 20 behaviors used to evaluate crew performance can be observed. The crew might be asked to evaluate their performance during this first 15 minutes discussing items covered during the pre-LOFT briefing. Later, when they view selected flight segments on the video, they will be better prepared to critique themselves.

Despite the fact that LOFT is not being conducted or designed as well as it could be, most crews evaluate it very favorably, as shown in the data presented in Figure 8.1. They provide reassurance that CRM programs are producing positive shifts in attitudes over time (Wilhelm, 1991). Crews find LOFT also has considerable merit as technical training (not surprising, considering the fact that most scenarios have a strong technical orientation and briefings and debriefings center on technical or procedural issues) and feel the training will be useful on the line, as shown in Figure 8.2 (Wilhelm, 1991).

Cockpit–Cabin Crew Interface

One area of realism that is hard to achieve in the LOFT environment is the interface between cockpit and cabin crew. Most crews observed during LOFT did not fully address the need for communication with flight service unless the problems presented involved events such as smoke in the cabin brought to their attention by the facilitator playing the role of a cabin crewmember. This problem may be due to the difficulty the cockpit crews have accepting that there is a need to consider flight service in a simulator. Many years of conditioning in simulator

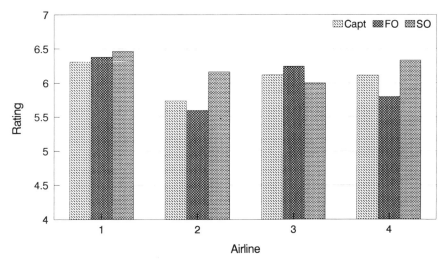

Figure 8.1 Average ratings for the item, "Overall, LOFT is an extremely useful training technique" in four airlines. Scale: 1, completely useless; 7, extremely useful.

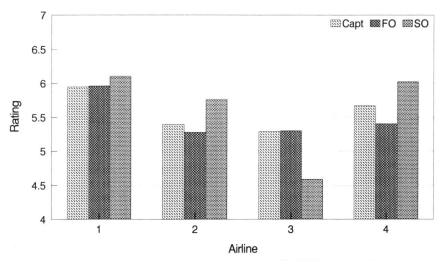

Figure 8.2 Average ratings by participants of the value of LOFT for technical (proficiency) training. Same scale as Figure 8.1.

training that has been maneuver-oriented and focused on individual proficiency make it hard for cock-pit crews to accept the presence of flight service as a part of the LOFT. (See the chapter by Helmreich, Wiener, & Kanki for further discussion of this issue.)

Advanced-Technology Aircraft and LOFT

The advanced-technology cockpit presents another area to be addressed in LOFT. It is a unique environment with its own potential problems for the crew as well as for LOFT designers and facilitators (Foushee & Helmreich, 1988; Wiener, 1988). One of the most common problems, often dubbed "automation fixation," was encountered during a line observation where a crew was led into this trap. On an arrival with good weather, the first officer tried to program the flight management system for the airport arrival and missed approach. He had difficulty entering the correct arrival identifier due to a change in the database. The captain became distracted and began watching the first officer. Both pilots had their heads down between 14,000 and 8,000 feet. This was an otherwise well-performing crew.

Although not unique to the latest "glass cockpit" technology, specific behaviors associated with advanced-technology aircraft are more likely to become an issue as the level of automation increases in cockpits. The behavioral differences between advanced-technology crews and standard cockpit crews has been examined in a field analysis of crew behavior by aircraft type and characteristics (Clothier, 1991a, 1991b). The need for LOFT scenarios uniquely designed to address automation issues is becoming more critical as the industry replaces older aircraft with advanced-technology aircraft incorporating high levels of automation (see the chapter by Wiener). Increased automation raises the question, "Who is in command?" Most of the flight management and autopilot system failures or malfunctions observed and available to the LOFT administrators do not address the kinds of problems that allow the best evaluation of the crew's performance in dealing with human factors issues of automation.

Some of the best automation problems observed were caused by simulator malfunctions rather than abnormalities designed into the LOFT. For example, while observing a LOFT in a Boeing 767 simulator, a computer malfunction caused the map display to shift several times, causing confusion for the crew. This was not a failure that could be duplicated by the LOFT facilitator, but was instead a random malfunction. Unfortunately, the LOFT facilitator interjected that he had not caused the problem, thus destroying the possibility of gaining a valuable training experience from the problem. The disorientation present would have required very effective crew coordination to resolve the anomalies presented by the map shift. The actions of the crew in this case raise serious questions about the level of crews' situational awareness when automation fails to do what is expected. Initially they did not revert to navigating using traditional instrumentation. It was only after the LOFT facilitator intervened that they took manual control of the airplane, ignoring the flight management system and navigation display.

The present advanced-technology cockpit is a reality, and LOFT designers must incorporate ways to address this new technology with its advantages and disadvantages. The advanced-technology LOFT should include the type of problem that requires pilot–computer interface—selected computer malfunctions at critical phases of flight. With the proper stress loading of external factors such as weather and/or ATC requirements, it becomes possible not only to evaluate CRM factors, but also to provide a research data base to answer questions posed by Wiener in his chapter.

Evaluator, Standardization, and Training

When Yen Ho was about to take up his duties as tutor to the heir of Ling, Duke Wei, he went to Ch'u Po Yu for advice. "I have to deal," he said, "with a man of depraved and murderous disposition. . . . How is one to deal with a man of this sort?" "I am glad" said Ch'u Po Yu, "that you asked this question. . . . The first thing you must do is not to improve him, but to improve yourself."

Taoist story of ancient China

One of the goals in a CRM/LOFT program is to verify that check airmen and LOFT facilitators are evaluating crews consistently. In initial training conducted by the NASA/UT Crew Research Project staff for these groups, the evaluations of different observers rating the same crew performance (a scenario designed as an average crew performance) ranged from poor to above average. This raises concerns regarding the level of standardization of evaluators overall and the criteria they use for evaluation within an organization. However, training evaluators does pay off, and after working with behavioral indicators, variations in ratings were narrowed considerably. In Helmreich & Wilhelm (1991) it is acknowledged that total agreement is seldom reached but that the realistic goal of assessment is not to achieve "perfection" but to determine the normative performance of crews. In particular, there was much greater agreement in evaluating the endpoint ratings of poor and exemplary performance after being trained to use behavioral indicators to aid in judgments. Not surprisingly, there was less consensus in the evaluation of crews slightly above or below average on specific aspects of crew coordination.

The variability we have found in evaluators before training and calibration shows how vital it is to train check airmen and LOFT facilitators and to examine the nature of their attitudes regarding crew coordination. Linking their training in evaluation of CRM with more traditional rating of technical skills helps to ensure that they are calibrated and to make evaluations more standardized across fleets within organization. The importance of training evaluators was outlined by Helmreich & Wilhelm (1987), and Butler, Helmreich, Wilhelm, & Taggart, (1991).

Though calibration of the evaluators is vital for research and for organizations' assessments of training and performance, equally important is the role check airmen and LOFT facilitators play as exemplars of the principles of CRM and as role models for command and leadership qualities (see the chapter by Helmreich & Foushee). Thus the key to an effective LOFT program to CRM impact is specialized training in CRM skills for check pilots, simulator instructors, and other management, instructional, and training staff (Taggart, 1991).

Training for these groups should include assistance in measuring performance changes and in designing annual recurrent LOFT programs. This training should be in addition to the baseline and recurrent CRM training that all crewmembers receive.

CONCLUSIONS ——————————————————————→

LOFT provides an environment where crews can see their actions as an integrated whole. The environment should provide them with a means of recognizing how the various functions of the aviation system depend on one another and how changes in any one part affect all others. It provides training in visualizing the relationship of individuals and teams to successful flight operations. The effective LOFT allows crews to act in a way that increases the overall safety of flight and requires a high degree of awareness of operational conditions and contingencies. It demonstrates the necessity to work effectively as team members and to build cooperative effort within a team. In its best form it requires accepting the existence of viewpoints and beliefs that are different and understanding what others really mean by their words and behavior.

A well-designed LOFT embodies consideration of both the technical and human factors aspects of resource management. While technical skill is primarily concerned with working with "things" (procedures or physical control), interpersonal skill involves working with people (the way an individual perceives and recognizes the situational assessments of other crewmembers' responses). Yet to design LOFT scenarios effectively, we must translate knowledge into action. We must distinguish among the areas of crew performance—of performing the technical activities, understanding and motivating individuals and groups, and coordinating all activities and interests of the team toward a common objective. This knowledge can provide us with the framework for building LOFT programs that meet high expectations.

LOFT designers and facilitators are always concerned about the role that they as individuals play in the development of CRM skills, but the line check pilot also plays a major role in the acceptance and reinforcement of the lessons of

LOFT. The changes that we are seeing in the training environment make it even more apparent that the check airman's CRM skills are an additional, critical element in fostering effective teamwork in the cockpit.

It should be the concern of those involved in the development and application of CRM and LOFT to watch the growth of the CRM skills within the organization as well as within crews, and to see that as an organization grows and learns, successes increasingly outweigh failures. This concept of growth is a vital part of the LOFT learning process. Crewmembers and management must both know that their performance develops, and that this development is limited only by their contributions. Especially, crews must see LOFT facilitators, check airmen, and management as individuals interested in and supportive of their growth in knowledge and CRM skills.

Effective LOFT includes reverse briefing, where crew involvement allows facilitators the opportunity to assess not only technical knowledge but also awareness of the human factors issues that form the basis for good CRM. LOFT design needs to encompass elements of choice that require total crew involvement in order for decisions to be made. Most importantly, debriefings must be conducted in a manner that lets crews recognize for themselves their most and least effective individual and crew behaviors.

Interpersonal skills and insight must be used to create individual satisfaction with the exercise of effective crew concepts both in LOFT and on the line, and to make the position of crewmember fulfilling for each individual. No CRM or LOFT program alone can do that, but with organizational and regulatory support, it is an attainable goal.

Observations of LOFT have provided an opportunity to look at the practical applications of concepts that were developed over 10 years ago. Guidelines and rules were developed before CRM programs had been introduced to airline crews. A new look at the design and goals of LOFT is needed.

As more airlines and military organizations move into CRM LOFT, some of the questions that we need to ask are:

1. Is full mission simulation the only answer?
2. Can CRM be reinforced through a less restrictive program involving shorter segments addressing specific CRM issues, as in SPOT?
3. Should a fixed amount of time or number of legs be dictated for LOFT, or should the merits of scenarios and training goals be the guiding factor for determining the design and execution of LOFT?
4. For airlines having fully integrated CRM and LOFT with an annual, single-visit training program, is pre-departure realism in LOFT important in setting the stage for later crew performance?
5. If the line check pilots are properly trained, can they effectively observe and evaluate CRM issues for the pre-departure phase of the operation during the line check?

These issues need to be addressed and the original model for LOFT reexamined. There is no question that the original model for conducting LOFT is still effective. It is ideal for research and for the design and conduct of LOEs in the simulator but may need to be expanded and modified as we learn from the experience gained over the past decade.

Acknowledgments

The research conducted at the University of Texas at Austin reported here was supported by NASA–Ames Research Center, Cooperative Agreement NCC2-286, Robert L. Helmreich, Principal Investigator, and by contract with the Federal Aviation Administration, BAA89-005. Special thanks are due Robert L. Helmreich for his many helpful comments on the early drafts of this chapter.

References

Butler, R. E. (1991). Lessons from cross-fleet/cross-airline observations: Evaluating the impact of CRM/LOFT training. In *Proceedings of the Sixth International Symposium on Aviation Psychology* (pp. 326–331). Columbus: Ohio State University.

Butler, R. E., Helmreich, R. L., Wilhelm, J. A., & Taggart, W. R. (1991). *Line/LOFT flightcrew evaluator workshop: The use of the Line/LOFT worksheet and behavioral indicators for evaluating flightcrews and LOFT administrators* (NASA/UT Technical Manual 91-4). Austin.

Clothier, C. (1991a). *Behavioral interactions in various aircraft types: Results of systematic observation of line operations and simulations.* Unpublished masters' thesis, University of Texas at Austin.

Clothier, C. (1991b). Behavioral differences in advanced technology and standard aircraft: Results of systematic observations of line operations and simulations. In *Proceedings of the Sixth International Symposium on Aviation Psychology* (pp. 332–337). Columbus: Ohio State University.

Federal Aviation Administration. (1989). *Cockpit resource management* (Advisory Circular 120-51). Washington, DC: Author.

Federal Aviation Administration. (1990). *Line operational simulations* (Advisory Circular AC 120-35B). Washington, DC: Autho.

Federal Aviation Administration. (in preparation). *Crew resource management* (Advisory Circular 120-51A). Washington, DC: Author.

Foushee, H. C., & Helmreich, R. L. (1988). Group interactions and flightcrew performance. In E. Weiner & D. Nagel (Eds.), *Human Factors in Aviation* (pp. 189–227). San Diego: Academic Press.

Ginnett, R. G. (1987). *First encounters of the close kind: The first meetings of airline flightcrews.* Unpublished doctoral dissertation. Yale University, New Haven, CT.

Hackman, J. R., & Helmreich, R. L. (1987). Assessing the behavior and performance of teams in organizations: The case of air transport crews. In D. R. Peterson & D. B. Fishman (Eds.), *Assessment for decision.* New Brunswick, NJ: Rutgers University Press.

Helmreich, R. L., & Wilhelm, J. A. (1987). Evaluating cockpit resource management training. In *Proceedings of the Fourth Symposium on Aviation Psychology* (pp. 440–446). Columbus: Ohio State University.

Helmreich, R. L., & Wilhelm, j. A. (1991). *Methodological issues in the use of the Line/LOS checklist and behavioral markers.* (NASA/University of Texas Technical Manual 91-1). Austin.

Helmreich, R. L., Wilhelm, J. A., & Gregorich, S. (1988). *Notes on the concept of LOFT: An agenda for research* (NASA/The University of Texas Technical Report 88-1). Austin.

Helmreich, R. L., Wilhelm, J. A., Kello, J. E., Taggert, W. R., & Butler, R. E. (1991). *Reinforcing and evaluating crew resource management: Evaluator/LOS instructor reference manual* (NASA/ University of Texas Technical Manual 90-2). Austin.

Huettner, C. (1981). In G. E. Cooper, M. D. White, & J. K. Lauber (Eds.), *Proceedings of a NASA/Industry workshop* (CP-2120). Moffett Field, CA: NASA–Ames Research Center.

Lauber, J. K., & Foushee, H. C. (1981). *Guidelines for Line Oriented Flight Training, Volumes 1 & II* (CP-2184). Moffett Field, CA: NASA–Ames Research Center.

Manske, F. A., Jr. (1987). *Secrets of effective leadership.* Columbia, TN: Leadership, Education and Development.

Nagel, D. (1988). Human error in aviation operations. In E. Weiner & D. Nagel (Eds.), *Human factors in aviation* (pp. 263–303). San Diego: Academic Press.

National Transportation Safety Board (1988). *Aircraft Accident Report: Continental Airlines, Inc. McDonnell Douglas DC-9-10, Stapleton International Airport, Denver, Colorado* (NTSB-AAR-88-9). Washington, DC: Author.

O'Hare, D., & Roscoe, S. (1990). *Flight deck performance: The human factor.* Ames, IA: Iowa State University Press.

Ruffell Smith, H. P. (1979). *A simulator study of the interaction of pilot workload with errors* (TM-78482). Moffett Field, CA: NASA–Ames Research Center.

Sears, R. L. (1986). *A new look at accident contributors and the implications of operational and training procedures.* IATA presentation, Geneva, Switzerland.

Taggart, W. R. (1991). Advanced CRM training for instructors and evaluators: Issues and methods. In *Proceedings of the Sixth International Symposium on Aviation Psychology* (pp. 356–361). Columbus: Ohio State University.

Taggart, W. R., & Butler, R. E. (1989). Validating and measuring the effectiveness of CRM and LOFT training programs. In *Proceedings of the Fifth Symposium on Aviation Psychology* (pp. 468–482). Columbus: Ohio State University.

Weiner, E. (1988). Cockpit automation. In E. Wiener & D. Nagel (Eds.), *Human factors in aviation* (pp. 433–461). San Diego: Academic Press.

Wilhelm, J. (1991). Crewmember and instructor evaluations of line oriented flight training. In *Proceedings of the Sixth International Symposium on Aviation Psychology* (pp. 362–367). Columbus: Ohio State University.

II

Perspectives

9

The Regulatory Perspective

Richard A. Birnbach
Federal Aviation Administration
Great Lakes Region
Des Plaines, Illinois 60018

Thomas M. Longridge
Federal Aviation Administration
Headquarters
Washington, D.C. 20041

HISTORICAL PERSPECTIVE ✈

Origins

Commercial aviation is generally considered to have been initiated in conjunction with the Air Mail Act of 1925, under which the U.S. Post Office began to contract with private carriers for airmail service on both domestic and international routes. As that system evolved, the government established rates of payment that were based on aircraft payload and awarded bonuses for the use of multiengine aircraft. As aircraft load capacity grew in response to this incentive, some airlines began to carry passengers in order to augment income. Thus was born the business of carrying passengers for profit.

In the United States, aviation safety regulations have often developed in reaction to disasters. Although some European nations had well-established governmental regulations pertaining to the licensing of pilots, in 1925 the United States still had no such requirements. Responding to public concern over an increasing number of well-publicized fatal accidents, Congress established the Air Commerce Act of 1926, which assigned both responsibility and regulatory authority for aviation to the Aeronautics Branch of the Department of Commerce, with the following objectives: (1) establish airworthiness standards and an associated system of aircraft registration, (2) administer examination and licensing procedures for aviation personnel and facilities, (3) establish uniform rules for air navigation, (4) establish new airports, and (5) encourage the development of civil aviation. Subsequent amendments to the Air Commerce Act authorized the Secretary of Commerce to investigate accidents and to define standards of safety. The Federal Aviation Act of 1958, which governs the current functions of the Federal Aviation Administration (FAA), retained all of these objectives.

Thus from the inception U.S. aviation regulatory authorities have had a dual mission. The Aeronautics Branch of the Department of Commerce and its successors, the Civil Aeronautics Administration (1938), the Federal Aviation Agency (1958), and the Federal Aviation Administration (1966), have all had the responsibility of both regulating safety in aeronautics and simultaneously promoting the efficient growth of the aviation industry. This dual responsibility may not be well recognized by the general public, but it represents a key aspect of the FAA's relationship with the aviation industry. Whether serving in the role of enforcer or enabler, the FAA shares goals with those over whom it maintains surveillance. Fortunately from the perspectives of both the FAA and industry, high standards of safety are jointly recognized as the first prerequisite to sustained growth in civil aviation. Historically, the FAA has been most successful in its regulatory role when it capitalizes on such common goals. This is particularly likely to be true with respect to any future regulatory initiative concerning crew resource management (CRM).

The Jet Era

When the first successful long-range jets began routinely flying in airline operations during the late 1950s and early 1960s, they quickly ended the era of long-distance train service and fast ocean-crossing passenger ships. As a result, the U.S. consumer soon had few alternatives for distant travel other than flying. In the same period, it became apparent that the then revolutionary new jet aircraft required new standards of pilot qualification. Thus, the newly created Federal Aviation Agency found itself in 1958 assuming its regulatory responsibilities during the era of emerging commercial jet aircraft.

The new agency responded to the introduction of jets by modifying previously established airman qualification rules to accommodate the special training needs of jet crews. At that time the principal focus concerned pilot proficiency required to cope with high-speed swept-wing handling qualities, high-altitude operation, high-speed long-range navigation, and particularly, jet powerplant characteristics. All these considerations, which were derived in part from the airworthiness standards established in certifying the new aircraft, entailed significant changes from the preceding era of propeller-driven aircraft. There was understandable concern that pilot qualification should specifically address the technical considerations associated with jet aircraft operations. The regulations which resulted emphasized teaching and testing air crewmembers as individuals, in order to ensure that each crewmember could competently execute the tasks required to operate fast swept-wing jets. This regulatory perspective on individual training and qualification has remained ever since, although the incidence of accidents primarily attributable to inadequate CRM, rather than to individual technical incompetence, is creating mounting pressure for change.

At the beginning of the passenger-carrying jet age, the vast majority of airline pilots had first been trained as military aviators. The values inculcated during prior military training migrated to the culture of civil aviation when military pilots became civilian commercial pilots, or when they became FAA inspectors. Among these values is respect for rank, for leaders who take charge and act decisively, and for subordinates who understand that it is usually not appropriate to question the decisions of their superiors. It was this cadre of FAA inspectors, in cooperation with their counterparts in the airlines, who developed the training, checking, operating practices, and cockpit crew culture which accompanied the introduction of jet transports. They brought to this task an attitude toward individual proficiency that required each captain to demonstrate the ability to handle nearly every conceivable situation that might be encountered in flight by him- or herself. Thus in many ways the rules and norms under which we currently operate are the product of the socialization process of their originators. This observation is not meant as a criticism, but rather to point out that as we strive for ways to improve our training and checking processes in the future, we should be cognizant of the power of attitudes and values in the establishment of standards of behavior.

FAR PARTS 121 AND 135 ✈

The organizationally varied history of aeronautical regulation, in which successive agencies adopted, then modified their predecessor's rules to meet the circumstances of the day, has resulted in a complex system of rules. Some Parts of the Federal Aviation Regulations (FARs) are directed at both commercial and general aviation, while others apply only to specific segments of the industry. The principle distinctions pertaining to commercial passenger service are based on the number of seats in an aircraft or its total payload. Part 121 applies to operators of aircraft that seat more than 30 passengers or have payload in excess of 7500 pounds—the large air carriers. Part 135 applies to operators of aircraft having 30 seats or less, or a payload under 7500 pounds—the commuter airlines. Until quite recently, operators with both categories of aircraft have been required to operate under both Parts 121 and 135, but FAA policy now permits certain operators to meet compliance requirements fully under Part 121, provided they do so in all of their operations.

Although Parts 121 and 135 have many requirements in common, they also exhibit some unusual differences. For example, while Part 121 requires a cabin attendant on aircraft seating 9 or more passengers, the comparable figure for Part 135 is 19 passenger seats. Part 121 requires weather radar equipment on all aircraft. Part 135 requires thunderstorm detection equipment on aircraft seating more than 10 passengers, but exempts from this requirement operations conducted entirely in Alaska or Hawaii. Parts 121 and 135 also differ with respect to allowable duty hours for a pilot and crew rest requirements, Part 121 being more restrictive. Among the most significant differences between Part 121 and 135 is airworthiness certification. Aircraft operated under Part 121 must be certified under FAR Par 25, while those operated under Part 135 may be certified under FAR Part 23. This distinction has important implications with respect to pilot proficiency, since the requirements of Part 25 regarding aircraft performance characteristics, instrumentation, and system redundancy are considerably more stringent than those of Part 23. The margin of error therefore tends to be smaller for Part 135 operations, particularly when one considers that they may often involve flight into airports which have less than a full repertory of equipment and navigation aids. Aircraft certified for Part 135 operations under Part 23 are likely to be characterized by more limited performance capability, less sophisticated cockpit instrumentation, and fewer back-up options in the event of equipment failure. The CRM training implications of this circumstance are obvious.

Another noteworthy difference between Parts 121 and 135 concerns dispatch. All scheduled Part 121 passenger-carrying flights are executed under the authority of an aircraft dispatcher licensed by the FAA. Operating out of a centralized dispatch facility with comprehensive information services, such as weather conditions at all points along the route of flight, fuel-to-destination, inoperable equipment on board, and status of enroute navigational aids, the dispatcher has authority to delay a flight's departure or redirect its route of flight if conditions so dictate. The dispatcher has instant communications access to the cockpit for the entire duration of a flight. Although some Part 135 operations are conducted on a similar basis, there is no regulatory requirement to do so. Under Part 135, the aircraft captain has full dispatch authority.

Flight Training Regulations

While the wording of those portions of Parts 121 and 135 pertaining to the regulation of training programs differs, they are very similar. All major airlines and commuters must have a training program which is approved by their designated FAA Principal Operations Inspector (POI). In order to foster standardization in criteria used to review an operator's program, the POI is provided with detailed guidance in the *Air Transportation Operations Inspector's Handbook* (FAA, 1988), which, as additional sections are written, is superseding its predecessor, the *Air Carrier Operations Inspector's Handbook* (FAA, 1986). The revised handbook provides guidance with respect to reviewing curricula, course materials, facilities, and record-keeping procedures. It categorizes flight training in terms of segments, modules, and lessons. For example, flight training segments might consist of ground school, simulator training, and aircraft training. The new handbook was written with particular emphasis on the importance of crew-oriented training in instructional curricula.

While the types of courses that must be included in Part 121 and 135 training programs are virtually identical, differences do occur in certain areas. For example, Part 121 requires the operator to meet programmed hours of instruction for both ground-based and aircraft-based training (but permits their reduction based on use of training devices and simulators). Part 135 does not employ the concept of programmed hours for training.

The content of flight training and proficiency checks also differs between the respective Parts. Part 121 requires training and practice on the maneuvers and procedures listed in Appendix E and proficiency checks on those listed in Appendix F (and Appendix H when conducted in a simulator). Under Part 135 the appropriate maneuvers and procedures are based on those required under FAR Part 61 for pilot certification.

Another notable difference between the regulatory provisions of these respective parts concerns initial operating experience (IOE). Following training and checking in an initial qualification curriculum, all Part 121 crewmembers must complete programmed hours of IOE in an aircraft under the supervision of a check airman. The check airman must certify their competence to perform their assigned duties or refer them for remedial action. Under Part 135 these requirements only apply to the pilot in command, not to the co-pilot.

As we proceed to develop recommendations for the implementation of CRM training and checking requirements, these differences between the traditional regulatory provisions of Parts 121 and 135 should be kept in mind. Part 135 represents a significant segment of the industry, and one whose operating circumstances clearly highlight the need for sound CRM practices.

Impact of Flight Simulators

One further difference between Parts 121 and 135 that stems from economic rather than from regulatory causes is the use of flight simulators to substitute for aircraft training and checking. Part 121 air carriers generally make extensive use of such resources for these purposes, while Part 135 operators historically have not. This circumstance is likely to be an important factor in any choice of CRM training strategy for Part 135.

No such problem exists for Part 121. Even during the 1970s, airlines and the FAA were quick to realize the benefits of simulator training. In 1981 the FAA published its Advanced Simulator Plan as Appendix H to Part 121, to encourage the use of advanced flight simulators and to specify their permissible use for training and checking, subject to flight simulator qualification conducted on each such device by the FAA. The flexibility inherent in flight simulators provides an opportunity for not only more efficient but more realistic training than would otherwise be available in the aircraft. For example, flight simulators are routinely employed today to train airline pilots to recognize and respond appropriately to windshear. Clearly there is a host of such abnormal and emergency procedures that can be fully exercised in a simulator, but only partially practiced in an aircraft. Simulators also provide an ideal environment for the development and exercise of CRM skills, but only if they are used for that purpose. Historically, their use has been mixed, some airlines having a long tradition of crew-oriented flight simulator training, while others only recently moving in that direction. In general, pilot professional organizations have strongly endorsed crew concept training. The FAA has formalized its recommendations on how such training should be conducted in two complementary publications, *Line Operational Simulations*, Advisory Circular 120-35B (FAA, 1990b), and *Cockpit Resource Management Training*, Advisory Circular 120-51 (FAA, 1989).

Regulatory Emphasis on Individuals

It is important to remember that the regulations concerning pilot qualification have always focused on individual performance. This individualistic orientation is reinforced by the physical characteristics of the aviation safety and operations system. For example, only one person can talk at a time on aeronautical two-way radios. Therefore, only one person, the pilot operating the radio, can express the thoughts of an entire aircrew when communicating with air traffic control. In the mind of the controller, the radio message is from the "captain," even though the speaker usually is the first officer. Conversely, the aircrew does not hear the "Boston Air Route Traffic Control Center," they hear a single voice that is directing their flight's routing, sometimes rather inconveniently. Pilots also tend to visualize a single air traffic controller rather than the air traffic control system. Similarly, pilots seem to assign airline training organizations the appearance of a particular check airman, and the FAA's safety and regulatory program may "look" just like the first FAA inspector a particular pilot may have met. These individuals are all part of an aviation system that assigns them specific responsibilities for compliance with safety rules. The air traffic controller, check airman, pilot, and FAA inspector are all subject to shared professional and personal risk when non-compliance with a safety standard is an issue. Because of the structure of the regulations and the physical characteristics of aviation operations, the investigations and remedial actions, as well as other "performance failure" issues, often seem to involve a "one against one" interpersonal struggle that ends with a clear winner and a clear loser.

An individual pilot retaking a failed checkride is subject to demotion or dismissal by the airline, or may be subject to official enforcement action by the FAA should he again fail the check. Individual air traffic controllers are reprimanded and sent to remedial training when compliance requirements are not met.

Individual FAA inspectors are reprimanded for any perceived performance deficiencies which involve the FAA's enforcement activities.

Designated Examiner Program

The Airline Deregulation Act of 1978 provided the first opportunity since 1938 for airlines to determine their own markets and set their own prices. Prior to deregulation, the FAA was actively seeking to downsize its inspector workforce. The fully compliant posture and excellent safety record of a well-regulated, stable industry suggested that safety would be better served by improved inspection management and automated information systems than by more inspectors. However, the rapid expansion of the airlines which accompanied deregulation upset these plans. The demands for air carrier inspector services quickly reached an all-time high. Most of the old hands were almost completely involved in certification of new pilots and new airlines on a full-time basis. Resources available for ordinary surveillance were limited. Because of the shortage of inspectors, the FAA reluctantly established a "designated pilot examiner" program, which allows airline employees to do the testing and checking which had traditionally been done by FAA inspectors. Under the current version of this program, an FAA Aircrew Program Manager (APM) is responsible for overseeing the technical performance of designated examiners—company employees approved by the FAA to serve as pilot license examiners. When serving in that capacity, these designated airmen function not so much as airline employees, but as representatives of the FAA Administrator. The APMs in turn are managed by the POI. Typically, a large airline will have one APM assigned for each aircraft type it flies, each of which will have a stable of designated examiners.

Although the designated examiner program is generally considered to have been successful, it obviously requires careful participant selection, conscientious management, and continuing surveillance to ensure its effectiveness. A designated examiner is in the unenviable position of reporting to two masters, only one of whom controls the paycheck. The structure of this system is presented here because it is a consideration for any future initiative involving the establishment of CRM standards for evaluation by check airmen.

THE RATIONALE FOR CRM TRAINING ──────── ✦

Joint Industry/Government Task Force Recommendations

In 1987 then FAA Administrator, T. Alan McArtor, directed the formation of a Joint Industry/Government Task Force to review the FAA's airline crew qualification standards. Among the products of this effort are the line operational simulation and cockpit resource management advisory circulars previously cited. Another is the Advanced Qualification Program (AQP), which is described later in this chapter. The joint task force, which has now been institutionalized under FAA auspices as the Aviation Training Subcommittee of the Aviation Rulemaking Advisory Committee, also recommended changes to the FARs that would mandate CRM team training for airline crews. While such regulatory changes have yet to be made, the FAA has concurred with the committee's rationale that in today's technological and operational environments, it is not sufficient to provide training that focuses only on an individual pilot's technical competence. While activities preparatory to the announcement of future rulemaking in this arena are under way, all the major airlines and some regional carriers already have CRM training programs in various stages of maturity.

While there appears to be universal agreement with respect to the benefits of CRM training, unanimity does not exist with regard to the desirability of elevating CRM to the status of pass–fail standards for proficiency checks. Indeed, even experts in this field are divided over the issue of the feasibility of any such strategy. From an FAA perspective, establishing proficiency check standards for CRM may be the surest way to bring about the uniform implementation of comprehensive CRM training programs throughout the industry. However, the feasibility of any such approach must be demonstrated prior to its consideration as a candidate for rulemaking.

Prior to discussing the appropriateness of pass–fail evaluation of CRM, a brief review of the FAA's perspective on flight standards is needed.

Application of Standards to Pilot Evaluation

A standard is simply a statement about expected performance. A proficiency check entails a set of qualification standards which together define minimally required competence to perform as pilot. Each qualification standard should contain explicit information in all three of the following categories: (1) the *behavior* to be observed; (2) the *range*, if any, of acceptable performance; and (3) the applicable *conditions*. To the extent that insufficient information is provided in any of these categories, the standard becomes increasingly subject to inconsistency in its application. The importance of well-formulated standards cannot be overstated, as they are the foundation of pilot qualification and certification.

For each of these categories—behavior, range, and conditions—there exist corollary issues that impact the usability of a standard. For example, the specification of behavior can vary in terms of its granularity, from tuning a navigation radio to controlling the approach phase of flight. Too narrow a perspective can lead to impractical evaluation requirements, while too broad a focus can preclude clearly definable behavioral specifications. For proficiency check purposes the boundaries of a particular standard should be selected so as to strike a balance between the need to observe an adequate sample of behaviors and the practical considerations associated with completing an entire set of such standards for the proficiency check.

The range of acceptable performance should be selected to reflect real-world operational requirements consistent with safety. Where applicable, tolerances should be selected so as to be clearly achievable by at least minimally competent airmen under the conditions specified. If not, such tolerance specifications are likely to be widely ignored. It should also be recognized, however, that as aviation tends to be very unforgiving of error, some standards may not allow for any range of tolerance in acceptable performance (e.g., lowering the landing gear). Such absolute standards should be employed only where failure to perform is critical to safety of flight.

The third category, specification of conditions, is among the most important for developing meaningful standards and is perhaps the area currently most in need of improvement in commercial aviation. This category identifies not only the media in which performance of the standard is to be observed, but the representation of internal and external conditions necessary for elicitation of critical behaviors. The former is selected from the universe of possible conditions occurring within the environment internal to the aircraft and may include specification of both functional and dysfunctional equipment, crew complement, aircraft configuration, fuel, gross weight, pertinent flight parameters, and any other such factor relevant to the behavior to be observed. Similarly, the external conditions for a given standard include such considerations as weather, route of flight, traffic density, airport, air traffic control, and any other such condition relevant to eliciting a representative sample of an airman's competency for proficiency check purposes on a given standard.

The most important consideration with respect to conditions is operational relevance. The conditions under which the proficiency check occurs should be highly representative of those which occur in both normal and abnormal operations. By way of illustration: A number of years ago an airline began experiencing crosswind landing problems in a newly acquired aircraft. The initial investigation focused on possible deficiencies in the flight simulator. In the final analysis, however, it was determined that airmen qualifying in the new aircraft simulator were simply never trained or checked on landing under a crosswind condition. When that condition was explicitly incorporated into the standard for proficiency check on landing, the problem disappeared.

Measurement Considerations

Sound measurement procedures are essential to the reliability and validity of the regulatory process for airman qualification and certification. Flight standards comprise the yardstick by which the competency of airmen is measured. Ideally, that yardstick should yield identical results when applied to identical behavior. To the extent it does not, the airman evaluation process lacks reliability. Unreliability in turn threatens the validity of the entire process.

Reliability refers to consistency in the measurement process, while validity is the extent to which a measure is in fact measuring what is intended. A measure can be completely reliable but nevertheless totally lacking in validity: for example, selecting airmen for hire based on eye color, or measuring flight aptitude based on skull diameter. Both selection practices can be done accurately and consistently, but neither has any true relationship to competence as a crewmember.

An unreliable measure, however, can never be valid because true variance in the measure cannot be distinguished from that variance attributable to error; that is, whatever relationship exists between the measure and the factor it purports to measure is lost within the error component. For example, if one were to measure the dimensions of a 10-foot room with a 5-foot elastic tape measure, the underlying true relationship between the measurement unit and the actual dimensions of the room cannot be validly determined due to the inherent error in the measuring device. Another example: check airmen who employ widely varying tolerance ranges for determining acceptable performance on a manual instrument landing system approach.

Maintaining reliability and validity in evaluation of airmen is therefore very important from a regulatory perspective, and a major consideration with respect to the incorporation of CRM into that process. The same guidelines on procedures for enhancing reliability and validity in current airman evaluation should apply to any future initiatives in CRM.

Such guidelines should not be complicated or difficult to implement. First, they should focus on clearly defined, observable behavior rather than inferences about underlying cognitive processes. The behavior that constitutes acceptable performance must be explicitly identified, so that no ambiguity exists with respect to what is to be observed for evaluation purposes. Compliance with this guideline not only enhances reliability among evaluators, it communicates to those being evaluated what is expected of them.

Second, the measurement environment should be standardized to the maximum extent feasible. Lack of standardized measurement conditions is the single greatest contributor to lack of reliability in test and evaluation. This simple dictum applies just as much to a proficiency check conducted in an advanced simulator as it does to a 10-minute oral exam. In either case, adherence to standardized measurement conditions can significantly enhance the reliability of the results. For this reason, it is absolutely essential that the condition set to be employed for any proficiency check that includes CRM be developed with great care.

Third, the measurement process must be calibrated, and quality control procedures for maintaining that calibration must be implemented. This guideline applies whether the primary measurement strategy consists of ratings by check airmen or automated measures of performance. Since virtually all proficiency checks in commercial aviation are currently conducted with human evaluators as the primary measuring instrument, it follows that calibration of check airmen for measuring CRM performance will be another essential requirement if CRM is to be formally evaluated in the future. This implies that any FAA-mandated requirement for CRM evaluation should be accompanied by a co-requirement for training and evaluation on a continuing basis of the human evaluators to be employed. This requirement should apply equally to FAA aviation safety inspectors and to company-employed check airmen.

Psychological Considerations

From a regulatory perspective, a primary goal of qualification and certification is safe performance in the operational environment. To the extent that behavior sampled during a proficiency check, or during a line check, is not representative of an airman's typical performance, the process has failed. The best means of achieving the generalization of performance standards to everyday operations is internalization of those standards by the pilot population, rather than their imposition by mandate. Internalized standards reflect a process of socialization applied to the cockpit environment—attitudes, values, expectations, and norms of behavior applied both to oneself and to others in that environment. It is important to recognize that even for the circumscribed environment of the cockpit, some form of socialization process will inevitably occur, regardless of whether an individual is consciously aware of it or whether an organization actively attempts to influence the course of its development. We believe that as part of our overall strategy for developing sound standards of performance—particularly for CRM behaviors—we must aggressively seek to influence this process in desirable directions.

The rationale for providing CRM training is well presented elsewhere in this volume and need not be detailed here. At least 60% of accidents in commercial aviation can be attributed to some form of preventable crew error. From our perspective, the case for formally incorporating CRM into the regulatory process for qualification and certification is well documented. New technology has produced a functional shift from pilot redundancy (co-pilot as back-up) to shared cockpit responsibilities. CRM skills are essential to the competent exercise of those responsibilities. Moreover, since the aircraft can only be safely flown with a full crew complement, training and evaluation should also be accomplished on that same basis.

The number of airlines in which CRM training has become standard has grown considerably within the past several years. Great progress has been made with respect to the socialization process as applied to fostering good CRM behaviors in aircrews. However, in the absence of a uniform regulatory requirement, considerable variability exists in the details of CRM training program implementation. Most significantly, nowhere is an airman's competence on CRM skills a formal consideration for qualification to occupy a crew position.

Any transition to the explicit incorporation of CRM factors in airman evaluation should only be accomplished with a recognition of the utility of internalized standards clearly in mind. Such an endeavor should therefore seek maximum buy-in from those who will be most affected. That would require a strategy of partnership between the FAA and industry, effective two-way communication, flexibility, and provisions to validate proposed methodologies prior to final rulemaking.

REGULATORY CONSIDERATIONS FOR CRM ──────── →

CRM Training: The Need to Demonstrate Proficiency

Given that the case for CRM training is well established, it does not necessarily follow that CRM should also be formally evaluated as part of a proficiency check. It has been argued, for example, that CRM training programs to date have been successful precisely because they have been conducted on a no-jeopardy basis, that is, free of the anxieties an evaluation setting can elicit. Would it therefore not be sufficient merely to establish a regulatory requirement that mandates CRM training and establishes some uniform guidelines on how that training should be conducted? Or should CRM be formally incorporated by FAR into both training and proficiency check requirements? The authors believe that because of the overwhelming evidence of its impact on flight safety, not only should CRM training be mandatory, but demonstrated proficiency in CRM ultimately should be a regulatory requirement for qualification and certification. However, there are sound reasons for proceeding on a gradual basis in the transition to any such requirement. In addition to the above considerations about the relative effectiveness of artificially imposed versus internalized standards, there are numerous practical issues which must first be resolved.

Perhaps the most pressing practical issue is the question of whether CRM can be meaningfully expressed in terms of standards which reflect explicit behavior, tolerance ranges, and conditions. Unless it can be empirically established that CRM standards can be applied with the same reliability and validity as standards for technical performance, CRM can never become a regulatory requirement for proficiency checks.

Research is continuing to determine the validity and reliability of evaluating CRM behaviors. A regulatory basis for obtaining these data is now firmly in place: the AQP, established by regulation with the publication of Special Federal Aviation Regulation 58 in October 1990 (FAA, 1990a), together with an accompanying AQP Advisory Circular, AC120-54 (FAA, 1991a). AQP is a voluntary 5-year test program which provides certificated Part 121 and 135 operators with an alternative to the traditional FARs for airman qualification and certification. Presently some of the largest Part 121 air carriers are among the participants in this new program.

CRM in the Advanced Qualification Program

From an FAA perspective, AQP contains all the necessary ingredients to permit the systematic development of flight standards for CRM and to determine empirically the reliability and validity of such standards. Of particular significance to that endeavor, AQP also provides the opportunity to reassess the specification of all flight standards and to incorporate CRM considerations into that process.

Although CRM is just as important an initiative outside AQP as it is within, the authors believe that the validation of CRM principles which AQP enables will ultimately have universal application. A synopsis of the CRM integration strategy for AQP may therefore be fruitful for the purposes of the present discussion.

Existing standards for airmen focus on technical performance in individual duty positions. Such standards were developed by the FAA based on years of practical experience and have been effective for the generations of aircraft on which they were based. As aircraft technology has evolved, however, some such standards have become of increasingly questionable relevance.

Figure 9.1 summarizes how the role of the pilot changes with increasing levels of aircraft automation. The emerging generation of highly automated fly-by-wire aircraft systems with glass cockpits is dramatically changing the role of the pilot from controller to systems manager. The modern cockpit places particular demands on such skills as information acquisition and processing, problem recognition, judgment, decision-making, crew communications, and shared responsibilities. All these clearly fall within the domain known as CRM. The impact of automation on crew coordination is discussed by Weiner in his chapter.

Other factors besides cockpit automation, of course, have also contributed to changes in pilot tasking, in particular changes to operational practices in the National Aerospace System. The changing role of the pilot warrants a complete reexamination of the standards which should be applied to a determination of competency to perform as an airman, at least with respect to the currently emerging generation of aircraft. AQP provides a systematic methodology for such a reexamination. That process starts with a detailed task analysis, explicitly documenting what the pilot must do to operate safely a particular make, model, and series of aircraft, together with the skills, knowledge, and attitudes needed for competent performance of each such task and subtask.

This approach permits CRM skills to be embedded in a task-specific con-

MANAGEMENT MODE	AUTOMATION FUNCTIONS	HUMAN FUNCTIONS

AUTONOMOUS OPERATION	Fully autonomous operation
	Pilot not usually informed
	System may or may not be capable of
	   being disabled
		Pilot generally has no role in operation
		Monitoring is limited to fault detection
		Goals are self-defined; pilot normally
		   has no reason to intervene

MANAGEMENT BY EXCEPTION	Essentially autonomous operation
	Automatic reconfiguration
	System informs pilot and
	   monitors responses
		Pilot informed of system intent;
		Must consent to critical decisions;
		May intervene by reverting to lower
		   level

MANAGEMENT BY CONSENT	Full automatic control of
	   aircraft and flight
	Intent, diagnostic and
	   prompting functions provided
		Pilot must consent to state changes,
		   checklist execution, anomaly resolution;
		Manual execution of critical actions

MANAGEMENT BY DELEGATION	Autopilot & autothrottle control
	   of flight path
	Automatic communications and
	   nav following
		Pilot commands hdg, alt, speed;
		Manual or coupled navigation;
		Commands system operations,
		   checklists, communications

SHARED CONTROL	Enhanced control and guidance;
	Smart advisory systems;
	Potential flight path and other
	   predictor displays
		Pilot in control through CWS or
		   envelope-protected system;
		May utilize advisory systems;
		System management manual

ASSISTED MANUAL CONTROL	Flight director, FMS, nav modules;
	Data link with manual messages;
	Monitoring of flight path control
	   and aircraft systems
		Direct authority over all systems;
		Manual control, aided by F/D and
		   enhanced navigation displays;
		FMS is available; trend info on request

DIRECT MANUAL CONTROL	Normal warnings and alerts provided; Routine ACARS communications performed automatically	Direct authority over all systems; Manual control utilizing raw data; Unaided decision-making; Manual communications

(Left axis: LEVEL OF AUTOMATION — from VERY HIGH at top to VERY LOW at bottom)

Figure 9.1 Impact of level of automation on pilot function. (From Billings, 1991.)

text, where appropriate. By identifying CRM behaviors in terms of the specific actions that should occur during the execution of a task, benefits for both training and evaluation purposes can be gained. In AQP such task-specific information will be employed to derive enabling, supporting, and terminal proficiency objectives which span the continuum, respectively, from the operation of an individual subsystem to integrated task performance. Proficiency objectives, in turn, may be allocated to indoctrination, qualification, and continuing qualification curricula, as appropriate to the entry level of the pilot.

Terminal proficiency objectives, together with their associated standards of satisfactory performance and conditions of measurement, constitute the new qualification standards to be employed in AQP. These new qualification standards will be determined on an aircraft make-, model-, series-, and variant-specific basis. All curricula will contain evaluation segments on which documentation of performance on such standards, including CRM standards, will be obtained. The resulting data will be forwarded in de-identified electronic digital format to the FAA for analysis and for the establishment of a permanent database on pilot proficiency.

Can CRM skills be effectively identified on a task-specific basis? We believe some such skills are already at least informally identified even in traditional training programs simply as procedures to be accomplished during a task, such as verbal acknowledgement by one crewmember of mode control panel changes executed by the other crewmember. In AQP such behaviors would be highlighted for training and checking purposes on CRM.

The authors believe that expressing CRM behaviors on a task-specific basis would not only facilitate the development of explicit standards for CRM, but would enhance the reliability and validity of the measurement process as applied to that domain. This approach does not preclude the application of global measures of CRM across all phases of flight, since clearly there do exist higher order CRM considerations, such as cockpit climate, which are indeed pervasive in their effect. The authors simply believe that our capacity to apply CRM principles to improved training and evaluation would be enhanced by augmenting such global information with task-specific data wherever it is feasible to do so.

Line-oriented flight training (LOFT) has been demonstrated to be among the most effective techniques for developing CRM skills (Helmreich, Wilhelm, Kello, Taggart, & Butler, 1991; Jensen, 1989; Lauber & Foushee, 1981), in part because it requires training to be conducted with a full crew complement under operationally realistic conditions. AQP extends this concept to line-oriented evaluation (LOE), in which qualification standards must include standards of performance in CRM. LOE will be conducted in a crew setting under realistic conditions. AQP provides, therefore, for CRM evaluation to be conducted under the circumstances best suited to its observation. However, until such time as an adequate database on CRM has been established, such CRM evaluation will continue to be conducted in AQP on a no-jeopardy basis. At least 5 years from program inception have been allocated to complete necessary data acquisition and analysis.

AQP was initially developed in close cooperation with industry, and this partnership continues to be a valuable source of mutual feedback on program effectiveness. From its inception, this interchange has been fostered by an active AQP Working Group sponsored by the Air Transport Association of America. Participants include all the major airlines, regional airlines, major aircraft manufacturers, training equipment manufacturers, representatives of the various pilot professional organizations, and members of the research community. As the industry proceeds with development of AQP and data pertinent to the presently proposed strategy for integrating CRM into training and evaluation are acquired, this group provides the mechanism for industry participation in future FAA decisions based on those data. We believe that the ultimate success of any future regulatory requirement for CRM evaluation will depend on industry's acceptance that such a requirement is in its best interest.

CONSIDERATIONS FOR THE FUTURE ────────────── ✈

It is unfortunate that those portions of the airline industry perhaps most in need of crew-oriented training and checking, the Part 135 regional and commuter airlines, are least equipped with resources for obtaining it. One of the FAA's major goals in AQP, therefore, is to create more opportunities for this type of training in that community.

AQP was designed to enable training centers, for example, to develop and conduct an individualized AQP program for certificated Part 121 and 135 applicants. Any such program would be subject to the same requirements for integration of CRM into training and evaluation as apply to the larger carriers and would thus provide a vehicle for expanding access to systematically developed CRM training for that segment of the industry.

A closely related initiative would be the development of a model AQP program focused on commuter aircraft. In recognition of the potentially significant front-end cost of analysis required to develop an AQP, such an initiative would seek to reduce that cost by establishing a generic AQP, together with FAA-approved templates created to simplify the process of customizing an AQP to match the individual applicant's circumstances. Any such model AQP would incorporate thorough integration of CRM into training and evaluation.

Flight Training Equipment

AQP has also been designed to provide significantly increased flexibility with respect to equipment which may be employed in flight training. Subject to justification on the basis of a documented front-end analysis, the FAA may approve use in a given curriculum of a wide range of such devices. With respect to CRM, this feature implies that training and proficiency evaluation on many technical tasks can be accomplished in lower order devices, thereby increasing the availability of higher order devices for crew-oriented training purposes. In AQP, LOFT may be conducted in certain flight training devices (as defined in Advisory Circular 120-45A, FAA, 1992) as well as full flight simulators. Although FAA qualification procedures for flight simulators (as defined in Advisory Circular 120-40B, FAA, 1991b) will remain unchanged in AQP during its initial 5-year test period, the built-in data acquisition features of AQP will ultimately provide a training effectiveness database that could be employed to refine such qualification criteria in the future.

AQP will, however, generate some immediate requirements for increased functionality in some aspects of flight training equipment. For example, the strong emphasis on crew orientation for evaluation as well as training will demand improved capacity to generate line operational scenarios tailored to the qualification standards they are intended to address. A much larger repertory of such scenarios will be required than presently exists for LOFT purposes. In addition, increased reliance on automated performance measurement capabilities in flight simulators to monitor aircrew technical performance would better enable human evaluators to focus on CRM performance. Currently, there is little or no use of such automated measurement technologies by air carriers.

Calibration of Evaluators

AQP specifically requires indoctrination, qualification, and continuing qualification for instructors and evaluators. Such curricula must specifically address techniques for training and evaluating CRM. The program also includes provisions for individually tracking evaluator-generated data on a continuing basis. Thus AQP not only contains the necessary mechanisms for calibrating evaluators but compared to traditional programs provides a significantly enhanced capability for surveillance of the evaluation process. Automated analysis of such data will be used to identify departures from calibration limits, which in turn can serve as a basis for directing on-site FAA surveillance.

Data Management and Analysis

AQP incorporates comprehensive database and analysis capabilities, a major objective of which is to provide an empirical foundation for increased understanding of CRM training and evaluation effectiveness. The integration of CRM, which begins with a detailed task analysis and culminates in proficiency objectives allocated to training and evaluation segments of flight training curricula, will be tracked in two complementary relational databases, the Program Audit Data Base and the Performance Proficiency Data Base. The former documents the products of the front-end analysis in which CRM factors are embedded within tasks and subtasks. The latter documents the observed results of evaluating performance relative to the proficiency objective standards derived from the supporting task and subtask analysis.

A major objective of AQP data management and analysis is to validate the extent to which the standards work as intended. When analysis of the Performance Proficiency Data Base suggests that this may not be the case, the information necessary to identify those areas of front-end analysis potentially in need of further refinement will be immediately available through the relational capabilities of the Program Audit Data Base. The process by which standards are derived and subsequently applied for measurement purposes is dynamic and self-correcting.

During its first 5 years, AQP requires that multipoint rating scales (e.g., 5-point Likert scales) be employed to grade performance on CRM standards but does not require the application of pass–fail criteria to such standards. This non-pejorative approach will permit an assessment over time of the effectiveness with which flight standards can be applied to evaluate CRM and a determination in particular of how the reliability and validity of such data compare with those obtained for AQP standards of technical competence. In that regard it should be reiterated that AQP provides for both technical and CRM standards to be derived within a single process which focuses on what the pilot actually does. CRM is not tacked on as a afterthought or as a supplementary training consideration. Consequently, the same audit trail from task analysis to qualification standards will be available for CRM as exists for technical behaviors.

CONCLUSIONS ⟶

From a regulatory perspective, the FAA clearly recognizes the value of CRM training for increasing aviation safety and is on record in a variety of its publications to that effect. Further, the FAA is interested in exploring the extent to which CRM may be feasibly extended from training application to proficiency evaluation. However, a major concern is the issue of whether reliable and valid standards of CRM performance can be established for pass–fail purposes. Under the AQP, a formal effort to acquire data directly pertinent to this issue is underway. The goals of that effort are to enable (1) increased precision in the specification of observable CRM behaviors, (2) the development of increasingly well focused CRM training strategies, and (3) the development of rigorous standards of CRM performance. To the extent these goals are achieved, the results are expected to have broad regulatory application to all flight training and proficiency check procedures.

References

Billings, C. E. (1991). *Human-centered aircraft automation: A concept and guidelines* (NASA Technical Memorandum 103885). Moffett Field, CA: NASA–Ames Research Center.

Federal Aviation Administration. (1986). *Air carrier operations inspector's handbook* (FAA order 8430.6C). Washington, DC: Department of Transportation.

Federal Aviation Administration. (1988). *Air transportation operations inspector's handbook* (FAA Order 8400.10). Washington, DC: Department of Transportation.

Federal Aviation Administration. (1989). *Cockpit resource management training* (Advisory Circular 120-51). Washington, DC: Department of Transportation.

Federal Aviation Administration. (1990a). *Special Federal Aviation Regulation 58 - Advanced*

Qualification Program (Federal Register, Vol. 55, No. 91, Rules and Regulations pp. 40262-40278). Washington, DC: National Archives and Records Administration.

Federal Aviation Administration. (1990b). *Line operational simulations* (Advisory Circular 120-35B). Washington, DC: Department of Transportation.

Federal Aviation Administration. (1991a). *Advanced qualification program* (Advisory Circular 120-54). Washington, DC: Department of Transportation.

Federal Aviation Administration. (1991b). *Airplane simulator qualification* (Advisory Circular 120-40B). Washington, DC: Department of Transportation.

Federal Aviation Administration. (1992). *Airplane flight training device qualification* (Advisory Circular 120-45A). Washington, DC: Department of Transportation.

Helmreich, R. L., Wilhelm, J. A., Kello, J. E., Taggart, W. R., & Butler, R. E. (1991). *Reinforcing and evaluating crew resource management: evaluator/LOS instructor reference manual* (NASA/ University of Texas Technical Manual 90-2). Austin: University of Texas.

Jensen, R. S., (1989). *Aeronautical decision making - cockpit resource management* (DOT/ FAA/PM-86/46). Washington, DC: Federal Aviation Administration.

Lauber, J. K., & Foushee, H. C. (1981). *Guidelines for line-oriented flight training* (Volume 1, NASA CP-2184). Moffett Field, CA: NASA–Ames Research Center.

The Accident Investigator's Perspective

Phyllis J. Kayten
Federal Aviation Administration
Washington, D.C. 20591

INTRODUCTION ✈

The aviation industry has always relied heavily on accident investigations to learn about and fix problems. Often, even if problems have been previously detected, it takes a push from the Federal government to effect change. Although in practice National Transportation Safety Board (NTSB) investigators were not the first to recognize cockpit resource management (CRM) as a possible method for reducing accident-causing behavior, the NTSB has played a major part in fostering the wide acceptance CRM concepts now enjoy in the regulatory, airline, and military environments. This chapter discusses the events which influenced the NTSB to converge on CRM as a deterrent to aircraft accidents and the mechanisms the Board employs to gain the aviation industry's acceptance of CRM. Since the NTSB investigates accidents in various transportation modes, "CRM" could be broadened to mean crew resource management, a term that is growing in popularity.

Legislative Background

The NTSB is the watchdog agency of transportation safety in the United States, responsible for determining the cause of all U.S. civil aviation accidents, as well as carefully selected accidents in other modes. The NTSB, as it exists today, was created by a succession of legislative actions, in many cases motivated by catastrophes (Bruggink, 1983; Corrie, 1986). Its earliest roots are found in the Air Commerce Act of 1926, which gave the Commerce Department the authority to determine the cause of aviation accidents. The NTSB was formally created by the Department of Transportation (DOT) Act of 1966, which created an umbrella executive department under which fell the existing Federal Aviation Administration (created by the Federal Aviation Act of 1958), the Federal Railroad Administration, the Coast Guard, and the Federal Highway Administration—and the NTSB, an independent agency attached to the DOT for administrative purposes. The Independent Safety Board Act of 1974 made the Board completely independent of the DOT or any other Federal agency.

International convention establishes certain minimum requirements for aircraft accident investigation. The participating states of the International Civil Aviation Organization are signatories to a convention which delineates rules of investigation and structure of reports (Annex 13 to the Convention on International Civil Aviation, which first met in Chicago, 1944).

NTSB's Power: Investigation, Reports, Recommendations

The NTSB has no enforcement or regulatory authority. The power of the NTSB lies in the impact of its investigative reports and on its recommendations and follow-up procedures.

Investigations

The NTSB "Go-Team", so called because its members typically launch to the site of an accident within 2 hours of notification, consists of highly skilled technical specialists who examine various aspects of the accident under the direction of an investigation manager, the Investigator-in-Charge. NTSB Go-Team members chair investigative groups which focus on airframe structures, aircraft powerplants, air traffic control, weather, survival factors, flight operations, and, occasionally, human performance.

The NTSB relies on a "party system" of investigation (Wandell, 1989) to ensure rapid development and exchange of factual information. The field phase of a major aircraft accident investigation can involve over 100 investigators, including about 12 NTSB investigators, the rest being party investigators, who represent the airline, aircraft and aircraft part manufacturers, pilots' union, the airport authority, flight attendants' union, air traffic controllers' union, maintenance workers' union, the Federal Aviation Administration, and others where appropriate.

Reports

The draft report, conclusions and findings, probable cause statement, and recommendations are written by NTSB staff and then discussed, modified, and approved by vote of the NTSB board members at a public "Sunshine" meeting, according to law. Often Board members consider issues of particular concern to them. These issues frequently reflect the particular expertise and experience of the board members (i.e., law, systems engineering, human factors, transportation policy). Over the years, the composition of the board has significantly affected the tone and content of reports, findings, and recommendations. The reasoning and deliberations leading to the decisions to word the final report, probable cause, and recommendations in particular ways can often be found only, if at all, in the transcript of the public board meeting.

Occasionally, the probable cause is worded to have a desired impact on the institutions which can effect change, and the manipulation of the probable cause statement has been a frequent subject of debate (Bruggink, 1988b; Davis, 1979; Lauber, 1983; Ramsden, 1983). The analyst who relies only on NTSB accident statistics for summaries of flightcrew-caused accidents will miss valuable information not accessible through any database search (Bruggink, 1988a).

Recommendation Follow-up

Recommendations made to agencies of the DOT (i.e., the FAA) require a response within 90 days of transmittal of the official recommendation letter (U.S. CFR 49, Section 1906). DOT agencies respond, and most often concur, because Congress pressures these agencies to either comply or supply reasonable justification for noncompliance. The NTSB has no authority to force any other agency, institution, or entity to implement a recommendation. Non-DOT agencies respond and frequently comply with NTSB recommendations because of public pressure (aided indirectly by media and by public speeches and state and Federal legislative testimony by Board members and staff).

The NTSB has a follow-up procedure that involves the writing of response replies, and in some cases providing individual staff assistance, until the recommendation is closed. When recommendations are closed, the Board members determine by vote an official classification: "Acceptable Action," "Unacceptable Action," "Reconsidered," or "Superseded" by a new recommendation. Congressional committees frequently ask for reports on the status of NTSB recommendations to the FAA and other government agencies.

NTSB recommendation and follow-up letters and the respondents' letters and supporting material are kept on file at the NTSB. A Safety Recommendation database, little used by outside researchers, provides useful insight into the complicated mechanisms of change.

HUMAN PERFORMANCE INVESTIGATION ——————— →

Human performance investigation is an evolving science; many would prefer to call it an art. The human performance investigation process has been described by several authors, and the scope of human performance investigation has both expanded and been refined over the last several years (Brenner, 1989; Danaher, 1984; Diehl, 1989; Kayten, 1989; Miller, 1977, 1979; Schleede, 1979; Stoklosa, 1981, 1983; Walhout, 1981a, 1981b, 1991). In early 1993, ICAO is expected to publish a Digest on Investigation of Human Performance, which should serve as an international guideline for investigation of human performance factors.

Before 1983, there was no separate human performance investigative division in the NTSB; this function was the responsibility of a Human Factors Division which handled investigation of both human performance and crash survivability. In the early 1970s the need for a greater emphasis on human behavioral issues was expressed by several factions, both within and outside the NTSB (Diehl, 1989; Kowalsky, Master, Stone, Babcock, & Rypka, 1974).

When then Acting Chairman Jim Burnett testified before Congress in 1982 (Burnett, 1982), he used three accidents to justify additional positions to fill a proposed human performance investigative division. All involved issues of command authority and crew assertiveness: the Eastern Airlines crash into the Florida Everglades (NTSB, 1973b); the Air Florida accident at the 14th Street Bridge in Washington, D.C. (NTSB, 1982); and an Allegheny Airlines accident in New Haven, Connecticut (NTSB, 1972). In late 1983, the Human Performance Division of the NTSB was formally established.

In general, human performance investigation encompasses six distinct areas of interest (Figure 10.1), and these interests overlap with those of other groups during the field phase of the investigation (particularly, the operations, survival factors, and ATC groups). Occasionally, during the field phase of an accident investigation, a human performance group will be formed to investigate a particular issue. This has seldom occurred; the first formal human performance group was formed in January 1981 for the investigation of a Cascade Airways Beech-99 accident in Spokane, Washington (Walhout, 1981a, 1981b; Stoklosa, 1981). This group found design issues in the approach chart, equipment design issues, and noted a high level of cockpit environmental noise, which precluded verbal communication between pilots without headsets.

More often, human performance investigators will join the Operational Factors Group during the field phase but will write a separate factual and analytic report for the record. Table 10.1 lists the type of data collected by a human performance investigator. Brenner (1989) describes two recent significant contributions by human performance investigators. The first was an analysis of the ability of the pilots of the two aircraft which collided in Cerritos, California (NTSB, 1987a) to see and avoid the other aircraft if alerted versus unalerted; the second was an analysis of pilot drug use as a contributing factor in a commuter crash near Durango, Colorado (NTSB, 1989a).

Human performance investigators work closely with the operational factors group and with the groups who transcribe and analyze the cockpit voice recorder (CVR) and flight data recorder (FDR) or digital flight data recorder (DFDR) information (Kayten & Roberts, 1985). Before the advent of FDRs and CVRs, efforts to learn the reasons for pilot errors were quite speculative (Walhout, 1983).

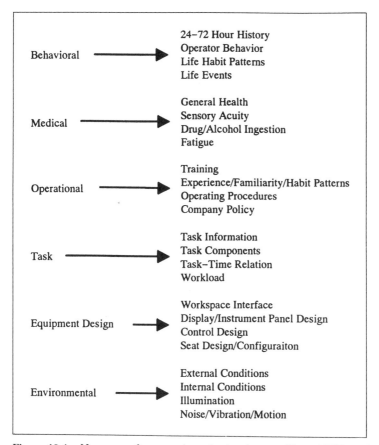

Figure 10.1 Human performance investigation factors. (From NTSB, 1983.)

Today, DFDR and CVR data are the primary resources for learning what happened in the accident sequence. The additional data listed in Table 10.1 help to determine why the human operators behaved as they did.

Some modern aircraft carry other flight data recording devices, such as Airborne Integrated Data Systems (AIDS), used generally by airlines for maintenance trending and analyses. These systems generally record many more parameters than DFDRs, but are not "crash-hardened." Such systems have been found to be valuable investigative tools when the aircraft is not destroyed in an accident, such as the Scandinavian Airline DC-10 accident at John F. Kennedy International Airport (NTSB, 1984c). There have been catastrophic occurrences in which the DFDR was destroyed but the AIDS recorder survived. The 1991 Airbus 320 controlled flight into terrain accident at Strasbourg, France, is a recent example.

Table 10.1
Data Collected by Human Performance Investigators

Category	Sources
Experience factors: Experience in similar situations	Logbooks; company records, personal records, certificates, licenses; interviews: company training personnel, fellow operators, frequent passengers
Equipment design factors	Display/control layout; manufacturer drawings: human factors design philosophy; company maintenance records, books, logbooks; training simulators
Sensory/perceptual factors: Light, sound, vibration, workload	National Weather Service observations; company records, pre-flight briefs; air traffic control reports/pilot reports; logbooks; simulator training records
Crew interaction factors: Age, experience, personality	FAA certificates; company and personal records, licenses, logbooks; interviews: fellow crewmembers, instructors; simulator training system records; operator manuals; CVR recording
Physiological and medical factors	Medical certification records, private physician record; postmortem examination; toxicological analysis; interviews: company and private physician, family, friends
Clinical factors: Job stability, life habits, recent events	Interviews: family, supervisors, colleagues, neighbors, friends; data from CVR

On October 11, 1991, new Federal regulations went into effect which require 28-parameter DFDRs on all carrier aircraft and require all aircraft with six or more passenger seats requiring two pilots to have a CVR. The international minimum standards for voice and flight data recording, first adopted by the ICAO in Annex 6 of the Chicago Convention on International Civil Aviation, have changed over the years and continue to be reexamined periodically by the ICAO Air Navigation Commission.

NTSB RECOGNITION OF CRM ——————————— ✈

Timing Is Everything

The NTSB first explicitly recognized the need for CRM-type training in its report on the December 28, 1978, crash of United Airlines Flight 173, in Portland, Oregon (NTSB, 1979b), although in earlier reports there are references to "teamwork" (NTSB, 1971), "inadequate flight management," "task-sharing" (NTSB, 1979a), "delegation of authority" (NTSB, 1973a), "failure to monitor flight instruments" (NTSB, 1973b; NTSB, 1976a), and "command authority and its inviolate nature" (NTSB, 1972). It is no coincidence that the Portland accident report, with its recommendation for "flight deck resource management indoctrination," followed closely on the heels of some very significant events in the history of CRM. Earlier investigative efforts lacked the vocabulary, analytical models, and tools to come up with focused statements and recommendations regarding CRM (Walhout, 1981b).

The significant events were the efforts of the research program in "human factors in aviation safety" at the National Aeronautics and Space Administration's (NASA) Ames research laboratory, begun in 1973 and summarized by Lauber (Cooper, White, & Lauber, 1980, pp. 3–16). These efforts include (1) a re-analysis of 62 jet transport accidents with significant resource management problems; (2) a confidential pilot interview study; (3) a working group which developed a conceptual framework for investigating human factors in aircraft accidents (Barnhart, Billings, Cooper, Gilstrap, Lauber, Orlady, Puskas, & Stephens, 1975), and NTSB's new chief of human performance investigation, who attempted to use this conceptual model (Schleede, 1979); and (4) the simulator study by Ruffell Smith, carried out in 1976 and published in 1979 (Ruffell Smith, 1979).

The CRM problems in the Portland accident were no more compelling than those in earlier accidents. These issues, however, had previously been treated in the framework of operational procedures and good airmanship; it was only after the NASA work that these problems were thought to have a unique training solution. The Ruffell Smith study and other simulator studies that followed showed that formal crew procedures could not always be expected to solve unexpected problems.

Some Early Treatments of Resource Management Problems

Trans International Flight 863—JFK Airport—10/8/70

On September 8, 1970, a Trans International Airlines (TIA) DC-8 on a ferry flight crashed on takeoff at John F. Kennedy International Airport, New York (NTSB, 1971). The NTSB investigation found that a foreign object had become trapped between the elevator and the stabilizer, which held the elevator in an approximate 5°–8° trailing edge-up position. The first officer was the pilot-flying, and the captain, according to TIA operating procedures, was responsible for making the rejected takeoff decision. The aircraft began to rotate at 80 knots, an abnormally low speed (computed rotation speed was 124 knots). The tail skid began dragging on the runway at 91 knots. The aircraft became airborne at 117 knots, and at this point there was no other reasonable alternative than to continue the take-off. The plane stalled and crashed shortly after take-off. All 11 crewmembers died; there were no passengers.

Although no human performance group was formed for this accident investigation, there was a thorough analysis in the report of why the pilots failed to reject the take-off in light of the information available to them. The analysis included discussion of (1) emphasis in flight manuals on the dangers of a rejected take-off, which might have prejudiced the crew against doing so; (2) the failure of the captain to monitor the take-off, and the failure of the first officer to offer any information to the captain about his difficulty in controlling the aircraft until after lift-off; (3) absence of a pre-take-off briefing and its impact on the preparedness of the crew.

Teamwork was discussed in the context of the need for a proper pre-flight briefing. The NTSB report quoted a Flight Safety Foundation *Accident Prevention Bulletin* article from April 1971:

> The best fail-safe provision in the cockpit is proper teamwork. Optimum teamwork however, is always preceded by a thorough briefing. . . . It is the solid basis of teamwork, from which mutual confidence and assistance develop into mutual cross-monitoring and cross-checking, without hesitation to call the other crew members' attention to any performance which is outside of given tolerances. This habit of mutual help, of early detection and elimination of each other's mistakes and errors, makes for the highest safety factor of a multiple crew. (NTSB, 1971, p. 17)

However, crew coordination and teamwork were not mentioned in the probable cause, which cited "an apparent lack of crew responsiveness to a highly unusual emergency situation, coupled with the captain's failure to monitor adequately the takeoff" (NTSB, 1971, p. 20). The Board recommended that the FAA

> review the subject of rejected takeoff procedures in air carrier operations with a view to: amplifying and clarifying these procedures; standardizing operation and flight manual procedures for each aircraft; reviewing the role each pilot plays in accomplishing a rejected takeoff; exploring the requirements for rejected takeoff training; providing flightcrews with more specific information regarding the dynamics of rejected takeoff conditions for the specific aircraft; and requiring a pretakeoff briefing of rejected takeoff and other emergency procedures that the crew may have to employ. (NTSB Recommendation No. A-71-039)

Rather than training, better standard operating procedures and briefings were the recommended solutions to this accident.

Mohawk Airlines—Albany, New York—3/3/72

Discussion of delegation of responsibilities found its way into the statement of probable cause in the report of a Mohawk Airlines accident in Albany, New

York, in 1972 (NTSB, 1973a). In this accident, the crew of a Fairchild-Hiller FH-227B turbojet aircraft experienced problems with the left propeller. The aircraft crashed into a house 3.5 miles short of the airport, killing the flightcrew and 14 of the passengers.

According to the NTSB report, the captain of the aircraft "apparently chose both to fly the aircraft and to attempt to withdraw the pitch lock, rather than to assign one or the other of these tasks to the first officer" (NTSB, 1973a, pp. 28–29). The first officer's failure to "follow the company altitude awareness procedures" (calling out altitude and airspeed in descent) and the captain's "failure to delegate any meaningful responsibilities to the copilot which resulted in a lack of effective task sharing during the emergency" were listed as contributory causal factors in the accident. The Board recommended to the FAA that

> Established pilot training programs and operations manuals should be revised to include guidance on time and task sharing in abnormal and emergency situations. Emphasis should be placed on the need of preplanning task and time sharing by the crew before an unusual or emergency situation arises. (NTSB Recommendation No. A-73-15)

The FAA responded on June 20, 1973, that this recommendation was not necessary, as "current air carrier training programs stress specific crewmember duties for abnormal and emergency situations." The NTSB, therefore, closed this recommendation as "Unacceptable Action" on August 13, 1973.

Eastern Air Lines—Florida Everglades—12/29/72

The Mohawk Airlines accident occurred only eight months before the crash of Flight 401 in the Florida Everglades (NTSB, 1973b), in which the crew permitted their fully operational Lockheed L-1011 to fly into the ground because they did not realize they had accidentally disconnected the altitude-hold feature of the autopilot. The entire crew of three focused only on a landing gear light that had failed to illuminate. This accident has come to represent the classic "CRM accident," yet the NTSB report concluded only, "The captain failed to assure that a pilot was monitoring the progress of the aircraft at all times" (NTSB, 1973b, p. 23), and the probable cause statement noted, "Preoccupation with a malfunction of the nose landing gear position indicating system distracted the crew's attention from the instruments and allowed the descent to go unnoticed." No corrective action was recommended.

Allegheny Airlines—Rochester—7/9/78 and New Haven—6/7/71)

Two Allegheny Airlines accidents, one in 1971 (NTSB, 1972) and the other in 1978 (NTSB, 1979a), provided ammunition for the NTSB to discuss the captain's command authority and the first officer's responsibility to question it. In the 1971 accident, the first officer survived and was able to give interesting insight into his decision process. In the second accident, both crewmembers survived and provided valuable testimony.

In the 1971 accident (NTSB, 1972), a Convair 340/440 crashed during a nonprecision instrument approach to Tweed–New Haven Airport. Twenty-eight people, including the captain, were killed; two passengers and the first officer survived. The NTSB determined the probable cause of the accident was

> the captain's intentional descent below the prescribed minimum descent altitude under adverse weather conditions without adequate forward visibility or the crew's sighting of the runway environment. *The captain disregarded advisories from his first officer that minimum descent altitude had been reached and that the airplane was continuing to descend at a normal descent rate and airspeed* [emphasis supplied]. The Board was unable to determine what motivated the captain to disregard prescribed operating procedures and altitude restrictions, and finds it difficult to reconcile the actions he exhibited during the conduct of this flight. (NTSB, 1972, pp. 1–2).

It can be surmised from the analysis section of the Board report that the investigators of this accident truly struggled with its cause. The report states that the Board found it difficult to imagine that an experienced airline captain would behave as this captain did. The report writers also struggled with the time-honored role and authority of the captain and the first officer's right and responsibility to question the captain's decisions or to take over. Allegheny Airlines' procedures stated:

> The first officer is designated as second in command, is directly responsible to the captain, and would assume command if the captain should become incapacitated. . . . All crewmembers must realize that the captain is in complete command of the airplane and his orders are to be obeyed, even though they may be at variance with written instructions. (NTSB, 1972, p. 22)

The captain was reported to have had an "authoritarian personality"; the first officer was a "quiet, submissive type, not one who would question a superior or his authority." The first officer stated that he had thought of taking over control but felt "it was better to have one person in full control of the airplane than to have two persons fighting over it" (NTSB, 1972, p. 29).

The NTSB report dedicated several pages to the concept of command authority, recognizing a dearth of guidelines regarding the circumstances and manner in which a flight crewmember should take affirmative action, and recommending in the body of the report that air carriers re-examine the relationship between the captain and other flight crewmembers with a view toward enunciating the responsibilities in circumstances where the aircraft is being operated unsafely. The Board formally recommended that the FAA

> review and revise where necessary the operations manuals of air carriers to clearly state management's operational control procedures with regard to the pilot-in-command and other crewmembers and the manner in which each crewmember is expected to execute his duty. (NTSB Recommendation No. A-72-137).

This recommendation was closed "Unacceptable Action" after the FAA responded in September, 1972, that it was "firm in its stand that adequate information is available and published which, if implemented, will assure continual assessment of pilot's operational control responsibility." The Board also recommended that the pilots' unions:

> implement a program within existing professional standards committees to provide an expeditious means for peer group monitoring and disciplining the very small group of air carrier pilots who may display any unprofessional (including hazardous) traits as exemplified by this accident. (NTSB Recommendation No. A-72-140)

This recommendation was eventually closed as "Acceptable Action." It is interesting to note that the pilots' unions are still struggling with how to deal with the "poor CRM" captains and first officers (McIntyre, 1989).

Both recommendations were reiterated in 1976 after an Alaska Airlines runway overrun accident in Ketchikan, Alaska (NTSB, 1976b). The reiteration of a recommendation is generally meant to indicate that the second accident would not have occurred if the first recommendation had been heeded.

The 1978 Allegheny accident bore some resemblance to the 1971 accident, and the NTSB report quoted generously from the earlier report, including the same excerpts from the flight operations manual regarding the complete command authority of the captain. In this accident, a BAC 1-11 overran the departure end of the runway at Monroe County Airport in Rochester, New York. The approach was too high and too fast, and the captain failed to initiate a go-around, even though he had sufficient aircraft performance capability to reject the landing well after touchdown. The NTSB listed as a contributing factor the first officer's failure to provide required callouts, but made no formal recommendations.

NTSB Special Study—ILS Approaches

If the 1978 Allegheny Airlines accident had occurred 3 years earlier, it would have been included in the NTSB's special study on flightcrew coordination procedures in air carrier instrument landing system (ILS) approach accidents (NTSB, 1976a). This study included a review of ILS accidents and incidents occurring between 1970 and 1975. Air carrier personnel and pilot union representatives were interviewed, and instrument approach procedures of various air carriers were compared. Additionally, U.S. Air Force training personnel were interviewed about their crew coordination procedures.

The special study found that flightcrew coordination procedures were either lacking or not followed in most of the accidents and made several recommendations regarding flightcrew coordination procedures. None of the recommendations addressed training; instead, the assignment of rigid areas of responsibility and strict checklist procedures were stressed.

NTSB's First Mention of CRM: United Airlines—Portland—12/28/78

On December 28, 1978, United Airlines Flight 173 crashed near the Portland International Airport after circling in the vicinity of the airport for an hour while the flightcrew tried to resolve a landing gear problem and prepare passengers for an emergency landing (NTSB, 1979b). Of the 81 passengers and 8 crewmembers aboard the DC-8, 8 passengers, the flight engineer, and a flight attendant were killed. The NTSB determined the probable cause was

> the failure of the captain to monitor properly the aircraft's fuel state and to properly respond to the low fuel state and the crewmember's advisories regarding fuel state. This resulted in fuel exhaustion to all engines. . . . Contributing . . . was the failure of the other two flight crewmembers either to fully comprehend the criticality of the fuel state or to successfully communicate their concern to the captain. (NTSB, 1979b, p. 29)

The NTSB report of the Portland accident became the first in which "flight deck resource management" was mentioned, although the accident had all the same ingredients as the Allegheny accident in 1971 (NTSB, 1972). The analysis stated, "this accident exemplifies a recurring problem—a breakdown in cockpit management and teamwork during a situation involving malfunctions of aircraft systems in flight" (p. 26).

One of the four recommendations made following this accident was to the FAA to

> issue an operations bulletin to all air carrier operations inspectors directing them to urge their assigned operators to ensure that their flightcrews are indoctrinated in principles of flight deck resource management, with particular emphasis on the merits of participative management for captains and assertiveness training for other cockpit crewmembers. (NTSB Recommendation No. AAR-79-47)

The NTSB closed this recommendation "Acceptable" on March 21, 1980, after the FAA issued Air Carrier Operations Bulletin 8430.17 Change 11, which included instructions regarding resource management and interpersonal communications training for air carrier flightcrew.

IMPACT OF NTSB ON DEVELOPING CRM, 1979–1986

From 1979 to the present, NTSB recommendations have continued to focus on crew coordination training. The Board has prodded the airlines to develop programs and urged the FAA to oversee and, more recently, to mandate CRM training. The following cases illustrate this process.

Downeast Airlines—Rockland, Maine—5/30/79

In May 1980, after a May 30, 1979, crash of a Downeast Airlines DHC-6 in Rockland, Maine (NTSB, 1980), the Safety Board issued two recommendations to the FAA on the subject of crew coordination:

> Require that 14 CFR 135 operators emphasize crew coordination during recurrent training, especially when pilots are qualified for both single-pilot/autopilot and two-pilot operations. These requirements should be outlined in an operator's approved training curriculum. (NTSB Recommendation No. A-80-42)
> Upgrade operations manuals of 14 CFR 135 operators to assure standardization by clearly delineating operational duties and responsibilities of all required cockpit crewmembers. (NTSB Recommendation No. A-80-43)

The FAA contested the necessity of making these changes, stating in a letter from Administrator Langhorne Bond to NTSB Chairman James King on August 20, 1980 that

> Section 135.329 of the FAR, entitled, "Crewmember training requirements," does in fact include provisions which, in our opinion, will result in effective crew coordination. Paragraph (e) of that section states:
> "(e) In addition to initial transition, upgrade and recurrent training, *each* training program must provide ground and flight training, instruction, and practice necessary to ensure that *each* crewmember:
> (1) Remain adequately trained and currently proficient for *each* aircraft, *crewmember position*, and type of operation in which the crewmember serves; and . . ."

With respect to Recommendation No. A-80-43, the FAA response was that flight manuals were not the appropriate vehicle for imparting the concept of crew coordination. The letter stated that Order 8430.1B, Inspection and Surveillance

Procedures Air Taxi Operators/Commuter Air Carriers and Commercial Operators, in Paragraph 111, entitled, "Altitude Awareness and Flightcrew Procedures During Instrument Approaches," "speaks specifically to cockpit vigilance during instrument approach operations" and that "FAA inspectors are required to ensure that these provisions are included in operators' training programs."

The NTSB responded in a letter dated January 8, 1981, that Section 135.329(e) of the FAR did not satisfy the first recommendation because, though it did address crew proficiency, it did not address crew coordination. The letter also suggested, in reference to the second recommendation, that "Order 8430.1B, paragraph 111, be amended to require that FAA inspectors monitor crew activities throughout the flight to ensure specifically that standardization and crew coordination are an integral part of all phases of flight."

On April 24, 1981, FAA Administrator J. Lynn Helms replied to NTSB Chairman King and proposed to add emphasis to crew coordination in a revision to Advisory Circular 135-3B and a revision to Section 135.329, Crewmember Training Requirements. The NTSB closed these recommendations as "Acceptable Alternate Action" on May 6, 1982, after the revisions were made.

Air Florida—14th Street Bridge, Washington, D.C.—1/13/82

On January 13, 1982, Air Florida Flight 90 departed from Washington National Airport bound for Fort Lauderdale, Florida, with 74 passengers and five crewmembers on board (NTSB, 1982). The flight's scheduled departure was delayed almost 2 hours due to heavy snowfall, which had necessitated the temporary closing of the airport. There was a significant delay between the de-icing of the aircraft and its take-off, and the plane took off with snow and/or ice on the airfoil surfaces and engine inlet probes. The aircraft's airspeed decayed during climb, and the aircraft reached full stall and struck the 14th Street Bridge connecting Washington, D.C., with Virginia at 4:01 p.m., in the height of rush hour traffic, then plunged into the ice-covered Potomac River, killing all but four passengers and one flight attendant on board. Four people in vehicles on the bridge were also killed. The Safety board listed as the probable cause

> the flightcrew's failure to use engine anti-ice during ground operation and takeoff, their decision to take off with snow/ice on the airfoil surfaces of the aircraft, and *the captain's failure to reject the takeoff during the early stage when his attention was called to anomalous engine instrument readings* [emphasis supplied]. Contributing to the accident were the prolonged ground delay between deicing and the receipt of the ATC clearance during which the airplane was exposed to continual precipitation, the known inherent pitchup characteristics of the B-737 aircraft when the leading edge is contaminated with even small amounts of snow or ice, and the limited experience of the flightcrew in jet transport winter operations.

The NTSB report of the Air Florida accident is a model for the thorough handling of human performance issues in future NTSB accident reports. The accident occurred during the period in which the concept of a Human Performance Division at the NTSB was being formulated, and the Air Florida accident provided a perfect showcase for its promotion. The accident represented the second time a human performance group was formed during the field phase of investigation.

After extensive simulations of the take-off, it was determined that ice had formed on a pressure probe in one of the engines, which caused a false indication of the thrust level. Tests confirmed that the crew had set the engine take-off thrust according to the false indication, causing a reduced thrust take-off.

Following this accident, investigators found several examples of similar occurrences, but in most of these, the flightcrews had rejected the take-off because they had observed that other engine indications did not agree with the engine pressure ratio indications. The same indications were available to the Air Florida crew. The Air Florida CVR transcript has been used so often to illustrate poor cockpit communication that most CRM training professionals can recite the following section by memory:

> Time 1559:58, FIRST OFFICER: God, look at that thing. That doesn't seem right does it?
> 1600:05, FIRST OFFICER: Ah, that's not right . . .
> 1600:09, CAPTAIN: Yes it is, there's eighty. (captain referring to 80 knots ground speed)
> 1600:10, FIRST OFFICER: Naw, I don't think that's right.
> 1600:19, FIRST OFFICER: Ah, maybe it is.
> 1600:21, CAPTAIN: Hundred and twenty.
> 1600:23, FIRST OFFICER: I don't know.

The first officer, who was the pilot-flying, continued the take-off even though he was clearly uneasy about something, which was most likely the disparity in engine instrument readings. He was unable to effectively communicate the problem to the captain.

One focus of this human performance investigation was the adequacy of the training for handling this situation. In reference to engine failures, Air Florida's training manual stated:

> Under adverse conditions to takeoff, recognition of an engine failure may be difficult. Therefore, close reliable crew coordination is necessary for early recognition.
> The captain *ALONE* makes the decision to "REJECT." (NTSB, 1982, p. 40)

The training manual also stated that "any crewmember will call out any indication of engine problems affecting flight safety" and "the decision is still the captain's, but he must rely heavily on the first officer." "The initial portion of each takeoff should be performed as if an engine failure were to occur."

This accident illustrated that written procedures stating that crew coordination must be accomplished are insufficient to foster such behavior. This accident scenario is used extensively as an example in CRM courses, the implication being that CRM training would have made the first officer more assertive and clear about his concerns and the captain more open to accept advice.

Lauber (1983), in a presentation to the Aviation Accident Investigation Symposium in Springfield, Virginia, characterized the NTSB report as a largely successful attempt to come to grips with the interaction problems between the captain and first officer.

> However, once again, the statement of probable cause fails to convey the lessons learned from this tragic accident. Instead of leading us to develop solutions to the problems uncovered, it leads us further into the adversarial morass in which the official finger is pointed at those "who did it." (Lauber, 1983, p. 7).

It should be noted that the NTSB causal statement also does not refer to a critical human factors aspect: the crew's lack of knowledge of the effects of engine probe icing on instrument readings (although the Board's first recommendation dealt with this subject). CRM has little or nothing to do with the initial imparting of technical knowledge. Had the first officer known about the symptoms of probe icing, he would undoubtedly have acted decisively without hesitation (G. M. Bruggink, personal communication, February, 1991).

United—Denver—5/31/84 and USAir—Detroit—6/13/84

Two 1984 non-fatal accidents involving windshear were employed by the NTSB to reinforce and further refine its recommendations regarding CRM. One involved a United Airlines B-747 which struck the ILS localizer antenna after takeoff in Denver in May (NTSB, 1985b), and the other, which occurred a month later, involved a USAir DC-9 which continued an approach into a severe weather cell over Detroit Metropolitan Airport, failed in attempting a missed approach, and landed 2,500 feet beyond the runway threshold, coming to rest in the grass on the side of the runway (NTSB, 1985a).

The NTSB capitalized on the Denver accident to portray effective crew coordination, saying,

> because United's training in flightcrew coordination techniques was designed specifically to result in the kind of effective communication and interaction that took place at the time of the takeoff rotation, the training can be credited with playing a significant part in that crew's coordination. . . . In the light of previous accidents in which the breakdown in

cockpit resource management was a contributing factor, the Safety Board believes that United's program in training in Cockpit Resource Management is a positive method to prevent this from being a factor in future accidents. All carriers will benefit by training all crewmembers in their respective roles. (NTSB, 1985b, p. 51)

In contrast, the Safety Board used the Detroit accident (NTSB, 1985a) to criticize USAir's training program, which at the time only offered a resource management–related course for its new captains. The Board saw

little indication that the captain provided leadership and planning guidance, while the first officer, by not articulating his uncertainties about the weather or discussing with the captain the feasibility of terminating the approach, failed to assist effectively the captain in the conduct of the flight. . . . Although air carriers are not required to train their crewmembers in this area, the Board believes that it would be a benefit to their crewmembers. (NTSB, 1985a, p. 43)

The USAir accident CVR transcript bore an uncanny resemblance to the transcript from Delta Air Lines' catastrophic windshear accident in Dallas, which occurred slightly more than a year later (NTSB, 1986b). As the USAir aircraft passed the outer marker, the captain said, "Smell the rain," and the first officer responded, "Yep, got lightning in it too" (NTSB, 1985a, p. 4). As the crew on Delta 191 began their before-landing check, the captain radioed to the tower, "Tower, Delta one ninety one heavy, out here in the rain, feels good." Twenty seconds later, the first officer said to the captain, "Lightning coming out of that one." The captain asked, "What?" The first officer repeated the sentence. The captain asked, "Where?" The first officer replied, "Right ahead of us." About 45 seconds later the airplane began to encounter the windshear.

As a result of the United and USAir accidents, the NTSB recommended that the FAA

conduct research to determine the most effective means to train all fight-crew members in cockpit resource management, and require air carriers to apply the findings of the research to pilot training programs. (NTSB Recommendation No. A-85-27)

The FAA's first two responses to this recommendation, in letters dated July 22, 1985, and December 9, 1986, referred to the FAA's initiation of selected projects within its Aviation Behavioral Technology Program, which included projects to optimize line-oriented flight training to enhance cockpit resource management, and to improve communications and coordination between cockpit and cabin crew. The letters also referred to the Pilot Judgement Training Program, which had progressed to the demonstration phase.

The Safety Board kept this recommendation in an open status until December, 1990. The final letter to the FAA on this matter, from Chairman James Kolstad to FAA Administrator James Busey, December 3, 1990, cited the Advisory Circular 120-51 on Cockpit Resource Management Training (dated December 1, 1989), and the issuance of the final rule for an Advanced Qualification Program (AQP) Special Federal Aviation Regulation (SFAR) in September, 1990, as the justification for closure.

In 1990, when USAir Flight 5050 crashed into Bowery Bay after an unsuccessful take-off abort at LaGuardia Airport, the NTSB again cited poor crew coordination and CRM (particularly the captain's failure to exercise command authority) and stated that even though the FAA Advisory Circular on CRM was only advisory, and issued after the accident, that USAir should have had better CRM training in place at the time of the accident (NTSB, 1990b).

Galaxy Airlines—Reno, Nevada—1/21/85

Galaxy Airlines' Lockheed Electra accident on January 21, 1985 (NTSB, 1986a), provided the impetus for NTSB to recommend that the FAA provide operators interim guidance in the principles of CRM so that operators could provide such training before the completion of the FAA's formal research (NTSB Recommendation No. A-86-019).

The FAA responded to this recommendation with an August 25, 1986, letter describing its contract with the Aviation Psychology Laboratory of Ohio State University for a study to examine the treatment of cockpit management methods and instruction at various airlines. A letter from the FAA dated May 5, 1987, stated that the draft report from this study was still in review, and 2 years later, in a letter dated April 14, 1989, the FAA stated that it was now developing a CRM handbook based on its review of the Ohio State study.

The NTSB, in a letter dated July 12, 1989, expressed its dismay over the 3 years it had taken to take this action, in which the operators still had very limited guidance. But in light of the advisory circular on CRM, then in draft, and related efforts, the NTSB classified the recommendation as "Open—Acceptable Alternate Action" and eventually closed the recommendation in August, 1990, based on the issuance of the CRM Advisory Circular 120-51.

Delta Air Lines—Dallas—8/2/85

The Safety Board used later accidents to further pressure the airlines to incorporate CRM into their training programs. In its report of the Delta Air Lines L-1011, which crashed after encountering a severe microburst on approach to Dallas–Fort Worth International Airport on August 2, 1985 (NTSB, 1986b), the NTSB noted that Delta did not provide CRM training, and stated:

> Although in this instance the lack of formal cockpit resource management and assertiveness training was not causal to the accident, the Safety Board believes that this training is necessary to ensure the proper exchange of

information among flightcrew members and should be provided by the air carrier companies. (NTSB, 1986b, p. 71)

No formal recommendation, however, was made to Delta at this time.

Piedmont—Charlotte, North Carolina—10/26/86

After an accident involving a Piedmont Airlines B-737 which continued an unstabilized approach and overran the runway, coming to a stop on the edge of railroad tracks beyond the airport property, the NTSB again cited the lack of effective crew coordination as a contributing factor (NTSB, 1987b).

The CVR showed that the first officer recited the landing checklist and stated that the speed brakes were in the manual mode. The NTSB report interpreted the remark about the speed brakes as a "subtle reminder to the captain that the required approach and landing procedures were not being adhered to" (NTSB 1987b, p. 32). The next and final statement recorded on the CVR was by the first officer, who stated quite clearly that they were going to "get the lights on the overrun," which they did. The Safety Board felt the first officer could have been significantly more assertive and informative before that point, when the accident might have been avoided.

The report stated that the Piedmont Airlines "did not provide, nor was it required to provide, training to its crewmembers in crew coordination or cockpit resource management" (NTSB, 1987b, p. 23). The NTSB also explained that Piedmont had previously had a program in "behavioral principles" that was part of their upgrade training for new captains, but had discontinued it 2 years before the accident because (according to the Human Performance Group Chairman's Factual Report) it was found to be ineffective and too expensive. The recommendation made in the Galaxy Airlines report (NTSB, 1986a), asking for the FAA to give interim guidance to air carriers on CRM concepts, was reiterated in this accident report.

1987 AND BEYOND ────────────────────────── ✈

NTSB Encourages the Institutionalization of CRM

In recent years, NTSB recommendations have aimed to cause the assimilation of CRM concepts into the everyday standard operation of airlines and the FAA. In the following cases, the FAA was urged to give standard guidance to all airlines for the incorporation of CRM into training programs and to require airlines to teach CRM according to these standards.

Northwest 255—Detroit—8/16/87

On August 16, 1987, Northwest Airlines Flight 255, an MD-82, crashed shortly after taking off from Detroit–Metro Airport, without the wing slats and flaps properly configured, killing 149 passengers, six crewmembers, and two people on the ground (NTSB, 1988b). One passenger, a 4-year-old girl, survived. The accident is considered a classic human error accident, and it contains several human performance issues, outlined concisely by Lauber (1989), including "task structure and the design and utilization of checklists" "warning systems: are they primary or secondary?" "hypothesis testing, mental set and conservatism," stress from a merger, and the flightcrew's concern about a possible flight delay.

The investigation represented a landmark in terms of the scope of the human performance investigation, and also in terms of the large proportion of the report dedicated to human performance issues. Witnesses at the NTSB public hearing regarding this accident included Earl L. Wiener, who testified about the effects of automated systems, including warning devices, on flightcrew performance, and H. Clayton Foushee, who testified on "the effects of interpersonal relationships on the performance of cockpit duties" (NTSB, 1988b, p. 44).

The NTSB report cited lack of cockpit discipline and "deference by a captain to a first officer" (p. 59). It also noted that "both crewmembers received single-crewmember training during their last simulator training and proficiency checks" (p. 62). It also criticized CRM training that is given only in the classroom (the type received by the accident crewmembers at Republic Airlines before the Republic–Northwest merger) and urged the FAA to give a high priority to its Aviation Behavioral Technology program. As a result of the Northwest 255 investigation, the NTSB recommended that the FAA

> Expedite the issuance of guidance materials for use by Parts 121 and 135 operators in the implementation of team-oriented flightcrew training techniques, such as cockpit resource management, line-oriented flight training, or other techniques which emphasize crew coordination and management principles"; (NTSB Recommendation No. A-88-69)

and that all Part 121 air carriers

> Review initial and recurrent flightcrew training programs to ensure that they include simulator or aircraft training exercises which involve cockpit resource management and active coordination of all crewmember trainees and which will permit evaluation of crew performance and adherence to those crew coordination procedures. (NTSB Recommendation No. A-88-71)

The air carrier responses were varied. They indicated that there was, at least, a heightened awareness among air carriers of the importance of CRM. Several airlines discussed limitations, such as the unavailability of simulators for the airline's aircraft fleet, and several small airlines reported sending their crew for training at larger carriers' training facilities. Several described their CRM training as classroom-only programs. On April 12, 1990, the NTSB closed out this recommendation to all air carriers as "Closed—Acceptable Action," as it had insufficient basis for finding any particular CRM program unacceptable.

Delta 1141—Dallas—8/31/88

On August 31, 1988, just a year after the Northwest 255 accident, Delta Air Lines Flight 1141, a B-727, crashed on take-off without the wing slats and flaps properly configured (NTSB, 1989c), prompting the Board to recommend that the FAA "require 14 CFR Part 121 operators to develop and use Cockpit Resource Management programs in their training methodology by a specified date" (NTSB Recommendation No. A-89-124). The FAA responded on April 12, 1990, that it was considering a notice of proposed rulemaking (NPRM) proposing this. The Board left the recommendation "Open—Acceptable Action," pending its review and comment on the NPRM.

Aloha Islandair—Molokai, Hawaii—10/28/89

The Board turned their attention to Part 135 operators after an Aloha Islandair DHC-6 Twin Otter accident in Molokai, Hawaii, on October 28, 1989 (NTSB, 1990c). The aircraft, flying under visual flight rules in darkness, crashed into terrain on a scheduled passenger flight from Maui to Molokai, killing the two pilots and all 18 passengers.

In addition to recommending that scheduled Part 135 operations (commuter) be conducted under instrument flight rules during darkness or visibilities of less than 3 miles (Recommendation No. A-90-137), the NTSB recommended that the FAA "require that scheduled 14 CFR Part 135 operators develop and use cockpit resource management programs in their training methodology by a specific date" (Recommendation No. A-90-135). The FAA responded in February, 1991, that they were considering amending the training requirements for all part 121 and 135 carriers, and that if adopted, they would require all who elected to follow the Advanced Qualification and Training program to include CRM in their programs.

Grand Canyon Airlines—Grand Canyon, Arizona—9/27/89

Grand Canyon Airlines Flight Canyon 5, a DHC-6 Twin Otter, crashed on landing to Grand Canyon National Park Airport after some apparent confusion between the pilots, causing a lack of coordination needed to execute a go-around (NTSB, 1991a). In the NTSB report, the Aloha Islandair accident (which had occurred a month later, but the NTSB report was released earlier) was cited, along with the Grand Canyon accident, as examples of poor crew coordination. The Grand Canyon accident was reported to

> further support the need for CRM training. In addition, it demonstrates the need for specific training for captains in the supervision of first officers, in decisionmaking regarding intervention when first officers are flying, and in the proper timing and execution of intervention. (p. 25)

Markair—Unalakleet, Alaska—6/2/90

Although the Board was unable to judge the quality of any CRM program when air carrier responses to the "Northwest 255" Recommendation No.

A-88-71 were received, they were able to make specific recommendations after FAA Advisory Circular 120-51 was formally released. On June 2, 1990, Markair Flight 3087, a B-737, crashed about 7.5 miles short of Runway 14 in Unalakleet, Alaska, while executing a localizer approach in low visibility (NTSB, 1991b). There were no passengers on board, and although there were no fatalities, the captain, first officer, and two flight attendants were injured. Poor crew coordination was cited, and the NTSB recommended that Markair "expand the Markair Cockpit Resource Management Program to conform to guidelines in FAA Advisory Circular 120-51" (NTSB Recommendation No. A-91-016). This recommendation remains open.

Recognition of Effective CRM

As the previously cited United Flight 663 windshear accident report (NTSB, 1985b) demonstrated, the NTSB and others have occasionally made use of positive examples of crew coordination to emphasize CRM training effectiveness. Other positive examples are discussed below.

Horizon Air—Seattle—4/15/88

On April 15, 1988, Horizon Air Flight 2658, a 37-passenger DeHavilland DHC-8, took off from Seattle–Tacoma Airport (NTSB, 1989b). Shortly after take-off, the crew noticed a power loss in the right engine, and the captain made a decision to return to Seattle for a precautionary landing. When the gear was lowered, a massive fire broke out in the right engine nacelle. Shortly after touchdown, the crew realized that all directional control and braking capability was lost. The aircraft struck several baggage carts and two jetways and came to rest against a third jetway. The airplane was destroyed, but there were no fatalities.

The CVR transcript provides a model for effective crisis management, and the Safety Board recognized the crew's coordination in their findings: "During the emergency, the flightcrew performed commendably and exhibited coordinated crew interaction in accordance with good CRM concepts which mitigated the seriousness of the emergency." Horizon Air was one of the first regional airlines to develop its own CRM course, a fact that was recognized at the Board's Sunshine meeting to consider the draft report.

United Airlines—Honolulu—2/24/89

On February 24, 1989, United Airlines Flight 811, a Boeing 747, took off from Honolulu with three flightcrew, 15 flight attendants, and 337 passengers on board (NTSB, 1990a). As the aircraft climbed through 22,000 feet, the forward lower lobe cargo door separated from the aircraft, and an explosive decompression ensued. Nine passengers were ejected from the aircraft and were never found. The crew made a successful emergency landing at Honolulu. This accident has been identified as a "good CRM" accident (Predmore, 1991), although no commendation was made in the NTSB report. Since the CVR transcript for this accident contained no information relevant to the reconstruction of the accident sequence of events, it is not printed in the published report, although it can be obtained through the NTSB's public docket. The communication patterns recorded in the transcript typify the types of communication encouraged in CRM training.

United Airlines—Sioux City—7/19/89

On July 19, 1989, United Airlines Flight 232, a DC-10, experienced an uncontained engine failure of the number 2 (center) engine, and engine fragments severed the hydraulic lines, rendering the airplane's hydraulic-powered flight control systems inoperative (NTSB, 1990d). The crew managed to fly the airplane using asymmetric thrust from the right and left engines, but a safe landing was virtually impossible. Still, the airplane touched down just slightly left of the centerline of the runway. Unfortunately, the right wing tip touched ground first, and the airplane skidded the right of the runway and cartwheeled into a cornfield, where it was destroyed by impact and fire. Miraculously, of the total 296 on board, 185 survived.

The United 232 accident has been publicized widely as one in which CRM training played a significant part in lessening the severity of the accident. Captain Al Haynes himself publicly attributed his success in landing the plane to United's resource management training (Haynes, 1991). The NTSB commended the crew in its report, concluding that their performance "greatly exceeded reasonable expectations." The report stated that the flightcrew's interactions were "indicative of the value of cockpit resource management training, which has been in existence at UAL for a decade" (p. 76).

As in the United 811 report cited above, since the CVR transcript only documents the last 30 minutes of the flight and was not felt to provide information relevant to the accident cause, it is absent from the report, but is available in the NTSB public docket. Predmore (1991) analyzed the communication patterns of both the United 232 and United 811 accidents. His graphic representation of the "efficient distribution of communications across multiple tasks and crewmembers" proves that crew communication is a measurable component of effective CRM.

NEW DIRECTIONS: EXPANSION OF THE CREW CONCEPT

Recently, the concept of the crew has started to undergo a transformation. Many airline training programs identify dispatch, maintenance, and cabin crew as resources to be added into the CRM equation. Pan American, and later Continental Airlines, have taught CRM concepts to maintenance personnel (Fotos, 1991a, 1991b). NTSB has identified several accidents in which coordination between flightcrew and air traffic controllers or between flightcrew and cabin crew was insufficient or inappropriate. Organizational factors have also been highlighted recently as significantly impacting the transfer of training from the classroom to the operational setting. These issues, discussed below, promise to be the new directions in the emphasis of CRM in accident investigation. Further discussion of the expansion of CRM beyond the cockpit can be found in the chapter by Helmreich, Wiener, and Kanki.

Cockpit–ATC Coordination

Eastern Air Lines—Florida Everglades—12/29/72

As Eastern Flight 401 (NTSB, 1973b) descended to 900 feet, the Miami approach controller asked, "Eastern, ah, four oh one how are things comin' along out there?" (p. 5). When the captain answered immediately with a request for a turn, the controller assumed the radar data block reading of 900 feet was an error, since he commonly experienced momentary deviations in the data block display. Less than a minute later, the aircraft crashed into the Everglades. One wonders how the outcome would have altered had the controller communicated his altitude reading to the crew. At the time, the Safety Board concluded that the Automated Radar Terminal Service (ARTS III) equipment, which processes transponder beacon data from the aircraft and displays aircraft identification, altitude, and speed, could have aided the controller in detecting the altitude deviation in time to take action to assist the crew. Implicitly the NTSB was suggesting an automated ground proximity warning for ATC, but explicitly they recommended that the FAA "Review the ARTS III program for the possible development of procedures to aid flightcrew when marked deviations in altitude are noticed by an Air Traffic Controller" (Recommendation No. A-73-46). The report did, however recognize air traffic control as a member of a "team":

> The Board recognizes that the ARTS III system was not designed to provide terrain clearance information and that the FAA has no procedures which require the controller to provide such a service. However, it would appear that everyone in the overall aircraft control system has an inherent responsibility to alert others to apparent hazardous situations, even though it is not his primary duty to effect the corrective action. (p. 14)

United Airlines—Kaysville, Utah—12/18/77

United Flight 2860, a DC-8 cargo flight, encountered electrical system problems on descent and approach to Salt Lake City Airport. The crew requested a holding clearance and then got clearance from the controller to leave the approach control frequency for a "little minute" (NTSB, 1978, p. 1). The minute became 7.5 minutes, during which the aircraft entered an area near hazardous terrain. When the flight returned to the ATC frequency, the controller gave the flight instructions to turn and climb, but the crew responded too slowly, and the plane crashed into a mountain.

The Safety Board cited imprecise communication and imprecise adherence to procedures as causal. In contrast to the Eastern 401 accident, the controller had a Minimum Safe Altitude Warning alert, signaling the aircraft's proximity to hazardous terrain. The report stated that, "considering the alternatives, . . . instructions for an immediate turn and climb with stress on the immediacy of the action would have been most appropriate" (p. 28).

Avianca—Cove Neck, New York—1/25/90

More recently, the Avianca Boeing 707 which crashed into a wooded residential area in Long Island, New York, on January 25, 1990 (NTSB, 1991c), raised the issue of ATC coordination between ATC and flightcrew, and in addition, between controllers. The Board found that the crew failed to adequately communicate their emergency fuel situation to ATC, and the controllers did not, nor were they required to, ask for clarification. There was a consideration of whether the handoff from the New York Center to New York's Terminal Radar Approach Control was adequate. The NTSB concluded that the handling of Avianca 052 was reasonable, but the mere implication raised the consciousness of the aviation industry with respect to controller "team" performance.

In December, 1990, the FAA released the draft National Plan for Aviation Human Factors (FAA, 1990), a joint endeavor of FAA, NASA, and industry to develop a coordinated approach to address the most pressing human factors problems in the airspace system. The plan identifies ATC team performance and team training as issues that must be addressed in the coming years.

Recently the FAA has begun to redesign completely the air traffic control curriculum, ab initio, at the academy in Oklahoma City, through facility-specific initial and recurrent training. CRM concepts have been targeted as an integral part of the training process at all levels. On October 22–24, 1991, an FAA Air Traffic Control Training Working Group sponsored a workshop on controller resource management in Austin, Texas, to exchange ideas with airline CRM training personnel, researchers, and members of the NASA/University of Texas Crew Performance Project. In October, 1992 the first groups of controllers were given facilitator training in preparation for a model training program to enhance team awareness.

Cockpit–Cabin Coordination

The extension of the crew concept into the cabin has been suggested by various components of the aviation industry. It was formally addressed by the chairperson of the National Air Safety Committee of the Association of Flight

Attendants in 1986 (Koan, 1986). Several airlines include flight attendants in at least a portion of their CRM training, and the Air Transport Association's Working Group on Flight Attendant Training is in the process of considering standards for flight attendant "CRM." NTSB, addressed cockpit–cabin coordination issues in several accident reports (NTSB, 1979b, 1984a, 1984b, 1985b, 1988a, 1990d).

In 1983, an Eastern Air Lines Lockheed L-1011 made a single-engine landing to Miami International Airport due to the omission of all the O-ring seals on the master chip detectors in the engine lubrication system. The pilots had shut down one of the three engines because of an indication of loss of oil pressure. Shortly after, the remaining two engines flamed out (NTSB, 1984a). The passengers stayed in the brace position for more than 10 minutes, because the flight attendants were unaware of the amount of time available for preparation. The NTSB recommended that Eastern Air Lines conduct joint training of cabin and cockpit crews to practice cabin–cockpit crew coordination (Recommendation No. A-84-043). Eastern responded that joint training was impractical. Eastern, instead, had flight attendants lecture new captains on the importance of good communication and coordination. The Safety Board closed the recommendation "Acceptable Action" on February 18, 1986.

On February 3, 1988, American Airlines flight 132, a DC-9-83, experienced an inflight fire below the main cabin floor during flight. The airplane touched down safely at Nashville, with minor injuries to 18 of the 131 on board as a result of the evacuation (NTSB, 1988a). Although there was ample evidence of smoke and heat in the cabin, the cockpit crew erroneously concluded that fumes rather than smoke were present in the passenger cabin. No inflight emergency was declared, and the airplane was not evacuated immediately on landing, exposing the crew and passengers unnecessarily to the threat of fire. The NTSB recommended that American Airlines

> Review and modify as needed training programs to require joint cockpit and cabin crew training with respect to emergency procedures; specific attention should be given to conducting periodic emergency drills in which cockpit/cabin crew coordination and communication are practiced. (Recommendation No. A-88-117)

American Airlines responded in a letter dated December 7, 1988, that it addressed cabin–cockpit coordination in its crewmember CRM course and in its "role playing during simulated emergencies (for flight attendants)," and did not consider joint crewmember training warranted. Although Board member Jim Burnett did not concur with the decision, the NTSB closed this recommendation as "Acceptable Alternate Action" on January 4, 1990.

The Safety Board has published a special investigation report on flight attendant training issues (NTSB, 1992). This report addresses the need for training and reinforcement of leadership skills, time management, and effective communication between flight attendants and the cockpit crew. The issue of cabin–

cockpit crew coordination will continue to be a visible one in the coming years, as more airlines expand their CRM training to the cabin.

Organizational Factors

Although several authors have discussed the safety impact of organizational factors, such as airline management and FAA oversight (Bruggink, 1985; 1988b; Reason, 1989a, 1989b) they have only recently been stressed by NTSB.

The Northwest 255 accident report (NTSB, 1988b) quoted Lautman & Gallimore (1987), who had studied air carriers with better than average and worse than average accident rates over a 10-year period. Lautman and Gallimore had found that the carriers with the lowest accident rates had management commitment to safety, which included the recognition of the importance of cockpit discipline and crew coordination.

In NTSB's report of Delta Air Lines Flight 1141, the Safety Board cited as contributing factors to the accident the airline's "slow implementation of necessary modifications" and "the lack of sufficiently aggressive action by the FAA to have known deficiencies corrected" (NTSB, 1989c, p. 94).

More recently, the ground collision between USAir Flight 1493 and Skywest Flight 5569 at Los Angeles International Airport on February 1, 1991, prompted the NTSB to assign primary cause to Los Angeles Air Traffic Control tower for implementing, and FAA evaluations, for allowing Los Angeles tower to implement, non-standard procedures which did not provide sufficient redundancy (NTSB, 1991d). This, the NTSB concluded, ultimately led the local controller to lose awareness of the traffic situation.

James Reason (1989a) analyzed several major disasters involving complex systems, including spacecraft, rail, military aircraft, off-shore oil platforms, and ferries, and concluded:

> These disasters were due to the adverse conjunction of a large number of causal factors, each one necessary but not sufficient to achieve the catastrophic outcome. Although the errors and violations of those at the immediate human—system interface often feature large in the post-accident investigations, it is evident that these "front-line" operators are rarely the principal instigators of system breakdown. Their part is often to provide just those local triggering conditions necessary to manifest systemic weaknesses created by fallible decisions made earlier in the organizational and managerial spheres. (p. 1)

CONCLUSIONS ————————————————————— ✦

There are many more accidents that illustrate good and poor CRM. This chapter has highlighted the accidents that have shaped the attitudes of those in the

United States who are in position to effect positive change: the air carriers, pilots' unions, and the Federal government. Accident reports have, to date, been instrumental in convincing several airlines to develop CRM courses, and NTSB recommendations have been a driving force in the FAA's development of advisory circulars and the SFAR on AQP.

Crew resource management is an evolving concept, and the crew concept is already expanding to encompass air traffic control, the cabin, dispatch, maintenance, and organizational decision-makers. Accident reports and recommendations will continue to focus on these issues, and will, hopefully, assist in prodding the appropriate decision-makers to make an already safe system even safer.

Acknowledgments

The author wishes to thank Gerard Bruggink, James Danaher, John Lauber, Julie Beal, Vicky D'Onofrio, and Rick Van Woerkem for their help in compiling and interpreting the historical material presented herein. The opinions expressed are those of the author and do not necessarily reflect the official policies of the Federal Aviation Administration or the National Transportation Safety Board.

References

Barnhart, W., Billings, C., Cooper, G., Gilstrap, R., Lauber, J., Orlady, H., Puskas, B., & Stephens, W. (1975). *A method for the study of human factors in aircraft operations* (NASA Technical Memorandum TM X-62, 472). Moffett Field, CA: NASA–Ames Research Center.

Brenner, M. (1989, September). *Human performance issues in two recent accidents.* Paper presented at the Annual Symposium of the International Society of Air Safety Investigators, Munich, Germany.

Bruggink, G. M. (1983). Civil aircraft accident investigation in the U.S. *International Journal of Aviation Safety, 1*(4), 349–354.

Bruggink, G. M. (1985, May). Uncovering the policy factor in accidents. *Air Line Pilot,* pp. 22–25.

Bruggink, G. M. (1988a, February). Accident reports: a neglected resource. *ICAO Bulletin,* pp. 20–24.

Bruggink, G. M. (1988b, June). Reflections on air carrier safety. *Flight Safety Foundation, Inc. Flight Safety Digest,* pp. 1–6.

Burnett, J. (1982). *Statement of Honorable Jim Burnett, Acting Chairman National Transportation Safety Board before the Subcommittees on Investigations and Oversight and Transportation, Aviation and Materials Committee on Science and Technology, House of Representatives, Regarding Aviation Safety, March 9, 1982.* 97th Cong., 2nd sess., No. 85.

Cooper, G. E., White, M. D., & Lauber, J. K. (Eds.). (1980). *Resource management on the flight deck: Proceedings of a NASA/Industry workshop held at San Francisco, California, June 26–28, 1979* (NASA Conference Publication 2120).

Corrie, S. J. (1986). In NTSB investigations, public disclosure of accident information is examined. In *Proceedings of the 17th Seminar of the International Society of Air Safety Investigators, Rotorua, New Zealand, October 6–9, 1986* (pp. 49–55). ISASI Forum, *19*(2).

Danaher, J. W. (1984). *Remarks made at the Aviation Accident Investigation Symposium, April 26–28, 1983, Springfield, Virginia* (NTSB/RP-84/01) (pp. 12–17).

Davis, T. H. (1979). The probable cause: A detriment to air safety? In *Proceedings of the 10th*

International Seminar of the International Society of Air Safety Investigators, Montreal, Quebec, Canada, September 24–27, 1979 (pp. 37–38). *ISASI Forum, 12*(3).

Diehl, A. (1989). Human performance aspects of aircraft accidents. In R. Jensen (Ed.), *Aviation Psychology*. Aldershot, England: Gower Press.

Federal Aviation Administration. (1990). *The national plan for aviation human factors* (NTIS No. PB01-100321). Washington, DC: Author.

Fotos, C. P. (1991a, August 26). Continental applies CRM concepts to technical, maintenance corps. *Aviation Week and Space Technology*, pp. 32–33.

Fotos, C. P. (1991b, August 26). Training stresses teamwork, self-assessment techniques. *Aviation Week and Space Technology*, pp. 33–35.

Haynes, A. C. (1991, August). United 232: Coping with the "one-in-a-billion" loss of all flight controls. *Avionics News*, pp. 30–61.

Kayten, P. J. (1989). Human performance factors in aircraft accident investigation. *Proceedings of the Second Conference, Human Error Avoidance Techniques, Herndon, Virginia, September 18–19, 1989* (SAE/P229/892688) (pp. 49–53). Warrendale, PA: Society of Automotive Engineers.

Kayten, P. J., & Roberts, C. (1985). The application of CVR and FDR data in human performance investigation. In *Proceedings of the 16th International Seminar of the International Society of Air Safety Investigators, September 3–6, 1985* (pp. 44–50). *ISASI Forum, 18*(3).

Koan, N. (1986). Cabin and cockpit crew coordination through communication. In *Proceedings of the Flight Safety Foundation, Inc. 39th Annual International Air Safety Seminar, October 6–9, 1986, Vancouver, Canada* (pp. 258–265). Arlington, VA: Flight Safety Foundation, Inc.

Kowalsky, N. B., Master, R. L., Stone, R. B., Babcock, G. L., & Rypka, E. W. (1974, June). *An analysis of pilot error-related aircraft accidents* (Technical Report NASA CR-2444). Washington, DC: NASA.

Lauber, J. K. (1983). *The investigation of human error in aircraft accidents: An historical perspective* (NTSB/RP-84/01). Presented at the Aviation Accident Investigation Symposium, April 26–28, 1983, Springfield, Virginia [The paper in the published proceedings is abridged].

Lauber, J. K. (1989). Anatomy of a human factors accident. *Proceedings of the 34th Annual Corporate Aviation Safety Seminar, Flight Safety Foundation, April 19–21, 1989, Dearborn, Michigan* (pp. 19–29). Arlington, VA: Flight Safety Foundation, Inc.

Lautman, L. G., & Gallimore, P. L. (1987, April–June). Control of the crew-caused accident. *Airliner Magazine*, pp. 1–7. Seattle, WA: Boeing Commercial Airplane Company.

McIntyre, J. (1989). The role of professional standards in cockpit resource management (CRM). In *Human error avoidance techniques: Proceedings of the Second Conference, Herndon, Virginia, September 18–19, 1989* (SAE/P-89/229) (pp. 39–41).

Miller, C. O. (1977, February 8). *Human factors accident investigation and the question of pilot decision-making*. Paper presented at the ALPA Symposium on Human Factors, Washington, D.C.

Miller, C. O, 1980, Spring). Human factors in accident investigation. *ISASI Forum, 13*(1) 16–25.

National Transportation Safety Board. (1971). *Aircraft Accident Report: Trans International Airlines Corp. Ferry Flight 863, Douglas DC-8-63F, N4863T, J.F. Kennedy International Airport, New York, September 8, 1970* (NTSB-AAR-71-12). Washington, DC: Author.

National Transportation Safety Board. (1972). *Aircraft Accident Report: Allegheny Airlines, Inc. Allison Prop Jet Convair 340/440, N5832, New Haven, Connecticut, June 7, 1971* (NTSB-AAR-72-20). Washington, DC: Author.

National Transportation Safety Board. (1973a). *Aircraft Accident Report: Mohawk Airlines, Inc., Fairchild Hiller FH-227B, N7818M, Albany, New York, March 3, 1972* (NTSB-AAR-73-8). Washington, DC: Author.

National Transportation Safety Board. (1973b). *Aircraft Accident Report: Eastern Air Lines, Inc.*

L-1011, N310EA, Miami, Florida, December 29, 1972 (NTSB-AAR-73-14). Washington, DC: Author.

National Transportation Safety Board. (1976a). *Special Study: Flightcrew Coordination Procedures in Air Carrier Instrument Landing System Approach Accidents* (NTSB-AAS-76-5). Washington, DC: Author.

National Transportation Safety Board. (1976b). *Aircraft Accident Report: Alaska Airlines, Inc., B-727-81, N124AS, Ketchikan International Airport, Ketchikan, Alaska, April 5, 1976* (NTSB-AAR-76-20). Washington, DC: Author.

National Transportation Safety Board. (1978). *Aircraft Accident Report: United Airlines, Inc., Douglas DC-8-54, N8047U, Near Kaysville, Utah, December 18, 1977* (NTSB-AAR-78-8). Washington, DC: Author.

National Transportation Safety Board. (1979a). *Aircraft Accident Report: Allegheny Airlines, Inc., BAC 1-11, N1550, Rochester, New York, July 9, 1978* (NTSB-AAR-79-2). Washington, DC: Author.

National Transportation Safety Board. (1979b). *Aircraft Accident Report: United Airlines, Inc., McDonnell-Douglas DC-8-61, N8082U, Portland, Oregon, December 28, 1978* (NTSB-AAR-79-7). Washington, DC: Author.

National Transportation Safety Board. (1980). *Aircraft Accident Report: Downeast Airlines, Inc., de Havilland DHC-6-200, N68DE, Knox County Regional Airport, Rockland, Maine, May 30, 1979* (NTSB-AAR-80-5). Washington, DC: Author.

National Transportation Safety Board. (1982). *Aircraft Accident Report: Air Florida, Inc., Boeing 737-222, N62AF, Collision with 14th Street Bridge, Near Washington National Airport, Washington, D.C., January 13, 1982* (NTSB-AAR-82-8). Washington, DC: Author.

National Transportation Safety Board. (1983). *Accident investigation of human performance factors.* Unpublished manuscript.

National Transportation Safety Board. (1984a). *Aircraft Accident Report: Eastern Air Lines, Inc., Lockheed L-1011, N334EA, Miami International Airport, Miami, Florida, May 5, 1983* (NTSB-AAR-84/04). Washington, DC: Author.

National Transportation Safety Board. (1984b). *Aircraft Accident Report: Air Canada Flight 797, McDonnell Douglas DC-9-32, C-FTLU, Greater Cincinnati International Airport, Covington, Kentucky, June 2, 1983* (NTSB/AAR-84/09). Washington, DC: Author.

National Transportation Safety Board. (1984c). *Aircraft Accident Report: Scandinavian Airlines System Flight 901, McDonnell Douglas DC-10-30 Norwegian Registry LN-RKB, John F. Kennedy International Airport, Jamaica, New York, February 28, 1984* (NTSB-AAR-84/15). Washington, DC: Author.

National Transportation Safety Board. (1985a). *Aircraft Accident Report: USAir, Inc., Flight 183, McDonnell Douglas DC9-31, N964VJ, Detroit, Michigan, June 13, 1984* (NTSB/AAR-85/01). Washington, DC: Author.

National Transportation Safety Board. (1985b). *Aircraft Accident Report: United Airlines Flight 663, Boeing 727-222, N7647U, Denver, Colorado, May 31, 1984* (NTSB/AAR-85/05). Washington, DC: Author.

National Transportation Safety Board. (1986a). *Aircraft Accident Report: Galaxy Airlines, Inc., Lockheed Electra L-188C, N5532, Reno, Nevada, January 21, 1985* (NTSB-AAR-86/01). Washington, DC: Author.

National Transportation Safety Board. (1986b). *Aircraft Accident Report: Delta Air Lines, Inc., Lockheed L-1011-385-1, N726DA, Dallas–Fort Worth International Airport, Texas, August 2, 1985* (NTSB/AAR-86/05). Washington, DC: Author.

National Transportation Safety Board. (1987a). *Aircraft Accident Report: Collision of Aeronaves de Mexico, S.A., McDonnell Douglas DC-9-32, XA-JED, and Piper PA-28-181, N4891F, Cerritos, California, August 31, 1986* (NTSB/AAR-87/07). Washington, DC: Author.

National Transportation Safety Board. (1987b). *Aircraft Accident Report: Piedmont Airlines Flight 467, Boeing 737-222, N752N, Charlotte Douglas International Airport, Charlotte, North Carolina, October 26, 1986* (NTSB/AAR-87/08). Washington, DC: Author.

National Transportation Safety Board. (1988a). *Hazardous Materials Incident Report: In-Flight Fire, McDonnell Douglas DC-9-83, N569AA, Nashville Metropolitan Airport, Nashville, Tennessee, February 3, 1988* (NTSB/HZM-88/02). Washington, DC: Author.

National Transportation Safety Board. (1988b). *Aircraft Accident Report: Northwest Airlines, Inc., McDonnell Douglas DC-9-82, N312RC, Detroit Metropolitan Wayne County Airport, Romulus, Michigan, August 16, 1987* (NTSB/AAR-88/05). Washington, DC: Author.

National Transportation Safety Board. (1989a). *Aircraft Accident Report: Trans-Colorado Airlines, Inc., Flight 2286, Fairchild Metro III, SA227 AC, N68TC, Bayfield, Colorado, January 19, 1988* (NTSB/AAR-89/01). Washington, DC: Author.

National Transportation Safety Board. (1989b). *Aircraft Accident Report: Horizon Air, Inc., De-Havilland DHC-8, Seattle-Takoma International Airport, Seattle, Washington, April 15, 1988* (NTSB/AAR-89/02). Washington, DC: Author.

National Transportation Safety Board. (1989c). *Aircraft Accident Report: Delta Air Lines, Inc., Boeing 727-232, N473DA, Dallas-Fort Worth International Airport, Texas, August 31, 1988* (NTSB/AAR-89/04). Washington, DC: Author.

National Transportation Safety Board. (1990a). *Aircraft Accident Report: United Airlines Flight 811, Boeing 747-122, N4713U, Honolulu, Hawaii, February 24, 1989* (NTSB/AAR-90/01). Washington, DC: Author.

National Transportation Safety Board. (1990b). *Aircraft Accident Report: USAir, Inc., Boeing 737-400, LaGuardia Airport, Flushing, New York, September 20, 1989* (NTSB/AAR-90/03). Washington, DC: Author.

National Transportation Safety Board. (1990c). *Aircraft Accident Report: Aloha IslandAir, Inc., Flight 1712, De Havilland DHC-6-300, Near Halawa Point, Molokai, Hawaii, October 28, 1989* (NTSB/AAR/90/05). Washington, DC: Author.

National Transportation Safety Board. (1990d). *Aircraft Accident Report: United Airlines Flight 232, McDonnell Douglas DC-10-10, Sioux Gateway Airport, Sioux City, Iowa, July 19, 1989* (NTSB/AAR-90/06). Washington, DC: Author.

National Transportation Safety Board. (1991a). *Aircraft Accident Report: Grand Canyon Airlines Flight Canyon 5, De Havilland Twin Otter, DHC-6-300, N75GC, Grand Canyon National Park Airport, Tusayan, Arizona, September 27, 1989* (NTSB/AAR-91/01). Washington, DC: Author.

National Transportation Safety Board. (1991b). *Aircraft Accident Report: Markair, Inc. Flight 3087, Boeing 737-2X6C, N670MA, Unalakleet, Alaska, June 2, 1990* (NTSB/AAR-91/02). Washington, DC: Author.

National Transportation Safety Board. (1991c). *Aircraft Accident Report: Avianca, The Airline of Colombia, Boeing 707-321B, HK 2016, Fuel Exhaustion, Cove Neck, New York, January 25, 1990* (NTSB/AAR-91/04). Washington, DC: Author.

National Transportation Safety Board. (1991d). *Aircraft Accident Report: Ground Collision of USAir, Inc. Flight 1493, Boeing 737-300, N388US, and Skywest, Inc. Flight 5569, Fairchild Metroliner (SA-227-AC), Los Angeles International Airport, February 1, 1991* (NTSB/AAR-91-XX). Washington, DC: Author.

National Transportation Safety Board. (1992). *Special Investigation Report: Flight Attendant Training and Performance during Emergency Situations* (NTSB/SIR-92/02). Washington, DC: Author.

Predmore, S. C. (1991). Microcoding of communications in accident investigation: Crew coordination in United 811 and United 232. *Proceedings of the Sixth International Symposium on Aviation Psychology.* Columbus: Ohio State University.

Ramsden, J. M. (1983, January 22). Safety of the DC-10. *Flight International*, pp. 209–220.

Reason, J. M. (1989a). *The contribution of latent human failures to the breakdown of complex systems*. Paper presented at the Royal Society Discussion Meeting on Human Factors in High-Risk Situations. London, England, June 28–29.

Reason, J. (1989b). *The human contribution to "organizational accidents"*. Draft paper for the Second World Bank Workshop on Safety Control and Risk Management, Karlstad, Sweden, November 6–9.

Ruffell Smith, H. P. (1979). *A simulator study of the interaction of pilot workload with errors, vigilance, and decisions* (NASA Technical Memorandum 78482). Moffett Field, CA: NASA–Ames Research Center.

Schleede, R. L. (1979, Winter). Application of a decision-making model to the investigation of human error in aircraft accidents. In *Proceedings of the 10th International Seminar of the International Society of Air Safety Investigators, Montreal, Quebec, Canada, September, 1979* (pp. 62–78). *ISASI Forum, 12*(3).

Stoklosa, J. H. (1981). Human performance factors in aviation accidents: an investigator's methodology. *ISASI Forum, 13*(4), 23–27.

Stoklosa, J. H. (1983). *Accident investigation of human performance factors*. Paper presented at the Second Symposium on Aviation Psychology, Ohio State University, Columbus, April 25–28.

Walhout, G. J. (1981a). Human performance investigation: An approach towards the assessment of human performance during accident investigations. *ISASI Forum, 13*(4), 21–22.

Walhout, G. J. (1981b). Remarks. *Third Human Factors Workshop on Aviation, Sponsored by the U.S. Department of Transportation, Federal Aviation Administration, March 18 & 19, Cambridge, Massachusetts* (FAA/ASF-81-5) (pp. 26–32).

Walhout, G. J. (1983). The role of aircraft recorders in human performance investigations, *Proceedings of Society of Automotive Engineers Second Aerospace Behavioral Engineering Technical Conference, Long Beach, California, October, 1983* (SAE/P-1321831414) (pp. 19–25). Warrendale, PA: Society of Automotive Engineers.

Walhout, G. J. (1991). Letter to the editor: Human factors checklists. *ISASI Forum, 24*(3), 1–2.

Wandell, W. V. (1989). Designation of parties to NTSB aviation accident investigation: A review. *ISASI Forum, 22*(2), 10–12.

11

Critical Issues for CRM Training and Research

Thomas R. Chidester
Crew Resource Management
American Airlines
Dallas-Fort Worth International Airport, Texas 75261

INTRODUCTION ✈

Crew resource management (CRM) training resulted from a co-occurrence of industry experience and research evidence suggesting problems inherent in integrating a collection of technically proficient individuals into an effective crew. Helmreich and Foushee have described accidents and research findings in their chapter that document the types of mistakes made by crews which are not effectively organized or led. This conclusion was most striking in the simulator study conducted by Ruffell Smith (1979), in which a number of B-747 crews had to complete an emergency scenario involving an engine failure early in a trans-Atlantic flight. The workload imposed by the scenario (completing abnormal procedures for the engine, deviating from track, choosing an airport, navigating, and dumping fuel) produced variability in performance far greater than expected by the researchers or the industry. The results questioned a very basic assumption—that any crew within an airline would handle a problem in essentially the same way and, if the problem were soluble, any crew would bring the flight to a safe conclusion.

That assumption was based on the degree of standardization of procedures and training and the level of proficiency demonstrated by each pilot or flight engineer in qualifying for his or her position. Instead, crews completing the Ruffell Smith scenario varied greatly in how, and how safely, they completed the flight. For example, several seriously overweight landings resulted from errors in fuel-dump calculations made by flight engineers, who were given several tasks to complete concurrently. It was as if each crewmember knew what he or she was supposed to do but did not know how the duties fit with those of other crewmembers. Viewed in the context of several accidents of the late 1970s that were attributed to crew coordination breakdowns and a review suggesting that these problems were common in accidents (Cooper, White, & Lauber, 1979), this research convinced the industry of a need for training focusing on how captains should lead and how first officers and flight engineers should perform as crewmembers.

Cooperation between the industry and a subset of the human factors community, organized primarily around National Aeronautics and Space Administration (NASA)–sponsored research efforts, grew as CRM training programs were implemented during the 1980s. United Airlines initiated its pioneering effort following the 1979 NASA workshop, *Resource Management on the Flightdeck* (Cooper et al., 1979), and virtually every major airline in the United States and many worldwide have followed suit. The research community has supported this effort by conducting simulation-based studies on issues critical to the industry (Chidester, Kanki, Foushee, Dickinson, & Bowles, 1990; Foushee, Lauber, Baetge, & Acomb, 1986; Wiener, Chidester, Kanki, Palmer, Curry, & Gregorich, 1991), by leading industry conferences on CRM training, and by participating in the development of guidelines for those implementing training (i.e., Federal Aviation Administration, FAA, advisory circulars). Both groups have benefited from this process. The industry has received answers to questions that otherwise would have been addressed through expensive trial and error, if at all. Researchers have gained operational credibility by learning the substance of cockpit tasks, and their understanding of human behavior has gained a degree of "ecological validity" unobtainable in the laboratory.

The relationship between the industry and the research community is now at a critical point. Many of the more basic questions of whether CRM training can have a positive effect are resolved, and relatively clear guidelines for implementing programs are in place. But the industry now faces a variety of constraints, recognizes that coordination problems are not limited to the cockpit, and is left with questions that need research answers. The human factors community, through the *National Plan for Aviation Human Factors* (FAA, 1990) developed by the FAA and NASA, is gaining the resources and defining a program to address industry questions. It is time for a new round of cooperation between the industry and the research community—one that involves focused questions from which both operational practices and scientific understanding can benefit. This chapter is intended to focus the debate on critical issues in CRM training. It is written with three goals: (1) to document what has been recommended by the FAA and by research evaluating CRM training effectiveness, (2) to describe the constraints airlines face in implementing CRM training programs, and (3) to highlight research issues that need greater attention.

RECOMMENDATIONS PROVIDED BY THE FAA AND NASA ⎯⎯⎯⎯⎯⎯⎯⎯⎯⎯⎯⎯⎯⎯⎯⎯⎯⎯⎯ ✈

Early attempts to implement CRM training programs proceeded with little guidance from either the FAA or the research community. Many airlines purchased off-the-shelf classroom programs from providers of management development training—then the closest analog to the crew coordination problems identified in the cockpit. As noted by Helmreich and Foushee in their chapter, these initial efforts met with mixed success, depending on the degree to which they were modified from a general or abstract management focus to the technical and interpersonal concerns of the cockpit. The anonymous, unpublished comments of one pilot going through training in 1991 may summarize the problems of initial mixed success:

> When this CRM training first started, I couldn't figure out what you were trying to do. I mean, the management games were interesting, but I had no idea how to use it in the cockpit. Now that you've focused more on real cockpit situations, I'm finding things I can use.

CRM training at each airline has evolved over a period of years, and this evolution has occurred in response to both the feedback of participating pilots and recommendations offered by researchers and the FAA.

FAA Recommendations

Crew coordination training has been implemented in a variety of forms, but a consensus on both form and content of training began to emerge during the 1986 conference on CRM training co-sponsored by NASA and the Military Airlift Command (Orlady & Foushee, 1987). The recommendations of that conference set the stage for the FAA Advisory Circular, *Cockpit Resource Management Training* (AC120-51, FAA, 1989), which was based largely on the work of Helmreich and Foushee. In the circular, the FAA recommended that training programs be broken into three phases: (1) an awareness phase in which crewmembers complete seminar instruction and group exercises to learn the basic concepts of CRM, (2) a practice and feedback phase in which crews fly a realistic simulation featuring aircraft problems in the manner in which they would occur on the line and receive feedback on their performance, and (3) a reinforcement phase in which the CRM concepts become a part of the organization's overall training and operating practices.

Awareness phase seminars focus on a series of topics which often include communication, decision-making, stress and workload management, leader and subordinate responsibilities, and management styles. Typically, seminars include participatory exercises in which crewmembers role-play various cockpit situations. In some cases, exercises are videotaped and subsequently reviewed and critiqued by the class. Some organizations have implemented this awareness phase but provided no feedback or reinforcement. In fact, most of the initial efforts to implement CRM training went no further than to provide a single seminar, and in some cases that seminar was provided only to captains, or aircraft commanders in the military.

Practice and feedback is typically provided in the form of line-oriented flight training (LOFT; Lauber & Foushee, 1981) completed during a recurrent training cycle following the awareness phase. Ideally this would occur immediately after initial awareness training, but the realities of simulator scheduling often result in some delay. So some degree of this practice and feedback is deliberately emphasized in awareness phase exercises. LOFT is a technique wherein a high-fidelity aircraft simulator is flown with a complete crew performing as if on an actual line flight (see the chapter by Butler). More recently, the term line-oriented simulation (LOS) has been used to describe the development of realistic flight scenarios for use in any simulator training event. In LOFT, crews complete all their preparations and paperwork, communicate with traffic control and "company" facilities, and perform all routine procedures required for a normal flight. The LOFT instructor simulates the other end of all communications in a manner intended to be consistent with normal practices. Typically, each LOFT includes an aircraft system failure or weather-related problem for the crew to solve while completing all normal duties. Some LOFTs consist of a single flight segment, while others contain multiple legs. Crew performance is videotaped and crews review the tape afterward, providing an opportunity for both instructor and self-critique.

Reinforcement requires integration of crew coordination into the recurrent training cycle and also requires performance evaluation. LOFT should become a permanent fixture in recurrent training. It is often combined with a classroom presentation focusing on one CRM curriculum area. In this way, crewmembers receive a short refresher at least every 12 months (some airlines have received special exemptions from the FAA to allow annual rather than semi-annual training for captains). Perhaps the most critical part of the reinforcement phase is ensuring that supervisory pilots (training or line check airmen) highlight crew coordination issues during evaluations of simulator-based proficiency checks or line checks. Helmreich, Chidester, Foushee, Gregorich & Wilhelm (1990) have argued that reinforcement by supervisors when it counts—when one must demonstrate competency to maintain one's rating—will quickly determine whether CRM skills are embraced and applied by crewmembers.

In summary, the FAA has recommended that each airline provide crewmembers with classroom training raising awareness of crew coordination issues, the opportunity to practice and receive feedback on performance as a crewmember, and regular reinforcement of CRM skills through recurrent training and integration of CRM concepts with technical proficiency training and evaluation. This last portion, integrating technical and crew coordination training, has been incorporated into FAA and industry efforts to develop the Advanced Qualification Program (AQP; see the chapter by Birnbach and Longridge). Each airline with a CRM program has developed or revised the program under the guidance of these recommendations, but few have yet been able to address each phase completely.

NASA Recommendations

In addition to the formal recommendations provided by the FAA through the Advisory Circular, the industry has also received some guidance directly from the research community. Research sponsored by NASA, evaluating the impact of CRM programs, has resulted in recommendations in two areas—general CRM program implementation issues, and specific problems in LOFT implementation. The major recommendations from those two areas are summarized in this section.

General Recommendations

Regarding CRM in general, Helmreich and his colleagues have described 12 characteristics associated with successful CRM programs, 6 dealing with initial implementation, and 6 dealing with long-term issues (Helmreich, Chidester, Foushee, Gregorich, & Wilhelm, 1990). These characteristics translate into the following recommendations:

1. *Organizational commitment.* Demonstrate commitment of the organization's management to the program. Cockpit crewmembers are quite sophisticated at determining whether a program was created merely to "fill a square." From the beginning, the organization should communicate why the program is needed and that commitment to the program derives from the highest levels of management. However, the program should not be sold as just a management program, particularly in organizations where pilot–management relations are strained. Obtaining the endorsement of the pilots' organization or union for the goals of the program and involving them in updating and revising the program greatly enhances credibility.

2. *Program goals.* Communicate the goals of the program prior to startup. Many misconceptions have surrounded CRM training, and some of them have come from mistakes made in early programs. CRM may be viewed as a threat to captains' authority, as veiled psychotherapy, or as management exercises with little to do with cockpit behavior. The organization should state from the outset what the program is intended to do, using pilot newsletters or other communication materials, and should continue with updates describing curriculum areas,

critical incidents and how they were dealt with, or topics regularly raised in the classroom.

3. *Assessment.* Assess the state of the organization prior to designing the program. One of the major problems with off-the-shelf programs is that they do not deal with issues unique to an organization. Survey research using standardized measures, review of incidents, focus groups, or discussions with union training or safety committees can reveal the particular needs of the pilot group within the organization.

4. *Customization.* Customize training to organizational needs. Whether an off-the-shelf or a custom program is selected, the critical issue is to make sure the program fits organizational needs. For example, an organization that has grown through merger and acquisition may need to emphasize standardization of procedures. Without an effort at customization, the training may quickly be viewed as irrelevant.

5. *Designing exercises.* Use exercises that actively engage participants and provide feedback (awareness and practice/feedback phases). While the issues surrounding CRM can be communicated in a traditional classroom lecture format, this type of instruction is not likely to have a significant behavioral impact on participants. Activities taken directly from management development training have been viewed as irrelevant in some pilot groups. Activities built around real incidents or slight variations from real incidents are perceived as highly involving, whether they accompany role-playing or class discussion.

6. *Training phases.* Recognize that initial training (awareness) requires practice and feedback phases. As recognized by the FAA, a single awareness phase seminar will not be sufficient for long-term behavior change.

Once a training program has been established, other, long-term issues come to the forefront:

1. *Integrate CRM with LOFT.* It is becoming clear that full-mission simulation combined with videotape-based debriefing is the most effective way to practice and reinforce CRM concepts.

2. *Stress the critical role of check airmen and instructors.* It is the check airman corps that clearly determines the extent to which CRM concepts taught in the classroom are translated into behavior on the line. This should be the first group trained in an organization implementing a new program, and specific training for this group should focus on how to assess, coach, and reinforce crew performance on the line or in the simulator. This can be accomplished by having check airmen evaluate vignettes of crew performance in the simulator. This is a good technique for "setting the standard" to be carried to the line. Abnormal and emergency situations occur rarely on the line, so a classroom environment with realistic vignettes can give check airmen the opportunity to think through and reach some consensus on what they want crews to do in the airplane.

3. *Select check airmen and instructors who support CRM concepts.* Recog-

nizing that check airmen set the standard and determine whether classroom concepts are put to use, those clearly opposed to CRM concepts following training should be placed in different roles.

4. *Institute quality control for CRM and LOFT training.* Considerable variability in crewmember acceptance of CRM training occurs even when it is conducted by the same instructors within a particular organization. It therefore becomes critical to monitor the formal training through participant evaluations of the training and through systematic observation. Classroom and simulator instructors and check airmen should participate in standardization meetings or receive checkrides. Use of a standard debriefing and evaluation form, such as the Line/LOS checklist (Helmreich, Wilhelm, Kello, Taggart, & Butler, 1991), can assist simulator and line personnel in debriefing.

5. *Consider similar training for cabin crews and other parts of the organization.* Several organizations have begun to extend CRM concepts to cabin and ground-based personnel. Data on the effectiveness of this strategy are lacking, but the concept appears worth considering for long-term implementation.

6. *Make provisions for CRM "boomerangs."* Every training program fails to reach, or is rejected by, some subset of crewmembers. Often, these crewmembers subsequently express more unfavorable attitudes toward crew coordination than they held prior to participating in training. In a sense, training has backfired or, in the terms of attitude-change research, the crewmember has "boomeranged." This may result from characteristics of the crewmember, or it may result from characteristics of the program. For example, a program perceived as an attack on captains' authority will likely result in a high percentage of that group rejecting its concepts. At the individual level, those with marginal communication skills may feel threatened by a program emphasizing the importance of communication and may harden their attitudes further in response to training. Most organizations are reluctant to deal with this issue if the crewmember in question has sound technical skills, and there are good reasons for this reluctance, given contractual provisions specifying how training "failures" or other disciplinary actions must proceed. In such cases, the best resort may be peer pressure, in the form of feedback from a professional standards committee (see also the discussion by Helmreich, Wiener, and Kanki in their chapter).

These recommendations require an organization to assess its commitment and ability to provide a comprehensive program. It is preferable to be able to view these requirements up front to make an honest determination of what the organization is willing to do, rather than to implement half-heartedly or to provide insufficient support for the program.

LOFT Recommendations

In reviewing data from hundreds of LOFT sessions reported using the Line/LOS checklist and in observing a number of sessions firsthand, Helmreich and his colleagues have noted several common problems with scenario design, instructor conduct of LOFT, and debriefing. Butler describes these in detail in his chapter, but a number of issues and potential solutions deserve attention here.

1. *Scenarios vary in relevance to CRM issues and difficulty of problem resolution and/or workload imposed.* Scenarios are rarely designed around specific training objectives. As a result, some clearly challenge leadership and crew coordination, while others provide purely technical exercises which can be resolved by reference to manuals. A more effective strategy for scenario development would generate a written set of objectives for each scenario. If the developer has a clear vision of the training goals, both technical and crew coordination, a better training tool will result. In any case, to benefit crew coordination maximally, problems should not have a simple "by-the-book" solution but instead should require tradeoffs and consideration of division of labor.

2. *Instructors vary the reality of LOFT simulation and events of the "approved" scenarios.* Instructors often do not allow a LOFT to continue uninterrupted to its conclusion, stepping in to coach the problem at hand rather than explaining issues during debriefing. This interrupts the flow of events and distracts from the goal of practicing the way the things would occur in the airplane. Further, many instructors vary the timing and number of abnormal events relative to the designed scenario. They may do this simply as a matter of personal preference, or they may be gauging the capabilities of the crew and attempting to provide them with a challenging scenario given their demonstrated skills. The negative aspects of this level of variability include the fact that scenario variants may or may not accomplish the goals of the original scenario and that management can lose track of what is actually being trained in LOFT. Much of the variability may be reduced if LOFT authors communicate objectives for the scenarios directly to the LOFT instructors, so instructors clearly understand the intended training outcomes. Without knowing those objectives, instructors may not recognize the effect of changing the timing or substituting or adding abnormals to a scenario.

3. *Debriefing periods generally do not meet their potential.* Instructors may not debrief effectively for a variety of reasons. They may not understand why the organization has implemented LOFT and may feel it detracts from proficiency training. They may not recognize the "markers" of effective crew coordination and therefore may be uncomfortable debriefing those skills. Or they simply may not have been trained in debriefing skills. This problem is particularly evident when crews have performed very well. Often instructors praise performance without referring to the videotape to show what the crew did well. This is disappointing because crewmembers may gain no understanding of why they were outstanding. Critical positive behaviors go unreinforced. A recommended method for improving debriefings is to communicate the scenario objectives to the

instructor, to specify the minimum debrief (such as reviewing the onset and resolution of the principal abnormal event of the scenario), and to provide an evaluation worksheet (such as the NASA/University of Texas Line/LOS checklist) to use in debriefing. The Line/LOS checklist includes a set of behavioral markers, so the debriefing can focus on the extent to which individuals or crews evidenced those behaviors.

4. *Behavior of supporting groups is not effectively simulated in LOFT.* In a real abnormal or emergency situation, a flight crew must deal with a variety of work groups external to the cockpit. Information must be obtained from and communicated to air traffic control (ATC), dispatch, maintenance or technical personnel, and the cabin crew. Communicating with each group interrupts the flow of events within the cockpit, so captains must set and enforce priorities of communication. And they must do this while ensuring that someone flies and navigates the aircraft and while working to resolve whatever problem prompted the emergency. Handled inappropriately, external communication becomes another (very insistent) source of workload, one that can become overwhelming. Few organizations simulate the behavior of those outside agencies effectively. The classic case is an abnormal procedure which requires the captain to brief the first flight attendant. I have seen a captain turn to his LOFT instructor and say, "Okay, I'm briefing the flight attendants," followed by the instructor acknowledging, "All right, that's complete." This exchange ignores the procedure to be followed by the flight attendant to obtain information necessary to prepare the cabin. Should the captain have to brief the flight attendants in a real emergency based solely on the experience in that LOFT, he or she will be unprepared for the questions that follow. The same can be said for dispatchers and air traffic controllers—their behavior is not accurately simulated in LOFT. This problem can be corrected using two approaches. First, LOFT instructors are too rarely familiar with ATC, dispatch, or flight attendant procedures, and that is correctable. Second, representatives of those groups are rarely involved in scenario design. Look to those representatives for review of existing or revised scenarios, or for information on how outside groups are trained to respond to the cockpit crew in a particular situation.

To summarize, a number of common problems have been encountered as organizations implement LOFT. Each of these can be resolved as new scenarios are designed or as LOFT policies and procedures are implemented or revised.

A relatively comprehensive set of recommendations has been provided by the FAA through advisory circulars and by NASA through information gained in research evaluating training effectiveness. Each organization implementing CRM has been more or less effective in implementing each recommended phase. What each has chosen to do—or to do first—reflects the type of constraints imposed on training by economic, regulatory, and logistical constraints. Some of those constraints are described in the following section.

CONSTRAINTS FACED BY AIRLINES ————————— ✈

Economic Constraints

Many of the constraints airlines face in their training departments are rooted in economics. Explaining the economics of the airline business is beyond the scope of this chapter. Crandall (1991) has described in detail the economic problems facing the industry. However, a few basic points are worth noting because they give some understanding of why airlines may appear to resist innovations that may improve training quality. First, though a small number of airlines produced record profits during the late 1980s, the airline business continues to produce a low return on investment relative to other industries. Because an airline is so capital-intensive (airplanes, facilities, and support equipment), operating profits are averaged over a large investment. Second, the airline industry has undergone fundamental change since 1978 due to deregulation. What had been a closely controlled, slow-growth or no-growth industry became highly competitive due to the birth of low-cost carriers. Those carriers that have made significant profits following deregulation have done so by averaging down their operating costs through growth—new employees were hired at lower, "B-scale" rates; newly acquired aircraft were more efficient. This allowed a small number of established carriers to compete with the new entrants who initially had a great cost advantage, particularly for labor. Growth requires airlines to compete for capital funds, often against investment opportunities in other industries, despite the relatively low rate of return. Third, even though the number of competing carriers has declined through merger, acquisition, or liquidation, competition among the remaining carriers is fierce. Airlines have not been able simply to pass along increasing costs to the consumer. For example, during 1990 and 1991, airlines increased their prices substantially less than their costs increased (e.g., fuel costs, which rose sharply following Iraq's invasion of Kuwait). Fourth, the profitability of any given airline has come to turn on cost and marketing advantages relative to its competition.

Each of these factors provides pressure to hold the line on operating costs. Training costs are a part of operating costs. An increment in training cost clearly reduces profit, but it may be more complex than a simple dollar-for-dollar subtraction from the bottom line. That incremental training cost may reduce or eliminate a cost advantage relative to a competing carrier, which can change the airline's marketing position relative to a competitor. The bottom line for those proposing to implement, improve, or revise CRM training is pressure to effect change in the most cost-effective manner.

Operational Constraints

There are also logistical and regulatory constraints which surround the training program structure into which a CRM program must fit. One must understand those programs from three perspectives: the career path of each pilot, the aircraft fleet, and the flight training department, including other programs which provide training across fleets.

Pilot Perspective

From the pilot's perspective, training is a career-long process. When pilots are hired by an airline, they undergo a basic indoctrination program, then move quickly to the ground and simulator instruction required to qualify for their first crew position (most commonly as flight engineer or second officer on a three-person aircraft). After passing oral and performance examinations, they begin to fly trips under the supervision of a check pilot (or check engineer), a process referred to as "initial operating experience" (IOE). They are then qualified to serve in that position for 12 months, when they must complete recurrent training and a proficiency check. That annual recurrent requirement will continue throughout their career, though its date will be adjusted when they change aircraft or crew positions.

Depending on pilots' seniority, they may move to another aircraft (transition) as flight engineer, or they may upgrade to co-pilot (often called first officer) on the same or a different aircraft. On upgrading to co-pilot, they will complete a generic course on the duties of their new position, followed by ground and simulator instruction specific to the aircraft. Examination and IOE follow just as in the initial crew position. As a first officer, most pilots transition to larger aircraft (which typically pay higher rates) as soon as their seniority allows, with most flying at least two aircraft prior to being able to upgrade to captain.

On upgrading to captain, pilots must complete generic and aircraft-specific courses and complete examinations and the IOE period in the new crew position. As captain, training becomes a series of recurrent cycles (with two proficiency checks per year) one on a regular line flight in the airplane and one in the simulator) and transitions to larger aircraft. It should be noted however, that there are some airlines which operate only a single type of aircraft. In those cases, crewmembers still go through recurrent and upgrade training, but transition training does not occur.

From the pilots' perspective, the behaviors required to ensure effective crew coordination change over the course of a career. As engineers or co-pilots, they must coordinate their duties with those of other crewmembers and provide support, assistance, and backup or redundancy as directed by the aircraft captain. As captain, they must lead and organize their crew in both normal and abnormal situations. Those behaviors, duties, and responsibilities differ in important ways, and CRM training should be keyed to those differences. In terms of constraints imposed on CRM training by the pilots' careers, CRM training should not interfere with the events required to obtain and maintain ratings but should facilitate changes in duties and responsibilities by crew position. Practically, this translates into a common interest between pilots and their airline. Both would tie CRM to other training events (such as recurrent or upgrade training)—pilots gaining assistance in transitioning to new crew positions and minimizing days in the training center, the airline making maximal use of training days. Pilots also may wish to avoid interrupting the ground or simulator program with a CRM training period.

Aircraft Fleet Perspective

An airline must provide qualification and recurrent training for each fleet (aircraft type) it operates.[1] In most airlines, the fleet's training management supervises all the ground school training (including classroom and computer-based instruction), simulator training, and proficiency checks required for a pilot to qualify for his or her new crew position. IOE may be managed by the fleet or by a flight standards department, depending on the airline. Recurrent training specific to the aircraft is also supervised by the fleet. While classroom CRM training is usually generic, administered and conducted across fleets, LOFT is conducted and administered by the fleet, typically with assistance from CRM experts in scenario design and instructor training.

From the fleet's perspective, the job is to provide the training required to supply a sufficient number of pilots to operate the airline. Like the pilots, then, fleet management will press for CRM training that facilitates, rather than inter-feres with, the process of qualifying and maintaining qualification. It is also the fleet that must implement LOFT, and any additional costs in terms of training time, training personnel, and equipment will be felt here. For example, when LOFT is added to recurrent training, each fleet's recurrent cycle increases by 4 hours—at least 2.5 in the simulator—unless the airline pursues an exemption to substitute LOFT for a proficiency check (PC) or to conduct annual (often called "single-visit") training. As of 1991, such exemptions had been granted to three carriers with the requirement that initial and recurrent CRM training and annual LOFT be provided. The transition to the annual PC creates logistical problems at the fleet level.

The fleets also experience difficulties due to growth, which creates problems for implementing LOFT. Specifically, whenever an aircraft is added to a fleet, additional captains and first officers must be trained to fill its crew positions. A new captain will come from the ranks of first officers, and one additional first officer must be trained to take his or her place. So first officers must be trained to fill the right seat on the new aircraft and to replace the upgrading first officer who becomes a captain. Even though those new crewmembers may come from other fleets, the growing aircraft fleet averages twice as many first officer as captain qualification cycles. The consequences of this ratio quickly multiply because an

[1]The names of the departments described here and specific functions assigned to each vary among airlines. I have tried be generally accurate while offering a description of the functions that must be performed at various levels.

average of seven to nine crews must be trained for each aircraft to cover its scheduled use. Down the line, the fleet will provide recurrent training to more captains than first officers. This may or not balance the two-to-one qualification ratio, but the regulations do not yet allow the mixing of crewmembers between qualification and recurrent LOFT periods. This creates problems for pairing crewmembers in both qualification and recurrent LOFT in every growing fleet. The regulations currently allow two captains or two first officers to be paired in qualification LOFT, and seat-qualified instructors often take the place of a line crewmember. In summary, aircraft fleets are pressed to provide high-quality training for qualification and requalification and to control costs associated with the practice/feedback phase of CRM training (LOFT).

Flight Training Department Perspective

It is typically at the flight training management level, where the programs of all the airline's fleets are supervised, that the economic, regulatory, and logistical constraints come together. In terms of economics, training time has significant value, and policies that increase it must be justified in terms of training quality or regulatory compliance. Training unit costs are greatly influenced by method of instruction—costs increase from computer-based instruction through classroom, training devices, and the simulator, to training in the airplane. This provides substantial pressure to choose the most effective and most cost-effective setting for each phase of training, whether technical or crew coordination. It is also at this level where concerns over crew-pairing restrictions for LOFT will be felt. Policy or regulatory prohibition against pairing two captains or first officers in LOFT must be justified at this level, and a plan for alternatives must be established and its costs justified.

Regulatory constraints surround the integration of CRM training with programs not provided by the aircraft fleet, such as security training, international procedures training, and any other areas required by regulation. Flight training management interfaces directly with the FAA's Principal Operations Inspector (POI) for the airline and must work with him or her to ensure that all training is in compliance with Federal Aviation Regulations (FARs). In terms of CRM program implementation, flight training management must see that each phase of CRM training complies with regulation. In most cases, because CRM requirements are advisory rather than regulatory, compliance of the program itself is rather straightforward. The focus instead is on what CRM training will add or replace in a qualification or recurrent program. If CRM replaces any training event previously conducted, that must be negotiated with the POI. In any case, management at this level will be pressed to maintain compliance with regulation and certification of pilots going through programs.

Logistical constraints surround the phasing in of CRM programs. There are several options for each phase. For awareness, for example, some airlines have implemented organization-wide, multi-day seminars over a short period of time, while others have linked seminars to other training events. If linkage to training events is chosen, how are exceptions, such as people who miss a recurrent cycle due to mid-year upgrade, to be handled? If organization-wide seminars, how will the reduction in pilot availability to fly the airline be handled and justified?

In putting together FAA and research recommendations for CRM training with economic, regulatory, and logistical constraints, flight training management will largely determine the form and implementation process of CRM training.

Summary

A number of constraints affect the ability to implement CRM training as recommended by the FAA. Economic realities provide pressure to hold the line on operating costs, and training is a part of that cost. Both pilots and training management have a substantial interest in seeing that CRM training is implemented in a manner that facilitates the certification process. Growing fleets suffer crew-pairing problems in implementing LOFT. And all phases of CRM implementation must work in compliance with regulations and pilot staffing levels. The question remains whether all the recommendations can be met within the constraints. That issue is addressed in the following section.

MATCHING THE RECOMMENDATIONS WITH THE CONSTRAINTS: IS THERE A CONFLICT? ———————— ✈

In general, the recommendations can be and have been met within operational and economic constraints. Each airline that has implemented a CRM program has come to its own conclusion on how best to do that. FAA recommendations for classroom-based programs have been addressed in some fashion by almost every airline in the United States. The most difficult recommendations, and those with substantially lesser compliance, surround practice/feedback or LOFT training. Only those few airlines which pursued and received exemptions for single-visit training have completely implemented qualification and recurrent LOFT with video-based debriefing. Despite this low level of current compliance, virtually every carrier plans to implement LOFT at some point in the near future, at least two in the context of an advanced qualification program (AQP).

This appears to be the substance of industry compromise between recommendations and constraints: that programs will be developed and phased in rather than implemented wholesale. This is a rational response by an industry with an extremely sound safety record.

One Airline's Program

American Airlines' CRM program represents one effort to comply with FAA recommendations within constraints. Combining the recommendations for awareness phase training with those for reinforcement, American has developed and implemented a career-long approach to classroom-based training and begun development of LOFT with video-based debriefing. The career-long approach begins with a one-half day introductory CRM course for new flight engineers during their first week with the company. The class introduces them to American's CRM philosophy and gives them an opportunity to work through scenarios they may experience as a flight engineer. Following 12 months of line experience, crewmembers return for their first recurrent CRM class, and they will continue to do so for the remainder of their career. Recurrent CRM brings crewmembers from all cockpit crew positions into a class focused on critical topics, such as decision-making, communication in time-critical situations, or working with groups outside the cockpit. The course is completely revised each year. Following upgrade to first officer, crewmembers attend a 1-day CRM program focusing on the duties and responsibilities of that position, and following upgrade to captain, they attend a 1.5 day CRM program. The captains' duties and responsibilities program is centered on leadership and crew coordination skills, and includes a 2-hour CRM session with dispatchers. Groups who must work effectively with the cockpit are brought into CRM through two programs, dispatchers in the captains' program and flight attendants in the recurrent training course. Through this combination of classroom programs, American has attempted to make CRM a part of all phases of flight training.

American has also worked to enhance reinforcement of CRM concepts and behaviors by providing special training for its check airmen. Check airmen attend the annual recurrent training program with line pilots, and newly selected check airman attend a two-day course on assessing, debriefing, and teaching effective crew performance. To comply with recommendations for practice and feedback, American has introduced video-based debriefing into qualification LOFT, beginning with a single fleet. The program is planned to be implemented on a fleet-by-fleet basis and ultimately expanded to recurrent training. American's program has evolved over time and represents one approach to phasing in a high-quality CRM program while meeting economic and operational constraints.

Summary

Most of the recommendations by the FAA and NASA can be implemented within constraints, though the majority of U.S. airlines have attempted a phased approach rather than wholesale implementation. One critical issue remains unresolved, however—how to deal with the uneven ratio of captains and first officers completing training cycles in a growing fleet. The industry needs some innovative and cost-effective ideas on how to best pair crewmembers for LOFT. Perhaps mixing crewmembers from qualification and recurrent cycles would be appropriate, though that is not yet permitted by regulation. That problem will continue with the implementation of AQP: it has served as a significant deterrent to those airlines that have not yet implemented recurrent LOFT, and it will deter some airlines from participation in AQP.

The economic and operational constraints that have driven or impacted CRM implementation over the past decade will not disappear in the near future. Each airline will have to balance its desire for the most effective program with the real constraints of the operating environment. In the next section, I argue that the industry continues to need assistance in striking that balance.

NEODS OF THE AVIATION COMMUNITY: A CALL FOR NEW RESEARCH DIRECTIONS ────────────────── ✈

Cooperation among the airline industry, the FAA, and the human factors research community needs to continue if a variety of issues are to be resolved over the next decade. However, both shifts in approach and more focused research may be necessary. The *National Plan for Aviation Human Factors* (FAA, 1990) provides the blueprint for addressing those needs. The following are issues that clearly need research attention.

Shifting Research Focus

Human factors research should continue to shift from justifying CRM as a useful concept to focusing on how to select crewmembers, what to train, and how to design cockpit procedures to optimize crew coordination. In the area of crewmember selection, the industry faces a number of challenges. Over the next decade, the pool of applicants reaching major airlines will shift from highly trained military pilots and high-time civilian pilots to applicants with significantly less experience. Ab initio training programs may be necessary to meet the demand for pilots, depending on the rate of growth of the industry. Airlines cannot select from the latter pool using current procedures. Today's applicants have proven themselves with substantial experience, and evidence of flying competence is apparent in applications and logbooks. Future selection boards will have significantly less information on which to base their judgments. The research community can address this need by working on non-discriminatory measures of aptitude for technical and crew coordination skills. There is also a need for procedures to evaluate the flying skill of low-time pilots. In an experienced applicant pool, tests of performance in the simulator clearly predict future technical ("stick-and-rudder") performance. This may not be the case among applicants with significantly less experience.

In the area of training, the industry needs operationally valid guidance toward developing CRM curricula. The human factors community, while providing valuable information on the form of CRM training, has provided far too little content. Helmreich, Wilhelm, Kello, Taggart, & Butler (1991) have clearly made a step in the right direction with their work on behavioral markers of crew coordination. That approach toward describing effective crew coordination in terms of cockpit behaviors has been utilized by several airlines to organize classroom exercises or performance evaluation and has been well received by pilots (cf. Langer, 1990). Researchers in a variety of areas would serve the industry well by assisting in the implementation of their concepts in the cockpit. Too few researchers have taken the step of determining how their ideas can be put to use by crewmembers. This may be only a matter of communication—management development training, for example, deliberately uses more abstract concepts and exercises. Pilots appear to have little patience with abstract ideas presented without tie to cockpit situations, and most people developing or implementing CRM programs are not academics. Researchers cannot assume that operational personnel will make the leap from abstract to concrete for them.

Research could also help resolve the problem of crew pairing in LOFT and, more importantly, in all phases of training. Part 121 of the Federal Aviation Regulations, which governs the training and operation of airlines, has provided no stipulation concerning crew pairing during simulator training other than during qualification LOFT. In moving to the AQP Special FAR (SFAR 58), the FAA has opened to debate generalizing crew pairing requirements to all simulator training. There is no research basis for determining whether this is the best course of action. Pairing a complete crew in LOFT provides the best or most realistic simulation of a line situation, and this should help crewmembers generalize their training to the line. However, that does not mean that all phases of training require a paired crew to be effective. There are reasons to suspect that working with a fellow captain, for example, would be preferable in some cases, providing opportunities to both observe and perform the same duties in the same session. In a sense, this is the same logic as part-task training: People can learn the pieces of the task separately, then learn how to put the pieces together. Research could provide guidance toward the most effective use of CBI, part-task trainers, fixed-base and motion simulators, and LOFT. Research could also determine where pairing a complete crew will best pay off.

In terms of designing cockpit procedures, the industry could use immediate guidance on standardizing procedures for use of automated systems. The airline industry prides itself on standardization—of training, cockpit procedures, division of labor, and performance evaluation. But it appears that cockpits are far less standardized in use of automated flight guidance and performance management systems than in other areas (Wiener, 1988). Wiener et al. (1991) conducted a full-mission simulation study on this subject, but it appears to have served more to define or describe how automation is being used—a critical starting point—than to offer solutions.

To date, the most guidance a CRM department can offer pilots on automation is to choose the level of automation appropriate to the situation. Every transport aircraft has some level of automation, ranging from "hands-on" flying through rate of turn and climb controls, radio or inertial navigation, to sophisticated lateral and vertical navigation functions. Those with the most sophisticated systems offer more choices. More sophisticated functions require "programming" (data entry) prior to use. In an abnormal situation, updating the system can become another source of workload. CRM departments, or the aircraft fleets themselves, can encourage pilots to take advantage of the system when it helps, and to back down a level of automation when programming creates unacceptable workload. Delta Air Lines, for example, has developed a philosophy of use for automated systems and implemented a training course for pilots transitioning to their first glass cockpit aircraft. This introduces pilots to benefits and potential problems with automation (see the chapter by Byrnes & Black). Communicating these messages to pilots is not the ultimate solution to the consequences of automation, but research may offer better procedures or possible changes to the pilot–flight management system interface.

Moving beyond the Cockpit

Human factors research should assist in developing policy and procedure for optimizing communication between the flight deck and other work groups. As noted in the discussion of LOFT recommendations, the behaviors of supporting workgroups and the interface between the cockpit and those groups are critical to resolving an emergency situation safely. These relationships are unstudied. In fact, in virtually every full-mission simulation study geared toward studying crew coordination (including my own, e.g., Chidester et al., 1990), the behavior of outside groups was a part of the manipulation, not a subject of investigation. This must change during the next decade. The unit of analysis should become the flight and cabin crew. Almost every safety problem encountered on one side of the cockpit door soon becomes a problem for the other. Coordination between these parts of the crew has been assumed in the operational community and unstudied by the research community. In fact, at American Airlines, we learned what the critical pilot–flight attendant issues were only by initiating our own program.

Dispatchers, by regulation, share responsibility with the captain for the planning, release, conduct, and termination of each flight, but their role has gone unstudied in human factors research. One need only look to the Avianca accident at JFK airport in New York, which resulted from fuel exhaustion (NTSB, 1991), to see the critical role of flight dispatchers. Avianca, as a non–U.S. carrier, does not operate under FAR Part 121 rules governing dispatch within the United States but contracted for dispatching services for its flights to the United States. They did not have the level of flight following typically provided by major U.S. carriers. However, we cannot simply assume that the increased level of dispatch support required under Part 121 eliminates the possibility of a similar situation. Do pilots know what to expect from their dispatcher in an unusual situation? How much assistance can dispatchers realistically provide? Again, coordination has been assumed in the operational community and unstudied by human factors researchers.

ATC needs to become a part of the crew coordination picture. The majority of ATC research has emphasized technology to solve the "party line" communication problem. The presence of multiple aircraft on each ATC frequency and in its associated airspace creates the opportunity for communication errors. Examples include missing clearances assumed to be directed to another aircraft and accepting clearances intended for someone else. A number of researchers are looking into alternative mechanisms for communicating between ATC and aircraft. However, it is likely a mistake to assume that technology will be the ultimate solution to human error in the air traffic system, just as automation was assumed to be the ultimate cockpit solution. Wiener (1988) points out that automation did not eliminate cockpit errors but changed their type and timing. Coordination among controllers is a known problem, and it has resulted in incidents involving loss of standard separation between aircraft. Miscommunication between ATC and cockpit crewmembers occurs many times a day, but at a relatively low rate given the high volume of communications (Morrow, 1991). Yet, prior to FAA initiatives in 1991, crew coordination training has gone largely untranslated to the ATC environment. Research should proceed on two fronts, coordination among controllers and optimizing pilot–controller communication in the present and future systems.

Other work groups, such as maintenance, ground support, and passenger service, interface with the cockpit on most if not all flights. Crisis teams may work with the cockpit crew in a security threat situation. Does each of these work optimally with the cockpit? Which ones directly impact flight safety? Is CRM training an appropriate solution to coordination problems? At least two carriers, Pan American and Continental, concluded that CRM training for maintenance personnel was needed and initiated such programs. Research could identify which of these areas need attention and what type of solution is appropriate.

Learning from Successful Crews

An opportunity to learn from accidents that did not happen is being missed by the human factors community. Most CRM-oriented research utilizes LOFT or full-mission simulation experiments and accident analysis as data sources. These are valuable but do not exhaust the opportunities to learn effective techniques or pitfalls to coordination. We may have as much to learn from successes as we have learned from accidents. In fact, CRM modules built around success stories have been very well received by crewmembers and provide positive examples of how crew coordination can work. The usefulness of these incidents may generalize beyond providing training examples, but few researchers have studied successes in detail. Predmore (1991) has provided a notable exception in his work on United flight 811, in which a Boeing 747 lost a cargo door, damaging two engines, and forcing an unscheduled return to Honolulu, and flight 232, in which a McDonnel-Douglas DC-10 lost all hydraulic systems and crash-landed at Sioux City, Iowa. This type of data may be rejected by some as merely isolated case studies, but Predmore's work demonstrates that systematic study is possible. Kanki, Lozito, & Foushee (1988) used detailed communication analyses to show that successful crews in a controlled simulation tend to communicate in the same way—to utilize a convention. For example, more successful crews tended to pair commands and acknowledgments. Are successful accident-avoiders systematically similar to successful simulation performers? Do they differ from crews less successful in simulation or involved in accidents? If so, these research results could greatly influence training in both the classroom and the simulator.

CONCLUSIONS ——————————————————— ✈

CRM training has grown from both the needs of the operational community and the abilities of the human factors research community. That cooperation has resulted in guidelines for training development grounded in sound research. Most of those recommendations have been heeded by a variety of military and civilian flight organizations, even though they continue to be phased in rather than adopted wholesale.

Cooperation among the airline industry, the FAA, and the human factors research community needs to continue if a variety of industry issues are to be resolved over the next decade. Some shifts in approach and more focused research may be necessary if the *National Plan for Aviation Human Factors* is to be successful. Issues that clearly need research attention include: (1) shifting from justifying CRM as a useful concept to focusing on how to select, what to train, and how to design cockpit procedures to optimize crew coordination; (2) optimizing communication between the cockpit and supporting outside groups; and (3) studying accidents that did not happen. Addressing these questions will make aviation safer and will increase our understanding of human behavior.

We should also recognize the place of CRM in aviation history. The growth of CRM training is not the first attempt to resolve problems resulting from needs for teamwork or coordination. For example, American Airlines moved to centralize all its cockpit training in 1964 following a detailed study of its operations and training. Prior to that time, training was decentralized, conducted in facilities located at or near a number of crew bases. The movement to centralized training was justified in terms of increasing safety and standardization, and that value for standardization of cockpit procedures and behavior was heavily emphasized and reinforced in the subsequent 28 years. As a result, even though the airline has doubled in size since 1984, standardization continues to be endorsed by pilots and check airmen as a primary means to effective crew coordination.

But American's efforts to emphasize standardization still were not the first dealing with what are now considered crew coordination problems. That honor probably goes to the debriefing between the Wright brothers following their first flight. Surely they discussed what worked, what didn't, what to try next, and who would fly the next leg.

Acknowledgments

The opinions expressed in this chapter do not necessarily reflect those of American Airlines' management or line personnel.

References

Chidester, T. R., Kanki, B. G., Foushee, H. C., Dickinson, C. L., & Bowles, S. V. (1990). *Personality factors in flight operations: I. Leader characteristics and crew performance in full-mission air transport simulation* (NASA Technical Memorandum No. 102259). Moffett Field, CA: NASA–Ames Research Center.

Cooper, G. E., White, M. D., & Lauber, J. K. (Eds.) (1979). *Resource management on the flight deck* (NASA Conference Publication 2120, NTIS No. N80–22083). Moffett Field, CA: NASA–Ames Research Center.

Crandall, R. L. (1991). Crandall explains cuts to shareholders, customers. *Flagship News, 47*(1). Fort Worth, TX: American Airlines, Corporate Communications.

Federal Aviation Administration. (1989). *Cockpit resource management training.* (Advisory Circular 120–51). Washington, DC: Author.

Federal Aviation Administration. (1990). *National plan for aviation human factors* (Publication No. PB91–100321). Washington, DC: Author.

Foushee, H. C., Lauber, J. K., Baetge, M. M., & Acomb, D. B. (1986). *Crew factors in flight operations III: The operational significance of exposure to short-haul air transport operations* (NASA Technical Memorandum 88322). Moffett Field, CA: NASA–Ames Research Center.

Helmreich, R. L., Chidester, T. R., Foushee, H. C., Gregorich, S. E., & Wilhelm, J. A. (1990). How effective is cockpit resource management training? Issues in evaluating the impact of programs to enhance crew coordination. *Flight Safety Digest, 9*(5), 1–17.

Helmreich, R. L., Wilhelm, J. A., Kello, J. E., Taggart, W. R., & Butler, R. E. (1991). *Reinforcing and evaluating crew resource management: Evaluation/LOS instructor reference manual* (NASA/University of Texas Technical Manual 90–2). Austin.

Kanki, B. G., Lozito, S. C., & Foushee, H. C. (1988). Communication indexes of crew coordination. *Aviation, Space, and Environmental Medicine, 60*, 56–60.

Langer, H. (1990, April 30). CRM value demonstrated, but research lags behind glass cockpit technology. *Aviation Week and Space Technology*, p. 67.

Lauber, J. K., & Foushee, H. C. (1981). *Guidelines for line-oriented flight training* (NASA Conference Publication 2184). Moffett Field, CA: NASA–Ames Research Center.

Morrow, D. (1991). *Collaboration in routine pilot–controller communication.* Paper presented to the SAE conference: Managing the Modern Cockpit - A Symposium for Line Pilots, Dallas, Texas.

National Transportation Safety Board. (1991). *Aircraft Accident Report: The Airline of Colombia, Boeing 707-321B, HK 2016 Fuel Exhaustion, Cove Neck, New York, January 25, 1990* (NTSB/AAR-91/04). Washington, DC: Author.

Orlady, H. W., & Foushee, H. C. (Eds.) (1987). *Proceedings of the NASA/MAC workshop on cockpit resource management* (NASA Conference Publication 2455). Moffett Field, CA: NASA–Ames Research Center.

Predmore, S. C. (1991). Microcoding of communications in accident analyses: Crew coordination in United 811 and United 232. *Proceedings of the Sixth International Symposium on Aviation Psychology.* Columbus: Ohio State University.

Ruffell Smith, H. P. (1979). *A simulator study of the interaction of pilot workload with errors, vigilance, and decisions.* (NASA Technical Memorandum 78482). Moffett Field, CA: NASA–Ames Research Center.

Wiener, E. L. (1988). Cockpit automation. In E. L. Wiener & D. C. Nagel (Eds.), *Human factors in aviation.* San Diego: Academic Press.

Wiener, E. L., Chidester, T. R., Kanki, B. G., Palmer, E. A., Curry, R. E., & Gregorich, S. E. (1991). *The impact of cockpit automation on crew coordination and communication: I. Overview, LOFT evaluations, error severity, and questionnaire data* (NASA Contractor Report 177587). Moffett Field, CA: NASA–Ames Research Center.

12

Training and Research for Teamwork in the Military Aircrew

Carolyn Prince
Eduardo Salas
Human Factors Division
Naval Training Systems Center
Orlando, Florida 32826

INTRODUCTION ✈

Military aviation has played a central role in the history of flight. Just 4 years after the Wright brothers had demonstrated their new invention at Kitty Hawk, the U.S. War Department began negotiations to build an airplane for military use. In 1910, the Navy made a cruiser available for ship take-offs and landings; this flying operation was successfully demonstrated the following January (Johnston, 1974). With the development of the seaplane in the same year, aviation's role in the Navy became assured. Military leaders' recognition of aviation's potential came while the rest of the world was still not certain that anyone had actually achieved manned, mechanically powered flight (Johnston, 1974). It was the demonstrated value of aviation in World War I that brought about vast improvements in aircraft, and it was the proven need for aviation by military forces that convinced manufacturers to mass produce airplanes for the first time (Biddle, 1991). In 1916, pilots acted only as observers for the ground forces, unable to do more than photograph the enemy from their position in the sky. In just two years, such progress had been made in equipping aircraft for battle that in 1918, American-built warplanes were an important force, and pilots were being hailed as heroes (Daniel, 1987). As described by Biddle (1991), military support of the nascent aviation industry was responsible for its growth and provided opportunities for the development of commercial aircraft.

Military aviators were among the pioneers in their new field. In the same year that commercial aviation marked its initial flight from London to France, Navy pilots completed the first trans-Atlantic flight. Major Smith-Berry, a military instructor, used a demonstration and explanation system of training that helped establish principles used in aviation training to this day (Neely, 1991).

CRM and Military Aviation: The Early Years

Despite the military's critical contributions to aviation and its early leadership in aircrew training, the innovation of cockpit resource management (CRM) training came from the world of civil air carriers, where the concept was developed and the programs were first instituted.

There are a number of reasons why airlines took the lead in this area. According to Lauber (1987), four events converged in the 1970s to stimulate the development of CRM. All four were directly related to the air carrier industry, and all signaled a need for training aircrews beyond technical flying skills. Three of these were the result of National Aeronautics and Space Administration (NASA) research efforts, including interviews with line pilots, analysis of information on jet transport accidents, and observations of failures of crew interactions among air carrier crews flying simulator scenarios. The fourth was the mounting public concern over aviation safety. This concern was triggered by the high number of fatalities in accidents caused by human error.

None of the important events outlined by Lauber (1987) pointed to the existence of a problem for the military. While NASA researchers were documenting problems in cockpit management for airline crews, the military had no significant research effort aimed at investigating cockpit interactions and resource use, nor did military mishap statistics clearly suggest the need for training to improve human interactions in the cockpit.

Results from statistical analysis of accidents depend on the information that is put into the statistical base. Mishap statistics reflect both the information available to the accident investigators and their training in probing for possible causation. The cockpit recording devices mandated for the airlines generally are not found in military aircraft, and military investigators are often unable to reconstruct crew interactions in the last minutes before a mishap, yet this may be the very evidence that certifies a problem in crew coordination. Leedom (1990) reported that the U.S. Army estimate of crew coordination–caused accidents was considerably higher in 1989 than it had been in 1973 (40% versus 11%) and much of this increase was due to inadequate identification of coordination as an accident cause in the 1970s.

Of the four reasons for the development of CRM given by Lauber (1987), aviation accidents was probably the most compelling. But, accidents as an impetus for development of CRM were clearly more powerful for civil aviation, where, with constantly increasing aircraft capacity, a single accident could account for the loss of several hundred lives. Military accidents rarely have an impact on the public mind, since they usually involve small numbers of people. This lack of specific evidence of human error and absence of public pressure made it highly unlikely that military leaders would be interested in the possible solution to a problem they did not think they had.

Although CRM includes in its definition software, hardware, and human resources, in practice many programs that are called CRM training address only crew interactions. Military leaders may not have seen a need for CRM training since the services already had a variety of ways to address interactions in the cockpit (Brown, 1987). For many years, the military had recognized the importance of the crew working together but had no clear agreement on how it could be obtained. Teamwork was encouraged in some instances by the consideration of the make-up of the crew; in others, by adding an item called aircrew coordination to the instructor pilot's checklist; and in still others, by conducting lectures on its importance. Povenmire, Rockway, Bunecke & Patton (1989) commented that Strategic Air Command (SAC) crews had already experienced aircrew coordination prior to the advent of CRM. Their observations of B-52 crews convinced them that the aircraft's high workload demanded coordination, which had been developed to some extent by making permanent crew assignments. In addition, coordination was expected to be positively affected by duty assignments that required crews to spend time together outside the cockpit.

Another reason that may have slowed the entry of CRM programs into the military is the way its organizations are structured. Their configuration does not lend itself to the easy adoption of a single program. An airline can dictate a training policy for its entire company, in some cases in response to regulatory action from the Federal Aviation Administration (FAA). But, just as the military is made up of more than one service, within each service there are a number of different organizations with a variety of missions. Each has a certain amount of autonomy in determining its training needs.

What Is Different Now?

Although the military community may be insulated from the shocking results of a single accident that takes hundreds of lives, its members feel the impact from any accident and suffer the loss of any single individual. With a heightened awareness of human error in the airlines, military mishap analysts began to document information identifying crew coordination errors as causal factors. It was soon clear that military aircrews were not immune from the human errors occurring in the airline cockpit (Leedom, 1990). The cost of replacing an aircraft is in the millions of dollars, repairs are increasingly expensive, and with the price of training constantly rising, the military investment in each aviator is substantial. Replacing a pilot or an aircraft is an expense best avoided. From a purely economic standpoint, the price of a program to reduce these replacements and repairs became reasonable.

Accident statistics and the establishment of CRM programs in the airlines began to reveal the problems with existing military training for coordination. For example, coordination training was neither standardized nor mandated in the

Army, and no measures of aircrew coordination had been developed (Leedom, 1990). Brown (1987) stated that CRM training was first considered for the Air Force as a way to take advantage of recent developments in training to update existing training for coordination.

The military establishment's interest in training to prevent errors increased when a second benefit of the training was suggested. As in the airlines, improving safety was a primary factor for instituting CRM training, but the possibility that this training would enhance mission effectiveness made it even more appealing. Research conducted by Povenmire et al. (1989) for the Air Force, and reported by Thornton, Kaempf, Zeller, & McAnulty (1991) for the Army, confirmed the relationship of coordination to mission effectiveness.

Training programs that were based on the CRM concepts from the airline industry were begun in the Air Force, the Army, and the Navy. The programs were generally referred to as aircrew coordination training (ACT) rather than CRM, although they were clearly patterned after existing CRM training programs. All three services established research projects in ACT in the late 1980s, and by 1990, the military services seemed to be firmly committed to a new era in coordination training.

Chapter Overview

This chapter presents elements of programs in the Army, Navy, and Air Force and each service's research to support the training in cockpit coordination. (Coast Guard crews participated, to some extent, in programs developed for other communities, and no Coast Guard research program has been established.) The chapter closes with a presentation of the future of the military services' efforts in ACT and the potential contribution that military aviation research can make. First, a comparison of the functioning of military aviation with that of civil air carriers lays the groundwork for what is to follow and gives a basis for understanding the challenges faced in adapting CRM to military use.

THE AIR CARRIER INDUSTRY AND MILITARY AVIATION ———————————————————————— ✈

The various aviation communities have much in common. They must all deal with navigation, with weather, and with controlling heavier-than-air equipment in flight. Pilots trained in one community (military aviation) routinely transition to another (commercial air carriers). The commonalities are important, but there are also differences that cannot be ignored. At the workshop on CRM in 1986, jointly sponsored by NASA and the Air Force Military Airlift Command (MAC), Cavanagh & Williams (1987) spelled out clear differences between military and airline cockpits which they believed warranted attention when developing CRM courses. They specified six categories of differences: purpose of the organization, qualifications of the crews, rank distinctions, responsibilities of the crews, and labor relations. The sixth category, miscellaneous factors, included training. These issues can be subsumed under three general categories: the task, the people, and the organization itself. The first category, task, is determined by the organizational purpose, and sets the requirements for the cockpit activities. It also determines much of the conditions of performance.

Task

Commercial air lines have as their charter the safe transport of people and freight from one location to another. Captains of these aircraft (and their crews) have to consider all flying tasks (e.g., fuel consumption, FAA regulations) and must attend to schedules and the comfort of their passengers. Safety of flight is always the primary consideration. Most military aircrews are expected to complete a mission that provides training for wartime objectives (e.g., air combat maneuvering, low-level bombing), and they must share their attention between requirements of that mission and safe conduct of flight. Military crews range in size from a single pilot to more than a dozen individuals. In some cases, the aircraft is used only as a convenient tool for transporting and positioning personnel so they may accomplish a special task, such as mine-sweeping. In others, the plane is used by the pilot alone as an instrument to outwit an enemy. This can be seen in the traditional "dogfight" of fighter aircraft. Military missions may include low-level, nap of the earth flight, gathering intelligence data, or serving as a simulated enemy for air combat maneuvering. The mission may be to bomb a target, defend other material resources from enemy attack, transport troops or supplies, or search for underwater threats. Many of the military-specific missions require heightened coordination. Cavanagh & Williams (1987) pointed out that the military not only requires more from its aircrews through increased duties, but it may place extra pressure on them to carry out special missions. In the Army's rotary wing aviation community, Leedom (1990) has stated that accidents occur under different conditions from those typically encountered in non-military flying. This is because much flight time for these military crews is spent in conditions that would be unusual or impossible for air carriers.

Task Environment

Naval aviators are routinely required to land on a rolling, pitching airfield atop a ship, and naval fixed-wing pilots are graded on every landing they make at sea. Although the grades are important and can add pressure on a pilot to perform well, they do not carry the same impact as that provided by the task itself: landing a fast-moving aircraft on a small, moving airfield in the middle of the ocean. This is a very demanding task under ideal conditions, with a fully operational aircraft, daylight, clear weather, and calm seas. But if any one of these conditions is degraded, the difficulty level rises. A disabled aircraft that is difficult to control, pitching seas, night time (especially night time) are normal conditions for carrier-based flight. Although it is the pilot who makes the landing and who receives the grades, he or she can be aided or hindered by the actions of others in the crew. Good support from a crewmember can come in the form of specific information on landing parameters, or in simply helping a pilot maintain confidence in his or her ability to land.

Military aircrew often fly in groups of planes and must coordinate as closely between aircraft as within the aircraft. The physical separation of the crews, with the need for mutual support, imposes additional requirements on maintaining group interactions. Communication within an aircraft, for example, may interfere with receiving communications from other aircraft. Flying close formation increases the pilot's workload and increases the demands of support from other crew members.

Mission Tasks

As part of their training, and as a fulfillment of job duties, fighter crews must practice air combat maneuvering. This type of flying usually occurs in short bursts of activity and requires high attentional skills from all the aircrew. Locking on to a target aircraft and getting the "kill" (and evading the same fate) is important preparation for combat; it is also a very engaging task. An attack aircrew, in maneuvering an aircraft to make a run where its weapons will be most effective, is engaged in an important task. It requires accurate positioning and precise timing. In such situations it is easy to lose sight of the primary responsibilities involved in flying the aircraft. Attention can be diverted from monitoring gauges, and a crew can easily descend to an unsafe altitude or come dangerously close to consuming too much fuel. Caution lights and warning sounds may go unattended, unable to pierce the crew's concentration. Even when a warning does come through to a pilot, he or she may have difficulty letting go of this absorbing task and reacting to a potential emergency in the cockpit. A crew performing in accord with one another will ensure that the work of the crew is divided in such a way that outside threats and mission tasks are given necessary attention and that the vital gauges for safety of flight are consistently monitored. They will also work out a method to make certain that the monitor will be able to gain the attention of the individual flying.

Decision Goals

There are some decisions that must be made in the cockpit that are clear-cut, generally accepted, and considered part of standard operating procedures. But many problems that occur do not have a single best solution. Any decision made in the cockpit under circumstances of ambiguity is tempered by the goal to be achieved. Military crews are in constant preparation for combat, and this is likely to cause them to select a riskier alternative than a crew of an airline, whose first consideration must always be safety of flight. Decision solutions also depend on the crew's specific circumstances. A more conservative decision may be made during a training mission and a more dangerous alternative may prevail during war, when completion of a mission may be extremely important. The addition of risk will certainly add to the importance of the decision-making process and may increase the need for coordination among the crew.

The captain of an airline flight is the single individual in charge, but a military flight may have two commanders, one who leads the mission and one who is responsible for safety of flight. With each mission having the dual goals of completing the mission safely and completing it effectively, there can exist opportunities for honest disagreement between the two.

Time Elements

Coordination can also be affected by the time the crew has to complete their tasks. Given the speed with which some military aircraft fly and the special circumstances of some tasks, such as take-off and landings from a carrier, there is no time in the cockpit during flight to allocate duties and to clarify ways of working together. As an example, an F-14 crew prior to take-off from a carrier (with the assistance of a catapult) needs to decide the minimum acceptable speed and altitude to continue the flight. There is no time to call for questions or pose suggestions as they hurtle off the bow of the ship toward the water.

Speed of the aircraft itself is not the only time factor. A characteristic of Army helicopter accidents (where low-level flight is common) is the amount of time that the crew has to react (in most cases less than half a minute) from the first sign of a problem until impact (Leedom, 1990). Leedom suggested that the time pressure for Army rotary wing crews, along with other differences in the type of flying required by the Army and the civilian aviation communities, makes implementation of much that is taught in current CRM programs questionable. With so little time to react to a problem, there may be no time for the crew to utilize principles to improve the processes of interaction.

Mission Alterations

A commercial airliner scheduled to fly from New York to Boston will not likely receive orders to fly instead to Washington, D.C. Military aircraft do not typically operate in established airways, and their mission may be changed at any time. Military crews may need to fly missions with minimal planning or divert to an airfield where none of the crew has been before. The conduct of some missions requires the aircrews to perform very different tasks in the cockpit. The bombardier/navigator in an attack aircraft needs to be able to switch back and forth between the role of co-pilot, backing up the pilot whenever needed, and a unique role in directing the bombing run. These non-standard aspects of a flight require the ability to plan for alternatives and the flexibility to switch goals and to re-plan.

Equipment

Certain equipment necessary for completing mission tasks in the military aircraft adds demands to the mission itself and may make crews more dependent on one another. Night vision goggles (NVGs), necessary for many low-level night missions, restrict the wearer's vision and peripheral sight. Yet flying low level at night requires a heightened knowledge of where the aircraft is in its environment. Military helicopter crews, to be tactically effective, must be able to fly close to the earth, just above the treetops. This type of flying requires constant vigilance in the daytime. At night the problems are compounded, since the type of terrain the crews have to overfly may not provide the contrast cues critical to NVG use (Leedom, 1990). Pilot and crew must all be attending to the mission and capable of communicating effectively and rapidly with one another.

Included in the equipment differences are the aircraft themselves. Cavanagh & Williams (1987) pointed out that cockpit communications for the military crews may be hindered by the physical layout of the cockpit and the ambient noise, and this is more likely to be a problem for military crews than for airline crews. During mine-sweeping operations, for example, the flightdeck crew needs to be in constant touch with the crew in the back of the helicopter in order to keep the aircraft properly positioned. Yet with the back of the aircraft open and the increased activities and dangers associated with handling the equipment in the back, communication is difficult. There may be a greater need for standard vocabulary and information transfer skills in the military cockpit to overcome equipment interference in communication.

People

The second category of differences between the civil air carrier world and military aviation is people. The services take individual aviators from the point of no experience with the aircraft, with the missions, or with the involvement of any others in the flight to the level of air combat engagements involving a number of aircraft (both friend and foe) that are part of a large strike force requiring coordination among multiple air and surface participants. Leedom (1990) reported that in the Army, ACT is given to students whose experience level in the cockpit is very low. He reasoned that this may require a training program with a format particularly sensitive to the special relationship between instructor and student.

Because military organizations in the United States provide ab initio training for large numbers of aircrews, military cockpits are likely to contain at least one inexperienced individual. Cavanagh & Williams (1987) pointed out that MAC pilots, when entering the command, may have only one fifth the number of hours that the newly hired airline pilot has. They also noted that promotion in MAC means accepting jobs not related to flying, so turnover is relatively rapid and experience level stays low. They contrasted this rapid turnover with the more stable position of the airline pilot and suggested this makes it difficult for flight crews in MAC to be as loyal or as knowledgeable about the organization's policy as is possible in the airlines.

Motivation for civilian aircrews is also likely to be different from military aircrews. Interviews conducted by Navy researchers with Marine reserve pilots, who fly both for commercial airlines and for the military, revealed that they consider the military aviation experience offers more of the fun of flying and camaraderie (Zalesny, Prince, Baker, & Salas, 1992). What effect this has on human interactions in the cockpit has not been established.

Organization

The third category that points up differences between the military cockpit and others, organizational issues, includes structures, responsibilities assigned outside the cockpit, and organizational activities. One notable structure existing in the military but not in the air carrier cockpit is military rank.

Rank and Position

Cavanagh & Williams (1987) described two situations based on rank that could occur in the military cockpit but would not occur in the airlines. The first, officer–enlisted relations, stemming from the long-held military tradition of separation of officer and enlisted ranks, they considered to be a possible inhibitor of assertiveness. The second, rank reversals (where the person of a lower rank may be the aircraft commander), they considered likely to add tension to cockpit relations. They also pointed out the formality that exists within the MAC cockpit may act as a barrier to effective communication. The formality is based at least partially on the recognition of rank differences. Others have commented on the problems military rank may introduce in the cockpit (Brown, 1987). Although not specifically referring to rank, Leedom (1990) noted that assertiveness, as it is generally taught in CRM programs, may interfere with Army regulations. Certainly these regulations would include considerations of rank and position. In some aviation communities there is an effort to overcome issues of rank in the cockpit by encouraging the use of call signs as terms of address once the canopy is closed. Although this helps to some degree, it does not erase the possibility of rank influencing behavior in the cockpit. Rank may be compounded by the position held by an individual (i.e. Commanding Officer, Executive Officer). Since people who are in positions of power within the squadron maintain flight status, they often fly with the subordinates whose jobs they control.

Additional Duties

Airline pilots are hired to work in the cockpit of an aircraft, usually first as a flight engineer, then as a flying crewmember. In the Navy and Marines, individuals are trained and assigned as aircrew but are given duties that may interfere with their flying. Because the work of a squadron must be done to support the personnel and the aircraft, pilots and other crewmembers take on the duties of Safety Officer, Legal Officer, and Maintenance Officer. They oversee Equal Employment Opportunity programs, make schedules, order aircraft parts, train subordinates, and give lectures. They hold inspections, sit on promotion boards, investigate accidents, fill out fitness reports, keep records, and make sure their buildings are painted and kept supplied with whatever is required. They may work on the engines or oversee others who do aircraft maintenance. They counsel subordinates, report to superiors, and support one another. When a crew goes out to fly, their other work remains for them to complete when they return.

Training

While the airlines have certain training requirements, they are in the business of providing transportation, and aircrew are hired to perform the duties that make that possible. Virtually every military flight in peacetime is a training flight; the military can be thought of as an organization whose major activity is training.

Training, for Navy and Marine pilots, begins in a small propeller-driven aircraft, with a student pilot in the front seat and an instructor pilot in the back. During the time a crew is flying as instructor and student, true coordination or resource management is rarely practiced. At the basic training level, a major objective is for the student to become capable of handling everything in the aircraft alone. If the instructor performs back-up duties or serves consistently as a competent co-pilot, the weak trainee may rely on that help and fail to achieve the competence expected. In initial training, the syllabus is clearly explicated, and the material to be covered is limited. Students are graded on each flight, and they make every effort to do as well as they possibly can on those graded items. Their concentration is on the items specified for the particular flight and on their own accomplishment of the tasks for the grades they need. Instructors are concerned with ascertaining the level of the student's ability and are less concerned with modeling good co-pilot behaviors. Even after pilots have earned wings, there is the need to become proficient on the equipment to which they will be assigned, and this means flying with still more instructors, continued concern over grades, and specific lessons to be learned on each hop. In the Navy and Marines, when pilots arrive at their assignment outside their initial training and fly as a "real" crew for the first time (rather than as instructor and student), there is often an uncomfortable period of adjustment to the presence of a crew.

MILITARY ACT/CRM PROGRAMS ✈

It was initially a concern for accident prevention that alerted military leaders to the possible value of CRM training. In the Army, Navy, and Air Force, human error factors began to be consistently identified as causes of accidents. In the Navy, it was the Naval Safety Center that initiated the largest training effort in a CRM-type program (Alkov, 1989). In the Army, the Army Aviation Safety Center (USASC) in conjunction with the U.S. Army Research Institute Aviation Research and Development Activity (USARIARDA) documented crew errors in the cockpit that were similar to those identified for the air carrier industry (Leedom, 1990). By 1989, all three services had at least one CRM-type program.

Just as military aviation is not a single entity but is separated into the different services, each separate service is divided into a number of different commands. Within those commands there are further divisions, and subdivisions down to the level of the squadron, each with its own commanding officer. Although military organizations are famous (or infamous) for their rule-bound structures, individual commanding officers have considerable latitude in how they may run their commands. It is perhaps for this reason that no single program has been applied service-wide that is recognizable in all its applications. Over the years, many squadron commanders informally have recognized a need for some type of training in ACT and have overseen its development. These programs, or certain elements of the programs, may be shared with other squadrons, or a program may be in use only until the person behind the program is transferred. Many of the programs are idiosyncratic, reflecting the singular ideas of one individual. Even without a program, most instructors attempt to introduce their students to some type of coordination concept, but since there is no clear definition or agreement on what constitutes aircrew coordination or how it should be taught, the training is highly individualistic.

Given such circumstances, an attempt at a comprehensive review of military programs to improve cockpit interactions is certain to fail to include several programs that someone would consider to have had a significant impact. This chapter presents instead at least one CRM-type program from each service for the years 1989 and 1990 and focuses on the similarities and differences among them. Relationships with programs developed for airlines are noted. Program materials are reviewed and the topics of decision-making and situational awareness from each program are presented in some detail.

Military CRM: Step One

The military services' rush to catch up with the need for training in coordination resulted in programs developed on the model common in the airlines, where courses were generally stand-alone lecture/discussion sessions, lasting 1 to 3 days. In many cases, little change was made to the program materials themselves. Videotapes developed for the airline courses were incorporated directly into military programs. By 1989, all three services had at least one CRM-type program that was instituted in more than a few isolated squadrons. Implementation was different in each service. In the Army, ACT was introduced to entry-level pilots and safety officers (Leedom, 1990); in the Navy, program implementation varied from squadron to squadron; and in the Air Force, the program purchased by one command was different from that purchased by another. These programs represent the military's initial step in CRM training.

Air Force

The Air Force was the first service to adapt the CRM model to their aircrew coordination training, and the first of its commands to do so was MAC. Within MAC there were several programs, but each had a strong similarity in structure and content to the others and was similar to some airline CRM programs (Keyes, 1990). According to Keyes (1990), course instruction was given primarily through lectures, videotapes, discussions, and exercises (including role-playing). A simulator session, mission-oriented simulator training (MOST), based on the line-oriented flight training (LOFT) that has been tailored for CRM training in the airlines, was recommended to complete the course. Course content included information designed to increase trainees' awareness of the need for coordination in the cockpit. This information was presented in accident statistics, mishap recreations, videotaped examples of good and poor communication, and discussions of role-playing. In the ACT program materials distributed by the Headquarters MAC (Moody, Stein, Allen, & Dean, 1988), the topics of communications, situational awareness, leadership/followership, decision-making, and mission analysis were introduced and information on each subject was provided.

The situational awareness and the decision-making sections from the program book distributed by Headquarters MAC (Moody et al., 1988) will serve as a sample of MAC program contents. In the program, definitions of situational awareness are given for both individuals and groups, and information is presented from accident statistics dramatizing the importance of awareness to ensure flight safety. Circumstances that concern a loss of situational awareness are listed, along with a solution for each. These solutions tend to be admonitions (e.g., "know yourself," "know your crews' limitations"). Information is provided on the difference between perception and reality, and on the most dangerous area of flight. A list of symptoms of loss of situational awareness is given, with hints for regaining it. The elements of situational awareness are presented (i.e., inquiry, advocacy, and analysis), and the consequences of these elements' absence is demonstrated with a videotape of a re-created accident. As originally developed, videotapes in this section were from airline accidents; accident reports were National Transportation Safety Board reports.

The decision-making section centers around five elements of decision-making: inquiry (open discussion and information gathering), advocacy (statements of opinions about necessary actions), conflict resolution (where opposing views are tested), review and feedback (where the decision-making is reviewed before the decision is implemented), and decide (implementing the plan, informing the crew of the decision made, defining the tasks required to carry out the decision, and monitoring the plan for a requirement for change). A model of decision-making, the synergy formula, is presented. This formula is based on the elements of decision making as defined by the program and is represented by *QPIDR*: *Q* (questioning), *PI* (promoting ideas), *D* (decide), and *R* (review, where the decision is announced and a report is gathered from the crew on that decision). The decision-making section includes lectures, discussion, and an exercise to demonstrate the superiority of group collaboration on a task. It ends with a group role-playing, which demonstrates the importance of each person's input into the decision-making process.

The Strategic Air Command was without a program in 1989 but had started investigation into the usefulness of such a program. Their efforts to determine the worth of ACT and to develop a program are described in this chapter under military research.

Army

The Army instituted a CRM-type program in two different training areas, initial entry rotary wing (IERW) training and training for safety officers (Leedom, 1990). One program used by some Army units is designed to change attitudes about decision-making, inter-personal communications, leadership, leader responsibilities, personal characteristics, resource management, and reactions. The course is divided into different sections based on the target attitudes and, as described by Leedom (1990), is limited to lecture and discussion, with training materials similar to those developed for civil aviation.

The situational awareness section from the program materials for one program used by some Army communities (Geis, Alvarado & Associates, 1989) provides information on the importance of situational awareness for safety of flight and lists the elements of situational awareness that the program developers considered important for training. The program describes the means of establishing situational awareness and gives clues to detecting its loss. The section on decision-making includes decision-making strategies and coping patterns. The program also presents a model for aircrews to use in problem-solving. The program materials describe hazardous thought patterns and the poor judgment chain. Corrective steps for breaking that chain are offered.

Coast Guard

The Coast Guard's need for CRM-type training has been fulfilled by contracting for the training with other organizations. One of the programs used in recent years was the CRM program described above for the Army.

Navy

The first CRM training program for the U.S. Navy was produced by program developers who had earlier developed a program for airline use. A superficial comparison of the two programs points up the large debt that military programs have owed to civil aviation CRM development. The airline program was described as being oriented toward a flight deck management (FDM) cycle (Krey and Rodgers, 1987). In the 1990 version of the Navy program (U.S. Navy, 1990) the trainee is presented with the aircrew coordination (AC) cycle. The two cycles, FDM and AC, are each illustrated by a triangle with planning as the base, challenge as one side, and response as the other. The subjects of aircrew coordination for the Navy and Marines are presented as: policy and regulation, command authority, communication, available resources, workload performance, decision-making, situational awareness, and operating strategy. The description of the airline program (Krey & Rodgers, 1987) contained the following subjects: policies, procedures, and company culture; communication; effective resource use; workload distribution; decision-making; and vigilance to challenges. Although workbook examples for the Navy program are from the airlines, there are a number of military mishap synopses included for discussion.

Situational awareness in this program has similarity to both the Army and the Air Force MAC programs described above. Situational awareness is defined, with the group level of situational awareness distinguished from the individual level. The importance of situational awareness is pointed out by linking it to accidents, the differences between perception and reality are presented, and the danger zone is identified. Causes and symptoms of poor situational awareness are given, and the elements of good situational awareness are discussed (i.e., experience and training, physical flying skills, spatial orientation, personal health, coordination, inquiry, assertiveness, and analysis). Information is presented for preventing the loss of situational awareness and for regaining it.

For decision-making, definitions are given and a model containing risk elements is presented. Trainees are instructed to consider the risks in each of these areas and to either cancel flight or try to remove risk elements before continuing. The decision-making process is described as being made up of inquiry, advocacy, conflict resolution, review and feedback, and decision. The synergy formula (QPIDR) is presented, followed by some hazardous attitudes with antidotes to each (e.g., "Follow the rules"; "Think first"). Finally, the poor judgment chain and recommended steps for breaking the chain are presented.

This program was designed to be taught by squadron members, both pilots and other aircrew. The implementation plan called for squadrons to send two individuals to an instructor training program to go through the training and develop the program they would teach from materials supplied during the training. Some instructors added exercises or videotapes to the program or included information that was specific to their community; others trimmed the program, discarding the parts they considered irrelevant or repetitive. In some squadrons the program was lengthened by adding a simulator session designed according to what the instructors wanted to demonstrate. For most squadrons, that option was not exercised. One community reduced the 2-day program to a session that lasts less than 3 hours by eliminating material considered to be irrelevant. The objectives of this shortened program include training pilots to: (1) describe coordination and its factors, (2) recognize individual traits that affect coordination, and (3) use an understanding of coordination in employing their aircraft (Person-System Integration, Ltd., 1990). Instructors lecture, lead class discussions, and show three videotapes of airline accident recreations.

AIRCREW COORDINATION RESEARCH IN MILITARY AVIATION ✈

The military's reaction to CRM programs was generally positive; however, it soon became apparent that additional work was needed in order to better fit the CRM training to the military mission. There was a clear need for tailoring programs to the communities and to the levels of experience of the aircrews, and a need for evaluation. These reasons led all three services to both program refinement and research.

Although there were some similarities in the need for research, specific reasons were different for each service. For the Air Force, it became important to demonstrate that there was indeed a link between performance and mission effectiveness. In the Army, there was a need to discover specifically what coordination problems were causing accidents and to determine how best to address those problems with training, given the special circumstances of the rotary wing tactical missions and the experience level of the aviators who were to receive the training. It was also important for the Army to establish a standard way to investigate crew coordination causes in Army mishaps (Leedom, 1990). The Navy had four major concerns that initiated their research: they wanted a program that would be skill-based, mission-specific, validated, and capable of being integrated into the on-going technical training.

Two common themes can be found in the three services' evolving ACT.

They are an emphasis on skill training instead of changing attitudes and an inclusion of some type of evaluation as part of the training.

Military Research: Step Two in CRM

As research began to reveal some information about coordination and its relationship to mission safety and effectiveness, the three services started moving to a different conceptualization of ACT. In the Air Force, research preceded program development; in the Army and Navy, research and program development were occurring simultaneously.

Air Force Research: Establishing the Link Between Coordination and Mission Performance

Safety issues, while always important, are not the only consideration for the military communities when determining the need for training. For scarce training dollars and for maximum efficiency in the training system, it is important that a program demonstrate potential for improving mission effectiveness as well. Povenmire et al. (1989) described an experiment conducted with B-52 crews to study both coordination in the cockpit and the mission effectiveness of the crews. Seven 6-person crews, ranked at the top or at the bottom of their squadrons by their operations officers, took part in the research. All crews flew a realistic mission in the full mission simulator for the B-52, the weapons system trainer. Performance of the crews was evaluated by expert observers who ranked crews on their mission performance and on their bombing accuracy. Crew communications, questionnaires, and the Line/MOST worksheets (an Air Force version of the Line/LOFT worksheet, Helmreich & Wilhelm, 1987; see also Helmreich, Wilhelm, Kello, Taggart, & Butler, 1990) were used to evaluate CRM performance. Analysis of the data showed that there was a high correlation between resource management behavior as measured by the Line/MOST worksheet score and both the mission performance rank and the bombing rank of the crews.

The result of the research with B-52 crews reported by Povenmire et al. (1989) was that, in general, crew awareness of mission progress was associated with effective mission performance. It was also clear that if the situational awareness of an individual who held a key position (in this case the electronic warfare officer) was enhanced with additional information from another key crew member, he could provide better options to the rest of the crew during the mission. This sequence was correlated with better mission performance for the entire crew.

After ascertaining that performance on the mission is related to aircrew coordination, SAC contracted to have a program developed. As described by Johnson, Shroyer, & Grewe (1991), the SAC program was planned to overcome deficiencies in many of the existing CRM programs. The program developers' primary criticism of the existing CRM programs was that they were not teaching skills. The SAC program was constructed with the intention of correcting this situation and it has departed to some degree from the more familiar programs.

According to Johnson et al. (1991), topics for this program were determined by a training requirements analysis, which was conducted through visits to selected SAC sites where interviews with SAC personnel gave program designers information on expectations, facilities, and objectives. Based on these data, the decision was made to center the program around five topics: communications, situation awareness, behavior styles, stress management, and mission management. Following the phase model suggested by the FAA (see, Prince, Chidester, Bowers, & Cannon-Bowers, 1992), the program begins with an awareness phase where information is presented to the trainee on interactive video disc. The second phase, practice and feedback, is conducted as a workshop with trained facilitators. This phase is taught with a briefing to refresh the awareness phase materials, a demonstration of objectives, a case study exercise, and exercises to build specific skills. The third phase, recurrent training, includes simulator training. To ensure integration of CRM skills in the community, there is a special, one-day training program for the designated instructors and evaluators which follows the regular practice and feedback phase of the CRM program. In this 1-day course, skills in observing and critiquing coordination are trained. The program has been designed to include evaluation opportunities.

Army Research: Devising Training for Unique Crew Requirements

Just as a review of accident causes was part of the initial conceptualization of CRM (Lauber, 1987), the review of Army aviation mishaps by the USARIAR-DA and USASC suggested that many Army rotary wing aircrews were performing less as integrated crews and more as a collection of individuals (Leedom, 1990). The review of Army mishaps revealed that the crews were suffering from some of the same problems found in civil aviation as documented in a FAA report on aeronautical decision-making (Jensen, 1989). Patterns of behaviors associated with mishaps included "failure to communicate critical information, poor management of crew resources, ambiguity over task assignment and task priorities, [and] lack of assertiveness by junior crew members" (Leedom, 1990). These were classified into four categories: information exchange in the cockpit, workload priority and distribution, cross-monitoring, and team relationship. The first two categories, communication and workload, accounted for the largest number of accidents in the Army tactical cockpit.

The second subtask for the Army research was accomplished with 20 aircrews flying a full mission scenario in the UH-60 Blackhawk simulator. Training scenarios and two rating instruments were developed for use with these simulations. The first rating instrument, known as the Aircrew Coordination Evaluation Checklist, was modified from the NASA Line/LOFT Check Airman

Worksheet (Thornton et al., 1991) to more specifically reflect the coordination tasks in the Blackhawk. The second evaluation method was keyed to certain events within the scenario. Crews were observed by specially trained instructors and rated on their performance. The results of an analysis of the recorded communications of the crews demonstrated a relationship between the interactions in the cockpit and mission performance (Thornton et al., 1991).

At the same time the accident analysis was being done, the Army had been reviewing the CRM programs they had initiated. Leedom (1990) reported that the coordination training programs in use were based on programs that were written for commercial transport flying and did not fit the Army requirements for several reasons. These included a format for the training that was different from the standard used in the Army and was therefore unfamiliar to the students. The contradiction between some of the programs' principles and Army regulations, and the difference in the Army's flying environment that does not allow application of some of the principles used in the air carrier cockpit, were also cited. Leedom (1990) pointed out that social and attitudinal factors are important in the airlines' CRM programs, but the stress imposed by the Army cockpit may weaken the influence of those factors. He suggested that the two categories of accident causes involving coordination that were most important in the Army, communication and workload, may be better trained using methods other than those used in the airlines where attitude change was the goal. In addition to the problems with the programs themselves, the Army researchers noted that one of the programs had been implemented for pilots who were still concentrating on developing basic "stick-and-rudder" skills and who may not be ready for coordination skills. It was also noted that training was implemented without simulator practice to reinforce its concepts, and coordination performance was not part of the standards that an aviator was expected to meet (Leedom, 1990).

Army researchers then began to explore a different approach to CRM training. Their approach was to introduce coordination at the task level by incorporating specific procedures into task standards, first specifying precisely what procedures for coordination would be carried out by each cockpit position for each task. This would be institutionalized by incorporating them into the task standards for each aircraft (Leedom, 1990). They began with the UH-60 (Blackhawk). Researchers and active Army personnel worked together to insert coordination into the *Aviation Training Manual* for the Blackhawk and presented their effort to the Army for evaluation.

The next task in the Army's research plan was to develop new accident investigation procedures that would help investigators uncover and document possible coordination causes. This was done with the CRM Accident Investigation Checklist, which was tested in three investigations and found to be effective in determining and categorizing aircrew coordination error (Pawlik, Simon, & Dunn, 1991).

*Navy Research: Developing a Methodology That Establishes
a Framework for ACT Systems*

Safety was the initial goal of the Navy's development of CRM-type training. When a program was made available to a large number of squadrons (Alkov, 1989), it was a positive start to addressing the problem of human error in the Navy cockpit.

Because of the great diversity in the types of aircraft and missions flown, this first CRM-type program for the Navy and the Marine Corps was accepted with more enthusiasm in some aviation communities than in others. Modifications to the program were made, both within and between communities, based on perceived relevance of the materials to the different aircraft missions and operating environments. Unfortunately, there were no research data that established the coordination needs of the community or the relative worth of the program elements that could be used to guide the modifications.

The Navy research goal, therefore, was to develop and demonstrate a methodology that could be used by the various aviation communities to build validated, mission-oriented, skill-based training for aircrew coordination which could be integrated with other aircrew training.

The ACT methodology for the Navy consists of (1) defining the needs for coordination skill behaviors among aircrews, (2) specifying the training objectives, (3) determining the most effective instructional strategies for training the identified behaviors, (4) training instructors in class facilitation as well as observation and provision of feedback, (5) developing an observation scale specific to the behavioral skills being taught (so both feedback to trainees and program evaluation are meaningful), and (6) devising evaluation that provides clear training information. Practice and feedback is considered a key component of behavioral skill training (Prince et al., 1992), and in order to provide opportunities for practice, the research includes investigation and development of a table-top trainer for eliciting coordination skills (Prince & Salas, 1991). The evaluation of effectiveness, to satisfy the Navy requirements, has been designed to include a number of levels of evaluation, including reactions to the program materials, attitude change, and a learning of the concepts, with an emphasis on demonstration of transfer of training of the behavioral skills to the cockpit (Cannon-Bowers, Prince, Salas, Owens, Morgan, & Gonos, 1989).

The introduction of extensive training that affects the functioning of such a large portion of an organization's population results in some type of organizational change. An additional element of the methodology is an investigation of the organizational issues that need to be confronted with the introduction of such a comprehensive program (Kozlowski & Salas, 1991). Navy research is being conducted to determine methods to anticipate its possible impact.

When the Navy research began, most of the existing programs had the goal of attitude change (Helmreich, 1987). However, research does not unequivocally support the assumption that specific attitudes will have a direct impact on specific behaviors (Fishbein & Ajzen, 1975), so the focus of change selected by the Navy researchers was skill behavior. This was based on the premise that training in skills to be used in the cockpit is the most direct method of achieving a detectable skill change in transfer of training (Prince et al., 1992).

Team research by Morgan, Glickman, Woodard, Blaiwes, & Salas (1986) and by Oser, McCallum, Salas, & Morgan (1989) with Naval tactical teams in training yielded results that supported the importance of team behavioral skills for team functioning. Morgan et al. (1986), using a team observation instrument to document critical team behaviors, were able to demonstrate differences in certain behaviors that could distinguish between effective and ineffective teams in training. Oser et al. (1989) concluded that it was possible to identify behaviors related to crew development and maintenance, to make discriminations of team effectiveness based on the behavioral observations of the teams, and to use these behaviors to define important dimensions for the teams studied.

In order to identify the skills that are necessary to train for coordination in aircrews, CRM literature and team training research were reviewed. Conference materials, relevant articles, and research reports on aircrew coordination were searched for the behavioral examples of the interactive skill dimensions that had been identified as necessary for effective crew performance. In addition, several CRM programs were attended and those program materials reviewed. Behaviors and the classification they were given were extracted from program materials and added to those identified in the literature review (Prince & Salas, 1989).

The seminal research in cockpit resource management by Ruffell Smith (1979) introduced the possibility of applying business management concepts to improve the functioning of cockpit crews (Lauber, 1987). Therefore, a review of management skills and their behavioral definitions used in management assessment and development conducted by Maher (1983) was used to select skills with behavioral definitions that appeared appropriate for the cockpit. These skills were communication, decision-making, interpersonal, assertiveness, leadership, perception, flexibility, organization and planning, and control and follow-up. A matrix was developed to compare the aircrew coordination skills identified in the CRM research review and the skills identified for effective management (Prince & Salas, 1989). The nine selected management skills and their behavioral definitions were listed across the top of the matrix with the skill dimensions that were identified from the CRM review along the side. All behaviors were placed in the appropriate cell of the matrix. All collected behaviors were included in the matrix; there were no behaviors that were not covered by the skills that were defined for the more traditional management situations. A second matrix was constructed with the managerial skills and the team skills and behaviors identified in Oser et al. (1989). Once again, all behaviors fit into the managerial skill categories.

Next, critical incident interviews with aircrews from one aviation community were conducted (Franz, Prince, Cannon-Bowers, & Salas, 1990). Behaviors in the incidents were added to the behaviors collected in the CRM literature review and were used to develop the Team Task Inventory form (Baker, Salas, & Prince, 1991). This form was sent to aviators in three squadrons. They were asked to rate each of the behaviors on importance to train, frequency of occurrence, criticality for mission accomplishment and safety, and difficulty. The responses of 134 aviators were analyzed, and they confirmed that most of the behaviors listed were very critical and very important to train. Seven skills resulted from the analysis of the responses: communication, decision-making, leadership, situation awareness (perception), mission analysis (organizing and planning), assertiveness, and adaptability/flexibility (see Table 12.1).

There were two surprises among the identified skills. Interpersonal skill behaviors were found to be critical for effectiveness in Navy tactical teams (Oser et al., 1989) and are critical in management but did not prove to be as important as the other skill behaviors for aviators. Interpersonal behaviors were not rated sufficiently high on any factor to retain that skill dimension. Adaptability, which was found to be important in the Navy team skills (Oser et al., 1989) and in management, was rarely identified in CRM program materials. The responses to the Team Task Inventory showed that adaptability behaviors were clearly considered necessary for the aircrews in the Navy and Marines (Stout, Prince, Bergondy, Baker, & Salas, 1992).

A behavioral observation scale, the Aircrew Coordination Observation/ Evaluation scale (ACO/E; Baker, Salas, & Prince, 1991) was developed from the analysis of the Team Task Inventory responses. Crews were then videotaped in a full mission simulator as they flew a realistic mission scenario, and the observation scale was used to classify the crews' behaviors. The ACO/E was refined in this process, and the skill definitions were modified according to the behaviors that were observed in the videotape analysis.

Finally, an investigation of mishaps was conducted to determine if deficiencies in the skill behaviors that crews had reported as important were responsible for Navy and Marine mishaps (Hartel, Smith, & Prince, 1991). Two hundred and sixteen mishap reports were analyzed for the behaviors that contributed to the mishap. Behaviors cited by the mishap investigators were coded and classified under the aircrew coordination skill dimensions. (Mishap investigators had not been aware of the seven skill dimensions when they completed their reports.) All behaviors that were cited in the reports clearly fit into the seven skill dimensions, and all skills were represented as causes for mishaps. The most frequently cited inadequacy of skill behaviors was found for situation awareness, followed by decision-making, mission analysis, communication, leadership, assertiveness, and flexibility. Differences in the kinds and numbers of citations were found among aircraft types and suggest that different emphases need to be placed on skills,

Table 12.1

Examples of Existing Task Components of Aircrew Coordination Training Dimensions

Mission analysis
  Define tasks based on mission requirements
  Structure tasks, plans, and objectives
  Identify potential impact of unplanned events
    on a mission
  Critique existing plans
  Devise contingency plans
  Question/seek information, data, and ideas
    related to mission plan

Decision-making
  Cross check information sources
  Anticipate consequences of decisions
  Use data to generate alternatives
  Gather pertinent data before making a
    decision
  Evaluate information and assess resources
  Identify alternatives & contingencies
  Provide rationale for decision

Communication
  Use standard terminology
  Provide information as required
  Provide information when asked
  Ask for clarification of a communication
  Make no response (Negative)
  Acknowledge communication (OK, Roger)
  Repeat information
  Reply with a question or comment
  Convey information concisely
  Use nonverbal communication appropriately

Adaptability/flexibility
  Alter flight plans to meet situation demands
  Alter behavior to meet situation demands
  Accept constructive criticism and help
  Step in and help other crew members
  Be receptive to others' ideas

Situational awareness
  Identify problems/potential problems
  Recognize the need for action
  Attempt to determine cause of descrepant
    information before proceeding
  Provide information in advance
  Note deviations
  Demonstrate ongoing awareness of mission
    status
  Demonstrate awareness of task performance
    of self

Leadership
  Determine tasks to be assigned
  Establish procedures to monitor and assess
    the crew
  Inform crew members of mission progress
  Verbalize plans
  Discuss ways of improving performance
  Ask for input, discuss problems
  Tell crew members what to do
  Reallocate work in a dynamic situation
  Focus crew attention to task
  Provide a legitimate avenue for dissent
  Provide feedback to crew on performance

Assertiveness
  Advocate a specific course of action
  State opinions on decisions/procedures even
    to higher-ranking crew members
  Ask questions when uncertain
  Make suggestions
  Raise questions about procedures

depending upon the community. This was confirmed by conducting interviews and surveys with six additional aviation communities, ranging from undergraduate aviation to helicopter transport to fighter aircraft. The same seven skills were identified, but some of the ratings of importance to train and criticality of the skill behaviors differed form one group to the next (Stout et al., 1992), and these differences could be related to the characteristics of the crews and the missions for the different communities.

Research and Skill Behaviors

The existence and importance of the skill behaviors for CRM have been confirmed by research that has been published since the initial identification of the skills. This includes research conducted by the Air Force, the Army, the Navy, and NASA.

Mission Analysis

Mission analysis, the skill in organizing and planning, is the first skill that must be exerted in an aircrew. Developing plans and strategies, assigning tasks, and prioritizing continue throughout a flight, but they are most critical at the beginning, particularly for crews that have not flown together before, and for any non-routine missions. The study reported by Ginnett (1986) documented differences in the kinds of behaviors of effective and ineffective leaders that were exhibited in the pre-flight brief. Effective leaders gave organized briefs and clarified important norms for the crews.

Orasanu (1990) reported that in an experiment conducted with commercial airline crews the captains of more effective crews made more plans and developed more strategies than did the captains of the less effective crews. Thordsen, Klein, & Wolf (1990) found that when Army rotary wing tactical crews did not have a clear understanding of the overall mission goals in a simulated mission, they were at a disadvantage when any changes in plans were required.

Assertiveness

Assertiveness is a topic covered in many CRM programs, and its absence has been cited as a causal factor in a number of accidents (Hartel et al., 1991; Leedom, 1990). As reported by Smith & Salas (1991), in the history of the study of assertiveness there has been uncertainty as to whether assertiveness could be considered a personality trait, an attitude, a skill, or some combination of the three. Smith & Salas (1991) describe a training experiment that investigated three different methods of training the specific assertive behaviors defined by the Navy research: lecture only; lecture and modeling of assertive behaviors; and lecture, modeling, and role-playing. They found that assertiveness behaviors could be trained only with a combination of lecture, modeling, and individual role-playing. They also found that the behavioral measures were not correlated with a personality inventory, with attitude scales, or with expressed confidence in task ability. The conclusion from this research was that task assertiveness is a trainable skill, but the training must include active practice and feedback.

Leadership

Finding leadership to be an important skill for crew interactions is hardly surprising. Ginnett (1986), in conducting research with airline crews, found that functional leader behaviors, generally performed by the captain of each crew studied, differed depending on the judged effectiveness of the captain. He found that more effective captains took an active role in involving the entire crew in the work of the group, addressed the interactions required on tasks, and clarified important norms for the crews. Thordsen et al. (1990) reported that crews who were "micromanaged" (where the commander was giving constant direction to the crew) in a simulated helicopter mission did less well than those who were not.

Communication

Starting with the work of Foushee & Manos (1981), to the analyses by Kanki, Lozito, & Foushee (1987), and continued by NASA researchers to the present, communication analysis has been making an important contribution to knowledge about crew coordination. An investigation of Army aviation accidents using a critical incident technique confirmed communication's role in Army accidents (Leedom, 1990). Hartel et al. (1991) found communication to be one of the interactive skills that was considered causal in a number of Navy and Marine aviation accidents. Oser, Prince, Morgan, & Simpson (1990) analyzed the communications of two-person helicopter crews in routine and non-routine segments of a simulated mission and found that the communication content varied depending upon the situation. In non-routine segments of the flight, all crews made more specific assignments, announcements of intended actions, and recommendations for future courses of action. This finding is similar to that reported by Orasanu & Fischer (1991), who found high-performing captains in three-person crews talked more in abnormal situations than low-performing captains. The finding contrasts with that found in a communications analysis of research using two-person airline crews, where it was reported that fewer commands were made during the abnormal phase than during the normal phase of flight (Orasanu, 1990). Research reported by Thornton et al. (1991) with Army helicopter crews demonstrated different numbers of commands being issued by the aircraft commander during two different non-routine segments of flight. This conflicting information suggests that there is more complexity to the interaction of communication and mission occurrences than a simple routine versus non-routine flight classification. Variables such as size of crew and type of situation may clearly have an influence on the communication in the cockpit.

Situation Awareness

Individual situation awareness is needed by every pilot; it is "the perception of the elements in the environment within a volume of time and space, the comprehension of their meaning and the projection of their status in the near future" (Endsley, 1989). Without this awareness, effectiveness and safety are both severely compromised. Situation awareness from the crew standpoint is also important for flight safety and effectiveness. In the analysis of Navy and Marine mishaps, a lack of situation awareness was found to be the most frequently cited causal factor (Hartel et al., 1991). One of the accident causes uncovered in the review of Army accidents (Leedom, 1990) was the failure to provide information on the situation to other crew members. Thornton et al. (1991) reported that in an experiment with Army tactical helicopter crews, lack of relevant and timely information was related to poor performance in navigation, in threat evasion, and in completing an instrument approach to landing. Orasanu (1990), in her analysis of crew communications for airline crews in a simulated flight, found that captains of effective crews did more alerting of the crews during routine flight, and both captain and first officer of the more effective crews demonstrated higher situation awareness than did the less effective crews.

Decision-making

Orasanu's (1990) analysis of communication by airline crews flying a full mission in a flight simulator found that the behaviors of captains of high-performing crews differed from those of lower-performing crews in providing rationales and in using more options in their decision-making. Hartel (1991), in a review of decision-making training, noted that the prescriptive models of decision-making used traditionally are not appropriate for the cockpit, where much decision-making occurs under stress and severe time limitations. She hypothesized that training crews in protocols that take the information processing tendencies exhibited by individuals under stress into account would improve decision efficiency for users. Hartel trained crews using the Problem Identification Validation (PIV) diagnostic method and found the teams trained with PIV solved the problem introduced in a simulated flight task quicker and with fewer errors than teams who did not receive the PIV training.

Adaptability

As noted previously, flexibility as a separate and distinct skill has not been as recognized as other skills for CRM. However, Hartel et al. (1991) in their analysis of Navy and Marine mishaps found adaptability was a distinct causal factor. Thornton et al. (1991) noted that differences in communication for two mission segments were likely due to differences in the tasks performed by the crews in response to dissimilar mission requirements. This indicates a requirement for crews to be flexible in their performance in the aircraft, changing their ways of responding to the task demands.

The identification and verification of the preceding taxonomy of skills for aircrew coordination has been one result of the Navy's research. Research on this taxonomy will continue, first to assure reliable measurement of the skills, and then to explore the specific relationships of these skills with other aspects of flight, including the mission, the size of the crew, the equipment, the environment, and the relationship of these skills with one another.

A major part of the challenge in the Navy research effort is the requirement to integrate CRM training with other existing aircrew training. The first version of the prototype program developed with the methodology from the Navy research was designed in modules, with each skill the subject of a module (Swezey, Llaneras, Prince, & Salas, 1991). These modules, lasting less than 2 hours each, are constructed to give some information about each skill, to demonstrate the skill, and then to supply the opportunity for active practice and specific feedback on the skill. They can be inserted in the regular training curriculum at any time and in any order. The second version of the methodology-based program takes the information and practice opportunities that are part of each module and integrates them further into the existing syllabus. Training for a specific coordination behavior is inserted in technical training sessions where it has the most relevance. Coordination skills can then be practiced and acquired along with technical skills as they are being practiced in the simulator. The expected result is that crewmembers will naturally employ the necessary coordination behaviors throughout their flying careers.

MILITARY AVIATION CRM AND RESEARCH: THE FUTURE ✈

The existence of military research in CRM has been initiated by the need to address the specific requirements of military aviation. The distinct characteristics of the military missions and the demands they make of crews, the difference in the experience levels of the military aviators, and the necessity of integrating CRM training into the existing training curricula all support the need for investigation and experimentation specifically designed for military aviation.

An important concern for the military is the determination of the most effective method for skill training in CRM. Moving to an emphasis on behavioral skills means training will need to be different from training for attitude change alone. It requires providing skill information and demonstration, as well as practice and feedback. Team training literature and management skill training provide some guidance, but there is still a need for research to determine the training strategies that will provide the best results. Research that has identified specific coordination behaviors and research that has resulted in behavioral measurement instruments have led to the development of LOFT-type scenarios that can be targeted to any specified skills in any mission. Next, the best method for providing feedback on the CRM skills must be established.

Feedback is an important part of CRM training, but the information that needs to be provided, the channel for that information, and the format of the information have not been determined by research. Training instructors to observe behaviors, document what they observe, and give feedback is another area of concern.

The military aviation communities are moving into the era of the advanced cockpit, with increased automation. Research must determine the changes that technological advances make in the management of crew and equipment resources and then, what training is needed to be able to take full advantage of the crew and the technology.

Just as with technical skill training, coordination skills will be enhanced with practice; a single program of training cannot assure that all aircrews achieve and maintain desired competence in the skills. The maintenance of CRM skills is an important issue for research. With technical flying skills, individuals are proud of their accomplishment, peers demand a certain level of accomplishment, and organizations provide rewards and sanctions for those skills. To ensure their continuing use, coordination skills will need to be treated in the same way, and it is a research task to determine how that will be done.

Organizational issues that will arise from the implementation of such a comprehensive training program have not been explored. The recognition by the Navy that the full acceptance of CRM-type training will affect the organization has led to the initiation of research to investigate the potential impact of the training. This is necessary to ensure program acceptance, maintenance, and reinforcement.

CONCLUSION ✈

Potential for the unknown to occur exists on every flight, and in the flight environment, the unknown can be dangerous in the extreme. Many of the flights required in military aviation include a greater proportion of unknowns than do routine flights in civil aviation. A thorough knowledge of the performance envelope of the aircraft, its systems, and the technical skills for handling some of the problems that could occur helps reduce the number of uncertainties. It has become apparent that in addition to the practice of technical skills, the practice of team skills can also be of value to the crew. Although improved performance will not eliminate aviation accidents, diligent practice of the effective CRM skills along with technical flying skills will diminish the area of the unknown.

In order for CRM to become a permanent part of the military aviation culture, its system of training must mature beyond the present level. This can be accomplished efficiently only with the active participation of research. Just as CRM was adopted by the military aviation communities well after it was developed in the airlines, military research on CRM issues has a relatively short history. Military research owes a large debt to those who pioneered in the CRM area, particularly the researchers performing under the auspices of NASA. Currently research in specific aircrew coordination training issues is continuing in the Army and Navy, while the Air Force is conducting directly related research. With this work, perhaps the military tradition of contribution to civil aviation will be extended to the area of CRM, and sharing of research results from both military and civilian areas will benefit all of aviation.

Acknowledgments

The opinions, views, and/or findings contained in this chapter are the authors' and should not be construed as an official position policy or decision of the organization with which they are affiliated, unless so designated by other official documentation. We gratefully acknowledge the support of PMA 205, OP 59, and the Office of Naval Technology.

References

Alkov, R. A. (1989). The U.S. Naval aircrew coordination training program. In *Proceedings of the Fifth International Symposium on Aviation Psychology* (pp. 483–488). Columbus: The Ohio State University.

Baker, D. P., Salas, E., & Prince, C. (1991). *Team task importance: Implications for conducting team task analysis.* Paper presented at the 6th Annual Meeting of the Society for Industrial and Organizational Psychology, St. Louis, MO.

Biddle, W. (1991). *Barons of the sky.* New York: Simon & Schuster.

Brown, D. (1987). Introduction to MAC CRM training. In H. W. Orlady & H. C. Foushee (Eds.), *Cockpit resource management training: Proceedings of the NASA/MAC workshop* (NASA-CP-2455) (pp. 132–134). Moffett Field, CA: NASA–Ames Research Center.

Cannon-Bowers, J. A., Prince, C., Salas, E., Owens, J. M., Morgan, B. B., & Gonos, G. H. (1989). Determining aircrew coordination training effectiveness. In *Proceedings of the Eleventh Interservice/Industry Training Systems Conference* (pp. 128–136). Fort Worth, TX.

Cavanagh, D., & Williams, K. (1987). The application of CRM to military operations. In H. W. Orlady & H. C. Foushee (Eds.), *Cockpit resource management training: Proceedings of the NASA/MAC workshop* (NASA-CP-2455) (pp. 135–144). Moffett Field, CA: NASA–Ames Research Center.

Daniel, C. (Ed.). (1987). *Chronicle of the 20th Century.* Mount Kisco, NY: Chronicle Publications.

Endsley, M. R. (1989). *Final report: Situation awareness in advanced strategic mission* (NOR DOC 89-32). Hawthorne, CA: Northrop Corporation.

Fishbein, M., & Ajzen, I. (1975). *Belief, attitude, intention and behavior: An introduction to theory and research.* Reading, MA: Addison-Wesley.

Foushee, H. C., & Manos, K. L. (1981). Information transfer within the cockpit: Problems in intracockpit communications. In C. E. Billings and E. S. Cheaney (Eds.), *Information transfer problems in the aviation system* (NASA Technical Paper 1875, pp. 63–71). Moffett Field, CA: NASA–Ames Research Center.

Franz, T. M., Prince, C., Cannon-Bowers, J. A., & Salas, E. (1990). The identification of aircrew coordination skills. *Proceedings of the 12th annual Department of Defense Symposium* (pp. 97–101). Colorado Springs, CO: U.S. Air Force Academy.

Geis, C. E., Alvarado, M. J., & Associates (1989). *Aircrew coordination training handbook.* Napa, CA: Geis–Alvarado & Associates, Inc.

Ginnett, R. (1986). *First encounters of the close kind: The first meetings of airline flight crews.* Unpublished doctoral dissertation. Yale University, New Haven, CT.

Hartel, C. E. J. (1991). *Improving team-assisted diagnostic decision making: Some training propositions and an empirical test.* Unpublished doctoral dissertation. Colorado State University, Fort Collins, CO.

Hartel, C., Smith, K., & Prince, C. (1991). *Defining aircrew coordination: Searching mishaps for meaning.* Paper presented at the Sixth International Symposium on Aviation Psychology. Columbus: The Ohio State University.

Helmreich, R. (1987). Theory underlying CRM training: Psychological issues in flightcrew performance and crew coordination. In H. W. Orlady & H. C. Foushee (Eds.), *Cockpit resource management training: Proceedings of the NASA/MAC workshop* (NASA CP 2455) (pp. 15–22). Moffett Field, CA: NASA–Ames Research Center.

Helmreich, R., & Wilhelm, J. (1987). *Reinforcing and measuring flightcrew resource management: Training captain/check airmen/instructor reference manual* (NASA/University of Texas Technical Manual 87-1). Moffett Field, CA: NASA–Ames Research Center.

Helmreich, R. L., Wilhelm, J. A., Kello, J. E., Taggart, W. R., & Butler, R. E. (1990). *Reinforcing and evaluating crew resource management: Evaluator/LOS instructor reference manual* (NASA/University of Texas Technical Manual 90-2). Austin: The University of Texas.

Jensen, R. S. (1989). *Aeronautical decision making–cockpit resource management* (DOT/FAA/PM-86/46), Washington, DC: Federal Aviation Administration.

Johnson, N. A., Shroyer, D. H., & Grewe, J. B. (1991). A new generation of crew resource management training. In *Proceedings of the Sixth International Symposium on Aviation Psychology* (pp. 404–409). Columbus: The Ohio State University.

Johnston, S. P. (1974). Flight, History of. *Encyclopaedia Britannica*, 15th ed., *Macropaedia*, 7, 380–406.

Kanki, B. G., Lozito, S., & Foushee, H. C. (1987). Communication indexes of crew coordination. In *Proceedings of the Fourth International Symposium on Aviation Psychology* (pp. 406–412). Columbus: The Ohio State University.

Keyes, R. J. (1990). *Cockpit resource management: A new approach to aircrew coordination training* (Research Report) Maxwell Air Force Base, AL: Airpower Research Institute.

Kozlowski, S. W., & Salas E. (1991). *An integrative multilevel model for the implementation and transfer of training interventions.* Unpublished manuscript.

Krey, N. C., & Rodgers, D. (1987). CRM training for Parts 91 and 135 operations (SimuFlite). In H. W. Orlady & H. C. Foushee (Eds.), *Cockpit resource management training: Proceedings of the NASA/MAC workshop* (NASA CP-2455) (pp. 158–169). Moffett Field, CA: NASA–Ames Research Center.

Lauber, J. K. (1987). Cockpit resource management: Background studies and rationale. In H. W. Orlady & H. C. Foushee (Eds.), *Cockpit resource management training: Proceedings of the NASA/MAC workshop* (NASA CP-2455) (pp. 5–14). Moffett Field, CA: NASA–Ames Research Center.

Leedom, D. K. (1990). *Aircrew coordination training and evaluation for Army rotary wing aircrews: Summary of research for fiscal year 1990.* Fort Rucker, AL: U.S. Army Research Institute Aviation Research and Development Activity.

Maher, P. (1983). An analysis of common assessment center dimensions. *Journal of Assessment Center Technology*, 6, 1–8.

Moody, R., Stein, J., Allen, L., & Dean, R. (1988). *MAC aircrew coordination training.* Scott Air Force Base, IL: Headquarters Military Airlift Command.

Morgan, B. B., Glickman, A. S., Woodard, E. A., Blaiwes, A. S., & Salas, E. (1986). *Measurement of team behaviors in a Navy environment* (Technical Report No. NTSC TR-86-014). Orlando, FL: Naval Training Systems Center.

Neely, P. (1991). *The Pilot.* New York: Simon & Schuster.

Orasanu, J. M. (1990). *Shared mental models and crew decision-making* (CSL Report No. 46). Princeton University: Cognitive Science Laboratory.

Orasanu, J. M., & Fischer, U. (1991). Information transfer and shared mental models of decision making. In *Proceedings of the Sixth International Symposium on Aviation Psychology* (pp. 272–277). Columbus: The Ohio State University.

Oser, R. L., McCallum, G. A., Salas, E., & Morgan, B. B. (1989). *Toward a definition of teamwork: An analysis of critical team behavior* (NTSC Technical Report No. 89-004). Orlando, FL: Naval Training Systems Center.

Oser, R. L., Prince, C., Morgan, B. B., & Simpson, S. S. (1990). *An analysis of aircrew communication patterns and content* (Technical report 90-009). Orlando, FL: Naval Training Systems Center.

Pawlik, E. A., Simon, R., & Dunn, Dennis J. (1991). Aircrew coordination for Army helicopters: Improved procedures for accident investigation. In *Proceedings of the Sixth International Symposium on Aviation Psychology* (pp. 310–325). Columbus: The Ohio State University.

Person-System Integration, Ltd. (1990). *F-14 Lecture Guide FABA 695 Crew Coordination* (Contract No. N00019-89-D-0050). Washington, D.C.: Department of the Navy, Naval Air Systems Command.

Povenmire, H. K., Rockway, M., Bunecke, J. L., & Patton, M. W. (1989). Cockpit resource management skills enhance combat mission performance in B-52 simulator. In *Proceedings of the Fifth International Symposium on Aviation Psychology* (pp. 489–494). Columbus: The Ohio State University.

Prince C., Chidester, T. R., Bowers, C., & Cannon-Bowers, J. (1992). Aircrew coordination: Achieving teamwork in the cockpit. In R. Swezey & E. Salas (Eds.), *Teams: Their training and performance*. Newark, NJ: Ablex.

Prince, C., & Salas, E. (1989). Aircrew performance: Coordination and skill development. In D. E. Daniel, E. Salas, & D. M. Kotick (Eds.), *Independent research and independent exploratory development (IR/IED) programs: Annual report for fiscal year 1988* (NTSC Technical Report No. 89-009) (pp. 45–48). Orlando, FL: Naval Training Systems Center.

Prince, C., & Salas, E. (1991). *The utility of low fidelity simulation for training aircrew coordination skills.* Paper presented at the International Training Equipment Conference, Maastricht, Netherlands.

Ruffell Smith H. P. (1979). *A simulator study of the interaction of pilot workload with errors, vigilance, and decisions* (NASA TM-78482). Moffett Field, CA: NASA–Ames Research Center.

Smith, K., & Salas, E. (1991). *Training assertiveness: The importance of active participation.* Paper presented at the 37th annual meeting of the Southeastern Psychological Association, New Orleans, LA.

Stout, R., Prince C., Bergondy, M., Baker, D., & Salas, E. (1992). *A methodology for determining aircrew coordination needs.* Unpublished manuscript, Naval Training Systems Center, Orlando, FL.

Swezey, R., Llaneras, R., Prince, C., & Salas, E. (1991). Instructional strategy for aircrew coordination training. In *Proceedings of the Sixth International Symposium on Aviation Psychology* (pp. 302–307). Columbus: The Ohio State University.

Thordsen, M. L., Klein, G. A., & Wolf, S. (1990). *Observing team coordination within Army rotary-wing aircraft crews.* (KATR90C2-90-05-Z). Yellow Springs, OH: Klein Associates Inc.

Thornton, R. C., Kaempf, G. L., Zeller, J. L., & McAnulty, D. M. (1991). *An evaluation of crew coordination and performance during a simulated UH-60 helicopter mission.* Unpublished manuscript, U.S. Army Research Institute Aviation Research and Development Activity, Fort Rucker, AL.

U.S. Navy. (1990). *Aircrew coordination workbook.* Link Training Services Division.

Zalesny, M., Baker, D., Prince, C., & Salas, E. (1992). *Organizational variables and aircrew coordination: Implications for team training.* Unpublished manuscript.

CRM: Cross-Cultural Perspectives

Neil Johnston
Aerospace Psychology Research Group
Trinity College
Dublin 2, Ireland

I think about my education sometimes. I went to the University of Chicago for a while after the Second World War. I was a student in the Department of Anthropology. At that time, they were teaching that there was absolutely no difference between anybody. They may be teaching that still.

Kurt Vonnegut, Jr.*

INTRODUCTION ✈

Cross-Cultural Perspectives

Despite these words, Kurt Vonnegut was awarded an honorary degree by the University of Chicago for the anthropological value of his novels. Vonnegut's writing testifies to the wide variability of the human condition and the impossibility of finding a definitive frame of reference from which to judge human behavior. Like a competent sociologist or anthropologist, Vonnegut has the gift of providing new perspectives on mundane behavioral events while integrating them into a credible social framework.

That is the challenge for this chapter, which seeks to provide insights into the variability of international aviation without losing sight of the fact that safe and efficient flight is a shared objective across the international aviation industry. However, while all in the international aviation community would readily affirm their commitment to operational safety and efficiency, there are differences in definitions, understandings, and choices as to the best means of achieving these objectives.

*From *Slaughterhouse-Five* by Kurt Vonnegut, Jr. Copyright © by Kurt Vonnegut, Jr. Used by permission of Delacorte/Seymour Lawrence, a division of Bantam Doubleday Dell Publishing Group, Inc.

Notwithstanding Vonnegut's tongue in cheek remark, our world is characterized by great economic, cultural and social diversity (Adler, 1990). For instance, the differing value systems of Muslim, Buddhist and Christian societies are integrated into radically different views of the world. In international aviation, cultural diversity is hidden by a high level of information exchange, advanced technology and the "language of aviation"; these sometimes imply that those involved in aviation are really tackling the same task in much the same way and using, by and large, similar methods and techniques. We may live in a "global village", but beneath the outward facade of conformity and consistency in aviation lie hidden the multiple perspectives and conflicting orientations common to all human activity.

The Cultural Context of Understanding and Meaning

Zulus have more than 30 words to describe the color brown (S. R. Trollip, personal communication, July, 1991) and the Inuit (Eskimo) similarly have an extensive vocabulary to describe the color white (Whorf, 1956 p. 216). Neither set of words can be rendered accessible to outsiders by the mere act of translation; meaning is also provided by the cultural and environmental context. It is the refined understanding of his environment that allows the Inuit to perform remarkable feats of long range navigation over many days, across vast distances, in almost featureless terrain (Irwin, 1985). This is achieved by a people whose indigenous logic would be considered deficient if judged against that of contemporary western cultures. And yet the efficiency and finesse with which the Inuit successfully exploit their unyielding environment is unrivalled (Lave, 1988). Now briefly consider how the specialized vocabulary of crew resource management (CRM) might be received in different cultures; indeed, might it not be the case that CRM training terminology could be unsuitable, or misdirected in some cultures?

Sociologists and anthropologists dedicate themselves to the study of social diversity. For these scholars the influence of culture and society predominates in shaping human behavior. They argue that social influences have a critical and subtle impact. This is partially revealed by the manner in which we all come to accept uncritically various actions, attitudes, practices, values, social arrangements, and definitions of "reality" as being normal and beyond challenge. Hofstede (1980a) suggests that culture be thought of as a "collective programming of the mind." This cultural programming determines "social realities" which themselves are then experienced as "facts of nature" (Miller, 1988, p. 267). Berger and Luckman (1966) argue that reality is a social construct we carry in our minds—a mental state which delimits those practices in our culture which define the "rules of the game" and provides a social framework of meaning from which we make our judgments of colleagues and foreigners. While we extend a fair measure of tolerance to the errors and quirks of the gauche and eccentric foreigner, it is still the foreigner who appears gauche and eccentric, not us! For the purposes of this chapter the reader is invited to consider that the perspective of gauche foreigners is normally appropriate when judged from the vantage point of their society.

The influence of culture extends well beyond social interaction. An American medical journalist resident in Europe consulted various physicians about a recurrent medical condition. She found that opinion varied between the American, French, British, and German doctors she consulted. She found a diversity in clinical practice which was determined more by national characteristics than by medico-scientific logic. Her research confirmed that cultural factors were a notable influence on interpretation of the medical literature (Payer, 1988). Yet the raw data of medical observation would initially strike us as being definitive, hard, incontrovertible information. Even time—something considered in technologically advanced Western societies to be an objective entity[1]—is perceived differently across various societies (Brown, 1987; Hofstede, 1980b). Brown discusses the implications of contrasting social understandings of time, describing a serious breakdown in relations between two teams of computer programmers (one Swiss, the other Italian) which derived from a cultural conflict over the "sense of time"; the "Swiss understood time as a precisely measured commodity, while the Italians saw time as more fluid and transitional" (p. 80). Here again we see how the meaning given to apparently objective entities is an artifact of culture (Bontempo, in press). Meaning transcends definition or direct translation. Roberts, Golder, & Chick (1980) even suggest that the meaning of "pilot error" will be a cultural variable. Now briefly consider the word "followership"—often used in U.S. CRM programs; this word is impossible to translate directly into most other languages, its intimation being embedded within a conceptual framework which is itself alien to many cultures.

Culture and CRM

The preceding remarks set the challenge and context for this chapter. Cross-cultural research projects rarely involve aviation, and the available cross-cultural literature has many limitations. It has, for instance, been strongly influenced by the values and imperatives underlying the North American academic tradition (Bond, 1988a; Cole, 1984; Hofstede, 1980b; Lonner, 1979; Moghaddam, 1987). The actual findings of cross-cultural research are also circumscribed by various restrictions. The literature mainly addresses basic research, methodological issues, or cross-cultural aspects of management training (Black & Mendenhall, 1990; Bond, 1988b; Hofstede, 1991; and Vertinsky, Tse, Wherung, & Lee, 1990).

[1]Of course this is merely the conventional wisdom of the Western layperson—modern physicists have a different conception of time (Hawking, 1988).

The search for pancultural psychological universals has not met with notable success (Amir & Sharon, 1987; Leung & Bond, 1989)—though, for instance, White & Baker (1991) take an ethological stance, suggesting that "dominance hierarchies" are an enduring human constant which "permeate . . . the basic concept of CRM." Schwartz & Bilsky (1987), Bond (1988b), and Kaplan (1991) also assess the prospect of finding cross-cultural universals. Others have sought to find universal aspects of organizational behavior across cultures (Adler, 1990; Evans, Sculli, & Hau, 1989; Smith & Tayeb, 1988). Typically, however, in suggesting that organizational differences between Thai and American management are minimal, Swierczek (1988) states that "the differences appear to be significant only in interactive situations, such as communications, conflict resolution, and interpersonal relations" (p. 80)—thus identifying differences in virtually everything of importance and relevance to CRM! South American and African countries are rarely considered in the literature. Given the relative geographical spread of accidents incidents (Figure 13.1), this is a significant deficiency, as both regions have a high incidence of crew-factor accidents.

From Figure 13.1 it can be seen that, collectively, emerging nations have a crew factor accident rate up to 8 times that of industrialized nations (Barnett and Higgins, 1989; Weener, 1990). In principle, areas with a high incidence of crew-caused accidents may require a CRM training response. However, while the need for CRM has been demonstrated in the United States, it does not necessarily follow that there is a need for CRM, as such, elsewhere—or that the U.S. analysis and model of CRM training is readily transferable. A link between CRM skill deficiencies and crew-caused accidents must first be established across the cultural regions

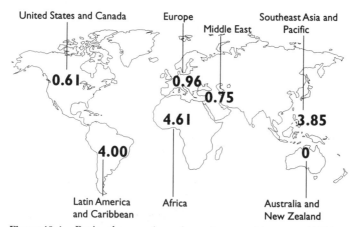

Figure 13.1   Regional comparison of crew factor accident rates (1980–1989). (Redrawn from Weener, 1990.)

of the world. A further problem arises when we look at CRM from a cross-cultural viewpoint; the assumptions and ideology underlying North American CRM training can themselves be viewed, and challenged, from the perspective of other cultures. Coming to definitive conclusions on these issues would require a substantial research program. In this chapter I merely consider:

1. Cross-cultural aspects of behavior on the assumption that CRM training is universally required
2. How effective implementation of CRM training might vary across cultures and organizations
3. Cross-cultural perspectives on existing CRM assumptions and practices.

Subsequently I briefly consider how CRM might be made culture-sensitive. My goals are to sensitize the reader to the impact of cultural imperatives and to establish the need for research.

CRM TRAINING: THE CROSS-CULTURAL CONTEXT ✈

What Is CRM?

CRM training seeks to assure the effective functioning of aircraft crewmembers through the timely and proficient use of all available resources (Federal Aviation Administration, FAA, 1989; Orlady & Foushee, 1987). The goal is safe and efficient flight. While resources vary from country to country, fellow crewmembers—the primary resource—are at least reasonably constant across international aviation. Central to the productive functioning of a crew are effective intra-cockpit communications and a shared view as to what constitutes appropriate crew behavior—in other words, an effective "team concept" (Cannon-Bowers, Salas, & Converse, 1990). Properly CRM trained cockpit teams will promptly solicit or provide relevant information in order to achieve effective and focused operational decision-making. In CRM training a key objective is to influence pilot attitudes and cockpit practices with a view to sustaining and improving overall cockpit communications and decision-making (Foushee, 1982, 1984; Hackman & Helmreich, 1984).

Cross-Cultural Universals and CRM Training

Most CRM programs differentiate between the orientation and attitudes of crew members toward the Task and Relationship dimensions of cockpit behavior. Figure 13.2 illustrates a task versus relationship model from Trollip & Jensen (1991). The intersection of high-task and high-relationship behaviors (labelled

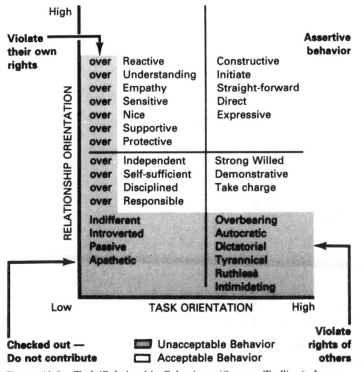

Figure 13.2   Task/Relationship Behaviors. (Source: Trollip & Jensen, 1991. Copyright © 1991 by Jeppesen & Co. Reprinted with permission of Jeppesen Sanderson, Inc.

"assertive") is preferred. Figure 13.2 is but one variant of similar models widely used in CRM courses. However, the descriptive terminology used by Trollip and Jensen raises important cross-cultural issues. For instance, the notion of "violating" the rights of either oneself or others would not be readily understood in most societies. Yet the basic idea of contrasting pilot attitudes to tasks and relationships seems to be a plausible training and educational tool. In the abstract it certainly appears to be a cross-culturally valid notion. Misumi (Misumi & Peterson, 1985) explored the dichotomy between task performance (P) and team maintenance (M) in extensive Japanese research. He demonstrated that effective Japanese supervisors achieve high scores on both P and M scales. Smith, Misumi, Tayeb, Peterson, & Bond (1989) report that "characterizations of P(Performance) and M(Maintenance) leader style have a similar factor structure [across four cultures]" (p. 97) and that "transcultural dimensions of leader style can indeed be identified, but that the skill of executing each style effectively varies by cultural setting" (p. 108). This suggests a need for CRM training which is compatible with the existing cultural milieu. CRM training may be either ineffective or widely rejected in the absence of such cultural compatibility (Scott-Milligan & Wyness, 1987). Smith and Tayeb (1988) review the impact of culture on leadership style, commenting that

> it could well be the case that leaders in organizations from all parts of the world do indeed need to attend both to the task at hand and also to the maintenance of good relationships within the work team. But how this is to be accomplished in each setting will be dependent upon the meanings given to particular leadership acts in that setting. (p. 162)

We thus return to the pervasive influence of culture—the ultimate source of meaning (Pepitone and Triandis, 1987). These remarks also affirm the importance of discerning the operational and safety connotations of the relevant culture, prior to determining the CRM training of choice.

Seeking Valid Cross-Cultural Comparisons

One problem with cross-cultural comparisons is that the level of diversity and complexity rapidly becomes daunting. Each culture sets a unique context for the formation of work groups. The social processes which contribute to group functioning may vary within a single culture and, indeed, from organization to organization within that culture. Structural factors, including the formal cockpit role structure, are relatively constant, though there are wide variations in process variables, role definition, and how cockpit roles are actually perceived. Aircraft operating philosophies differ considerably, and while "standard operating procedures" (SOPs) are widely used in aviation, there is definitional diversity and varied application by crewmembers. SOPs themselves are subject to cultural and sub-cultural variation (Degani & Wiener, 1991).

In a sea of cross-cultural relativism the issue of what constitutes appropriate and safe cockpit behavior is clearly relevant. The question also arises as to what constitutes an effective cockpit crew and how one might recognize such a crew in action. And, above all, how can one obtain the magic definition which specifies the normative aspects of CRM? Which culture, if any, "sets the standard"? These issues were addressed by Captain Hisakki Yamamori in a stimulating address to the 1986 NASA/MAC CRM Workshop (Yamamori, 1987), when he observed that

> [the] behavior [of American pilots] contrasted with the behavior of Japanese pilots at our seminar in Japan where the Japanese tended to behave in a more group-oriented fashion. . . . Japanese modesty is not seen as a virtue in the American culture. In the team discussions during CRM semi-

nars, I felt that the Americans did not easily accept another person's opinion, whereas Japanese tended to accept a person's opinion whether right or wrong in order to preserve harmony within the group. . . . Although I saw these differences in our cultures, I realised that, in the cockpit situation, neither the Japanese way of behavior nor the American way are the best way. I don't think that any culture whether it is Japanese, American, or any other—fits in with the cockpit environment. And in this sense, CRM is culture free. (p. 79)

Hofstede's Approach to Cultural Differences

Issues such as effective communications, superior leadership, the effective formation of work groups, shared responsibility, the willingness of subordinate crew members to speak out, adherence to rules and procedures, the building of shared mental models, coping with novel decision-making situations, and so forth are among the topics addressed by CRM training. How can such diverse factors be productively considered across cultural boundaries? A similar challenge was faced by Professor Geert Hofstede, who conducted a systematic study of work-related values across more than 50 countries (Hofstede 1980a, 1991). His substantial study is one of the largest cross-cultural research programs ever undertaken. It offers a number of significant cross-cultural insights relevant to CRM.

Hofstede determined that national cultures can be scaled and differentiated across four basic dimensions. Each culture can then be given a distinctive overall position within the resulting framework. The use of average survey response rates to characterize different cultures along a number of dimensions can certainly lead to anomalies. However, most people subscribe to the notion that individuals have a shared range of characteristics which aggregate to a national *persona*. It was the subjective content of such supposed national characteristics that Hofstede sought to clarify. He proposed four cultural dimensions.

1. *Power distance (PDI)*. This considers the habitual exercise of power within a culture. It refers to the manner in which superiors and subordinates expect, and accept, the unequal distribution and exercise of power. It concomitantly refers to those social inequalities accepted to be proper and legitimate. In a *high power-distance* culture (e.g., India) social inequality is readily accepted and leaders are expected to be autonomous and decisive, while their subordinates are expected to know their place and implement their leader's directives. In a *low power-distance* culture (e.g., Austria) superiors and subordinates view and treat each other as colleagues; here information tends to be much more freely offered by subordinates who are, in any case, more likely to be consulted spontaneously by their managers.

2. *Uncertainty Avoidance (UAI)*. This dimension addresses the ease with

which cultures cope with novelty, ambiguity, and uncertainty. *High uncertainty-avoidance* cultures (e.g., Japan, Greece) seek clarity and order in social relationships, favouring rules and regulations. Strict codes of behavior, inflexibility, and intolerance can underlie a desire to avoid unstructured and unpredictable situations. Alternatively, in *low uncertainty-avoidance* cultures (e.g., Denmark) uncertainty is viewed as a natural part of life, and a pragmatic view of rules and regulations is customary. Such societies are relatively tolerant and adaptable.

3. *Individualism (IDV)*. This dimension considers the cultural emphasis given to individualistic, as distinct from collectivist, social mores. In strongly *individualistic cultures* (e.g., the United States) primacy is given to personal initiative and individual achievement, in contrast to group achievements. The entitlement of the individual to hold and express personal opinions is highly valued. In *collectivist cultures* (e.g., Iran) the social framework is much tighter and social obligations to clan, class, or group are exchanged for the protection and promotion of one's interests as part of the collective. In collectivist cultures membership in a group implies a moral and personal commitment to the group—hence being a good group member is valued highly, whereas in individualistic cultures good leaders generate higher social prestige.

4. *Masculinity (MAS)*. In *masculine* cultures (e.g., Italy, Australia) ambition and performance are valued. These are measured by money and material success. *Machismo*, forceful behavior, and drive are the order of the day. In *feminine* cultures (e.g., Sweden) a more ecological approach is normal, with public service and a high quality of life considered desirable social goals. *Masculine* cultures tend to have clearly defined sex roles with men expected, and expecting, to fulfil a dominant social position.

These four dimensions distinguish elements of culture whose daily manifestations seem natural and compellingly obvious from within those cultures. Table 13.1 records values for Hofstede's four indices for 50 countries and 3 regions. Hofstede statistically combined his raw PDI, UAI, IDV, and MAS survey scores to group these countries into characteristic clusters. He then isolated a number of "culture areas" "on the basis of which we can explain partly similar mental programming of their citizens" (Hofstede, 1980a, p. 333). Various country clusters and culture areas are illustrated in Table 13.2; Japan is the only country in a unique culture area.

Applying Hofstede's Findings to Aviation

Hofstede's cultural dimensions have potential implications when CRM training requirements are considered.

1. *Power Distance. High Power Distance* seems likely to provide the most potent source of CRM problems, since it is closely associated with social stratifica-

Table 13.1

Values of IDV, PDI, UAI, and MAS Indices for 50 Countries and 3 Regions[a]

Country	Code	IDV	PDI	UAI	MAS	Country	Code	IDV	PDI	UAI	MAS
Arab*	ARA	38	80	68	53	Jamaica	JAM	39	45	13	68
Argentina	ARG	46	49	86	56	Japan	JPN	46	54	92	95
Australia	AUL	90	36	51	61	Korea (South)	KOR	18	60	85	39
Austria	AUT	55	11	70	79	Malaysia	MAL	26	104	36	50
Belgium	BEL	75	65	94	54	Mexico	MEX	30	81	82	69
Brazil	BRA	38	69	76	49	Netherlands	NET	80	38	53	14
Canada	CAN	80	39	48	52	Norway	NOR	69	31	50	8
Chile	CHL	23	63	86	28	New Zealand	NZL	79	22	49	58
Colombia	COL	13	67	80	64	Pakistan	PAK	14	55	70	50
Costa Rica	COS	15	35	86	21	Panama	PAN	11	95	86	44
Denmark	DEN	74	18	23	16	Peru	PER	16	64	87	42
East Africa**	EAF	27	64	52	41	Philippines	PHI	32	94	44	64
Ecuador	ECA	8	78	67	63	Portugal	POR	27	63	104	31
El Salvador	SAL	19	66	94	40	South Africa	SAF	65	49	49	63
Finland	FIN	63	33	59	26	Singapore	SIN	20	8	8	48
France	FRA	71	68	86	43	Spain	SPA	51	57	86	42
Great Britain	GBR	89	35	35	66	Sweden	SWE	71	31	29	5
Germany (West)	GER	67	35	65	66	Switzerland	SWI	68	34	58	70
Greece	GRE	35	60	112	57	Taiwan	TAI	17	58	69	45
Guatemala	GUA	6	95	101	37	Thailand	THA	20	64	64	34
Hong Kong	HOK	25	68	29	57	Turkey	TUR	37	66	85	45
Indonesia	IDO	14	78	48	46	Uruguay	URU	36	61	100	38
India	IND	48	77	40	56	U.S.A.	USA	91	40	46	62
Iran	IRA	41	58	59	43	Venezuela	VEN	12	81	76	73
Ireland	IRE	70	28	35	68	West Africa***	WAF	20	77	54	46
Israel	ISR	54	13	81	47	Yugoslavia	YUG	27	76	88	21
Italy	ITA	76	50	75	70						

[a] See Table 13.2.

Table 13.2

Country Clusters: Shared Characteristics between 50 Countries and 3 Regions[a,b]

Group	Country or region	Group	Country or region
1	Guatemala	4	Philippines
	Panama		Malaysia
			India
	Chile		
	Yugoslavia		Singapore
	Uruguay		Hong Kong
	Portugal		Jamaica
	El Salvador		
	Korea (South)	5	Austria
	Peru		Israel
	Costa Rica		
			Ireland
2	Indonesia		New Zealand
	West Africa***		Canada
	Iran		Great Britain
	Thailand		Australia
	East Africa**		United States
	Taiwan		
	Pakistan		Italy
			Switzerland
3	Japan		Germany
			South Africa
	Colombia		
	Ecuador	6	Denmark
	Venezuela		Sweden
	Mexico		Norway
			Netherlands
	Belgium		Finland
	France		
	Greece		
	Argentina		
	Spain		
	Arab*		
	Brazil		
	Turkey		

[a] Key to Tables 13.1 and 13.2: *Indices*—IDV, Individualism; UAI, Uncertainty avoidance; PDI, Power distance; MAS; Masculinity. *Regions*—*Arab: Egypt, Iraq, Kuwait, Lebanon, Lybia, Saudi Arabia, U.A.E.; **East Africa: Ethiopia, Kenya, Tanzania, Zambia; ***West Africa: Ghana, Nigeria, Sierra Leone.

[b] Derived from data in Hofstede, 1980a, 1984, 1991.

tion, perceptions of social status, and the value systems of both leaders and followers. In high PDI countries, junior crewmembers are more likely to fear the consequences of disagreeing with leaders, possibly with good reason. Leaders are themselves likely to feel comfortable with paternalistic behavior and leadership by directive. Leaders, rather than followers, will tend to initiate communication. This is a useful reminder that leadership does not exist in a social vacuum—it is directly related to the incumbent social embodiment of "followership" or "subordinateship." Unresponsiveness to legitimate authority could arise with *Low Power Distance*—especially if associated with high individualism.

2. *Uncertainty Avoidance. High UAI* tends to generate rigidity and strong adherence to the formality of rules and regulations. This could manifest itself in a preference for clear guidance and a belief in the merits of explicitly controlling subordinates. High UAI is associated with social acceptance of aggressive behavior, strong task orientation, ritual behavior, and written rules. If formal goals are not achieved, there is potential for dispute over the "rules" or rule adherence, rather than about the operational objectives to which the rules are directed. Alternatively, *low UAI* could conceivably be associated with a permissive and indulgent approach to rules and standard operating procedures.

3. *Individualism (IDV)*. Individualism and collectivism are intimately associated with the predominant value systems of society at large. In *high IDV* societies, individual decision-making is normal and preferred to group decisions. Individual initiative and leadership are highly valued. In *low IDV* societies, group decisions are felt to be better than decisions made by individuals. Personal initiative is not encouraged. Social identity and position are determined by membership in various in-groups. Here the implications for cockpit communications and CRM should be obvious.

4. *Masculinity*. This relates to beliefs regarding the gender division of social roles. High MAS societies tend to have a belief in the "independent decision-maker," and leaders value their decision-making autonomy. Decisiveness, interpersonal directness, and *machismo* are common in high MAS societies. Again, there are implications here for CRM.

These four general cultural tendencies do not exist independently; they interact with each other. By way of illustration, Figure 13.3, from Hofstede (1984), plots Power Distance against Individualism for the 50 countries and 3 regions listed in Table 13.1. We see here a general tendency to form distinctive clusters and a strong (negative) correlation between power distance and individualism; countries with large power distances tend to be collectivist, and vice versa. This dichotomy is a potentially valuable point of departure when considering CRM training requirements.

Rieger & Wong-Rieger (1988) included Hofstede's cultural dimensions in their investigation of airline management in nine cultures. The salient dimensions

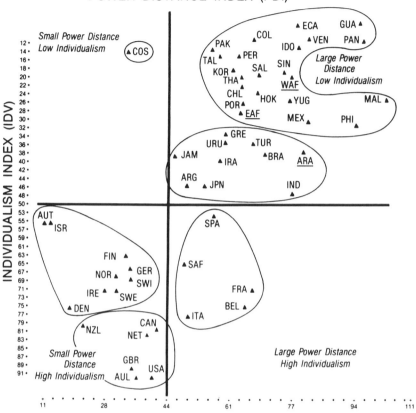

Figure 13.3 Power distance × individualism–collectivism plot for 50 countries and 3 regions (see Table 13.1 for country codes). (Source: Hofstede, 1983.)

in Hofstede's analysis were supported by their findings. Redding & Ogilvie (1984) considered Hofstede's findings in their airline study of six airlines drawn from Europe, North America, Asia, and the Pacific. Redding and Ogilvie sought to determine the influence of hierarchy upon the "openness of the communication process" (p. 46) in the cockpit. They found sufficient evidence "to argue that perceptions of psychosocial climate in these airlines are in reality different" (p. 54). They found that the "status consciousness one would anticipate in high power distance cultures is, in fact, evident" (p. 53), and that "a cultural value of egalitarianism conveyed in low power distance scores is strongly related to perceiving no barriers to communications due to status" (p. 55). Data from the NASA/University of Texas CRM research project (R. L. Helmreich, personal communication, October, 1991) lends support to these findings, suggesting that captains in one airline from a high power distance/low individualism culture are "less open to input from other crew members [than those in U.S. and European carriers]." Redding and Ogilvy's final conclusions were cautious:

> There is thus *some* evidence that (a) societal values about the distribution of power are brought into the cockpit, (b) that they influence the climate in which communications take place and (c) that the more open flow of communications is conducive to better cockpit performance.
>
> This conclusion must, however, remain tentative. . . . Further work will clearly be needed. [emphasis in original] (p. 55)

These findings reflect the difficulty of deriving definitive information from cross-cultural research and the hazards of reaching premature conclusions. Indeed the cross-cultural literature is replete with cautious conclusions, and debate continues as to the validity of research findings (Bond, 1988a; Hofstede, 1980a; Pepitone & Triandis, 1987; Sharon & Amir, 1988). On the other hand, the realities of producing CRM courses cannot await a resolution of academic debates. It would certainly appear reasonable to use Hofstede's data as a point of departure, though a healthy regard as to its possible limitations would be prudent.

Hofstede's conclusions are supported by other studies, though few are as comprehensive as his pioneering work. In particular, the individualism–collectivism dimension has been widely applied and accepted (Gudykunst, Yoon, & Nishida, 1987; Hui & Triandis, 1986). Hofstede's central argument is that, given the distinctive cultural breakdown in work-related values, efficient work practices and group processes are likely to vary from country to country (Hofstede, 1980b, 1983, 1991). To be effective, the organization of work and management practices must reflect the social mores of the relevant culture. Triandis (1980) endorses these sentiments, stating that in recent years "it has become very clear that one cannot take a psychological method and use it in another culture without drastic modification" (p. 7). It would clearly be foolish to tackle cross-cultural problems of management and group functioning by blindly using a narrow and predefined repertoire of conceptions, prescriptions, and tools.

THE EFFECTIVE IMPLEMENTATION OF CRM TRAINING ➜

The discussion moves further into uncharted waters when we consider barriers to CRM training implementation. There has been almost no research on CRM training needs outside the United States—exceptions being research involving British pilots by Wheale (1984) and Harris & Muir (1986). The tenor of this research contrasts with that conducted in the United States and serves to alert the reader to cultural subtleties in the manifestation of central CRM issues. Similarly, there is little information on the implementation of CRM training outside of the United States, though Margerison, McCann, & Davies (1987, 1988) provide a valuable review of their Australian experience. Scott-Milligan & Wyness (1987) address cross-cultural issues which arose when introducing CRM training in New Zealand. Their experience is instructive.

> [Cultural insensitivity] has been a major deterrent in accepting courses from Europe and North America. . . . "Synergy" for example, a word used frequently in North American CRM training, has been resisted quite strongly. . . . Resistance is not limited to words, as a strong European accent does not engender acceptance either. . . . With the obvious advantage of hindsight we strongly suggest that [an] analysis of in-house requirements should occur prior to leaping on the CRM bandwagon. (pp. 379–380)

This minor "cultural incompatibility" involves countries within the same "country cluster" (Table 13.2) but was sufficient to adversely impact CRM training implementation (see also Davidson, 1987, p. 89). These remarks also alert us to potentially serious obstacles to CRM implementation *across* Hofstede's culture areas.

How Might CRM Training Requirements Vary?

In a society where highly effective working groups are natural, existing CRM training directed to promote effective group functioning might be largely superfluous—or even provocative. On the other hand it is possible that, in such a society, effective cockpit leadership and followership might merit explicit attention. Alternatively, in a socially stratified society characterized by high power distance, CRM training might seek to ameliorate the excesses of abrasive leadership styles, explicitly seeking to promote effective cockpit group processes and communications.

The point here is obvious: the desired form and substance of CRM training may be as much of a variable as is culture itself. Not only will CRM training requirements vary from culture to culture, but it is more than likely that in larger countries it will be productive to tailor CRM training to specific airline subcultures. Indeed, even in smaller countries the sub-culture of the national airline can deviate markedly from that of other airlines. Many airlines recruit pilots from limited backgrounds such as the military, or a particular foreign country. The sub-culture of such airlines might differ markedly from that anticipated on the basis of Hofstede's analysis.

Corporate and Operational Culture

These observations raise a host of issues associated with airline corporate and operational sub-cultures—topics addressed more by anecdote than by research. Wheale (1984) states that "the influence of an airline is reflected in the fact that 83 percent of the [surveyed] pilots believe that company policy affects co-ordination and interaction on the flight deck" (p. 39). Operational goals and orientations of pilots across different airlines within a single culture can vary widely (Johnston, 1986), and relationships between pilots within airlines also vary (Hynes, 1990). Hence, to ensure effective implementation, CRM training must nest appropriately and harmoniously within the prevailing corporate culture.

CRM training is ultimately concerned with sustaining or modifying fundamental operational practices and pilot communications styles. If the desired pilot attitudes and dispositions are not endorsed and supported by the surrounding organizational environment, CRM training may simply fail to make an impact (Hackman, 1987). An example here would be incompatibility and tension between the management style applied to the major cockpit resources (the pilots) and the espoused pilot CRM style; anecdotal evidence suggests that this may indeed be a problem in a number of airlines. As Hynes (1990) observes, "We need improvements in Managing Cockpit Resources, before we will see the full benefit of CRM training programs" (p. 33). If CRM training is critically influenced by corporate and operational culture, successful implementation will be intimately associated with core organizational processes. These transcend the immediate operational setting and are a function of both operational and corporate management practices. For example, Vandermark (1991) discusses the impact of corporate culture on the implementation of a joint pilot–flight attendant CRM program. He explicitly addresses CRM "as planned organizational change" (pp. 92–93), demonstrating how the CRM program forms an integral and fully consistent part of the airline's management culture. This would appear to be a key factor in its success.

Airline Induction and Airline Culture

The optimal organizational position is to avoid any need for planned change, by ensuring that pilots join an airline whose existing management and cockpit practices are consistent with desired CRM behavior. Training would then aim to integrate new pilots into the existing culture and assure effective cockpit management practices. It would not necessarily be a "conventional" CRM course (Johnston, 1991). Such training is proposed in the FAA's Advanced Qualification Program (FAA, 1991), while similar influences can be detected in training proposed for the Boeing 777 (Boeing, 1990).

Planned "corporate socialization" is not always well received in strongly individualistic societies, so it is all the more significant that a number of very successful U.S. corporations are known to have a strong internal culture, which they explicitly seek to foster (Peters & Waterman, 1982; Schein, 1990). Pascale (1985) suggests that such corporate cultures provide "an awesome internal consistency which powerfully shapes behavior" (p. 29), while Wilkins (1984) and Nooij (1985) consider how such internal cultures are best conveyed to new employees. Many European airlines, and especially those with *ab initio* training programs, explicitly seek such carefully crafted pilot training (Harms, 1988; Johnston, 1989). Such airlines increasingly seek to integrate the principles of CRM across the entire training curriculum, and especially at the point of airline entry (Johnston, 1991). This important *rite of passage* provides a unique and cost-effective opportunity to impart corporate values and operating philosophies, so obviating the subsequent need for dedicated (and expensive) CRM courses. Nooij (1985) reviews such training within an *ab initio* setting.

Consultation with Pilots

During CRM development pilots are often consulted about their CRM training needs and prospective course content. This is one of the methods by which CRM is tailored to an airline's sub-culture. There is often formal participation by pilot representatives and, in many airlines, such a process of consultation will be judged essential. It is reasonable to anticipate that an agreed "problem definition" and shared approach to the training will be a natural precursor of successful implementation (Margerison, McCann, & Davies, 1987; chapter by Byrnes and Black). Similarly, a number of airlines have reported that they recruit CRM training facilitators from the line pilot group rather than from the ranks of instructors or check airmen.

However, it is not always the case that operational management deems consultation and participation to be either proper or desirable. Consultative management techniques are not common in societies characterized by high power distance and/or low individualism. In such cultures the average—and often the more effective—manager may be a "benevolent autocrat" who sees little need for participative management. In many countries it is not considered normal or appropriate to enter into discussions with pilot representatives on such matters. Here again we meet a cultural gulf with implications for CRM implementation.

Sources of Expertise and CRM

The corpus of knowledge on human factors and CRM is concentrated heavily in a very small number of the most developed nations of the world. In particular, the growing expertise of CRM practitioners in the United States contrasts markedly with the situation in other countries. This is a significant barrier to

implementation, as operational personnel do not always have the necessary expertise in training group and communications skills, while external experts—even if
available—often lack the operational insights required to make training credible
and effective. Indeed, in most countries it is difficult for interested pilots to keep in
contact with developments in CRM training practice. An attempt to overcome
such problems of communications and human factors education was recently
initiated by the International Civil Aviation Organization (ICAO), through the
continuing publication of a number of Human Factors Digests (for examples see
ICAO, 1989a, 1989b, 1991).

Regional Differences

Inter-Cultural CRM Training

A number of airlines employ cockpit and cabin crew recruited from different countries and distinct cultures. In such airlines the need for inter-cultural CRM
training arises. This is a specialized subject, presenting a unique challenge. It will
not be considered here. However, as the following pilot report illustrates, inter-
cultural issues are relevant to CRM: "young ethnic F/O continually chatting to
passengers on PA at inappropriate times, despite my gentle hints re priorities (as a
non-national I am aware of political implications if I remonstrate too obviously
with F/Os)" ("Does the Left," 1991). The prerequisites for success in inter-
cultural training are specifically considered by Ooi (1991). Initial information
from the NASA/University of Texas CRM research team (R. L. Helmreich,
personal communication, August 1991) indicates that, in each of two surveyed
airlines, different nationalities reacted differentially to specific components of the
same CRM training. This lends some support to the notion that distinct cultural
groups may have differing CRM training needs.

Cultural Understandings

Regional differences in mapping the human factors domain also impacts on
CRM implementation. There is, for instance, a marked difference in how human
performance training is perceived outside the United States. In the United States,
CRM is normally seen as the primary vehicle through which to address human
factors issues impacting on pilots. Other countries, notably those in Europe, see
human factors and CRM as overlapping, viewing them as close but distinct
relatives. CRM training in Europe often has a different tenor from that found in
the United States (Johnston & Mauriño, 1990). There is, for instance, formal and
examinable training in human factors at the basic training stage, and while this
anticipates CRM training, it is not CRM training as such.

In this context it should also be noted that a number of accidents in the
United States which have been held to demonstrate the need for CRM are not

always viewed in the same light by outside observers. For example, the 1982 Air Florida accident in Washington is extensively quoted as demonstrating the need for CRM training—for example, by Trollip & Jensen (1991; see also the chapter by Kayten). Observers outside the United States would agree that the cockpit voice recorder provides evidential testimony to a lack of CRM skills. However, they would also question the basic knowledge and airmanship of the pilots, who both appear to demonstrate an unacceptable level of ignorance regarding appropriate operational behavior in adverse weather conditions. While this observation raises the debatable issue of how causal factors can be best categorized (Wasserman, Lempert, & Hastie, 1990), it also demonstrates cultural differences in the isolation of salient casual factors (Payer, 1988; Senders & Moray, 1991).

Psychological Tests and CRM Performance Appraisal

Margerison *et al.* (1988) are among those reporting the successful use of questionnaires to assist pilots with feedback on personal psychological profiles and preferred working relationships. Most CRM practitioners would support this training method, though it is again important to note that such direct feedback, even if handled sensitively, is not the norm in most cultures. This is another issue calling for a fair measure of cross-cultural insight. It is not simply a matter of developing sensitivity to the content or delivery of feedback—it also relates to the absence in many countries of the Western concept of individual identity. Some Eastern societies do not even think in terms of individual "personalities," a person's identity being understood as the aggregate of the individual and his social milieu (Hofstede, 1980a, p. 215). Basic social processes in collectivist cultures are patterned differently from those typifying individualistic societies. The critical point is that these social processes rarely lend themselves to the management techniques and interventions common in individualistic Western cultures (Hofstede, 1980b, 1991). The evidence thus indicates that current methods of providing personal feedback will prove intrinsically unsuitable in collectivist cultures, where saving face and preserving harmony is at a high social premium (Pun, 1990). In these countries violating social norms and expectations during CRM training will lead to discord and unease.

Barriers to Implementation

The remarks above have implications for the effective implementation of CRM training, especially in circumstances where there is a distinct cultural gap across Hofstede's individualism–collectivism and power distance dimensions (Figure 13.3). What is acceptable and practical in countries scoring low on individualism and power distance will differ markedly from that found necessary and desirable in countries scoring high on individualism and power distance (Hofstede, 1983, 1984). This is not to deny the potential value of CRM training across cultures. However, it does mean that the CRM training might differ markedly from that currently in vogue—even to the extent that the training of preference may display little similarity to contemporary CRM programs. In any case this would not be an appropriate test of such new CRM programs, which should rather manifest operational relevance—and be capable of successful implementation—while making a positive contribution to air safety. These must be considered the definitive tests.

However, in considering these remarks it should be kept in mind that the highly structured cockpit working environment may, in actual fact, offer a special setting wherein any such "cultural negatives" are singularly amenable to the counter-impact of appropriate procedures, work mores, and sub-cultural values (Ooi, 1991; Swierczek, 1988). Paradoxically, it may yet be determined that the interaction of technology and precise cockpit role definition can provide unique training opportunities to help ameliorate "cultural negatives" (Lave & Wenger, 1991). A number of writers outside aviation have identified the interaction of technology and culture as key determinants of management style (Tanaka & Gakushuin, 1973; Evans, Hau, & Sculli, 1969). There is no information available on the relevance of this intriguing possibility to aviation. This underlines our ignorance of such matters and further emphasizes the need for research.

CRM REVISITED: A CROSS-CULTURAL CRITIQUE — ✦

The discussion has, by and large, proceeded on the basis that CRM training is appropriate and necessary across the world's aviation industry, albeit with appropriate cultural variations. However, a consequence of taking a cross-cultural perspective on any subject is that one's very point of departure can be challenged. The cross-cultural challenge to CRM which I briefly outline below is twofold. I wish first to consider the ready transfer of current CRM to all countries and second to suggest that the basic connection between CRM deficiencies and human factors accidents in the United States may not always be valid elsewhere.

Can CRM Be Effective beyond the Borders of the United States?

The United States scores highest on Hofstede's individualism dimension (Table 13.1). It should therefore come as no surprise that a number of aviation accidents have been attributed to the impact of this strong individualism—the "right stuff" of aviation folklore. Foushee & Helmreich (1988) open by considering the historical context of the "right stuff," quoting from Wolfe (1979)—itself a notable celebration of the fruits of American individualism. Foushee and Helmreich then proceed to demonstrate the necessity and desirability of CRM training, making a case that is certainly compelling. But is their argument applicable beyond the borders of the United States? Specifically, is existing CRM training suitable and generally compatible with all the world's cultures and, second, are international cockpit management and safety problems directly comparable?

The Academic Debate

Within the literature on cross-cultural psychology, the point is consistently—even stridently—made that American psychology dominates the academic world. However, while it has "become an American export commodity" (Koch, quoted by Jahoda, 1988, p. 93), it has been widely suggested that "many of our psychological theories are little more than elaborations of Western 'folk models'" (p. 90). Kohn (1989) and Sharon & Amir (1988) are among those who discuss the difficulty of cross-culturally replicating the empirical studies on which we rely. The limitations and cultural parochialism of U.S. social psychology are frequently noted, for instance by Moghaddam (1987) and several contributors to Bond (1988a). In introducing a special issue of the *Journal of Cross Cultural Psychology*, Lonner (1987) observes that

> the general failure to replicate, in Israel, six relatively simple yet representative United States social psychological studies is not very encouraging to those who would like to believe that social psychology is a generalizable science. The United States and Israel are culturally much more similar than they are different; what would have happened if the attempt had been made in, for instance, Indonesia, or Sri Lanka, or Chad? (p. 381)

Mann (1980) claims that "many of the standard social psychological experiments . . . become distorted, even ludicrous, in many non-western culture settings" (p. 197). Hofstede (1980b) affirms that the "United States has been the world's largest producer and exporter of management theories" (p. 52), observing elsewhere (Hofstede, 1984) that "almost without exception, the cultural assumptions that went into these packages have not been explored" (p. 91). Hofstede presents a cross-cultural challenge to a number of Western management thinkers, questioning the notion that their theories are universal (Hofstede, 1980a, 1984, 1991). It would be fair to say that contemporary academic and management training literature supports these sentiments.

Applying the Academic Critique to CRM

One example should suffice to illustrate the application of these criticisms to CRM. It is difficult for those of us from cultures sustaining an acute sense of individual identity to recognize that, in other cultures, the very essence of one's identity is defined by virtue of being a member of a group or collective. Geertz, quoted by Jahoda (1986), observes that

> the Westerner's conception of the person as a bounded, unique, more or

less integrated motivational and cognitive universe, a dynamic centre of emotion, judgment, and action organized into a distinctive whole and set against both other such wholes and against a natural and social background is . . . a rather peculiar idea within the context of the world's cultures. (p. 22)

In a collectivist society, the combination of personal identity and normal social processes will ensure that many current CRM training techniques will be deflected, or that their intended application will be subverted. This would not be conscious or planned—it would merely be the outcome of a natural response to alien training techniques which did not relate intelligibly to the prevailing culture. Even if we take the universal need for some kind of CRM training as a given, it remains possible that current training techniques and methods will be found ineffective in a some cultures—since they are predicated on assumptions which lack universal validity (Guptara & Murray, 1990). While cockpit management training for pilots in all countries may be required, the import of these remarks is that many current CRM training techniques will simply not transfer across the entire globe (Pun, 1990). Indeed, the training of preference in some countries could conceivably be so different from that used in the United States as to merit a different name.

Why Is CRM Required Outside the United States?

We now move to the relationship between aviation accidents and CRM failures. Cooper, White & Lauber (1979), Foushee & Manos (1981), Murphy (1980), and Ruffell Smith (1979) provide persuasive evidence for the connection between CRM deficiencies and crew-error accidents among U.S. carriers. My purpose here is not to challenge their findings, but to suggest that their conclusions should not be arbitrarily applied to the rest of the world.

The categorization of data and examination of evidence must necessarily be consistent with a theory or descriptive framework. Just as the developed world exports its management theories, it also generates most of the statistical analyses from which we derive our conclusions on the role of human failure. There is *prima facie* evidence that this categorization and statistical analysis may be incomplete, and that particular care is necessary when deducing the international incidence of CRM deficiencies. There may be a significant difference between the major causal factors at work in the more and less developed parts of the world. This clearly has immediate relevance to any purported need for CRM training. While I know of no similar treatment of this topic, this is not the place to argue the case in detail, and the discussion following is necessarily brief and allusive.

Figure 13.1 provides a comparative illustration of the relative regional breakdown of crew factor accident rates. Barnett & Higgins (1989) endorse the general import of this figure, adding that "the flag carriers of the Communist bloc and Third-World nations averaged [1977–1986] eight times the death risk per flight as those from industrialized First-World nations" (p. 1); they further observe that "in terms of safety, the dichotomy 'first world' vs. 'second-and-third worlds' has a strong statistical basis" (p. 12). It is widely accepted that human failure consistently figures as the major contributor to these accidents, and some proponents of CRM accordingly argue for the wider international availability of CRM training.

Barnett and Higgins ask the question, "Could it be that it is not size but rather the politico-economic status of the 'mother country' that is the primary correlate of safety performance?" (p. 11). It should be noted that their analysis only considered "30 U.S. domestic airlines and 80 international flag carriers" (p. 1). Captain H. Caesar (personal communication, August, 1991) confirms the regional accident imbalance. In Figure 13.4 he provides a comparison of global figures for percentage accumulated accidents and percentage fleet size. These demonstrate that, when we widen the statistical base and consider the cumulative record from 1959 to 1988, operators with smaller fleets are shown to be at higher risk over this period (see also Learmount, 1991).

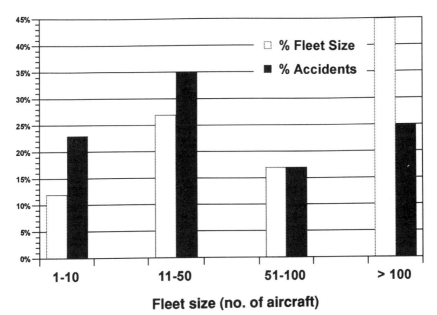

Figure 13.4 Total operational losses 1959–1988. Percentage fleet size and percentage accumulated accidents: jet aircraft of 20 Tonnes or greater. (Source: Captain Heino Caesar, personal communication August, 1991.)

Additional information is contained in Figure 13.5 (Weener, 1990). This compares the accident rates of "industrialized" and "emerging" nations for one short-range aircraft type and one intercontinental type. Figure 13.5a confirms that the "industrialized" and "emerging" nation accident dichotomy applies to the short-range aircraft type. However, Figure 13.5b shows that accident rates and trends are virtually identical for "industrialized" and "emerging" nations operating the intercontinental airplane type. Weener further notes that a comparison of operators "show[s] accident rates that seem to depend on route structure and, we suspect, airport and airway infrastructure" (p. 4). Furthermore, the natural tendency to associate regional statistics with the carriers of that region may occasionally be misleading; Stoller (1990) states that *"irrespective of the nationality of the airline,* more fatal accidents occurred over Latin America than over any other region of the world. No one we questioned about this could give [an] explanation" (p. 82, emphasis added). Learmount (1991) reports that larger carriers in South America have "a safety record comparable with companies of other regions." Lautman & Gallimore (1987) report a survey of 12 operators with an above average safety record, observing that corporate, and particularly operational, management probably plays a critical role in the success of the surveyed operators. Taylor (1988) notes that one particular Asian airline had three accidents in 1984 involving the approach and landing phase; he reports

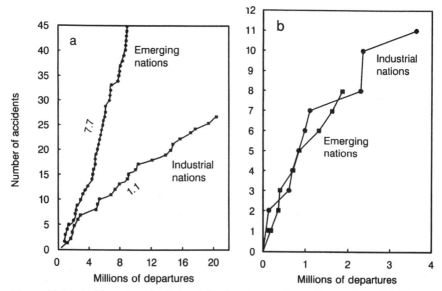

Figure 13.5 Accident rates for industrialized nations and emerging nations. (a) Short-range airplane type, 1969–1989. (b) Intercontinental airplane type, 1970–1989. (Source: Weener, 1990.)

that the International Air Transport Association Safety Advisory Committee agreed "that the remedy lay in a *programme by the flight operations management* to address the causative factors *rather than individual pilot action*: (p. 160, emphasis added). Both Stoller (1990) and Barnett & Higgins (1989) establish that a small number of regional carriers figure disproportionately in the accident statistics.

What are we to make of such information? Socio-politico-economic factors appear to impact on safety, though the salient influences seem to impact particularly on smaller operators and, in certain circumstances, on airlines "visiting" the poorer regions of the world. Why should this be so? And what are the implications for CRM training? Pending detailed investigation, one can only speculate as to the answer. Though risky, I believe that there is merit—in the context of this discussion—in such speculation. These speculations are advanced in the form of four loosely formed hypotheses.

1. That the underlying causes of human factor accidents will vary across the regions of the world—with a distinct division between developed and emerging nations.
2. That the correlation between socio-politico-economic factors and accidents in the less-developed regions of the world hides a number of distinct influences. First is an absence of investment in infrastructure and training, second a lack of regulatory expertise and independent monitoring of operators, and third a lack of suitable corporate and operational management expertise.
3. That, collectively, these tend to militate against remedial/preventive system safety action.
4. Where there is a marked asymmetry in the incidence of accidents, aspects of the prevailing culture (e.g., high power distance, low individualism) will be found to combine with socio-politico-economic deficiencies so as to actively conspire against effective long-term remedial action.

The key point here is that the codification of human factor accidents is normally shaped by causal categorizations determined in the developed world. These tend, in turn, to drive our inferences as to the required remedial action. However, if my hypotheses are even approximately accurate, it would be risky and presumptuous to apply an expensive "CRM solution" without paying attention to underlying factors. While CRM training has an important role to play, in some cases the critical air safety investment may be elsewhere. This is both a caution and plea for more research.

CONCLUSION ✈

Determining CRM training needs and requirements must start with the reality of cockpit practices, pilot attitudes, and procedural adherence as they exist within the relevant airline and culture. A culturally sensitive "problem definition" should be supplemented by a specification of desired training goals and operational outcomes. It will be necessary to attend to naturally occurring cultural strengths and weaknesses, noting their impact on cockpit management. Pilot attitudinal dispositions and practices—the operational sub-culture—will also be highly relevant. Unfortunately, this approach to the problem of cultural relativism merely replaces one problem with an even bigger one! For who is to diagnose the specific CRM training needs of specific cultures and airlines? And by what yardstick can one assess and measure effective crew functioning?

These are really questions for the research community, though considerable information is already available (FAA, 1989; Foushee & Helmreich, 1988; Helmreich, Chidester, Foushee, Gregorich, & Wilhelm, 1989; Jensen, 1987; Orlady & Foushee, 1987; Oser, McCallum, Salas, & Morgan, 1989). The NASA/University of Texas research team led by Professor R. L. Helmreich is intimately involved in assessing these issues. Researchers at the U.S. Naval Training Systems Center are among those reporting steady progress in determining the essentials of effective team building (Glickman, Zimmer, Montero, Guerette, Campbell, Morgan, & Salas, 1987; Salas, Dickson, Converse, & Tannenbaum, 1992). Most CRM research is based in the United States, though Ooi (1991) and Lester (in progress) report current research into cross-cultural aspects of CRM.

Notwithstanding legitimate concerns, there has to be a point at which academic and research issues are disregarded and practical action is initiated. This is not to deny the existence of real uncertainties and problems. However, for most aviation industry training we ultimately rely on the insights and skills of highly experienced operational personnel, often aided by external specialists. Even in the face of apparently intractable cultural uncertainties, in many countries a prudent and operationally well-informed team of specialists can anticipate success when developing CRM training. The essential elements will be management commitment, sufficient development time, and a fair measure of insight into the nature of the prevailing cultural and sub-cultural imperatives. The objective throughout must be to support and sustain cultural strengths while simultaneously moving to ameliorate the negative impact of cultural mores on flight safety.

In concluding, it must be observed that however alien and exotic the cross-cultural sentiments expressed above may appear to the reader, they do not reduce to sophistry or idle academic musings. Consider, for instance, the cultural and mental world occupied by the cockpit crew of a B-747 at Seoul airport in 1980 who "chose to die in the burning airplane after a landing short accident" (T. Ueda, personal communication, September, 1991). There *are* fundamental cultural issues which must be addressed if CRM is to prove globally successful. Perhaps the most daunting problems are the absence of research and suitable specialist expertise to guide those across the various cultural regions of the world who wish to develop effective CRM courses. However, for all the potential problems, CRM remains an essential component of our operational defences, and *effective* CRM must always remain a high priority—regardless of one's cultural point of origin.

Acknowledgments

I thank the numerous colleagues who reviewed drafts of this chapter. There are too many to list individually, though special mention is due to Nick McDonald, Patrick Lester, and Captains Oscar Elizalde Alcorta, Daniel Mauriño, Harry Orlady, Hans Sypkens, and Tsuneo Ueda for their detailed and highly constructive comments. I am also obliged to Captain Paul Russell of the Boeing Aircraft Company, Captain Heino Caesar, and Professor Geert Hofstede for providing various illustrations and observations. My thanks also go to the editors. Their comments and suggestions greatly improved early drafts of this chapter. I would particularly like to acknowledge the efforts and contribution of those respondents who do not have English as their first language.

References

Adler, N. J. (1990). *International dimensions of organizational behaviour.* New York: P.W.S. Publishing Company.

Amir, Y., & Sharon, I. (1987). Are social psychological laws cross-culturally valid? *Journal of Cross-Cultural Psychology, 18,* 383–470.

Barnett, A., & Higgins, M. K. (1989). Airline safety: The last decade. *Management Science, 35,* 1–21.

Berger, P. L., & Luckmann, T. (1966). *The social construction of reality.* Harmondsworth, England: Penguin.

Black, J. S., & Mendenhall, M. (1990). Cross-cultural training effectiveness: A review and a theoretical framework for future research. *Academy of Management Review, 15,* 113–136.

Boeing Commercial Aircraft Company. (1990, October). Cockpit management techniques. *Boeing Flight Operations Safety Seminar, Paris.* Seattle, WA: Author.

Bond, M. H. (Ed.). (1988a). *The cross-cultural challenge to social psychology.* San Francisco, CA: Sage.

Bond, M. H. (1988b). Finding universal dimensions of individual variation in multicultural studies of values. *Journal of Personality and Social Psychology, 55,* 1009–1015.

Bontempo, R. N. (in press). Cultural differences in decision making. *Commentary: Special issue on judgment and decision making.* Singapore: National University.

Brown, R. J. (1987). Swatch vs. the sundial: A study in different attitudes towards time. *International Management, 42*(12), 80.

Cannon-Bowers, J. A., Salas E., & Converse, S. A. (1990). Cognitive psychology and team training: Training shared mental models of complex systems. *Human Factors Society Bulletin, 33,* 1–4.

Cole, M. (1984). The world beyond our borders. *American Psychologist, 39,* 998–1005.

Cooper, G. E., White, M. D., & Lauber, J. K. (Eds.). (1979). *Resource management on the flight deck* (NASA Conference Publication 2120). Moffett Field, CA: NASA–Ames Research Center.

Copeland, L., & Griggs, L. (1986). Getting the best from foreign employees. *Management Review, 75*(6), 19–26.

Davidson, J. (1987). Introduction to Trans Australia Airlines CRM training. In H. W. Orlady & H. C. Foushee (Eds.), *Cockpit resource management training* (NASA Conference Publication 2455) (pp. 88–89). Moffett Field, CA: NASA–Ames Research Center.

Degani, A., & Wiener, E. L. (1991). Philosophy, policies and procedures: The three P's of flightdeck operations. In *Proceedings of the Sixth International Symposium on Aviation Psychology* (pp. 184–191). Columbus: Ohio State University.

Does the left know what the right is doing? (1991, November). *Feedback*, Farnborough, England: CHIRP, Royal Air Force Institute of Aviation Medicine.

Evans, W. A., Sculli, D., & Hau, K. C. (1989). Cross-cultural factors in the identification of managerial potential. *Journal of General Management, 13*, 52–59.

Federal Aviation Administration. (1989). *Cockpit resource management training* (Advisory Circular 120–51). Washington, DC: Author.

Federal Aviation Administration. (1991). *Advanced qualification program* (Advisory Circular 120–54). Washington, DC: Author.

Foushee, H. C. (1982). The role of communications, socio-psychological, and personality factors in the maintenance of crew co-ordination. *Aviation, Space and Environmental Medicine, 53*, 1062–1066.

Foushee, H. C. (1984). Dyads and triads at 35,000 feet: Factors affecting group process and aircrew performance. *American Psychologist, 39*, 885–893.

Foushee, H. C., & Helmreich, R. L. (1988). Group interaction and flight crew performance. In E. L. Wiener & D. C. Nagel (Eds.), *Human factors in aviation* (pp. 189–227). San Diego, CA: Academic Press.

Foushee, H. C., & Manos, K. L. (1981). Information transfer within the cockpit: Problems in intracockpit communications. In C. E. Billings & E. S. Cheaney (Eds.), *Information transfer problems in the aviation system* (NASA Technical Paper 1875) (pp. 63–71). Moffett Field, CA: NASA–Ames Research Center.

Glickman, A. S., Zimmer, S., Montero, R. C., Guerette, P. J., Campbell, W. J., Morgan, B. J., & Salas, E. (1987). *The evolution of teamwork skills: An empirical assessment with implications for training* (Technical Report 87-016). Orlando, FL: Naval Training Systems Center, Human Factors Division.

Gudykunst, W. B., Yoon, Y., & Nishida, T. (1987). The influence of individualism–collectivism on perceptions of communication in ingroup and outgroup relationships. *Communication Monographs, 54*, 295–306.

Guptara, P., & Murray, K. (1990). The art of training abroad. *Training and Development Journal, 44*, 13–18.

Hackman, J. R. (1987). Group-level issues in the design and training of cockpit crews. In H. W. Orlady & H. C. Foushee (Eds.), *Cockpit resource management training* (NASA Conference Publication 2455). Moffett Field, CA: NASA–Ames Research Center.

Hackman, J. R., & Helmreich, R. L. (1984). *Assessing the behaviour and performance of teams in organisations: The case of air transport crews* (Tech Report #5). New Haven, CT: Yale School of Organization and Management.

Harms, D. (1988). *Ab initio* training at Bremen. In *Report of the 7th General Flight Training Meeting, New Orleans*. Montreal: International Air Transport Association.

Harris, J. R., & Muir, H. C. (1986). *Leadership on the flight deck: The influence of crew social relations and crew member experience on leadership style effectiveness in civil aviation flight crews*. Summary Report. Cranfield, England: Cranfield Institute of Technology, Applied Psychology Unit.

Hawking, S. W. (1988). *A brief history of time*. New York: Bantam.

Helmreich, R. L., Chidester, T. R., Foushee, H. C., Gregorich, S., & Wilhelm, J. A. (1989). *Critical issues in implementing and reinforcing cockpit resource management training* (NASA/UT Technical Report 89-5). Austin: University of Texas.

Hofstede, G. (1980a). *Culture's consequences: International differences in work-related values.*

Beverly Hills, CA: Sage.

Hofstede, G. (1980b, Summer). Motivation, leadership and organizations: Do American theories apply abroad? *Organizational Dynamics*, 42–63.

Hofstede, G. (1983, Fall). The cultural relativity of organizational practices and theories. *Journal of International Business Studies*, 75–89.

Hofstede, G. (1984, January). Cultural dimensions in management and planning. *Asia Pacific Journal of Management*, 81–99.

Hofstede, G. (1991). *Cultures and organizations: Software of the mind.* Maidenhead, England: McGraw-Hill.

Hui, C. H., & Triandis, H. C. (1986). Individualism–collectivism: A study of cross-cultural researchers. *Journal of Cross-Cultural Psychology, 17,* 225–248.

Hynes, M. K. (1990). Administrative considerations of the management of cockpit resources (pilots) in the complex labor relationship environment of the 1990's. *ISASI Forum Proceedings,* pp. 26–34.

International Civil Aviation Organization. (1989a). *Human factors digest No. 1: Fundamental human factors concepts* (Circular 216-AN/131). Montreal: Author.

International Civil Aviation Organization. (1989b). *Human factors digest No. 2: Flight crew training: Cockpit resource management and line-oriented flight training* (Circular 217-AN/132). Montreal: Author.

International Civil Aviation Organization. (1991). *Human factors digest No. 3: Training of operational personnel in human factors* (Circular 227-AN/136). Montreal: Author.

Irwin, C. (1985). Inuit navigation, empirical reasoning and survival. *Journal of Navigation, 38,* 178–190.

Jahoda, G. (1986). Nature, culture and psychology. *European Journal of Social Psychology, 16,* 17–30.

Jahoda, G. (1988). J'Accuse. In: M. H. Bond (Ed.), *The cross-cultural challenge to social psychology.* San Francisco, CA: Sage.

Jensen, R. S. (1987). *Cockpit resource management training* (Final Report, Contract No. DTFA01-80-C-10080). Arlington, VA: Systems Control Technology, Inc.

Johnston, A. N. (1986). Organizational and motivational aspects of air carrier pilot decision making. In *Proceedings of the Third International Pilot Decision Making conference* (pp. 36–57). Ottawa: Transport Canada.

Johnston, A. N. (1989). A review of airline sponsored *ab initio* pilot training in Europe. In *Proceedings of the Fifth International Symposium on Aviation Psychology* (pp. 33–38). Columbus: Ohio State University.

Johnston, A. N. (1991). *An Introduction to APT.* Dublin, Ireland: Aer Lingus Training Document.

Johnston, A. N., & Mauriño, D. (1990, May). Human factors training for aviation personnel. *ICAO Journal,* 16–19.

Kaplan, M. (1991). Issues in cultural ergonomics. In J. A. Wise, V. D. Hopkin, & M. L. Smith (Eds.), *Automation and systems issues in air traffic control.* Heidelberg: Springer-Verlag.

Kohn, M. L. (Ed.). (1989). *Cross-National Research in Sociology.* London: Sage.

Lautman, L. G., & Gallimore, P. L. (1987, April–June). Control of the crew caused accident. *Boeing Airliner,* pp. 1–6. Seattle, WA: Boeing Commercial Aircraft Company.

Lave, J. (1988). *Cognition in practice: Mind, mathematics and culture in everyday life.* Cambridge University Press.

Lave, J., & Wenger, E. (1991). *Situated Learning.* Cambridge, England: Cambridge University Press.

Learmount, D. (1991, November). Small airlines less safe. *Flight International, 140,* p. 8.

Lester, P. T. (in preparation). *A multi-national study of pilot attitudes and values.* Unpublished manuscript, University of Hawaii.

Leung, K., & Bond, M. H. (1989). On the empirical identification of dimensions for cross-cultural comparisons. *Journal of Cross-Cultural Psychology, 20,* 133–151.

Lonner, W. J. (1979). Perspectives on cross-cultural psychology. In A. J. Marshella, R. G. Tharp, & T. P. Ciborowski (Eds.), *Perspectives in cross-cultural psychology* (pp. 17–45). New York: Academic Press.

Lonner, W. J. (1987). Introduction to the special issue. *Journal of Cross-Cultural Psychology, 18*(4), 379–382.

Mann, L. (1980). Cross-cultural studies of small groups. In *Handbook of cross-cultural psychology* (Vol. 4, pp. 155–209). Boston: Allyn and Bacon.

Mann, L. (1988). Cross-cultural studies of small groups. In M. H. Bond (Ed.), *The cross-cultural challenge to social psychology.* San Francisco, CA: Sage.

Margerison, C. J., McCann, R., & Davies, R. (1987). Aircrew team management program. In H. W. Orlady & H. C. Foushee (Eds.), *Cockpit resource management training* (NASA Conference Publication 2455) (pp. 90–107). Moffett Field, CA: NASA–Ames Research Center.

Margerison, C., McCann, R., & Davies, R. (1988). Air-crew team management development. *Journal of Management Development, 7,* 41–54.

Miller, J. G. (1988). Bridging the content–structure dichotomy: Culture and the self. In M. H. Bond (Ed.), *The cross-cultural challenge to social psychology.* San Francisco, CA: Sage.

Misumi, J., & Peterson, M. F. (1985). The performance–maintenance (P–M) theory of leadership. *Administrative science quarterly, 30,* 198–223.

Moghaddam, F. M. (1987). Psychology in three worlds. *American Psychologist, 42,* 912–920.

Murphy, M. R. (1980). Analysis of eighty-four commercial aviation incidents: Implications for a resource management approach to crew training. In *Proceedings of the Annual Reliability and Maintainability Symposium* (pp. 298–306).

Nooij, G. J. N. (1985). Implementing non-technical skills: A cultural problem. In *Report of the XVIth Conference of the Western European Association for Aviation-Psychology.* Helsinki: Finnair Training Center.

Ooi, T. S. (1991). *Cultural influences on flight operations.* Paper presented at the SAS Flight Academy International Training Conference, Stockholm, Sweden.

Orlady, H. W., & Foushee, H. C. (Eds.). (1987). *Cockpit resource management training* (NASA Conference Publication 2455). Moffett Field, CA: NASA–Ames Research Center.

Oser, R., McCallum, G. A., Salas, E., & Morgan, B. B. (1989). *Toward a definition of teamwork: An analysis of critical team behaviours* (Technical Report 89-004). Orlando, FL: Naval Training Systems Center, Human Factors Division.

Pascale, R. (1985). The paradox of "Corporate Culture": Reconciling ourselves to socialization. *California Management Review, 27,* 26–41.

Payer, L. (1988). *Medicine and culture.* New York: Henry Holt.

Pepitone, A., & Triandis, H. C. (1987). On the universality of social psychological theories. *Journal of Cross Cultural Psychology, 18,* 471–498.

Peters, T. S., & Waterman, R. H. (1982). *In search of excellence.* New York: Harper and Row.

Pun, A. S. L. (1990). Managing the cultural differences in learning. *Journal of Management Development, 9*(5), 35–40.

Redding, S. G., & Ogilvie, J. G. (1984). Cultural effects on cockpit communications in civilian aircraft. *Flight Safety Foundation Conference, Zurich.* Washington, DC: Flight Safety Foundation.

Rieger, F., & Wong-Rieger, D. (1988). Model building in organizational/cross-cultural research: The need for multiple methods, indices, and cultures. *International Studies of Management and Organisation, 18,* 19–30.

Roberts, J. M., Golder, T. V., & Chick, G. E. (1980). Judgement, oversight and skill: A cultural analysis of P-3 pilot error. *Human Organization, 39,* 5–21.

Ruffell Smith, H. P. (1979). *A simulator study of the interaction of pilot workload with errors, vigilance, and decisions* (NASA Technical Memorandum 78482). Moffett Field, CA: NASA–Ames Research Center.

Salas, E., Dickson, T. L., Converse, S. A., & Tannenbaum, S. I. (1992). Towards an understanding of team performance and training. In R. Swezey & E. Salas (Eds.), *Teams: Their training and performance.* Norwood, NJ: Ablex.

Schein, E. H., (1990). Organizational culture. *American Psychologist, 45,* 109–119.

Schwartz, S. H. (in press). *Toward a universal content and structure of values: Extensions and cross-cultural replications.* Jerusalem, Israel: Hebrew University.

Schwartz, S. H., & Bilsky, W. (1987). Toward a universal structure of human values. *Journal of Personality and Social Psychology, 53,* 550–562.

Scott-Milligan, F., and Wyness, B. S. (1987). Cockpit resource management: An antipodean view. In *Proceedings of the Fourth International Symposium on Aviation Psychology* (pp. 379–383). Columbus: Ohio State University.

Senders, J. W., & Moray, N. P. (1991). *Human error: Cause, prediction, and reduction.* Hillsdale, NJ: Erlbaum.

Sharon, I., & Amir, Y. (1988). Cross-cultural replications: A prerequisite for the validation of social psychological laws. In M. H. Bond (Ed.), *The cross-cultural challenge to social psychology.* San Francisco, CA: Sage.

Smith, P. B. (in press). Organizational behaviour and national cultures. *British Journal of Management.*

Smith, P. B., Misumi, J., Tayeb, M., Peterson, M., & Bond, M. (1989). On the generality of leadership type measures across cultures. *Journal of Occupational Psychology, 62,* 97–109.

Smith, P. B., & Peterson, M. F. (1988). *Leadership, organizations and culture.* London: Sage.

Smith, P. B., & Tayeb, M. (1988). Organizational structure and processes. In M. H. Bond (Ed.), *The cross-cultural challenge to social psychology.* San Francisco, CA: Sage.

Stoller, G. (1990, July). The world's safest airlines. *Condé Nast Traveler,* pp. 80–88.

Swierczek, F. W. (1988). Culture and training: How do they play away from home? *Training and Development Journal, 42,* 74–80.

Tanaka, Y., & Gakushuin, U. (1973). Toward a multi-level, multi-stage model of modernization: A cross-cultural social-psychology approach. *International Journal of Psychology. 8,* 205–214.

Taylor, L. (1988). *Air travel: How safe is it?* London: BSP Professional Books.

Triandis, H. C. (Ed.). (1980). Introduction to Volume 1. *Handbook of cross-cultural psychology.* Boston: Allyn and Bacon.

Trollip, S. R., & Jensen, R. S. (1991). *Human factors for general aviation.* Englewood, Colorado: Jeppesen Sanderson.

Vandermark, M. J. (1991). Should flight attendants be included in CRM training? A discussion of a major air carrier's approach to total crew training. *International Journal of Aviation Psychology, 1,* 89–94.

Vertinsky, I., Tse, D. K., Wehrung, D. A., & Lee, K. (1990). Organizational design and management norms: A comparative study of managers perceptions in the People's Republic of China, Hong Kong and Canada. *Journal of Management, 16,* 853–867.

Vonnegut, K. (1972). *Slaughterhouse 5.* London: Jonathan Cape.

Wasserman, D., Lempert, R. O., & Hastie, R. (1990). *Hindsight and causality.* Boulder, CO: University of Colorado, Center for Research on Judgment and Policy.

Weener, E. F. (1990). Control of crew-caused accidents: The sequel. *Boeing flight operations regional safety seminar, New Orleans.* Seattle: Boeing Commercial Aircraft Company.

Wheale, J. L. (1984). *A preliminary survey of crew co-ordination and personal interaction on the flight deck of commercial transport aircraft* (Divisional Record BSD/F/4). Farnborough, England: Royal Air Force Institute of Aviation Medicine.

White, G., & Baker, L. J. V., (1991). Inappropriate functioning of the cockpit dominance hierarchy as a factor in approach/landing accidents. In *Proceedings of the Sixth International Symposium on Aviation Psychology* (pp. 706–711). Columbus: Ohio State University.

Whorf, B. L. (1956). Science and Linguistics. In J. B. Carroll (Ed.), *Language, thought and reality: Selected writings of Benjamin Lee Whorf.* Cambridge, MA: MIT Press.

Wilkins, A. L. (1984). The creation of company cultures: The role of stories and human resource systems. *Human Resource Management, 23,* 41–60.

Wolfe, T. (1979). *The right stuff.* New York: Farrar, Straus and Giroux.

Yamamori, H. (1987). Optimum culture in the cockpit. In H. W. Orlady & H. C. Foushee (Eds.), *Cockpit resource management training* (NASA Conference Publication 2455) (pp. 75–87). Moffett Field, CA: NASA–Ames Research Center.

Keeping CRM Is Keeping the Flight Safe

Hisaaki Yamamori
Takao Mito
Japan Airlines
Tokyo International Airport
Haneda Ota-ku, Tokyo 144, Japan

INTRODUCTION ✈

It has been over 30 years since the aviation industry entered the jet age. Japan Airlines put their first DC-8 jetliner into service between Tokyo and San Francisco in August, 1960. In order to learn valuable lessons from our experience in the jet age, our Flight Safety Department has examined the records of accidents and incidents experienced in the past three decades in terms of the trend and nature of these occurrences. This work resulted in our being able to pick out 10 safety fundamentals pertaining to human factors that underlie the causes of many accidents and incidents.

These fundamentals were called the Safety Ten (Figure 14.1), and they were the catalyst for our Flight Operations Department to develop a safety campaign effective from April, 1990, through December, 1991. These 10 items are not unique, but rather common. However, the theme of this campaign was the challenge of developing them into instrumental planning.

"Keeping CRM Is Keeping the Flight Safe" was selected as the top item of the Safety Ten because lack of cockpit resource management (CRM) was seen in most of the incidents and accidents examined. This verified to us that CRM is the most essential factor in keeping the flight safe. Let us now describe the Japan Airlines CRM seminar.

Since 1986, 2,300 crewmembers have attended the CRM seminar at Japan Airlines. Our report is based on the results from those crewmembers who have completed the CRM seminar. Our CRM objectives are:

1. Getting the crew to work together as a team under all circumstances.
2. Getting crewmembers to understand how they communicate with one another.
3. Understanding the process of decision-making and CRM.

"SAFETY TEN"

1. **KEEPING CRM IS KEEPING THE FLIGHT SAFE.**
2. SOP IS ABC.
3. BE COOL, IN NO HURRY AND NO HASTE!
4. A WISE MAN NEVER COURTS DANGER.
5. MONITOR THE INSTRUMENTS AND THE OUTSIDE!
6. WHEN IN DOUBT, SPEAK OUT!
7. ONE MAN'S FAULT IS ANOTHER'S LESSON.
8. FIXATION LEADS TO TUNNEL VISION.
9. EVEN A GOOD AIRMAN MAKES A MISTAKE.
10. CHECKLISTS ARE ANCHORS OF SAFETY.

Figure 14.1 *"Safety Ten".* Motonari Mohri, A Samurai general, conquered the whole western part of Japan in the mid-16th century, the age of civil strife, though he had been only a native Samurai leader in Aki state (the current Hiroshima Prefecture). In the rivalry of local Samurai leaders he felt a sense of crisis in governing his country, which had grown too fast, and he asked his three sons to band together against their enemies like a bundle of three arrows, which he demonstrated couldn't fail. His teaching of "three arrows" was handed down to posterity as his family precept. The legend seems to tell us the importance of cockpit resource management, which Motonari would agree with if he were in the aviation world today.

In initiating a unique human factors-based training program at Japan Airlines, we decided that a frame of reference was needed. We used the Grid® theory, which was developed by Scientific Methods, Inc., as a basis of understanding and identifying cockpit behavior (Blake & Mouton, 1982; Blake, Mouton, & United Airlines, 1990).

In order to utilize the human resources available and the leadership required for cockpit effectiveness, it is necessary to recognize the different styles of interpersonal relationships and the effects that those styles have on the actions of other crewmembers. The Grid was developed as the frame of reference because it is a method of learning that is easy to understand. The ultimate goal is to understand how the behavior of each crewmember influences cockpit effectiveness. This framework provides a basis for understanding differences between people and a means to comprehend how and why individuals behave as they do (see also Blake & Mouton, 1968, 1983; Carroll & Taggart, 1987; Mouton & Blake, 1984).

THE GRID FRAMEWORK ⟶ ✦

One reason we selected the CRM training program was its use of the Grid. We found that other researchers, such as Robert Helmreich (1980), proposed a similar "dimensions" theory. Helmreich states that group and individual reactions can be divided into goal orientation and group orientation. Another characteristic of Helmreich's theory that is similar to the Grid is that these two dimensions are orthogonal, that is, a high score on one dimension does not necessarily mean a low score on the other.

Whenever a crewmember thinks about his responsibilities, at least two basic considerations are involved. One is degree of concern for performance. He must have some concern for actual flying performance, safety, and other aspects of flight. Performance can be visualized on a 9-point scale on a horizontal axis, where 9 represents high concern for performance and 1 low concern for performance. The second consideration is the crewmember's degree of concern for people, those with whom the crewmember interacts in his work activities. Concern for people is also rated on a 9-point scale, again with 9 showing high concern and 1 low concern.

These two concerns make up the Grid framework, as depicted in Figure 14.2 (Blake, Mouton, & United Airlines, 1990, p. 20). Grid makes possible the study of the different ways in which these two concerns interact with one another. The four corners and the midpoint represent five theoretical types of thinking about resolving dilemmas in achieving production through people.

Within the Grid framework, 81 different positions can be identified, but there are five clear-cut, straightforward fundamental positions, corresponding to the plots (1,1), (5,5), (9,1), (1,9), and (9,9). The numbers 1 to 9 on the indices represent low and high degrees of concern and do not represent specific amounts. The first digit always represents the horizontal axis (concern for performance), and the second the vertical (concern for people). This theory provides a solid basis for understanding the available alternatives.

The (9,1) position on the Grid represents the thinking of a person who has high concern for performance and low concern for people. The (9,1) approach is a "tough," authority-obedience type of leadership. People are viewed as tools of

---

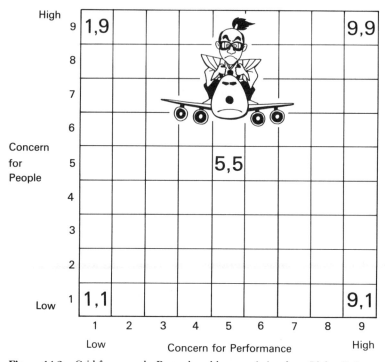

Figure 14.2   Grid framework. Reproduced by permission from Blake, Robert R., and Mouton, Jane S. (Scientific Methods, Inc.) and Command/ Leadership/Resource Management Steering Committee and Working Groups (United Airlines), *Grid Cockpit Resource Management* (2nd ed.), p. 20. Copyright © 1990 by Scientific Methods, Inc.

production, not contributing beings who can be called upon to think or solve problems. Communication tends to be one-way, and incoming communication is expected to indicate compliance.

At the (1,9) position, low concern for performance is joined with high concern for people, just the opposite of the (9,1) approach. The (1,9) orientation emphasizes the overriding importance of good relations. Communication is at the very heart of good relationships. Discussion does not need to be work-related.

Low interest in performance in the (1,1) approach is coupled with equally low interest in people. A (1,1)–oriented crewmember is thought of as staying on the job in order to go on to retirement. Communication tends to be on a message-passing basis.

In a (5,5)–oriented approach, an individual adjusts to the system and to the comfortable tempos that others have come to adopt. This crewmember does not push for better results even though the results obtained are less than what might have been accomplished by a different approach. Communication techniques such as compromise, accommodation, and adjustment are used to resolve differences in ways that avoid conflict.

The (9,9) theory shows a person who has high concern for performance fused with high concern for people. This synergistic result of the two brings about a different approach, getting better results than other Grid styles. The (9,9) approach to crew leadership is based on involvement, participation, and commitment. Communication is an open, candid, and free exchange between crewmembers. No one needs to be on guard in order to avoid risking misunderstanding by the others.

Figure 14.3 depicts the five fundamental styles on the Grid framework. Whether or not they know their Grid styles, crewmembers apply one of these approaches or a combination of them every time they speak to a captain, colleague, or subordinate. At the time they may, of course, be unaware of this; their actions may be so ingrained or habitual that they perform without a moment's introspection.

A major reason for crewmembers to learn the Grid is to clarify the ap-

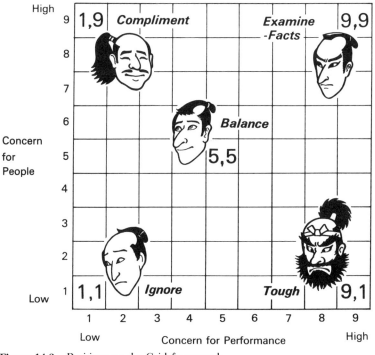

Figure 14.3 Positions on the Grid framework.

proaches they have been using, as contrasted with others that might provide a sounder and stronger basis for our actions. This enables them to test their natural inclinations against behavioral scientific findings.

Sound Cockpit Teamwork

The first topic of the CRM seminar is how a cockpit should operate in order to function in a truly professional manner. There are eight items concerning cockpit management, behavior, and performance.

1. Captain's authority
2. First officer and flight engineer roles and responsibilities
3. Training and development
4. Inquiry
5. Advocacy
6. Conflict
7. Problem definition
8. Critique

Problems associated with each item can be approached in a variety of ways. Five possible approaches corresponding to the five Grid alternatives are described in the course. For example, Figure 14.4 refers to captain's authority.

Alternatives are chosen according to what participants think would be sound practice in an effective cockpit. For each item, participants rank the alternative that represents the soundest way to operate a cockpit as a 5. A rank of 4 is placed by that alternative which is the best back-up in case the soundest choice is not available. The remaining alternatives are ranked as well, with 1 marking that alternative which is the least acceptable method of operating in a cockpit.

The focus of this activity is on values, with the team being aided to think through the soundest way for teamwork to take place in the cockpit.

Each alternative must be used in order to broaden the choices of considerations that make available a full range of possible actions. If, for each of the 8 items, the answers chosen as the most sound are the ones representing the same Grid style, the score for that style is the maximum 40 points (5 points × 8 items). If the answers chosen for each of the 8 items are the least sound for the same Grid style, the score for that style is the minimum 8 points (1 point × 8 items). Since each item is ranked 1–5, the total points for each item always sum to 15.

Figure 14.5 indicates that at Japan Airlines, regardless of crew composition, captains, including foreign International Air Service Company (IASCO) pilots, first officers, and flight engineers (second officers) all agree that the (9,9) orientation represents the soundest style of cockpit management. The (5,5) orientation of cockpit management was chosen as the second best, while the (1,1) approach was selected as the least sound for operating a crew.

SOUNDEST		ACTUAL
A_____	The Captain seeks to establish a warm and friendly atmosphere in the cockpit. This minimizes the need to exercise authority. Agreements come in an easy way since there is cohesion among crew members.	A_____
B_____	The Captain exercises authority so as to maintain a balance between the needs for effective performance and the desires of other crew members. He retains responsibility for ultimate decisions but understands that it is important to take the views of others into account.	B_____
C_____	The Captain makes effective use of authority by directing the effort in such a manner as to maximize crew involvement and participation. In this way he gains the use of all available resources toward the objective of excellence. When time is a critical factor, he does not hesitate to decide or choose a course of action.	C_____
D_____	The Captain rarely exercises authority as for the most part the flight operates itself. Other crew members offer relevant information if necessary.	D_____
E_____	The Captain feels accountable only to himself. Since the responsibility is his, he expects his decisions to be accepted as final. He asks for information from the other crew members only when necessary.	E_____

Figure 14.4   How should a cockpit operate with respect to the captain's authority?

		9,9	9,1	5,5	1,9	1,1
Captain	Japanese	40.0	21.7	28.6	19.6	10.1
	Foreigner (IASCO)	40.0	19.2	28.9	21.0	10.9
First Officer		40.0	19.4	29.3	20.7	10.6
Flight Engineer (2nd Officer)		40.0	19.6	28.7	21.3	10.4

Figure 14.5   Seminar participant scores for least to most sound (range 8–40).

In our CRM seminar, participants are also asked to assess the same eight items according to their sense of how they actually operate on a typical day-to-day operational basis. Again, they are asked to arrange all the items in order from *most* (5) to *least* (1). Data from our CRM seminar results show that the actual cockpit environment is far different from what is agreed to be the soundest cockpit environment. Comparing Figure 14.6 with Figure 14.5 shows that actual cockpit culture does not attain the ideal (9,9) cockpit culture, but is better than the least desirable (1,1) style of management.

This indicates that the theory is not being put into practice. The (9,9) style of cockpit management which CRM participants agree is the most effective style is rarely seen in the actual conditions of flight operation. Revealing these data causes seminar participants to consider what must be done to strengthen their own performance and the cockpit environment if excellent professional results are to be achieved.

Through CRM seminars, participants learn to recognize the weaknesses of their culture and to provide constructive methods to make it possible to create an ideal, (9,9)-style cockpit culture. When the attitudes and thinking of an ideal culture can be seen in contrast to those that actually exist, conditions are favorable for change.

Comparing Style of Performance Values

The next CRM topic of concern is what crewmembers see as the best way to solve problems with other crewmembers. Forty situations are described. Each situation is followed by two alternatives; each Grid style is paired with each of the others. The cockpit managerial behavior described involves crewmembers' in-

		9,9	9,1	5,5	1,9	1,1
Captain	Japanese	33.1	18.9	28.9	22.9	16.2
	Foreigner (IASCO)	30.5	20.5	28.5	22.7	17.8
First Officer		26.5	22.1	29.4	22.5	19.5
Flight Engineer (2nd Officer)		27.9	19.9	29.7	24.0	18.5

Figure 14.6 Seminar participant scores for actual operation.

teractions in planning, organizing, directing, and controlling the behavioral aspects. The example in Figure 14.7 shows 2 of the 40 questions.

A participant shows his preference by weighing each alternative against the other on a 3–0, 2–1, 1–2, or 0–3 basis. Each participant selects the answer he prefers as representing the more effective way to manage. The highest score available for any Grid style statement is 48 points, the lowest 0.

Figure 14.8 shows that captains including foreigners (IASCO), first officers, and flight engineers (second officers) prefer the (9,9) theory most. The (5,5) style is preferred second, and the other preferences in order are (9,1), (1,9), and (1,1).

In evaluating the cultural aspects of a cockpit, the CRM seminar first achieved agreement on what would be the soundest cockpit culture. When complex aspects of cockpit management are evaluated, the (9,9) cockpit orientation is endorsed as the theory that makes the most productive use of a cockpit's crewmembers.

Gap Lecture

In the last part of the CRM seminar, participants are given feedback on the performance values and Grid styles to compare results between the pre- and post-

---

A Captain can reduce resistance to authority by

A___ emphasizing the positive aspects of authority to crew members.

B___ moving with extreme caution to avoid disrupting the routine.

A Co-pilot or Flight Engineer should

A___ realize that since the Captain has sole responsibility for the flight, he should not contribute his opinions unless asked.

B___ maximize overall performance of the flight by active participation and input to the operation.

Figure 14.7 Sample situations: What is the best problem-solving style in a cockpit?

		9,9	9,1	5,5	1,9	1,1
Captain	Japanese	41.9	21.9	30.7	19.3	6.2
	Foreigner (IASCO)	42.2	23.4	29.2	18.8	6.4
First Officer		42.0	19.4	30.7	20.4	7.5
Flight Engineer (2nd Officer)		42.6	21.1	30.3	18.7	7.3

Average of all crewmembers
who believe the 9,9 value   **42.2**   (42.2 out of total possible 48 is 88%)

Figure 14.8   Seminar participant scores for preference Grid theory (range 0–48).

seminar data. One part of the data summation is to gain a new perspective on the values one holds toward performance that affects the action of the other crewmembers.

According to seminars held throughout Japan Airlines, pre-seminar data results show that 76% of the participants believe the (9,9) performance value is the most effective style. However, at the end of the seminar, new insight has been gained by each participant who re-assesses his performance values. The post-seminar data results show an increase to 87% for those who believe the (9,9) value is the most effective (see Figure 14.9). This is a clear indication that cockpit attitude toward effective behavior has been strengthened and crystallized.

Another important issue involves how crews see their own actual behavior

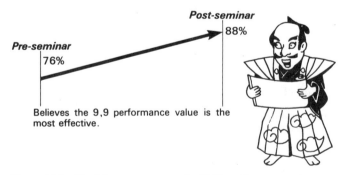

Figure 14.9   Participant assessment for (9.9) performance value pre- and post-seminar.

in the cockpit. This encompasses the issue of self-deception. Unless crewmembers understand and are aware that they may come across to other crewmembers in a way that is less than effective, there is probably not much motivation for behavior change, since the operating assumption of these crewmembers is that they are already as effective as possible. The statistics in Figure 14.10 show that on average 55% of the participants who complete pre-seminar study work believe that their operating style is about as effective as possible. However, at the end of seminar, this percentage drops to less than 18%. This indicates that considerable progress has been made toward stripping away self-deception. The importance of this in the areas of both attitudes and behavior is that at the end of the seminar, attitudes about effective cockpit behavior have been strengthened, while at the same time, a better picture is developed for how each crewmember actually operates in the cockpit.

The greatest significance exists in the fact that while a (9,9) performance

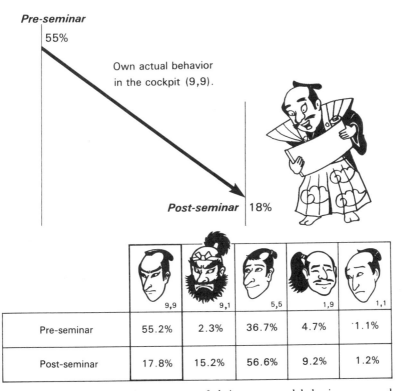

	9,9	9,1	5,5	1,9	1,1
Pre-seminar	55.2%	2.3%	36.7%	4.7%	1.1%
Post-seminar	17.8%	15.2%	56.6%	9.2%	1.2%

Figure 14.10 Participants' assessment of their own actual behavior, pre- and post-seminar.

value shifts upward, in terms of what the individuals regard as the best way to do things, the (9,9) style shifts down, further away from what people actually do. As shown in Figure 14.11, the two-way shift from pre- to post-seminar indicates a greater perception of the gap which exists between the crewmembers' perceived performance value and their actual Grid styles. Thus crewmembers have a greater readiness to face up to the implications of the gap.

The message of this finding is quite important. To improve the safety level, crewmembers must understand and be aware of the large gap between what they should be doing and what they are doing in the cockpit. There must be a willingness and a conscious effort from all crewmembers to close this gap between reality and ideal. After the seminar, almost all crewmembers agree that the (9,9) style has the best performance value. However, this belief does not necessarily carry over to behavior in the cockpit. Why does a crewmember have difficulty performing according to his preferred (9,9) behavior?

A major factor that affects behavior is culture, which includes many influences outside our control. A conceptualization of the total situation is summarized in Lewin's Formula, $B = f(PV \times C)$, where B represents behavior, a function of

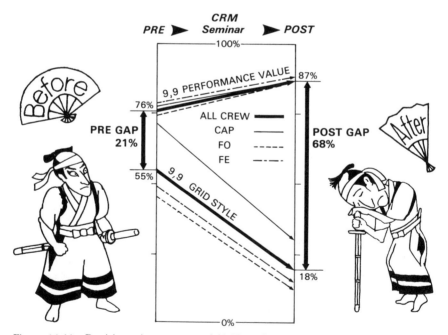

Figure 14.11 Participants' assessment of (9.9) performance value and their own actual behavior, pre- and post-seminar.

Lewin's Formula

$$B = f(P.V \times C)$$

B   : Behavior

P.V : Performance Value

C   : Culture

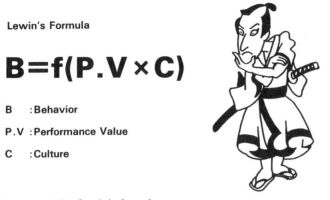

Figure 14.12   Lewin's formula.

the interdependence between performance value (PV) and cultural background (C). (See Figure 14.12.) If a person's cultural background does not agree with his performance value, behavior will be affected. There must be some kind of compromise between performance value and cockpit culture to get the behavioral results that will produce the safest and most efficient working environment in the cockpit. So we must first realize how our culture affects our behavior before we can begin to change our attitude and actions in the cockpit. When everyone in a cockpit crew has an understanding of the behavioral scientific theories of management, a cockpit has the foundation on which to build excellence.

POST-TRAINING QUESTIONS AND ANSWERS ⟶ ➤

After crewmembers have finished their four-day CRM seminar, they have a question-and-answer session. Ever since CRM was introduced as a part of our crew training program, the same questions seem to keep popping up. We have selected for discussion a few of these questions and would like to share them with the reader.

Question 1. Do you think that during some critical phases of the flight, (such as a decision to go or no-go at takeoff, or go-around during final approach), it might be better to exercise a (9,1) style? A frequent misconception is that a direct decisive action taken by an individual is a (9,1) action. However, some crises can be anticipated, and therefore procedures can be planned to handle them. Under such conditions, this would be (9,9)-style leadership, because each person knows the responsibilities he must perform and understands who is to take what action.

If one person initiates an action because he is in the best position to do so, has the experience and competence, and others cannot contribute to relieving the crisis, then this is a single-person (9,9) action. Perhaps the judgment is that there is no time for input in discussion or that the action must be taken by the captain. Such action is not inappropriate and should not be considered (9,1) action. However, it would be highly important for the captain and the rest of the crew to brief each other on the circumstances later and to understand why the action was taken and how in the future such a condition could be spotted earlier. Such a (9,9)-style briefing would help prevent a need for an anomalous action as well as provide greater opportunity for an earlier resolution. The key difference between the two styles is that the (9,1) style has adopted the assumption "I'm right," and therefore no longer involves inquiry, whereas the (9,9) style is still trying to determine "What's right" and in doing so, is using inquiry.

Question 2. This CRM program was developed by the researchers of United Airlines and Scientific Methods, Inc. (UAL/SMI). Despite differences in culture, are you able to successfully adapt a Western-style concept to the Asian way of thinking? From our experience of working with American pilots in the UAL public seminars, we feel that American pilots are more task-oriented than Japanese pilots. Their behavior contrasted with the behavior of Japanese pilots at our seminar in Japan, where the Japanese tended to behave in a more group-oriented fashion. As a result of this observation, we see America as a task-oriented society. Western people seem more aware of themselves as individuals rather than as part of a group. American culture seems to encourage the individual, independent self, while Japanese culture encourages the development of the group-oriented, dependent person.

The Japanese sense of modesty is not seen as a virtue in American culture. In team discussions during CRM seminars, we felt that Americans did not easily accept another person's opinion, whereas Japanese tended to accept a person's opinion, whether right or wrong, in order to preserve harmony within the group. Because they are competitive and tend to view situations in terms of winning or losing, Americans will sometimes aggressively support their own opinion, even if they know they are not entirely correct. In contrast, Japanese will usually become silent and non-supportive of their own ideas if they see some opposition to them. Another important point is that Japanese are often conformists who need to identify with a group. Japanese will rarely try to stand out and be creative in a group situation. This is because we want to achieve a sense of harmony. It is part of our history and our culture. About 1,400 years ago, a famous Japanese prince called Shotoku Taishi said, "Harmony is to be respected." His words and this thought are still in the Japanese mind today.

Of course, the Japanese are also competitive people. However, they differ from Americans in that their competition is directed toward outside groups or organizations. While the Japanese are very competitive toward each other in their own minds, they will never express that competition verbally.

In Japanese society, acceptance is highly valued and is achieved through a person's effort for his group. His efforts, whether useful or not, are seen as having merit and will earn him respect and promotion, even if he has little real ability. Although we saw these differences in our cultures, we realized that, in the cockpit situation, neither the Japanese way of behavior nor the American way is the best way. We do not think that any culture, whether Japanese, American, or any other, fits in with the cockpit environment. In this sense, CRM is culture-free (see also Yamamori, 1987).

There are many situations where authority must be shown in the cockpit. There are also times when cockpit authority must be questioned or challenged. And it is in this type of challenge situation that crewmembers react differently based on their cultural background. Authority is rarely challenged in a group-oriented society. But as we in the airline industry know, this kind of attitude has led to many fatal accidents. On the other hand, in a task-oriented society those in authority may fail to listen to the opinion of others when their authority is challenged. This, too, has led to fatal accidents.

Let us explain this through the use of a Grid. As we said earlier, our feeling is that American pilots are task-oriented and Japanese pilots are mostly group-oriented. Both, of course, have the same goal in mind, the goal of ultimate safety.

Even with the same program and objectives, if the culture is different, there will be different approaches to the goal. However, since the cockpit environment is culture-free, it is not as important to think of a person's cultural background as it is to think of the approach to the goal of ultimate safety. Crewmembers should look at their individual safety goals and compare them to their behavior to see if it matches their own safety goals. One of the objectives of the CRM seminar is to point out to participants the difference between what they believe to be optimal behavior and their actual behavior. Becoming aware of a discrepancy between their actions and their safety goals helps crewmembers change their behavior.

Question 3. Please explain the need for a behavioral change in the cockpit; also, what do you think about the demand for a behavior change-based recurrent training course? First, we would like to explain the need for behavioral change. Let us look at official accident investigation reports that state, "This accident would have been preventable if the crewmembers had been working together more effectively." And "The commission wishes to emphasize that the accident sequence was triggered by the captain's failure to exercise positive flight management." And "Continuing . . . contributing causal factors were the captain's failure to delegate any meaningful responsibilities to the first officer, which resulted in a lack of effective task sharing during the emergency." These statements clearly point out that aviation accidents for the most part can be prevented with better cooperation and a more effective working relationship between crewmembers. The relationship of people working together has a direct effect on safety.

Of course, crewmembers clearly understand the importance of "stick-and-rudder" technical skills, but it is equally important to recognize that resource management skills such as communication and interpersonal skills have an important place in the cockpit. The question now is how we apply this aspect of training. For this, we should first understand and make a distinction between sound and unsound behaviors. In order to make this distinction it is necessary to study the science of human behavior.

We feel that the first important step toward recognizing the need for human skills training was taken when Japan Airlines adapted the CRM program. We realized, however, that generally people are strongly opposed or resistant to any changes in behavior, even if the need for change is recognized. Since we have been conditioned for so many years to our habits, attitudes, and culture, it will be a great challenge to change these aspects. Both individuals and groups such as cockpit crews and company organizations resist change. This process of change takes a tremendous amount of time and effort by both management and flight crews. Speaking psychologically, we can say that a behavioral change has occurred if reliable differences are observed between behaviors before and after learning. At most, one can expect individual change in knowledge or behavior at the end of a CRM seminar. In order to reinforce new knowledge and behavior, recurrent training is required. The learning process for human behavior, as in other disciplines, requires constant reinforcement to ensure more permanent change.

For example, when learning to play golf, it is important not only to read the golf manual written by a professional player, but also to get out onto the driving range and practice the swing. It is obvious that you cannot learn to play golf just by reading a book on the subject. Theory must be put into practice. Even if you watch a professional golfer in a slow-motion video, you can only learn the outline of the golf swing. To get a real understanding and feel for the game, you must actually go out and do it. Therefore, a recurrent training program like line-oriented flight training (LOFT) is absolutely necessary for the crew to go out and get a feel for the new behavioral leadership styles learned in the CRM seminar.

Question 4. What types of comments did you receive from participants who completed the CRM seminar at Japan Airlines? A management pilot commented, "I imagined that my actions in the cockpit were the best based on my judgment, but after the CRM seminar, I understood that many of my judgments were based on habitual thinking on how other crewmembers would think." Another participant expressed his opinion on the study of cockpit culture, "The open and candid discussions resulted in our examining old habits and problems that previously were not discussed. Old habits were brought to light. The important ideas are that the CRM seminar created a culture in which critique and inquiry were the correct and responsible things to do." Other comments include: "The CRM seminar makes us aware of our personal strengths and weaknesses. By helping us understand ourselves, we can objectively evaluate our personal skills and, by doing so, hopefully improve our performance in the cockpit." "I recognize the importance of critiquing. The CRM seminar opened my eyes to the human factors side of flight safety. Understanding how and when to effectively critique other crewmembers is a useful resource in handling effective communication skills in the cockpit culture." "Effective performance in the cockpit requires not only the captain giving orders, but the crewmembers working together to create a synergistic atmosphere." "Human behavior is nurtured by the environment and culture it lives in, so it is important to have the support of the management to help CRM grow and thrive within the company. Without management support, CRM would be just another required training program."

Question 5. How do you plan to put the concepts learned in the CRM seminar to practical use after it is finished? After the seminar, LOFT is provided on a recurrent basis. LOFT puts the theory of CRM into practice under operational circumstances by simulating a line flight. Management of human factors not only requires all the crewmembers involved to have the common basis of understanding the CRM concept prior to undergoing LOFT, but also gives them a chance to see themselves objectively.

Technical skills must be learned in order for a pilot to be skillful in handling an airplane; therefore recurrent training is needed in order to help maintain high technical levels. Likewise, human error management skills must be learned much as the training of take-off and landing skills requires a flight simulator or an airplane. However, the training of human error management skills requires an environment in which these skills are realistically tested. LOFT is best able to provide us with this environment and fits our need for a continuing periodic training session that would encourage and reinforce CRM concepts. LOFT deals with instructing crewmembers how to find the best solution for an unexpected situation by the use of teamwork as well as "stick-and-rudder" technical skills. The CRM concept followed by LOFT effectively solves such problems which require behavioral scientific knowledge as crew intercommunication and interaction.

Question 6. Did you see any attitude or behavioral change in crewmembers after they completed the CRM seminar? We would like to try to answer this in general terms. Figure 14.13 shows the transformation of a human being on four levels. The figure illustrates relative difficulty levels and the time required to bring about change in the following four areas.

1. Knowledge
2. Attitude
3. Individual behavior
4. Group or organizational behavior

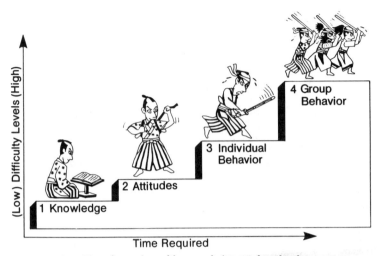

Figure 14.13   Transformation of human being on four levels.

It is not difficult to bring about change in the area of knowledge. Knowledge is constantly being obtained when we read a book, attend a seminar, or see or hear something new. However, how does one think about changes in attitudes? Because there are underlying factors behind attitudes, for example feelings, likes, and dislikes, changes in attitudes do not take place as easily as changes in knowledge. The imperfect link between attitudes and behavior indicates that it is far more difficult to accomplish a change in individual behavior, and creating such a change will require much more time. The reason is that through their experiences, people have formed their own type of behavior which gives them a feeling of comfort. It is also true that people need more time and experience to change their behavior as they grow older. This idea can be compared to a drop of ink which is enough to discolor a cup of water, while the same drop is too little for a bottle of water. What is meant is that the level of change in behavior depends on the cumulative amount of experience of an individual. Finally, the amount of effort made is the key to realizing behavioral change.

Since attainment of change in individual behavior is very difficult, it would be an even more difficult and longer process for a group or an organization to change its behavior. Conscious effort and awareness of the need to change are the keys to individual and group behavioral change (modification).

Question 7. The CRM concept is considered to apply to a three-person cockpit, as studied by NASA in 1979 and introduced in UAL in 1982. I'm afraid that it might not apply to a two-person cockpit. This is a wrong idea. Lauber stated (1980, p. 3), "one of the principal causes of incidents and accidents in civil jet transport operations is the lack of effective management of available resources by the flight-deck crew. It is further argued that present aircrew training programs could be augmented to improve flight-deck management." The goal of CRM training is to let crewmembers know in such circumstances (1) that accomplishment of a task requires the interaction of two or more people, (2) what leadership or communication styles are observed as human behavioral characteristics, and (3) how those leadership styles affect other people in performing their work and bringing about different outcomes.

Generally speaking, performing a job can be described as accomplishing something through the interaction of many other people. Therefore, we can define one's ability as the power to accomplish something. For this reason, we make an effort to learn the knowledge and skills that are required for our job. Then, do knowledge and skills provide you with the power to accomplish something? "Knowing something" refers to having knowledge. "Being able to do something" refers to having skill. However, If one cannot accomplish something by making use of those two elements, one can not be said to have a power or ability.

We often see great differences in the manner of performing a job or accomplishing a subsequent output among those who have the same knowledge and skills. One major factor contributing to such a difference is the attitude and behavioral characteristics that are peculiar to each individual. Especially during interaction with other people who are involved in a task, one's attitude and behavioral characteristics will manifest themselves in one's speech, action, or response. Some behavioral characteristics contribute effectively to putting knowledge or skills to practical use. On the other hand, knowledge or skills, no matter how excellent, may meet with rejection from the other people concerned. This means that the type of behavioral characteristics one has will help determine one's ability to perform rather than one's knowledge or skills. Traditionally, however, education and training programs have emphasized the importance of knowledge and skill, rather than behavioral characteristics.

CRM training aims at making the crewmembers aware of the most basic concepts of behavioral science by use of the Grid theory, which leads them to have a common understanding of the effectiveness of human behavioral characteristics and thus to find concrete clues to reinforce their ability to do their job. Consequently, CRM training has nothing to do with the crew size, whether two-person or three-person.

Question 8. What is being planned for CRM concepts to make them standard, everyday practice? Critique is thought to be a vital element for CRM to be a daily practice, because it is a technique in which we continuously learn from our own experience in order to improve ourselves. That is, critique helps us find ways to improve ourselves by taking a serious examination of what we do and say. Those who have finished the CRM seminar may better understand what critique is by the statement, "Critique is a continuous activity which qualifies us to solve problems in a (9,9) style." The repeated process of critique should help reinforce CRM skills. Another key element for critique to be useful is continuous learning. Therefore, CRM/LOFT should be a recurrent training program. This will help reinforce CRM skills to the point where they become a daily habit in the cockpit environment.

Question 9. If the CRM seminar has made some pilots self-skeptical or suffer a loss of self-confidence in their management style, will it make them more indecisive and feel insecure about flying? As mentioned before, a person's speech, action, or response is a reflection of his behavioral characteristics. This is supported by the general concept that social behaviors are shaped, intentionally or not, by one's basic thought hidden far beneath one's conscious mind. One point of view argues that the type of behavior to assume is of no concern, because it is an issue of one's values or likes and dislikes. Another view insists that an ideal type should be chosen based on comprehensive study to identify an optimum behavioral style. The CRM seminar is provided to support the latter view.

To best realize this view, first of all, it is necessary to learn a theory supported by the behavioral sciences and to be able to envisage a behavioral style of one's own or others in the light of that theory. (The Grid is a tool for learning this.) The theory leads to learning whether "concern for product" inherently conflicts with "concern for people." Thus crewmembers can come to realize an effective behavioral style which they had been unaware of before.

Second, people need to modify their biased assessment of themselves. In general, people are liable to estimate themselves considerably better than they really are. This is demonstrated by the data obtained in the seminar. Self-deception, self-justification, or self-rationalization may sound excessively harsh, but this is a very normal mental process that people experience and employ. In all events, if we desire to change ourselves toward better behavior in order to accomplish a better job, we must see ourselves exactly as we really are. If convinced by Grid theory that there is a disparity between the ideal (9,9) behavioral style and their own true style, crewmembers seem naturally motivated to try to close the gap between the ideal and their present style. Here, the important point is that crewmembers will not be motivated to change unless the gap is realized by themselves through their own self-initiated study of the theory. We feel confident that participants do not fall into self-skepticism and have a loss of self-confidence because the CRM seminar is managed on the basis of a spontaneous, self-developmental training theory.

As we have noted, the behavioral style in which "concern for product" is compatible with "concern for people" is called the (9,9) type in the seminar. The distinguishing feature of the (9,9) style is that it is a leadership style which places importance on teamwork that produces a synergy effect. That is, a leader, the captain, advocates his opinion openly and frankly and also encourages others to do so in order to benefit from a variety of opinions and ideas. During this discussion process, if he finds some opinion better than his own, he is willing to accept it and abandon his own. It would be wrong to assume that this behavior is indecisive. Rather, this can correct mistakes or misunderstandings and is important in preventing human error from taking place.

Question 10. Is CRM/LOFT a standard course of training approved by the Japan Civil Aviation Bureau (JCAB)? Since the total performance of a crew needs to be reinforced by improving crew coordination and communication in the cockpit to accomplish a higher level of safety, CRM/LOFT has been used at Japan Airlines since 1984 as a complement to the training program. In addition, negotiation took place with the JCAB authorities to change the current position of CRM/LOFT into an approved recurrent training program. We made the case to them that the current training and evaluation environment was focused mainly on a procedure-oriented session for trainees, and this did not provide the crewmembers enough opportunities to make important judgments and decisions. We also pointed out that the current training emphasized only individual skills and could not cope with poor crew coordination or deteriorated team performance under stressful situations. Briefly, current rules or procedures with which the crewmembers are qualified dealt only with individual skills or proficiencies. We do not deny that these are important. However, competent individuals do not always form a well-functioning team.

Because different individuals make up different crews, today's excellent crew does not promise that tomorrow's crew will also be excellent. Therefore, the CRM/LOFT training is focused on interpersonal skills which require individuals to demonstrate the desired crew effectiveness.

A difficult issue in seeking JCAB approval was how to evaluate team performance. Some said that interpersonal skills should be evaluated by the same standards as technical skills. The answer to this is not easy, but let us consider a LOFT scenario which involves an engine fire. Assume that the first officer mistakenly shuts down the normal engine instead of the engine on fire, which results in both engines being completely shut down. In such a case, is it correct to determine that the cause was the captain's inadequate supervision of the first officer, although no problem would have occurred if the captain were flying with another first officer? Is a re-check required for the first officer? How about the flight engineer? If we think team performance is so important, is it not natural that rules and standards should challenge this theme? However, we can also say that such a problem is mostly the responsibility of airlines which must make a continuous effort to reflect contemporary requirements of training and evaluation, rather than rule makers or authorities. CRM/LOFT was approved by the JCAB as recurrent training on March 29, 1988.

Question 11. Do you think CRM skills can be practiced outside of the cockpit environment? The following three sets of skills required in CRM are not confined to the cockpit.

1. Interpersonal and communication skill
2. Leadership and management skill
3. Planning and problem resolution skill

Since the team management type referred to in CRM, the so called (9,9) style, is the captain's ideal cockpit management for safety and efficiency, it can also be applied when performing a ground job because the (9,9) type always seeks excellence. If such behavioral training is effective for flightcrew training, it should also be effective for all other organizations where people must work together as a team.

Acknowledgments

We would like to acknowledge Barbara Kanki of NASA and W. R. Taggart of Resource Management and NASA/University of Texas for the many articles and research papers that provided us with the information for writing this chapter. We would like to especially thank Captain J. E. Carroll, former Vice President of United Airlines, for assistance in our work in CRM and the human side of flight safety.

References

Blake, R. R., & Mouton, J. S. (Scientific Methods, Inc.). (1968). *Corporate excellence through GRID organization development.* Austin, TX: Gulf Publishing Company.

Blake, R. R., & Mouton, J. S. (Scientific Methods, Inc.). (1983). *Consultation: A handbook for individual and organization development* (2nd ed.). Austin, TX: Addison-Wesley.

Blake, R. R., Mouton, J. S. (Scientific Methods, Inc.), & Command/Leadership/Resource Management Steering Committee and Working Groups (United Airlines). (1982). *Grid cockpit resource management.* Austin, TX: Scientific Methods, Inc.

Blake, R. R., Mouton, J. S. (Scientific Methods, Inc.), & Command/Leadership/Resource Management Steering Committee and Working Groups (United Airlines). (1990). *Grid cockpit resource management* (2nd ed.). Austin, TX: Scientific Methods, Inc.

Carroll, J. E., & Taggart, W. R. (1987). *Cockpit resource management: A tool for improved flight safety.* In H. H. Orlady & H. C. Foushee (Eds.), *Proceedings of the NASA/MAC Workshop on Cockpit Resource Management* (pp. 40–46) (NASA Conference Publication 2455). Moffett Field, CA: NASA–Ames Research Center.

Helmreich, R. L. (1980). *Social psychology on the flight deck.* In G. E. Cooper, M. D. White, & J. K. Lauber (Eds.), *Resource Management on the Flight Deck* (pp. 17–30) (NASA Conference Publication 2120). Moffett Field, CA: NASA–Ames Research Center.

Lauber, J. K. (1980). Resource management on the flight deck: Background and statement of the problem. In G. E. Cooper, M. D. White, & J. K. Lauber (Eds.), *Resource Management on the Flight Deck* (pp. 3–16) (NASA Conference Publication 2120). Moffett Field, CA: NASA–Ames Research Center.

Mouton, J. S., & Blake, R. R. (Scientific Methods, Inc.). (1984). *Synergogy: A new strategy for education, training, and development.* Austin, TX: Jossey-Bass.

Yamamori, H. (1987). Optimum culture in the cockpit. In H. H. Orlady & H. C. Foushee (Eds.), *Proceedings of the NASA/MAC Workshop on Cockpit Resource Management* (pp. 75–87) (NASA Conference Publication 2455). Moffett Field, CA: NASA–Ames Research Center.

15

Developing and Implementing CRM Programs: The Delta Experience

Robert E. Byrnes
Reuben Black
Delta Airlines
Hartsfield Atlanta International Airport
Atlanta, Georgia 30320

INTRODUCTION ✈

The complexities of creating and implementing an effective crew resource management (CRM) program are formidable. Yet if aviation operators could foresee the myriad benefits of a successful CRM program, few would resist the challenge and opportunity for positive change and increased safety. Knowing that a lack of CRM skills contributes to a high percentage of aircraft accidents and incidents seems a most compelling argument for having a CRM program based on self-interest. Yet many operators currently have no program, or worse, have an inadequate program which pays lip service to impending regulatory requirements for CRM and the Advanced Qualification Program (AQP).

The purpose of this chapter is to share with the reader the evolution of CRM at Delta Air Lines, a large and complex company with over 9,000 pilots on its current seniority list. Many facts suggest that the Delta Crew (we believe "crew" is more accurate than "cockpit") Resource Management Program has been highly effective. Academia, the National Transportation Safety Board (NTSB), NASA, and the Federal Aviation Administration (FAA) have endorsed this program as prototypical, and our crewmembers have enthusiastically accepted it. We believe that the knowledge we gained can be generalized to almost any size or type of aviation operation, given the desire and wherewithal to do so. Not only has our program increased safety, but it has proven to be an investment which has more than paid for itself.

The hypothesis that safer flight operations result from CRM training is reinforced by the statistics in our database. Frequently overlooked, however, are the ancillary benefits derived from an effective CRM program, the most important of which is increased job satisfaction and higher self-esteem of crewmembers. Use of CRM skills on the job generates what we think of as a positive adaptive spiral. The creation of a cohesive team exercising effective communications skills, inter-personal diplomacy, appropriate assertiveness, and team-oriented decision-mak-ing generates positive reinforcement and respect within the team. This reinforce-ment tends to increase the likelihood that these behaviors will be repeated over time and will be generalized to the pilot's personal life. The net result is a palpably happier and more efficient crew, one which interacts more effectively with each other, cabin crewmembers, and passengers. This change in crewmember attitude is not only obvious to observers, but is easy to measure if a database is created. We will show you how. Additionally, this chapter addresses topics we believe are critical to the success of an effective CRM program. They include:

1. Corporate cultural influences
2. Methodology and research
3. Curriculum development
4. Module development
5. Preparation of course materials
6. Facilitator selection and training
7. Check airman and management training
8. Classroom facilities
9. Line-oriented flight training (LOFT)
10. Impact of automation on CRM training

THE CORPORATE CULTURE ──────────────── ✈

When a decision to have a CRM program is reached, the first issue is who will create and implement the program. While it was tempting simply to write a check and buy an existing "off-the-shelf" program, our research indicated that acceptance of the program depends on the unique orientation of the end user, the pilot. While some existing programs cover most of the skill bases, they suffer three liabilities. First, they are frozen in the time frame in which they were written, while CRM research is dynamic and ongoing. Second, they do not factor in the past experiences and type of flying of the crewmembers addressed, which erodes credibility. Finally, "canned" programs are not responsive to the wishes and inputs of the crewmembers and therefore are not "owned" by them.

Delta Air Lines is widely thought of as a conservative, "Southern" com-pany. In reality, its 1987 pilot force was composed of former Chicago & Southern, Northeast, Western, and original Delta Air Lines pilots: four distinct cultures. Moreover, approximately 90% of this pilot force was college-educated with mili-tary backgrounds. It was impossible for our Flight Operations Department to predict just what attitudes and interpersonal skill deficits prevailed. Although we had enjoyed an impeccable 25-year safety record, the summer of 1987 produced a disastrous series of highly publicized "incidents" involving breakdowns in crew discipline, crew coordination, and communications. Delta Air Lines became the butt of Johnny Carson jokes on national television, a powerful incentive for self-evaluation, not to mention the powerful pressure exerted by the FAA and our senior management.

Delta's Flight Operations Department decided to form an ad hoc committee consisting of pilot executives, line check and proficiency check airmen, representatives from the Air Line Pilots' Association (ALPA), and highly regarded line pilots possessing unique educational and on-the-job skills. This committee was directed to survey our entire line operation from the jumpseat, to analyze the highly publicized "incidents" we had experienced, and to decide the nature and scope of the problem. In a series of highly charged meetings, the committee arrived at several painful conclusions. Many of our pilots exhibited deficits in human skills areas of communications, assertiveness, interpersonal diplomacy, and management of available resources. We considered ourselves a "captain's airline"; the captains were not standardized, and the subordinate crewmembers did not know what to expect from one flight to the next. As a consequence, copilots and flight engineers tended to "go with the flow," neither asserting their opinions on operational matters nor communicating their displeasure when individual captains did not "follow the book." In short, there was very little group participation in decision-making or bidirectional communication between crewmembers regarding operational procedures or technique. What communication there was tended to come from the captain down the chain of command. Subordinates believed that assertive suggestions would be met with hostility and, in a disputed situation, company backing could not be expected. While this anachronistic holdover from propeller days had produced a previously outstanding safety record, the increasingly complex environment of the late 1980s had rendered this approach obsolete. The "incidents" we suffered were directly attributable to team management problems in the cockpit. These problems had been previously articulated by Trans Australia Airlines at the NASA/MAC Conference on CRM in 1986 (Margerson, McCann, & Davies, 1986).

1. *Lack of support.* Where one crewmember fails to back up another during high workload situations.
2. *Standard operational procedures ignored.* Where the captain and crew fail to complete a checklist under time or other pressures.
3. *Stress problems.* Where a crew experiences difficulty in adapting to unusual emergency situations.
4. *Judgment problems.* Where management of priorities and cockpit distractions distort the judgment process.

5. *Emotional problems.* Where aggression or extreme submissiveness in the cockpit affect personal relations, or where there is a carryover, for example, of domestic worries and conflict to the job.
6. *Discipline problems.* Where corners are cut and there is inadequate control of operations in the cockpit.
7. *Leadership problems.* Where the captain does not delegate adequately.
8. *Communication problems.* Where there are misunderstandings or lack of conversation control.

Another compelling problem was identified. We had not accomplished the complete melding of the Delta, Northeast, and Western Airline cultures. It was fairly obvious to our ad hoc committee that something needed to be done to facilitate the blending of three cultures into a standardized Delta culture. We needed to borrow the best from all three to obtain standardized operating procedures. This would make it difficult (and unimportant) for pilots to determine the employment origin of their peers, based on how each operated the equipment. An opportunity needed to quickly blur the dividing lines between these cultures, perhaps in a non-cockpit setting in which each could offer opinions while becoming acquainted with the history and traditions of the other companies. The theory was that if pilots who think they are different are put in a room where self-expression is encouraged, they will discover more similarities than differences. Common desire for safety and excellence would inevitably evolve into mutual respect and desire for future unity of purpose.

All these problems—different cultures, non-standardization, tradition of "captain's airline," and shortcomings in human skills—suggested an experiential seminar-type program based on cockpit resource management. The NASA/MAC workshop on CRM training (1986) had produced a series of recommendations which convinced the ad hoc committee that CRM training would be the answer, but it had to be CRM training tailored to our specific problems. Lecturing our pilot force was deemed inappropriate and self-defeating. What we needed was training where each pilot could become more fully aware of how interpersonal skills affected safety and why a Delta flight crew must function as a team. If during this process we could break down old barriers and provide an opportunity for each pilot to contribute input into the operation, so much the better.

The ad hoc process produced two directives from Delta management. First, a new Flight Standards Department was created which was responsible for system procedural standardization, quality control, and selection and training of line check airmen. Second, a CRM program was to be created and implemented as rapidly as possible. Rapidity dictated research into existing and "off-the-shelf" programs. Unfortunately, none of these programs met what we strongly believed were our unique needs. It soon became obvious we had to bite the bullet and create our own.

METHODOLOGY AND RESEARCH ────────────── ✈

Delta embarked on this very ambitious program in October, 1988. A senior member of the ad hoc committee was assigned responsibility for creating and implementing a "second generation" CRM program at Delta. Fortunately, this pilot had worn many hats at Delta: line pilot, System Manager–Flight Training, Chief Pilot, ALPA Professional Standards Chairman, and ALPA negotiator. His was a long history of advocacy for increased emphasis on human factors in pilot training. His background provided our effort with a leader possessing great credibility with management, the union, and the line pilot.

STEP ONE: Find a leader who is respected by all. It must be one who has "been there," possessing line experience. It must be one who believes in the efficacy of the project. Above all, it must be one with facile CRM skills of diplomacy, assertiveness, decision-making, team building, and resource management.

The CRM chairman's first major task was appointment of a Steering Committee. The makeup of this group was crucial. Aware that others had experienced problems in this area, we wanted to be sure that every facet of our operation was represented. We therefore created slots on the committee not by name, but by position. We needed a line check airman, a Flight Training Department pilot, a line pilot, a pilot representing ALPA, a base chief pilot, a retired pilot, a ground training representative, and—since we believed that the definition of flight crew included flight attendants—we asked our Flight Attendant Department to send a representative. This list of people, solicited initially by position, ended up containing one Ph.D., a Ph.D. candidate, an M.S. in Education, and a member of the Human Factors Society.

STEP TWO: Appoint a steering committee representing as many facets of flight operations as possible. Selection by position creates balance, credibility, and creativity. It also guarantees that all flight operations departments "own" the end result.

Of particular importance to the committee was the experience of Trans Australia Airlines (TAA) in developing their Aircrew Team Management Program. Their definition of the human factors problems most matched the problems which caused our 1987 "incidents." Through trial and error, TAA had established what we believed were several self-evident principles essential for an efficient and successful program. First, the committee had to thoroughly understand the problem and establish goals with timetables. Second, we needed to become intimately familiar with established research at NASA and other airlines before incorporating unique inputs from our own pilot force. Third, the training had to be conducted by our own line pilots trained in facilitation skills in order to preserve credibility. Fourth, the training had to be experiential as opposed to didactic, using videotaped role-playing exercises, team games, and skill practice. Fifth, participants had to be given an opportunity to comment on and rate the training to generate meaningful changes and to correct mistakes. Last, training aids such as videos, slides, room layout, charts and other materials had to be of the highest quality.

STEP THREE: Establish goals and create a timetable. The committee established the following goals for our program:

1. Enhance safety through optimized team performance.
2. Promote crew/team development.
3. Promote individual professional development.
4. Increase job satisfaction.
5. Promote personal growth.
6. Develop and enhance crew decision making skills.
7. Develop improved communication skills.
8. Encourage modification of the corporate "shell" to accommodate new behaviors.
9. Create a mechanism to remedy problem behaviors.

Our second concern was how to justify the cost to senior management. We believed it was possible to measure scientifically the result of our training effort, not only to satisfy the "bean counters" but also to advance the sum total of human factors knowledge. From the outset, we believed that CRM training had to be an ongoing process integral to our annual training cycle. Scientific measure of its value would provide needed ammunition to convince skeptics, both on the line and in management, to continue emphasis on human skills training long after the immediacy of the 1987 "incidents" faded. Indeed, the December 14, 1987, FAA Advisory Circular 1.2 had stated, "In order to be effective, CRM training must be accomplished in several phases over time" (FAA, 1987, p. 2).

The concern for verification led us to Robert Helmreich at NASA/University of Texas (UT), the pioneer of database verification in CRM training. Other airlines had used various criteria to judge training effectiveness, none of which our Steering Committee felt were reliable and valid. We believed Helmreich had the answer to verification. CRM research indicated three factors determine pilot performance: psychomotor skill, personality, and attitude (Helmreich, 1987). Psychomotor ability is genetically determined, while personality is changeable only through long-term psychotherapy. Therefore, what is malleable is attitude, and attitude can be measured using the NASA/UT *Cockpit management attitudes questionnaire (CMAQ)* (Helmreich, Wilhelm, & Gregorich, 1988). Using a pre/post-seminar design, it was possible to measure the change in Delta pilot attitudes vis-à-vis cockpit management in such areas as communications and coordination, command responsibility, and recognition of stressor effects. Pre-CRM training responses from individuals are linked to post-training responses to determine if attitudes change for each scale and, if so, how much, and in which direction.

Our committee decided to send our pilots a questionnaire which included questions from the *CMAQ*, a 50-question survey of opinions concerning our flight operations and quality of life, and a Team Skills Survey designed by Richard Hackman at Harvard which, among other things, measures attitude and opinions about team performance. 7,000 mailed surveys produced 3,794 replies, a clear indicator that our pilots were in favor of change. These de-identified data were fed into the NASA/UT database, and from this information powerful group statistics emerged which verified the findings of the ad hoc committee. It clearly indicated our needs in terms of seminar course content. For example, over 90% of our pilots believed that they were invulnerable to outside personal stress when on the job. Additionally, we found that our pilots were poor communicators, lacked assertiveness, were unclear about command responsibility, and in general were unhappy with the way cockpits were run on the airline.

Many other benefits accrued from the survey. We were able to compare our attitudes and opinions with other airlines and the military, between pilot domiciles (cultures), by status in the crew (captain, first officer, second officer), by equipment flown, by educational and aviation background, by age and length of airline experience.

We decided to measure each seminar with the *CMAQ* to assess on-the-spot change. We also decided to resurvey the entire airline in 5 years to measure durability of change brought about by our approach to CRM training.

STEP FOUR: Create a database, not only to measure the success of the effort, but also to contribute to the sum total of existing human factors knowledge. In the long run, a database may provide many financial benefits, such as reduction in insurance premiums or facilitation of an AQP application.

One of the most compelling ideas common to CRM literature indicates that to be effective in the long term, CRM training must consist of increased awareness, practice and feedback, and reinforcement (see FAA, 1987). Seminars provide only increased awareness of the value of good attitudes toward resource management and interpersonal skills. What then about practice/feedback and reinforcement? Our Committee drew these conclusions:

1. CRM principles had to be incorporated into every aspect of our flight operation and pilot training, beginning with new hire training and ending with retirement.
2. CRM principles had to be actively adopted and practiced by all proficiency and line check airmen.
3. The best opportunity for practice/feedback and reinforcement occurs in a flight simulator during recurrent LOFT. (The next most effective opportunity occurs on a line check if the line check is crew (as opposed to individual)–oriented.)

To maximize the impact of LOFT, certain techniques must be utilized by a simulator instructor trained in facilitation skills. At a minimum, the crew must observe and self-critique video playback of good and poor CRM-related events occurring during the simulation. To maximize the reinforcement effect of a line check requires a line check airman trained in observation of team interaction, not only in the cockpit during multiple legs, but during team formation, layover, and debriefing. Both LOFT and line check maximization techniques could be the subject of a separate chapter, and the lasting success of any CRM program is totally dependent on the utilization of LOFT and line checks with motivated and highly trained check airmen. Recent research by Helmreich indicates that positive attitude change created by a CRM seminar returned to baseline at an airline without a continuing LOFT program (see the chapter by Helmreich and Foushee).

STEP FIVE: Include in program planning not only a classroom experience, but provide for extensive check airman training, videotaped LOFT (if possible), and a system utilizing multiple leg line checks. Planning must also include provisions for inclusion of CRM into new hire and recurrent annual training. We believed that absent this type of comprehensive program, an isolated single classroom experience is, in the long term, a relative waste of time, effort, and money.

CURRICULUM DEVELOPMENT ⟶

STEP ONE: Evaluate available resources (money and time), the long-term commitment and needs of the organization, and establish realistically achievable goals.

Our committee decided on a long-range program which included two experiential CRM seminars, extensive check airman training, videotaped LOFT, multiple-leg line checks, inclusion of CRM issues in recurrent, initial equipment, and new hire training. Moreover, we decided that while remaining faithful to principles established by those who developed programs before us, our program would be a "second generation" CRM program with three key directions, again articulated by Hackman:

> To take seriously the fact that cockpit crews are teams, and to design CRM training so that crew members become increasingly skilled as team members.
>
> To recognize that the captain is a team leader, and to help captains become as competent in leading teams as most of them are in the technical aspects of flying.
>
> To acknowledge that organizational and regulatory contexts bear powerfully on the degree to which the lessons learned in CRM courses will

take root and prosper on the line, and to begin the never-ending process of "tuning" the contexts within which crews operate so that they actively support effective teamwork and crew coordination. (J. R. Hackman, letter to Delta Air Lines, April, 1989)

This approach dictated what we perceived as a "second-generation" approach. First-generation programs contained traditional human skill subjects such as stress management, communications, leadership, and the like. We were convinced that to achieve maximum impact a CRM program had to include small group skills such as team formation and situational leadership. Pilots needed to learn that a cockpit crew is a team and its performance is not a simple function of the competence and motivation of individual members. Rather, crew performance is usually either significantly better or worse than that which would be predicted by simply looking at the qualities of the members as individuals. Also implied is that there can be no lasting change in what Hackman calls the "cockpit shell," absent a change in the outside forces which impact the crew most strongly, the "corporate shell" (Hackman, 1987; his chapter). Crews needed to be aware of the often invisible influences of the organization on team performance and to have an awareness of how pilots can improve the "shell" in which they operate. Clearly, if the company and its flight operations department do not believe in and practice appropriate human and team skills, their pilots will not undergo a lasting attitude change. In our case, if management attitudes about being a "captain's airline" did not change, neither would the pilots. The Steering Committee defined "management" as line and training check airmen, because this group is the primary human contact point between pilots and Delta management.

In a smaller company, this definition may vary. However, the point is that CRM is effective only when its principles are unconditionally adopted at the top of an organization and flow down through the organization.

The "second-generation" approach led us into uncharted territory. For example, if we posited team/small group performance as essential to complete CRM training, what about the influence of automated "glass cockpit" aircraft on traditional team performance? (See the chapter by Wiener). We contacted Earl Wiener at the University of Miami, who has studied the impact of cockpit automation extensively. His opinions confirmed our concerns, resulting in the inclusion of a curriculum item on workload management. His continuing research has subsequently impacted all pilot training at Delta.

The analysis of seminar content, based on "second-generation" thinking, timing, and available assets led us to establish a two-phase approach to the training which would include a seminar and LOFT session in each phase, with the two phases 6 months apart. The first phase, Phase A, would include traditional CRM skill subjects covered by most existing CRM programs. However, a recurring theme would be how these skills or lack thereof would affect team as well as individual performance in the cockpit.

After a 6-month hiatus, each pilot would return to our training center for Phase B training covering team/small group issues as well as material to be developed on automation and workload. The LOFT following this session would be high-impact, with multiple problems requiring excellent team performance based on Phase B modules.

Concerns with our management "shell" prompted us to schedule the first 6 months of training for check airmen. Not only did this provide an opportunity to conduct the training in depth, but it also allowed the curriculum to be fine-tuned for credibility and accuracy. During this 6 months the formidable job of facilitator selection and training was to be accomplished. The goal was to have a polished, professional product before any line pilot participated. The detailed feedback we received from our check airmen proved to be of crucial importance before facing our most critical audience, the line pilots.

STEP TWO: Evaluate pilot survey results to determine skill areas unique to the operation and adjust curriculum emphasis and/or content based on this analysis.

Our survey indicated surprisingly strong denial about how personal stress affects pilot performance. It also disclosed a near total misunderstanding of crewmember diplomacy, particularly how and when to be assertive. Command authority was a gray area, particularly with captains. Definite cultural differences in responding verified the suspicion that we were four different airlines rather than one. Our pilots were not happy with how cockpits were being run, how checklists were constructed, and how management communicated or rather, how they failed to communicate. These results heavily impacted the ultimate emphasis and content of the curriculum. They also began the process of modifying the corporate "shell," particularly in the area of management communications.

STEP THREE: Research other programs. Attendance and participation by those who will write and facilitate your program is especially helpful.

Our Steering Committee was fortunate to attend CRM programs at United Airlines, Pan American, and Alaska Airlines. We were particularly impressed with the work of Captain David Harris at Alaska and were subsequently able to hire him to train our facilitators and act as program administrator. Participation in another company's seminars provides several important learnings, not the least of which is a heightened awareness of the unique cultural bias of your own pilot group. Observing others through the filter of your own company background makes what not to do very clear.

STEP FOUR: Consider acquiring consultants.

We were very lucky. The commitment of our company and the compelling urgency of our need allowed us to obtain help from academic experts. They were and are invaluable. Robert Helmreich and his staff at NASA/UT Austin, J. Richard Hackman of Harvard, Earl Wiener of University of Miami, and Bob Ginnett of the Air Force Academy were our primary consultants. They assisted in database creation and interpretation, curriculum development, and module creation (including starring in videos), and, most important, they provided our effort with badly needed credibility. These consultants were suggested to us by Clay Foushee, Chief Scientific and Technical Advisor for Human Factors at the Federal Aviation Agency, who was most helpful in assisting us. We think our involvement with consultants was a win–win situation, because we believe they learned from us as well. But the bottom line on consultants is that they shorten the time needed to produce a program of high quality. They are an insurance policy against failure to produce the desired result. Their experience with other programs is worth the price of admission alone. However, we did not use them as managers, writers, or administrators. Rather, we used them as advisors and "sounding boards" on an as-needed basis while assuming total responsibility for the end product ourselves. This approach worked well for all concerned, preserving cordial relationships which are ongoing.

STEP FIVE: Keep the pilot group informed of progress with curriculum development and proposed training scheduling.

To help the pilot population "own" the program, that is, to be favorably disposed upon arrival at the training site, it is immensely helpful to periodically communicate progress prior to commencement of the program. Our effort took the form of publication of progress reports in company publications with tear-off comment forms which could be returned to the committee. Our Vice President–Flight Operations included progress reports in his "road show" talks with our pilot group. We were careful to publicize the makeup of the Steering Committee and to state that the training was being researched and written by Delta personnel based on personal experience. We used the pilot survey results to "sell" the need for the program and to emphasize the fact that pilots' responses were, in part, designing the curriculum.

MODULE DEVELOPMENT ✈

Although the Steering Committee wanted two 8-hour classroom sessions for Phase A, economic considerations dictated one 8-hour session and one 4-hour session. The enormous expense of daily training pay for several thousand pilots continued to counterbalance "blue sky" planning during the entire CRM process. Phase B evolved into one 8-hour classroom session followed by a LOFT.

STEP ONE: Select modules for inclusion in the seminars. We decided on these modules for Phase A.

1. *Traditions.* Responding to the concern that there were deep cultural divisions between pilot groups, a module was needed which would promote bonding and unity of purpose. A catalyst was needed to prompt pilots from the

different cultures to feel equally Delta while maintaining pride in their company of origin. The ultimate objective of this module was to create a bonded team atmosphere for the training to follow.

2. *Foundations.* A short module designed to answer the question, "Why are we here?" The safety rationale of human skills versus technical skills had to be convincingly implanted to provide motivation for the hard work to follow. We had to prove that human and team skill failures caused most accidents. Fortunately (and unfortunately), there were many accident reports which underlined specific human skill failures to which participants could relate. These included Air Florida at Washington National (assertiveness), United at Portland, Oregon (communications and situational awareness), TWA near Dulles (decision-making), and the terrible 747 ground collision at Tenerife (conflict resolution, stress management, and communications). For further information on these accidents, see the chapter by Kayten. Analysis of aircraft accidents engenders powerful motivation in most pilots. However, the challenge of this module was how to convince participants that the need for CRM skills relates to more than the occasional catastrophic, safety-related event. Rather, how do these skills apply to the every-day operational situation to make crews more effective in all phases of their job?

3. *Crew dynamics.* We wanted to establish the basis and definition of "command authority" as a starting point leading into team issues. We defined the most important team issues to be principles of good leadership/followership, the concept of situational leadership, how to recognize differing leadership styles, and crewmember skills in diplomacy. We hoped to teach coping skills effective in dealing with dysfunctional management extremes.

4. *Communications.* Based on survey results, this module needed the most punch. It needed to impart heightened awareness of the importance of effective communications in flying safety and crew efficiency. Participants needed to understand the necessary components of, and barriers to, effective communications. Elements of effective assertive statements particularly needed definition. Woven throughout the module had to be our concern with changing Delta pilots' attitudes toward the team approach to decision-making and toward defusing the notion that the captain is always right. Therefore, subordinates had to learn how to resolve conflict when the team approach malfunctioned.

5. *Decision dynamics.* Preliminary research identified four concerns with decision-making. What is the basic decision-making process model used by pilots? How are bad decisions made? What identifiable factors have negative potential for causing bad decisions? And finally, what are the potential benefits and liabilities of habitual routines used by pilots? Other than the basic model of decision-making, a preliminary search of the aviation literature bore little fruit. The Steering Committee hoped this was an area in which we could contribute significantly to human factors knowledge through synthesizing research from other disciplines. By borrowing the concept of heuristics and applying it to cockpit usage, this indeed happened (Maher, 1991). How the concept of situational

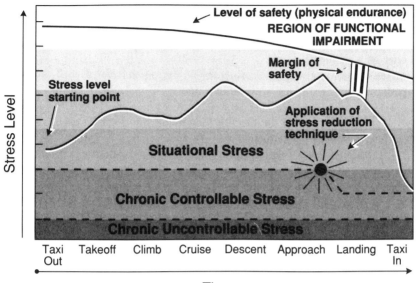

Figure 15.1   The stress of flight. (Source: Delta Air Lines, Inc.)

awareness affected decision-making had to be included in the module at some point. Debate over this module involved all the aspects of decision-making. We hoped we were practicing what we were hoping to preach.

6. *Stress management.* To counter prevailing pilot attitudes of personal invulnerability, this module needed to make the points that the effects of stress are cumulative and that stress can cause dysfunctional behavior leading to disastrous results in the cockpit. (See Figure 15.1.) It had to impart effective techniques to ameliorate stress. The challenge implied was to overcome pilots' strong tendency for denial and defensiveness. Understanding the mind–body connection underlies the acceptance that stresses of flying and stresses experienced in our personal life add up. We needed to communicate these facts without excessive reliance on psychological terms, since survey input indicated that pilots harbored intense dislike for a "holding hands in a hot tub" (psychotherapeutic) approach to problem-solving.

Phase B was scheduled 6 months after Phase A. Reviewing A seemed to be a logical beginning for B. The remainder of this 8-hour training covered crew effectiveness. Its learning objectives included:

1. Awareness of major influences on crew effectiveness and ways crew can make constructive contributions to these influences.
2. Clarification of ways in which skills in managing crew performance can be

developed, particularly skills in managing the level of effort applied to the work.

3. Development of crewmember knowledge of how to build and maintain the crew as a performing unit.
4. Increased awareness of the influences of the organizational shell on team performance.

STEP TWO: Divide the Steering Committee into working groups having primary responsibility for particular module writing.

Several members of the committee had recognized expertise in given areas, making selection of work groups an easy process. Work groups were instructed to construct a research plan and time line for committee approval. A separate work group was designated as the clearing house for all modules. Its task was to put the material in a format appropriate for inclusion in a working manual for classroom facilitators and to contract with other Delta departments for production and acquisition of needed training materials, videos, handouts, and equipment necessary to present the modules.

A lesson plan format was created which assured that each seminar class would receive an identical training experience. Strict time allotment was included so that each facilitator would stay on schedule.

Work groups presented their proposed material to the entire committee for revision prior to submission to the clearing house group. Within each work group, the role of "expert" lay with the person either having the most knowledge concerning the material to be taught or with training experience with similar material. However, the work group as a whole was responsible to the committee for the academic purity of their module. Exposing the entire committee to the preliminary material of each work group provided not only critique on the material, but also input on how each module could be connected to its predecessor.

STEP THREE: Decide on overall strategy of the seminar.

From strategy decisions flow direction and content of the individual modules as well as the logistical and equipment needs required to implement the strategy. We had previously decided upon experiential learning. This method suggested the use of role-playing exercises, videotaped problem-solving, team competitive games, group decision-making, and above all an opportunity for each participant to observe and practice the skills we were trying to teach. For example, to teach team formation experientially, a team must be formed by the participants. We decided to limit each seminar to 30 participants, divided into five teams of 6 pilots each, seated at round tables identified by colors. Table assignments were preselected by the facilitator so that each contained (ideally) two captains, two first officers, and two second officers. Insofar as possible an attempt was made to place pilots from different domiciles (cultures) at each table. Although wearing name tags was required, crew position was not identified. Each team member was required to listen to the pilot on his right give a short autobiography which did not include flying or airline experience, then to stand up and introduce this participant to the table by reciting all remembered biographical material such as hobbies, marital status and number of children, location of home, and so on. This process involved almost all the CRM skills we would attempt to impart. More importantly, it experientially demanded the process of team formation by involving a common experience, sharing areas of common interest, eliminating stranger anxiety, and eliciting a sense that "we're all in this together," that is, bonding. It also provided many good laughs as pilots attempted to utilize unfamiliar public speaking skills while trying to remember information heard only once in the buzz of conversation which filled the room.

To promote a sense of relevance, extensive use of video and audio tapes of airline accidents and incidents was made. We had each team analyze Delta's "incidents" of 1987. Insofar as possible, we blended this material into the syllabus at spots appropriate to emphasize a point under discussion. Nothing impacts an airline pilot with greater force than listening to a voice recorder tape of an accident. If this is coupled with a discussion of the particular CRM skill failure of the crew, the point is vividly made. If the pilots are then immediately placed in a videotaped role-playing of a similar set of circumstances where the skill under discussion is required, learning is assured.

The Steering Committee also believed that to teach concepts and skills having a psychological orientation, we had to avoid reliance on lecturing and psychological terms (which our critique sheets labeled "psychobabble"). To teach the effect of stress is was necessary to place the pilot under stress while videotaping his or her reactions. Although the cumulative nature of stress is a concept from psychology and physiology, it is easy to demonstrate the concept without spending a lot of time defining it. We connected our pilots to a galvanic skin response recorder while asking them to perform uncomfortable tasks such as singing from a piece of sheet music. The skin conductor was hooked to an audio device which hummed at frequencies proportional to the subject's apparent stress. This dramatic demonstration produced not only learning, but also much-needed humor to lighten a very serious subject.

Strategic use of the learning theory of modeling was inserted into the material at every opportunity. For example, pilots tend to be reticent self-disclosers, while we know that self-disclosure is an effective communications opener and stress reducer. Furthermore, we believe this is essential to flight safety, particularly if the pilot is not feeling well or is undergoing traumatic personal stress in his life. We encouraged our facilitators to disclose sensitive personal material when appropriate during the stress module. By observing a fellow pilot reveal his own problems without loss of peer respect, we hoped this behavior would be modeled as acceptable and useful.

Another strategy employed was the use of a female flight attendant to read accident reports on video. Not only did this spark hostility in the group, but it opened up the entire subject of the pilot–cabin attendant relationship, including surfacing pilot feelings on the subject of gay male flight attendants. By escaping from the ordinary platitudes about pilot–flight attendant conflict, it was easy to broach the subject of the proper place of flight attendants in the safety equation of the entire crew, rather than just their place as airborne waiters and waitresses. As an aside, the most laudatory comments about the success of our CRM program at Delta come from flight attendants. They report that they are treated with more respect, feel more a part of the crew, and are included much more often in crew briefings since CRM. They were so impressed that they have included selected CRM subjects in their own leadership program. Our management "shell" responded by directing that the flight attendant briefing be included on all "Before Start" checklists in the aircraft, thereby endorsing the CRM crew concept.

Our pilot survey brought home the point that pilots believed communications between management and the line pilot were seriously flawed. We attempted to use the seminars to correct this perception by assigning every table team the job of creating "Harry's List" (referring to our Vice President of Flight Operations, Harry Alger). This list of complaints/suggestions was compiled and edited, and each significant item was answered by Alger on videotapes distributed to each pilot domicile. Not only did this opportunity to "ventilate" reduce tensions, it was used as an example of "win–win" conflict resolution, the assertive statement, open communications, self disclosure, and team formation.

The last significant strategy used involved the selection and use of line pilots as seminar facilitators. The committee was aware that professional facilitators would probably have done a better job in the classroom, but several considerations added up to a mandate to take on the Herculean task of selecting and training 30 line pilots responsible for the entire success or failure of a multi-million dollar program. The bottom line in our thinking was credibility. We believed that pilots will not respond to a classroom instructor in human skills unless he or she has experienced the situations in which these skills were critical. Moreover, we believed the pilot classroom reactions to the material might be incomprehensible to a non-pilot. To guarantee a two-way flow of information we decided to use at least two pilot facilitators in each class. If one facilitator ran into a personality conflict with a participant, a quick switch usually solved the problem.

FACILITATOR SELECTION AND TRAINING ────── →

"Facilitator" is the term widely used in CRM for the person who guides the learning process in both workshop and simulator sessions. The term is used because the process is truly self-learning. The leaders simply facilitate the process by keeping the group on task.

The critical nature of the proper selection and adequate training of facilitators was obvious from the outset. The chairman of the Steering Committee had at every opportunity addressed groups of pilots to describe the upcoming program and provide progress reports. It was made clear not only that our own people would write the program but that it would be taught/facilitated by pilots. During each presentation and in each CRM article in our pilot publications, a request was made for interested volunteers. Each volunteer was requested to write a letter to the chairman expressing interest, citing prior experience, general background, and source of motivation. During 1988, over 90 letters were received. Six months before the first workshop was scheduled, the volunteers were sent a letter outlining what would be expected of them, along with a simple form asking for biographical information. Fifty responses were received, and from that number 30 were invited to participate in a 2-day Facilitator Workshop. There were two objectives for this meeting: First, the volunteers were given a preview of the workshops that they would be conducting to see just what would be involved; second, this workshop allowed the committee and our new CRM Manager, Captain David Harris, a chance to evaluate the volunteers.

The workshop sessions previewed our written modules. Volunteers were asked for stand-up, spoken critique. Next, volunteers were asked to present a short speech to the group on a subject of their choice. The participants were then ranked by perceived speaking ability, personality, appearance, and enthusiasm. A list of six "stars" was selected to begin training for the first Phase A seminars.

Each selectee was given a *Facilitator's Guide* covering facilitation skills, and a *Facilitator's Manual* which contained the entire CRM course. The first seminars were given to check airmen and management personnel. Facilitator trainees attended their first seminar (led by the CRM Manager and a member of the Steering Committee) as participants, the second seminar as observers, and in subsequent seminars progressively took over the job of facilitating one module at a time as a co-facilitator. Their performance was videotaped and critiqued by the CRM Manager. When members of this first group were certified as qualified, the other 24 volunteers were put through the same process. By the first line pilot seminar in June, 1989, all facilitators were trained and certified.

One important element of success was tight lesson plan control. Module lesson plans followed strict formats which included time lines. This forced facilitators to stay on track during each phase of the workshop, a process which guaranteed that subjects near the end received their scheduled time. Lesson plans were modified for workability as the seminars progressed. However, no changes were allowed without approval of the Steering Committee.

Efficient communication flow between facilitators and the CRM Manager emanated from two "logbooks." The first was a notebook of instructions and letters from the CRM Manager and/or the Steering Committee amplifying or clarifying a particular concept or module facilitators found difficult to teach. The other contained material entered by facilitators at the end of each seminar covering practical suggestions based on actual classroom experience, logistical problems and how to solve them, pitfalls to avoid, jokes and anecdotes that worked, and general impressions of how to do the job better. This notebook proved very popular among the facilitators. It undoubtedly improved performance and standardization.

Many benefits accrued from training check airmen and management personnel before training line pilots. Our consultants believed that check airmen would be the most resistant to CRM training and most critical of the program. This turned out to be the case. But by the time the first line pilot showed up for CRM training, his facilitator was a seasoned, battle-scarred veteran using material sifted and modified by the most scathing critiques imaginable.

Placing the facilitators' job in perspective, in 6 months they conducted workshops for over 7,400 pilots, conducting two and sometimes three simultaneous seminars 7 days a week. Additionally, during Phase A each facilitator trained himself to conduct Phase B, which began the day after the last Phase A seminar. Complicating the process were ongoing contract negotiations at Delta, a stressful time for all. Facilitators quite often found themselves in the role of counselor, mediator, company spokesperson, and conciliator. Such pressure on a daily basis took a toll which made it necessary to create a means of stress reduction for facilitators.

The process which evolved created a facilitators' group meeting on the last day of each month. At least one representative from senior management attended, along with members of the Steering Committee having expertise in counseling and stress management. These meetings provided an opportunity to ventilate frustrations and to make suggestions for change. Facilitators invariably left these meetings feeling highly valued, that pet peeves had been aired to one empowered to rectify them if appropriate, and that most peers shared similar feelings of "burnout." In one meeting, intensive training in defusing anger and conflict in groups proved especially useful. Fortunately, the attrition rate for facilitators was insignificant. Their monumental contribution shifted the mindset of an entire major airline.

CHECK AIRMAN AND MANAGEMENT TRAINING ── ✈

If the concepts and practices of CRM are to become standards of operation in any organization, it follows that check airmen will necessarily play a central role in the process.

(Helmreich, 1987, p. 19)

Ironically but understandably, check airmen taken as a group can be the most resistant to the personal change suggested by a comprehensive CRM training program. They are the "top of the food chain" of the pilot group and as such tend to believe that the skills which brought recognizable success are adequate. As "captains' captains," suggestions for change can be interpreted as criticism of past performance. Therefore, since CRM is all about changing attitudes, one must first clear this hurdle of defensiveness before any meaningful learning can take place. To make matters more complicated, the tense atmosphere which prevailed at Delta in 1987 placed many egos on the line. Our committee was painfully aware that resistance was to be expected. Not only were our check airmen expected to accept CRM, they were expected to teach, model and judge others in the use of CRM skills. This proved to be our most serious challenge. We therefore decided to present the entire course to our check airmen first. They were required to participate in the seminars as line pilots would and to complete both phases of the program back to back. Placing them in workshops with peers provided an opportunity to justify the need for the training to each other. It also provided us with highly constructive criticism from a very perceptive source. By responding positively to these suggestions, their "ownership" of the program was enhanced.

Check airmen cannot be expected to teach and evaluate CRM skills on the line and in LOFT without additional in-depth training. Responding to check airman concerns, a special training course was created specifically to teach evaluation. A 1-day, 8-hour training program was developed that has since been expanded into a 2-day program. In addition, CRM evaluation is reinforced annually in an 8-hour training program for all line check airmen. CRM evaluation and facilitation skills are now part of initial and recurrent training for all Flight Training Department instructors.

CLASSROOM FACILITIES ✈

Facilities needed for a CRM seminar are not much different than for any workshop. Classrooms should be comfortable, well lighted, and properly air conditioned. We planned our workshops for a maximum of 30 pilots divided into groups of six, seated at round tables. Fortunately, Delta had just opened a new ground training facility which had round tables, comfortable tilting chairs on rollers, and the latest state-of-the-art video equipment. However, a successful program does not require these trappings. What is required is the message to participants that those conducting the workshop have done their best to provide a comfortable learning atmosphere. The timeliness and volatility of the material will soon render other considerations irrelevant.

Considerable attention needs to be directed to slides and video presentation. Educational experts recommend that any given video be 7 to 9 minutes in length and followed up with group discussion or critique. One important ingredient of such a presentation is timing. A facilitator should not have to spend a great amount of time turning on video players and rewinding tapes. We put all video segments on one tape in sequential order separated by colored leaders. When finishing a tape segment one simply lets the tape run until the color changes, knowing that when it is restarted it will be properly positioned.

Our CRM Manager developed a checklist of supplies needed to conduct a given workshop. The facilitator was required to check the stock at the beginning of each seminar. At the end of the day, replenishment of the supplies from the storeroom was the final checklist item. Supplies were stored in kit form, so that each kit contained all the items needed for the entire day. This not only saved much time but also gave the facilitator a sense of support at the end of a long day.

LOFT ✈

Much has been written elsewhere in this book (see the chapter by Butler) about LOFT. Our comments will be restricted to our approach to LOFT and how it may be unique.

In a large airline, standardization of instruction becomes a significant problem. To forestall the temptation for each LOFT writer and simulator instructor to place a personal interpretation on the content and presentation of LOFT, our committee wrote a LOFT manual. It contains a step-by-step procedure for the construction of each scenario, a review process internal to the Flight Training Department, and detailed instructions and proscriptions covering how each session is to be conducted, briefed, and debriefed. Every instructor is given formal schooling on an annual basis in how to maximize the experience for the participants. LOFT debriefings are facilitated, that is, the crews self-debrief using excerpts from the videotape. Events in the tape can be electronically marked by the instructor when significant CRM events occur, so that the entire tape need not be replayed.

LOFT scenarios are rated by the participants as to difficulty, training value, realism, and impact. These evaluations are placed in a database to enable analysts to weed out less effective scenarios and to define just what types of scenarios are most effective. An attempt is made to correlate scenario content with CRM classroom material presented in annual recurrent training. All LOFT sessions are conducted with a complete crew of line pilots to ensure team issues are an integral part of the experience.

THE IMPACT OF AUTOMATION ON CRM TRAINING ✈

Early in the process of conducting CRM seminars, it became apparent that the experiences of crews operating highly automated aircraft, particularly the

Boeing 757 and 767, were different from those who operated less automated, older aircraft in terms of communication, team dynamics, situational awareness, and workload management (Wiener, 1989). Beginning with initial training, our pilots perceived operating these aircraft as highly stressful. Contrary to the aims of the designers, they believed that workloads approached unsafe levels in critical situations. They could not understand why personal confrontations with the other member of a two-person crew seemed to happen with a frequency never experienced in the older aircraft.

This feedback prompted a complete re-evaluation of the training and line operations of these aircraft. Among the findings was that our airline did not have a philosophy of automation. Absent such a philosophy, a vacuum was created filled by individual bias and the custom of usage. In our case, the philosophical vacuum was filled by the ubiquitous belief that if the company bought it, automated equipment was to be used and used all the time. In practice, older captains with no computer background were expected to master the flight management system (FMS) prior to the first simulator training period. No attempt was made to demonstrate that, for example, a B-767 flies like a B-727 (or any other airplane) when the ''magic'' is turned off. Indeed, from the first training period in the simulator, a trainee was expected to use all the automation and to master it before the checkride. This process created a failure rate higher than had ever been experienced at Delta. Moreover, many older pilots avoided upgrading to the B-757/767 because of fear of failure. But most importantly, our feedback in CRM seminars indicated that after training, pilots believed there was a 3–6-month period in which they were only marginally competent, and during this period stress levels skyrocketed. This was reported to be creating personal problems, confrontations with fellow crewmembers, and potentially unsafe situations on the line when automation anomalies occurred. Younger, computer-literate co-pilots tended to assume incompetence when the captain was slow to reprogram the FMS, and since on an automated aircraft ''the power resides in the box,'' serious confrontations of command authority, or worse, total abdications of authority were reported.

The response to this feedback was immediate. One working group created a ''Delta Air Lines Philosophy of Automation,'' accepted by all departments and taught in annual recurrent training (see Appendix), while the Flight Training Department totally revised the approach to simulator and flight training on the B-757/767. Before a pilot can attend ground school on an automated aircraft for the first time, he or she must first attend a generic automation school called ''Introduction to Aviation Automation,'' in which the general principles of automation and computerization are contrasted with old methods of navigation and systems management.

The first two simulator sessions in initial training are now conducted without use of the FMS, following which an extensive training regimen is conducted on state-of-the-art FMS training devices. When simulator training is resumed, pilots have learned the FMS but are capable of flying the aircraft in a non-automated as well as automated mode. They are encouraged to downgrade the level of automation whenever doubt or confusion exists. Current feedback indicates complete amelioration of the problems, and the failure rate in initial training resembles that on all other types of aircraft.

This is but one example of an ancillary benefit derived from a CRM training course where both the "cockpit shell" and the "corporate shell" are modified through effective two-way communication. However, the hidden potential for automation problems yet to be experienced will demand continuing theoretical and practical research, if the next generation of aircraft is to be introduced without creating additional human factors deficits.

EPILOGUE ✈

While the research design used to verify our CRM effort as effective suffers the liabilities of all large social psychology projects in terms of provable cause and effect, in early 1992 it can be reported that Delta has not experienced additional highly publicized operational "incidents." Quarterly air carrier discrepancy reports have declined significantly, the number of FAA violation cases defended by our Legal Department has dwindled, and Johnny Carson has moved on to other subjects. The database at NASA/UT tells us our pilots' attitudes changed significantly for the better vis-à-vis the importance of human and team skills in cockpit safety, and that this change has remained stable over time. Our new hires are indoctrinated in the importance of CRM skills as part of their initial training, and each pilot is refreshed on an annual basis in recurrent training and LOFT.

Delta Air Lines bet many millions of dollars on CRM. We believe that Delta, its crewmembers, and the traveling public will continue to win in the years ahead.

APPENDIX: DELTA AIR LINES STATEMENT OF AUTOMATION PHILOSOPHY ✈

The word "Automation", where it appears in this statement, shall mean the replacement of a human function, either manual or cognitive, with a machine function. This definition applies to all levels of automation in all airplanes flown by this airline. The purpose of automation is to aid the pilot in doing his or her job.

The pilot is the most complex, capable, and flexible component of the air transport system, and as such is best suited to determine the optimal use of resources in any given situation.

Pilots must be proficient in operating their airplanes in all levels of automation. They must be knowledgeable in the selection of the appropriate degree of automation and must have the skills needed to move from one level of automation to another.

Automation should be used at the level most appropriate to enhance the priorities of Safety, Passenger Comfort, Public Relations, Schedule, and Economy, as stated in the Flight Operations Policy Manual.

In order to achieve the above priorities, all Delta Air Lines training programs, training devices, procedures, checklists, aircraft and equipment acquisitions, manuals, quality control programs, standardization, supporting documents, and day-to-day operation of Delta aircraft shall be in accordance with this statement of philosophy.

References

Federal Aviation Administration. (1987). *Advisory Circular 120-51 (Draft 1.2)*. Washington, DC: Author.

Hackman, J. R. (1987). Group level issues in the design and training of cockpit crews. In H. W. Orlady & H. C. Foushee (Eds.), *Cockpit resource management training: Proceedings of the NASA/MAC workshop* (NASA Conference Publication 2455). Moffett Field, CA: NASA–Ames Research Center.

Helmreich, R. L. (1987). *Theory underlying CRM training: Psychological issues in flight crew performance and crew coordination* (NASA Conference Publication 2455), San Francisco, CA: Author.

Helmreich, R. L., Wilhelm, J. A., & Gregorich, S. E. (1988). *Revised version of the Cockpit management attitudes questionnaire (CMAQ), and CRM seminar evaluation form* (NASA/UT Technical Report 88-3), Austin.

Maher, J. W. (1991). Why pilots are least likely to get good decision making precisely when they need it the most. In *Proceedings of the Sixth International Symposium on Aviation Psychology.* Columbus: Ohio State University.

Margerson, C., McCann, D., & Davies, R. (1986). *Aircrew team management program* (NASA Conference Publication 2455). pp. 94–95, San Francisco, CA: Author.

Wiener, E. L. (1989). *Human factors of advanced technology ("glass cockpit") transport aircraft* (NASA Contractor Report No. 177528). Moffett Field, CA: NASA–Ames Research Center.

III

Conclusions

16

Airline Pilot Training Today and Tomorrow

Harry W. Orlady
Orlady Associates
Los Gatos, California 95032

INTRODUCTION ✈

This chapter addresses recent behavioral developments in training in the context of regulatory requirements that affect airline flight training. It assumes that pilots already have the technical skills and knowledge traditionally required of an airline pilot. This chapter also assumes that advanced technology aircraft (ADVTECH) are the transports of the immediate future, and that they will continue to play an important part in air transport for at least the next 20 years (Billings, 1991). During this period most pilot training will involve these aircraft.

The training process furnishes the primary interface between manufacturers, the companies that buy transport airplanes, the environment in which they must be operated, and the pilots that fly them. The environment in which these airplanes must be operated has become more complex. The airplanes have become both more sophisticated and more expensive. These interfaces—between the manufacturers, the airline companies, the pilots, and the environment—and the pilot training associated with them have become even more important.

In addition, over the years airline pilot training has become increasingly expensive. Working rules have become intricate, airplanes and training aids have become even more highly developed, and the airplanes must be operated in an increasingly complex aviation system. Acceptance of full utilization of simulation by the operators, the pilots, and the Federal Aviation Administration (FAA) has alleviated some of that expense, but it has by no means eliminated the real world economics involved in airline pilot training.

There have also been major changes in pilot training. Both regulators and operators recognize, and now explicitly state, that airplanes are flown not by individuals but by crews. This is an important and a major change, as other chapters in this book have stated.

THE AVIATION SYSTEM ————————————————— ✈

The airline transport industry is an important segment of a very complex aviation system. Many parts of the system and its major sub-systems have training implications. The regulatory or quasi-regulatory agencies, the research community, the manufacturers, the operators (including pilot and flight attendant unions), and several unofficial overseers of air transport operations such as the Air Transport Association of America (ATA) and consumer groups, can directly or indirectly influence training. Although this chapter is largely based upon U.S. experience, all these elements have their counterparts in other countries, oftentimes with different nomenclature.

The International Civil Aviation Organization (ICAO)

Aviation is truly international. Its inherent lack of terrestrial boundaries creates an obvious need for coordination and cooperation in aviation matters among the nation states that are directly involved in aviation operations.

ICAO was founded in 1947 to meet this need. It is a specialist agency of the United Nations and has had a major effect on the development of solutions for aviation's political and technical problems in the post–World War II era. It now has 166 contracting states as members. ICAO's principal aviation training activities lie in its development of uniform standards and recommended practices (SARPs) and in its Technical Assistance Programs for those countries that need them.

Each ICAO member state agrees to follow ICAO's SARPs unless the state gives formal notice that it is unable to comply with a specific SARP for internal reasons. These are rare events (D. Maurino, personal communication, December 12, 1991). Taylor (1988) contains an excellent summary of the role of ICAO and other international organizations involved in aviation.

Aviation in the United States

Interested Parties

In the United States, the FAA, the air traffic control system (ATC)—which is managed and operated by the FAA—the airlines, pilot-representing organizations, and the manufacturers of transport aircraft all play important roles in pilot training. To a considerably greater extent than formerly, the manufacturers of the other hardware and software used by the airlines, various research institutions, Congress, and the general public can also affect training. This amalgam of interests would create an almost impossible mixture of legitimate conflicts if their basic goals were not essentially the same. This does not mean that integration of the traditional goals of safety and efficiency always follows without difficulty.

Regulatory Agencies

The chief regulatory agency in the United States, and the overseer of all U.S. airline training activities, is the FAA. Organizationally, the FAA is a part of the U.S. Department of Transportation (DOT). The DOT is headed by the Secretary of Transportation, who is a member of the President's Cabinet.

Basic training philosophy, as well as specific training requirements for the U.S. aviation industry, is developed by FAA headquarters in Washington. Minimum standards are set there, usually with an industry consensus and within the broad international consensus established by ICAO's member states. While these minimum standards can be modified, they can be modified only with a specific exemption from the FAA. Because the FAA supervises the day-to-day operation of each airline and must approve all operating manuals and all training, it plays a very large role in airline training.

A recent FAA reorganization has been of particular interest to anyone involved in pilot training. In this major reorganization, the FAA created a high-level division headed by the Chief Scientific and Technical Advisor for Human Factors. This division functions at the top of the organization and affects all other divisions. It is a very graphic illustration of the recognition and growing importance of human factors in aviation operations. Another illustration of its importance is the development of a *National plan to enhance aviation safety through human factors improvements* (ATA, 1989; Foushee, 1990). This National Plan was prepared by the ATA's Human Factors Task Force in cooperation with 10 other major civil aviation organizations, including the FAA.

The Individual Airline

Ultimately each airline, whether it is a trunk, a regional, or a commuter airline, is responsible for the safety of its operations and therefore the adequacy of its training. As straightforward as that sounds, even within highly regulated countries such as the U.S., there are considerable differences in the quality of training and in operating practices, even among similar-appearing airlines (Degani & Wiener, 1991; Lautman & Gallimore, 1987).

There are several reasons for these differences. Air transport is a relatively young industry. It was created by a group of highly individualistic entrepreneurs who operated during difficult and dynamic times. They were blessed with very adaptable pilots whose adaptability was a requirement for both pilot and corporate success. Despite growing maturity, the air transport industry continued to be volatile in the ensuing years, largely because of the substantial growth of the industry, increased competition, the expansion of its geographic horizons, and the major technical developments which resulted during World War II.

SAFETY AND EFFICIENCY IN THE AVIATION SYSTEM
———————————————————————————————————— ✈

The paramount importance of safety in air transportation is acknowledged by all segments of the industry. Entirely apart from moral issues, airlines can no longer survive if they are not safe. Neither can they survive if their operations are inefficient. This is particularly true in a deregulated environment.

John Lauber, an aviation psychologist, formerly a research scientist at the National Aeronautics and Space Administration's (NASA) Ames Research Center and now a member of the National Transportation Safety Board (NTSB), has put it this way: "It is also clear that safety considerations have absolute veto power— no matter how economically beneficial a bit of technology might be. If it introduces, or is perceived to introduce, adverse safety consequences, it won't fly" (Lauber, 1991).

While there have been significant improvements in the safety and reliability of air transport, the industry is still faced with the fact that human error (or the failure of human beings in critical roles to always perform as expected) is involved in from 60% to 80% of its accidents (Lautman & Gallimore, 1987). This percentage has been true since the DC-3 days, despite a remarkable expansion in air transport. The industry's safety record has improved when measured in almost every way that safety can be measured, with the single exception of the item directly related to expansion, the absolute number of accidents or fatalities.

Formerly permissible safety standards are no longer acceptable. The industry seems fairly close to achieving the maximum number of accidents or fatalities, each month or each year, that the public will tolerate without inducing political and often emotional and unproductive action.

This chapter includes a discussion of the critical safety issue because training is a crucial part of the safety equation. It has become increasingly essential that training be done well. It is a requirement for survival.

The Role of Those Who Oversee

A great many organizations (some governmental and some from the private sector) monitor or oversee air transport safety, occasionally from quite different perspectives. While today any airline that survives must operate efficiently, its ultimate test, and the ultimate test of the adequacy of its training, is the safety of its operations.

The Federal Aviation Administration

As we have noted, the FAA is the chief governmental overseer of airline operations in the United States. Historically, it has decentralized its supervision of the airlines. Because of this decentralization, once basic policies were established, they were frequently subject to considerable interpretation by strong-minded individuals (principally FAA officials and airline operating executives). This has resulted in differences in the specifics of required training among the airlines.

The enforcers of FAA rules and guidelines are usually the FAA inspectors in the field. They are led by the Principal Operating Inspector (POI) for a specific airline. The development of effective training programs for POIs and the inspectors who work for them is a major task for the FAA.

The National Transportation Safety Board

While there is no question that the FAA, because of its regulatory and enforcement responsibilities, is the chief day-to-day overseer of all air transport operations in the United States, the NTSB has a special role. It has been given separate and independent investigatory powers by the U.S. Congress. The NTSB is an autonomous agency whose mission is to analyze selected accidents and incidents that occur in the U.S. transportation system, to determine the causes of these accidents and incidents, and to make recommendations based on its analysis and expertise. However, other than moral and occasionally powerful political persuasion, the NTSB has no enforcement capabilities. It has often been critical of its sister agency, the FAA.

Confidential and Non-Punitive Incident Reporting

A sometimes overlooked asset of the aviation system in the United States is the Aviation Safety Reporting System (ASRS). It is operated by NASA and funded by the FAA. One of the major changes in recent years has been the growth of confidential and non-punitive incident reporting systems, and the ASRS has become an acknowledged leader in this movement.

For a great many years aviation safety experts have believed that they could learn a great deal about preventing aircraft accidents from aviation incidents (Allen, 1966; Bruggink, 1983; Orlady, 1982b). This hypothesis got considerable and influential support when on December 1, 1974, TWA's Flight 514 crashed just outside our nation's capital, killing all the people on board.

At the time of this crash, information was available which might have prevented it. An innovative program of confidential, non-punitive incident reporting had just been inaugurated on United Airlines as a part of its Flight Safety Awareness Program. The second incident reported in this new program occurred just 6 weeks before the TWA accident and was almost a dress rehearsal for the TWA accident. Pilots involved in the United incident reported the same ATC clearance received by TWA's 514 six weeks later and had the same misunderstanding regarding the details of that clearance—the same misunderstanding that led to the TWA crash.

The information regarding the United incident might have prevented TWA's tragic accident and saved the lives of a great many people. That information had been circulated to United's pilots and to the FAA. However, at this time there was no program to expeditiously make such information known industry-wide.

Developments following the investigation of that crash led directly to the ASRS in the United States (Reynard, Billings, Cheaney, & Hardy, 1986). It was formed in order to make the safety lessons that could be learned from otherwise unavailable aviation incidents effectively available to all interested parties, to identify valid real world problems, and to stimulate appropriate research. Similar programs are now flourishing in several other countries. The United Kingdom's Confidential Human Factors Incident Reporting Programme (CHIRP) is an outstanding example. CHIRP is operated by Britain's Institute of Aviation Medicine. While it frankly admits it has borrowed much from the ASRS, CHIRP has made its own very real contributions to increased aviation safety.

There is little doubt that pilots will furnish data regarding their "unwanted occurrences" if they can do so without jeopardy to themselves and their careers. To date, over 235,000 reports have been sent to the ASRS. The facts and factors involved in these "unwanted occurrences" are frequently otherwise unavailable. These data have important training implications and the potential for making a significant improvement in aviation safety.

The day-to-day supervision of the ASRS is a special activity of NASA. It supervises the ASRS through an interagency agreement with the FAA which finances nearly all of the ASRS operation. NASA is also responsible for coordinating ASRS research activities with other elements of the aviation industry. It accomplishes the ASRS administrative function by contracting the day-to-day operation of the ASRS to an outside organization. Because NASA has no enforcement responsibilities, it is in a very good position to obtain uniquely straightforward data.

Virtually every report made to the ASRS is an "unwanted occurrence," and virtually every "unwanted occurrence" represents a breakdown or a weakness in the aviation system. All this makes the ASRS an important part of the system. It provides a heretofore unavailable mechanism to identify real-world problem areas. Unfortunately, the reporting process by itself seldom will identify the root cause of the problems reported. A major task is to identify the causes of the anomalies reported with precision and then to develop effective means of alleviating them. This problem is recognized in the *National Plan to Enhance Aviation Safety through Human Factors Improvements*.

Using ASRS data intelligently is a big challenge to researchers, for these data present some very real problems. For example, while there are a great many relevant variables in the aviation system, none of the reports can be fully investigated because of the importance of maintaining confidentiality. The aviation system is very complex, and simply tallying the anomalies or averaging numbers of incidents which have different root causes seldom provides definitive answers.

Other Organizations

The Air Line Pilots' Association (ALPA), which represents a majority of the airline pilots in the United States, maintains a large Air Safety and Engineering Department. In the course of its many activities the Engineering and Air Safety Department spends considerable effort in the training area—usually through its training committees, which are active at both local and national levels. ALPA spends a considerable portion of its dues dollars on its Air Safety and Engineering Department, as does the Allied Pilot's Association (APA), which represents the pilots of American Airlines.

Other organizations that monitor the safety of airline operations include the cabin crew unions, the U.S. Congress, various representatives of airline passengers, and the general and aviation press.

Aviation Research with Training Ramifications

Much aviation research has training ramifications. In the United States, the chief aviation research agency is NASA. NASA is split into two not entirely equal components, one dealing with space activities and the other with aviation. In the latter NASA conducts or supervises a great deal of the aviation research conducted in this country. Much of this research is done in-house, although a substantial amount is also done by universities and other organizations through NASA grants and contracts under NASA supervision. This research involves both present and future aviation activities. Anyone dealing with airline training must keep selectively well informed of NASA's aviation research. For example, NASA performed or has been responsible for many of the studies on line-oriented flight training (LOFT) and cockpit resource management (CRM) which have led to their current emphasis in this country and around the world. (See the chapter by Helmreich & Foushee.)

The FAA conducts or finances a considerable amount of research on its own. In accordance with its overall responsibilities, this research covers the entire gamut of aviation. Because the FAA has sole responsibility for the ATC system, a great deal of the research it funds or conducts is devoted to ATC problems.

Government research in aviation includes that done by a separate group within the DOT known as the Research and Special Programs Administration. Virtually all this research is done at the Volpe National Transportation Systems Center at Cambridge, Massachusetts. The Research and Special Programs Administration does research for all of the Federal government's transportation modes.

The Volpe Center was formerly called the Transportation Systems Center. It employs systems analysts, engineers, computer scientists, programmers, and human factors psychologists to support the research and analytic needs of the various transportation modes (M. S. Huntley, Jr., personal communication, October 15, 1991).

The manufacturers of both transport aircraft and their systems also do important research with training applications. Classic examples are the ground proximity warning system (GPWS) and the traffic alert collision avoidance system (TCAS). Other aviation research is conducted by individual airlines and some universities. Universities are inclined to specialize in single-pilot general aviation activities both because of their interest and because of the difficulty of performing meaningful research in the complex air transport system with the facilities available to them.

A basic problem for the air transport industry, researchers, and the FAA is to ensure that research aimed at industry problems deals with the real world in which the industry operates (Helmreich, 1990). The final report of the Training Sub-Committee of a recent NASA/FAA/Industry Workshop (Norman & Orlady, 1988) stated, "It is equally important that members of the scientific community (which includes the universities) interested or involved in air carrier operations receive sufficient training or indoctrination in those operations to ensure that their recommendations and research are responsive to real-world needs and problems." The report did not state how this task could be accomplished, but it is clear that it will take substantial funds, cooperation, and valuable time from the airlines, research organizations, and the universities to accomplish it.

In many cases the training ramifications of a given research study are serendipitous (Lauber, 1987). For example, two influential NASA studies, Ruffell Smith, (1979) and Foushee, Lauber, Baetge, & Acomb (1986), have both led to major training innovations. The training ramifications of these studies were not envisioned when setting the original research objectives.

AIRLINE PILOT TRAINING ————————————————————→

Airline operating philosophy, policies, and procedures are key ingredients in any operation. Degani & Wiener (1991) have called them "the three P's of flight-deck operations." All three are an integral part of pilot training. Differences in the definition and implementation of the "three P's" lead to substantial differences in the operational quality of airlines and their operations (Lautman & Gallimore, 1987; Weener, 1991).

Traditional Pilot Training

Traditionally, airline pilot training has been concerned with developing and maintaining technical skills. There are four basic types of training for these skills. Each assumes a reasonably well qualified pilot who has the skills and knowledge that are appropriate for his or her position.

The first training is for new hires. For some it includes an upgrading of skills and knowledge, but its main purpose is simply to teach the aviator what he or she needs to know to fly the company's airplanes on the company's routes. The second type of training has been called upgrade training. Here the purpose is to prepare the pilot for a change in status, such as from co-pilot to captain. A third type of training is transition or conversion training on a specific aircraft. Its objective is to teach pilots how to fly a sometimes different airplane safely and efficiently in the company's line operations.

A fourth type of traditional airline pilot training is recurrent training. It affects all pilots. Recurrent training in the United States is mandated by Federal Aviation Regulations (FAR) at specified times—traditionally every 6 months for captains and annually for first officers. Its purpose is to ensure that the pilot has maintained his or her proficiency and the skills and knowledge required to fly as an airline pilot on a specific type of equipment. A secondary purpose is to reinforce knowledge of the latest operational information affecting the specific equipment involved. Historically the second annual period of recurrent training includes required proficiency checks for both captains and first officers.

In the United States, the intervening time between sessions of recurrent training is one of the issues currently being re-examined. It is a subject that is highly controversial. Several airlines are already operating under modifications of the usual rules. The most common modification substitutes one 3- or 4-day session of training annually for the more usual two periods of 2 days with each period 6 months apart. A condition for FAA approval of this modification has been assurance that the airline would place considerable emphasis on CRM during each annual training period. Critics claim that periods of 13 months and beyond are too long for any pilot to be absent from a flight training center.

Specific details of required maneuvers for pilot initial, transition, recurrent, and upgrade flight training and for proficiency checks are stated in Appendixes E and F of FAR 121.424 and FAR 121.441. Any modifications of compliance with these appendixes require an official exception. Air taxi and commuter airline training requirements are found in FAR 135.

In many countries there is no ready source of previously trained potential airline pilots. Therefore, airlines have had to start ab initio training on their own.

Dedicated, airline-specific ab initio training for prospective airline pilots started in Europe in the 1950s (Johnston, 1991). It is a fifth type of training and is a new concept for a great many U.S. and Third World airlines. Clearly, ab initio training for airline pilots can be done very successfully. It may become the norm of the future.

Generic Changes in Pilot Training

Over the past decade there have been many changes in training for airline pilots. Several of them have been truly generic. For example, virtually all persons and institutions involved in training now recognize that flying a current transport airplane in today's environment is a team task. This was not always true. Former FAA Administrator Allan McArtor, one of the leaders in this movement, put it succinctly at a meeting of airline executives in Kansas City in August, 1987. Among other things he said, "Individuals don't crash, flight crews do." Regulators did not always speak this way, and neither has most of the rest of the industry.

In what may be the most important generic difference of all, the role and responsibility of the first officer has been substantially increased. This is true whether he or she is the pilot-flying (PF) or the pilot-not-flying (PNF). This change has been expounded in NTSB accident reports, by the FAA, and by a great many carriers.

A graphic example of the effect of this new emphasis on the role and responsibilities of the second in command may be seen in a comparison of an early ASRS study by Orlady (1982a) with a NASA study done 9 years later by Degani, Chappell, & Hayes (1991). In the first study, captains detected a significantly larger number of anomalies than did first officers. It made virtually no difference whether they were the PF or the PNF. This indicated, among other things, that the captains in the first study were much more effective monitors than their first officers. The missed items reported in this study were all straightforward operational items. Most of them were altitude deviations. All the anomalies reported were well within the knowledge of the first officers. Their detection could not be attributed simply to the greater experience of the captains.

In the second study Degani et al. found no difference between the detection performance of captains and first officers in the altitude deviations they were examining. As in the earlier study, it made virtually no difference whether the pilot who first detected the anomaly was the PF or the PNF.

This expansion of the responsibility of first officers was stressed by many airlines, the NTSB, the FAA, NASA, and pilot unions during the interim period between the studies. All of them emphasized the need for first officers to be more assertive and for captains to encourage this kind of behavior. An example of this approach from a non-U.S. carrier is given in an excerpt from the "Briefs of evidence to and memorandum by Royal Commission" by Captain Cooper, Vice Chairman Overseas Branch Council New Zealand Airline Pilots Association

(NZALPA) during the Royal Commission's investigation of the crash of Flight 901 at Mt. Erebus. Captain Cooper, reflecting on the policy of Air New Zealand and NZALPA, stated, "It is the inherent responsibility of every crew member, if he be unsure, unhappy or whatever, to question the pilot in command as to the nature of his concern. Indeed, it would not be going too far to say that, *if a pilot in command were to create an atmosphere whereby one of his crew members would be hesitant to comment on any action, then he would be failing in his duty as pilot in command*" (Vette with McDonald, 1983, emphasis supplied). A great many airline flights were not operated in accordance with this philosophy during the period of the first study.

Human Factors in Pilot Training

There is no question but that human factors will play an increasingly important role in pilot training and in all aviation operations. Human factors has become a truly international concept and is now recognized as a "core technology" in aviation, in much the same manner as are such disciplines as meteorology, aerodynamics, navigation, communication, and others. Several aspects of human factors are of direct concern to anyone involved in flight operations. Most of them have training ramifications.

Internationally, the ICAO Assembly set the foundations for a program for aviation human factors for all nations 6 years ago (1986) by passing Assembly Resolution A26-9. ICAO's Air Navigation Commission further defined the objective of this resolution, stating that its purpose was "to improve safety in aviation by making States more aware and more responsible for the importance of human factors in civil aviation through the provision of practical human factors materials and measures, developed on the basis of experience within States" (ICAO, 1989). The passage of this resolution is an example of real leadership by ICAO. It has already had considerable influence on the content of pilot training programs.

Three years later, the ICAO Council enacted a revision to the 1989 update of ICAO's Annex I. Annex I now requires that all pilots in the future be familiar with "human performance and limitations" as they relate to their flying activities and the formal privileges of their license. This new ICAO provision provides a challenge to many ICAO contracting states. Provision of appropriate background and testing material in the effective implementation of this regulation is not an easy task despite the production of a series of excellent *Human Factors Digests* by ICAO.

It is of considerable interest that U.S.S.R. delegates (now members of the Russian Commonwealth of Independent States) have been a driving force behind ICAO's human factors efforts. They were a major influence in the implementation of Resolution A26-9. It is also important to recognize that the revision to Annex I involving pilot knowledge of human performance and limitations had been steadfastly supported by the International Federation of Airline Pilots delegate and by a great many states. There is little doubt that increased recognition of the importance of human factors in aviation is truly a broadly based international movement.

Great Britain has been one of several leaders in the area of the effective implementation of human factors knowledge for pilots. In compliance with the ICAO Recommended Practice and a European Civil Aviation Commission syllabus, the United Kingdom Civil Authority (like an increasing number of ICAO member counterparts) now specifically requires a human performance and limitations examination for all prospective private and commercial license holders. Green, Muir, Jones, Gradvell, & Green (1991) was written specifically to help U.K. pilots meet their new requirement.

In the United States, the importance of human factors is implicit in the FAA's reorganization, the consensual development of a *National plan,* and the positive continuing influence of the ATA's broadly based Human Factors Task Force. The task force included the pilot unions—ALPA and APA—the manufacturers, the DOT and FAA, and the Regional Airlines Association. All of them emphasize the significance of human factors development in U.S. aviation.

One of the most elementary aspects of human factors in aviation deals with human limitations. While this seems obvious, on occasion basic human limitations have been overlooked. They are now specified in the update of ICAO's Annex I. A second aspect that continues to be important deals with operation in a changing aviation environment that is often foreign to the people who temporarily live or work in it.

A third aspect of aviation human factors is involved with the design and manufacture of the aircraft and its subsystems. In addition to basic human limitations, there is also concern about primarily physical attributes—the placement and adequacy of seats, controls, displays, lighting characteristics, cockpit environment, and so on, as well as potential cockpit workload and the training ramifications of the new design.

A fourth aspect of aviation human factors becomes a major consideration after an aircraft and its subsystems have been manufactured. At this point, manuals, procedures, checklists, and specific training become an important part of the human factors spectrum. The distinction between the human factors involved in manufacturing and the human factors involved in the implementation of a safe and efficient operation after an airplane has been manufactured has not always been recognized.

At a slightly different level, while training should not be used as a dumping ground for poor design (as has sometimes happened), neither should an operation based on inadequate training, unsatisfactory manuals, or inferior procedures, or one that trangresses basic human limitations, be used to malign what is essentially a good aircraft or system. This has also happened on occasion.

A fundamental truth is that once an airplane is purchased, whether it is a good airplane or whether it is marginal, it becomes the responsibility of the airline that purchased it to fly this new piece of equipment safely and efficiently in its day-to-day operations. This can only be done with effective training (Orlady, 1989b).

Other Recent Changes in Pilot Training

Most of the changes that have occurred in flight operations and in training over the years have been evolutionary rather than revolutionary. This is not surprising, since change and technological innovation have always been an inherent part of air transport. The industry has gone from lighted cans of kerosene to the first runway lights; from the old loop and then the Adcock four-course radio ranges to very high frequency omnidirectional radio ranges and category III instrument landing systems; from straight wings and "suck, squeeze, bang, and push" (intake, compression, power, and exhaust) piston engines to swept-wing airplanes and smooth, rotating turbine power. Now global positioning systems are becoming an operational reality. They are satellite-based and so accurate that they have approach and landing applications. In this very dynamic industry, there is nothing new about technological change (Orlady, 1990).

Frequently, major evolutionary changes are accompanied by a "shakedown period." For example, when the industry changed from piston to jet-powered airplanes and from straight wings to swept wings, nobody—operators, regulators, or pilots—really knew how train for or operate the new airplanes optimally in day-to-day line operations.

These new airplanes also had minor problems, and in a very few cases, major problems. Pilots and mechanics had to learn and depend on new cues and learn to disregard old, dependable cues that were often overlearned. There was frequently disagreement about optimum procedures. Appropriate simulators and training facilities were often not available, and flight and ground instructors, check airmen, and the FAA were all new to the airplane (Orlady, 1990).

Perspective in these matters is important. While such occasions may be rare, we need to identify valid problems quickly. We also need to identify those problems that are simply a part of the "shakedown period." The present era of increased automation and the "glass cockpit" is no exception. There are considerable data to suggest that at least some of the problems identified during the introduction of airplanes with these characteristics have been "shakedown" problems.

The demanding profession of airline piloting, even with good training, will also have rare failures. For reasons that are far from clear, a few pilots lose the motivation, skills, and knowledge required for their position in spite of a long period of satisfactory performance. In other cases a very few people, including some trainers and regulators, have difficulty adapting to changing conditions and a changing environment. This happened in the early days when pilots first had to learn to fly on instruments. It also happened when large parts of the industry transitioned from piston airplanes to jets. The only acceptable program that deals with either of these adaptability problems in an ever-changing operation is one that provides the flexibility and sensitivity needed to give people in this very gray area as much help as most of them richly deserve.

NEW TRAINING CONCEPTS

In the United States, and in many other countries of the world, LOFT and CRM have almost become buzzwords. In several countries the terms, and even the concepts, are still contentious. It is my belief that much of the dispute about CRM and LOFT involves more semantics than substance, but there is no question that there is far from total international agreement on this nomenclature and the meaning, content, and even the efficacy of these concepts.

Line-oriented Flight Training

In the United States, the concept of LOFT was originated by Northwest Orient Airlines under the leadership of Captain Tom Nunn. Northwest called this new type of training coordinated crew training or CCT. It was approved by the FAA on February 5, 1976, with an exemption from FAR 121.409 (FAR Exemption No. 2209, and Advisory Circular 120-35, July 13, 1978; Nunn, 1981). However, as an example of the difficulty of making categorical statements about the origins of training advancements, many Lufthansa pilots maintain that they have been using something like LOFT for a great many years.

During this same period NASA scientists at the Ames Research Center, including Charles Billings, John Lauber, Clay Foushee, and Miles Murphy, were becoming increasingly concerned regarding the effects of intra-crew behavior on our accident rate. They were stimulated and encouraged by Ruffell Smith's (1979) classic study of the relationships between pilot workload and errors, vigilance, and decision-making and developed a program which had several common elements with the innovative training started by Nunn.

A new and important training concept had been developed independently by the two separate groups. While both parties had somewhat different goals, both had recognized a very real problem and independently of each other developed solutions which had a great deal in common. It was an example of the less than optimal communication system that we occasionally find in the air transport industry, despite what is basically a very good record in any area involving effective training and safer flight operations.

Unfortunately the terminologies used in describing LOFT and full-mission simulation have been used interchangeably. Tom Nunn made the distinction between the two very clear at a NASA/Industry Workshop held at the Ames Research Center in January, 1981 (Lauber and Foushee, 1981, pp. 27–28). Among many other things he stated:

> LOFT is *not* full-mission simulation. LOFT *utilizes* full-mission simulation to create a real-world environment [for training] but full-mission simulation has many uses beyond original LOFT concepts. Traditional LOFT is entirely a training concept. Full-mission may be used as a vehicle for check-rides, navigation training, specific emergency procedures training, experimental evaluations and other purposes. The primary thrust of LOFT is not specific procedure training and (it) is certainly not intended for flight checking. A proper distinction between any type of full-mission simulation and LOFT must be maintained.

Although the distinction can become very gray, particularly when LOFT is integrated with the "training to proficiency" concept, the LOFT exercise should not include any type of check or final evaluation.

As the name implies, LOFT is a form of training. It begins as a simulated line trip—with dispatch, load planning, and any other paperwork included. Specific problems are introduced as the flight continues with no "simulator freezes" or other interruptions, so that the entire crew can see the ultimate consequences (good or bad) of their actions.

LOFTs are videotaped at some carriers so that they can be played back for the crew at debriefing. Because of the videotape, a skilled instructor can involve the entire flight crew in an effective discussion of flightcrew performance much easier than is possible without such realistic feedback. This feedback enhances the training exercise's potential (Hawkins, 1987; chapter by Butler).

In the United States, most videotapes are erased at the conclusion of the training session to be sure that performance during a LOFT session will have no later checking or disciplinary ramifications. Under these conditions, a LOFT session is seen by the pilots entirely as a learning situation. However, in some other countries, there is a belief that routine erasure at the conclusion of a LOFT exercise can diminish the training potential of that session—that lessons learned, both good and bad, can and should be shared. Further discussion of LOFT and its techniques can be found in the chapter by Butler.

Although training was not a part of the original interest of his study, Ruffell Smith noted in his final report that "special training in resource management and captaincy [should] be developed and validated. Such training should include the use of full mission simulation of scenarios that are representative of actual situations. Special emphasis should be given to those situations where rapid decisions and safe solutions for operating problems are required" (Ruffell Smith, 1979).

This training need, which anticipates both LOFT and CRM, had not been previously recognized by many operational personnel.

Today it should be remembered that LOFT is still a new training technology. Modifications and improvements are still being made. While LOFT has full FAA conceptual support, there is not always agreement on some of its details. The report of a NASA/Industry workshop on LOFT is required reading for anyone interested in implementing a LOFT program (Lauber and Foushee, 1981).

In any total flight operations training program there are two basic problems for both the FAA and the carriers it supervises. The first is to ensure that the flightcrew is capable of handling all the problems it might reasonably be expected to encounter. It is not easy to develop appropriate LOFT scenarios that meet all these conditions. The second, and entirely separate, problem is what to do with a crewmember whose performance is not satisfactory. There is no question that if the checking aspect is not a part of the LOFT process, a more productive training situation is created. The strategy presently being used is simply to require more training before the mandatory checking period. So far this approach seems to have worked well. However, the checking/training dilemma associated with the "training to proficiency" concept still leaves many people—pilots, operators, and the FAA—at least slightly uneasy. The FAA recognizes this problem and has indicated that a great deal of importance will be accorded to "evaluators" in any approved Advanced Qualification Program (Office of the Federal Register, 1990). The Advanced Qualification Program (AQP) concept is discussed later in this chapter and in considerably more detail in the chapter by Birnbach & Longridge.

Cockpit Resource Management

Many of the concepts of cockpit resource management, which is now often known as crew resource management to ensure that other relevant operational individuals are included (FAA, 1991), have been around for many years and have been routinely used by good pilots. However, until recently the individuality of the checking and licensing process, plus the "one-man-band" tradition of the captain's role, prevented official acceptance (by either the FAA or most airlines) of the CRM philosophy as an important part of aviation safety. The phrase "cockpit resource management" is actually an extension of the older phrase "cockpit management" and probably was originated by Lauber, who has defined CRM as "the effective utilization of all available resources—hardware, software, and liveware—to achieve safe, efficient flight operations" (Lauber, 1987). This was several years ago and is still a good and useful definition.

A problem for many has been the proliferation of names or acronyms for programs having essentially the same content. For example, a major airline and a pioneer in the implementation of the ubiquitous CRM concept called it Command,

Leadership, Resource Management or C/L/R. In its *Introduction to Command/Leadership/Resource Management* United Airlines wrote

> Representatives of management and ALPA have studied and continue to examine this problem (effective cockpit resource management) in depth. Their investigations have led to three important conclusions:
>
> 1. Piloting skills, systems knowledge, intellectual curiosity, mental and physical health, and a thorough knowledge of the aviation environment are the base upon which effective Command/Leadership/Resource Management can be built.
> 2. C/L/R cannot be a one-shot approach. It has to be a coordinated, long-range program. It must therefore be an integral part of the entire training effort: new hire training, transition and upgrade programs, and recurrent training.
> 3. C/L/R training should include all members of the flightcrew in every phase of each individual's career.

Another major airline (American) took a slightly different approach and listed the following seven principles of cockpit resource management in its publication *Flight Deck* (1981):

Principles of Flight Deck Management

> 1. Appropriate delegation of tasks and assignments of responsibilities.
> 2. Establishment of a logical order of priorities.
> 3. Continuous monitoring and cross checking of essential instruments and systems.
> 4. Assessment of problems with care and avoidance of preoccupation with minor ones.
> 5. Utilization of all available data to conduct an operation.
> 6. Clear communications among crew members of all plans and intentions.
> 7. Assurance of sound leadership by the pilot in command.

Illustrating the common theme that permeates this activity, Wiener (1989) wrote:

> Generically the term "cockpit resource management" (CRM) refers to the manner in which the crew conducts a flight, not as two or three highly trained individuals, but as one team. CRM refers to the manner in which the individual crew members support each other, the roles played by the captain as pilot in command, and the role of the first officer, and flight engineer if a three-pilot crew. It is an encompassing term which includes crew coordination, communication, the use of human and inanimate re-

sources both within and without the cockpit (e.g. company radio, ATC), role definition, the exercise of authority by the captain, and assertiveness by the other crew member(s).

This was a nearly decade later.

Finally, a draft of a FAA CRM Advisory Circular (FAA, 1991) defines not *cockpit* but *crew* resource management as

> the effective utilization of resources available to the aircrew—information, equipment and personnel (themselves and others)—expressed in terms of individual and collective cognitive, interpersonal and motor skills; knowledge and attitudes. The scope of safe operations must include a realistic set of conditions that include the external environment (weather, ATC, dispatch, weather service, navigation aids, etc.) as well as aircraft abnormalities and emergencies.

While this quotation is from a late FAA draft of its CRM Advisory Circular, there may well be further modifications of this definition in future drafts.

Advanced Qualification Program

The FAA's AQP represents a major agency effort to demonstrate maximum flexibility in order to take full advantage of the skills and knowledge of individuals, and also to meet the ever-increasing costs of airline pilot training. All of this without derogating its basic responsibility for safe and efficient public transport by air.

The AQP objectives have the solid support of the ATA Task Force on Human Factors, of ALPA and APA, and of many others. It is completely consistent with the broadly supported *National plan to enhance aviation safety through human factors improvements* (ATA, 1989; Foushee, 1990). Several airlines have already applied to participate and at least one has achieved FAA approval for an AQP program (Langer, 1992). While consensus has not yet been reached on many of the details of an effective AQP program, the importance of AQP in the field of airline pilot training can hardly be overstated.

AIRLINE PILOT TRAINING TODAY AND TOMORROW

Today there are at least two kinds of required training: (1) Training for technical skills, which includes basic "stick-and-rudder" skills and such traditional disciplines as meteorology, aerodynamics, power plants, navigation, and so on; and more recently (2) training for those behavioral and resource management skills which are also required in order to fly safely and efficiently in today's environment. While CRM, which is getting a great deal of attention today, is primarily concerned with behavioral and resource management skills, this by no means implies that a high level of technical skills is not also required.

There have been changes in the professional airline pilot's job. Today's professional pilots must not only know the technical aspects of their job (i.e., their airplane, their procedures, aerodynamics, meteorology, etc.) but they must also know basic human factors as they relate to the job of being an airline pilot (Orlady, 1989b). This concept of the pilot's job is reinforced by virtually all organizations concerned with air transport safety.

At a minimum, today's pilots must recognize that both they and their fellow crewmembers are human beings with human strengths and human limitations. Today's pilots need special behavioral and resource management skills, and they must understand small-group performance as it is reflected in improved crew coordination and performance. One of the prime tasks of today's professional airmen (pilots and managers alike) is to take advantage of human strengths to prevent or control human weaknesses, including outright mistakes (Orlady, 1989b). This principle is now recognized at virtually all relevant levels of operational authority. It is also recognized that these interpersonal and largely behavioral concepts require specific training.

Regulation in the United States

"There is a consensus among training experts, both within and outside the industry, that regulatory requirements (and those training practices that are based solely upon them) have not kept up with advancing technology" (Norman & Orlady, 1988). The FAA, which ultimately sets the minimum standards for all airline training done in the United States, is fully aware of this problem. Its AQP, which is discussed in considerably more detail in the chapter by Birnbach & Longridge, is an innovative method of dealing with this issue. While the regulators in other countries may have taken a different approach, most of them have recognized the basic problem of ensuring that required training keep up with advanced technology in an important and very dynamic industry.

The Manufacturers' Role

There seems little doubt that manufacturers will play a larger role in pilot training than they have in the past. There are several reasons for this. One of the most important is that there is growing recognition that the general training requirements needed for pilots to operate new equipment safely and efficiently should be considered an integral part of the design process. While training requirements need not be specific, the designers of new aircraft and their systems should consider the skills and knowledge that will be required to operate their new aircraft and systems safely and efficiently. They should also consider the amount and kind of training necessary to acquire the skills and knowledge that will be required of the pilots who fly their aircraft and the mechanics who maintain them.

Another basic reason for the larger training role of the manufacturers is that the training capability of the buyers of ADVTECH aircraft can vary considerably. Because the training process provides the interface between the manufacturer and the operator, and because airline pilot training has become even more complex and important, the only way that the manufacturer can be assured that high-quality training is always available is to provide it. The moral and economic stakes are too high to do otherwise.

Air Carrier Management

It seems obvious that any serious discussion of pilot training and CRM has implications for both pilots and managers (Orlady, 1989b). The functions of each group are absolutely crucial. It is essential that the training aspect of airline operational management be viewed in this context. For many pilots, airline training begins with air carrier management. Flight instructors and check pilots have a special role and are dealt with separately below.

A basic requirement for any flight operations management is to be able to communicate effectively with its pilots. It is particularly important when major changes, such as the FAA's AQP, are being developed. Several years ago, Captain Eric Jackson (1975) of Aer Lingus stated a basic principle of effective communication when he wrote:

> there . . . is an *absolute requirement* to consult, discuss, justify and defend all procedures, changes and rules where the pilot is professionally and personally involved. This makes constant liaison necessary . . . with the maximum exchange of information, views and policies absolutely vital. [emphasis supplied]

While this specific approach may need slight modification for some airlines, it is worth noting that it can do two important things. First, it can help ensure that pilots understand the reasons for their procedures and the reasons and rationale for any changes. Second, it almost certainly secures pilot interest and, hopefully, positive involvement in the consistent utilization of the basic principles and of the process and procedures being developed.

One of management's first tasks is to develop a clear understanding of the way it wants its flight operations conducted. Unfortunately, not all managements have done this. A specific operating philosophy must be stated clearly and without equivocation. This is more difficult than it may appear (Degani & Wiener, 1991). This operating philosophy must then be communicated effectively to trainers and pilots (Orlady, 1983).

Both management and training are concerned with the specifics of basic operating procedures as they are established by the manufacturer (and as they may be modified by the airline). They should be equally concerned with the manner in which their operating practices and procedures are implemented.

Operating practices and procedures include the "monitored approach," the "fail safe crew," and the basic "crew concept." They also include procedures for the handling of "obvious" and "subtle" incapacitation, the use of the "two communication rule" (which states that any crewmember should have a high index of suspicion any time he or she does not receive an appropriate response to any operational communication or to any deviation from standard operating procedures or a standard flight profile), and the development of clear distinctions between PF and PNF duties. All these practices or procedures are part of Degani and Wiener's "three P's," and they all have training implications.

An equally important requirement is to ensure that training pilots, check airmen, other supervisory pilots, and higher levels of flight operations management follow the rules and procedures that have been promulgated. In the elegant language of the academics, the "theory espoused" must also be the "theory practiced" whenever and wherever management is involved. While this sounds relatively simple and blatantly obvious, the "theory practiced" by some parts of management sometimes varies from the "theory espoused" (Bolman, 1979).

Flight manuals, equipment manuals, checklists, and operational bulletins are all important communications media. They should be useful documents that reflect the character and operating philosophy of the airline. They reflect the airline's operational procedures and its training. It takes considerably more than simply the issuance of manuals or directives from the top of an "operational Mount Olympus" to communicate effectively to pilots (Orlady, 1983).

In recent years, teaching, and then implementing, general company policies and specific operating philosophy have become an important part of CRM. They are becoming an integral part of airline pilot training. Teaching, and then implementing, general company policies and the company's specific operating philosophy in all fleets in a consistent, organized, and effective manner is not an easy task where this has not been a part of the company's tradition.

While most carriers perform their own training, the practice of contracting at least some of that training to another airline, to the manufacturer, or to a training organization is growing. This is done usually because the airline does not have the facilities (simulators, instructors, etc.) to do the training in house at that time. In addition, it has become a less and less attractive alternative to take an airplane out of line service to do training, because to do so has become extremely expensive. A major and continuing problem is to be sure that the airline's philosophy, policies, and procedures are reflected in contracted training and evaluation.

An increasing number of airlines have anticipated a continuing need for high-quality airline pilot training and have developed specialized "training centers" whose services are available for hire. These airlines maximize the use of expensive training equipment, and many of them are marketing their training capabilities. Several, particularly in Europe, consider their flight academies as separate profit centers and provide training ranging from ab initio to aircraft-type training (Hopkins, 1991). There is no reason to anticipate a diminution of these efforts.

Role of the Flight Instructor and the Check Pilot

The increasing emphasis on CRM principles is making the role of the flight instructor and the check pilot (or "evaluator" in AQP terminology) more complex. Not only are the roles of flight instructors and check pilots changing, but both jobs are becoming more difficult. The teaching, and then the evaluation or assessment, of airline pilots must now include the behavioral aspects of airline flight operation. Flight instructors and check pilots are real keys in effective pilot training. There is now even more emphasis on selection procedures for both, with considerable concern for the ability to teach CRM principles (Helmreich, Chidester, Foushee, Gregorich, & Wilhelm, 1989).

Inevitably, both flight instructors and check pilots will require special training. No longer will technical skills be enough. The FAA has given considerable emphasis to the importance of both instructors and evaluators (check pilots) in its Notice of Proposed Rulemaking (NPRM) dealing with AQP. As this chapter is being written, methods for evaluating individuals in team performance and in an individual's ability to perform as a team member have not been validated. The development of suitable criteria and the validation of workable methods has been given and needs a very high priority (Helmreich et al., 1989).

Training Organizations

A new provision under the AQP program is the formal establishment of FAA-designated "training centers." They are defined under a FAA NPRM as: "An independent organization that provides training under contract or other arrangement to certificate holders. A training center may be a certificate holder that provides training to another certificate holder, an aircraft manufacturer that provides training to certificate holders, or a non-certificate holder that provides training to a certificate holder."

Such training centers will be staffed with people who have been approved by the FAA. Approved training centers will be authorized to furnish both flight instructors and evaluators for carriers for CRM and for specific airplanes for specific carriers. This will formalize a process that has grown over the past few years.

While many manufacturers will have approved training centers, it seems probable that most manufacturers will concentrate on initial qualification and recurrent training for their airplanes.

Purely training organizations are already playing an increasing role in commuter airline operations. There is little doubt that they will play a continuing and growing role in both U.S. and foreign airline trunk transport as well.

Training in the Future

Without doubt there will be many changes for the line pilot. Computer-based training (CBT) is one of them despite some of its obvious limitations. Today, even the best CBT seems to adapt much better to needs in the technical training area than it does in areas requiring behavioral and other kinds of skills and knowledge.

Unfortunately, many early CBT programs did not provide realistic training because they were essentially single-path trainers. These training devices had only one way to accomplish a specific goal. They became little more than a "punch the right button so you can get to the next step" training device. They did not have the alternatives that were available in the airplane and therefore did not simulate their part of the real world. It is not at all surprising that pilots gave early CBT a poor reputation.

Fortunately, there have been substantial advances in virtually all CBT areas, and there is little doubt that its use will continue to increase. Among the advantages attributed to CBT are the following: (1) it is more economical than lecture-type instruction; (2) it ensures that all trainees receive the same and the correct information; (3) it does not require large numbers of expert instructors; and (4) somewhat controversially, it reduces undesirable pressure on trainees by permitting them to proceed at their own pace.

Critics maintain that even the best CBTs do not actually reduce the time pressure on trainees because there are usually expected and sometimes even published time limits for each section (Curry, 1985). The critics also maintain that the classroom interface with other students and a live instructor in the older classical ground school environment provides a valuable educational exchange that is impossible with CBT. The most successful training programs seem to have some of each.

From virtually the beginning of the ADVTECH era, pilots have complained that they did not get enough basic system training, and in particular that they did not get enough in flight management systems (FMS). One answer seems to be increased use of part-task trainers, which are sometimes called flight training devices (FTDs). The FAA has established seven different levels of complexity required in FTDs (FAA, 1992a) and in addition has four levels of fidelity for full-flight simulators (FAA, 1992b). The level of fidelity required for the most effective teaching and the best use of limited fidelity are both still controversial. This raises an important question because, almost inevitably, increased fidelity means increased costs. In addition, there is considerable evidence that in some cases unneeded fidelity can actually decrease training effectiveness by causing unnecessary distractions.

There have been major advances in the use of FTDs in pilot training. They are considerably less expensive than full-flight simulators, and there is a great deal of evidence that they can be very efficient teaching devices. There seems little doubt that the use of FTDs as well as the use of CBT and full-flight simulators will continue to grow.

One of the most recent developments, perhaps stimulated by the success of "zero flight time" training programs, has resulted in a 50-page document approved by the representatives of 12 nations and called *International Standards for the Qualification of Airplane Flight Simulators.* It was adapted unanimously by 120 delegates in January, 1992, in London and will be offered to ICAO as a new international flight safety standard.

The document was developed by "United Kingdom, U.S., French, Dutch, German, Swiss, Swedish (representing other Scandinavian countries), Canadian, Australian, and Soviet regulatory authorities." If it is adopted by ICAO, it could reduce the considerable workload of aircraft manufacturers, simulator makers, and regulatory authorities worldwide in qualifying the increasing number of simulators that are a growing part of the international aviation system. Shifrin (1992) has speculated that "eventually, the agreement could lead to reciprocity among regulatory agencies around the world, allowing an inspection of a simulator by the regulators of one country to be acceptable to those of another."

SUMMARY AND CONCLUSIONS ─────────────── ➔

The Team Concept and the Importance of Effective Monitoring

The "team concept" and the importance of effective monitoring (including monitoring of the automatics) will continue to be stressed in training. It is one of the major changes of this era.

For a great many years it has been important for pilots to monitor the operation that they supervise, whether they are the PNF or the PF (either manually or with partial or full use of the automation available to them). However, this concept was not given official recognition. This is no longer true.

Increased Responsibility for the Second-in-Command

The increased responsibility of the second-in-command is now acknowledged by all elements of the industry. It is very close to being a required element in proficiency checks for both captains and co-pilots.

Measuring Team Performance Skills

Today, training programs can no longer emphasize only the technical aspects of flying. They must also deal effectively with the various types of crew management techniques that are essential to safe flight operations (FAA, 1989). It is inevitable that the checking of individual performance which is required by the FAA and is inherent in each company's overall responsibility will also include individual team performance skills as soon as suitable measures for measuring team performance and the individual's ability to operate as an effective team member can be created and validated (Helmreich, Kello, Chidester, Wilhelm, & Gregorich, 1989).

Cockpit Workload

Cockpit workload is an important and elusive concept (Wiener, 1985; Wiener & Curry, 1980). What is often forgotten is the importance of training in evaluating the workload that is imposed on operating pilots. A task that is very difficult for a poorly trained person can be a simple task for one adequately trained (Orlady, 1991).

Individual Needs

There will be a greater effort to identify and meet individual needs as part of the move toward the "training to proficiency" concept. While these needs may or may not be job-related, they do affect pilot behavior and the efficiency of the training process.

Individual needs can vary depending on recent and total experience, motivation, airline philosophy (particularly in cases of airline sales or mergers), individual capability, an elusive characteristic called "computer literacy," and many other things. Effective training to meet these sometimes different needs can be important and economical.

In a similar fashion, an accurate and specific diagnosis of the individual's need for special training and for the type of training needed can be very difficult to identify. Everyone loses if an airline pilot's career is unnecessarily terminated. The FAA's AQP may provide more flexibility in meeting individual needs than is presently feasible.

While the "training to proficiency" concept deals with individual needs, it is a mistake to believe that it will eliminate all proficiency problems, for it obviously will not. The only answer may very well put some apparently permanent proficiency problems back into the gray area of the collective bargaining arena where such problems probably belong.

The "Recalcitrant Trainee"

A similar and very real problem is that of the so-called "recalcitrant trainee," or the trainee who does not seem to fit in with or comprehend the trend toward the "team approach" to safety and efficiency in air transport. Such pilots have been called the "wrong stuff," as opposed to pilots who apparently have adapted very well and are now called the "right stuff" (Helmreich & Wilhelm, 1989). While this may not always be an apt metaphor, it seems inevitable that there will be a small number of individuals who do not have and cannot or will not acquire the additional skills that are becoming essential in this era (Helmreich, Chidester et al., 1989; Johnston, 1987). Fortunately, the number of such individuals is very small.

Pilots Like New Technology

We know that pilots like and use new technology (Orlady, 1991; Wiener, 1985). This was true in the DC-3 days and is certainly true today. While we do not suggest that there have not been and will not be problems in the future, including inevitable "shakedown problems," air transport will continue to be an industry driven by new technology. The importance of good training is bound to increase.

Automation Does Not Reduce Training Requirements

One of the great myths associated with increased automation in air transport operations is that automation reduces training. This is simply not true. Automation has created training requirements that add to the previous requirements.

Increased automation is a welcome tool and is used by pilots to make flight safer and more efficient. However, the skills and knowledge associated with taking full advantage of increased automation must be added to the training curriculum. All the former skills and knowledge of professional pilots are still required.

It is simply not possible to monitor a system effectively without knowing how the system is planning to accomplish its task (Billings, 1991). Unfortunately, present training does not always ensure that pilots have this information. For a further discussion of the effect of automation on training, see the chapter by Wiener.

Manual Skills Still Required

A high level of manual piloting skills is still required. This means, almost by definition, that manual skills must be part of the training and evaluation program. There can be many reasons for skill deterioration, including such items as scheduling or even motivation, but in most cases of manual skills deterioration the problem is simply lack of practice. A great deal of the problem of maintaining manual skills can be minimized by company philosophy regarding the use of automation and the importance of maintaining manual skills.

Pilots Need More System Knowledge

At many airlines, pilots want and need more systems knowledge, including better training in the use of such systems as the FMS. It seems inevitable that there will be increased use of CBT and FTDs to accomplish this.

Training Is Necessary and Expensive

Training is both necessary and expensive. It is inevitable that efforts will be made to keep all the associated costs under control. This does not ease the problems of the trainers or the pilots. It is however, a fact of life.

Training may well become more cost-efficient. This could include an increased use of home computers and perhaps even more home study. These later possibilities would undoubtedly create collective bargaining problems regarding the responsibilities of each party in a changing world. They are entirely separate from the collective bargaining problems associated with a lack of proficiency.

The industry has gone from doing all training on scheduled days off to the present system of bidding for required training in place of flying regularly scheduled trips. There is no reason that the collective bargaining problems associated with making training more cost-efficient cannot be solved to the advantage of both parties by achieving suitable provisions in the Working Agreements which govern their activities.

What Really Causes Our Accidents?

Lauber (1988) raised an interesting question at an aviation conference during a discussion of ADVTECH accidents, incidents, and human errors when he asked, "Are these examples of automation-caused problems, or are they simply human performance accidents which just happen to involve automatic systems, but which are otherwise not fundamentally different from any other human performance accident?"

David Meister (1989) raised the same question in much more general terms when he noted that

> it is possible that most behavioral problems do not change, but appear in a new guise only when one concentrates on the molecular hardware/software interface details in which they are wrapped. There may be few "new" problems, if one analyzes these problems at a higher system level. (p. 91)

These comments raise extremely important questions for anyone interested in present and future airline pilot training and, of course, in aviation safety. There is little question that we are in a new transport era. ADVTECH aircraft are characterized by enhanced performance, improved noise control, considerably advanced economic characteristics, "glass cockpits," the automation of many subsystems formerly the province of the flight engineer, further automation of pilot controlling and navigational tasks, noteworthy advances in the display of cockpit information to the flight crew, and, for many aircraft, significantly extended operating ranges.

What seems far from clear is whether or not these "new" airplanes have alleviated our old problems, brought us entirely "new" problems, or are only giving us the same old problems in new clothes. My belief is that at least part of the truth lies in affirmative answers to each of these questions. Clearly, it would be a great mistake to blithely assume that the only problems we have today are the "new" ones caused by ADVTECH airplanes and increased automation and to further assume that we have solved all of our old problems.

These final comments assume that basic problems such as company philosophy, communication with the pilot group, and the establishment of appropriate procedures have been solved. In this chapter I have been primarily concerned with the quality and effectiveness of the training that pilots receive and with its considerably broadened content. The 1990s will be an innovative and dynamic decade in air transport. For a great many of its operating personnel it can well be called "the training decade."

Acknowledgments

While there is no question that the author of this chapter is responsible for all the statements within it, including any errors or misstatements, it would be completely inappropriate not to acknowledge the contributions produced by many discussions with a great many people over a long period of time. Many of them (especially Bob Helmreich and Earl Wiener) have also been such prolific writers on subjects dealing with training, operating practices, and aviation safety that to deal adequately with their contributions by references would make a such a record unacceptably long.

The following list is admittedly incomplete. However, it does illustrate the range of individuals and the disciplines that are concerned with the broad aspects of flightcrew performance and aviation safety. The author is particularly grateful to these individuals for both their friendship and their continuing concern. Their names are listed to provide at least a meager acknowledgment of the contribution that they have made to this chapter: Jerry Berlin, Charles Billings, Rolf Braune, Gerry Bruggink, Bill Dunkle, Earl Carter, Del Fadden, Clay Foushee, Dick Gabriel, Curt Graeber, Rex Hardy, Dick Harper, Neil Johnston, George Kidera, John Lauber, Les Lautman, Jerry Lederer, Linda Orlady, Lawson White, and the late Bill Ashe, Lloyd Buley, Ted Linnert, and Clancy Sayen.

References

Air Transport Association of America, Human Factors Task Force. (1989). *National plan to enhance aviation safety through human factors improvements.* Washington, DC: Author.

Allen, B. R. (1966). Incident investigation: The sleeping giant. In *Summary of Flight Safety Foundation's 19th International Air Safety Seminar, Madrid.* Arlington, VA: Flight Safety Foundation.

American Airlines. (1981, March). Flight crew responsibility. *Flight Deck.* Dallas, TX: Author.

Billings, C. E. (1991). *Human-centered aircraft automation: A concept and guidelines* (Tech. Memorandum 103885). Moffett Field, CA: NASA–Ames Research Center.

Bolman, L. (1979). Aviation accidents and the "theory of the situation." In *Resource management on the flight deck, Proceedings of a NASA/Industry workshop* (pp. 31–58). Moffett Field, CA: NASA–Ames Research Center.

Bruggink, G. M. (1983). Reflections on the Potomac. *International Journal of Aviation Safety, 1*, 5–12.

Curry, R. E. (1985). *The introduction of new cockpit technology: A human factors study* (Tech. Memorandum 86659). Moffett Field, CA: NASA–Ames Research Center.

Degani, A., Chappell, S., & Hayes, M. (1991). Who or what saved the day? A comparison of traditional and glass cockpits. In *Proceedings of the Sixth International Symposium on Aviation Psychology* (pp. 227–234). Columbus: The Ohio State University.

Degani, A., & Wiener, E. L. (1991). Philosophy, policies, and procedures: the three P's of flight-deck operations. In *Proceedings of The Sixth International Symposium on Aviation Psychology* (pp. 184–191). Columbus: The Ohio State University.

Federal Aviation Administration. (1989). *Cockpit resource management training* (Advisory Circular No. 120-51). Washington, DC: Author.

Federal Aviation Administration. (1991). *Crew resource management training* (CRM Advisory Circular Draft No. 2.5). Washington, DC: Author.

Federal Aviation Administration. (1992a). *Airline flight training device qualification* (Advisory Circular 120-45A). Washington, DC: Author.

Federal Aviation Administration. (1992b). *Airline simulator qualification* (Advisory Circular 120-40B). Washington, DC: Author.

Foushee, H. C. (1990, August). *National plan for aviation human factors.* Presentation to the Society of Automation Engineers G-10 Committee, Monterey, CA.

Foushee, H. C., Lauber, J. K., Baetege, M. M., & Acomb, D. B. (1986). *Crew factors in flight operations: III. The operational significance of exposure to short haul air transport operations* (NASA Tech. Memorandum 88322). Moffett Field, CA: NASA–Ames Research Center.

Green, R. G., Muir, H., James, M., Gradwell, D., & Green, R. L. (1991). *Human factors for pilots.* Hants, England: Gower House.

Hawkins, F. H. (1987). *Human Factors in Flight.* Hants, England: Gower House.

Helmreich, R. L. (1990). *Studying flight crew interaction: The intersection of basic and applied research.* Presented at the dedication of the NASA–Ames Research Center Human Performance Research Laboratory, Moffett Field, CA.

Helmreich, R. L., Chidester, T. R., Foushee, H. C., Gregorich, S., & Wilhelm, J. A. (1989). *Critical issues in implementing and reinforcing cockpit resource management training* (NASA/UT Tech. Report 89-5). Moffett Field, CA: NASA–Ames Research Center.

Helmreich, R. L., Kello, J. E., Chidester, T. R., Wilhelm, J. A., & Gregorich, S. E. (1989). *Maximizing the operational impact of line oriented flight training (LOFT): Lessons from initial observations* (NASA/UT Tech. Report 89-6). Moffett Field, CA: NASA–Ames Research Center.

Helmreich, R. L., & Wilhelm, J. A. (1989). When training boomerangs: Negative outcomes associated with cockpit resource management programs. In *Proceedings of the Fifth International Symposium on Aviation Psychology.* Columbus: The Ohio State University.

Hopkins, H. (1991, March). Market focus. *Flight International,* pp. 35–37. London.

International Civil Aviation Organization (1989). *Human factors digest No. 1* (Circular 216-AN/131). Montreal: Author.

Jackson, E. A. (1975). Relations with pilots in developing rules and procedures. In *20th Technical Conference: Safety in flight operations* Montreal, PQ: International Air Transport Association.

Johnston, N. (1987). Remedial training: Will CRM work for everyone. In H. W. Orlady & H. C. Foushee (Eds.), *Cockpit resource management training* (NASA Conference Publication 2455). Moffett Field, CA: NASA–Ames Research Center.

Johnston, N. (1991). Human factors training seminar/workshop: An overview. In *Proceedings of the*

Sixth International Symposium on Aviation Psychology (pp. 44–52). Columbus: The Ohio State University.

Langer, H. A. (1992, January–February). Meeting the challenges together. *The Cockpit.* Chicago, IL: United Airlines.

Lauber, J. K. (1987). Cockpit resource management: Background studies and rationale. In H. W. Orlady & H. C. Foushee (Eds.), *Cockpit resource management training* (NASA Conference Publication 2455). Moffett Field, CA: NASA–Ames Research Center.

Lauber, J. K. (1988). *Airline safety in a transitional era.* Paper presented at the Annual Airline Operational Forum of the Air Transportation Association of America, Williamsburg, VA.

Lauber, J. K. (1991). Principles of human-centered automation: challenge and overview. In *Proceedings of AIAA/NASA/FAA/HFS Conference Challenges in Aviation Factors: The national plan.* Arlington, VA.

Lauber, J. K., & Foushee, H. C. (1981). *Proceedings of a NASA/Industry workshop: Guidelines for line-oriented flight training, Vol. 2* (NASA Conference Publication 2184). Moffett Field, CA: NASA–Ames Research Center.

Lautman, L. G., & Gallimore, P. L. (1987). Control of the crew caused accident. *Flight Safety Foundation Safety Digest.* Arlington, VA: Flight Safety Foundation.

Meister, D. (1989). *Conceptual aspects of human factors.* Baltimore: John Hopkins University Press.

Norman, S. D., & Orlady, H. W. (1988). *Flight deck automation: Promises and realities.* Final report of a NASA/FAA/Industry workshop held at Carmel Valley, California. Moffett Field, CA: NASA–Ames Research Center.

Nunn, H. T. (1981). Line-oriented flight training—Northwest Airlines. In J. K. Lauber & H. C. Foushee (Eds.), *Proceedings of a NASA/Industry workshop: Guidelines for line-oriented flight training, Vol. 2* Moffett Field, CA: NASA–Ames Research Center.

Office of the Federal Register. (1990). *Special Federal Aviation Regulation 58: Advanced Qualification Program* (Federal Register, Vol. 55, No. 91, Rules and Regulations pp. 40262–40278). Washington DC: National Archives and Records Administration.

Orlady, H. W. (1982a). *Flight crew performance when pilot flying and pilot not flying duties are exchanged* (Contractor Report 166433). Moffett Field, CA: NASA–Ames Research Center.

Orlady, H. W. (1982b). *Incident reporting, behavior, and safety in civil aviation.* Paper presented at the 17th Annual Symposium of the Civil Aviation Medical Association, Toronto, Canada.

Orlady, H. W. (1983). Resource management training for the small operator. In *Second Symposium on Aviation Psychology.* Columbus: The Ohio State University.

Orlady, H. W. (1989b). *The professional airline pilot of today: All the old skills—and more.* Paper presented at the International Airline Pilot Training Seminar conducted by VIASA Airlines and the Flight Safety Foundation, Caracas, Venezuela.

Orlady, H. W. (1990). The 1990s: a training decade. In *Proceedings of FAA Training Technology Symposium,* Oklahoma City, OK: FAA.

Orlady, H. W. (1991). Advanced cockpit technology in the real world. In *Proceedings of the Royal Aeronautical Society Conference "Human Factors on Advanced Flight Decks."* London.

Reynard, W. D., Billings, C. E., Cheaney, E. S., & Hardy, R. (1986). *The development of the NASA Aviation Safety Reporting System* (NASA Reference Publication 1114). Moffett Field, CA: NASA–Ames Research Center.

Ruffell Smith, H. P. (1979). *A simulator study of the interaction of pilot workload with errors, vigilance, and decisions* (Tech. Memorandum 78482). Moffett Field, CA: NASA–Ames Research Center.

Shifrin, C. A. (1992, March). Representatives from 12 nations draft international standards for simulators. *Aviation Week and Space Technology,* pp. 42–43.

Taylor, L. (1988). *Air travel: How safe is it?* Oxford, England: Blackwell Scientific Publications.

Vette, G., with Macdonald, J. (1983). *Impact Erebus.* Aukland, New Zealand: Hodder and Stoughton.

Weener, E. F.(1991). *Control of crew-caused accidents: The Sequel.* Seattle, WA: The Boeing Commercial Airplane Group.

Wiener, E. L. (1985). *Human factors of cockpit automation: A field study of flight crew transition* (NASA Contractor Report 177333). Moffett Field, CA: NASA–Ames Research Center.

Wiener, E. L. (1985). Beyond the sterile cockpit. *Human Factors, 27,* 75–90.

Wiener, E. L. (1989). *Human factors of advanced technology ("glass cockpit") transport aircraft* (NASA Contractor Report 177528). Moffett Field, CA: NASA–Ames Research Center.

Wiener, E. L., & Curry, R. E. (1980). Flight deck automation: Promises and problems. *Erognomics, 23,* 995–1011.

Wiener, E. L., Curry, R. E., & Faustina, M. L. (1984). Vigilance and task load: In search of the inverted "U". *Human Factors, 26,* 215–222.

The Future of Crew Resource Management in the Cockpit and Elsewhere

Robert L. Helmreich
Department of Psychology
University of Texas at Austin
Austin, Texas 78712

Earl L. Wiener
Department of Management Science
University of Miami
Coral Gables, Florida 33124

Barbara G. Kanki
Aerospace Human Factors Research Division
NASA–Ames Research Center
Moffett Field, California 94035

INTRODUCTION ✈

The first skirmishes over the usefulness of human factors training have been fought and won. Initial doubt about its relevance, concerns about "brainwashing" and "psychotherapy," and resistance to new ideas have been largely overcome. CRM is now accepted as a proven concept that is on its way to becoming an integrated and required part of all flight training. Does this mean the war is won and that it is time to turn to other pursuits? The answer to this rhetorical question is emphatically No! We have learned enough to know how much more there is to learn before we achieve the potential benefits from applying human factors concepts. We must refine and extend our knowledge of both the basic behavioral issues and the best means of delivering training.

In many ways CRM, its advocates, and its creators may be embarrassed by success. In spite of the fact that many barriers were placed in the path of CRM implementation, there is no denying that CRM training and its traveling companions such as line-oriented flight training (LOFT) have, in one decade, found their place in aircrew training. And they have done so in an industry that is conservative by nature, one that at the very least demands proof that anything added to a training program have measurable merit. Furthermore, this has occurred not during economic good times, but during a dismal period of airline economics, when "bottom-line" thinking has prevailed. Only about half the U.S. carriers that we worked with in the last decade still exist in their original form!

Obviously, airlines and other aviation organizations have looked at the price tag of CRM training and have decided that it is worth the money. Now the expertise of the first generation of CRM researchers and applications persons is being sought by non-cockpit and non-aviation domains. More will be said about this shortly.

As researchers in the field, we are amazed at the rapidity with which these new concepts have been accepted. The challenge of the second decade of CRM will not be acceptance, but refinement. The question that we will be asked will not be whether CRM training is effective as a concept, but whether there is not some better way of doing it. Ask any airline pilot about the CRM training program and he or she will say something like, "I believe in the concept; I'm glad my company is doing it; it was long overdue; but I didn't like the games" (or what have you).

The challenge will lie not so much in the classroom as outside its walls. As many of the chapters in this volume point out, the bright future of CRM training will be in developing the ancillary functions: human factors–centered LOFT, line checks, proficiency checks, and recurrent training. These challenges must be faced in an evolving, non-stationary aviation environment. Consider the partial list of factors below that are at work in the industry. Each has its implications for cockpit management.

• Mega-carriers are developing today, merging and mixing not only the cultures within the airlines of a nation, but those of other nations. We have just begun to see the leading edge of globalization.

• Flightdeck automation will continue to increase. Already there are features in the B-747-400, A-320, and MD-11 that were not present in the first generation of glass cockpits. The B-777 will take automation a step further. As Wiener points out in his chapter, crew coordination and communication in the glass cockpit may be modulated by the degree and usage of automation, a point being examined in a lengthy project by Wiener, Chidester, Kanki, Palmer, Curry, & Gregorich (1991).

• The promulgation of the Federal Aviation Administration's (FAA) Advanced Qualification Program (AQP) will bring CRM training into the canon law of training regulations. Until now, CRM training has been at the pleasure of the airlines. Those wishing to submit their fleets for AQP approval also have to propose CRM training, as well as ancillary activities such as crew evaluation, database management, plans for line-oriented simulation (LOS), and recurrent human factors training.

• Manufacturers are becoming purveyors of CRM training. Already Airbus Industrie is offering its customers a form of CRM training that they call aircrew integrated management (AIM) as part of its training package (North, 1992). Other airframe manufacturers may follow suit.

• The inevitable presence of legal liability has reared its head. In recent years, as Kayten points out in her chapter, the National Transportation Safety Board (NTSB) has recognized crew coordination and communication failures as causal in numerous aircraft accidents and has recommended that the FAA require CRM training as a counter-measure. Failure of carriers to offer CRM training has recently been offered in courts of law as evidence of negligence on the part of the airline. Obviously, in the future the mere presence of a CRM program will not deter the lawyers: they will probe into the nature of the program and whether is achieves its goals.

It is very clear that the scientific and airline communities will be under considerable pressure in the next decade. No one will be allowed to rest on the laurels of merely having put into place a first-generation CRM or LOFT program. The half-life of any technology, any training approach, any set of procedures is exceeding brief in the aviation industry. CRM and LOFT programs are no exception.

ISSUES IN CRM ✈

Enabling and Integrating CRM

It seems counterproductive to delay introduction of human factors training until crewmembers are experienced in line operations. A more useful approach should be to include basic instruction in human factors theory and applications as part of the curriculum for ab initio training. Current training practices that are rooted in tradition and regulation stress individual learning and proficiency leading to solo flight. It is certainly appropriate to train and demand personal mastery and proficiency, but this individualistic focus is rarely re-examined, even when the flying task becomes serving within a multi-person crew. Early exposure to CRM could serve to build and reinforce positive habits from the beginning of an aviator's career. In contrast, current training strategies involve trying to change old, less adaptive attitudes and behaviors regarding crew coordination. Making CRM part of initial training could also prevent it from being viewed as some form of "soft" supplement to the "real," technical tasks of flying.

In the approach to CRM adopted by most organizations, both initial and recurrent training are separated from aircraft-specific technical instruction, and CRM courses are often facilitated by line pilots from outside training departments. CRM LOFT is usually conducted as an optional adjunct to proficiency training and checking and, indeed, is sometimes perceived as competing for scarce simulator resources. We feel that this approach can and should change. In future, mature programs, specific CRM concepts will be stressed and integrated into all aspects of instruction, including ground school and systems training as well as instruction in specific maneuvers. One of the requirements of the FAA's AQP, described in the chapter by Birnbach & Longridge, is the integration of CRM concepts into all training. Although simple in concept, achieving this integration is

a complex process that requires fine-grained re-analysis of the tasks and sub-tasks surrounding the operation of an aircraft. A subcommittee of the Air Transport Association's AQP Committee, chaired by Captain Kevin Smith of United Airlines, has spent more than a year addressing this issue. The committee was composed of line pilots, experts in instructional systems design, and research psychologists. The committee reached a general consensus that this type of integration can be achieved, although disagreements remain regarding optimal approaches and levels of analysis.

An example of the process of defining human factors and technical tasks involved in a particular maneuver is shown in Table 17.1. The analysis was conducted by Captains Kevin Smith and William Hamman of United Airlines. The table shows a partial listing of the factors surrounding a take-off in an advanced-technology aircraft with an engine failure at V_1 and terrain obstructions in the flight path. As the analysis indicates, successful completion of the maneuver requires not only a number of coordinated technical activities by the crew, but also recognition and practice of CRM concepts. Effective training and evaluation of the maneuver must address both. The challenge is to develop training that integrates CRM and technical components and allows students to recognize the essential characteristics of both.

Table 17.1

Technical and Human Factors Tasks Involved in Take-off with Engine Failure at V_1: Advanced-Technology Aircraft[a]

Technical tasks	Human factors tasks
Take-off briefing	Establish open communications
Perform take-off roll	Identify potential problems, such as terrain
Rotate to establish climb profile	Provide guidelines for crew action
Maintain wings level and directional control	Specify PNF duties with regard to automation
Initiate turn for terrain avoidance	Address consideration of risk
Disconnect autothrottle	Interpret control and performance instruments
Altitude hold	Interpret propulsion information
Check flaps setting	Workload managed and activities coordinated
Fight fire if needed	Avoid "tunnel vision" focus on one issue
Notify tower of emergency	Workload distribution is communicated
Configure aircraft	Task assignment acknowledged
Set automation as appropriate	Risk is managed and reduced
Perform navigation	

[a] From Kevin Smith and William Hamman, United Airlines.

In practice, the integration of human factors and technical elements is a complex and lengthy process. Simply to define integration for the V_1 cut involved the following steps:

1. Decomposing the maneuver into the following segments: (a) briefing, (b) brake release to rotation, (c) rotation to 500' above ground level (AGL), (d) acceleration at 500' AGL to second segment climb.
2. For each maneuver segment, defining formal objectives that specify desired outcomes.
3. Flying and videotaping the maneuver in an appropriately configured simulator for in-depth analysis.
4. Developing a matrix relating each observable, technical activity to a set of enabling CRM-related behaviors (the behavioral markers described in the chapter by Helmreich & Foushee).
5. Preparing an instructor's guide that specifies both human factors and technical behaviors for the maneuver.

Obviously, to achieve this type of integration will require a serious commitment of time and talent on the part of training organizations.

The Evaluation Controversy

To accomplish the integration and enhancement of CRM, the definition and evaluation of human factors behaviors must be as reliable and valid as that of technical maneuvers. As Gregorich & Wilhelm point out in their chapter, comprehensive assessment strategies are in their infancy. Birnbach & Longridge note in their chapter that assessment of the human factors as well as technical aspects of crew performance is a stated objective of the new U.S. Special Federal Aviation Regulation AQP and is essential to its success. Perhaps the criticality of assessment can be stated in the form of four axioms regarding effective CRM implementation.

1. To be accepted, practice of CRM concepts must be accorded the same status as adherence to technical standards that are continually measured and reinforced.
2. If the concepts of CRM cannot be reinforced, there is no point in committing resources to training. CRM will not be treated with the same seriousness as technical issues.
3. CRM concepts cannot be reinforced if they cannot be reliably assessed.
4. Instructors and evaluators must be trained and skilled in assessment and reinforcement of human factors practices.

The issue of performance evaluation has proved to be one of the most contentious aspects of initiating the AQP. In reality, there are two issues contributing to this controversy. One involves concerns regarding the ability to achieve reliable assessment of human factors issues, while the other centers on concerns about shifting from current pass—fail evaluation to multi-level grading standards for technical proficiency.

We feel that substantial progress has been made in refining the assessment of human factors behaviors, and that evaluators given systematic training and calibration in performance assessment can achieve high levels of reliability. Experience with the design and delivery of such training indicates that valid assessment is an attainable goal (Helmreich, Wilhelm, Kello, Taggart, & Butler, 1991). Further support for this contention is derived from longitudinal data collected in organizations employing such assessment as an adjunct to traditional checking and LOFT data from expert observers conducting parallel assessment (Butler 1991; Clothier, 1991a, 1991b; Helmreich, Butler, & Wilhelm, 1992).

Debate over the appropriateness of multi-level grading versus binary pass—fail evaluation seems to be rooted more in U.S. tradition and policy than in inherent problems in making finer assessments. There is certainly awareness that a rating of "satisfactory" covers a range of performance from marginal to exemplary. One of the concerns is that more detailed grading could provide the basis for the award of damages in litigation surrounding an accident (for example, discovering that the captain's assessments, while satisfactory, were below the organization's average). The AQP's requirement for grading crew performance but maintaining the evaluations in anonymous databases will allow analysis of fleet and organizational trends and detailed feedback and reinforcement while preventing additional exposure of the organization on the basis of an individual's rated performance.

It should be noted that limiting assessment to a pass—fail criterion is by no means a universal practice. Many organizations outside the United States have long used more refined grading practices. Cathay Pacific in Hong Kong, for example, grades all aspects of enroute checking on a 5-point scale, with four graduations in the "passing" range. Qantas Airlines has recently initiated an assessment standard that includes eight defined points (a 5-point scale with plusses and minuses), with seven falling in above-minimally-acceptable standards.

The adoption of more sophisticated assessment strategies that not only define the range of acceptable behaviors but also integrate human factors behaviors would benefit the individual crewmember by giving more meaningful feedback and the organization by identifying more precisely areas of strength and areas needing additional training. Furthermore, the inclusion of human factors elements should provide more accurate indication of causal factors in cases where performance is not up to standards. For example, when a crew fails an instrument approach during a check, the root cause is seldom a lack of "stick-and-rudder" skills or a lack of awareness of proper procedures. Instead, the failure is frequently the result of poor CRM practices, for example in deficient practice of specific human factors behaviors such as the behavioral markers that define preparation, planning, vigilance, and workload management. In other words, through lack of preparation and planning and workload management, the crew "got behind the aircraft." If the root causes are isolated, the remedial training required to return the crew to proper standards of performances can be more focused and more effective.

While many instructors deal with both human factors and technical issues, current training practices have not formally addressed this integration. On the basis of research and operational experience in airlines working toward integration and evaluation of human factors, we feel that this is an attainable goal. As noted above, achieving it will require substantial effort, resources, and time, but the payoff in terms of more effective training, efficiency, and safety should be large.

The Globalization of CRM

The research and operational viewpoints presented in this book are drawn primarily from the United States. The concept of a global community is drawing nearer, aided by the growth of air transport, but in reality not only laypersons but also behavioral scientists view the world through lenses ground by their own cultures. The body of systematic, cross-cultural research into the determinants of social behavior is small, and cross-cultural research on flightcrew behavior is even more limited. It is easy and comforting to think of the flightdeck as an environment that transcends national boundaries. However, the insights in the chapters by Johnston and Yamamori & Mito should cause us to reexamine the universality of this assumption. Yamamori and Mito suggest that there is enough common ground to allow successful translation of a particular approach to CRM training from the United States to Japan, despite recognized cultural differences between the countries in modal attitudes regarding such issues as optimal means of dealing with authority figures and resolving interpersonal conflict. Johnston, in contrast, is more concerned with cultural diversity and discusses modal, cultural differences in styles of interaction and, by implication, personality. He further notes great variability in resources available (for example, navigational aids) and operating environments in different regions of the world. He suggests that these environmental factors may be major determinants of the level of air safety, perhaps more critical in some regions than human factors.

We can better understand these issues in the context of the input, process, outcome model of crew performance outlined by Helmreich & Foushee in their chapter. In terms of valued outcomes, there are certainly no cultural differences; organizations and crews in every culture share the primary goals of safe and efficient flight operations and secondary goals of positive attitudes and morale. In contrast, there is overwhelming evidence for dramatic differences in input factors such as resources and support, organizational cultures, regulatory policies, methods of pilot selection and training, and standards for proficiency and proficiency evaluation. Since these input factors directly impact the way crews work and interact, we should expect significant differences in group processes between cultures.

Despite these expected differences, basic group process factors (team formation and management, interpersonal relations, communications and decision-making, situation awareness, workload management, etc.) are conceptually generic. CRM as a strategy is universally sound, although tactics may vary based on cultures and operating environments. In our view, the definition of effective behaviors from a human factors viewpoint should be similar throughout the world. With the possible exception of areas of command authority, we would expect little disagreement regarding what constitutes an effectively managed flightdeck in Africa, South America, the United States, or the Commonwealth of Independent States. Even though differences in input factors may result in significant differences in the way these behaviors are prioritized and carried out on the flightdeck, it does not follow that CRM is more or less relevant in one culture than another.

If we interpret "CRM relevance" to mean the effectiveness of specific forms of CRM behaviors, this issue can arise within a single culture and even within a single flight. Among the complex and multiple input factors that affect all crew performance, some occur so often and in such predictable ways that certain CRM strategies assume nearly universal status. However, there are always factors (e.g., changes in task, mission objectives, environment, personnel, etc.) that carry the potential to alter the appropriateness of specific behaviors. High-frequency strategies are tied no less to normal conditions than low-frequency strategies are tied to abnormal conditions. While there are likely to be universal CRM principles, it is an error to assume that specific CRM behaviors are context-free. For example, a catastrophic structural failure at crusing altitude may instigate an immediate and total reprioritization of actions and redistribution of work that deviates significantly from typical "good" CRM practices.

What are typical conditions for one flying organization may not be typical conditions for another, and large differences in "normal" operating conditions may also contribute to performance diversity. A crew that must fly with minimal navigation aids, degraded airway facilities, and challenging weather and terrain will necessarily adopt CRM strategies that may appear different from those of their counterparts flying in a resource-rich aviation system. But we believe the differences are more of form than of function.

The existence of input and group process differences does imply, as Chidester notes in his chapter, that it is essential for training to reflect the culture in which it is imbedded. Although Chidester focuses on cultural differences among U.S. airlines such as those rooted in history, economic health, and the impact of mergers, this "subculture" issue is a critical one in an era when mergers and takeovers have increased diversity not only among airlines but within them as well. Clearly, the tailoring of CRM programs to fit training needs caused by operating conditions as well as the philosophy and characteristics of an organization and its personnel is required in order to ensure that CRM is relevant in spite of differences resulting from national cultures, subcultures, and the availability of resources.

Given this perspective, the apparent divergence of Johnston's and Yamamori and Mito's viewpoints may be less dramatic than first reading would indicate. CRM training that is centered on defining and dealing with abstract concepts of personality or interpersonal style will necessarily be differentially applicable in different cultures, and changing styles will be more or less relevant depending on the culture's modal patterns of interpersonal interaction. However, what Helmreich and Foushee defined as the third generation of CRM training, experiential learning that is focused on group process factors and specific behaviors, should be more globally relevant. Nonetheless, to achieve comparable impact, training must reflect the constraints that are imposed by national or regional culture. What we see as an ultimately achievable goal is a state where cultural differences, be they organizational or national, are minimized on the flightdeck and where observers can note a common level of effectiveness in both human factors and technical proficiency in the cockpit.

Dealing with Training Failures: Reactive and Proactive Strategies

The existence of a small but significant minority of crewmembers who reject CRM training and concepts has been shown by research and is a matter of concern (Helmreich & Wilhelm, 1989). As Chidester notes in his chapter, these individuals pose a major challenge for organizations. Given compelling evidence for the role of human factors in accidents and incidents, it is reasonable to assume that these individuals may be the most significant threat to safety in flight operations. In addition, other crewmembers come to question an organization's commitment to CRM concepts when such individuals are allowed to continue behaving in defiance of what is being taught. However, as long as such crewmembers demonstrate technical proficiency meeting regulatory requirements, it is difficult if not impossible to remove them from flying status.

This rejection of CRM training has been identified by Helmreich & Wilhelm (1989) both through participant evaluations of seminars and through negative shifts in attitudes regarding cockpit management (a "boomerang" effect). Several causal factors have been identified, including organizational cultures, group dynamics in particular training classes, and personality characteristics of individuals. The demonstration of a significant link between personality and acceptance of CRM training suggests that, given current instructional techniques, personality may be a limiting factor in the success of CRM (e.g., Helmreich & Wilhelm, 1989, 1991; chapter by Chidester). A further implication is that refinements in pilot selection strategies may be needed.

One approach that has been used is for management to send individuals to be "fixed." Sometimes this has involved putting the individual through a CRM course for attitude adjustment. In other cases the individual has been sent for psychiatric or psychological assessment only to return with a document that certifies him or her to be "sane."

More recently, several carriers have begun to adopt an integrated, cooperative approach to dealing with pilots having problems with CRM concepts. These involve company management, pilot organizations' professional standards committees, internal human factors/CRM staff, and appropriate outside consultants. This multi-dimensional approach, coupled with the benefit of peer pressure and positive group norms, seems to hold the greatest promise for the future. More research and experimentation will be needed to arrive at optimal solutions to this vexing problem.

New Strategies for Crew Selection

Approaches to pilot selection have been generally successful in identifying individuals with appropriate cognitive and psychomotor skills. The importance of personality factors has been less recognized, and much of the effort in this area has centered on the screening out of candidates with actual or potential psychopathology (e.g., Chidester, Helmreich, Gregorich, & Geis, 1991). In the future, however, a more sophisticated strategy should center on selecting in those with attributes associated with effective team performance as well as strong individual skills. This does not mean that screening to identify and eliminate those with disabling deficiencies should cease. Instead, the new strategy is predicated on the notion that appropriate psychological tests can be validated as predictors of effective crew performance and can discriminate among normal individuals. In other words, useful tests must identify those with personality profiles associated with effective performance. Select-in approaches define the bases of successful performance as consisting not only of exemplary technical competence and motivation but also interpersonal skills that can enhance group processes.

Successful select-in strategies must also be dynamic, taking account of changing conditions in aviation. With increasing cockpit automation, requirements for pilot aptitude are shifting from emphasis on "stick-and-rudder" skills to interpersonal programming and monitoring capabilities—in short, management skills. Paralleling changes in the flying environment are changes in the rewards associated with flight—with automatic flight, the satisfaction is gained from precise and correct management of the flight guidance system, rather than precise manual handling of the aircraft's controls. At the same time, with a computer serving as the third, "electronic crewmember" on most flightdecks, needs for effective communications and active monitoring by the remaining humans may become even more important. Selection must be based on continual reassessment of the skill mix required for optimum performance, attributes associated with job satisfaction in the changing environment, and how the individual will respond to training.

EXTENDING CRM CONCEPTS BEYOND THE COCKPIT

CRM is growing in popularity in aviation and elsewhere. In the years to come, there will surely be an increasing demand on persons knowledgeable in CRM program development to participate in the introduction of CRM training into non-cockpit domains. There is nothing inherent in CRM concepts that restricts them to the cockpit, or to aviation in general. The success that CRM has enjoyed in the last decade in the cockpit could clearly be exported to other high-risk domains, such as nuclear power production, military operations, high-technology medicine, law enforcement, construction, and shipping, just to name a few.

Likewise, there is nothing inherent in CRM concepts that restricts them to high-risk enterprises. Already some airline managements have observed the impact of CRM programs in their own organizations and have concluded that they could benefit from similar training, adapted to their needs. We see little reason why CRM-like training could not also benefit a wide variety of low-risk enterprises, such as government operations, retailing, service industries, education, and traditional professions. With the current interest in total quality management (TQM) that has swept the United States, it would be conceivable for CRM training to be embraced as a pathway toward TQM. As Helmreich and Foushee point out in their chapter, CRM shares a common heritage with both social psychology and many approaches to management training but has a sharper focus.

At this writing, only a handful of airlines and military units have embraced the idea that the concepts of CRM go far beyond the cockpit and extend into every component of organizations where success requires effective interpersonal coordination and communication. Programs that have been initiated and enthusiastically received have included dispatchers, maintenance personnel, and flight attendants. In addition, the FAA, basing its decision on research data from the cockpit domain, has decided that CRM training should become an integral part of initial and recurrent qualification for air traffic controllers.

We now discuss very briefly some of the existing extensions of CRM training and the potential for others. What follows is not meant to be a thorough examination of the applications. Unfortunately, very little has been written on non-flightcrew applications, so both we and the reader will have to wait for some time for the authors of these programs to publish information about their works. A welcome exception is Vandermark's (1991) article describing the joint training of pilots and flight attendants at America West Airlines.

Aviation Applications

We are already seeing the migration of CRM concepts within the aviation industry. CRM training is being implemented in aircraft maintenance and in cockpit–cabin communications.

Maintenance

To date, the experience with modifying and extending cockpit CRM training to maintenance personnel has provided empirical data regarding attitude and behavioral impact. The first maintenance CRM course was developed by William R. Taggart for Pan American Airlines personnel (Taggart, 1990). The impact of the training was measured by participant evaluations of the training, and changes in attitudes regarding crew coordination and management were measured using an adaptation of the *Cockpit Management Attitudes Questionnaire* (CMAQ; Helmreich, Wilhelm, & Gregorich, 1988). Overall reactions were more favorable than those in most pilot courses, and significant positive attitude change was noted.

More recently, Continental Airlines has initiated a program for its maintenance and technical operations personnel under the direction of Captain Frank Tullo (Fotos, 1991). The initial training is based on the airline's CRM course and consists of a 2-day workshop. Program goals include increasing the efficiency of maintenance activities, the reliability of aircraft, and safety on the shop floor. Although the groups involved in maintenance are more diverse than cockpit crews, basic issues of communication and team coordination are highly similar.

Under FAA sponsorship, the program was evaluated by James Taylor of the University of Southern California (Taylor, 1992). Taylor used similar measures of participant evaluations and further modified Taggart's revised CMAQ to include two new scales measuring goal attainment. The results at Continental also showed highly favorable reactions to the training and significant attitude change in the desired direction. This study is of particular importance because objective performance data were available to serve as criteria for evaluating the operational impact of the training. Preliminary data are highly encouraging. Significant positive changes between pre- and post-CRM attitudes were found on maintenance performance measures such as number of ground damage incidents, number of flight diversions caused by human error, days lost due to personal injury, and departures within 5 minutes of scheduled time. In addition, significant correlations were found between post-training attitudes and performance measures.

Cockpit–Cabin Communication

In 1989 an American Airlines MD-80 landed at Nashville with an underfloor fire due to spillage of a hazardous chemical in the cargo compartment. What was remarkable about this incident was that the cabin flight attendants had repeatedly called the cockpit on the interphone to report smoke coming from below the floor, and their calls were ignored. The captain was aware of problems with the aircraft's auxiliary power unit that had resulted in cabin fumes on a previous flight and was skeptical about the flight attendants' warnings. Even when a dead-heading fellow pilot called from the cabin and repeated the warning, the cockpit crew still showed little concern and did not take steps to expedite the approach and landing.

In its list of recommendations included in the incident report (NTSB, 1988, 1989), the Board included the following to American Airlines:

> Review and modify as needed training programs to require joint cockpit and cabin crew training with respect to emergency procedures; specific attention should be given to conducting periodic emergency drills in which cockpit/cabin crew coordination and communication are practiced. (Class II, Priority Action) (A-89-117)

It became obvious to many of those involved in early CRM program development that the training was seriously truncated: CRM training did not extend aft of the cockpit door. The following NASA Aviation Safety Reporting System (ASRS) report, though less dramatic than the example above, illustrates the hazards of deficient cockpit–cabin communication.

> During the descent into Tulsa the seat belt sign was turned on at approximately 12,000 feet MSL and supporting announcement was made to include, "landing in about 10 minutes." At about 7000 feet I picked up the passenger announcement hand mike to make the flight attendant's (F/A's) "prepare for landing" announcement, and simultaneously the "A" [lead] F/A knocked on the door very vigorously. I unlocked the door thinking something was wrong, and she came in and asked if we would like a beverage. I (Capt.) emphatically replied, "We're landing now", and she returned to the cabin. At that point I replaced the passenger announcement handset on its hook without officially making an announcement. Two of the three F/A's were standing when we landed [a serious breach of safety, as well as a Federal Aviation Regulation violation –Eds.]. The equipment that I am currently flying is a new model that is an expanding fleet. The

manpower requirement to pilot the aircraft is also increasing rapidly with a constant flow of newly transitioned pilots arriving weekly. The F/A's rely on the "prepare for landing" announcement, which is supposed to be given five minutes before landing. However, with the experience level in the cockpit, it is inappropriate to divert attention away from the very busy approach and landing phase to make an announcement at that time. I believe the announcement should be made at 10,000. (ASRS Report No. 163059)

Some airlines struggled with this question, but the cost and practicality of bringing flight crew and cabin crew together for joint training were too imposing. A compromise was struck by several carriers that joined cabin supervisory personnel with flight crews during training sessions. An exception, mentioned previously, was the program at America West, which brought flightdeck and cabin crews together in the first day of what it chose to call aircrew team dynamics (ATD) training. The second day concentrated on conventional cockpit problems. At the time of Vandermark's writing (1991), approximately 325 pilots and 716 flight attendants had been trained in ATD.

A further commitment of this company to full-crew CRM can be seen from the fact that during LOFT sessions, a flight attendant is present in the simulator and plays a role dictated by the script. Another person, not the LOFT instructor, plays the part of air traffic controller. These LOFTs appear to be on the forefront of realism.

In July 1992, Southwest Airlines introduced extended crew training for new captains as part of their upgrade program. Based on NASA- and FAA-sponsored research into critical crew behaviors, the additional training involves the new captains along with flight attendants, maintenance personnel, ground operations personnel, crew schedulers, and dispatchers. Problem-solving drills and experiments are used to help prepare the new captain for management responsibilities and to augment the training of other participants.

It is difficult to forecast the future of cockpit–cabin CRM training. We would like to forecast that other airlines will follow the example of American West and Southwest, but we have little basis for such a prediction. The high cost is a barrier that may never be surmounted. Once airlines have invested in the initial programs of a day or more for cockpit crews, it is unlikely that they will send them back for extensive training with cabin crews. Probably the subject of communications with the cabin will be addressed in recurrent training, but this is at best a compromise, a weak substitute for the richness of face-to-face contact and role-playing between the two cultures. It bears repeating that Vandermark noted that one of his most significant findings was that both pilots and flight attendants reported that they did not have a good understanding of what the other crew members did during a flight. In its report on the F-28 accident in Dryden,

Ontario, discussed in the chapter by Helmreich & Foushee, the Commission of Inquiry recommended regulation to require training for flight attendants in basics of flight operations and joint CRM training (Moshansky, 1992).

Air Traffic Control

It is somewhat surprising that "controller resource management" did not develop in conjunction with cockpit resource management. The history of crew-related causes of accidents and incidents that served as a catalyst for human factors training in the cockpit domain is paralleled in air traffic control (ATC). The same analytic strategy employed to identify problems is applicable in the ATC setting, and the information gained can be used to guide curriculum development.

Outside of reports generated from incident records, systematic research in this work environment is just beginning. Full mission simulation research into human factors issues has focused on aircrew performance. Pilot–ATC communications formed part of the experimental environment, but the communications made by the "controllers," while realistic, were scripted and performed by experimental confederates. However, there is increasing interest in conducting research into pilot–controller communications (see the chapter by Kanki & Palmer) as well as controller performance itself.

One impressive beginning is an investigation conducted by Human Technology (1991) that analyzed the communication of enroute air traffic controllers using both field and simulation data. Three communication links were studied: (1) within-team (i.e., controller to controller in the same facility team), (2) ground–air (i.e., controller to pilot), and (3) ground-line (i.e., controller to controller in different facilities). The following questions were asked: Are there variations in communication processes that distinguish radar controllers from radar associate controllers, more experienced controllers from less experienced, and higher rated controllers from lower rated controllers? Paralleling work in cockpit crew communication and the research by Morrow, Lee, & Rodvold (1991) into controller–pilot communication, this study took an inductive approach in searching for patterns of communication that were associated with contrasts of interest. It delineated speech patterns that distinguish differences relating to (1) performance, (2) types of teams, (3) workload conditions, and (4) aspects of their tasks. For example, speech patterns characterizing ground–air communications were found to be very different from controller–controller communications because the controller–pilot task is concerned primarily with implementing control actions (e.g., managing arrivals, departures, etc.), and communications can be described by a small number of speech categories, highlighting commands and acknowledgments. In contrast, controller-to-controller communications show a wide variety of speech types, as these tasks are primarily cognitive (e.g., maintaining situation awareness). However, it was also clear in ground-line communications that the primarily cognitive task shifts toward a greater emphasis on operations when traffic volume and complexity increase. The top-rated teams were characterized by patterns that were consistent with each type of task demand as well as shifts in task focus.

These analyses provide a basis for better understanding how top-rated controller teams accomplish their tasks. It is important to extend exploratory research to define the dimensions of behavior related to performance effectiveness—associated communication principles. These principles can then be adapted and incorporated into human factors training for controllers.

Just as research progress has been made, progress has also been made in promoting awareness in the ATC community and in developing strategies for developing and implementing CRM programs. A controller resource management conference was held in October, 1991, that had as its goals (1) defining the issues and/or problems related to controller resource management in the operational environment, (2) specifying the outcomes and objectives to be achieved through the program, and (3) outlining suggested training approaches and/or organizational implementation strategies. These issues were addressed by five working groups representing the FAA Academy, en route, terminal, supervisory, and management components of the ATC community. Although controller resource management training has not been implemented formally across the national ATC system, plans are being developed to integrate CRM into all aspects of technical training.

Non-Aviation Domains

The Merchant Marine Industry

There is probably no enterprise that could profit from human factors considerations more than merchant shipping. The accident figures are incredible: on the average, about 370 merchant vessels are lost at sea each year—one a day! Regulations concerning staffing, qualifications (other than the officers), training, crew communication, and operations are almost non-existent. At a joint safety meeting between aviation and maritime experts in London in 1990, the two domains seemed a century apart, and those from the maritime world readily admitted it (Royal Aeronautical Society, 1990).

Crew communication may readily deteriorate when a pilot boards the ship to bring it into harbor. A discussion of human error in merchant marine operations (Maritime Transportation Research Board, 1976) describes the situation

> The in-depth survey contained numerous responses pointing out ambiguities in the responsibilities of the pilot and captain in pilotage water. When asked if a dangerous incident had ever resulted from a conflict between the pilot and the captain, 40% of those responding to the question answered "yes". The interviews provided numerous incidents of confusion or contra-

dictory orders from the pilot and master that resulted in casualties or near-casualties. (p. 8)

The potential for CRM and other human factors areas to contribute to the alarming situation in the maritime industry is great, but whether it will ever be realized is difficult to say. To date safety standards in the maritime world seem to be resistant to even the most potent forces: loss of life, loss of capital equipment, and financial liability.

Production

Probably first among the high-risk production industries that could benefit from CRM is power production, particularly nuclear power. Growing from the experiences of the Three Mile Island accident and other incidents in nuclear power plants (National Research Council, 1989), programs that parallel CRM training have been implemented for control room crews in several plants. Dr. John Kello of Davidson College has worked on adaptation of a number of concepts from the cockpit to the control room, including a "nuclear" version of the CMAQ. The use of full mission simulation that parallels LOFT, including videotaped feedback, is also becoming widespread in nuclear control room training.

Additional parallels in the need for comprehensive human factors training have been noted among bridge crews in marine operations and in teams controlling complex processes in petrochemical refineries and chemical operations. Douglas Schwartz of Flight Safety International has been leading an effort to adapt cockpit CRM courses for the petrochemical environment.

A common factor in all of these environments is that equipment has become increasingly reliable with the major source of error remaining the human operator (Weener, 1990). In addition, the potential for economic loss and adverse publicity due to accidents is high in all of these settings. As Helmreich & Foushee note in their chapter, it seems somewhat paradoxical that training based on long-standing notions of managerial development should become more widely endorsed in the aviation community than they are in industry. However, as they point out, the greater behavioral specificity of the latest programs appears to increase their relevance to participants, ease of translation into practice, and behavioral impact.

Medicine

One of the more intriguing extensions and applications of CRM concepts and training is in medicine. Faculty in anesthesiology departments at several medical schools have been struck by the parallels in communication patterns between operating room teams and cockpit crews and the existence of similar problems of between- and within-group coordination. In the operating room, there are four distinct roles—surgeon, anesthesiologist, surgical nurse, and anesthesia nurse. Effective communication among these groups regarding patient status and planned actions is essential, yet the flow of information needed for decisions is often imperfect. The choices that need to be made in this setting are seldom clear-cut. Status differentials and definitions of leadership can also impede communication. In addition, automation in terms of monitoring equipment and displays has proceeded in a haphazard manner, resulting in a proliferation of displays that are not integrated and are often difficult to monitor (Kennedy, Feingold, Wiener, & Hosek, 1976).

Dr. David Gaba of Stanford University and his colleagues have developed a training seminar that parallels initial CRM awareness training in aviation. They have also embraced the concept of LOFT and have developed an operating room simulation that includes a mannequin patient, surgeons, nurses, and anesthesiologists (Howard, Gaba, Fish, Yang, & Sarnquist, 1992). Paralleling practices in LOFT, simulations are videotaped to provide participants with concrete feedback on their behaviors.

At the University of Basel in Switzerland, Dr. Hans-Gerhard Schaefer has launched a comprehensive research program to examine input and process issues in the operating room. This program involves assessment of personality and attitude factors among all operating room personnel, along with the use of video recording of operating room behavior. The goals of this program are multiple: to understand critical performance issues in this environment, to improve selection practices, and to develop relevant training to optimize team performance.

SYSTEMS APPROACHES AND RESEARCH CHALLENGES ━━━━━━━━━━━━━━━━━━━━━━━━━━━━━━━━━━ ✦

The model of crew performance presented by Helmreich & Foushee (Figure 1.2) suggests that the extent to which crews practice effective CRM is determined not only by their knowledge and acceptance of the concepts but also by a number of external forces including organizational, regulatory, and environmental factors. The example provided by Canada's investigation into the complex determinants of a seemingly simple accident caused by a crew's failure to de-ice illustrates how the systems approach can inform our knowledge (Moshansky, 1992). Systems analyses also lead to a conclusion that simple fixes such as a single CRM seminar that only address a piece of the puzzle will not produce large and lasting change in crew behavior.

Most research into issues surrounding CRM is limited in that it considers only a limited number of factors beyond personality, training, attitudes, or behaviors. If investigations examine broader organizational or environmental issues, they often fail to look at individual and crew factors (see the chapter by Kanki & Palmer). The fact that research is limited in scope is itself determined by multiple

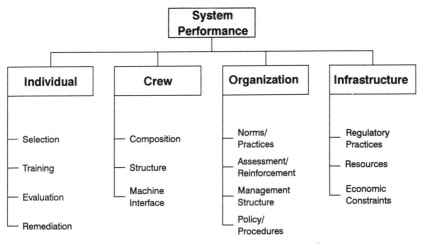

Figure 17.1 Components of integrated research into system performance.

factors, including the increasing specialization of training in the behavioral sciences and increasingly limited resources for research. Nonetheless, future research needs to address contextual factors as well as specific variables under investigation. Figure 17.1 shows graphically issues that need to be integrated in research to understand the determinants of system performance. What is needed is a multidisciplinary collaboration that brings a variety of theoretical and methodological expertise to bear on understanding behavior in its complex context.

CRM and the U.S. *National Plan for Aviation Human Factors*

The recently completed U.S. *National Plan* (FAA, 1990) provides a comprehensive conceptual framework for research into all aspects of human factors as they relate to the aviation system. However, the plan does not provide mechanisms for conducting and utilizing the work. There are also difficulties posed because researchers are not familiar or comfortable with large, collaborative research and have different methodological and theoretical orientations. Shotgun marriages between subdisciplines of the behavioral sciences are neither common nor necessarily destined to succeed.

Nevertheless, the *National Plan* defines the universe of aviation research in several very important ways. First, it recognizes that applied human factors projects can accomplish a wide range of both scientific and applied objectives. Specifically named are the following topics:

1. Automation and advanced technology
2. Aviation system monitoring

3. Basic scientific knowledge of human performance factors
4. Human performance measurement
5. Information transfer
6. Controls, displays, workstation designs
7. Training and selection
8. Certification and validation standards

   While any one project may primarily serve one objective, an integrated program of research will address multiple, related objectives that support each other, often in a phased sequence. For instance, the development of human performance measures in phase 1 may be required in order to conduct basic science research in phase 2. A phase 3 project may take the results from phase 2 and translate its findings into training materials. Clearly CRM research has profited greatly from its multi-objective approach, and examples of how these categories interrelate are numerous. For example, CRM research may begin with information from NTSB accident reports or aviation system monitoring data (e.g., ASRS). The information can help to identify critical research questions on such topics as automation and information transfer. Basic research typically implies the development of methods to assess human performance and concludes with a phase that is focused on new training practices and/or selection applications. However, basic research can also direct itself toward the perceptual issues related to control, display, and design issues and how they influence crew interaction; or toward regulatory objectives (certification and validation standards). In order to achieve the maximum value across a vast and complex system, researchers cannot be satisfied with confining themselves to narrow objectives; rather they must utilize insights and information from one body of research to the next.

   A second critical feature of the *National Plan* is its farsighted inclusion of all parts of the aviation system, namely (1) the flightdeck, (2) ATC, (3) flightdeck–ATC integration, (4) aircraft maintenance, and (5) airways facilities maintenance. As we witness the transition from cockpit resource management to crew resource management, the *National Plan* maps out new areas in which CRM research can prosper. Given an integrated plan, it should be possible for research accomplished in one environment to provide technology transfer to other environments; if not at the level of specific findings, at least in terms of methodology and lessons learned. The history of CRM research and program development in the flightdeck environment provides an unquestionable advantage for those just starting out in other environments.

IMPLICATIONS FOR EDUCATION ─────────────→

   The rarity of integrated approaches to research into human performance is a reflection of educational practices. Graduate training in the behavioral sciences has become increasingly specialized and narrow. The result is that few degree programs produce graduates capable of approaching problems on multiple levels. One of the greatest benefits of activities such as the *National Plan* would be to foster the development of graduate programs that could produce a new generation of renaissance-person researchers. Should it prove possible to achieve an integration of the disparate components of psychology, the results should provide better data with more applicability and could also lead to a more sophisticated psychology of individual and group behavior.

SUMMARY ✈

The sum of research and operational experience reported by the authors of this volume represents a true success story in meeting a national need for safety and efficiency in aviation. We have learned a lot about the contribution of human factors and human factors training to team and organizational effectiveness and about the technology of changing human behavior. The cockpit crew is like a small organization. As Hackman notes in his chapter, it is created, does something, and dissolves—and we can measure its successes and failures.

There are several important lessons to be learned and re-learned in this experience. One is that collaboration in the pursuit of a shared goal is synergistic and more effective than individual efforts. The CRM concept of team action is seen in the sharing of ideas, methods, and findings among the academic and government research communities and the air carriers, who are fierce competitors in the marketplace. Another lesson is that the impact of research is much greater when investigators define their roles to include the interpretation and implementation of findings instead of seeing their job as complete when a report is delivered.

Aviations's experience with the development, implementation, and refinement of CRM training is not only useful in its own right but can serve as a general model for research and operational collaboration in many endeavors. Like the space program, industry experiences with CRM may have many spin-offs and applications for education, industry, and government.

References

Butler, R. E. (1991). Lessons from cross-fleet/cross airline observations: Evaluating the impact of CRM/LOS training. In *Proceedings of the Sixth International Symposium on Aviation Psychology* (pp. 326–331). Columbus: Ohio State University.

Chidester, T. R., Helmreich, R. L., Gregorich, S., & Geis, C. (1991). Pilot personality and crew coordination: Implications for training and selection. *International Journal of Aviation Psychology*, *1*, 23–42.

Clothier, C. (1991a). Behavioral interactions across various aircraft types: Results of systematic observations of line operations and simulations. In *Proceedings of the Sixth International Symposium on Aviation Psychology* (pp. 332–337). Columbus: Ohio State University.

Clothier, C. (1991b). *Behavioral interactions in various aircraft types: Results of systematic observation of line operations and simulations.* Unpublished Masters' thesis. The University of Texas at Austin.

Federal Aviation Administration. (1990). *The national plan for aviation human factors* (NTIS No. PB01-100321). Washington, DC: Author.

Fotos, C. P. (1991, August 26). Continental applies CRM concepts to technical, maintenance corps. *Aviation Week and Space Technology,* pp. 32–33, 35.

Helmreich, R. L., Butler, R. E., & Wilhelm, J. A. (1992). Final report on the cross-airline, cross-fleet human factors observation project (NASA/UT/FAA Technical Report 92-5).

Helmreich, R. L., & Wilhelm, J. A. (1989). When training boomerangs: Negative outcomes associated with cockpit resource management programs. In *Proceedings of the Sixth International Symposium on Aviation Psychology* (pp. 92–97). Columbus: Ohio State University.

Helmreich, R. L., & Wilhelm, J. A. (1991). Outcomes of crew resource management training. *International Journal of Aviation Psychology, 1,* 287–300.

Helmreich, R. L., Wilhelm, J. A., & Gregorich, S. E. (1988). *Revised versions of the cockpit management attitudes questionnaire (CMAQ) and CRM seminar evaluation form* (NASA/The University of Texas Technical Report 88-3). Austin.

Helmreich, R. L., Wilhelm, J. A., Kello, J. E., Taggart, W. R., & Butler, R. E. (1991). *Reinforcing and evaluating crew resource management: Evaluator/LOS instructor reference manual* (NASA/University of Texas Technical Manual 90–2). Austin.

Howard, S. K., Gaba, D. M., Fish, K. J., Yang, G., & Sarnquist, F. H. (1992). Anesthesia crisis resource management training: Teaching anesthesiologists to handle critical events. *Aviation, Space, and Environmental Medicine, 63,* 763–770.

Human Technology (1991). *Analysis of controller communication in en route air traffic control: Report to the Federal Aviation Administration.* McLean, VA: FAA.

Kennedy, P. J., Feingold, A., Wiener, E. L., & Hosek, R. (1976). Analysis of tasks and human factors in anesthesia for coronary bypass. *Anesthesia and Analgesia, 55,* 374–377.

Maritime Transportation Research Board. (1976). *Human error in merchant marine safety.* Washington, DC: National Research Council, Author.

Morrow, D. G., Lee, A. T., & Rodvold, M. (1991). Collaboration in pilot–controller communication. *Proceedings of the Sixth International Symposium on Aviation Psychology* (pp. 266–271). Columbus: Ohio Sate University.

Moshansky, V. P. (1992). *Commission of Inquiry into the Air Ontario Accident at Dryden, Ontario: Final report (Volumes 1–4).* Ottawa, ON: Minister of Supply and Services, Canada.

National Research Council. (1989). *Human factors research and nuclear safety.* Washington, DC: National Academy Press: Author.

National Transportation Safety Board. (1988). *Hazardous Materials Incident Report: In-flight Fire; McDonnell Douglas DC-9-83, IN569AA, Nashville Metropolitan Airport, Nashville, Tennessee, February 3, 1988* (NTSB/HZM-88/02). Washington: Author.

National Transportation Safety Board. (1989, December 5). *Safety Recommendation A-89-110 through -120.* Washington, DC: Author.

North, D. M. (1992, March 23). Airbus pilot training center stresses task-sharing, good communications as key to flying advanced aircraft. *Aviation Week and Space Technology,* pp. 63–64.

Royal Aeronautical Society (U.K). (1990). Safety at sea and in the air: taking stock together. *Proceedings of the Royal Aeronautical Society Symposium.* London: Author.

Taggart, W. R. (1990). Introducing CRM into maintenance training. *Proceedings of the Third International Symposium on Human Factors in Aircraft Maintenance and Inspection.* Washington: Federal Aviation Administration.

Taylor, J. (1992). *The effects of crew resource management (CRM) training in maintenance: An early demonstration of training effects on attitudes and performance.* Washington: Federal Aviation Administration.

Vandermark, M. J. (1991). Should flight attendants be included in CRM training? A discussion of a major air carrier's approach to total crew training. *International Journal of Aviation Psychology, 1,* 87–94.

Weener, E. F. (1990, December). *Control of crew-caused accidents.* Paper presented at Third Annual Society of Automotive Engineers symposium on human error, Dallas, Texas.

Wiener, E. L., Chidester, T. R., Kanki, B. G., Palmer, E. A., Curry, R. E., & Gregorich, S. E. (1991). *The impact of cockpit automation on crew coordination and communication: I. Overview, LOFT evaluations, error severity, and questionnaire data* (NASA Contractor Report 177587). Moffett Field, CA: NASA–Ames Research Center.

Richard A. Birnbach is the Assistant Division Manager, Flight Standards Regional Office, Great Lakes Region, FAA. Previously he served as the Manager of the Air Carrier Training Branch at FAA headquarters, where he was responsible for the development and oversight at a national level of FAA policies, procedures, and regulations on airline training and qualification for aircrew personnel. Mr. Birnbach attended St. Louis University. He served as a pilot in the U.S. Army, with ratings in both rotary and fixed-wing aircraft. Following combat duty in Vietnam, he was an instructor pilot at the Army Aviation Center, Fort Rucker. He has been an active civilian pilot since 1960 and has worked as an FAA aviation safety inspector since 1970 in a variety of air carrier and general aviation capacities. He is an author of the FAA's *Air Carrier Operations Inspector's Handbook* and was responsible for the development of FAA policies regarding airline use of computer-enhanced weather forecast systems to control flight operations. Prior to his assignment to FAA headquarters, Mr. Birnbach was responsible for DC-9 aircrew certification for an air carrier. Mr. Birnbach also led the FAA team that approved the first U.S. operation of helicopters under instrument flight rules in support of petroleum exploration in the Gulf of Mexico. He served as the FAA's principal inspector for oversight of urban helicopter operations at New York Airways. His hobbies include restoring and flying antique aircraft. His most recently completed restoration is a 1939 Aeronica Cabin Monoplane.

Reuben Black has recently served as Assistant Vice President–Flight Operations at Delta Air Lines, serving as Chief Pilot for over 9,000 pilots at Delta. Captain Black now flies the L-1011 internationally. He served as the first Chairman of Delta's CRM Steering Committee and was responsible for facilitating the construction of that program by the 14-member committee. He also organized and implemented the initial Joint Safety Department at Delta. A 30-year veteran pilot at Delta, he is current in the L-1011 and holds ratings on the DC-9, B-727, DC-8, B-767, B-757, and L-1011. He has been a line check airman on the B-727, B-767, B-757 and L-1011 and a proficiency check airman on the DC-8. Captain Black has served on Delta's management team as a Chief Pilot; System Manager–Flight Training; System Manager–Line Operations; Director–Safety, Standards, and Training; Director–Flight Operations; as well as his present position as Chief Pilot.

Roy Butler is a research fellow at the University of Texas. He is currently working with the NASA/University of Texas Aerospace Crew Research Project, directing a program to evaluate crew performance in line and LOFT operations across airlines and fleets. His responsibilities include calibration training for the project expert observers and selected management and check pilots at the airlines working with this project. He retired from Pan American World Airways in 1990 as the System Director, Flight Training, and Boeing 747 captain. At Pan Am he had the overall responsibility for managing the International Flight Academy. During his 25-year tenure at Pan Am he held positions as Director, B-747 training, CRM project manager, and senior training captain and check airman. He holds type ratings on the Boeing 707 and 747, the Lockheed L-1011-500, and the Airbus A-310. His involvement with CRM and LOFT began in 1985 when he began developing a model for LOFT and planned the introduction of CRM training for pilots at Pan Am. He began his flying career in 1952 when he entered the Naval Aviation Cadet pilot training program at Pensacola, Florida. After completing flight training, he served as an all-weather night fighter pilot in the Marine Corps. He joined Pacific Airlines in 1957, where he flew the DC-3, Martin 202/404, and F-27. In 1961 he left Pacific Airlines to join the Lockheed Missiles and Space Company in Sunnyvale, California, as a pilot. At Lockheed he entered an 18-month Manufacturing Technical Training Program, and after completion of this training assignment he was assigned to the Special Products Division as a project coordinator. During this period, as a part of his training assignment at Lockheed, he completed his education at San Jose State University with a major in physics.

Robert E. Byrnes has a primary interest in applying a clinical psychology background to the aviation industry. He is currently an international captain, flying the L-1011 at Delta. He served as Chairman of the CRM Steering Committee at Delta, succeeding Captain Reuben Black, and as Delta's representative to the NTSB Accident Investigation Board (Human Performance Committee) for the Delta Flight 1141 accident at Dallas–Fort Worth Airport. He has been a line check and proficiency check airman on the Lockheed 100, Convair 880, DC-8, DC-9, and B-727. Captain Byrnes is the author of scripts and seminars on stress management, communications skills, human factors in automation, psychological intervention with stress-impaired pilots, simulator behavioral testing, and pilot selection and testing strategies. He is president of Human Performance Associates Inc., a consulting firm in Boca Raton, Florida, and conducts a private practice in psychotherapy and marital/family counseling.

Thomas R. Chidester is Manager of Crew Resource Management Training for American Airlines. He received his Bachelor of Sciences degree from the University of Houston (1982) and his Master's (1984) and Ph.D. (1986) from the University of Texas at Austin and completed a National Research Council Research Associateship in support of the Crew Factors research program at NASA–Ames Research Center

(1986–1988). Dr. Chidester served as a Research Psychologist with the Aerospace Human Factors Research Division at NASA–Ames (1988–1990), a position he left to join American. Dr. Chidester's research has focused on the importance of individual personality to performance in aerospace operations, including individual differences in responses to short-haul and long-haul flight operations and individual differences in personality within the pilot population influencing responses to training in cockpit resource management and performance in full-mission simulation of flight operations. Dr. Chidester's work for American focuses on applying human factors research to training for cockpit crewmembers, flight attendants, and flight dispatchers.

H. Clayton Foushee was appointed Managing Director of Procedures, Standards, and Training at Northwest Airlines in June, 1992. He was named Chief Scientific and Technical Advisor for Human Factors for the FAA in June, 1989. In this capacity he served as scientific and technical advisor to the FAA Administrator and Executive Board and is the agency focal point on human performance issues. He headed a joint effort of the FAA and NASA, with Department of Defense assistance, to implement a comprehensive National Aviation Human Factors Plan. Prior to his appointment at the FAA, Dr. Foushee was Principal Scientist of the Crew Research and Space Human Factors Branch at the NASA–Ames Research Center in the San Francisco Bay Area, where he headed a research program on team and organizational factors in both aviation and space.

He is a magna cum laude graduate of Duke University in 1975 and received a Ph.D. in social psychology from the University of Texas in 1979. After his doctoral studies, he became a National Research Council Fellow at Ames Research Center and received a permanent NASA assignment in 1981, where he began a program of research into factors that influence crew behavior. He has participated in a number of government and industry activities, including the *NASA*/U.S. Air Force Military Airlift Command Workshop on Cockpit Resource Management and the Joint Government/Industry Task Force on Flightcrew Performance. His work to develop team and organizational performance enhancement techniques includes space shuttle operations, planning for the international Space Station Freedom, commercial airlines, the military, the nuclear power industry, and surgical teams.

Robert C. Ginnett is a senior research and program associate and the Director of Research for the Colorado Campus of the Center for Creative Leadership. In addition to administering and conducting research on leadership and teamwork, he conducts seminars for senior leadership levels in private industry and the Federal sector. He has conducted research in a variety of team settings including commercial and military aircrews, surgical teams, product development teams, and top management teams. In his current research he is studying space launch and quality improvement teams. Prior to joining the Center for Creative Leadership, he was a tenured professor at the U.S. Air Force Academy and the Director of Leadership and Counseling Programs. He received his B.A. in psychology from the University of Maryland, an

M.B.A. from the University of Utah, and a Ph.D. in organizational behavior from Yale University. He has published numerous articles on the leadership of teams and has recently co-authored a book on leadership.

Steven E. Gregorich received his Ph.D. in social psychology from the University of Texas at Austin in 1991. Since 1990 he has been in residence at NASA–Ames Research Center as a project associate with the San Jose State University Foundation. During the past 6 years he has conducted both experimental and field research in the areas of personality, motivation, attitude change, training, and human performance. His current research interests concern CRM training program assessment and human performance within the domains of aviation and science.

J. Richard Hackman is Cahners-Rabb Professor of Social and Organizational Psychology at Harvard University. He received his undergraduate degree in mathematics from MacMurray College in 1962 and his doctorate in social psychology from the University of Illinois in 1966. He taught at Yale until 1986, when he moved to Harvard. Professor Hackman conducts research on a variety of topics in social psychology and organizational behavior, including the performance of work teams, social influences on individual behavior, and the design and leadership of self-managing units in organizations. His most recent book, *Groups That Work*, was published in 1990 by Jossey-Bass.

Robert L. Helmreich is professor of psychology at the University of Texas at Austin. He received his Ph.D. in personality and social psychology from Yale University in 1966. He has conducted research on group processes and performance sponsored by NASA, the Office of Naval Research, and the FAA, as well as research on personality and motivation sponsored by the National Science Foundation and the National Institute of Mental Health. He is a fellow of the American Psychological Association and the American Psychological Society and former editor of the *Journal of Personality and Social Psychology*. He was chair of an FAA working group to develop the *National Plan for Aviation Human Factors*. He is a member of the National Academy of Sciences Committee on Space Biology and Medicine and Committee on Human Factors. He is Director of the NASA/University of Texas/FAA Aerospace Crew Performance Project investigating issues in crew selection, training, and performance evaluation in both aviation and space environments.

A. Neil Johnston joined the ab initio pilot training program of Aer Lingus, the national airline of Ireland, directly from school. He is now a Boeing 737 captain with Aer Lingus. He was the founding chairman of the Human Performance Committee of the International Federation of Airline Pilots' Associations. He is currently chairman of the Human Factors Working Group in the International Air Transport Association (IATA). He represents IATA on the Human Factors and Flight Safety Study Group at the International Civil Aviation Organization. He was awarded a B.A. with First Class Honours by the Open University in 1986 and is a Consulting Editor to the *Interna-*

tional Journal of Aviation Psychology. His interests include the marriage of theory to practice in aviation and pilot training. He has been intensively involved in various innovations in pilot training, working both for Aer Lingus and as an independent consultant.

Barbara G. Kanki is currently a staff research psychologist in the Aerospace Human Factors Research Division of NASA–Ames Research Center and a principal investigator in the Crew Factors research group. Dr. Kanki received her graduate degree from the Behavioral Sciences Department at the University of Chicago, where she specialized in the areas of communication and group dynamics. She came to Ames Research Center in 1985 as a National Research Council post-doctoral associate and began work in the aeronautical domain by studying the relationship between crew communication and aircrew performance, using both full-mission simulation and field research methods. Although much of the Crew Factors research focuses on the study of aircrew team performance and training in air transport operations, the work generalizes to other domains in the aviation system, such as aircraft maintenance, as well as to ground-based space operations. As such, the program has grown to include payload and orbiter processing teams for NASA shuttle missions and other teams, such as aquanauts and mountaineering teams, whose work environments are analogous to space operations in critical respects.

Phyllis J. Kayten is currently Deputy Chief Scientific and Technical Advisor for Human Factors for the FAA. She received her B.A. (1971) from Brandeis University, and her M.A. (1976) and Ph.D. (1978) in developmental psychology from the State University of New York at Stony Brook. From 1981 to 1983, she was employed by Ship Analytics, Inc., where among other things, she conducted research on the equivalence of simulator training to real-world experience for the acquisition of merchant marine deck officer skills. In November, 1983, she became an original member of the NTSB's newly formed Human Performance investigative division, where she investigated accidents in the aviation, railroad, highway, and marine modes. From 1986 to 1990, she served as special assistant to John K. Lauber during his first term as NTSB board member. She is a member of the Human Factors Society, the American Psychological Society, the Association of Aviation Psychologists, and the International Society of Air Safety Investigators, and an associate member of the Society of Naval Architects and Marine Engineers.

Thomas M. Longridge is the Manager of the Advanced Qualification Program Office, Air Transport Division, Headquarters, FAA. He received his Ph.D. in human engineering from the University of Arizona in 1975. He joined the FAA in 1989. From 1985 to 1989 he was employed as the technical team leader for flight simulation research at the Army Research Institute Aviation R&D Activity, Ft. Rucker, Alabama. From 1977 to 1985 he was employed as a flight simulation research psychologist at the Air Force Human Resources Laboratory, Williams AFB,

Arizona. Previously, he served as an associate professor of behavioral science at the U.S. Air Force Academy.

Takao Mito graduated from the Aeronautical Engineering Department of Osaka Prefecture University in 1962, and then entered Japan Airlines as an engineering staff member. He worked in maintenance and operation engineering in J.A.L. and flight operations in Japan Asia Airways, J.A.L.'s subsidiary, before being assigned to the Flight Safety Department, where he is a staff director promoting crewmember safety awareness as an editor of J.A.L.'s in-house flight safety magazine.

Judith Orasanu joined the Crew Factors group at NASA–Ames Research Center in 1991, where she is conducting research on crew problem-solving and decision-making. She went to NASA after working for 6 years at the U.S. Army Research Institute's Basic Research Office. In that position she developed a program on planning, problem-solving, and decision-making that examined reasoning in everyday settings. Her involvement with that program laid the foundation for her research on crew communication and problem-solving begun while she was a Visiting Fellow at Princeton University from 1989 to 1990. Prior to joining the Army Research Institute, Dr. Orasanu was a Senior Research Associate at the National Institute of Education, where she managed research programs on literacy and bilingualism from 1979 to 1983. Dr. Orasanu received her Ph.D. in experimental psychology with an emphasis on psycholinguistics and memory from Adelphi University in 1975. She was awarded a Postdoctoral Fellowship at the Rockefeller University, where she studied culture and cognition in the Comparative Human Cognition Laboratory, and then worked as a research associate in the Experimental Psychology Laboratory studying cognitive processes in language comprehension, focusing on metaphor.

Harry W. Orlady retired from United Airlines after 39 years as a pilot and after flying 10 different types of aircraft ranging from the Boeing 247 and the DC-3 to the Boeing 747. He has completed several studies in pilot ground and flight training as well as studies in the aviation human factors, aeromedical, and aviation safety fields. While with United, Orlady received several United and industry aviation awards. He has presented nearly 100 papers or lectures on flight training and operational safety in aviation. Since retirement he has served as a Senior Research Scientist for the Aviation Safety Reporting System (ASRS). He has also served as a research contractor to the ASRS, as an independent contractor to NASA–Ames and to private research firms, and as a consultant to the FAA in its certification of the Boeing 747-400 and the McDonnell-Douglas MD-11.

Captain Orlady is an elected Fellow of the Aerospace Medical Association. He was a member of ICAO's Medical Study Group, IATA's Human Factors Study Group, and the Steering Committee for IATA's Istanbul Technical Conference on Human Factors. Currently, Captain Orlady is a member of the Human Factors Society, the Association of Aviation Psychologists, the Aerospace Medical Association, the Society of Automotive Engineers, the SAE Human Behavioral Technology and G-10 Committees, and the ICAO Flight Safety and Human Factors Study Group.

Mark T. Palmer is an Assistant Professor of Communication Studies at Northwestern University and a National Academy of Sciences, National Research Council Associate at NASA–Ames Research Center (1990–1992). Dr. Palmer's past research has focused on the cognitive and communicative processes by which social actors comprehend and enact their interpersonal and goal-oriented relationships in face-to-face encounters. In the aviation context, this research centers on the relationship between dynamic patterns of communication (e.g., speech acts, information-seeking and provision, topical focus, planning) with changing patterns of task-related activities.

Carolyn Prince received a Ph.D. degree in industrial/organizational psychology from the University of South Florida. She has worked in the area of management selection and development, where she conducted management task analyses, developed assessment materials for management selection, designed management skill training programs, and trained assessors to observe, document, and rate managerial skills. Some of the organizations for which she performed these tasks include the FAA, the Department of Transportation, General Motors, Federal Express, and Prudential Life Insurance. Since joining the Human Factors Research and Development Division at the Naval Training Systems Center she has worked exclusively in the area of aviation and has been the principal investigator for the aircrew coordination research from its inception.

Eduardo Salas is a Senior Research Psychologist in the Human Factors Division of the Naval Training Systems Center (NTSC). He holds an M.S. in industrial psychology from the University of Central Florida and a Ph.D. in industrial/organization psychology from Old Dominion University, Norfolk, Virginia. He is the principal investigator for NTSC's research and development program on team training and performance, and project manager of the research on aircrew coordination training for Navy and Marine aircrews. Dr. Salas has conducted research in team and individual training design, training evaluation, job/task analysis, skill acquisition, and personnel psychology. His most recent project responsibilities are in the aircrew coordination training area and as laboratory director for the Tactical Decision Making Under Stress Project.

Earl L. Wiener is a professor of Management Science at the University of Miami. He received his B.A. in psychology from Duke University and his Ph.D. in psychology and industrial engineering from Ohio State University. He served as a pilot in the U.S. Air Force and U.S. Army and is rated in fixed wing and rotary wing aircraft. Since 1979 he has been active in the aeronautics and cockpit automation research of NASA's Ames Research Center. Dr. Wiener is a fellow of the Human Factors Society and the American Psychological Association and has served as president of the Human Factors Society. He currently serves on NASA's Aerospace Research and Technology Subcommittee and the FAA's Research, Engineering, and Development Advisory Committee. He is the co-editor (with David Nagel) of *Human Factors in Aviation*, published in 1988 by Academic Press.

John A. Wilhelm received the Master of Arts degree from the University of Texas at Austin in 1971. He has worked with Robert L. Helmreich on various research projects since the early 1970s. These projects have been based primarily on data collected in field settings as diverse as underwater habitats and supertankers. In recent years, the field settings have been primarily in aviation and space-related analog environments. Mr. Wilhelm's special interest is in the compilation and analysis of the datasets produced in these diverse research settings. He has seen the tools of his trade change from mainframe batch-mode processing to the rapidly evolving personal computer environment. A second interest is in teaching these computer-based technical tools to the many undergraduate and graduate students who have worked on the research projects across the years. One of these students was Steven Gregorich.

Hisaaki Yamamori graduated from the Civil Aviation College in 1959. Upon graduation, he entered Japan Airlines and became a Douglas DC-4 co-pilot. In 1966 he became a CV-880 captain, and then captained the DC-8 and B-747. He is currently captain for the B-747-400. In 1982 he attended a United Airlines CRM seminar and LOFT training program. He later brought CRM/LOFT to Japan Airlines. He was director of the Flight Safety Department and recently was promoted to Vice President, secretariat of the Flight Safety Committee.

Index